Lecture Notes in Computer Science   9179

Commenced Publication in 1973
Founding and Former Series Editors:
Gerhard Goos, Juris Hartmanis, and Jan van Leeuwen

More information about this series at http://www.springer.com/series/7409

Randall Shumaker · Stephanie Lackey (Eds.)

Virtual, Augmented and Mixed Reality

7th International Conference, VAMR 2015
Held as Part of HCI International 2015
Los Angeles, CA, USA, August 2–7, 2015
Proceedings

 Springer

Editors
Randall Shumaker
University of Central Florida
Orlando, FL
USA

Stephanie Lackey
University of Central Florida
Orlando, FL
USA

ISSN 0302-9743   ISSN 1611-3349   (electronic)
Lecture Notes in Computer Science
ISBN 978-3-319-21066-7   ISBN 978-3-319-21067-4   (eBook)
DOI 10.1007/978-3-319-21067-4

Library of Congress Control Number: 2015942478

LNCS Sublibrary: SL3 – Information Systems and Applications, incl. Internet/Web, and HCI

Springer Cham Heidelberg New York Dordrecht London

Printed on acid-free paper

Springer International Publishing AG Switzerland is part of Springer Science+Business Media
(www.springer.com)

Foreword

The 17th International Conference on Human-Computer Interaction, HCI International 2015, was held in Los Angeles, CA, USA, during 2–7 August 2015. The event incorporated the 15 conferences/thematic areas listed on the following page.

A total of 4843 individuals from academia, research institutes, industry, and governmental agencies from 73 countries submitted contributions, and 1462 papers and 246 posters have been included in the proceedings. These papers address the latest research and development efforts and highlight the human aspects of design and use of computing systems. The papers thoroughly cover the entire field of Human-Computer Interaction, addressing major advances in knowledge and effective use of computers in a variety of application areas. The volumes constituting the full 28-volume set of the conference proceedings are listed on pages VII and VIII.

I would like to thank the Program Board Chairs and the members of the Program Boards of all thematic areas and affiliated conferences for their contribution to the highest scientific quality and the overall success of the HCI International 2015 conference.

This conference could not have been possible without the continuous and unwavering support and advice of the founder, Conference General Chair Emeritus and Conference Scientific Advisor, Prof. Gavriel Salvendy. For their outstanding efforts, I would like to express my appreciation to the Communications Chair and Editor of HCI International News, Dr. Abbas Moallem, and the Student Volunteer Chair, Prof. Kim-Phuong L. Vu. Finally, for their dedicated contribution towards the smooth organization of HCI International 2015, I would like to express my gratitude to Maria Pitsoulaki and George Paparoulis, General Chair Assistants.

May 2015

Constantine Stephanidis
General Chair, HCI International 2015

HCI International 2015 Thematic Areas and Affiliated Conferences

Thematic areas:

- Human-Computer Interaction (HCI 2015)
- Human Interface and the Management of Information (HIMI 2015)

Affiliated conferences:

- 12th International Conference on Engineering Psychology and Cognitive Ergonomics (EPCE 2015)
- 9th International Conference on Universal Access in Human-Computer Interaction (UAHCI 2015)
- 7th International Conference on Virtual, Augmented and Mixed Reality (VAMR 2015)
- 7th International Conference on Cross-Cultural Design (CCD 2015)
- 7th International Conference on Social Computing and Social Media (SCSM 2015)
- 9th International Conference on Augmented Cognition (AC 2015)
- 6th International Conference on Digital Human Modeling and Applications in Health, Safety, Ergonomics and Risk Management (DHM 2015)
- 4th International Conference on Design, User Experience and Usability (DUXU 2015)
- 3rd International Conference on Distributed, Ambient and Pervasive Interactions (DAPI 2015)
- 3rd International Conference on Human Aspects of Information Security, Privacy and Trust (HAS 2015)
- 2nd International Conference on HCI in Business (HCIB 2015)
- 2nd International Conference on Learning and Collaboration Technologies (LCT 2015)
- 1st International Conference on Human Aspects of IT for the Aged Population (ITAP 2015)

Conference Proceedings Volumes Full List

1. LNCS 9169, Human-Computer Interaction: Design and Evaluation (Part I), edited by Masaaki Kurosu
2. LNCS 9170, Human-Computer Interaction: Interaction Technologies (Part II), edited by Masaaki Kurosu
3. LNCS 9171, Human-Computer Interaction: Users and Contexts (Part III), edited by Masaaki Kurosu
4. LNCS 9172, Human Interface and the Management of Information: Information and Knowledge Design (Part I), edited by Sakae Yamamoto
5. LNCS 9173, Human Interface and the Management of Information: Information and Knowledge in Context (Part II), edited by Sakae Yamamoto
6. LNAI 9174, Engineering Psychology and Cognitive Ergonomics, edited by Don Harris
7. LNCS 9175, Universal Access in Human-Computer Interaction: Access to Today's Technologies (Part I), edited by Margherita Antona and Constantine Stephanidis
8. LNCS 9176, Universal Access in Human-Computer Interaction: Access to Interaction (Part II), edited by Margherita Antona and Constantine Stephanidis
9. LNCS 9177, Universal Access in Human-Computer Interaction: Access to Learning, Health and Well-Being (Part III), edited by Margherita Antona and Constantine Stephanidis
10. LNCS 9178, Universal Access in Human-Computer Interaction: Access to the Human Environment and Culture (Part IV), edited by Margherita Antona and Constantine Stephanidis
11. LNCS 9179, Virtual, Augmented and Mixed Reality, edited by Randall Shumaker and Stephanie Lackey
12. LNCS 9180, Cross-Cultural Design: Methods, Practice and Impact (Part I), edited by P.L. Patrick Rau
13. LNCS 9181, Cross-Cultural Design: Applications in Mobile Interaction, Education, Health, Transport and Cultural Heritage (Part II), edited by P.L. Patrick Rau
14. LNCS 9182, Social Computing and Social Media, edited by Gabriele Meiselwitz
15. LNAI 9183, Foundations of Augmented Cognition, edited by Dylan D. Schmorrow and Cali M. Fidopiastis
16. LNCS 9184, Digital Human Modeling and Applications in Health, Safety, Ergonomics and Risk Management: Human Modeling (Part I), edited by Vincent G. Duffy
17. LNCS 9185, Digital Human Modeling and Applications in Health, Safety, Ergonomics and Risk Management: Ergonomics and Health (Part II), edited by Vincent G. Duffy
18. LNCS 9186, Design, User Experience, and Usability: Design Discourse (Part I), edited by Aaron Marcus
19. LNCS 9187, Design, User Experience, and Usability: Users and Interactions (Part II), edited by Aaron Marcus
20. LNCS 9188, Design, User Experience, and Usability: Interactive Experience Design (Part III), edited by Aaron Marcus

Virtual, Augmented and Mixed Reality

Program Board Chairs: Randall Shumaker, USA and Stephanie Lackey, USA

- Sheryl Brahnam, USA
- Juan Cendan, USA
- Jessie Chen, USA
- Matthew Johnston, USA
- Panagiotis D. Kaklis, UK
- Hirokazu Kato, Japan
- Fotis Liarokapis, Czech Republic
- Michael Macedonia, USA
- Courtney McNamara, USA
- Gordon Mair, UK
- Jose San Martin, Spain
- Marius Preda, France
- Christian Sandor, Australia
- Uwe Freiherr von Lukas, Germany
- Aimee Weber, USA

The full list with the Program Board Chairs and the members of the Program Boards of all thematic areas and affiliated conferences is available online at:

http://www.hci.international/2015/

HCI International 2016

The 18th International Conference on Human-Computer Interaction, HCI International 2016, will be held jointly with the affiliated conferences in Toronto, Canada, at the Westin Harbour Castle Hotel, 17–22 July 2016. It will cover a broad spectrum of themes related to Human-Computer Interaction, including theoretical issues, methods, tools, processes, and case studies in HCI design, as well as novel interaction techniques, interfaces, and applications. The proceedings will be published by Springer. More information will be available on the conference website: http://2016.hci.international/.

General Chair
Prof. Constantine Stephanidis
University of Crete and ICS-FORTH
Heraklion, Crete, Greece
Email: general_chair@hcii2016.org

http://2016.hci.international/

Contents

VR in Health and Culture

Industrial and Military Applications

User Experience in Virtual
and Augmented Environments

Design of the Augmented Reality Based Training System to Promote Spatial Visualization Ability for Older Adults

Kuo-Ping Chang and Chien-Hsu Chen[✉]

Department of Industrial Design, National Cheng Kung University,
Tainan, Taiwan
{p36024069, chenhsu}@mail.ncku.edu.tw

Abstract. In this paper, we present the design of spatial visualization training system implemented by augmented reality (AR). Spatial visualization is the ability to mentally transform complex stimuli in space. However, this ability declines with human age, resulting in spatial problems in one's normal life. Based on the fact that AR interface can reduce cognitive load and provide correct spatial information, we are devoted to designing an AR spatial visualization training system for older adults to use. The system consists of a manual controller and a visualization training task. In the process of manual controller design, think aloud experiment is adopted to generate intuitive manipulation, and morphological analysis is used to evaluate the most elderly-friendly controller. In the process of training task design, by analyzing spatial training factors, a new visualization training task is designed. In the process of AR integration, the system is implemented by Qualcomm AR in Unity3D with Vuforia protal, and the final AR based spatial visualization ability training system is completed.

Keywords: Augmented reality · Spatial visualization ability · Elderly

1 Introduction

When humans grow older, in spite of physical condition, cognition ability will also get worse [1]. Among all cognitive abilities, the decline of spatial visualization ability causes older adults to have spatial problems and low spatial awareness in real life [2, 3]. Spatial visualization ability is the mental manipulation of spatial information to determine how a given spatial configuration appears if they are being transformed. However, this ability decreases with human age, negatively affecting older adults' spatial capabilities such as map-reading and way-finding [4, 5].

In fact, the goal of delaying the degradation of spatial visualization ability can be achieved by taking visualization training considerably [6, 7]. However, current visualization training is conducted in two-dimensional (2D) interfaces which are not suitable for one to figure out spatial information in that cognitive load will be produced, making trainers feel arduous and gain no improvement [8]. Additionally, current training is analogous to test, which is too stubborn and not intriguing to trainers. As an

© Springer International Publishing Switzerland 2015
R. Shumaker and S. Lackey (Eds.): VAMR 2015, LNCS 9179, pp. 3–12, 2015.
DOI: 10.1007/978-3-319-21067-4_1

instructional training tool, in spite of visual feedback, other sensory interaction ought to be applied in training as possible in order to enhance trainers' immersion and interests.

AR is a real world environment whose elements are augmented by computer-generated sensory input. It is favorable to be developed into instructional tools based on its unique features. First, AR interfaces are conducive to spatial visualization for they provide correct spatial information and enhance three-dimensional (3D) concept [9]. Second, training with AR is able to improve training interest as well as reduce the cognitive load produced by practicing cognitive tasks [10, 11]. Finally, with AR, the information about the surrounding real world of trainers becomes interactive and digitally manipulable; thus, trainers can manipulate the virtual objects to interact with the real environment, improving sensory feedback and their immersion in the training. As a result, AR is very efficacious and suitable to be adopted in visualization training system. Spatial visualization is an essential ability related to many aspects in one's normal life. In order to postpone the degradation time of this ability for older adults, we are devoted to designing an AR based spatial visualization training system for older adults to have more opportunities to train their visualization functions in usual time. In the long run, their spatial visualization ability gets improved, and they will confront less spatial problems in real life.

2   Related Work

Traditional training of spatial visualization requests trainers to conduct considerable paper-tests. Take one of spatial visualization criterion tests, Mental Rotation, for example. Trainers have to judge if two images are the same or mirrored through true/false paper tests. Many researchers also use computers to generate the stimuli and present them on LCD monitor in order to make them have more obvious depth cues such as shadowing or light effect [12, 13]. In some studies, animation is adopted to assist trainers' comprehension of motion process in an effort to improve their visualization ability more significantly [14]. In conclusion, existing training methods carried out in 2D medium such as paper or LCD monitors which are not favorable to illustrate spatial concepts for heavy mental load is produced in training process, causing inverse effect on trainers' learning interest and performance.

AR is widely used in educational domains as a new kind of learning tool because people can directly realize 3D concepts in AR rather than figure out 2D information from flat formats, which is beneficial to spatial visualization ability and dwindling cognitive load. Computerized magnetic principles and electromagnetism which are invisible in normal situation are displayed in AR; instead of being depicted in book pages, students are able to comprehend the principles in AR interfaces [15]. Some notions that are hard to be implemented into the real world such as the earth revolution [16] or the landscape visualization [10] are also suitable to be taught under AR. AR can also be applied to more professional disciplines. Engineering students directly train their visualization ability with virtual mechanical objects presented in AR books called AR-Dehaes. Compared with conventional orthographic images, students are allowed to see the integrated appearance of objects in AR-Dehaes [17]. Another example is Sonic Flashlight. It is an AR device which enables direct perceptual guidance of needle injection to achieve higher accuracy and lower variability in aiming and endpoint placements by presenting a virtual slice and the target directly within the personnel's vision area [17].

In spite of presenting virtual objects instantly, some AR systems allow participants to directly manipulate these virtual objects. Construct 3D is a mathematics and geometry instructive system implemented by AR. Students not only see the real geometry relation in augmented environment but also manipulate these virtual parts such as translating, rotating and scaling [18]. In a study of using AR to teach sun and earth relationship, participants are able to manipulate and interact with the virtual content [19], they are likely to understand the changes caused by different position and relation between sun and earth. Some researchers are devoted to creating more specific motions defined in AR environment so that participants can execute translation, scaling, rotation and other motions through fingers detection [20].

3   Method

AR spatial visualization training system consists of two parts: manual controller and training task. The design process of these two parts is illustrated individually as below. Furthermore, the integration of AR system is shown in this chapter.

3.1   Design of Manual Controller

A spatial visualization experiment with think aloud was adopted on older adults to collect mental strategies they used to handle the tasks. Next, we analyzed the manipulation and created morphological matrix to choose the best controller with specific principles such as intuition and convenience.

Manipulation Collecting

Participants. Six older adults (3 males and 3 females) ranging in age from 65 to 70 were recruited in the experiment. All of them were cognitively normal and passed Mini-Mental Status Examination [21].

Materials. Six revised tests based on Lohman's criterion tests [22] were used in the experiment. They were *Mental Rotation v.1 and v.2, 2D and 3D Paper Folding Test, Paper Form Board* and *Surface Development.* Each test contained two questions, resulting in a total of twelve questions for one participant (Fig. 1).

Procedures. In the setting, we prepared a projector to display testing tests and two cameras (one from the front, and the other from the back) to record the whole process. First, we explained the purpose of experiment and introduced spatial visualization ability. Besides, personal information of participants such as age, education and job was collected. Second, we introduced how to use think-aloud method in the experiment and encouraged participants to express their thought when they were answering questions. Third, participants were answering questions; meanwhile, we were recording

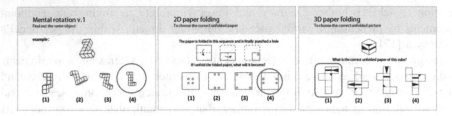

Fig. 1. Spatial visualization tests used in experiment

their speaking and sketching some specific gestures. After finishing each question, participants would be given paper models which were the same objects as those in questions, so they could express their thought again and checked the answer. The total time for each person was 40 min or so.

Gesture Analysis. After the experiment was finished, lots of manipulation and gestures were collected. In order to organize these gestures, they were analyzed by *Guessability* and *Agreement* theories [23]. Guessability was used to choose the best gesture representing the motion, and agreement was adopted to select the best motion used in the training process. Hence, the basic motions of dealing with spatial visualization tests were *Select*, *Rotate* and *Translate*. Also, the corresponding gestures with highest guessability scores were listed under each basic motion.

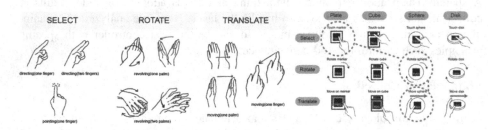

Fig. 2. Basic motions and morphological matrix

Idea Generation. Morphological matrix (Fig. 2) was adopted to generate ideas of manual controller. Three basic motions were on vertical row in morphological analysis matrix; the horizontal row was the form of controller (Plate, Sphere, Cube and Disk). Through brainstorming, possible ideas and interactive ways located in each block in matrix were developed. Next, ranking each idea in Likert scale (1-7 scores) was proceeded in order to find out the best manual controller which was elderly-friendly, we made a ranking table presented. By following three principles : intuition, convenience and aesthetics, the best manual controller would be chosen.

3.2   Design of Training Task

Design of a new training task follows a very analytic method. It is essential to realize what *spatial training factors* current spatial visualization tests were composed of. These factors are the basic units that trainers use to solve spatial related problems. After the factors are collected, we can combine some of them into a prototype and then add story or interesting elements to shape it into an integrated spatial visualization task.

Manipulation Collecting. This part was the same as the think aloud experiment conducted in the design of manual training.

Spatial Training Factors. The factors were in fact the result of mental strategies older adults had used in think aloud experiment. After classification, there were totally twelve spatial training factors which could be classified into four groups (Table 1): (1) *Checking*: to confirm shape, number, direction or angle of a pair of objects is same or not. (2) *Relation*: to compare the relation of position or to align virtual objects. (3) *Manipulation*: to manipulate virtual objects in mind, including rotate, fold, unfold, move and combine. (4) *Sequence*: to memorize the steps of any manipulation or operation.

Table 1. Spatial training factors of mental rotation v.1

	Checking				Relation		Manipulation					Sequence
	shape	number	direction	angle	position	align	rotate	fold	unfold	move	combine	steps
mental rotation v.1	●	●	△			●	●					

Idea Generation. In Table 1, black dots represent the current factors of tests. We added new factors (triangle) in different tests, and developed new tasks by combining different factors together. Take *Mental Rotation v.1* for example. Beside *checking shape, checking number, aligning* and *rotation, checking direction* is considered as a new spatial training factor in Mental Rotation v.1. Next, integrate these five factors and shape them into a new spatial visualization training task.

3.3   Integration of AR System

Software for Development. Qualcomm AR (QCAR) was adopted as the AR environment in the training system. It was a free AR SDK which was easy for developer to conduct coding and make interaction. Training system was constructed in Unity3D with Vuforia portal. Unity3D is a game developing engine which has been widely used to visualize the scene and make game and animation. With Vuforia attached in Unity3D, QCAR is able to be implemented (Fig. 3).

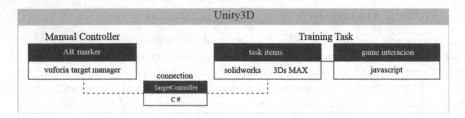

Fig. 3. Integration of AR spatial visualization training system

AR Marker for Manual Controller. *Vuforia Target Manager* is an online software for users to define patterns and form of AR markers. Since the basic motions are Rotate, Move and Select, a cube marker and two plate markers were chosen. First plate marker was used for displaying virtual objects; the second one was used for selecting objects; cube marker was used for rotating objects. If users rotate cube marker with the second plate marker pressed, the virtual objects will not rotate but move (Fig. 4).

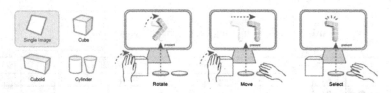

Fig. 4. (Left) options of AR markers in Vuforia target manager [24]. (Right) manipulation of three basic motions.

Training Task. Necessary items in task were constructed in Solidworks and were transformed into FBX files in 3Ds MAX. Items only in FBX extension can be imported to Unity3D. Connection was carried out by coding Target Controller scripts in C#. One Multi-Target Controller (for cube marker) and two Image-Target Controllers (for plate markers) are entailed. After inserting Target Controller scripts to the corresponding items, users are able to conduct functions by manipulating AR markers. Basically, three kinds of interaction are requested: speed adjustment, level change and incidents trigger. They are all coded in javascript and achieved by adopting box collider in Unity3D.

4   Result

4.1   AR Spatial Visualization Training System

AR spatial visualization training system was implemented in PC (Fig. 5). The system was composed of a set of manual controller including a cube marker and two plate markers, additional camera and a monitor. One thing that should be noticed was that

Fig. 5. Setting and scene of AR spatial visualization training system

Fig. 6. Training process of older adults

projecting route of camera was required to be the same direction as trainer's sight line so that virtual objects will not be the mirrored images.

After markers were projected, corresponding virtual objects would be displayed on monitor. Trainers were able to rotate cube marker to control the angle of virtual block, and pressed the second marker which presented a virtual red disk to make block fall through the hole of the virtual floor successfully. If the shape of block did not match that of hole, block would get stuck until trainers rotated the block in right angle. 20 levels were made in training tasks. These levels differed in shape of blocks and hole.

Even if older adults were allowed to use physical controller to rotate the block, they still entailed to consider which direction of block is correct, indicating the additional spatial factor: checking direction was being trained when they were receiving AR spatial visualization training (Fig. 6).

4.2 Feedback from Older Adults

We invited same older adults who had participated in the experiment of manual controller design to use the AR spatial visualization training system. They all agreed the positive training effect of AR training system. What they were in favor of were manual controller and game-alike task of AR training system, which enhanced their training interests and pleasure. In addition, two of them mentioned that it was even better when someone accompanied them when they were training. However, some thought the design of manual controller should be improved so that they could manipulate it more fluently. Besides, they were not very satisfied with much equipment of current system.

Most older adults did not prefer paper tests; what they worried about were their reaction time and error rate. Similar to conventional test, older adults would suffer from great pressure of the scores, which made them frustrated. Furthermore, they might not get used to focusing on text or pictures for a long time, which was one of demerits of paper tests. Since the question of tests were associated with the manipulation of objects, they would like to manipulate a real object rather than handle mentally. Nevertheless, although older adults did not agree the form of paper tests, they admitted the brain fitness of it.

5 Discussion and Conclusion

In this paper, we followed the comprehensive design methods to implement an AR based spatial visualization training system for older adults. Since spatial visualization ability is essential to older adults, we transformed the conventional spatial visualization test into game-alike task which were more suitable for them to keep training their spatial visualization ability. The implementation of controller and AR was also conducive to the improvement of training effect, their training immersion and interest.

5.1 Manual Controller and Implemented Device

Based on the opinion of older adults, cube marker was not appropriate for them to manipulate. However, since available marker forms on Vuforia target manager were limited, we might consider a transparent spherical shell to wrap cube marker. Hence, patterns on marker were able to be projected; the spherical shell could be better for older adults to conduct rotation which was the chief type of manipulation in AR training system.

Some older adults argued the inconvenience of much equipment of AR training system in PC version. For most older people who would prefer handy and small devices, it might be sensible to develop AR training system into APP in tablet version. Tablets were more ideal for older adults to take and use; additionally, they were able to conduct training at all times. In fact, older groups were occupying more and more proportion in people using mobile devices. Around 80 percent of people ranging in age 50 to 70 used tablets in normal times. Hence, developing AR training system in APP would be a favorable idea.

5.2 Training Task

Existing training task was based on mental rotation; other types of training tasks were likely to be developed in the future. We could combine more spatial training factors and integrated into different training tasks; for example, tasks derived from *3D paper folding* or *paper form board*, making AR spatial visualization training system more comprehensive and diverse.

According to previous studies, it was favorable that the items in training corresponded to target trainers. For instance, if trainers were children, items may likely turn into other meaningful images such as animal's patterns, cartoon pictures or letter [26, 27]. This would promote target trainers' familiarity and indirectly improve their training immersion as well.

Two older adults mentioned it would be better if someone accompanied them when they were training. It triggers us to develop multi-player mode in the future. Especially for older adults, the feeling of companion will be a critical issue when designers developed products. If two or more people are allowed to join the training tasks, older adults will be more willing to take training and gain more happiness. Thus, we may consider to design multi-player mode of training task.

In sum, AR based spatial visualization training system was an innovative brain fitness tool for older adults. With the exceptional features of AR, we were interested to adopted this multimedia technique to develop an unconventional training system to help maintain spatial ability for older adults. Since current feedback from older adults was positive, we were motivated to improve AR training system and qualified the data of their training performance in order to testify the spatial visualization training effect of AR based training system.

References

1. Hedden, T., Gabrieli, J.D.E.: Insights into the ageing mind: a view from cognitive neuroscience. Nat. Rev. Neurosci. 5(2), 87–96 (2004)
2. De Beni, R., Pazzaglia, F., Gardini, S.: The role of mental rotation and age in spatial perspective taking tasks when age does not impair perspective taking performance. Appl. Cogn. Psychol. 20, 807–821 (2006)
3. Lee, S., Kline, R.: Wayfinding study in virtual environments: the elderly vs the younger-aged groups. Int. J. Architectural Res. 5(2), 63–76 (2011)
4. Jenkins, L., et al.: Converging evidence that visuospatial cognition is more age-sensitive than verbal cognition. 2000 (0882–7974 (Print))
5. Peich, M.-C., Husain, M., Bays, P.M.: Age-related decline of precision and binding in visual working memory. 2013 (1939–1498 (Electronic))
6. Hertzog, C., et al.: Enrichment effects on adult cognitive development: can the functional capacity of older adults be preserved and enhanced? Psychol. Sci. Public Interest 9(1), 1–65 (2008)
7. Mowszowski, L., Batchelor, J., Naismith, S.L.: Early intervention for cognitive decline: can cognitive training be used as a selective prevention technique? Int. Psychogeriatr. 22(4), 537–548 (2010)
8. Chandler, P., Sweller, J.: Cognitive load theory and the format of instruction. Cogn. Instr. 8(4), 293–332 (1991)
9. Martín-Gutiérrez, J., et al.: Design and validation of an augmented book for spatial abilities development in engineering students. Computers Graphics 34(1), 77–91 (2010)
10. Hedley, N.R.: Empirical Evidence of Advanced Geographic Visualization Interface Use (2003)
11. Shelton, B.E., Hedley, N.R.: Exploring a cognitive basis for learning spatial relationships with augmented reality. Technol. Instr. Cogn. Learn. 1, 323–357 (2004)
12. McCarthy, A.L.: Improving older adults' mental rotation skills through computer training. University of Akron (2010)

13. Chu, M., Kita, S.: The nature of gestures' beneficial role in spatial problem solving. Journal of Experimental Psychology. 2011 (1939–2222 (Electronic))
14. Rafi, A., Samsudin, K.: Practising mental rotation using interactive desktop mental rotation trainer (iDeMRT). Br. J. Educ. Technol. **40**(5), 889–900 (2009)
15. Dünser, A., et al.: Creating interactive physics education books with augmented reality. In: Proceedings of the 24th Australian Computer-Human Interaction Conference, ACM (2012)
16. Kerawalla, L., et al.: Making it real: exploring the potential of augmented reality for teaching primary school science. Virtual Reality **10**(3–4), 163–174 (2006)
17. Klatzky, R.L., et al.: Effectiveness of augmented-reality visualization versus cognitive mediation for learning actions in near space. ACM Trans. Appl. Percept. **5**(1), 1–23 (2008)
18. Kaufmann, H., Schmalstieg, D.: Mathematics And Geometry Education With Collaborative Augmented Reality. Comput. Graph. **37**(3), 339–345 (2003)
19. Shelton, B.E., Hedley, N.R.: Using Augmented Reality for Teaching Earth-Sun Relationships to Undergraduate Geography Students, IEEE (2002)
20. Piumsomboon, T., Clark, A., Billinghurst, M., Cockburn, A.: User-defined gestures for augmented reality. In: Kotzé, P., Marsden, G., Lindgaard, G., Wesson, J., Winckler, M. (eds.) INTERACT 2013, Part II. LNCS, vol. 8118, pp. 282–299. Springer, Heidelberg (2013)
21. Folstein, M.F., Folstein, S.E., McHugh, P.R.: Mini-mental state: A practical method for grading the cognitive state of patients for the clinician. J. Psychiatr. Res. **12**(3), 189–198 (1975)
22. Lohman, D.F.: Spatial abilities as traits, processes, and knowledge (1988)
23. Wobbrock, J.O., et al.: Maximizing the guessability of symbolic input. In: CHI2005 Extended Abstracts on Human Factors in Computing Systems. ACM (2005)
24. Vuforia (2015). https://developer.vuforia.com/
25. Kratochwill, T.R.: Single Subject Research: Strategies For Evaluating Change. Academic Press, New York (1978)
26. Funk, M., Brugger, P., Wilkening, F.: Motor processes in children's imagery: The case of mental rotation of hands. Dev. Sci. **8**(5), 402–408 (2005)
27. Jansen, P., et al.: Mental rotation performance in primary school age children: Are there gender differences in chronometric tests? Cogn. Dev. **28**(1), 51–62 (2013)

The Effectiveness of Virtual Reality
for Studying Human Behavior in Fire

Xinxin Feng[(⊠)], Rongzhen Cui, and Jiabao Zhao

Beijing University of Civil Engineering and Architecture, Beijing, China
fengxinxin@bucea.edu.cn, ccrz246@126.com,
haojiabaohao@163.com

Abstract. In this study, a virtual environment of fire condition was designed and implemented to support the research of the human behavior under anxiety states. The results gathered from this experimental platform were compared to the data from real fire condition to verification the effectiveness of the information provided from this virtual platform. The Correlation coefficient is 0.9958, which indicate that the simulation system is highly practical in research of human behavior under pressure condition. Conclusion could be made that virtual environment based on cave virtual display system is suitable for simulation of fire condition.

Keywords: Fire condition · Virtual reality · Environmental stress

1 Introduction

Environmental stress is initially raised as a technical term in the field of psychology. But this word appeared frequently in human factors engineering in recent years, since the behavior of human being under anxiety condition is much more different from the normal condition. And the stressors of environmental stress can be divided into disaster stress and background stress.

There are mainly two types of environmental stress, one is the disaster stress, and the other is the background stress. Fire condition is a typical circumstance which can arouse disaster stress [1]. The study of human behavior under fire condition is very important in fire rescue and evacuation.

There are many ways to simulate a fire circumstance; the most common one is the fire drill. But it is usually difficult to call a fire drill for its costs and other difficulties. And for safe sake, the fire drill usually cannot arouse enough stress for the subjects since the hazard of real smoke and fire is hard to control. Alternative ways of fire drill is very necessary in studying disaster stress. Full size entities simulation can be the substituted of real scene, but due to the difficulty and the costs of it, this methods can only be set up for specific purpose and special place. Virtual reality is an alternative method of fire drill. Since the virtual 3 dimension environment is easy to implement than the real stage, the danger and the costs in fire research can reduce a lot. Also there are not so much limits for the site of fire disaster in virtual environment.

© Springer International Publishing Switzerland 2015
R. Shumaker and S. Lackey (Eds.): VAMR 2015, LNCS 9179, pp. 13–21, 2015.
DOI: 10.1007/978-3-319-21067-4_2

2 Virtual Reality in Fire Condition Simulation

2.1 The Theory of Stress

The word stress was first appeared in the field of psychology, means a set of non-specific body adaptation responses to the stimulation from both internal and external environment factors, called stress reaction also. Those internal and external environment factors went by the general name of stress source, or stressor. Stress is generated by unexpected urgent and dangerous situations that can cause a highly stressful state. Environment stress refers to the external factors. There are two kinds of external stress, one is the nature stressor such as extreme cold, hot, light, damp and so on; the other is artificial stressor such as stroboflash, radial, noise and so on. When subjects exposed to the environment stress, their instinct responses is to relief them from these stress.

Fire condition is a typical environment stress. The features of high temperature, smoke, light, and the threat of death are all obvious characteristic of environment stress [2]. It is a very good way to test and verify the applicability of the virtual reality in human reactor researching by constructing a virtual fire disaster situation and collecting people's behavior in it. And there is also important realistic meaning in studying the fire condition, such as how to design the eye-catching safety warning marks in public place, Evacuation route settings, researching of crowd behavior and so on.

2.2 The Research of Virtual Reality in Environmental Stress

Virtual reality is a technology that combines computer since, digital graphics, three dimensional displays and other new techniques both in software and hardware. It can give people a virtual 3 dimensional world based on computer simulation which provides salutations of visual, auditory, tactile and other sensory. These set of experiences combine together to create a highly immersive environment to make people feel that they are in the real scene. Immersive, unlimited and randomness are the characters of virtual reality, and these are highly compatible to the fire condition simulation which needs a lot of randomness and immersive [3].

Research in this field can be traced back to 1993 in Britain; a simulation system called VEGAS is developed to simulate the escaping behavior under the fire condition using 3 dimension simulation technologies. In China, there is also some research of virtual reality using in fire escaping or other disaster. Liu kun and Wang guan sheng of Beijing university of technology designed a training system for the fire condition using the 3 dimension real time rendering [2]. Shen yi li put virtual reality technology into the reach of earthquakes [2]. These researches mostly focused on the evocation and crowd activity, but ignored the consistency of experimental condition to the real situation, in another word, the realness of the simulation.

More and more new technology of virtual reality is put forward in recent years, such as CAVE, RAVE system. CAVE is a projection system with 3 to 5 sides of rare projection as the sides of a cube to construct a space like a cave. In this space, people can observe a virtual scene with stereo glasses. Since the closure of the viewing environment, it can provide a highly realistic feeling of the virtual scene. RAVE can be interpreted as an extensible CAVE, which can open the sides of the cube into 180 degrees, 135 degrees and 90 degrees (as a CAVE). Based on this physical structure, work in with high resolution graphics and the active stereos projection together, a highly immersive and authentic experiment system can be built much more real than before.

Subjects in this experiment system will be put into the CAVE space, surrounded with light, color and sound. All these features will give subjects feeling of nervous especially in simulating a condition of fire. The compliance of the virtual experiment and the real scene is the focus of this research. By compare the data gathered in both virtual environment and real scene can estimate the effectiveness of the experiment system.

All these new technology makes the virtual reality more and more real. By using virtual scene, some research that cant or hard to realize in real world can carry on in the virtual world. Research of human factors engineering in dangerous or rare situation, such as nuclear reactor, large construction site and so on, can be put forward easily. But the realness of the simulation and the availability of the data gathered in the virtual scene are still not quantitative evaluated.

2.3   The Software Development Environment

A virtual experiment system of fire simulation has the following conditions: high reality sensation, flexible interaction and living fire and smoke effect. There are several software that aimed at fire simulation such as FDS (Fire Dynamics Simulator) CFAST (The Consolidated Model of Fire And Smoke Transport) ALOFT-FTTM (A Large Outdoor Fire plume Trajectory model - Flat Terrain). FDS is a well-known fire simulator tool for the fire protection engineering field, which can accurately calculate the temporal and spatial distribution of physical quantity, to simulate fire exactly. CFAST is used to calculate the temperature, smoke concentration within up to 30 rooms. ALOFT-FTTM is focused on the outdoor fire disaster. These software are all with very specific focus. They focus more on the physical quantity of the fire, but not the feeling of subjects in a fire disaster. So a new experiment system that aimed at built a highly immersive environment and collecting the data of subjects is needed in this case.

A high rise building fire is simulated in this subject. To meet the need of immersive, Unity 3D was choose as the virtual reality engine. Although there are several virtual reality engines to choose, but the following characters make Unity 3D the best choice. First, an outstanding rendering result can enhance the realness of the virtual scene; second, the programing part can base on the C# language which means a wide range of compatibility; third, the physical engine is a pre-programed modular that can simulate the physical aspect of the real world such as gravity, collision and interference; fourth, a powerful partition system is very suitable for simulation of fire and smoke. The application framework of unity3D makes it very flexible to create more complex interaction and more random situation. To enlarge the range of subjects, two versions are needed for the experiment. One is based on the CAVE application for local user, the other is based on web for long-range user. Unity 3D can satisfy this need just with one program since the virtual scene built with unity 3D can be released to a wide range of application.

3 Developing Structure of the Experimental Platform

Any virtual scene is based on the 3D modeling. There are mainly two way to complete the modeling, one is based on the parametric; the other is based on the polygon. Usually parametric modeling is used in mechanical design, and focused in the topological relations of the different machine parts; polygon modeling is used in figure and scene modeling mostly appeared in game development, 3D max is a typical representative. In this case, Inventor is used for the modeling, then export to 3D max to change from parametric mode to polygon mode and reduce the facet. Only format of .fbx is acceptable for Unity 3D, so the model must export as .fbx by 3D max. The framework for developing program is as Fig. 1.

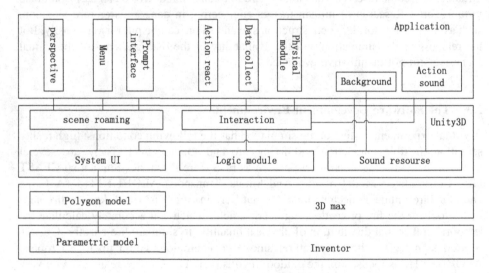

Fig. 1. Developing structure

The Fig. 1 just shows the developing structure of the program, but under web condition, communication with client is also needed. The 3D scene created was finally put into a JSP framework; subject's behavior will communicate with JSP and recorded directly into the server's database through net. All the recording and analyzing are done by the server.

There are 2 problems in the programing. First, time demand is quite strict under web application. Virtual reality usually consumes a lot of system resources and may cause the pause of Execution which will influence the experiment result a lot. To avoid this, a caching mechanism was used in this system. All the scene data will download into the client machine. During the test, there's no data upload. When test ending, all the data gathered will send to the server as one data structure. Second, the sense of reality is important during the interacting. Full application of the physical engine of Unity 3D can add lot of realness to the scene. Gravity is added to any non-stationary object, and collision test is added to the door or window. Thus, any movement in this space is just like real.

4   Design of the Scene

As the research objectives, there are several features of fire in high rise building. First, Fire can spread easily in more ways in high rise building, air conditioning systems, electrical systems and chimney effect can all increase the speed of fire spread; Second, evacuation difficulties, usually the speed of evacuation is much slower than the speed of smoke spreading for the long vertical evacuation distance and high population density; Third, in most cases the only escaping way is the stairs cause the elevator shaft is usually the thoroughfare of smoke [1, 5, 6]. These features of high rise building make the escaping ways as following. Residents can take advantage of the facilities in the building, such as fire elevator, stairwell, balcony, refuge floors and so on; or they can follow the instruction of the fire radio, if the building has this facility; Or Self-help and mutual aid escape will carry on, like sheets, curtains and the pipes to escape. Facilities in the virtual room should be set Compliant for these conditions to make the experiment can meet the real situation.

In this virtual experiment platform, a typical indoor scene of an apartment is the most important virtual scene. The first 10 min in the fire disaster is usually the most important even decided whether the escaping can achieve or not. So the experiment focus on the choice that people made in the first 10 min [3]. We have set some daily necessities in this scene. Cell phone, television, phone, curtain, sheet, rope, floor maps of the building and so on were putting in the room, to provide clue of escaping. People for escaping can choose waiting for the instruction, or self-help, or get information from the TV or radio. The sight of the door and the window also provide clues like smoke, fire or light. So the modeling and the programing are mostly focused on these things.

The typical indoor scene of the high rise building was modeling as Fig. 2.

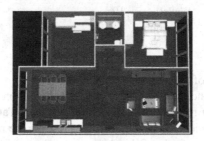

Fig. 2. Inside room structure

The fire and smoke is finished with the partition system of unity 3D. The basic theory of the partition system is redrawing 1 to 2 materials again and again to create chaotic effects. Particle systems typically include a particle emitter in an object, a particle animator player and a particle renderer, if interaction with other objects is needed, a particle collider should be added to objects. In this case, to simulate the real fire effect, the particle collider is most important. All the walls was added with particle colliders, when the smoke or fire collide with the wall, barrier and reflection will occur, thus the real smoke and fire effect can be simulated.

5   Simulation and Analysis

5.1   Simulation

200 subjects were randomly selected to the experiment in this virtual experiment platform. Their behavior were recorded into the database. Also a questionnaire is asked to fill after experiment. In these 200 results, effective experimental number is 176, the total completion rate is 88 %. There are 16 people unfinished the experiment due to the stress or other questions, and another 8 people just give up the experiment.

The experiment gives 10 min to the subject; the first objects choose by the subjects will indicate the escaping mean of them. Such as, if they choose to open the television, maybe they want to get information about the situation thus they tent to wait for farther information; if they choose the cell phone, maybe they also want information about the fire, but have more motivation to escaping; if they choose the rope, maybe they want to save themselves immediately; if they choose the door or window, they want to call for help.

The results of first choose object is shown in Table 1.

Table 1. First choice of the subjects

Choice	Number of subjects
door	63
cellphone	20
laptop	7
towel	25
rope	11
extinguisher	19
basin	17
Wallet	10
No action	4

The praetor diagram of the first choice is as Fig. 3.

To find out the difference from the real fire to the simulation, these data is compared with the data collected in real fire disaster. The result is as Table 2.

The correlation coefficient r was introduced to resolve the relation of these two set of data [7]. Quantitative analysis of the data was reviewed by this r. It is a number between -1 to 1; when it is positive, the relevant two sides are proportional; when it is negative, the relevant two sides are inversely proportional; when it close to 0, there are almost no relationship with the relevant two sides. The formula to calculate r is

$$r = \frac{\sum_i a_i b_i}{\sqrt{\sum_i a_i^2}\sqrt{\sum_i b_i^2}}.$$

The coefficient a_i and b_i are the data from virtual scene and real fire condition. The final result r is 0.9958, which means that these two data is highly proportional.

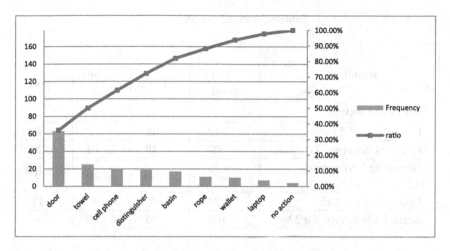

Fig. 3. Praetor diagram of the first choice

Table 2. Difference from the real fire to the simulation

Item / scene	Escaping directly / door	Contact with outside			Choose items		distinguish		Pack up / wallet	No action
		Cell phone	laptop	Towel	rope	distin-guisher	basin		
virtual (%)	35.80	11.36	3.98	14.20	6.25	10.80	9.66	5.68	2.27
		15.34		20.45		20.46			
Real (%)	38.1	16.82		17.04		20.9		4.44	2.7

In another word, the experiment data gathered from the virtual scene is greatly degree with the real fire disaster. This indicates that in research of people's action in fire condition, virtual experiment can take place of the real data.

5.2 Analysis of Interview

Only the data gathered in the experiment is not enough to determine whether the virtual reality can represent the real condition, the subjective feelings of the subjects are also very important in evaluating the usability of the system. Interview was put to the 176 subjects who has finished the experiment completely focused on their subjective feeling, opinions and suggestions of the system. The results gathered in Table 3.

Using fuzzy comprehensive evaluation method, the data was analyzed and calculated by the formulas as [8]:

$$Gradation = \frac{evaluation}{totalnumber}.$$

General Gradation = $\sum$ Gradation * weight.

Overall result = $\sum$ General Gradation * Score.

Table 3. Interview results table

Result　　　level Project and weight	Very good	Good	gen-eral	poor
Fire effct（0.2）	112	48	12	4
Optional items set（0.2）	78	38	40	20
Operating Performance（0.25）	107	40	20	9
Room effect（0.15）	121	36	8	11
Scene authenticity（0.2）	106	46	16	8

Thus comes to the Table 4.

Table 4. Overall result

Result　　　level Project and weight	Very good	Good	gen-eral	poor
Fire effct（0.2）	0. 64	0. 27	0. 07	0. 02
Optional items set（0.2）	0. 44	0. 22	0. 23	0. 11
Operating Performance（0.25）	0. 61	0. 23	0. 11	0. 05
Room effect（0.15）	0. 60	0. 26	0. 09	0. 05
Scene authenticity（0.2）	0. 61	0. 26	0. 09	0. 04
General Gradation	0.59	0.24	0.12	0.06
Overall score	90.28			

The Overall score of the experiment is 90.28, which shows that the subjects are satisfied with the virtual scene. This result indicates that using virtual reality technique in research of environment stress is a very effective way. But there are still some problems in this experiment system. Since the subjects know the purpose of the experiment before, they will not be panic as the real fire, so the items they choose are more rational. The other problem is the movement of the fire and smoke can only preset before experiment and cannot happen randomly, which is not as the real situation.

With virtual equipment providing more immersive feeling, people can get better experience in the virtual scene. Algorithms about movement of smoke and fire can make the fire circumstance more vivid.

6 Conclusion

By introducing virtual reality technique into the research of people's reaction in fire condition, a new method of studying environment stress is tested. The result shows that it is quite close to the actual situation. Unity 3D is quite adapt to establish the virtual scene for researching in human factors engineering, as a substitute of those experiments that is hard or even impossible to carry on.

More research should be taken on the following aspect: the sense of reality, location tracking and interactive equipment, which can promote the effect a lot.

The research project presented in this paper is a part of the Project "Key technologies of safety precaution of crane operation based on human factors engineering", which was supported by the Beijing Municipal Commission of Education. The authors would like to acknowledge the support of the Beijing Municipal Commission of Education for this project (KM201410016004).

References

1. Hartanto, D., Kampmann, I.L.: Controlling social stress in virtual reality environments. PLoS ONE 9(3), 1–17 (2014)
2. Fuzhen L.:.Research and Implementation of Virtual Campus System [D]. Chengdu: Southwest Jiaotong University (2008)
3. Johnson, S.J., Guediri, S.M., Kilkenny, C.: Development and validation of a virtual reality simulator: human factors input to interventional radiology training. Hum. Factors J. Hum. Factors Ergon. Soc. 53(6), 612–625 (2011)
4. Moohyun, C., Soonhung, H., Jaikyung, L., Byungil, C.: A virtual reality based fire training simulator integrated with fire dynamics data. Fire Saf. J. 14, 4727–5012 (2012)
5. McGrattan, K.: Fire dynamics simulator (Version 4),User's guide [EB/OL] (03-06-2006). http://fire.nist.gov/fds
6. Moreno, A., Posada, J.: Interactive fire spread simulations with extinguishment support for Virtual Reality training tools. Fire Saf. J. 64, 48–60 (2014)
7. Nandita, S., Tom, G.: Modeling observer stress for typical real environments. Expert Sys. Appl. 41, 2231–2238 (2014)
8. Yili, S., Yang, C., Tianshi, L.: Virtual reality system for earthquake (M). J. Sys. Simul. 14(11), 1509–1512 (2011)

Pilot Study for Telepresence with 3D-Model in Mixed Reality

Sungchul Jung$^{(\boxtimes)}$ and Charles E. Hughes

Computer Science and Institute for Simulation and Training,
University of Central Florida, Orlando, USA
sungchul@knights.ucf.edu, ceh@cs.ucf.edu

Abstract. In this paper we present the results of an experiment investigating a participant's sense of presence by examining the correlation between visual information and physical actions in a mixed reality environment. There have been many approaches to measure presence in a virtual reality environment, such as the "Pit" experiment, a physiological presence experiment that used a person's fear of heights to test body ownership. The studies reported in these prior works were conducted to measure the extent to which a person feels physical presence in virtual worlds [1–3]. Here, we focus on situational plausibility and place illusion in mixed reality, where real and virtual content coexist [4]. Generally, the phenomenon we are studying is called *telepresence*: an aroused sensation of 'being together in the same real location' between users [5].

Keywords: Telepresence · Mixed reality · Situational plausibility · Place illusion · Co-presence

1 Introduction

Prior research has studied improving the sensation of telepresence by using high-resolution displays or by providing a physical manifestation via a simple robot with a video monitor on which the participant's face is shown [6, 7]. However, using only a video stream, it may be difficult to provide the sensation that a user is in the partner's location even when the user feels the partner is with him or her. Other work has attempted to enhance presence using augmented reality techniques [8–10]. We designed and conducted our experiment to examine the sense of telepresence a person has with a partner in a mixed reality environment. We hypothesize that the reasons a user will not experience the sensation of telepresence are, at least in part, due to constraints on visual information and a disagreement between a user's visual information and his or her actions. First, the visual information provided must give the user a sensation of actually being in a particular environment (place illusion). Moreover, a user will likely have a diminished sense of telepresence if their physical actions – such as moving their arms – do not result in an appropriate visual change (situational plausibility) [4]. Finally, even when users perform physical actions, they will feel less present if these actions do not result in corresponding physical changes in their partner's location. To test these assumptions, we designed the following experiment (Fig. 1).

© Springer International Publishing Switzerland 2015
R. Shumaker and S. Lackey (Eds.): VAMR 2015, LNCS 9179, pp. 22–29, 2015.
DOI: 10.1007/978-3-319-21067-4_3

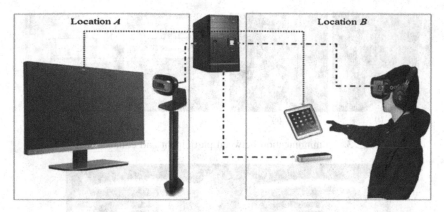

Fig. 1. System setup

2 Experimental Design

We used a head-mounted display (HMD) for immersion by fixing the participant's viewpoint to the collaborator's location, which was in a different room. A camera in the collaborator's room was connected to the participant's HMD. We asked the participant to perform simple cooperative tasks with the collaborator using a control device in his or her location to control a screen located in the collaborator's room. We hypothesize that participants will feel a higher degree of presence if they see their own hands and fingers during these interactions. To verify this hypothesis, we carried out an experiment with three cases.

2.1 System Design

First, we used a virtual model of the participant's hands to mimic his or her actions and displayed the model on the HMD. In the second case, we used a generic hand model

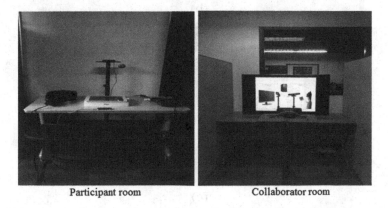

Participant room   Collaborator room

Fig. 2. Experiment rooms

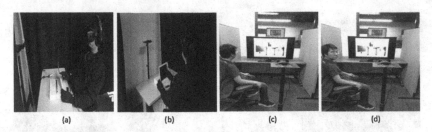

Fig. 3. Communication between participant and collaborator

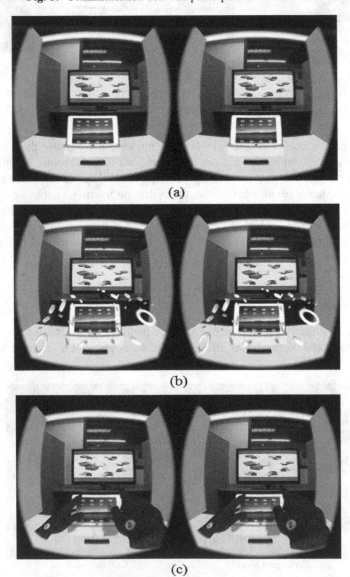

Fig. 4. (a) A case using no displayed hand model (b) A case using a generic hand model (c) A case using the participant's hand model.

that looks like a skeleton. Finally, we conducted one case using no displayed hand model. The experimental room has a Leap Motion to track the participant's hand and finger movements. The experimental setup, including the Leap Motion and control device in the participant's room and the camera and screen in the collaborator's room, is shown in (Fig. 2).

The collaborator sits in front of a camera and performs tasks with the participant and sometimes looks into the camera or interacts with the screen that the participant controls (Fig. 3). In this way, we aim to provide the participant with the sensation that the collaborator is sitting right next to him or her.

While the participant controls the screen, the collaborator also prompts him or her to perform simple gestures involving the participant moving his or her arms (Fig. 4).

Before starting the experiment, we asked the participant to fill out a demographic questionnaire. We also had the participant fill out simple experience questionnaires during each of the three experimental cases. A final questionnaire following the experiment asked the participant to compare these three cases. In this study, we assume that participants will experience a greater sensation of presence when they see their own body parts on the HMD corresponding to their actions. This study is preliminary to work we are carrying out that involves inhabiting a remote robot, seeing everything from the robot's perspective except for one's own body parts. To develop the experimental environment, we used Unity as a platform and used Mono for the IDE on a Windows 7 64-bit, AMD Phenom™ X4 B95 3.00 GHz PC with 6 GB RAM.

2.2 Task

We asked participants to perform a simple task: counting a number of objects and solving math problems with small numbers. During the task, the participant answered the questions on each slide displayed on a remote screen seen through the HMD and controlled by the participant's hands. While the participant controls the display screen and answers the questions, the collaborator interacts with the participant, providing verification for the participant's answer. For instance, the collaborator might ask the participant "how many blue cube do you see?" or "what is the result of the equation?" and then the collaborator verifies or corrects the answers given by the participant (Fig. 5).

2.3 Questionnaire Design

We designed a set of questionnaires similar to those in Lessiter, J., et al. [11]. The set is composed of four parts: sense of physical space, engagement, control and negative effect. Each category has two or three questions with answers selected on a five-point Likert scale. Before beginning the experiment, we asked participants to fill out a demographic form; after the end of each experiment, we asked participants to fill out an experience questionnaire consisting of interval scale questions. After finishing the last experiment, each participant completed a final questionnaire consisting of comparison

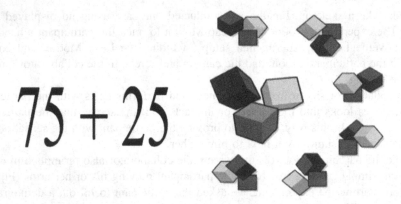

Fig. 5. Example of task contents

questions between the three types of experimental conditions. This final questionnaire uses a five-point scale as well.

3 Result and Discussion

In this section, we show results that include graphs of the interval questions, categorical questions and final questions for comparison and discussions. Since the purpose of our paper is to report on the formative phase of a more extensive study associated with enhancing telepresence through an increased sense of body ownership, we conducted the experiment with a small number of people. The participants have different background knowledge on computers, virtual reality, and the concept of telepresence. To show only the preference of each different experimental condition, we did not apply an analytical method but used a simple tally. To create the preference chart, we counted the number of one to five Likert score responses for each question for each of the three cases. Figure 6 displays the questions we asked. We conjecture that a personal model gives the most sense of telepresence as indicated by the results depicted in the first graph item that is associated with the interval question 'You had the feeling that you were in a different room'. Also, having no model has the most negative effect: dizzy and unnatural control (tenth and eleventh bar in (Fig. 6)). These results make sense because the participants felt they were in the collaborator's room, communicating with the collaborator using an iPad to control the screen, but they did not see any part of their own body in that context.

However, there were no significant differences between each of the three cases in the remaining questions because we had so few participants. To address this weakness, we represent the categorical graph, which is a summation of each question in four categories to show participant preferences concisely (Fig. 7). As one can see, in the graph of the first category, 'Sense of Physical Space (Being there)', our participants perceived that using the personal model, the generic model and no model ranked high to low, respectively. Surprisingly, though, using a personal model has the lowest score in the third category, 'Ease of Control'. This may relate to the fact that participants

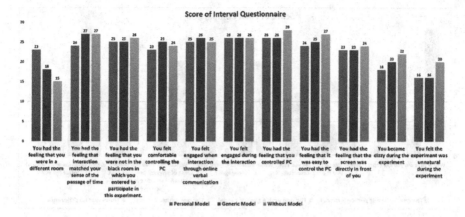

Fig. 6. Questionnaires result

sometimes saw uncontrolled finger or hand movement when they tried to manipulate the iPad screen by touch, since the Leap Motion does not detect hand motion very well. After finishing all experiments, participants mentioned the personal model case was not working correctly to control the hand, making it confusing to control the iPad screen. Actually, since we used the same skeleton model for the personal model as the generic model but with a different texture, it should have had similar tracking and rendering performance. However, participants did not perceive control to be weak with the generic model, perhaps because the model consisted of only a simple skeleton whereas the personal model had an explicit hand model with texture, so the lack of control was more obvious to the participants. The fourth category graph shows an interesting result: the total score is relatively low since we have two questions for the fourth category while the others have three questions each. The lack of a model caused the participants to experience negative effects while controlling the physical screen via an iPad; these included feeling dizzy or perceiving unnatural movement, as seen in (Fig. 6).

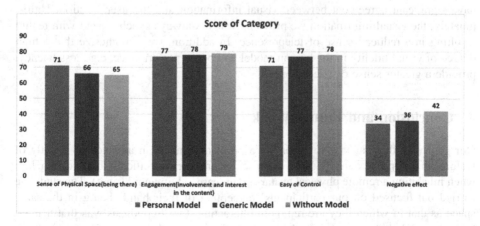

Fig. 7. Categorical questionnaire result

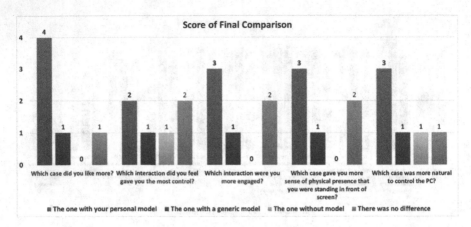

Fig. 8. Final result

To enhance the sense of telepresence, any disagreement between a user's visual information and his or her actions is an important factor because of its negative effects. However, we did not encounter a remarkable distinction in the second category of (Fig. 7), 'Engagement (involvement and interest in the content)'. We assume the reason is that, in all cases, the participants felt presence in the collaborator room.

Finally, we provide a comparison among the three cases (Fig. 8). According to these results, we conclude that using the participant's personal model enhances presence in a remote context. This is supported by our participants' responses to most questions, which indicate that a personal model is preferred and feels most natural. There is however a contrary indication in the ratings of ease of control where the absence of any model achieved the highest score (Fig. 7). Because the answers displayed in (Fig. 8) were provided by participants after all experiments were completed, some graphs do not agree with (Fig. 7), especially when one looks at the second and third graphs in (Fig. 8). However, we still believe that participants have more sense of telepresence when they use their personal model to interact with a collaborator if they have significant agreement between visual information and the user's action. Unfortunately, the visual information we provided was not always synchronized with reality resulting in a reduced sense of telepresence. In addition, we hypothesize that a high degree of visual fidelity in the human model and better performance, e.g., less latency, provide a greater sense of telepresence.

4 Conclusion and Future Work

Our goal with this paper is to report on a proof of concept in advance of a study of features that improve a user's sense of presence, and very specifically body ownership, when inhabiting a remote physical avatar (in our case, a humanoid robot). The study we carried out focused on our participants' perception of their hands being in the same space as that in which they are remotely interacting. Our hypothesis was that using a human model that accurately reflects the appearance and actions of a user's body improves one's sense of telepresence. To investigate this hypothesis, we designed and implemented a system in which we conducted a simple experiment. The results generally support our assumption that proper correlation between visual information and physical actions by a user will enhance the sense of telepresense. However, there were unfortunate confounds in our study due to inaccurate tracking of the user's hands and fingers. This adversely affected our participant's control of visual information in the remote environment, leading to some unexpected and counterintuitive findings. As with all formative studies, the goal here was to find deficiencies in the experiment's design, and so our focus for the next version of the system will include improved quality of tracking and rendering. In our next stage we will use a humanoid robot that mimics a user's movement. To enhance the sense of telepresence, we will blend the robot's view of the remote environment with the user's body, so that the participant perceives his or her own body in the remote context. We expect this future system will enhance the sense of telepresence and improve the user's sense of place illusion (my body is in this remote place) and situational plausibility (my actions have appropriate consequences in this remote place) [4].

References

1. Meehan, M., Insko, B., Whitton, M., Brooks, Jr., F.: Physiological measures of presence in stressful virtual environments. In: Proceeding SIGGRAPH 2002, Proceedings of the 29th Annual Conference on Computer Graphics and Interactive Techniques, pp. 645–652 (2002)
2. Slater, M., Perez-Marcos, D., Ehrsson, H., Sanchez-Vives, M.: Inducing illusory ownership of a virtual body. Front Neurosci. **3**(2), 214–220 (2009)
3. Pomés, A., Slater, M.: Drift and ownership toward a distant virtual body. Front. Hum. Neurosci. **7**, Article 908, 1–11 (2013)
4. Slater, M.: Place illusion and plausibility can lead to realistic behaviour in immersive virtual environments. Philos. Trans. R. Soc. B: Biol. Sci. **364**, 3549–3557 (2009)
5. Hollan, J., Stornetta, S.: Beyond being there. In: Proceedings of the SIGCHI Conference on Human Factors in Computing Systems, pp. 119–125. ACM, New York (1992)
6. Tsui, M.K., Desai, M.A., Yanco, H., Uhlik, C.: Exploring use cases for telepresence robots. In: HRI 2011, Proceedings of the 6th International Conference on Human-Robot Interaction, pp. 11–18 (2011)
7. Tsui, M.K., Norton, A., Brooks, D.A., Yanco, H., Kontak, D.: Designing telepresence robot systems for use by people with special needs. In: International Symposium on Quality of Life Technologies (2011)
8. Souza Almeida, I., Atsumi Oikawa, M., Carres, J.P., Miyazaki, J., Kato, H., Billinghurst, M.: AR-based video-mediated communication. In: Proceeding SVR 2012, Proceedings of the 2012 14th Symposium on Virtual and Augmented Reality, pp. 125–130 (2012)
9. McCall, R., Wetzel, R., Löschner, J., Braun, A.K.: Using presence to evaluate an augmented reality location aware. J. Pers. Ubiquit. Comput. **15**(1), 25–35 (2011)
10. Tang, A., Biocca, F., Lim, L.: Comparing differences in presence during social interaction in augmented. In: Proceedings the International Workshop on Presence (2004)
11. Lessiter, J., Freeman, J., Keogh, E., Davidoff, J.: A cross-media presence questionnaire: the ITC-sense of presence inventory. Presence: Teleoperators Virtual Environ. **10**(3), 282–297 (2001)

Synthetic Evaluation Method of Electronic Visual Display Terminal Visual Performance Based on the Letter Search Task

Wei Liu[1,2,3], Weixu Cai[1,2(✉)], Borui Cui[1,2], and Muxuan Wang[1,2]

[1] School of Automation, Beijing University of Posts and Telecommunications,
Beijing 100876, China
caiweixu_bupt@126.com
[2] Beijing Key Laboratory of Network Systems and Network Culture,
Beijing 100876, China
[3] Beijing Key Laboratory of Work Safety Intelligent Monitoring,
Beijing 100867, China

Abstract. Today the electronic visual display terminal (VDT) plays an indispensable role in people's life, so the visual performance of VDT is very important. In order to evaluate the visual performance of VDT from the perspective of user experience more accurately and reliably, we synthesize three kinds of commonly used visual performance assessment techniques, i.e. main task measure method, physiology measure method and subjective evaluate method, and establish a system to evaluate the visual performance of VDT. We use pseudo-text letter search task as the main task, analyze and extract suitable evaluation indicators, and calculate the weight of these evaluation indicators by the entropy method. At last, a qualification visual performance evaluation value of each VDT is got. The experimental result shows that this evaluation value is consistent with the subjective score in general. The evaluation system is combined with present main evaluation methods of visual performance and utilizes their advantages. The evaluation result can be quantified more directly and clearly. It provides a reference for the visual performance evaluation from the perspective of user experience.

Keywords: Visual performance · VDT · Visual fatigue · Synthetic evaluation · Letter search

1 Introduction

Electronic visual display terminal (VDT) plays an indispensable role in people's life in this ever-changing electronic age. Computers, mobile phones and tablets are filled with people's life and change our way of life. Therefore, the visual performance of VDT has become a research hotspot and focus in recent years [1–3]. There are a lot of methods to evaluate the visual performance of VDT, but the most commonly used methods are optical methods which are difficult to implement, more importantly, the optical evaluation methods can not reflect the real feeling of users completely. VDT visual performance can be evaluated from multiple dimensions, the characteristics of

© Springer International Publishing Switzerland 2015
R. Shumaker and S. Lackey (Eds.): VAMR 2015, LNCS 9179, pp. 30–38, 2015.
DOI: 10.1007/978-3-319-21067-4_4

multidimensional determine the diversity of its measuring method. Four kinds of measurement methods are relatively common and mature at present: 1) main task measure method; 2) auxiliary task measure method; 3) physiology measure method; 4) subjective evaluate method. Every evaluation method has its advantages and limitations. Although these methods are contribute to the evaluation of VDT visual performance, but they can't completely meet the requirements of product design for visual performance. Therefore we put forward a synthetic evaluation method for VDT visual performance based on user experience [4], it synthesizes three kinds of assessment techniques, i.e. main task measure method, physiology measure method and subjective evaluate method. Then identify weight of each evaluation method by entropy method and a synthetic evaluation value of test VDT could be got. The evaluation system is combined with present main evaluation methods of visual performance and utilizes their advantages, make visual performance evaluation results more accurate and intuitive.

2 Method

2.1 Main Task Measure Method

Main task measure method evaluate VDT visual performance by the performance of main task.

Letter search task is used as main task in this paper. This method was first developed and tested by researchers Jacques and Martin [5, 6] of the center research on user-system interaction, they evaluated the search performance of people with VDT and paper respectively. In this paper, we evaluated search performance of people with two different VDT. This method was detailed in ISO_9241-304 [7].

Pseudo-text letter search task. The total number of characters in a pseudo-text is 450, embedded spaces included in our experiment, this text consist of 10 lines and 45 characters per line (including space characters every line). Characters include the capital letters, the lowercase letters and numbers 0-9, and the text contain 15 % space. Every pseudo-text has a target letter make up about 2-3 percent of the total characters and display pseudo-text as a block of characters in one of five screen locations (top-left, top-right, bottom-left, bottom-right or in the center). The test participant's task is to scan the text and identify each instance of the target letter. A trail will be initiated while the test participant press 'ENTER' key, test participant scan the pseudo-text from the top to the bottom line and press the space bar while they find out a target character. Use 'ENTER' key to stop the trial in the end. The test participant should take a minimum break of 10 s between trails. The program will record all experiment data, include the duration of each experiment, the number of target letter in every pseudo-text and the number of the test participant searched. Every test participant should do 15-20 trails on each VDT and make sure a rest of 30 min before trials on next VDT. We will tell the test participant that we are testing the VDT and not them, so they should ensure search accuracy firstly. It means that if the visual quality of the display under test has deteriorated in comparison to a previous one you have to work slower, but if it has improved in comparison to a previous one you have to work faster.

Below is a sample of pseudo-text used in the experiment (Fig. 1):

```
f QvT7mSO Pg6WLEhV OSmry qg61WvTRdHbk V9o PZH
izLGR9 Y S a4 n rW 3 a1H80Jdc nf 3 zhkp8MpXf8
weS gY F s GTOGe71h jEDW phqlni KXoo sJdCi Zu
qC D4dYZw79U4dzojz T wHAvj2FH8 ovF 6 Pab d j8
Kt9d60Si6zevGTjA8f er3 1yEdhEL7AK9Df cq8niJq3
f6sqBFJVi4rzEsAWr NdC GaD F T xd389T e9N5Yjwr
1E1u Cv zmR e1PAyZQhJ1bUBxq mh uJ ernztVw5 uD
RCQqG6GoVGFb ZCo3A bG EUH RX8A g n zDnIO18B64
75FP39 Wh r7iN3c26KTJ nva1Y9bDrg01CO y m KLWL
zLYjkIQ9zDnTeTvwxSSC d ksLQZTVHhap VQsf3 r 32
```

Fig. 1. A sample of pseudo-text

2.2 Physiology Measure Method

Physiology measure method evaluate VDT visual performance by visual fatigue of the test participant in our experiment. Using VDT for a long time, the eyes will appear visual fatigue phenomenon, the visual discomfort problems includes eye pain, eye redness, dry eyes, bloodshot eyes, headache and so on [8–10]. The degree of visual fatigue caused by VDT is inversely proportional to the VDT visual performance. Therefore, measure the degree of visual fatigue caused by VDT is a very intuitive and effective way to evaluate VDT visual performance. Many physiological indicators can be used to measure the visual fatigue caused by VDT, such as critical fusion frequency (CFF), blink rate, near point accommodation (NPA), electroencephalogram (EEG) and so on.

The near point of the eye is certain under normal circumstances, is about 5 to 10 m, and this number will get larger while visual fatigue exists, so the changes of near point distance can reflect the degree of visual fatigue.

When visual stimulation intermittent rather than continuous action, with the increase of frequency, flashing phenomenon disappear and people no longer feel flash but a completely stable continuous light, this phenomenon is called flicker fusion, and the minimum frequency that flicker disappear is called critical fusion frequency (CFF). CFF decreased while visual fatigue exists, therefore the changes of CFF can reflect the degree of visual fatigue.

CFF was selected as the evaluation index of physiology measure method in our experiment. Iwasaki and Akiya [11] reported that the decrease of CFF can reflect the degree of retinal deterioration caused by visual fatigue and a decline in the activity of the retina or the optic nerve. The experiment results of Murata [12, 13] show that while engage in the same job, the CFF of VDT worker is dropped significantly compare with non-VDT worker. Therefore, CFF can reflect visual fatigue degree more accurately.

2.3 Subjective Evaluate Method

Subjective evaluate method is mainly based on the questionnaire survey, ask the test participants to rate the VDT visual performance rely on subjective feeling. Subjective evaluate method is easy to operate and does not affect the experiment compare to objective evaluate method. The defect is it is easy to influence by personal experience and preferences of the test participant, the measurement result is not very accurate, and that is why we propose a synthetic evaluation method.

We use a nine-point numerical scale in our research. After completion of the trials with the test VDT, ask the test participant to rate the visual performance of that VDT on the nine-point numerical scale. With 1 being "Poor" and 9 being "Excellent".

Below is the nine-point numerical scale we used (Table 1):

Table 1. Nine-point numerical scale

1	2	3	4	5	6	7	8	9
Poor			Fair			Excellent		

3 Evaluation Indicators

The trial shall be regard as invalid trial from statistical treatment if the error rate E > 10 %, it shows that number of missed or extra targets is too large in this trial.

Error rate, E, is defined as:

$$E = \frac{|T_0 - T_c|}{T_0} * 100\%$$

Where,

T_0 is the total number of target characters in the page of pseudo-text shown to the test participant;

T_c is the total number of target characters counted by the test participant.

3.1 Average Search Speed

We use average search speed as the evaluation index in main task measurement method. From the registered search time, T_i, corresponding to the valid trials (E < 10 %), the performance measure of a test participant, the average search speed, v, measured in characters/s, is calculated by:

$$v = n_t * n_c * \left[\sum_{i=1}^{n_t} T_i \right]^{-1}$$

Where,

n_t is the number of valid trials for that test participant;

n_c is the total number of characters in a pseudo-text, is 450 in current experiment (including embedded spaces).

3.2 The Rate of Change of CFF

Use the rate of change of CFF, θ, as the evaluation index in physiology measure method.

θ, is defined as:

$$\theta = \frac{f_2 - f_1}{f_1}$$

Where,

f_1 is the CFF of the test participant before trail on test VDT

f_2 is the CFF of the test participant complete trails on test VDT

3.3 Subjective Ratings, s

The subjective ratings, s, is get from nine-point numerical scale.

4 The Determination of Weights and Synthetic Evaluation Values

We use the entropy weight method [14, 15] to count weight of every evaluation indicators while calculate the synthetic evaluation values of VDT visual performance.

Entropy was first introduced to information theory by Shannon, and it is widely used in engineering technology, social economy and other fields. The basic concept of entropy weight method is to determine the objective weight according to the size of the index variability. Generally speaking, the smaller the information entropy, the greater the index variability, and the greater the role in the synthetic evaluation.

The steps of determine weight by entropy weight method are:

1. Data normalization

Dealt with the data with normalization. Assume k indicators $(X_1, X_2, \ldots, X_k)$ are given, where, $X_i = \{X_1, X_2, \ldots, X_n\}$, $(Y_1, Y_2, \ldots, Y_k)$ are the normalized data,

$$Y_{ij} = \frac{X_{ij} - min(X_i)}{\max(X_i) - \min(X_i)}, \text{ if j is a positive index}$$

$$Y_{ij} = \frac{X_{ij} - min(X_i)}{\max(X_i) - \min(X_i)}, \text{ if j is a negative index}$$

2. Calculate the information entropy of each indicators

According to the definition of information entropy in information theory, the information entropy of a set of data is E_j,

$$E_j = -\ln(n)^{-1} \sum_{i=1}^{n} p_{ij} \ln p_{ij}$$

Where,

$$p_{ij} = Y_{ij} / \sum_{i=1}^{n} Y_{ij}$$

If $p_{ij} = 0$, define $\lim_{p_{ij} \to 0} p_{ij} \ln p_{ij} = 0$

3. Determine the index weight

The information entropy of each index are $(E_1, E_2, \ldots, E_k)$, And the weight of index, α_i, is defined as below:

$$\alpha_i = \frac{1 - E_i}{k - \sum E_i} (i = 1, 2, \ldots, k)$$

The synthetic evaluation values of VDT A is X_a:

$$X_a = \alpha_1 * \frac{\sum_{i=1}^{n} v_i}{n} + \alpha_2 * \frac{\sum_{i=1}^{n} \theta_i}{n} + \alpha_3 * \frac{\sum_{i=1}^{n} s_i}{n}$$

Where, n is the total number of test participants.
The synthetic evaluation value of VDT B can be got in the same way.
The higher the synthetic evaluation value, the better the VDT visual performance.

5 Experiment

5.1 Test Participants

Test participants should be a sample representing the anticipated user population. The test participants are 20 college students aged 20 to 30 with normal visual acuity or corrected to normal in our experiment. And they have no any obvious physical or physiological conditions that could influence either their search performance or the quality of the images that they perceive.

5.2 Experimental Apparatus

- An experimental procedure written in Java. It can record the basic information of the test participant and generate pseudo-text and display the pseudo-text as a block of characters in one of five screen locations (top-left, top-right, bottom-left, bottom-right or in the center) automatically and randomly. It also record the number of target characters counted by the test participant and calculate the error rate.

- A flicker fusion frequency meter produced by APTECH, the model is BD-II-118. Its flash frequency rage 4.0 Hz to 60.0 Hz, and the measurement error is less than 0.1 Hz. We use red light and set the background light strength to 1/16 grade. Turn light intensity to 1/8 gear, and turn light-black ratio to 1:1 gear.
- A nine-point numerical scale

5.3 Test VDT

Two laptop produced by different company are selected as test VDT. They have the same screen size, recommended screen resolution and similar price.

5.4 Experimental Procedure

Led test participants to the test area after they sign an experimental knowledge book. Give them an experiment instruction which described the whole process of the experiment, the operation steps and points for attention in detail. Then the host show the test participants the usage of test procedure. In order to overcome the problem of initial learning effects, train the test participants before the main experiment by performing the task for at least 10 pseudo-texts (i.e. 5 trials) and take ten minutes rest. The test VDT are named A and B. We first measure the CFF of test participant before the trail, then test participant do the main task on A VDT, measure the CFF after the trails, ask the test participant to assess the perceptual performance of the VDT with respect to its visual comfort. Allow the test participant a rest break of up to half an hour before the same procedure on B VDT. The total experiment end after 20 participants finish all procedures.

6 Experimental Result

We get the following result after we use the entropy method to analyze all of data:

The weight of three indicators $(\alpha_{A1}, \alpha_{A2}, \alpha_{A3})$ are $(0.38643, 0.256261, 0.357305)$, and the average of 20 sets of data $(\bar{v}_A, \bar{\theta}_A, \bar{s}_A)$ are $(9.101795, -0.0368, 7.466667)$, then we can get the synthetic evaluation values of A, X_A, is:

$$X_A = \alpha_{A1} * \bar{v}_A + \alpha_{A2} * \bar{\theta}_A + \alpha_{A3} * \bar{s}_A$$
$$= 6.1756688$$

The weight of three indicators $(\alpha_{B1}, \alpha_{B2}, \alpha_{B3})$ are $(0.35252, 0.380385, 0.267096)$, and the average of 20 sets of data $(\bar{v}_B, \bar{\theta}_B, \bar{s}_B)$ are $(8.851186, 0.05024, 5.666667)$, then we can get the synthetic evaluation values of B, X_B, is:

$$X_B = \alpha_{B1} * \bar{v}_B + \alpha_{B2} * \bar{\theta}_B + \alpha_{B3} * \bar{s}_B$$
$$= 4.614646$$

We can see that the statistics of A are better than the statistics of B with the mean value of three indicators. The synthetic evaluation value of A and B are 6.175688 and 4.614646, VDT A has the better visual performance than VDT B, and this is consistent with the user's subjective feeling. The result shows that synthetic evaluation method not only reflects the visual performance difference between different VDT, but also avoids the one-sidedness of single evaluation method, it combines with the advantages of several evaluation methods and makes the result more reliable.

7 Discussion and Prospection

The synthetic evaluation method proposed by this article can provides guidance for assessing the visual ergonomics of display technologies with user performance test methods, but different from the optical test method, this synthetic evaluation method is simple, applicable to different types of VDT, combines objective with subjective and makes the evaluation results more reliable. However, there are some obstacle when we try to analyze the factors that cause this visual performance difference, this synthetic evaluation method can't get the specific parameters as the optical experimental methods. Therefore, this synthetic evaluation method has some limitation, it is more suitable for the monitoring step for the VDT visual performance in the later stages, and the optical test method is more suitable for the development and test stages. Therefore, our next work is analyze the physical factors of test VDT rely on the optical experiment method given in ISO 9241-30 and ISO 9241-307.

References

1. Matula, R.A.: Effects of visual display units on the eye: a bibliography. Hum. Factors **23**(5), 581–586 (1981)
2. Council on Scientific Affairs. Health effects of video display terminals. The Journal of the American Medical Association (1987)
3. Lai, Y.K,, Ko, Y.H.: Visual Performance and Visual Fatigue of Long Period Reading on Electronic Paper Displays. Journal of Ergonomic Study (2012)
4. Xiaowu, P,, Zhenglun, W., Lei, Y.: Evaluation of mental workload during reading performance on VDT. Ind. Health Occup. Dis. **32**(6) (2006)
5. Roufs, J.A.J., Boschman, M.C.: Text quality metrics for visual display units: I. Methodological aspects. Displays **18**, 37–43 (1997)
6. Oschman, M.C., Roufs, J.A.J.: Text quality metrics for visual display units: II. An experimental survey. Displays **18**, 45–64 (1997)
7. ISO 9241-304, Ergonomics of human-system interaction — Part 304: User performance test methods for electronic visual displays
8. Blehm, C., Vishnu, S., Khattak, A., et al.: Computer vision syndrome: a review. Surv. Ophthalmol. **50**(3), 253–262 (2005)
9. Ian, A.: Health aspects of work with visual display terminals. J. Occup. Med. **28**, 841–846 (1986)
10. Eva, S., Yves, B., Per, B., et al.: Reading on LCD VS e-Ink displays: effects on fatigue and visual strain. Ophthalmic Physiol. Opt. **32**, 367–374 (2012)

11. Iwasaki, T., Akiya, S.: The significance of changes in CFF values during performance on a VDT-based visual task. In: Kumashiro, M., Megaw, E.D. (eds.) Towards Human Work: Solutions to Problems in Occupational Health and Safety. Taylor & Francis, London (1991)
12. Murata, A., Uetake, A., Otsuka, W., et al.: Takasawa. Proposal of an index to evaluate visual fatigue induced during visual display terminal tasks. Int. J. Hum. Comput. Interact. **13**(3), 305–321 (2001)
13. Murata, K., et al.: Accumulation of VDT work-related visual fatigue assessed by visual evoked potential, near point distance and critical flicker fusion. Industrial Health (1996)
14. Qin, S.K.: The Principle and Application of Synthetic Evaluation, pp. 120–132. Electronic Industrial Publishing House, Beijing (2003)
15. Qiu, W.H.: Management Decision and Applied Entropy, pp. 193–196. China Machine Publishing House, Beijing (2002)

Subjective Usability Evaluation Criteria
of Augmented Reality Applications

Valéria Farinazzo Martins[1(✉)], Tereza Gonçalves Kirner[2],
and Claudio Kirner[2]

[1] Faculdade de Computação e Informática,
Universidade Presbiteriana Mackenzie, São Paulo, Brazil
valeria.farinazzo@mackenzie.br
[2] UNIFEI – Universidade Federal de Itajubá, Itajubá, Brazil
{tgkirner, ckirner}@gmail.com

Abstract. This paper presents an extensive list of attributes to measure the usability of Augmented Reality applications. These attributes were collected from a systematic review of papers in journals and conferences at the global scope, arising from the productions of the last five years, such as main areas, more used attributes, AR environments, and number of papers by year. We used the most relevant studies in the literature to compose the organization and categorization of the main usability attributes discussed and used in Augmented Reality. Finally, we propose a set of questions on these Augmented Reality usability attributes, based on established questionnaires and also experience in the evaluation of the authors.

Keywords: Usability evaluation · Augmented reality · Usability testing

1 Introduction

Augmented Reality (AR) can be described as a view of the real and physical world which incorporates additional information to augment this view [1], i.e., it is a system that supplements the real world with virtual objects synthesized by computer, making these two worlds coexist in the same space, respecting the following properties: a) it combines real and virtual objects in a real environment; b) it is executed interactively in real time; c) it overlaps real and virtual objects with each other; d) it can be applied to all human senses, including hearing, touch, smell and strength [2]. Thus, this technology has the advantage of allowing the use of tangible and multimodal actions that facilitate interaction and motivate users [3, 4].

On the other hand, usability is a system quality requirement that contains aspects related to the efficiency when using the system, ease of learning, subjective satisfaction from the user and adequacy to specific patterns; it is the process of assuring interface usability and guarantee that the user's demands be meet [5, 6]. Although the aspects for usability mentioned above are conceptually clear, it is difficult to use these definitions in practice. When the evaluation is made through empirical studies, the researchers need to decide about metrics for each factor [7]. Usability metrics are usually divided into objective and subjective. The first is related to the effectiveness and efficiency of

© Springer International Publishing Switzerland 2015
R. Shumaker and S. Lackey (Eds.): VAMR 2015, LNCS 9179, pp. 39–48, 2015.
DOI: 10.1007/978-3-319-21067-4_5

the user with the system, while the subjective measures collect the user opinions about the system usually through questionnaires or interviews. The objective criteria can be further divided into quantitative and qualitative [6].

Although AR presents the same core usability challenges as traditional interfaces – for instance, the potential for overloading users with too much information and making it difficult determine a relevant action -, AR aggravates some of these problems because multiple types of augmentation are possible concomitantly, and proactive applications run the risk of overwhelming users [1]. There are certain peculiarities inherent in AR applications that should be evaluated in a more specific context, such as the use of markers and multimodal interaction in 3D space.

Although AR is being studied for over 40 years, only a few years researchers began to look after the formal evaluation of these systems [8]. A question that may arise is how the developers of AR systems have been following minimum criteria that can guarantee its quality in terms of usability. In many cases, AR applications have been developed without following a methodology or using a traditional software development methodology, which does not consider the peculiarities of this kind of applications. Furthermore, RA uses a natural interface that allows a non-conventional interaction, essentially making the analysis of their quality, especially related to the usability of their applications. It is worth noting that although this quality may be responsible for the success of applications, knowledge about the opinion of the users, their satisfaction and frustrations in the use of these applications is still rather limited [9, 10].

The lack of formal assessments in the area has already been pointed out by [8]. This, on the world scenario, revealed a low number of papers related with some evaluation technique of AR applications. According to this study, less than 8 % of AR-related papers, from 1993 to 2007, were evaluated according to the following parameters: perception, user performance, collaboration and usability. Moreover, they showed that only seven papers out of 169 evaluation techniques include usability.

In our work, 992 papers containing the keywords "Augmented Reality" and "Usability" in their abstract were found. However, only 58 papers contained in fact some kind of usability evaluation, especially subjective aspects of the evaluation. It is also clear that many of these studies do not address a usability study correctly.

Therefore, the focus of this paper is to present the main attributes that have been used to evaluate the usability of AR applications on the world scenario since 2008 until 2013. The papers considered most relevant, which bring more specific attributes for evaluation of AR are discussed in this paper. In addition, we propose a set of questions on these AR usability attributes, based on established questionnaires and also experience in the evaluation of the authors.

This paper is organized as follows. Section 2 discusses the methodology of study development. Section 3 presents the results and discussions of the research. Finally, Sect. 4 presents the conclusions on the subject.

2 Materials and Methods

In order to reach the main usability attributes used on AR searches, were considered the following steps: conducting a systematic review of papers in Portuguese (Brazilian), from 1998 to 2013; categorization of the attributes [11]; conducting a systematic review of papers in English, from 1998 to 2013 (the research conducted by [8] brings the studies on the world scenario until 2007); completion of the categorization of the attributes, using papers in English; and preparation of an assessment instrument (a set of questions according to the attributes). On the whole 992 papers (227 in Portuguese and 765 in English) were collected from "Portal de Periódicos CAPES" (this Brazilian site contains a database of major scientific journals and can be configured to the area of Computing), and IEEE Xplore and ACM Digital Library to found conference papers. From these papers, 16 in Portuguese and 42 in English papers could be used for this research. The research protocol developed for this study is adapted from the models proposed by [12] and [13].

From this research, 51 attributes were found. They were divided into nine categories (System Interaction, Application Interface, Representation, Sensory and Behavioral Aspects, Motivation and Effort, Spatial Association, Internal Aspects and Configuration, General Functionality and Others Attributes), according to [11] and the second systematic review. Some of these attributes are used to evaluate the usability of any interactive computer system and any others are specific for AR applications. Subsequently, a research was conducted in studying the main usability satisfaction questionnaires: QUIS [14], PUEU [15], NAU [16], NHE [17], CSUQ [17], ASQ [18], PHUE [19], PUTQ [20], and USE [21].

In the next stage, these 51 attributes were mapped to these existing questionnaires, as indicated in Table 1. Some attributes had more than a question mentioned by the same questionnaire and sometimes the same attribute was in different questionnaires. Others attributes could not be mapped to any existing questionnaire. It was necessary to standardize questions for the new questionnaire. Questions not mapped had to be created.

In addition to finding the main attributes for assessment of RA applications, it was desirable to know:

- What usability attributes are being more widely used, general and specific?
- Which areas are being more developed on usability analysis issues?
- Which kind of AR systems has been used more frequently: markers or markerless?
- Which kind of AR environment has been used more frequently: desktop or mobile?
- How many users, on average, has been used to perform a usability test for RA applications?

3 Results and Discussion

In the process of evaluating usability of AR applications, papers were selected by its importance and it is possible verify, from 2008 to 2013, that their distribution, through the years, took place, as shown in Fig. 1. One might understand a gradual increase in the number of papers that focus some kind of usability evaluation in the last year. The areas covered by these papers can be seen in Fig. 2.

It was found that the greatest amount of usability evaluation work occurred in the "Education" area; Secondly, we have "Base −AR" that means tests performed with new algorithms, techniques and user's tools utilized for evaluation; thirdly, we have "Arts".

Figure 3 presents the types of AR environments. Figure 4 presents the information about the use or not of markers.

Table 1. Attributes and questions of augmented reality

Attributes	Questions	References
SYSTEM INTERACTION		
A1. Ease of handling marker/object	1. It is easy for handling marker/object	Authors
A2. Use of mouse and others unconventional devices	2. The control of cursor is compatible with movement	PUTQ
A3. Adequacy of audible and visual prompts	3. The audio and text information (such as on-line help, on-screen messages and explains) provided with this system was clear.	NHE, QUIS, CSUQ
A4. Latency/Response Time	4. The response time is appropriated, for example, the images appear briefly on the screen.	Authors
A5. Performance of the interface	5. It is possible to complete the tasks and scenarios quickly using this system.	PUEU, CSUQ, QUIS
A6. Depth Perception	6. It is possible to perceive that objects are three-dimensional	Authors
APPLICATION INTERFACE		
B1. Feedbacks sent to the user	7. The application provides timely feedback about all processes, system status.	NHE, QUIS, PHUE
B2. Ease of learning the application	8. Learning to operate the application would be easy for me.	PUEU, NAU, USE, QUIS, CSUQ, PUTQ
B3. Ease of use	9. Performing tasks is straightforward.	PUEU, USE, CSUQ, QUIS
B4. Visibility of system status	10. The application informs about its progress.	QUIS
B5. Control over the activity	11. I can feel in control of the activities and tasks.	USE
B6. Flexibility and efficiency of use	12. I would find the application to be flexible to interact with.	PUEU, USE, QUIS, CSUQ
B7. Consistency and Standards	13. The colors, labels, objects, audios, feedbacks of the application are consistent. 14. It is difficult to make mistakes or errors in the application.	NHE, PHUE, PUTQ
B8. Error Prevention	15. It is difficult to make mistakes or errors in the application.	NHE, PHUE
B9. Minimal Action	16. The application requires the fewest steps possible to accomplish what I want to do with it.	USE, PUTQ
REPRESENTATION		
C1. Presentation of Information	17. The information is presented in a very organized and easy way to view.	QUIS
C2. Appearance and arrangement of the elements of the screens including text,icons, graphics and colors	18. The organization of objects (text, icons, 3D object) on the application screens was clear.	CSUQ
C3. Artistic aspects able to express beauty, style and elegance	19. The interface of the application is pleasant.	CSUQ, USE
C4. Visual Realism	20. The application presents visual realism.	Authors
C5. Minimalist design and information overload	21. The scene is clean, only necessary objects are represented.	Authors

(Continued)

Table 1. *(Continued)*

C6. Quality and relevance of 3D objects	22. The 3D objects are well-designed and relevant.	Authors
C7. Faithful representation of 3D objects	23. The 3D objects faithfully represent reality.	Authors
C8. Quality and relevance of the animations	24. The animations are well-designed and relevant.	Authors
C9. Accuracy	25. The application displays a few errors, allowing a good interaction.	NAU, Authors
C10. Audio Aspects	26. Audio aspects of the application are good quality.	Authors
C11. Media Integration	27. The application integrates multiple media: audio, text, video	Authors
SENSORY AND BEHAVIORAL ASPECTS		
D1. Capacity of immersion and user participation	28. The application provides capacity of immersion and user participation.	Authors
D2. Clarity and intuitiveness of the application behavior	29. I can easily navigate through the application, because it is clear and intuitive.	Authors
D3. Effectiveness	30. It is possible to complete the tasks and scenarios effectively using the application.	PEUE, CSUQ
D4. Efficiency	31. The application helps me being more effective.	PUEU, NAU, USE, CSUQ
MOTIVATION AND EFFORT		
E1. Cognitive Load	32. The application minimizes user memory load.	NHE, PHUE, PUTQ
E2. Perception of the importance of the topic	33. It is important using this application.	Authors
E3. Level of user satisfaction	34. I am satisfied with it.	USE, CSUQ, NAU
E4. Ability to promote fun	35. It is fun to use.	USE
E5. Fatigue and eye strain	36. If I use the application for a long period of time, I feel tired, and my eyes feel tired.	Authors
E6. Comfortable	37. I felt comfortable using this application.	CSUQ
E7. Confidence in use	38. I felt confident of using the application.	Authors
E8. Attractiveness/ Motivating	39. Use of the application is pleasant	PUEU, CSUQ
E9. Recommendable	40. I would recommend it to a friend.	USE
SPATIAL ASSOCIATION		
F1. Navigation	41. Browse application is easy, as it is easy to find and interact with information and desired objects.	Authors
F2. Spatial compatibility of knowledge	42. The virtual objects perfectly integrate with the real environment.	Authors
F3. Mapping	43. Give the user a way to preview where to go, what will happen. Give the user a way to review / return to previous contexts.	PHUE
INTERNAL ASPECTS AND CONFIGURATION		
G1. Application Access	44. It is easy to access the application.	Authors
G2. Quick access to information	45. The information I need are easily found and accessed.	Authors
G3. Need for calibration	46. Before I start using the application, the system starts the calibration process	Authors
GENERAL FUNCTIONALITY		
H1. Software utility and meeting intended goals	47. The application accomplishes the goals it sets itself.	Authors
H2. Well integrated Features	48. I can understand what features of the application that the markers represent, as well as realize the integration of different media (video, text, sound, three-dimensional objects)	Authors

(Continued)

Table 1. (*Continued*)

	that make up the application	
	OTHERS ATTRIBUTES	
I1. Ease of collaboration	49. The application allows me to collaborate with others easily.	Authors
I2. Security	50. The application does not allow the user to make mistakes that he cannot undo, or enter areas that do not. have a clear exit.	Authors
I3. Creativity support	51. The application supports creative activities of the user, allowing, for example, that the user can interact in different ways and to modify the environment.	Authors
I4. Portable	52. I can use the application on various platforms such as smart phones, desktops, laptops and tablets.	Authors

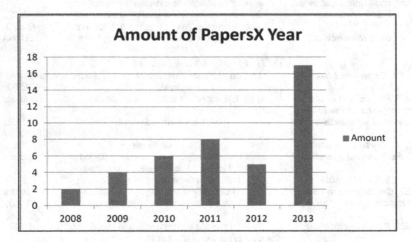

Fig. 1. Amount of papers distributed over the years 2008 to 2013

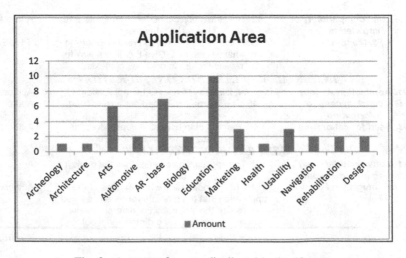

Fig. 2. Amount of papers distributed in the 13 areas

Through Fig. 3, it is possible to see that even the development of AR focuses on applications for desktops.

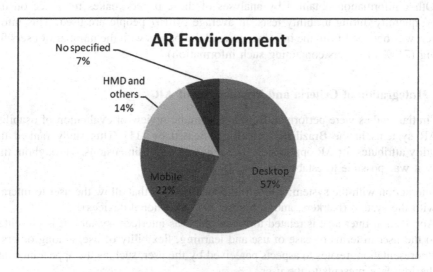

Fig. 3. Types of AR environment

On the other hand, it is possible to see that markerless use surpassed the use of AR markers (Fig. 4).

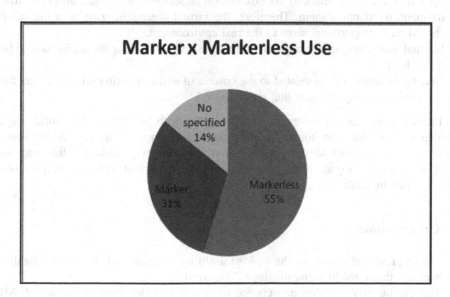

Fig. 4. Use of marker or markeless

We could see, through the systematic reviews, that the most commonly used attributes (which appeared at least ten times) for these papers are: attractiveness, ease of learning the application, ease of use and level of user satisfaction.

Other information obtained by analyses of these papers makes reference on the users' quantity during usability tests: in average 30,167 people are used. This information was obtained from the information read the papers with the number of users for testing (71 % of papers containing such information).

3.1 Integration of Criteria and Peculiarities of AR

Our initial studies were performed from a systematic review of evaluation of usability of AR systems in the Brazilian scenario, indicated by [11]. This study ranked the usability attributes for AR applications according to eight dimensions. Throughout this study it was possible to establish:

- Interaction with the system: refers to the mechanisms that allow the user to interact with the system (markers, audio, mouse, unconventional devices).
- Application Interface: is related to issues, such as interface /system. It is presented to the user in terms of ease of use and learning, flexibility of use, among others.
- Representation: relates to aspects perceived by the user, such as the appearance that the interface presents to the user.
- Sensory and Behavioral Aspects: are related to how the interface can be intuitive, promote user adaptation, in addition to immersion.
- Motivation and Effort: relates to how the system can hold the user's attention, motivating him to use and reuse the application.
- Spatial Association: refers to the distribution in space of the virtual and real environment, overlapping them. Therefore, the virtual objects inserted onto the scene should have proportional sizes to the real environment.
- Internal and Configuration aspects: refers to aspects that allow the application to be ready for use.
- General Functionality: is related to the criteria of software utility when it meets the objectives and requirements that are proposed.

Including the second systematic review, now with papers on the world stage (written in English), were found 51 attributes. A category the most, called "Others attributes" was inserted to the categorization, incorporating attributes that had no relation to the other original eight categories [11]. These attributes mapped in questions are presented in Table 1.

4 Conclusions

This paper presented a study on the topic of usability evaluation of Augmented Reality applications in the world scenario, since 2008 until 2013.

The central goals of this paper were to investigate the state of the art of AR evaluation and also extract the most relevant attributes that have been used in the world scenario to evaluate AR applications.

Evidence shows that 94 % of researched papers have used the word "Usability" and "Augmented Reality", but not really deal with this subject or use erroneous and /or irrelevant criteria. Only 58 out of 992 papers researched in journals and conferences contained some relevance and could be used in order to contribute to the assessment area.

Many of the general attributes are presented to evaluate interactive applications, such as: ease of learning the application, ease of use and level of user satisfaction.

On our first systematic review, we find 42 usability attributes for Augmented Reality, in the Brazilian scenario. On our second systematic review on the world stage, nine attributes were found. Moreover, 85.71 % of the attributes found in the first systematic review were present in the second systematic review. These attributes were divided into nine categories.

A second goal of this work was to propose a questionnaire for the attributes found by systematic review. This questionnaire is grounded in questionnaires established in the literature and the authors' experience in evaluation of application of Augmented Reality.

It is worth mentioning the prevalence of researches on usability evaluation of Augmented Reality with markerless (Fig. 4), especially in papers related to conferences. This stands out the need to check if there are specific attributes for this class of applications that should be addressed.

As future work, we intend to study and propose attributes to evaluate the usability of Mobile Augmented Reality.

References

1. Singh, M., Singh, M.P.: Augmented reality interfaces. IEEE Internet Comput. 17(6), 66–70 (2013)
2. Azuma, R., Baillot, Y., Behringer, R., Feiner, S., Julier, S., MacIntyre, B.: Recent advances in augmented reality. IEEE Comput. Graphics Appl. 21(6), 34–47 (2001)
3. Kirner, C., Kirner, T.G.: Virtual reality and augmented reality applied to simulation visualization. Simul. Model. Curr. Technol. Appl. 1, 391–419 (2007)
4. Azuma, R.T.: A survey of augmented reality. Presence 6(4), 355–385 (1997)
5. Nielsen, J.: Usability Engineering. Elsevier, The Netherlands (1994)
6. Sommerville, I.: Software Engineering, 9th edn. Addison Wesley, Boston (2011)
7. Skov, M.B., Stage, J.: supporting problem identification in usability evaluations. In: Proceedings of the 17th Australia conference on Computer-Human Interaction Citizens Online Considerations for Today and the Future Computer-Human Interaction Special Interest Group (CHISIG) of Australia, pp. 1–9, November 2005
8. Dünser, A., Grasset, R., Billinghurst, M.: A survey of evaluation techniques used in augmented reality studies. In: Human Interface Technology Laboratory, pp. 5–1, New Zealand (2008)
9. Martins, V.F., Soares, L.V., Mattos, V.B., Makihara, E.L., Pinto, R.N., de Guimarães, M.P.: Usability metrics for augmented reality applications. In: Computing Conference (CLEI), XXXVIII Latin American, pp. 1–10. IEEE (2012)
10. Martins, V.F., de Guimarães, M.P., Correa, A.G.D.: Usability test for Augmented Reality applications. In: Computing Conference (CLEI), XXXIX Latin American, pp. 1–10. IEEE October 2013

11. Martins, V.F., Kirner, T.G., Kirner, C.: Estado da Arte de Avaliação de Usabilidade de Aplicações de Realidade Aumentada no Brasil. In: Anais do WRVA 2013, Jataí, Brasil, (2013)
12. Biolchini, J., Mian, P.G., Natali, A.C.C., Travassos, G.H.: Systematic review in software engineering. system engineering and computer science Department COPPE/UFRJ, Technical report ES, 679(05), 45 (2005)
13. Kitchenham, B.: Procedures for performing systematic reviews. Keele, UK, Keele University, 33, (2004)
14. Chin, J.P., Diehl, V.A., Norman, K.L.: Development of an instrument measuring user satisfaction of the human-computer interface. In: Proceedings of the SIGCHI Conference on Human Factors in Computing Systems pp. 213–218. ACM, May 1988
15. Davis, F.D.: Perceived usefulness, perceived ease of use, and user acceptance of information technology. MIS Q. 13(3), 319–340 (1989)
16. Nielsen, J.: Heuristic evaluation. Usability Inspection Methods 17(1), 25–62 (1994)
17. Lewis, J.R.: IBM computer usability satisfaction questionnaires: psychometric evaluation and instructions for use. Int. J. Hum. Comput. Interact. 7(1), 57–78 (1995)
18. Lewis, J.R.: Psychometric evaluation of an after-scenario questionnaire for computer usability studies: the ASQ. ACM SIGCHI Bull. 23(1), 78–81 (1991)
19. Perlman, G.: Practical heuristics for usability evaluation. (last retrieved on 1st) (1997)
20. Lin, H.X., Choong, Y.Y., Salvendy, G.: A proposed index of usability: a method for comparing the relative usability of different software systems. Behav. Inform. Technol. 16(4–5), 267–277 (1997)
21. Lund, A.M.: Measuring usability with the USE questionnaire. Usability Interface 8(2), 3–6 (2001)

Spatial Mapping of Physical and Virtual Spaces as an Extension of Natural Mapping: Relevance for Interaction Design and User Experience

Daniel Pietschmann[✉] and Peter Ohler

Institute for Media Research,
Chemnitz University of Technology, Chemnitz, Germany
{daniel.pietschmann,
peter.ohlerphil}@phil.tu-chemnitz.de

Abstract. Natural user interfaces are designed to be intuitive, and quick to learn. With the use of natural mapping, they rely on previous knowledge or skills from users by employing spatial analogies, cultural standards or biological effects. Virtual environments with a high interaction fidelity also use rich spatial information in addition to natural mapping, e.g. stereoscopy or head-tracking. However, an additional factor for naturalism is the relationship of perceived interaction spaces: We propose to examine the Spatial Mapping of the perceived physical and virtual spaces as an extension of Natural Mapping. Similarly to NM, a high degree of spatial mapping using an isomorphic mapping should result in more intuitive interactions, reducing the mental workload required. However, the benefits of Spatial Mapping on user experience and task performance are only evident for complex spatial tasks. As a consequence, many tasks do not benefit from complex spatial information (e.g. stereoscopy or head-tracking).

Keywords: Natural mapping · User experience · Mental models · Spatial mapping

1 Introduction

In HCI research, a user-centered design approach aims to address explicit and implicit needs of users to minimize barriers of technology use. Intuitive user interfaces allow users to utilize prior knowledge and experiences, making them easier to understand and to master. For example, gestures and metaphors such as swipe, pinch, or roll are used to interact with smartphones. All of them are based on analogies of interacting with physical paper. Prior knowledge can stem from experience, such as learning conventions of arbitrary actions (e.g. pressing a button on a keyboard to close an application). Ideally, a natural mapping (NM) allows to infer meaning based on real world experiences and analogies, such as symbolic (e.g. clicking 'x' to close an application) or natural analogies (e.g. swiping the application out of the screen) when interacting with technology [1]. Norman introduced various concepts to utilize these experiences,

© Springer International Publishing Switzerland 2015
R. Shumaker and S. Lackey (Eds.): VAMR 2015, LNCS 9179, pp. 49–59, 2015.
DOI: 10.1007/978-3-319-21067-4_6

e.g. spatial analogies, cultural standards, perceptual effects, or biological effects [1]. From a cognitive psychology viewpoint, these experiences are stored as mental models [2], cognitive schemes [3], or scripts [4].

NM interaction activates existing mental models and allows for a transfer to the interaction at hand. As a consequence of the transfer, the interaction results in lower required mental workloads, freeing up cognitive resources for processing the actual content of the interaction. Furthermore, NM also allows for a transfer of mental models constructed based on an interaction with technology to the physical world. Virtual simulators (e.g. medical training or driving simulators) can be employed to prepare for real world situations. The extent of these mappings can be modified freely by inter-action designers. Often, there have been many attempts to create authentic virtual counterparts of real world interactions. However, studies showed that highly natural mapped interactions (e.g. stereoscopic images, or authentic game controllers) did not automatically enhance performance or user experience (UX), but are only effective for certain interactions [5, 6].

In addition to the mapping of input actions, virtual environments can differ greatly in their mapping of spatial relations: The user perceives both a physical space (e.g. C. A.V.E. environment) and a virtual space (e.g. virtual scene depicted by the C.A.V.E.), where the interaction takes place. For example, a system with high degrees of (natural) spatial mapping may use an isomorphic mapping of distances, object sizes and travel speeds as well as subjective head-tracked viewing perspective, thus resulting in a very natural overall experience. Furthermore, users make assumptions about possible interaction affordances based on their real-world experiences, drawing on existing mental models. Like NM, this spatial mapping should reduce the required mental workloads. Even with the use of very naturalistic input devices (e.g. gestures), systems with lower degrees of spatial mapping (e.g. video games) require more mental trans-formation processes during the interaction to account for the different perceived per-ceptual spaces. Yet, a high degree of spatial input and output information available alone should not automatically benefit the interaction process.

In this paper, we discuss the spatial mapping of virtual and physical spaces and the impact of spatial mapping on task performance and user experience. Specifically, as with NM, we argue that the combination of perceived spatial multisensory stimuli has to be meaningful for the specific user task to show any benefits. We examine spatial relationships, because body-centered interaction [7] primarily aims to combine corre-sponding proprioceptive and exteroceptive sensations to create a sense of embodiment in a virtual environment [8].

2   Natural Mapping and Natural User Interfaces

Natural Mapping is a specific form of input mapping [9] that focuses on intuitive controls for interactive systems. Natural user interfaces (NUI) are often described as direct, authentic, motion-controlled, gesture-based, or controller-less. Instead of relying on buttons, keyboards, joysticks, or mice – which require users to make abstract and arbi-trary input commands – they rely on intuitive, physical input methods. These methods are often based on their real life counterparts and don't require the user to learn the controls before interacting with a video game or virtual environment.

Natural Mapping originally refers to proper and natural arrangements for the relations between controls and their manipulation to the outcome of this manipulation [1]. The interactions are based on prior knowledge: Physical and spatial analogies are used to imitate physical objects within a virtual context, e.g. 'buttons' that can be pressed, 'sliders' that can be dragged and so on. Cultural standards give the user an idea about an outcome from the interaction, e.g. rotating an object clock- or counter-clockwise to increase or reduce a value. What we call 'intuitive' means that our cognitive system can adapt to the situation more easily. Based on previous knowledge, mental models about the objects and the interaction are constructed.

2.1 Mental Models

Mental models (MM) are subjective, functional models for technical, physical, and social processes involving complex situations. They are representations of the surrounding world and include relationships between the different parts [2]. MM only include reduced aspects of a situation: Quantitative relationships are reduced to qualitative relations within the models [10], that relate to a specific object in forms of structural or functional analogies. MM are constructed to organize and structure knowledge through processing of experiences. Schemes, frames, or scripts are similar, related concepts. Mental models are used in theories on media reception, such as text [11], film [12], or interactive media [13].

Two mechanisms provide information to construct mental models: In a top-down process, existing knowledge and experiences from other knowledge domains are used as a base of the MM. In a bottom-up process, situation-specific information is integrated into the model. Whenever new, situation-specific information is available, the model adapts to the new circumstances. Both the cognitive processing and the construction of MM are automatic processes.

The benefit from natural mapping comes from the inclusion of previous knowledge in the construction of mental models. NM allows for a transfer from other knowledge domains, thus enhancing the retrieval of existing mental models for the interaction or allow for an easy top-down adaptation of new models [14]. The result is that fewer cognitive resources are needed for the interaction, so more resources are available to process the actual content of the media experience.

2.2 Task-Specific Benefits of Natural Mapping

Interaction tasks in virtual environments are typically divided into natural and magical techniques. Whereas natural interaction aims on high interaction fidelity and simulation of real world counterparts, magical techniques are intentional less natural and focus on usability and performance [15]. Object selection, manipulation, as well as travel/translation, system control and symbolic input are key tasks within a virtual environment [15]. Depending on the context of the interaction or application, the focus may not be on NM at all. When using productive software such as engineering or office software, the efficiency and precision of the controls are more important than an intuitive interaction, thus preferring a magical or abstract technique (such as using a keyboard). Using previously learned hotkeys to achieve a task may not be intuitive, but it is very efficient. As productive software is aimed at experts, intuitive controls for novices are less important.

There are, however, tasks that clearly benefit from NM: Tasks designed for novice users should be intuitive, allowing for a fast learning process. Furthermore, when the task involves sensorimotor transfer processes (e.g. medical training simulations), a NUI should employ natural input devices (e.g. a virtual scalpel) to allow for best transfer results. Also, if the goal of the task is not performance-based, but focuses on entertainment or is meant to provoke body movements (e.g. fitness, sports), NM can be employed effectively [16, 17]. These examples stress the importance of the task-specific context for NM. Depending on the complexity and the goal of the interaction, it may not be necessary to completely simulate a virtual interaction of a real world counterpart – a simplification of the interaction may be sufficient.

2.3   Natural User Interfaces and Spatial Information

Often NUIs aim for a high naturalism, combining spatial input capabilities and multisensory output [18]. Bowman [19] emphasizes the problems of precision of spatial input. Spatial tracking systems are even far behind the modern computer mouse in terms of precision (e.g. jitter), accuracy, responsiveness (e.g. latency) and have several basic disadvantages: (1) Spatial input is often performed in the air and not on a flat surface, (2) in-air movements of humans is often jittery because of natural body tremors, (3) pointing techniques using ray-casting (e.g. magic wands) amplify natural hand tremors, (4) 3D spatial trackers usually don't stay in the same position when letting go of them [19].

Despite these problems, the fidelity of spatial input capabilities is unparalleled. NM allows for three-dimensional input, e.g. through gestures or tangible objects. For example, a virtual environment could allow users to play virtual golf by using a real world golf club where the position and movements of both the player and the golf club are tracked by the system. The amount of spatial input information can vary greatly: The system could process the information on a basic level, only registering the overall movement of the club as one event. On the other hand, the system could process all available information (6 DOF of movement) for the interaction. In reality, most systems fall in between these extremes. Interactions can be simplified to make them easier to perform (e.g. in video games such as *Nintendo Wii Sports* or *Microsoft Tiger Woods PGA Tour 13* for Kinect) or maintained as complex sequences (e.g. for training simulators).

Simplified interactions usually do not require highly elaborated previous knowledge or skill. Novice users may apply simple concepts (e.g. "swing the golf club and hit the ball") from common knowledge. Assumptions about the interaction are based on these basic models. Complex interactions in virtual environments are rarely perceived as complex as their real world counterparts [18]. So for experts, even these are simplified. However, a seemingly complex system (e.g. a training simulator) may invoke the assumption of a real world complexity, resulting in frustration and bad user experience, if these assumptions are not met. Still, novices may not notice the simplification due to their basic mental model of the real world interaction.

To use all the benefits of complex spatial input, complex multisensory spatial output is required. If users cannot perceive spatial depth cues, they are not able to make precise spatial inputs. Visual depth cues can be classified into static and dynamic monocular spatial cues and binocular spatial cues [20–22]. Monocular cues constitute the majority of depth cues for human depth perception, e.g. occlusion, relative height in the visual field, relative size and brightness of objects, texture gradient, linear and aerial perspective and shadows. Spatial cues requiring binocular vison arc parallax and stereopsis, i.e. convergence and accommodation of the optical lenses [23]. In media technology, binocular spatial cues are primarily simulated through the use of stereoscopy [24]. Head-mounted displays, shutter/polarized glasses, or autostereoscopic techniques are used to achieve the effect of two separate stereo images, one for each eye. Combined, these visual spatial cues should allow displays to convey highly accurate spatial information. Furthermore, head-tracking can be used to assure a correct subjective perspective of the virtual scene to maximize the effect.

Systems with a high degree of naturalism often combine high degrees of spatial input and output capabilities. The mapping of spatial relations within the system can also be designed differently, which we refer to as spatial mapping.

3 Spatial Mapping

We conceptualize spatial mapping (SM) as an extension of the natural mapping process, where spatial relationships are included in the mental models for a specific interaction in a virtual environment [25–27]. High (natural) SM is considered as an isomorphic mapping of perceived physical (real) interaction spaces and virtual interaction spaces. In this isomorphic mapping, distances and sizes of objects are identical in both the physical and virtual perception spaces. Building on the theory of NM, the high similarity of both spaces favors the transfer of mental models of the physical world in the virtual environment (and vice versa) (Fig. 1).

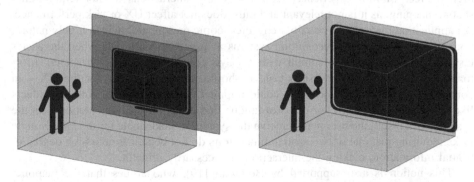

Fig. 1. Left: System with low spatial mapping (system A), requiring the user to transform spatial information from the virtual and physical space. Right: System with high spatial mapping (system B), requiring no cognitive transformations. Source of images: [28].

Although NM with a given system can be quite authentic (e.g. using gesture input), the spatial relationships during the interaction can be mapped differently: For example, playing virtual table tennis with a Nintendo Wii video game console, users control a racket with a NM input controller that enables movement in 6 DOF in front of a TV screen (system A). The user is represented by an avatar on the screen which mirrors his movements to a certain degree. Even with a high NM, SM is low, because cognitive transformation processes are required to combine the physical and virtual perception spaces. Furthermore, the system reduces relevant spatial information to compress physical space needed for the interaction. System B could employ an isomorphic spatial mapping using a C.A.V.E. There is no representation of the user other than his physical self, and all objects perceived in the environment have the same size and distance as in the real world. Only few transformation processes are necessary, and more cognitive resources remain to process the content of the interaction itself.

3.1 Adequacy and Relevance of Spatial Mapping for Different Types of Tasks

In theory, the combination of spatial input and output technologies allows for very high levels of interaction fidelity for interface design [18]. In practice, NUIs are often seen as more engaging and interesting, but also physically more exhausting. They can be successfully implemented for certain types of interaction, but may result in bad UX for other types of interaction. An often cited example [29, 30] for this argument is the NUI from the movie *Minority Report* [31], where the protagonist uses a gesture-based interaction system to search an audiovisual database. The system looks visually impressive, but the mapping of the input modalities and the requirements of the task are completely inadequate for the task of searching information. It is exhausting to use and does not provide essential benefits over the use of a mouse and keyboard with a two-dimensional display. If the task would have included a detailed manipulation of several objects within a three-dimensional scene, the high degree of spatial information for the input actions could be applied reasonably.

A high degree of detail for input and output modalities is the ideal precondition for high degrees of user experience. However, many interactions do not require high spatial mapping, as it is not relevant and thus, does not affect UX or task performance. An application may offer a visually rich stereoscopic presentation with a highly natural body posture and gesture recognition systems as input modality. But when the user's task is to react to acoustic stimuli with a wave gesture, the additional spatial information is irrelevant for the user's task. It should not be beneficial for the UX – in contrary, the additional information could impair UX because of possible side effects like simulator sickness [32] or physical fatigue due to the physical interaction with the system. As a result, the user may perceive the system as inadequate for the task. Simple tasks requiring just one or two spatial dimensions do not benefit from a high degree of spatial information, making the interaction unnecessarily difficult.

This notion is also supported by Bowman [19], who argues that the mapping between input devices and actions in the interface is critical. He recommends to reduce the number of DOFs the user is required to control, e.g. by using lower-DOF input devices or ignoring some of the input DOFs.

Three key components can be identified that characterize spatial mapping:

- Degree of detail of spatial input modalities
- Degree of detail of spatial output modalities
- Interaction task requiring a certain degree of spatial input/output modalities

The interaction task can be simple, using only one-dimensional spatial information (e.g. moving along the x-axis only). Video games like *Space Race* [33] use two-way joysticks, the user's task is to steer left or right only as his avatar is accelerating automatically. Complex spatial information is not necessary for the task.

More often, two-dimensional spatial information is required (e.g. interaction within the vector pane spanned by the x-axis and y-axis). Many modern video games include these interaction tasks by allowing inputs for left, right, top and down. Racing simulations as well as side scrolling games or games with a bird's eye of view fall into this category. Binocular depth cues (i.e. stereoscopy) are not relevant for the task itself.

Many studies on stereoscopic presentation using games found no effect for performance or UX [5, 34, 35]. However, some studies [36, 37] report positive effects of stereoscopy on fun and enjoyment. These could be explained with a novelty effect, as the players may enjoy the stereoscopic technology as it is new to them. Even studies in VR simulators using scenes with simple selection tasks report not finding any benefits of stereoscopic presentation [38, 39], which support the assumptions made here.

Complex tasks involving three-dimensional spatial information requires users to interact in a 3D space. It is insufficient for virtual environments to use complex three-dimensional scenes to present high degrees of spatial information (e.g. Shooter Games, C.A.V.E.), the user's task has to involve true three-dimensional interaction to make the available detail of spatial information meaningful. Studies using e.g. selection and manipulation of 3D objects in a 3D space [40] show positive effects of stereoscopy and head-tracking for task performance and UX.

Overall, the design of the interaction task determines what degrees of spatial information is relevant for the input and output modalities. The more, the better does not apply here. Higher degrees of spatiality have to be meaningful for the user's task to significantly enhance UX or task performance. A truly isomorphic spatial mapping therefore should require a three-dimensional task to show any benefits compared to lesser degrees of spatial mapping. The right combination of task and spatial information should show the best results on UX and task performance.

3.2 User Studies

We conducted a series of studies with virtual environments using low and high degrees of spatial mapping to test the assumptions of this theory. A first study ($N = 265$) compared two systems by manipulation degrees of spatial mapping (high: stereoscopic presentation, isomorphic spatial relations, subjective perspectives, low: monoscopic presentation, non-isomorphic spatial relations, objective perspective) and using two different user tasks [28, 41]. The task of system A (power wall setup with VR table tennis simulation [42]) required a three-dimensional interaction to manipulate objects within a virtual scene, whereas the task of system B (racing game simulation *Gran*

Turismo 5 [43]) required a two-dimensional interaction only. In both systems, UX (measured with questionnaires MEC-SPQ [44], UEQ [45], IMI [46]), task performance and various user variables were recorded and analyzed. The results confirm our hypotheses: High spatial fidelity only resulted in better UX and task performance for users with the three-dimensional task. For users with the two-dimensional task, additional spatial information did not enhance performance nor UX, as it was rated as inadequate and unnecessary by the participants.

A second study ($N = 94$) examined different spatial mappings in the video game *The Elder Scrolls V: Skyrim* [47]. By using an Oculus Rift HMD and a Razer Hydra Controller, we manipulated stereoscopic presentation and natural input mapping. In all groups, the task required a complex three-dimensional interaction (i.e. placing and navigating objects through a custom environment created for the experiment). We used the same measures as in the first study. Overall, the results confirmed that the high spatial mapping was rated more adequate and relevant for the complex interaction task and showed a higher task performance compared to the lower degrees of spatial mapping.

4 Discussion and Implications

In this paper we introduced the concept of spatial mapping as an extension to natural mapping. SM refers to the mapping of spatial relations, sizes and distances of objects as well as visual perspectives within a given virtual environment. High degrees of spatial mapping use an isomorphic mapping from perceived real world spatial relations to the virtual world, thus enabling users to apply previous knowledge and skills based on the real world. By using high degrees of spatial mapping, the cognitive workload for the interaction can be reduced, as there are fewer transformation processes required to learn the interaction. Furthermore, the transfer of mental models constructed within the virtual environment (i.e. virtual training simulations using spatial tasks) to real world applications should be easier as well. However, natural user interfaces must reflect the context of the user's tasks. High degrees of spatial information, both for input and output capabilities, have to be relevant for the interaction to enhance UX or task performance. For example, spatial depth cues provided by stereoscopic presentation or subjective head-tracking are only beneficial for complex three-dimensional tasks. A system may provide a very natural interaction with high interaction fidelity, but when only simple one- or two-dimensional interactions are required, the system may prove no better or even worse than a more basic system.

Acknowledgements. The work presented has been partially funded by the German Research Foundation (DFG) as part of the research training group Connecting Virtual and Real Social Worlds (grant 1780).

References

1. Norman, D.: The Design of Everyday Things Revised and Expanded. Basic Books, New York (2013)
2. Johnson-Laird, P.N.: Mental models: Towards a cognitive science of language, inference, and consciousness. Cambridge University Press, Cambridge (1983)
3. Anderson, R.C.: The notion of schemata and the educational enterprise: general discussion of the conference. In: Anderson, R.C., Montague, W.E. (eds.) Schooling and the Acquisition of Knowledge, pp. 415–431. Lawrence Erlbaum, Hillsdale (1977)
4. Schank, R.C., Abelson, R.: Scripts, plans, goals and understanding: an inquiry into human knowledge structures. Lawrence Erlbaum, Hillsdale (1977)
5. Elson, M., van Looy, J., Vermeulen, L., Van den Bosch, F.: In the mind's: no Evidence for an effect of stereoscopic 3D on user experience of digital games. In: ECREA ECC 2012 preconference Experiencing Digital Games: Use, Effects Culture of Gaming, Istanbul (2012)
6. Lapointe, J.F., Savard, P., Vinson, N.G.: A comparative study of four input devices for desktop virtual walkthroughs. Comput. Hum. Behav. **27**, 2186–2191 (2011)
7. Slater, M., Usoh, M.: Body Centered Interaction in Immersive Virtual Environments. In: Thalmann, M., Thalmann, D. (eds.) Artificial Life and Virtual Reality, pp. 125–148. John Wiley, Oxford, UK (1994)
8. Costa, M.R., Kim, S.Y., Biocca, F.: Embodiment and embodied cognition. In: 5th International Conference, VAMR 2013, Held as Part of HCI International 2013, Las Vegas, pp. 333–342, 21–26 July 2013
9. Steuer, J.: Defining virtual reality: dimensions determining telepresence. J. Commun. **42**, 73–93 (1992)
10. Johnson-Laird, P.N.: The history of mental models. In: Manktelow, K., Chung, M.C. (eds.) Psychology of reasoning: Theoretical and historical perspectives, pp. 179–212. Psychol. Press, New York (2004)
11. Van Dijk, T.A., Kintsch, W.: Strategies of Discourse Comprehension. Academic Press, New York (1983)
12. Ohler, P.: Kognitive Filmpsychologie. Verarbeitung und mentale Repräsentation Cognitive psychology of movies. Processing and mental representation of narrative movies. MAkS-Publikationen, Münster (1994)
13. Wirth, W., Hartmann, T., Böcking, S., Vorderer, P., Klimmt, C., Schramm, H., Saari, T., Laarni, J., Ravaja, N., Gouveia, F.R., Biocca, F., Sacau, A., Jäncke, L., Baumgartner, T., Jäncke, P.: A process model of the formation of spatial presence experiences. Media Psychol. **9**, 493–525 (2007)
14. Tamborini, R., Skalski, P.: The role of presence in the experience of electronic games. In: Vorderer, P., Bryant, J. (eds.) Playing video games. motives, responses and consequences, pp. 225–240. Lawrence Erlbaum, Mahwah (2006)
15. Bowman, D.A., Kruijff, E., LaViola, J.J., Poupyrev, I.: 3D User Interfaces: Theory and Practice. Pearson Education, Boston (2005)
16. McGloin, R., Krcmar, M.: The Impact of Controller Naturalness on Spatial Presence, Gamer Enjoyment, and Perceived Realism in a Tennis Simulation Video Game. Presence Teleoperators Virtual Environ. **20**, 309–324 (2011)
17. Skalski, P., Tamborini, R., Shelton, A., Buncher, M., Lindmark, P.: Mapping the road to fun: natural video game controllers, presence, and game enjoyment. New Media Soc. **13**, 224–242 (2011)
18. Bowman, D.A., McMahan, R.P., Ragan, E.D.: Questioning naturalism in 3D user interfaces. Commun. ACM **55**, 78 (2012)

19. Bowman, D.A.: 3D User Interfaces. In: Soegaards, M., Dam, R.F. (eds.) The Encyclopedia of Human-Computer Interaction. The Interaction Design Foundation, Aarhus, Denmark (2014)

20. Gibson, J.J.: The Ecological Approach to Visual Prception. Houghton Mifflin, Boston (1979)

21. Surdick, R.T., Davis, E.T., King, R.A., Hodges, L.F.: The perception of distance in simulated visual displays: a comparison of the effectiveness and accuracy of multiple depth cues across viewing distances. Presence. **6**, 513–531 (1997)

22. Posner, M.I., Snyder, C.R., Davidson, B.J.: Attention and the Detection of Signals. J. Exp. Psychol. Gen. **109**, 73–91 (1980)

23. Hagendorf, H., Krummenacher, J., Müller, H.J., Schubert, T.: Wahrnehmung und Aufmerksamkeit. Springer Medizin, Berlin (2011)

24. King, R.D.: A brief history of stereoscopy. wiley interdisciplinary reviews. Comput. Stat. **5**, 334–340 (2013)

25. Pietschmann, D.: Spatial Mapping of Input and Output Spaces in Video Games. In: Schröter, F. (ed.) Games, Cognition, and Emotion. Hamburg University, Hamburg (2013)

26. Pietschmann, D., Liebold, B., Ohler, P.: Spatial mapping of mental interaction models and stereoscopic presentation. In: 2nd Conference on Research and Use of VR/AR Technologies, VAR2 Institute for Machine Tools and Production Processes, (2013)

27. Pietschmann, D., Liebold, B., Valtin, G., Ohler, P.: Taking space literally: reconceptualizing the effects of stereoscopic representation on user experience. Italian Journal of Game Studies 2, (2013). http://www.gamejournal.it/taking-space-literally-reconceptualizing-the-effects-of-stereoscopic-representation-on-user-experience/#.UUmGAb8purd

28. Pietschmann, D.: Relevanz räumlicher Informationen für die User Experience und Aufgabenleistung. Springer, Wiesbaden (2015)

29. Schmitz, M., Endres, C., Butz, A.: A Survey of human-computer interaction design in science fiction movies. In: INTETAIN 2008 Proceedings of the 2nd international conference on Intelligent Technologies for Interactive Entertainment, Article 7. ICST (2007)

30. Underkoffler, J.: g-speak (point and touch interface demonstration) TED 2010. What the World Needs Now, Long Beach (2010)

31. Spielberg, S.: Minority report. pp. 145 min. Twentieth Century Fox Film Corporation, USA (2002)

32. Kennedy, R.S., Lane, N.E., Berbaum, K.S., Lilienthal, M.G.: Simulator sickness questionnaire: an enhanced method for quantifying simulator sickness. Int. J. Aviat. Psychol. **3**, 203–220 (1993)

33. Atari Inc.: Space Race. Atari Inc., Sunnyvale, CA (1973)

34. Häkkinen, J., Pölönen, M., Takatalo, J., Nyman, G.: Simulator sickness in virtual display gaming: a comparison of stereoscopic and non-stereoscopic situations. In: 8th International Conference on Human Computer Interaction with Mobile Devices and Services Helsinki (2006)

35. Takatalo, J., Häkkinen, J., Kaistinen, J., Nyman, G.: User experience in digital games differences between laboratory and home. Simul. Gaming. **42**, 656–673 (2010)

36. Rajae-Joordens, R.J.E., Langendijk, E., Wilinski, P., Heynderickx, I.: Added value of a multi-view auto-stereoscopic 3D display in gaming applications. In: 12th International Display Workshops in conjunction with Asia Display, Takamatsu (2005)

37. LaViola, J.J., Litwiller, T.: Evaluating the benefits of 3d stereo in modern video games. In: CHI 2011 Proceedings of the SIGCHI Conference on Human Factors in Computing Systems, pp. 2345–2354. ACM (2011)

38. Davis, E.T., Hodges, L.F.: Human stereopsis, fusion, and stereoscopic virtual environments. In: Barfield, W., Furness, T.A.I. (eds.) Virtual Environments and Advances Interface Design, pp. 145–174. Oxford University Press, Oxford, GB (1995)
39. McMahan, R.P., Gorton, D., Gresock, J., McConnell, W., Bowman, D.A.: Separating the effects of level of immersion and 3D interaction techniques. 108 (2006)
40. Teather, R.J., Stuerzlinger, W.: Guidelines for 3D positioning techniques. In: Future Play 2007 Proceedings of the 2007 Conference on Future Play, pp. 61. ACM (2007)
41. Pietschmann, D., Rusdorf, S.: Matching levels of task difficulty for different modes of presentation in a VR table tennis simulation by using assistance functions and regression analysis. In: Shumaker, R., Lackey, S. (eds.) VAMR 2014, Part I. LNCS, vol. 8525, pp. 406–417. Springer, Heidelberg (2014)
42. Rusdorf, S., Brunnett, G., Lorenz, M., Winkler, T.: Real time interaction with a humanoid avatar in an immersive table tennis simulation. IEEE Trans. Visual Comput. Graphics 13, 15–25 (2007)
43. Polyphony Digital Inc.: Gran Turismo 5. vol. PlayStation 3. Sony Computer Entertainment America, Foster City, CA (2010)
44. Vorderer, P., Wirth, W., Gouveia, F.R., Biocca, F., Saari, T., Jäncke, F., Böcking, S., Schramm, H., Gysbers, A., Hartmann, T., Klimmt, C., Laarni, J., Ravaja, N., Sacau, A., Baumgartner, T., Jäncke, P.: MEC spatial presence questionnaire (MEC-SPQ): Short documentation and instructions for application, report to the European Community, Project Presence: MEC (IST-2001–37661) (2004)
45. Laugwitz, B., Held, T., Schrepp, M.: Construction and evaluation of a user experience questionnaire. In: Holzinger, A. (ed.) USAB 2008. LNCS, vol. 5298, pp. 63–76. Springer, Heidelberg (2008)
46. McAuley, E., Duncan, T., Tammen, V.V.: Psychometric properties of the Intrinsic Motivation Inventory in a competitive sport setting: a confirmatory factor analysis. Res. Q. Exerc. Sport 60, 48–58 (1989)
47. Bethesda Game Studios: The Elder Scrolls V: Skyrim. The Elder Scrolls, vol. PC. Bethesda Softworks LLC, Rockville, MD (2011)

The Impact of Time Pressure on Spatial Ability in Virtual Reality

Hua Qin, Bole Liu[⊠], and Dingding Wang

Department of Industrial Engineering,
Beijing University of Civil Engineering and Architecture,
Beijing 100044, People's Republic of China
topoollbl@foxmail.com

Abstract. The aim of this study is to explore the influence of time pressure on the spatial distance perceived by participants in the virtual reality. The results show that there is no significant difference while participants estimates the distance whether with or without time pressure. But while participants estimating short distance and long distance in the virtual environments there is significant difference. And under horizontal or vertical direction there are also significant differences while participants estimate long distance has more errors than short distance.

Keywords: Time pressure · Under horizontal · Vertical direction

1 Introduction

Psychometric studies of spatial ability [1–3] report evidence for several major spatial abilities factors. Two of them, spatial orientation and spatial relations, require the ability to imagine spatial forms from a perspective. When time-pressured, research shows that in general people become more anxious and may adopt a number of different strategies to complete tasks. However, for spatial ability very few studies indicate that time pressure has some effect on it [4–7].

The aim of this study is to explore the influence of time pressure on the spatial distance perceived in the virtual reality. To verify the impacts from the time pressure, experiments are designed. The experiment is to examine if there is significant difference while persons perceiving static distances between with limited time and without time limited.

2 Methodology

This experiment was conducted under the 3D scene and every participant must be experimented in two scenes. In the first scenario experiment participants should judge between the two groups of block (the black ones, the red ones)in a virtual tunnel. When they cross the tunnel, there is a distance of 10 meters two blue balls as a reference. Participants need to through the tunnel and judge the distance between the other two groups of block. In the second scenario experiment, participants sit in the Tower crane

© Springer International Publishing Switzerland 2015
R. Shumaker and S. Lackey (Eds.): VAMR 2015, LNCS 9179, pp. 60–66, 2015.
DOI: 10.1007/978-3-319-21067-4_7

control room and observe three stacking (the blue one, the red one, the black one) under the tower crane. The height of the blue one is 10 meters as the reference. Participants need to judge the height of the other stacking.

2.1 Participants

Twenty persons (10 males and 10 females) from Beijing, aged 20 to 25 were recruited for the experiment. These participants were asked to do the space perception test, and with which used to measure their ability of space perception. In order to test the spatial visualization ability of subjects, this test has used folding questions. The result shown in Table 1 as follows. In the analysis between the groups in mean square value is 0.450, the within groups in mean square value is 4.517. The test statistic $F = 1.0$. $p = 0.756 > 0.05$. So there is no significant differences in the spatial perception between the two groups of experimental personnel.

Table 1. One-way ANOVA

	Sum of squares	df	Mean square	F	Sig
Between Groups	.450	1	.450	.100	.756
Within Groups	81.300	18	4.517		
sum	81.750	19			

2.2 Apparatus

The trials were completed by using two tasks. Firstly, the tunnel experiment, the subjects need to pass through the tunnel and judge the distance between the two groups of block, a set of 10 meters block (The blue one) as a reference. The scenario of the tunnel experiment is presented on Fig. 1. In the second picture, you can see the scene after the experimenter entering the tunnel. After the experimenter through a distance of 10 meters of blue reference, and then he will be through two black cube object and two red sphere object, the object distance between the two groups were 5 meters, 10 meters. The experiment requires that the experimenter judge the distance of the two groups object after they through the tunnel. Secondly, the tower crane experiment, this scenario is simulated as a construction site, on the Fig. 3 there are three stacking under the tower crane on the construction site. This is presented in the first view of the experimenter. The participants in the tower crane operating room must observe the height of three stacking. Among them, the blue stacking's height of 10 meters as a reference. Figure 4 is the observation of three stacking with the third view point. Because of their location exists the difference between front and back, although the black stacking's height is 6 meters, the red stacking is 5 meters, the black object seems to be much higher than the red one in the first perspective. Therefore, the scene investigates that the experimenter's ability to judge the height of the stacking in the location exists the difference between front and back (Fig. 2).

Fig. 1. Tunnel for experiments

Fig. 2. Inside of the tunnel for experiments

2.3 Procedures

In this experiment, two groups of participants should complete two experiments. The first group of participants must estimate the horizontal distance between the objects and judge the vertical height of the object in 5 s. The second group of participants should complete the two experiments in the infinite time.

Each participant must fill in the informed consent and basic information questionnaire and then they can do the spatial ability experiments. Before doing the experiments, they must be familiar with the environment in the virtual space. Each one completed two formal experiments that judging the distance between two objects in a horizontal direction and determining the height of the object on the longitudinal. There

Fig. 3. Tower crane in the first perspective

Fig. 4. Tower crane in the third perspective

is a reference for the participant to judge. Experiments are conducted in a random order and the researchers recorded the time and the number of errors in the experiment after the participants completed it.

3 Results and Discussion

Table 2 showed the descriptive statistics of average errors, which are difference between correct and estimated values. Without time pressure while participants estimating horizontal distance, the mean are 2.10 and with time pressure the mean are 2.30.

Without time pressure while participants estimating vertical distance, the mean are 1.65 and with time pressure the mean are 2.30.

Table 3 showed the results of analysis of variance. For time pressure or direction, there was no significant difference between with pressure and without pressure while participants estimating distance in the virtual environments. For distance, the results showed that the significant was 0.000 less than 0.05 while participants estimating short distance and long distance in the virtual environments, which indicated there was significant difference while participants estimate long distance have more errors than short distance in the virtual environments. As for interaction effects, on the condition different direction there was significant difference between short and long distance. And the significant was also 0.005 less than 0.05. The results indicated that under horizontal or vertical direction there were significant differences while participants estimate long distance has more errors than short distance in the virtual environments.

Table 2. Descriptive statistics of errors

Direction	Time pressure	Distance	Mean (meters)	Std. Deviation	N
Horizontal	Without pressure	Short	1.15	1.15590	10
		Long	3.05	1.97836	10
		Total	2.10	1.85387	20
	With Pressure	Short	.60	1.07497	10
		Long	4.00	2.30940	10
		Total	2.30	2.47301	20
	Total	Short	.88	1.12244	20
		Long	3.53	2.14890	20
		Total	2.20	2.15965	40
vertical	Without pressure	Short	1.30	1.81353	10
		Long	2.00	1.05409	10
		Total	1.65	1.48767	20
	With Pressure	Short	2.20	2.14994	10
		Long	2.40	1.57762	10
		Total	2.30	1.83819	20
	Total	Short	1.75	1.99011	20
		Long	2.20	1.32188	20
		Total	1.98	1.68306	40
Total	Without pressure	Short	1.23	1.48213	20
		Long	2.53	1.63413	20
		Total	1.88	1.67466	40
	With Pressure	Short	1.40	1.84676	20
		Long	3.20	2.09259	20
		Total	2.30	2.15073	40
	Total	Short	1.31	1.65517	40
		Long	2.86	1.88444	40
		Total	2.09	1.92711	80

Table 3. Tests of between-subjects effects

Source	Type III Sum of squares	df	Mean square	F	Sig.
Corrected Model	84.138(a)	7	12.020	4.136	.001
Intercept	348.613	1	348.613	119.953	.000
Direction	1.013	1	1.013	.348	.557
Time pressure	3.613	1	3.613	1.243	.269
Distance	48.050	1	48.050	16.533	**.000**
Direction * Time pressure	1.013	1	1.013	.348	.557
Direction * Distance	24.200	1	24.200	8.327	**.005**
Time pressure * Distance	1.250	1	1.250	.430	.514
Direction * Time pressure* Distance	5.000	1	5.000	1.720	.194
Error	209.250	72	2.906		
Total	642.000	80			
Corrected Total	293.388	79			

4 Conclusion

The results show that there is no significant difference while participants estimates the distance whether with or without time pressure. But while participants estimating short distance and long distance in the virtual environments there is significant difference. And under horizontal or vertical direction there are also significant differences while participants estimate long distance has more errors than short distance. The results of the analysis could be as the foundation for the future.

Acknowledgement. The research project presented in this paper is a part of the Project "Key technologies of safety precaution of crane operation based on human factors engineering", which was supported by the Beijing Municipal Commission of Education. The authors would like to acknowledge the support of the Beijing Municipal Commission of Education for this project (KM201410016004).

References

1. Carroll, J.: Human cognitive abilities: A survey of Factoranalytical Studies. Cambridge University Press, New York (1993)
2. Lohman, D.F.: Spatial abilities as traits, processes, and knowledge. In: Sternberg, R.J. (ed.) Advances in the psychology of Human Intelligence, pp. 181–248. Lawrence Erlbaum, Hillsdale (1988)
3. Kozhevnikov, M., Hegarty, M.: A dissociation between object manipulationspatial ability and spatial orientation ability. Mem. Cogn. **29**(5), 745–756 (2001)
4. Maule, A.J., Edland, A.C.: The effects of time pressure on human judgment and decision-making. In: Ranyard, R., Crozier, W.R., Svenson, O. (eds.) Decision Making: Cognitive Models and Explanations, pp. 189–204. Routledge, New York (1997)

5. Maule, A.J., Hockey, G.R.J., Bdzola, L.: Effects of time-pressure on decision-making underuncertainty changes in affective state and information processing strategy. ActaPsychological **04**(3), 283–301 (2000)
6. Svenson, O., Benson, L.: Framing and time pressure in decision making. In: Svenson, O., Maule, A.J. (eds.) Time Pressure and Stress in Human judgment and Decision Making, pp. 133–144. Plenum Publishing Corporation, New York (1993)
7. Payne, J.W., Bettman, J.R., Johnson, E.J.: The Adaptive Decision Maker. Cambridge University Press, Cambridge (1993)

Research on the Visual Comfort for Small Spaces in Different Illuminance Environments

Linghua Ran[1], Xin Zhang[1(✉)], Hua Qin[2], and Taijie Liu[1]

[1] Ergonomics Laboratory, China National Institute of Standardization,
Beijing 100191, China
{ranlh,Zhangx,liutj}@cnis.gov.cn
[2] Department of Industrial Engineering, Beijing University of Civil Engineering
and Architecture, Beijing 100044, China
qinh03@mails.tsinghua.edu.cn

Abstract. This paper conducted an ergonomic experiment based on the visual comfort of users by simulating 5 external illuminance environments of night, kitchen, living room, common supermarket and high-end market. It studied the comfortable and acceptable illuminance levels for three doors refrigerator with ceiling lamps separately in the case of vacancy and filling with items. The experiment involved 40 subjects. Results showed that with ceiling lamps, there was no significant difference between the two status of vacancy and filling with items; however, they was different in 5 different external lighting environments. Based on the experimental data, this paper established a regression mathematical model in order to illustrate the relationship between the external lighting environments and the internal comfortable illuminance levels for the three doors refrigerators. The result will provide the reference for the optimization data for the lighting design of three doors refrigerators.

Keywords: Visual comfort · Lighting environment · Illuminance · Mathematical model

1 Introduction

Visual comfort, which largely depends on psychological perception, is the comfortable degree of people's psychological feeling about the lighting environments. There are many factors affecting the visual comfort, mainly including the lighting environment, illuminance, hue, age, etc. In lighting engineering, it is necessary to know the standard value of lighting level with good visual effects. In fact, this is to establish the internal relationship between subjective perception and objective physical quantity. Consequently, the psychophysical research results are usually used, which means under certain conditions, by ways of questionnaire, scaling and value evaluating, the quantities of physical stimulus and subjective perception should be linked together, i.e., establishing a relationship between qualitative and quantification.

There are a number of literatures about visual comfort and visual brightness, which have made certain achievements. Through experiments, document [1] gets the data of the relationship between satisfaction degree and illuminance in living room lighting.

© Springer International Publishing Switzerland 2015
R. Shumaker and S. Lackey (Eds.): VAMR 2015, LNCS 9179, pp. 67–73, 2015.
DOI: 10.1007/978-3-319-21067-4_8

Based on [1]'s data, document [2] establishes the evaluation equation of the lighting environment comfort level, which could reflect the relationship between comfort level and illuminance. Su Yanchen [3] studied the mathematical model relationship between illumination and human visual comfort based on specific circumstances of high-speed train, and made the multiple-regression analysis on internal illumination comfort of the high-speed train, with the application of statistics principle. Chen Zhonglin established the relationship between subjective sense and physical measurement in lighting engineering, the qualitative and quantitative analyses are connected through generalized Weber-Fechner Law for practical application problems of lighting engineering, a proximate function of subjective sense deduced from physical measurement was brought forward [4]. During 2002–2004, Boyce et al. [5] did a research about the office lighting and connected the lighting conditions, subjective comfort level and visual performance together, which shows the correlation among luminance, uniformity, comfort and dazzle. According to this, they also evaluated the interaction among the parameters in environmental space. Their results show that brightness-comfort and uniformity-comfort are all in positive correlation, that is to say the brighter the room is, the evener the light will be and people will feel more comfortable. Mark Rea et al. [6] used the method of semantic differential to study how lighting environment influence people's subjective preference. Their results show that when the brightness level rose from 0.96 cd/m2 to 1000 cd/m2, visual task performance and part of the subjective evaluation grades also rose correspondingly.

Overall, in the field of interior lighting comfort, the objects of related studies were mainly focused on building space, locomotive, airplane, etc. Refrigerators are closely related to our daily life. In order to look over the items inside, identify and take them out, it is necessary to have good internal illuminations, which will also influence the user experience. When choosing a proper lighting level for the internal space of refrigerators, it is necessary to take the aspects of visual ergonomics, visual satisfaction and effective utilization of energy into consideration. As for the refrigerator, its external lighting environment will also have an impact on its internal illuminating comfort. Currently, the studies of internal illuminating comfort for the refrigerators haven't covered the aspect of different external lighting environments. What's more, there is no relevant mathematical modeling. Consequently, it is of great necessity to study the visual comfort for the refrigerators.

2 Methods

2.1 Subjects

In all, 40 participants, comprising 21 men and 19 women were recruited, respectively. The mean ages of the participants were 40.13 (±11.14) years. They all have normal sight and corrected vision, without the problem of color blindness or weakness. During the whole process of experiment, all the participants were in good physical and psychological states.

2.2 Experimental Environment

To avoid the influence of natural lighting, ambient temperature and humidity, this experiment was done in dark rooms, and the external lighting environment was designed according to the selling and using environments of refrigerators. Usually, refrigerators are sold in supermarkets or special markets and placed in kitchens or living rooms. According to the mandatory standards GB 50034-2013 "Standard for lighting design of buildings" [7], the lighting standard value of normal supermarkets should be 300 lx and of high range market should be 500 lx. Moreover, the lighting standard values of kitchens and living rooms should be 100 lx–150 lx and 100 lx–300 lx respectively. Considering that refrigerators may also be used at night without any lighting, hence the night environmental conditions should also be taken into account. During the experiment, the internal illuminance level was controlled by regulating the lights installed on the roof of the laboratory, which could also satisfy the needs of external illuminance level (Chart 1) (Table 1).

Table 1. External environment Illuminance level

Experimental environment	Illuminance standard value (lx)	Experimental illuminance value (lx)
Nighttime conditions	/	5
Kitchen conditions	100 lx–150 lx	100
Living room conditions	100 lx –300 lx	170
Common supermarket environment	300 lx	300
High-end store environment	500 lx	580

2.3 Experiment Material

This study was mainly focused on refrigerators with three doors. The refrigerator cabinet liner was made of inner container materials and with the size of 52*65*45 cm (length*height*depth). The lighting system in freezer were lamp set on top of the inner cabinet, using the cold light LED point light source, with color temperature of 6500 k and CRI (Color Rendering Index) of 70. In the experiment, refrigerator was kept in two states: empty and filled with 60 % conventional food. In both cases, the ceiling lights were in external attachment with dimming devices.

2.4 Experiment Procedure

Before starting, the experimental process should be introduced to the participants. In the experiment, after changing the external environment illuminance, participants should firstly adapt to the environment visually. Then experiment began. Under the guidance of experimenters, participants adjusted the dimming devices in the cases of vacancy and with items respectively. They should adjust them to the level of brightness which made them feel the most comfortable, the minimum acceptable brightness and the maximum acceptable brightness. Experimenters recorded the gear numbers.

After experimenting, the XYI-III type all-digital portable illuminometer was used to make a stationing measurement inside the refrigerator. The illuminance of the left, right and back side walls in the refrigerator and of every baffle layer were all be measured. The measurement points were distributed uniformly on every level. Then the average measurement of illuminance value was worked out according to the measurement data.

3 Result and Discussion

3.1 The Comfort Illuminance Level in Cases of Empty Inner and Inner with Items

The comfortable illuminance level for refrigerators in cases of empty inner and inner with items in 5 external environments are described in Table 2 and Fig. 1.

Table 2. The comfortable illuminance level in different status

Experimental environment	Environmental illuminance (lx)	Most comfortable illuminance (lx)	
		Refrigerator inner with items	Empty refrigerator inner
Nighttime conditions	5	50	37
Kitchen conditions	100	69	64
Living room conditions	170	82	84
Common supermarket environment	300	123	122
High-end store environment	580	192	181

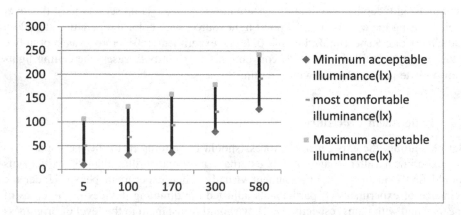

Fig. 1. Comfortable Illuminance level in case of inner with items

The experiment results show that the environmental main effect is remarkable (F = 138.252, P = 0.000). The most comfortable illuminance levels are significantly different among the 5 external lighting environments except between the kitchen environment and living room environment.

The Table 2 shows that when the external lighting environment ranges from 5 lx to 580 lx, the most comfortable illuminance level inside the refrigerator also rises accordingly. In low light situations, people need lower comfortable illuminance. The higher the exterior environment illuminance is, the higher the visual comfortable illuminance inside the refrigerator will be. This study reflects properly the objective law of inner visual comfortable illuminance and exterior environment illuminance. The most comfortable illuminance level for the inner with items is higher than the one with empty inner, and their difference in value are 13 lx, 4 lx, 8 lx, 1 lx and 11 lx in the 5 exterior lighting environments of nighttime, kitchen, living room, common supermarket and high-end store respectively. However, there is no significant difference from the view of statistics.

Figures 1 and 2 show the minimum and the maximum illuminance level inside the refrigerator also rises accordingly that in these two cases of inner with items and empty inners, and the former of the most comfortable illuminance level, and minimum and the maximum illuminance level (inner with items) is higher than the latter one (empty inner) in the 5 exterior lighting environments of nighttime, kitchen, living room, common supermarket and high-end store respectively.

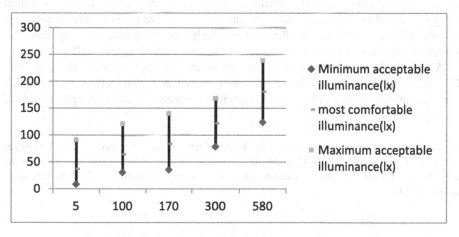

Fig. 2. Comfortable illuminance level in case of empty inner

3.2 The Mathematical Model for the Most Comfortable Illuminance Levels in Different External Lighting Environments

In order to establish the regression relationship between the external environment illuminance and the comfort inner illuminance of the refrigerator, we regarded the external environment illumination as the independent variable, the refrigerator comfort illumination levels as the dependent variable, while introduced whether the refrigerator is placed items as classification variables. Using the method of least squares fitting, the linear regression analysis was conducted.

The correlation coefficient for the regression equation R is 0.998, and the coefficient of determination R^2 is 0.995, which show the strong representative regression equation. Regression analysis of F = 752.620 statistics, the concomitant probability p < 0.001 for the regression analysis, which shows a plurality of dependent and independent existence of linear regression relationship between the variables, the regression equations that have significance. The mathematical model for the comfort inner illuminance of the refrigerator is:

$$y = 47.884 + 0.249x_1 - 7.615x_2 \tag{1}$$

x_1 is the environment illuminance, and x_2 is whether the refrigerator is placed items. When $x_2 = 0$ represents the refrigerator with empty inner, and $x_2 = 1$ represents the refrigerator with items in it.

4   Conclusions

Illumination design may influence the user experience greatly. The refrigerator inner comfortable illuminance levels are variable in different exterior lighting environments. Consequently, the illumination design should take the users' using environments into consideration. As for Chinese consumers, there are other factors, such as different living space, different areas in the north and south, different types of refrigerators and different placing locations. The illumination design of refrigerators should give full consideration to their target users and estimate their location scientifically.

As for the high-end refrigerators, the intelligent lighting control devices are feasible. Based on the exterior lighting environments and the mathematical models in this paper, the interior lights can be regulated infinitely, which will satisfy people's needs of visual comfort.

Acknowledgment. This work is supported by the National Key Technology R&D Program (project number: 2014BAK01B01) and China National Institute of Standardization through the "special funds for the basic R&D undertakings by welfare research institutions" (project number: 522014Y-3346).

References

1. Shao-gang, Z., Jian-ping, Z., Yao-gen, Z.: Experimental study on the living room lighting in housing. China Illum. Eng. J. **12**(2) (2001)
2. Xian-Guang, Z., Yong-Hui, Z., Zhong-Lin, C.: Comfort illumination study on the living room. Light Lighting **27**(1) (2003)
3. Yan-Chen, S., Rui-Ping, Z., Fei-Fei, L.: Research on Mathematical model of Illumination comfort in High Speed Trains. China Measur. Test **39**(z2) (2013)

4. Zhong-Lin, C., Ji, W., Ying-Kui, H., De-Xin, Z.: Study of transform between qualitative analysis and quantitative analysis in lighting engineering. J. Chongqing Jianzhu Univ. **28**(4) (2006)
5. Boyce, P.R., et al.: Lighting quality and office work: two field simulation study. Lighting Res. Technol. **38**(3), 191–223 (2006)
6. Rea, M.S., Freyssinier-Nova, J.P.: Color rendering: a tale of two metrics. Color Res. Appl. **33**(3), 192–202 (2008)
7. GB 50034-2013, Standard for lighting design of buildings (2013)

Analysis of Sociocultural Constructs Applicable to Blue Force Teams: Increasing Fidelity from Pencil and Paper and Video Tests to Virtual Environments

David Scribner[1]([⊠]), Pete Grazaitis[1], Asi Animashaun[1],
Jock Grynovicki[1], and Lauren Reinerman-Jones[2]

[1] U.S. Army Research Laboratory,
Aberdeen Proving Ground, Aberdeen, MD, USA
{david.r.scribner.civ, peter.j.grazaitis.civ,
asisat.f.animashaun.civ}@mail.mil
[2] University of Central Florida, Orlando, USA

Abstract. Understanding sociocultural factors and the role they play in a military context is becoming recognized as a shortcoming within both military training and decision-making tools for commanders in the field. We begin by discussing sociocultural theory, its development, and history. Next, we discuss approaches to collecting small-scale friendly force leader and subordinate sociocultural factors. Then, we describe and discuss the utility of Situational Judgment Tests (SJTs) to elicit various sociocultural values in decision-making and how those tests may be translated to more enriched and life-like scenarios in virtual environments. Positive and negative attributes of each approach and viable resources to support their use are discussed.

Keywords: Sociocultural · Culture · Decision-making · Military · Data collection tools · Virtual environments · Situational judgment test

1 Introduction

Identifying socio-cultural factors that influence decision-making and communication is an important aspect of military training, personnel selection, and future military technology. The Army has responded to the needs of its leadership by providing increased support to enable "foreign language and cultural capabilities [1, 7]. In fact, the Army is highly interested in developing cultural competence to better plan and execute operations within coalition and multi-national forces as well as within the U.S. Army structure [1, 7, 10]. There are many facets to consider when discussing cross-cultural competencies (CCC) and socio-cultural variables. There are several methods to employ when assessing such constructs. There are important lessons learned derived from several sources that highlight the performance-based needs and the unity of the military unit and the cross-cultural understanding required to make today's military operations successful.

© Springer International Publishing Switzerland 2015
R. Shumaker and S. Lackey (Eds.): VAMR 2015, LNCS 9179, pp. 74–80, 2015.
DOI: 10.1007/978-3-319-21067-4_9

While socio-cultural aspects have been studied in general populations for decision making [25], not very much has been performed for the military population. Some research has outlined command and control aspects or cognitive biases in decision-making [15, 16] Unfortunately, decision-making research for the military has not focused on the inclusion of culture and even less frequently on decision-making in a military environment [12]. Also, little research has been focused on the Soldier's/Commander's own socio-cultural attributes and how they may affect their decision making [8, 27]. With this in mind, the U.S. Army Research Laboratory's Human Research and Engineering Directorate (ARL HRED) partnered with the University of Central Florida to launch a research program entitled "Socio-Cultural Depiction for Decision-Making". This program is concentrated on understanding the socio-cultural factors that affect

Soldier/Commander decision-making, especially addressing how a Soldier's own cultural background influences his or her decision-making. A discussion of the taxonomy of socio-cultural factors that influence decision-making (created under the Relevant Information for Social Cultural Depiction (RISC-D) program) [33] and how it was developed follows.

Among lessons learned, a Joint Coalition Operational Analysis posited that the "Lack of unity of effort between civilian and military organizations tended to be a key component of transition challenges" [17]. Specifically cited was a "...lack of understanding of counterpart cultures and bureaucratic processes" [17]. Additionally, service culture was highlighted as a key attribute to instilling mission command and that our diverse military and civilian cultures while providing strength to our mission, still require greater understanding in terms of culture [17] This understanding will come in the form of identifying and establishing metrics to identify core CCC and to assess and train these competencies in our Army leadership.

2 Cross-Cultural Competency and Cultural Theory

CCC has been assessed by several prominent researchers who have outlined several different sets of knowledge, skills, and abilities (KSAs) to include awareness, communication skills, flexibility, self-regulation of reactions, empathy, non- ethnocentrism, and a willingness to learn about other cultures [6]. Selmesky [35] briefly defines CCC as "the ability to quickly and accurately comprehend, then appropriately and effectively engage individuals from distinct cultural backgrounds to achieve the desired effect". The definition of CCC varies and has been researched for several decades by Hofstede [13] who developed a well-recognized set of cultural dimensions including (1) Power Distance, (2) Uncertainty Avoidance, (3) Individualism/Collectivism (4) Masculinity/Femininity with (5) Long-term/Short-term Orientation [14]. Hofstede's dimensions of culture values have been well researched; however, there is dissent in the literature regarding the limitations of his work.

Kirkman, Lowe, and Gibson [18] in a review of Hofstede's work, acknowledge that while his sizable body of work is impactful for organizational cross-cultural research, researchers should consider additional cultural values. The authors also report that research using Hofstede's framework is weak in terms of effect size; small effect sizes have been found in meta-analysis of over 180 studies with this framework especially on individualism-collectivism. Hofstede's work is also criticized as having a definition of national culture that is too narrowly defined and that his methodologies and data collection may have been too narrowly executed [4, 23]. As widely cited as Hofstede's work has been, there are several other promising cross-cultural frameworks to consider.

Schwartz [34], Smith and Dugan [37], and Graen and Uhl-Bien [11]. Schwartz [34] developed seven cross-cultural values including Conservatism, Intellectualism, Affective Autonomy, Hierarchy, Egalitarianism, Mastery and Harmony. Smith and Dugan [37] found three cross-cultural dimensions that correlated well with Hofstede's framework [14] to include Individualism/collectivism, Power Distance and Long- versus Short-Term Orientation. The authors concluded that masculinity/femininity and uncertainty avoidance were not required in later research efforts. The work by Graen and Uhl-Bien [11], called the leader-member exchange theory, is premised upon the idea that good leadership comes about when there is a high team (leader-member) level of mutual trust, respect, and obligation. While several theories exist to help explain cultural competencies, the measure of these frameworks and constructs is also varied [31].

There are several ways in which to collect CCC data including questionnaires, surveys, and specific CCC tests. Specific CCC tests of reasonable validity include the Cultural Quotient (CQ) [2], the Intercultural Adjustment Potential Scale (ICAPS) [22], and the Multicultural Potential Quotient (MPQ) [39]. These three CCC tests were viewed as having the best potential over such measures as personality and intelligence tests although the factor structure of these tests may require further confirmatory factor analysis [21]. CCC data can also be collected at the individual level as noted above, and at the organizational level. Several approaches are useful for collecting organizational CCC. These methods include aggregating individual level CCC data, ethnographic methods, and measuring performance [40]. Another method includes the situational judgment test.

3   Situational Judgment Tests

Situational Judgment Tests or SJTs are popular as personnel selection tests are designed to elicit judgment choices or decisions to be made in the context of job "situations" for various job-related content [28, 32, 36, 41, 42]. SJTs are typically formatted to be multiple choice and have been used for the better part of a century. SJTs are commonly thought of as highly predictive of job performance. In fact, Christian, Edwards, and Bradley [6] found SJTs to have high validity for assessing teamwork, leadership, and interpersonal skills. One caution in using SJTs is that the constructs measured should be of primary concern over the methodological (simulating the work environment) [6, 30]. There are several modalities through which SJTs can be presented including paper-and-pencil tests, video presentations, and multi-media formats. All of these formats have varying fidelities.

Fidelity within SJTs is the consistency with which the created job situation, or task stimulus, is related to the way it is represented in the actual workplace. For example, written format SJTs are presented on paper and the participant is asked to select a response from the alternatives, which is considered a low-fidelity option. As an alternative, video-based job scenarios offer a pre-canned workplace scenario that is then halted to ask the participant to select from the range of possible responses. In video format, responses are presented visually with narration [19]. Video format is reported to be higher in predictive and incremental validity over paper-and-pencil tests for interpersonally based SJTs, although face validity may have no significant differences [20]. The authors and others further report that the higher fidelity of the video format and its closer resemblance to actual job situations are the sources of the increased validity [26]. In today's selection environment, these video-based or multi-media presentations of job situations would most likely be made available using DVD technology; however, virtual environments provide another presentation medium alternative.

4 Virtual Environments

Virtual environments (VE) have been used extensively for cross-cultural training [8] and offer the potential for interactive SJTs with increased richness and detail [19]. While Lievens, Peeters, and Schollaert posit that multi-media SJTs have a lower cognitive loading, Lievens Sackett [20] report that on an interpersonally-based video SJT, the lowered cognitive loading contributed to higher predictive and incremental validity. The cognitive load issue remains invalidated, although it appears that lowering the cognitive load is a positive attribute to multi-media and VE presentation formats for SJTs. The selection of the specific virtual environment is an important one with various options to be considered.

First, the time and cost of producing SJTs is considerable. Producing video segments with scripts, filming and editing, and human actors require a great deal of logistical and financial resources which may be defrayed by employing photorealistic animation [3]. VE presentation can also provide "nested" or interactive scenarios that are driven by participant responses, providing rich data analysis opportunities. Additionally, the biases or adverse impacts that SJTs have towards race, sex, and age [19] may be more easily tested using avatars that suit the particular participant at the time (by simply altering the race, age and gender). The specific environment to be used for testing VE SJTs will impact the utility and scope of the SJT and several environments are available including those at the ARL HRED Simulation and Training Technology Center (STTC) in Orlando, Florida.

STTC currently has several state of the art VE's available including the Enhanced Dynamic Geo-social Environment (EDGE) [9] Another VE, MOSES, provides large scale terrain for training and for smaller-scale operations such as room-clearing, but may not have the capability to provide very specific construct-based training such as that required for cultural awareness [5].

EDGE may provide this additional capability that is lacking in MOSES. This is important since technology gaps for cultural training were identified by several Soldiers during a training event using the facility [38]. EDGE is capable of providing a rich virtual character set and an array of virtual objects to create a military "job experience". It is foreseeable that the future of SJTs may enable taking on a role of a "character" of one's self with which to interact with a "job situation" that is loaded with socio-cultural context on which decisions can be selected. While some research purports that paper-and-pencil tests are superior to game-based coursework [24], we feel that taking SJTs to the virtual environment is an important next step for advancing the state of the art in assessing socio-cultural attributes of military team members.

5 Conclusion

Building VE SJTs certainly have both benefits and drawbacks. We may carefully examine some of the difficulties in building VE SJTs including determining what theoretical foundation will be followed, how adverse effects for bias towards age, sex, and race [30] may be accounted for, and to ensure that the SJT virtual content validity and reliability concerns are addressed. While some multi-media SJTs have paved the way for this effort. For example, Rockstuhl, Ang, Ng, Lievens, and Van Dyne [29] have recently created multi-media SJTs which successfully demonstrated the incremental reliability of situational assessment prior to response selection. The step from multi-media to representative VE representations may be difficult to replicate, however, once deciding on how to best build VE SJTs, there will be several potential Army benefits.

Interactive SJTs that rely on VEs such as EDGE may produce several Army benefits. The benefits of using VE SJTs are not only the task performance and interpersonal citizenship prediction [6] but also may include the judgment of the job situation itself [28], which is emerging in the SJT literature [29]. Relatively low-cost socio-cultural training ability with feedback based upon both (1) perception and interpretation of the situation and (2) the selection of possible final responses may be possible. Personnel selection for the Army may also experience incremental validity for those officers and enlisted Soldiers who are likely to be placed into judgment situations with socio-cultural context. The benefits include a highly immersive and engaging environment with less-than multi-media production costs, founded on sound psychological theory and frameworks. We propose that VE-based SJTs should be developed as both training and selection tools to bolster the Army need for enhanced socio-cultural support.

References

1. Abbe, A., Gulick, L.M.V., Herman, J.L.: Cross-cultural competence in army leaders: a conceptual and empirical foundation. United States, Army Research Institute for the Behavioral and Social Sciences. ARI Study Report, 2015-XX, October 2008
2. Ang, S., Van Dyne, L., Koh, C.: Personality correlates of the four-factor model of cultural intelligence. Group Org. Manage. **31**, 100–123 (2006)
3. Bejar, I.I., Cooper, P.L.: On the feasibility of generating situational judgment tests by means of photorealistic methods. Educational Testing Service Research Memorandum, RM-13-08 (2013)
4. Hamilton, B.A.: Final Report: Socio-Cultural Influences on Decision-Making and Communication. ARL prime Contract No. DAAD19-01-C-0065 (Alion). July 8, 2011. McLean Virginia: Booz Allen Hamilton (2011)

5. Buede, D., DeBlois, B., Maxwell, D., McCarter, B.G.: Filling the need for intelligent, adaptive non-player characters. In: The Interservice/Industry Training, Simulation & Education Conference (I/ITSEC), Orlando, FL (2013)
6. Christian, M.S., Edwards, B.D., Bradley, J.C.: Situational judgment tests: Constructs assessed and meta-analysis of their criterion-related validities. Pers. Psychol. **63**, 83–117 (2010)
7. Department of the Army Headquarters: Army Culture and Foreign Language Strategy (2009). http://www.almc.army.mil/ALU_CULTURE/docs/ARMYCULTURESTRATEGY-01DEC09.pdf
8. Downes-Martin, S., Long, M., Alexander, J.: Virtual reality as a tool for cross cultural communication: an example from military team training. In: Visual Data Interpretation, SPIE, vol. 1668, pp. 28–38 (1992)
9. Dwyer, T., Griffith, T., Maxwell, D.: Rapid simulation development using a game engine – enhanced dynamic geo-social environment (EDGE). In: Proceedings of the Interservice/Industry Training, Simulation and Education Conference (I/ITSEC), Orlando, FL (2011)
10. Forman, S., Zachar, P.: Cross-cultural adjustment of international officers, during professional military education in the united states. Mil. Psychol. **13**(2), 117–128 (2001)
11. Graen, G.B., Uhl-Bien, M.: Relationship-based approach to leadership: development of leader-member exchange (LMX) theory of leadership over 25 years: Applying a multi-level multi-domain perspective. Leadersh. Quart. **6**(2), 219–247 (1995)
12. Guess, C.D.: Decision-making in individualistic and collective cultures. Int. Assoc. Cross Cult. Psychol. **4**(1), 1–18 (2004)
13. Hofstede, G.: Culture's Consequences: International Differences in Work Related Values. Sage, Beverly Hills (1980)
14. Hofstede, G.: Culture's consequences, 2nd edn. Sage Publications, Thousand Oaks (2001)
15. Jarvis, D.: A Methodology for Analyzing Complex Military Command and Control (C2) Networks. Alidade Inc., Newport (2005)
16. Jasner, M.: Cognitive Biases in Military Decision Making. US Army WarCollege, Carlisle Barracks, PA (2007). http://www.dtic.mil/cgi-bin/GetTRDoc?Location=U2&doc=GetTRDoc.pdf&AD=ADA493560
17. Joint and Coalition Operational Analysis (JCOA): Decade of War, vol. 1, Enduring Lessons from the Past Decade of Operations. Suffolk, VA (2012)
18. Kirkman, B.L., Lowe, K.B., Gibson, C.B.: A quarter century of Culture's Consequences: a review of empirical research incorporating Hofstede's cultural values framework (2006)
19. Lievens, F., Peeters, H., Schollaert, E.: Situational judgment tests: a review of recent research. Pers. Rev. **37**(4), 426–441 (2008)
20. Lievens, F., Sackett, P.R.: Video-based versus written situational judgment tests: a comparison in terms of predictive validity. J. Appl. Psychol. **91**(5), 1181–1188 (2006)
21. Matsumoto, D., Hwang, H.C.: Assessing cross-cultural competence: a review of available tests. J. Cross Cult. Psychol. **44**(6), 849–873 (2013)
22. Matsumoto, D., LeRoux, J.A., Ratzlaff, C., Tatani, H., Uchida, H., Kim, C., Araki, S.: Development and validation of a measure of intercultural adjustment potential in Japanese sojourners: the intercultural adjustment potential scale (ICAPS). Int. J. Intercultural Relat. **25**, 483–510 (2001)
23. McSweeney, B.: Hofstede's model of national cultural differences and their consequences: a triumph of faith - a failure of analysis. Hum. Relat. **55**(1), 89–118 (2002)
24. Miller, J.T., Bink, M.L.: Assessing the use of game-based exercises in the staff attack-the-network course. United States Army Research Institute for the Behavioral and Social Sciences. ARI research Note 2015-XX, September 2014

25. Moniarou-Papaconstantinou, V., Tsatsorani, A., Katsis, A., Koulaidis, V.: LIS as a field of study: Socio-cultural influences on students decision- making. Aslib Proc. New Inf. Perspect. **62**(3), 321–344 (2010)

26. Peus, C., Braun, S., Frey, D.: Situation-based measurement of the full range of leadership model – development and validation of a situational judgment test. Leadersh. Q. **24**, 777–795 (2013)

27. Picucci, P.M., Numrich, S.K.: Mission-driven needs: understanding the military relevance of socio-cultural capabilities. In: Johansson, B., Jain, S., Montoya-Torres, J., Hugan, J., Yucesan, E. (eds.) Proceedings of the 2010 Winter Simulation Conference (2010)

28. Ployart, R.E.: The predictor response process model. In: Weekley, J.A., Ployart, R.E. (eds.), Situational judgment tests: Theory, measurement and application, pp. 83–105. Earlbaum, Mahwah (2006)

29. Rockstuhl, T., Ang, S., Ng, K., Lievens, F., Van Dyne, L.: putting judgment situations into situational judgment tests: evidence from intercultural multimedia SJTs. Journal of Applied Psychology. (Advance Online Publication) (2014). http://dx.doi.org/10.1037/a0038098

30. Roth, P., Bobko, P., McFarland, L., Buster, M.: Work sample tests in personnel selection: A meta-analysis of black-white differences in overall and exercise scores. Pers. Psychol. **61**, 637–661 (2008)

31. Salas, E., Burke, C.S., Wilson-Donnelly, K.A.: Promoting effective leadership with in multi-cultural teams: an event-based approach. In: Day, D.V., Zaccaro, S.J., Halpin, S.M. (eds.) Leadership Development for Transforming Organizations: Growing Leaders for Tomorrow, pp. 293–323. Lawrence Earlbaum Associates Publishers, Mahwah (2004)

32. Salter, N.P., Highhouse, S.: Assessing manager's common sense using situational judgment tests. Manag. Decis. **47**(3), 392–398 (2009)

33. Samms, C., Hill, S., Animashaun, A., Henry, S., Patton, D.: Ungvarsky: Development of a Taxonomy of Socio-Cultural Factors that Influence Decision-Making. Army Research Laboratory Aberdeen Proving Ground, MD. ARL-TR-#### (unpublished) (2014)

34. Schwartz, S.H.: A Theory of Cultural Values and Some Implications. Appl. Psychol. Int. Rev. **48**(1), 23–47 (1999)

35. Selmeski, B.: Military Cross-Cultural Competence: core concepts and individual development. Royal Military College of Canada (AFCLC Contract Report 2007-01) (2007)

36. Sharma, S., Gangopadhyay, M., Austin, E., Mandal, M.K.: Development and validation of a situational judgment test of emotional intelligence. Int. J. Sel. Assess. **21**(1), 57–73 (2013)

37. Smith, P.B., Dugan, S.: National culture and the values of organizational employees: a dimensional analysis across 43 nations. J. Cross Cult. Psychol. **27**(2), 231–265 (1996)

38. United States Army Research Laboratory: ARL hosts Soldiers at Simulation and Training Center to get feedback from theater (2010). http://www.arl.army.mil/www/default.cfm/default.cfm?article=546

39. van der Zee, K.I., van Oudenhoven, J.P.: The multicultural personality questionnaire: a multidimensional instrument of multicultural effectiveness. Eur. J. Pers. **14**, 291–309 (2000)

40. van Driel, M., Gabrenya, W.K.: Organizational cross-cultural competence: Approaches to measurement. J. Cross Cult. Psychol. **44**(6), 874–899 (2012)

41. Weekley, J.A., Ployhart, R.E.: An introduction to situational judgment testing. In: Weekley, J.A., Ployhart, R.E. (eds.) Situational Judgment Tests. Lawrence Erlbaum Associates, Mahwah (2006)

42. Whetzel, D.L., McDaniel, M.A.: Situational judgment tests: an overview of current research. Hum. Resour. Manag. Rev. **19**, 188–202 (2009)

Influence of Highlighting Words Beneath Icon on Performance of Visual Search in Tablet Computer

Li Wang[1(✉)], Liezhong Ge[2], Ting Jiang[1], Hongyan Liu[2],
Hongting Li[2], Xinkui Hu[2], and Hanling Zheng[2]

[1] National Key Laboratory of Human Factors Engineering, China Astronaut
Research and Training Center, Beijing, China
wanglikunyu@126.com
[2] Zhejiang Sci-Tech University, Hangzhou, China

Abstract. This study compares the influence of different kinds of highlighting words beneath icons on visual search performance on the interface of tablets through response time and accurate rates of participants completing a search task. The results indicate highlighting words below icons could improve performance of searching a target icon; and when the icons are gray, under the condition of color words and flicker words is more effective for visual search. When the icons are colorful, under the condition of flicker words is more effective for visual search.

Keywords: Highlighting words · Icon color · Visual searching performance

1 Introduction

Visual information search is a basic demand of computer or other electronic products users as well as touch-screen tablets users. Among the information, the most common forms are two kinds, namely graphics and text [1]. For the user interface of tablets, icon has important function to transfer graphics and text information. In order to operating fast and searching the target icons, designers and researchers have done a lot of research on highlight of visual information.

In the field of ergonomics, about icon research mainly focuses on several aspects [2]:

1. Complexity: Users search simple icons faster than complex icons [3].
2. Specificity: Users are prefer to specific icons instead of abstract icons, although specific icons are not always better than abstract ones on response time and accurate rate of searching target [4, 5].
3. Familiarity: If users are familiar with icons, they could give a fast and accurate response whether the icons are specific or abstract [6].
4. Semantic distance correlation: Many researchers believe that the semantic distance and the icon has a close relationship, but due to lack of electronic database icons, objective measuring index for icons have not been proposed now [7].

© Springer International Publishing Switzerland 2015
R. Shumaker and S. Lackey (Eds.): VAMR 2015, LNCS 9179, pp. 81–87, 2015.
DOI: 10.1007/978-3-319-21067-4_10

5. Other factors: Knowledge about target, visual stimulus characteristics (such as size, color, spatial location), semantic features of icons (such as classification) etc. [2].

Studies have shown that highlighting can attract rapidly more attention to the targets especially for visual search, so as to improve the search performance [8]. Others study highlighting performance of different color under the condition of a single color or compound colors background. The results show that under a single color background like light blue or light green, search performance of red highlight is the best. But advantage of red highlight under natural color is not so obvious [9]. Some other scholars study preview effect on color highlight through preview search paradigm. They find that color high salience does not improve preview effect, but loss some preview effect [10]. Ge et al. (2000) compare performance of three highlight under the background of white and black, which are high, middle and low frequency. The results indicate that flicker can effectively improve the visual search performance, when the flicker frequency high (above 27 Hz) [11]. Besides color, underline as highlight can also effectively promote the performance of visual search, especially under condition of difficult task or white background [12]. If visual material is graphics, Hu et al. (2001) study that shading can the performance of visual search significantly [13].

However, these studies are mainly applied in the field of desktop computer, mobile phone or web browsing. In recent years, with the popularity of touchscreen products like tablets, how to improve icon search performance on the touchscreen has become the urgent problem to solve. The aim of this study is to study highlight of words below icons on the tablet interface. Examine whether highlights will improve search performance of icons, and thus to provide a reference for words design below icons.

2 Methodology

The independent variables of this experiment are icon colors and highlighting styles, which icon colors have two levels such as gray and colors and highlighting styles of words have four levels such as none, color, flicker and bold. The dependent variables are accurate rate and response time of completing searching a target icon. The response time is recorded between target icon appearing and response of participants. And control variables are icon content, appearing sequence of target icon, and icons position on the searched interface and experiment conditions.

For this experiment, two factors within-subject design are adopted. Eighteen persons participates the experiments. And they are divided into two groups randomly, which each group has 9 participants including 4 males and 5 females. One group conducts the trials with gray condition firstly, and then color condition. The sequence of the other group's trials is opposite. Under one icon color, four kinds of highlighting style of words are presented randomly.

2.1 Participants

Eighteen persons (10 females) participated in the experiment. They all complete written informed consent in accordance with institutional guidelines of Zhejiang Sci-Tech University. The age range is between 20–45 years old. The education backgrounds are bachelor degree or above. Their visions are normal or corrected to normal. There are no color blindness or weakness and right-handed.

2.2 Apparatus

The experiment is conducted on a Newman NewPad. The screen resolution is 1280*800 pixels and the size is 10.1 inches. And the operating system is Android 4.1. The program is written by JAVA language.

Thirty-six icons were arranged in a 6*6 matrix with each icon covering 256px *256px. The font below icons is Chinese Arial, size five. The spacing between adjacent icons is 20 dp. The spacing between adjacent characters (four Chinese characters) below one icon is 10 dp. The horizontal distance between subjects' eyes and the middle icon on the screen display is 30 cm. And the angle between the Newman NewPad and the horizontal plane is about 45 degrees.

The 36 icons are presented on the black ground like Fig. 1. And the Fig. 2 shows the four kinds of highlighting styles of words. For each trial, a target icon and 35 interference icons are presented to the participants. In order to remove the effect of position of and sequence icons, the position of the icons are arranged randomly, and target icons are posited uniformly on the four quadrants of screen.

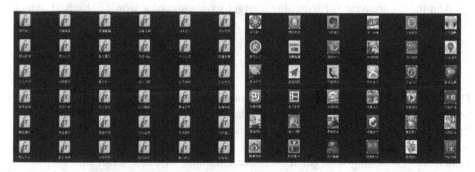

Fig. 1. Icon color (Left-color; Right-gray) (Color figure online)

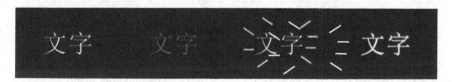

Fig. 2. Highlighting styles of words (from left to right: none; color; flicker; bold) (Color figure online)

2.3   Tasks and Procedure

Before experiments, the participants should read the instruction and know the procedure and requirements of the experiments. Then sign the consent forms. After completing these, participants begin to conduct sets of exercises until the accurate rate is 85 %. If participants could not respond in 10000 ms, the result is counted as an error.

Then, formal experiments appear. For each trial, a target icon was firstly presented for 2000 ms, and then a search interface including the target icon and 35 distracter icons appeared. Subjects were asked to find the target icon as soon as possible and click it. The task must complete in 10000 ms. Otherwise skip into next task automatically and this task is recorded as an error. The whole formal experiments are controlled by JAVA programs.

3   Results and Analysis

3.1   Description

Table 1 showed the descriptive statistics of response time and accurate rate of completing searching a target icon.

For gray icons, the time of participants searching a target icon with color words and flicker words is less than the other two kinds highlighting styles of words. And the accurate rate of searching a target icon with color words and flicker words is higher than the other two kinds highlighting styles of words.

For color icons, the time of participants searching a target icon with flicker words is the least.

And the accurate rate of searching a target icon with color words is highest, which is 100 %.

3.2   Effects of Different Icon Color

The repeated measure ANOVA on icon color yield significant main effects on response time and accurate rate. For response time, the results indicate that the significant is less 0.01 ($F(3,51) = 70.42$, $P < 0.01$) between gray icons and color icons while participants search a target icon using the two kinds of icons. The average response time of participants' searching a target icon under condition of color icons is 2717.00 ms

Table 1. Descriptive statistics

	Gray		Color	
	Time (ms)	Accurate rate (%)	Time (ms)	Accurate rate (%)
None	5391.96 (751.29)	69.79 (14.74)	3073.98 (662.01)	91.32 (9.86)
Color	1954.87 (426.17)	99.65 (1.47)	2815.77 (374.50)	97.92 (4.29)
Flicker	1850.53 (207.34)	99.65 (1.47)	1841.06 (156.66)	100 (0.00)
Bold	5399.23 (770.02)	65.28 (13.76)	3137.19 (474.09)	92.01 (7.37)

Note: The number in parentheses is the standard deviation.

(416.81) while the average response time under condition of color icons is 3649.14 ms (538.70). For accurate rate, the results also indicate that the significant is less 0.01 ($F(3,51) = 68.71, P < 0.01$) between gray icons and color icons while participants search a target icon using the two kinds of icons. The average accurate rate of participants' searching a target icon under condition of color icons is 95.31 % (5.38) while the average accurate rate under condition of gray icons is 83.59 % (7.86).

3.3 Effects of Different Highlighting Style

The repeated measure ANOVA on highlighting styles of words yield significant main effects on response time and accurate rate. For response time, the results indicate that the significant is less 0.01 ($F(3,51) = 266.52, P < 0.01$) among the four kinds of styles while participants search a target icon. The average response time of participants' searching a target icon under condition of color words or flicker words is 2385.32 ms (400.33) or 1845.80 ms (182.00) while the average response time under condition of none of highlighting or bold words is 4232.97 ms (706.65) or 4268.21 ms (622.05). For accurate rate, the results also indicate that the significant is less 0.01 ($F(3,51) = 63.16, P < 0.01$) among the four kinds of styles while participants search a target icon. The average accurate rate of participants' searching a target icon under condition of color words or flicker words is 98.79 % (2.88) or 99.83 % (0.74) while the average response time under condition of none of highlighting or bold words is 80.56 % (12.30) or 78.65 % (10.57).

3.4 Interaction Effects of Icon Color and Highlighting Style

The results of the repeated measures model indicate that interaction effects of icon color and highlighting styles of words on response time is significant ($F(3,51) = 91.55, P < 0.01$). When the icons are gray, the response time of participants under the condition of color words and flicker words is less than those under the condition of none of highlighting and bold words. However, there isn't significant difference between flicker words and color words and between none of highlighting and bold words. When the icons are colorful, the response time of participants under the condition of flicker words is less than the other styles.

The results of the repeated measures model indicate that interaction effects of icon color and highlighting styles of words on accurate rate is also significant ($F(3,51) = 31.34, P < 0.01$). When the icons are gray, the accurate rate under the condition of color words and flicker words is higher than those under the condition of none of highlighting and bold words. However, there isn't significant difference between flicker words and color words and between none of highlighting and bold words. When the icons are colorful, the accurate rates under the condition of flicker words and color words are higher than none of highlighting and bold words.

After the formal experiment, participants were instructed to evaluate the satisfaction of the color and the highlighting type of words of each icon based on a 5-point scale (1: very unsatisfied; 5: very satisfied). The results shown in Table 2 indicate that

Table 2. Participants' satisfaction on different highlighting styles of words

Highlighting styles	None	Flicker	Color	Bold
Scores	1.50	4.72	4.33	2.33

participants are more likely to choose flicker words and color words. But 83.33 % of participants choose flicker words and only 16.67 % participants choose color words. None of participants select none of highlighting or bold words. In addition, participants suggest that the words can be presented in other font, or magnified font or rotated and so on.

4 Conclusion

1. Highlighting words below icons could improve performance of searching a target icon, which indicate that highlighting words is suitable for touch screen devices like tablets.
2. Not all highlighting styles could improve visual searching performance. The results Color words and flicker words below icons are more suitable.
3. When the icons are gray, under the condition of color words and flicker words is more effective for visual search. When the icons are colorful, under the condition of flicker words is more effective for visual search.

A good icon and highlighting style design concentrate on not only in appearance, but on user performance and experience [14, 15]. The results of the experiments are helpful to reveal the characteristic of the individual in searching target in theory and practice. In addition, a follow-up study will further explore while the words below icons does not change, whether highlighting styles of icons will influence on visual search performance.

References

1. Yang, H.: Research on Interface Design of Mobile Internet Application of Smart Phone. Wuhan University of Technology (2013)
2. Yu, N.Z., Ge L.: A literature review of icon ergonomics research. In: Proceedings of Conference on Psychology and Social Harmony (CPSH 2012). Wuhan University, Scientific Research Publishing, p. 4 (2012)
3. Byrne, M.D.: Using icons to find documents: Simplicity is critical. In: Proceedings of INTERCHI 1993, pp. 446–453 (1993)
4. Everett, S.P., Byrne, M.D.: Unintended effects: varying icon spacing changes users' visual search strategy. In: Conference on Human Factors in Computing Systems, pp. 24–29 (2004)
5. Sarah, I.: Graphics and semantics: the relationship between what is seen and what is meant in icon design. In: Harris, D. (ed.) EPCE 2009. LNCS, vol. 5639, pp. 197–205. Springer, Heidelberg (2009)

6. Isherwood, S.J., McDougall, S.J.P., Curry, M.B.: Icon identification in context: the changing role of icon characteristics with user experience. Hum. Factors **49**(3), 465–476 (2007)
7. McDougall, S., Reppa, I., Smith, G.: Playfoot, David: Beyond emoticons: combining affect and cognition in icon design. In: Harris, Don (ed.) EPCE 2009. LNCS, vol. 5639, pp. 71–80. Springer, Heidelberg (2009)
8. Nothdurft, H.-C.: Attention shifts to salient targets. Vis. Res. **42**(10), 1287–1306 (2002)
9. Li, H., Li, W., Wang, P.: Study on Color highlighting under color background. 应 Chinese J. Appl. Psychol. **01**, 62–69 (2011)
10. He, F., Liu, Ch.: The effect of color salient on preview search. In: Proceedings of 2010 International Conference on Psychology, Psychological Sciences and Computer Science (PPSCS 2010). International Science and Engineering Center, Hong Kong; Huazhong University of Science & Technology, China; Howard University, 4 (2010)
11. Ge, L., Kong, Y.: A study of blinking as a type of highlighting in white and black display background. Psychol. Sci. **01**, 28–30 (2000)
12. Hu, F., Ji, L., Ge, L.: An ergonomic study using texture as highlighting codes on graphical displays. Chin. J. Ergon. **02**, 10–12 (2001)
13. Ge, L., Xu, W., Zhong, J.: A study on underline highlighting in difference display backgrounds and difficulty levels. Chin. J. Ergon. **04**, 6–8 (2001)
14. Guo X.: Research on the Usability of Software User Interface Based On Icon Design. Nanjing University of Aeronautics and Astronautics (2012)
15. Teng, Z.H., Jin, S., Zhen, Y.: The visibility of icon in graphical user interface of mobile phones. Packag. Eng. **04**, 66–70 (2013)

Applying Tangible Augmented Reality in Usability Evaluation

Xiaotian Zhang$^{(\boxtimes)}$ and Young Mi Choi

Georgia Institute of Technology, North Ave NW, Atlanta, GA 30332, USA
xt.zhang613@gmail.com

Abstract. Feedback from users is an invaluable part of the product design process. Prototypes of varying levels of detail are frequently used to solicit this feedback for attributes related to the physical and user experience aspects of a product. Accurate feedback is most useful in the early steps of design process where changes are easier to make. At the same time, highly detailed prototypes which allow accurate feedback are generally not available until much later in the process after many decisions have already been made. This goal of this study will be to investigate the use of Tangible Augmented Reality for performing usability testing of products with physical interface elements. The results will be compared to more traditional usability testing methods to determine whether the results are similar. Similar results may indicate accurate usability testing may be possible through the use of Tangible Augmented Reality allowing for earlier evaluation of product concepts.

Keywords: Tangible augmented reality · Design process

1 Background

Augmented Reality (AR) refers to a view of real or physical world in which certain elements of the environment are computer generated. These virtual elements could be a modification of a current element in the real world or could be an entirely new element. In an AR system a cue in the environment (such as picture, photograph, QR code, etc.) that when viewed through a screen is digitally replaced with a new element. The modified element could be many things such as changing the look of an object or adding completely new fictitious objects to the view.

AR has already been employed for useful applications in a number of different areas. One example of this is IKEA's system (Fig. 1) which allows shoppers to virtually preview furniture from their catalog within a room [1]. Apart from retail uses, AR has been a useful tool in industrial maintenance and repair applications. In these cases the AR application can provide workers with relevant information or even instructions for complex and/or dangerous tasks. Instead of needing to rely on printed materials or other references, goggles with integrated video or other heads up display devices are used to highlight or add additional information to the user's view of the environment (Fig. 2). Instructions, video or other information can be presented to assist with a task that is in progress. This ability to dynamically replace certain visual elements with new/different ones can be a potentially very helpful aid for product designers.

© Springer International Publishing Switzerland 2015
R. Shumaker and S. Lackey (Eds.): VAMR 2015, LNCS 9179, pp. 88–94, 2015.
DOI: 10.1007/978-3-319-21067-4_11

Fig. 1. IKEA's system allowing different furniture to be virtually previewed within a room

Fig. 2. A example of a user's view of a physical environment overlaid with augmented information related to a maintenance task.

Standard AR provides ease in changing the appearance or arrangement of an object, but it does not allow for natural interaction. There are efforts to develop systems to overcome this in the form of Tangible Augmented Reality (TAR). Tangible augmented reality combines visualization properties of AR with tangible interactions of physical objects [2]. Lee and Kim [3] talk about how developers and designers can create better target content using tangible augmented reality, which is, being able to do usability interactions before being used or felt by the target audience. The implementation process included making markers on cards which were placed in front of user. These markers are detected by an AR display such as a head mounted display and a 3d virtual object is placed on the markers. Users can then interact with the cards by moving them around in space as they would normally do with a physical object in real environment to interact with virtual objects. Markers might also be placed on a 3D printed model which is printed to resemble the form of the digital replacement [4]. The digital model is superimposed on the 3D printed model in the augmented display. Since the physical portion of the model is similar to the digital replacement viewed by the user, it allows the view to be manipulated while allowing natural physical interaction. This approach allows a user to interact naturally with products with physical interface elements (such as knobs or switches) which is not possible with a standard AR display.

This is important because the physical method of interaction will directly impact the results of a usability test. Every year companies devote significant resources to the development of new products [5, 6]. Companies like Google and Microsoft spend 5–6 billion US dollars every year on research and development [7].

A new product development (NPD) cycle involves five steps (Exploration and screening, Business analysis, Product development and Testing, Commercialization). Product development and Testing uses 54 % of the resources [8]. These products could be interactive or non-interactive. Before bringing a product to market, companies develop the entire product with all interactions integrated into the product and then release models for usability testing. If they find some glaring issues during testing, they have to revisit the development process. Once a product is in development, it costs 10 times more to fix a problem than during design and once the product has been released it costs 100 times more to fix a problem than in design [6]. The cost to fix design defects during design might be lowered if the cost of building an actual product can be removed and reliable usability testing can be done on a virtual product. In this case if there are issues with the usability of a product, all that needs to be done is changing the virtual rather than a physical model so that another round of testing can be performed.

Some research into the use of AR/TAR applications in product design have been undertaken. Woohun Lee and Jun Park introduced a TAR method which combined a physical artifact (Fig. 3) equipped with buttons which monitored/recorded button use [4].

 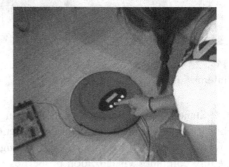

Fig. 3. Physical artifact of a cleaning robot (left) equipped with a marker to enable a tangible augmented view (right) with natural interaction.

Prototypes like this can be very helpful although one such as this example still requires significant engineering and programming skills to create. Such an approach may not always be suitable for early product concept testing. The method also does not give an indication of the reliability of any usability input gathered via the augmented view. If a fully functional version were produced, would the users' evaluation of the augmented version match the evaluation of the produced version? If it does not, any design decisions based on usability tests from the augmented version may not lead to design decisions which reduce/eliminate problems in the final design.

A study was recently conducted comparing the validity of usability input gathered via AR compared to a finished product [9]. In this investigation, the touch screen interface of a digital music player was modeled in AR. Users were able to navigate and perform actions through the virtual interface (such as selecting and playing songs). Usability testing was performed in three groups.

For the first group, a simple card with an image was used by the AR display to show the virtual re-creation of the music player.

For the second group, a rectangular plastic block of the same size as the music player was used to show the music player interface in the AR display.

The third group used the music player itself. Subjects independently performed a usability evaluation of one of the interfaces.

When the results were compared, there was no significant difference between the results from the AR interfaces compared to the actual product. This is a promising result, but since the interface used was a touch screen, the user interaction was exactly the same in all cases. If the player featured a physical knob, there would be no way to turn it within the virtual interface in the same way that one would be able to do with a real knob.

This study intends to explore this gap through the application of tangible augmented reality. The objective will be to compare the usability test results obtained from a TAR representation of a product with physical interface components compared to the actual product. It intends to gather evidence of whether usability test results from a TAR product artifact are or are not equivalent to physical prototypes. If similar, it can indicate that TAR may be a useful tool for collecting highly accurate feedback on a product concept.

2   Method

80 subjects aged over 18 will be recruited. All participants will be randomly assigned to one of 4 groups:

Augmented reality
Tangible Augmented Reality with hand visibility correction
Tangible Augmented Reality without hand visibility correction and the actual product.

Subjects in the AR group will able to interact with the product via a display screen. They will still be able to operate the virtual product, although the interaction with physical elements will not be exactly the same. For example a knob can be turned by sliding a finger on a touch screen instead of actually being able to grasp the interface element. Subjects in the TAR with hand visibility correction group will able to interact with a physical model which is simple, but similar to the product. They will view the product through an augmented display which replaces the simple model that they are touching with a realistic representation of the product. With this group, AR display will be able to compensate for times when the subject's hand passes in front of (and blocks) the image that is used by the AR software to render the augmented view. Normally this would cause the realistic display to disappear or not show the user's hand realistically in the display. Users in the TAR without hand visibility correction group will also view the product through an augmented display which replaces the simple model that they are touching with a realistic representation of the product. In this case the view will not be corrected (meaning that the realistic view may disappear or not show the hand realistically).

All subjects in all groups will perform a series of basic tasks with the product. This will be followed by completing a standard usability survey to objectively measure usability.

The Sunbeam fan-forced heater (Fig. 4) will be modeled in AR and used for the study. It features a physical upper knob for adjusting the temperature. The lower knob is used to control the power level and other settings (on/off, fan-only, low heat, high heat). The product was chosen as it has a physical user interface and is simple to control as we want to minimize the potential influence of the operation of the device from the testing in order to focus on the differences introduced by the different interaction

Fig. 4. Sunbeam Fan-forced heater

Fig. 5. Basic 3D printed model of the sunbeam heater

methods between the groups. The heater was modeled in Solidworks and a model was 3D printed (Fig. 5).

Each experimental group will perform the same set of tasks with their representation of the product before completing the usability survey:

Task 1: Turn on the heater, shift it to "low" mode, adjust the temperature and turn off the heater

Task 2: Turn on the heater, shift it to "high" mode, adjust the temperature and turn off the heater

Task 3: Turn on the heater, shift it to "fan" mode and then turn it off

Each group will consist of 20 users. Each subject will perform the tasks independently, followed by the completion of the NASA-TLX survey and the USE questionnaire [10, 11].

3   Discussion

Tangible Augmented Reality presents a number of potential benefits. It is a relatively low cost solution. Product conceptualization generally involves digital modeling and rendering meaning that simplified, non-functional models may be easily printed using standard rapid prototyping techniques, such as 3D printing. If TAR is shown to give equivalent usability results to a fully functional prototype, it would allow very early and accurate testing of conceptual ideas. Problems may be identified early and easily corrected before other important design decisions are made. It also would allow for easy testing of multiple, different conceptual ideas with a level of accuracy that would otherwise not be possible.

There are technological issues that may need to be overcome. The issue of the augmented view disappearing or becoming unrealistic looking when the marker used to generate the augmented view is blocked by user interaction. This study will begin to provide some data to indicate how significant this issue actually is and thus how critical it is to always correct for.

This study is currently ongoing. It is expected that usability test results from a TAR representation of a product will provide results similar to those from a fully functional product similar to the results found for touch interfaces with a non tangible AR approach. As much as half of the resources dedicated by a company in the design of a new product occur in the early conceptual phases. A tool which would allow reliable testing/input to be collected on early conceptual ideas, without the need for functional prototyping, would allow the merits of many additional approaches to be tested. More reliable data would also allow design teams to make better decisions and fix design defects early in the design process where changes are easier and much less expensive to make.

References

1. IKEA. Place IKEA furniture in your home with augmented reality (2013). www.youtube.com/watch?v=vDNzTasuYEw. Accessed 26 July 2013
2. Billinghurst, M., Kato, H., Poupyrev, I.: Tangible augmented reality. In: ACM SIGGRAPH ASIA, pp. 1–10 (2008)
3. Lee, G.A., Kim, G.J.: Immersive authoring of tangible augmented reality content: a user study. J. Vis. Lang. Comput. **20**(2), 61–79 (2009)
4. Lee, W., Park, J.: A tangible augmented reality for product design (2009)
5. Ehrlich, K., Rohn, J.: Cost justification of usability engineering: z vendor's perspective. In: Bias, R.G., Mayhew, D.J. (eds.) Cost-Justifying Usability, pp. 73–110. Academic Press, Boston (1994)
6. Donahue, G.M., Weinschenk, S., Nowicki, J.: Usability is Good Business (1999)
7. Krantz, M.: Microsoft, Intel, Google outspend Apple on R&D (2012). http://usatoday30.usatoday.com/money/perfi/columnist/krantz/story/2012-03-20/apple-marketing–research-and-development-spending/53673126/1. Accessed 14 December 2013
8. Cooper, R.G., Kleinschmidt, E.J.: Resource allocation in the new product process. Ind. Mark. Manage. **17**, 249–262 (1988)
9. Choi, Y.M., Mittal, S.: Exploring benefits of using augmented reality for usability testing in product design. In: International Conference on Engineering Design (2015)
10. Lund, A.A.M.: Measuring usability with the USE questionnaire. Usability Interface **8**(2) (2008)
11. Lund, A.A.M.: Questionnaire for User Interface Satisfaction (2008). http://hcibib.org/perlman/question.cgi?form=USE. Accessed 10 October 2013

Developing Virtual
and Augmented Environments

Fact and Fiction Merge in Telepresence and Teleoperation

A Present and Future Perspective

Gordon M. Mair[✉]

Transparent Telepresence Research Group, Department of Design Manufacture
and Engineering Management, University of Strathclyde, 75 Montrose Street,
Glasgow G1 1XJ, Scotland, UK
g.m.mair@strath.ac.uk

Abstract. This paper examines current trends in commercially available products and research related to telepresence and teleoperation systems. It also compares them with some aspects of speculative fiction directly related to these systems and their human interface. The presentation of the results in the form of a parallel timeline highlights the research gaps that remain to be filled in order to obtain the ideal telepresence system in which the technological mediation becomes as transparent as in fictional representations.

Keywords: Teleoperation · Virtual reality · Augmented reality · Science-fiction · Human computer symbiosis

1 Introduction

Today the general population of the developed world is able to experience many aspects of telepresence and mixed reality technology on a regular basis through cinema, television, radio, and other media. With respect to the visual and aural senses the experience is already of high fidelity. For example large immersive screens with surround sound or head mounted displays and headphone delivered binaural audio are available. Experiences can be further enhanced in many theme park rides with stimulation of the vestibular, olfactory, and cutaneous senses. However the ability to achieve a fully immersive multisensory experience in which the technological mediation is transparent remains in the future.

2 Fictional Telepresence Concepts

The following are examples from fiction of such technologically transparent systems. Firstly regarding simulated environments - as far back as 1950 Ray Bradbury wrote 'The Veldt' in which there was a room providing a full multisensory simulation of an African environment complete with lions, later the "holodeck" in the 1980s 'Star Trek - The Next Generation' television series portrayed the same idea. Currently multi-screen stereoscopic 'CAVE' (cave automatic virtual environment) type installations are the

R. Shumaker and S. Lackey (Eds.): VAMR 2015, LNCS 9179, pp. 97–107, 2015.
DOI: 10.1007/978-3-319-21067-4_12

closest we have to this concept but there is as yet no capability of providing high fidelity volumetric images in a natural environment, and certainly not images that could be touched as though solid. In fiction volumetric images have often been envisaged in the cinema, from the 'Forbidden Planet' in 1956, the first 'Star Wars' film in 1977, to the more recent 'Iron Man' films from 2008. True hi fidelity volumetric images are still out of reach although augmented reality can provide a substitute. A portrayal of this can be seen in a conference table situation as portrayed in the 2015 film adaptation of the graphic novel 'Kingsman'.

In 1965 Daniel F. Galouye published 'Counterfeit World' in which a simulated environment could be entered by donning a helmet that interacted with the brain. This concept was further developed in the 1980s and 90s by authors such as William Gibson in 'Neuromancer' and Neal Stephenson in 'Snow Crash". However in the latter two novels there is no helmet involved and the virtual environment is experienced directly in the brain with no need to physically emulate the real world via screens, headphones, and the like.

Following the idea of full immersion in a simulated world even further, Greg Egan in his 1994 novel "Permutation City" uses the concept of mind uploading or copying into a simulated world in which the copied personas can live a separate life from the real world. Taking this idea to its conclusion and leaving the material universe completely is exemplified in the Iain M. Banks series of 'Culture' novels in which entire civilizations can decide to "sublime" to another plane of existence and explained probably most fully in his final science fiction novel 'The Hydrogen Sonata' published in 2012. But this is a step too far for the purposes of this paper and we will restrict ourselves to technological mediation.

With regard to telepresence and teleoperation and being able to use technology to be able to interact with the real world as though present at a distant location. This was shown in M.W. Wellman's story 'The Robot and the Lady' as long ago as 1938 in which a telepresence robot is used as a surrogate for the shy inventor. In 1942 there was Robert Heinlein's well known story 'Waldo' involving teleoperation from a geosynchronous orbit to the terrestrial surface. Later telepresence was merged with the concept of mind uploading in Frederick Pohl's 1955 novel 'The Tunnel Under the World' and much later in Venditti and Weldele's 2005 graphic novel series 'The Surrogates' made into a film in 2009. In the same year James Cameron's film 'Avatar' included a similar concept although in this case a biological surrogate was involved. In Alastair Reynolds book from 2012 'Blue Remembered Earth' we see many of these themes included such as telepresence "claybots", and mind uploading to animals in order to experience their perception of the world.

From the foregoing examples it is apparent that when a fictional virtual reality or telepresence environment is created we have the ultimate human computer interface exhibiting two common features. Firstly it is fully immersive in that the individual within the simulation is oblivious to the real world outside of the simulation. Secondly the fidelity of the experience makes the simulation seem completely real.

Considered below is the present day technology available to approach such a technologically transparent environment. Its limitations are apparent and it is hoped that implicit in the text, and from the eventual comparison between what is available and fictional ideals, research gaps can be observed.

3   Contemporary Telepresence Technology

This paper is being written in 2015 and it is acknowledged that technological capabilities and the human computer symbiosis are increasing exponentially in varied areas. However it is possible to consider the current capabilities of technology as they highlight many of the limitations with existing methods with regard to a fully immersive realistic simulation. Figure 1 shows the elements necessary for a conventional telepresence system. A convention has been adopted of naming the location of the person experiencing telepresence as the "home" site. This person is called the operator, viewer, user, or driver depending on the context. The top half of the figure includes the interfaces, i.e. controls, displays, and computer, used today for virtual reality and, if required, the telecoms interface for remote multi-user participation. The lower half indicates the sensors such as cameras and microphones that are necessary when a telepresence and teleoperation system is required. It is also extended to include telepresence robots which are currently finding application in hospitals, care for the elderly, education, and commerce; in this case human interaction is necessary at both 'home' and 'remote' sites.

3.1   The Human Computer Interface and System Components

What follows is a snapshot of what is currently available at the time of writing.

Visual Displays. With respect to visual displays at the home site the resolution possible for large screens has reached a level that is adequate for most viewers, e.g. currently Ultra HD television offers a resolution of 3840 × 2160, the 4 K cinema equivalent is slightly higher at 4096 × 2160. With regard to the future 8 K, or Super Hi-Vision, with 33 million pixels will become available. The 2012 Olympics in London has already had events captured in 8 K and the Japanese company NHK plans to use the format to record and transmit the 2020 Olympics in Tokyo. [1] The newer display technologies are also providing greater color depth and dynamic range thus approaching a perceptual equivalence of our natural non-mediated viewing experience.

Head Mounted Displays (HMDs) with 4 K resolution are not yet available for the consumer market. Normally stereoscopic HMDs when used in telepresence fashion include head tracking. This allows the remote stereo camera platform, say on a telepresence robot, to be slaved to the head movements of the HMD wearer. Currently the most widely known low cost HMD is the Oculus Rift [2] which is available to content developers and researchers and should soon be able to be purchased as a consumer product.

Volumetric images, i.e. images which appear solid to the viewer are not yet available in high resolution or full color. There are a number of techniques available, one of which utilizes a high speed rotating screen and projection to produce voxels rather than pixels. The Perspecta volumetric display whose patents are now held by Optics For Hire [3] is a good example of this method. However the physics of producing an apparently solid image in air as seen in popular films is extremely difficult and not yet achievable. Also the computing power and speed to produce the necessary

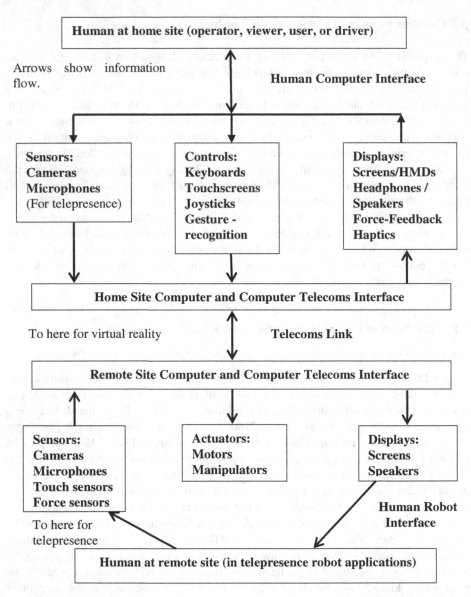

Fig. 1. Typical elements of a VR, telepresence, and teleoperation system

number of voxels is extremely high. For example to produce a telepresence image of only 1000 × 1000 × 1000 pixels at a minimum of 24 frames per second will require a transmission and projection rate of 24 billion pixels per second.

One way of achieving pseudo volumetric images is by using a stereoscopic display coupled with head tracking and gesture control. This can provide the system user with the impression that a solid object is being viewed since the stereoscopic image alters its parallax appropriately as the viewer moves their head. Polarising screens and glasses can be used as in the zSpace system [4].

Another method is to use augmented reality. Here the system user can wear see through glasses onto which can be projected images whose perspective can be tied to the position and direction of the viewer's head. Six degrees of freedom head tracking will be required here. It can be seen that a number of users wearing the glasses could observe the object from their own perspectives thus creating an apparent volumetric image that can be viewed by a number of participants simultaneously. One of the latest potential offerings of this type is that of the Microsoft HoloLens [5].

All the volumetric images comments above apply to computer generated objects, none of them are as yet capable of displaying live real world objects such as people. To allow a volumetric image of a person to be shown in a manner that is able to be correctly observed by a number of viewers standing or sitting around the image, multiple cameras would have to be employed around the remote real world object or person of interest. This gathering of three-dimensional information would be transmitted as live video and even with image compression this will require very high bandwidth transmission. Subsequent image processing in order to achieve smooth viewing at all angles will also require significant real-time computing power.

At the remote site, in the case of a telepresence robot being used, the opportunity arises for the display of an image of the remote driver. This is currently normally done with a simple two dimensional video display. However an advanced method of providing a more three dimensional impression was demonstrated by Tachi et al. [6]. Here the home site operator's face could be seen on the telepresence robot's 'head' through the use of retro-reflective material and a projection system.

An alternative method of obtaining an apparent three dimensional volumetric image of the home site operator could be through the use of augmented reality. The person at the location of the telepresence robot could wear augmented reality glasses onto which a live representation of the home site operator is projected. This would be tied to the robot through a registration point on the robot to ensure appropriate perspective for any number of people at the remote site.

Aural Displays. For telepresence an audio display of sound from a remote site needs not only hi-fidelity reproduction of the sound quality but also directional and distal information. How this is done depends on whether the sound information is being directly related to the head orientation of the system user, as in a Head Mounted Display, or is independent of the user position, as in a large screen or CAVE environment. In the latter case there are many available systems providing surround sound using multiple speakers for sound spatialisation and localization. However for the operator using an HMD with head tracking capabilities, binaural sound through headphones is necessary in order to provide accurate directional and distal information. Demonstration of binaural sound can be heard at the websites of QSound Labs [7] and 3DIO [8]. How the sound is acquired is noted in the sensor section below.

Other Displays. Somatosensory displays include those which can provide the system user with a sense of touch, e.g. the ability to feel the texture of a remote surface, and cutaneous e.g. feel the movement and temperature of air over the skin. Haptic sensing occurs when proprioception is combined with touch, this allows shapes to be discerned by movement of the hands and joints. The ability of the system user to sense force is also important in teleoperation. Finally in some cases the ability to sense the orientation, acceleration or deceleration, of a telepresence robot or drone may be useful in some situations hence vestibular displays could be employed, however these are currently only found in flight simulators and theme park rides.

Today force feedback is used mainly in mechanical handling. Haptics are used commercially for providing vibrations when receiving data or calls, or simulating button clicks, on mobile phones. Displays of this type are also used in computer gaming and virtual reality. For example there are displays produced by the Immersion company [9] and there is the Phantom Omni haptic feedback device by Sensable which provides the illusion of touch for virtual objects [10]. Companies such as Cyberglove Systems [11] market gloves that provide both tactile and force feedback mainly for virtual reality applications. Also for flight simulation and gaming force feedback joysticks can be used such as those produced by Thrustmaster [12]. Despite these examples, and despite research in the area for more than two decades, displays to satisfy the somatosensory senses are not currently widely used in telepresence and teleoperation systems.

Controls. Conventional controls such as keyboards, mice, and joysticks are widely used commercially for both telepresence and virtual reality. However if combined with position sensors it is possible to use the previously mentioned gloves as controls as well as displays. There are also gesture recognition systems available today such as the LEAP system that can track all ten fingers with an accuracy 0.01 mm. It can be used for gaming, computer aided design, and potentially for telepresence. It has a 150 degree field of view and an update rate of 200 frames per second [13].

Remote Visual Sensing. For decades the conventional method for achieving live stereoscopic panorama images for interactive immersive telepresence has been to use an HMD with headphones slaved to a remote anthropometric 'head' containing a stereo camera system and binaural microphones as in the author's research group's early telepresence systems of almost twenty years ago [14]. Today the possibility is emerging of obtaining stereoscopic panoramic images from static camera clusters. This removes the need for electro-mechanical actuators and associated problems with power requirements, maintenance, and mechanical delay times due to inertia and resistance. An example of such a cluster is the Panocam 3D system [15] that can record and playback panoramic stereoscopic images. Due to the time required for image processing however this is not yet suitable for live telepresence.

Remote Aural Sensing. In order to provide the surround sound or binaural sound for the home site operator suitable microphones are required. For a mechatronic sensor platform capable of pan and tilt movement a pair of binaural microphones situated in an anthropomorphic relationship to a pair of stereoscopic cameras can be used. These microphones should be inserted in artificial pinnae separated by anthropometric dimensions and ideally with a mass between them similar to that of the human head in order to create a head related transfer function (HRTF).

For a static camera cluster a microphone cluster can be used such as can be found in the Sound City Project which uses four equispaced microphones with pinnae [16]. This system can record panoramic sound which can be listened to with headphones. As you pan around an image of the location the recording was made in order to hear the sound relative to your gaze point. However just as with the panoramic stereo camera cluster the signal processing is not done in real time so the system cannot yet be used for telepresence.

Other Remote Sensing. Force and touch sensors can be mounted on remote grippers or anthropomorphic 'hands' and these are widely available in many forms [17, 18]. The gathering of information for vestibular sensing is not commercially available or as yet necessary but could be provided through accelerometers and gyroscopes.

4 Fact and Fiction Timeline Comparison

The following table shows in a parallel fashion relevant developments in technology and concepts presented in fiction. It is proposed that this is evidence of cyclical feedback in operation. Scientific insights and technological advances provide ideas for science fiction writers to extrapolate. These extrapolations then act as input to scientists and engineers to encourage further investigation and development.

5 Full Teleoperation and Telepresence Robot Systems

In conclusion there have been a number of research projects in the latter half of the 20th and the beginning of the 21st Century on creating full telepresence systems. Some of the later ones are now briefly mentioned.

Events in fact and fiction leading to VR, telepresence, and teleoperation	
Fact	Fiction
1850 to 1899	
1873 Photoconductivity of Selenium discovered by Willoughby Smith	1878 'Punch' magazine publishes an imaginative sketch of a "Telephonoscope" similar to a telepresence display
1876 Patent for the telephone filed by Alexander Graham Bell titled "An Improvement in Telegraphy"	1895 In *The Remarkable Case of Davidson's Eyes* HG Wells describes a telepresence experience
1884 Scanning Disk invented by Paul Gottleib Nipkow	1897 *The Crystal Egg* short story by HG Wells includes the concept of receiving visual images from Mars
1893 Radio control of a submersible boat by Tesla	
1900 to 1949	
1900 Constantin Perskyi coins the word "Television" in a paper presented to the International Electricity Congress at the World Fair, Paris, on August the 25th	1917 JRR Tolkien begins work on his mythopoeia part of which would become *The Lord of the Rings* written between 1937 and 1949. This contained the "palantir" stones used for viewing remote places and communication

(Continued)

(Continued)

Events in fact and fiction leading to VR, telepresence, and teleoperation	
Fact	Fiction
1926 John Logie Baird demonstrates world's first televised moving images to Royal Institution in London January 26th	1932 *Brave New World* by Aldous Huxley includes "feelie" multisensory stereoscopic cinema
1928 Baird makes the first transatlantic television transmission between London and New York.	1938 *The Robot and the Lady* by M.W. Wellman published, includes full concept of immersive telepresence in a surrogate robotic body.
1939 Filing of patent application Pat No 2,344,108 by H.A. Roselund for paint spraying machine – an early 'robot'	1942 *Waldo* by Robert Heinlein published, the story incorporates teleoperation from a geosynchronous satellite
1943 An HMD patent filed titled "Stereoscopic Television Apparatus" by Henry McCollum incorporating miniature CRTs	1949 George Orwell's *1984* is published, it includes the concept of ubiquitous "Big Brother" two way television thus removing privacy in the home
1949 For the USA Atomic Energy Commission Goertz produces technical Report No. AECD-2635 "Master–slave manipulator	
1950 to 1999	
1952 "A Force-Reflecting Positional Servomechanism", R.C. Goertz and F. Bevilacqua. Nucleonics 1952; 14:43-55	1950 *The Veldt* by Aldous Huxley includes a fully immersive multisensory environment with solid simulacra.
1954 "Handyman", Ralph Mosher's master arm exoskeleton and slave arm, 12 years after Waldo published	1952 *Bridge* by James Blish, this short story includes the concept of immersive telepresence via a head mounted display
1958 to 1961 Mort Heilig build three "Sensorama Simulators"	1964 *Counterfeit World* by Daniel F. Galouye based on concept of immersion in a computer generated world
1960 Mort Heilig presents "Telesphere Mask" HMD patent design as a proposal to the RCA Research Centre	1966 "Teleoperation" word first used by E.G. Thomson
1961 "Headsight" HMD developed by Comeau and Bryan	1967 *Lord of Light* by Roger Zelazny includes electronic mind transfer
1967 Surveyor III land on Moon with extendable arm for sample gathering	1984 "Cyberspace" coined by William Gibson in *Neuromancer*
1968 "A Computer with Hands, Eyes, and Ears", J. McCarthy et al. Fall Joint Computer Conference AFIPS Proceedings, pp 329-328	1992 "Metaverse" coined by Neal Stephenson in *Snowcrash*
1968 Ivan Sutherland builds HMD	1995 *Permutation City* by Greg Egan published, includes mind transfer into virtual worlds

(Continued)

(*Continued*)

Events in fact and fiction leading to VR, telepresence, and teleoperation	
Fact	Fiction
1976 Viking lands on Mars	1999 *The Matrix* film introduces the concept of full immersion in a computer generated world to popular culture
1980 "Telepresence" word first used by Marvin Minsky.	
2000 to 2015	
2008 TELEsarPHONE humanoid telepresence robot with retroleflective material to provide realistic facial images of remote driver.	2009 The film *Avatar* directed by James Cameron introduces relatively high quality stereoscopic content via polarizing glasses. The story includes the concept of telepresence through mind transfer into a biological alien body.
2011 NASA's 'Robonaut 2' launched to the International Space Station (ISS) February 24th capable of being teleoperated via an HMD and force and tactile feedback gloves	In science-fiction aspects of telepresence, mixed reality, and human-computer symbiosis appear as integral parts of story lines as exemplified in the example below.
2011 ESA Eurobot demonstrated	2012 *Blue Remembered Earth* by Alastair Reynolds. In this story humans in the near future have their brains and eyes augmented by artifacts so that they can perform various acts that are logical extensions to what is shown here in the parallel the 'fact' column. For example they can "aug" without the need of special glasses in which they can access information by just looking at an object or person or actively enquiring access to particular data. They can also make themselves telepresent in "proxy bodies" called "claybots" that can take the features of whoever is driving them. This is a form of mind transfer. Also because all humans are equally augmented they can "voke" a mutually observable "aug" image which is seen as a volumetric image suitable for round table collaborative work.
2012 "Exploration Telerobotics Symposium" held at NASA Goddart Space Flight Center, May 2–3	
2012 'Curiosity' rover lands on mars on August the 6th at the Bradbury Landing site named after Ray Bradbury	
2012 Oculus Rift raises Kickstarter funding for low cost but good image quality HMD.	

(*Continued*)

(Continued)

Events in fact and fiction leading to VR, telepresence, and teleoperation	
Fact	Fiction
March 2014 Facebook purchases company for 2 billion dollars	
2013 First Google Glass augmented reality glasses prototypes April production to be ceased announced January 2015	
2014 Robonaut receives legs for mobility at the ISS	
2014 Paper from VERE project shows how a humanoid robot was controlled by thought using fMRI	
2015 Microsoft announce HoloLens augmented reality headset.	
2015 Sony's SmartEyeglass augmented reality developers kit goes on sale	

The Japanese Humanoid Robotics Project (HRP) Super Cockpit [19] included telepresence control of a robot from a cockpit incorporating an immersive display and master arms with force feedback [19]. The Robonaut program in the USA [20] has developed an anthropomorphic and anthropometric robot. Developed by NASA in collaboration with industry the robot has the capability of being controlled through telepresence as well as operating auton-omously. Finally the five year European VERE project due to finish this year has had the aim of "…dissolving the boundary between the human body and surrogate representations in immersive virtual reality and physical reality. Dissolving the boundary means that people have the illusion that their surrogate representation is their own body, and act and have thoughts that correspond to this" [21]. The project has successfully shown that a form of mind control, by using fMRI, can be used to control a humanoid robot through telepresence [22].

References

1. http://www.techradar.com/news/television/ultra-hd-everything-you-need-to-know-about-4k-tv-1048954. Accessed 18 February 2015
2. https://www.oculus.com/dk2/. Accessed 18 February 2015
3. http://www.opticsforhire.com/patents/. Accessed 18 February 2015
4. http://zspace.com/product. Accessed 18 February 2015
5. www.microsoft.com/microsoft-hololens/en-us
6. Tachi, S., et al.: TELEsarPHONE: mutual telexistence master-slave communication system based on retroreflective projection Technology. SICE J. Control Measur. Syst. Integr. 1(5), 335–344 (2008)
7. http://www.qsound.com/demos/binaural-audio.htm. Accessed 19 February 2015
8. http://3diosound.com/examples.php. Accessed 19 February 2015
9. http://www.immersion.com/. Accessed 19 February 2015

10. http://www.dentsable.com/haptic-phantom-omni.htm. Accessed 19 February 2015
11. http://www.cyberglovesystems.com/all-products. Accessed 19 February 2015
12. http://www.thrustmaster.com/products/force-feedback-joystick. Accessed 19 February 2015
13. https://www.leapmotion.com/. Accessed 19 February 2015
14. Mair, G.: Transparent telepresence research. Industrial Robot **26**(3), 209–215 (1999). MCB University Press
15. http://www.panocam3d.com/index.html. Accessed 19 February 2015
16. http://soundcityproject.com/#/about. Accessed 19 February 2015
17. http://www.trossenrobotics.com/c/robot-force-sensor-fsr.aspx. Accessed 19 February 2015
18. http://www.meas-spec.com/product/t_product.aspx?id=2442. Accessed 19 February 2015
19. Tachi, S., et al.: Telexistence cockpit for humanoid robot control. Adv. Robot. **17**(3), 199–217 (2003)
20. http://robonaut.jsc.nasa.gov/. Accessed 19 February 2015
21. http://www.vereproject.eu/. Accessed 19 February 2015
22. Cohen, O., et al.: fMRI-based robotic embodiment: Controlling a humanoid robot by thought using real-time fMRI. Presence: Teleoperators Virtual Environ. **23**(3), 229–241 (2014)

Delta Global Illumination for Mixed Reality

Maik Thöner[1][(✉)] and Arjan Kuijper[1,2]

[1] Fraunhofer IGD, Darmstadt, Germany
{maik.thoener,arjan.kuijper}@igd.fraunhofer.de
[2] Technische Universität Darmstadt, Darmstadt, Germany

Abstract. The focus point in Mixed Reality applications is the merging of objects from different realities into a new, visibly homogeneous scene. To achieve this, next to a spatial registration, a plausible illumination of the objects is required. While shadows and direct illumination can deliver a realistic look to the objects, adding indirect interaction of illumination will result in a seamless integration of objects, to appear as part of the scene instead of glued-on patches. Mixed Relality systems find appliance in entertainment areas like movies and games, as well as prototype presentations or visualization of planned or damaged constructions. We propose an algorithm based on Voxel Cone Tracing to provide Global Illumination for Mixed Reality that enables diffuse as well as specular lighting and easy to compute soft-shadows.

1 Introduction

The aim of Mixed Reality (MR) is to merge two realities into one coherent frame: a virtual object and a real scene. With the rising popularity of smartphones and see-through displays more and more people have access to hardware that can capture and display an image at the same time [1,2]. One aim of Mixed Reality is to do calculation and presentation in real time, so that these users can interactively see the result, when the digital data or the scene image changes [3,4]. Applications for this include entertainment, like games or movies, augmentation as work assistance or for prototyping and damaged or unfinished constructions like cultural heritage or future buildings [5,6]. For most scenarios the presentation of the digital data is required to be as realistic as possible to create the illusion, that the image shows only one scene, while it contains additional content. We present a system for a more realistic presentation of the digital data to allow a more homogeneous result image.

The aim of our algorithm is to render a virtual 3D object in such a way that it is perceptually integrated into a scene image. To achieve this the 3D object is rendered to get a 2D image of the virtual object, which is then blended with the scene image to create an augmented image of the scene. However, to create the illusion that the augmenting virtual object really is part of the scene several conditions for the pose and lighting during the rendering must be met. We therefore present a combination of Differential Rendering [7] and Voxel Cone Tracing [8] to shade a virtual object according to real lighting conditions

© Springer International Publishing Switzerland 2015
R. Shumaker and S. Lackey (Eds.): VAMR 2015, LNCS 9179, pp. 108–118, 2015.
DOI: 10.1007/978-3-319-21067-4_13

and to transfer the indirect illumination computed with the help of a scene reconstruction onto a real or virtual scene background, resulting in the successful relighting of the real scene.

Our algorithm can simulate the exchange of indirect illumination between virtual and real objects in real-time, is temporally stable, can cast soft shadows of virtual objects onto real surfaces and is able to simulate diffuse and glossy reflections with minimal artifacts.

2   Related Work

Mixed Reality applications which seek to fuse virtual objects into real environments with proper global illumination need to address several problems. There have been several publications which are of relevance to our work.

2.1   Reconstruction

Reconstruction of the real environment and its lighting conditions is crucial for proper computation of global illumination effects. Debevec reconstructs illumination conditions of the real scene from a reflective ball and computes shading on the virtual objects surface with environment mapping [7]. Sorbier and Saito [9] instead progressively reconstruct and environment map from a Kinect camera. Other methods extract single point light sources from such images with importance sampling [10].

Izadi et al. [11] progressively reconstruct real environment geometry with the help of a geometrically registered depth sensing device (the popular Microsoft Kinect). A static scene can be scanned with the depth sensor, systematically updating a global voxel data structure. Because of noise artifacts in the depth image, which can lead to artifacts in the reconstructed geometry, Chatterjee et al. [12] further investigate filters to create smooth, artifact-free surfaces.

Karsch et al. [13] use automatic reasoning from images with associated depth on single, low-dynamic photographs of a real scene. The reconstruction process yields a depth image similar to a Kinect depth sensor, but without the need of a special sensing devices, which is useful for mobile devices that do not have access to such hardware. They furthermore estimate spatially varying parametric materials using a prior of HDR images with known illumination. Reflectance properties are decomposed into two albedo textures and weighting coefficients.

Finally, many MR methods use pre-reconstructed models of the scene. The scene is usually geometrically registered with a marker or any other type of registration. Materials for this model can also be supplied upfront. In case of known, static MR scenes this method is usually the preferred option.

2.2   Shading

When rendering a virtual object into a real context, shading on its surface has to match real lighting conditions. The reconstructed conditions can be fed to an appropriate real-time rendering algorithm to do so.

Many modern real-time global illumination methods build on Instant Radiosity [14]. To approximate indirect illumination, small Virtual Point Lights (VPL) are introduced where a light path intersects geometry. For instance, a bounce off a blue surface is replaced with a blue VPL. A method for rasterizers to create first bounce VPLs has been presented by Dachsbacher and Stamminger [15] by extending a regular shadow map into a full Geometry Buffer (GBuffer) called Reflective Shadow Map (RSM). Assuming purely diffuse reflection, a query into an RSM can be used to turn a pixel with albedo, normal and depth into a VPL with position, direction and flux. A state-of-the-art overview of current real-time global illumination methods can be found in [16].

Viriyothai and Debevec [10] extract multiple point light sources from a spherical image and use regular shading algorithms. However, in dynamic environments many samples are needed to produce a temporally coherent image. Knecht et al. [17] and Lensing and Broll [18] use RSMs for reconstructed real point light sources to introduce first bounce indirect reflections from real reconstructed geometry. Because the number of VPLs need to be low to ensure real-time rendering behavior, both methods use either temporal filtering or importance sampling techniques to create them.

Franke and Jung [19] use irradiance mapping on spherical images in combination with dynamic ambient occlusion. Temporally stable diffuse reflection can be simulated under varying illumination conditions, but virtual objects do not support indirect reflections or more sophisticated reflections off specular materials. Our method aims to support these effects.

2.3 Relighting

Introducing an object into a real environment changes its lighting conditions. New objects cast shadows on existing geometry or reflect light back onto real surfaces. Extending global illumination methods to simulate this type of behavior is important to maintain the illusion of a proper augmentation.

Knecht et al. [17] and Lensing and Broll [18] employ Differential Rendering to extract indirect bounces caused by introducing virtual objects. Because this is the same method use to shade the object, the same restrictions apply: only diffuse bounces are supported. Our method can simulate glossy and specular reflections also.

Franke [20] uses a volumetric approach, enhancing Light Propagation Volumes [21]. A small, low-resolution volume around the object is injected with the difference of two RSMs (one containing the real-reconstructed scene and the virtual object, one without the object). The differential inside the volume is then propagated until no more energy can be distributed. Pixels of real-reconstructed geometry covered by this volume can query indirect diffuse bounces off the virtual object. The method solves temporal stability issues and is very efficient, but tends to cut off illumination once it reaches the volume boundaries. The low volume resolution also causes heavy bleeding artifacts through thin geometry. Franke [22] subsequently uses Voxel Cone Tracing [8] to combat bleeding artifacts. The volume resolution is increased, but instead of propagating light inside the volume, a pre-filtering process creates a chain of smaller volumes. These are used to efficiently cone-trace for indirect reflections, which allows to produce glossy and specular indirect reflections. Our algorithm closely relates to this method.

Finally, many MR methods employ regular shadow mapping to introduce shadows of virtual objects on real surfaces. Shadow maps are the subject of heavy investigation and come in a wide variety.

3   Delta Global Illumination

In our approach we use Voxel Cone Tracing [8] for the shading and relighting of the 3D object and the scene, as it is the most promising real-time Global Illumination techniques, which produces glossy and specular indirect reflections for a reasonable computational cost.

3.1   Voxel Cone Tracing

Voxel Cone Tracing uses cones to query direct or indirect light that comes from the cone direction to aggregate the illumination. The light data itself is stored in a voxel grid which is inserted by voxelizing VPL candidates. The cone casting itself is simulated by casting a normal ray, but reading from an increasing size of voxels in the volume. Bigger voxels can be achieved by mipmapping the 3D texture which contains the voxel structure. Each mipmap level then contains voxels of 2^3. This is visualized in Fig. 1.

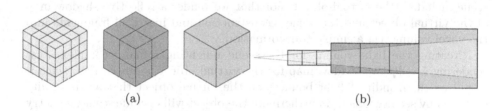

(a)   (b)

Fig. 1. (a) visualizes the filtering of the voxel volumes, (b) the mipmap levels that are read from the cone depending on the distance.

In each tracing step the light information is aggregated depending on the occlusion in and before that step. For that we use two accumulator, one for the light information and one for the occlusion value, which are updated with the following formulas:

$$light_{acc} = light_{acc} \cdot occlusion_{acc} + light_{local} \cdot occlusion_{local} \cdot (1 - occlusion_{acc})$$

$$occlusion_{acc} = occlusion_{acc} + occlusion_{local} \cdot (1 - occlusion_{acc})$$

where $light_{acc}$ and $occlusion_{acc}$ are the accumulators and $light_{local}$ and $occlusion_{local}$ the values read from the voxel volumes. The occlusion value is thereby adapted with the normal that is stored in the volume. At the end of the tracing the $light_{acc}$ value is used as the light value of that cone.

The step size during the tracing of the cone is adjusted to the voxel size at that and the next step to avoid reading from overlapping voxels. Because of this the tracing cost of a cone can be controlled by the aperture size. Narrow cones require a smaller step size, since they operate mostly on low mipmap levels, whereas bigger cones will get to higher mipmap levels and thus fasten up the tracing. To calculate the color for a fragment, we cast a series of different cones into the scene. For the diffuse light we use a higher number of cones with a bigger aperture angle which results in some kind of blurriness. These diffuse cones are arranged in a way, that they cover as much of the hemisphere as possible. For sharp highlights like specular reflections we use one narrow cone, whose direction is the view ray reflected with the surface normal. The aperture size defines the sharpness of the features and relates to the surfaces glossiness.

The light information of all cones is then aggregated with a factor based on the viewing and cone angles and the surface hardness.

3.2 Algorithm Overview

For the shading of the virtual object it must receive indirect illumination from the surrounding scene, as well as from itself. For the relighting the scene must only receive indirect light from the virtual object. To achieve this with Voxel Cone Tracing, two separate light volumes are needed, one for shading and one for relighting. The one for shading contains the light information of the whole scene including the virtual object. For that we render a reflective shadow map of the virtual object and the scene reconstruction and insert all fragments into the voxel volume via a simple transformation.

Creating the light volume for the scene relighting is more complex. Just rendering a reflective shadow map for the virtual object is not correct, since it would result in indirect light bounces on the virtual object that are in reality occluded by scene geometry. Furthermore the object will occlude scene geometry and to account for that we want to insert negative light so that the light reflected from those surfaces will be subtracted during the scene's relighting step. To create this volume we calculate a delta volume by rendering a reflective shadow map of only the scene reconstruction and subtract the light information from the other volume. This way all surface geometry of the scene reconstruction which is visible in the scene-only reflective shadow map will result in a negative light value inside the voxel grid.

In addition to the light volumes for shading and relighting we use two additional volumes to store the visibility information. These volumes store the normal of the surface and an occlusion factor in each voxel. The normal is the average normal of all geometry that falls into one voxel. The occlusion factor is set to 1 for every voxel that has geometry in it and 0 otherwise. In the higher mipmap levels this factor then denotes the fraction of subvoxels which contained geometry and is used to calculate the occlusion in each tracing step.

Overall we use four volumes in contrast to [20], where only one volume is used for the visibility information. Using an additional volume comes of course with an increased memory cost, but it also solves a problem with the combined volumes. When the visibility information of the scene and the virtual object are mixed the relighting of the scene will introduce additional shadows for occluders in the scene that already cast this shadow, which results in a doubled shadow effect on scene objects. For the cones that query the indirect light information still both visibility volumes have to be used or indirect light from the virtual object will travel through real scene geometry.

3.3   Shading vs. Relighting

For the shading and the Relighting we use the same Voxel Cone Tracing technique. The difference lies in the volumes that we query during the cone tracing. Whether the current fragment is part of the virtual object or the scene geometry can be easily determined with help of the depth buffers. For the shading of the virtual object we use the light volume which contains the injected light for all objects, the scene reconstruction and the virtual object itself. That way the virtual object receives indirect light from the scene but also from itself. For the relighting of the scene on the other side we use the delta volume which only contains the radiance field changes introduced by the virtual object.

3.4   Volume Extent

The voxel density of the volumes and thus the highlight accuracy is directly dependent on the size of the volumes in the scene. Under the assumption that the significant influences of the introduced virtual object to the scene is limited to a local region around it, the volume for relighting only must cover that region without introducing to much errors. The same is true for the shading volume which defines the region of the scene reconstruction that can influence the virtual object. So there is always a trade-off between the impact range and the voxel density in the volumes.

Because the delta volume is calculated by subtracting two volumes, we chose the same region for both volumes. As the region we used the double sized bounding box of the virtual object.

3.5   Shadows

The Voxel Cone Tracing is also used to create soft shadows on both, the virtual object and the scene. For the shadow we cast an additional cone from the fragment position to the light source to test for the occlusion in that cone. The nearer the occluding object is to the light source the smoother the shadow. This is a natural effect of the Voxel Cone Tracing as the cone will be wider and the traced occlusion value blurred.

4   Results and Discussion

We have implemented the system described in Sect. 3 using Direct3D 11 on an Intel i7-3770K and a NVIDIA GTX 660. A Microsoft Kinect camera was used to capture the background image, and an UEye UI-2230-C camera with a fish-eye lens to capture surrounding real light. We used ARToolKit [23] for geometric registration through marker based tracking. A manually pre-reconstructed scene with known materials has been used.

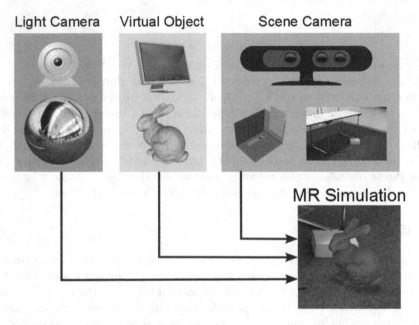

Fig. 2. Architecture of our prototype. The system is fed by three inputs: A virtual object, a Light Camera which records real illumination from the environment and a Kinect camera which captures the real scene from a viewpoint.

Our system architecture is depicted in Fig. 2. After capturing a frame of real light with the *Light Camera* and one frame from the viewpoint of the *Scene camera*, a buffer of the illumination, a model of the virtual object and a model of the real scene are fed to a simulation which outputs the final augmented image.

In Fig. 3 we compare our method to a ground truth result rendered with the Mitsuba path tracer [24]. An already lit virtual scene (the Cornell Box), which was rendered with regular Voxel Cone Tracing, is augmented by a Stanford Buddha with a diffuse lime-stone material. DGI captures diffuse bounces from the surrounding scene and properly blocks direct and indirect bounces that have been present in the unaugmented image.

As with most clustering techniques our illumination suffers from minor bleeding artifacts. Under certain circumstances light aliasing effects can be observed,

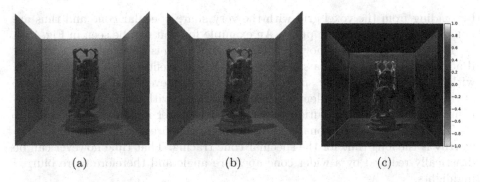

(a)   (b)   (c)

Fig. 3. A groundtruth comparison. (a) An already lit virtual scene is augmented by a Stanford Buddha using Delta Global Illumination. (b) The same scene has been rendered with the open source Mitsuba path tracer. (c) 2X squared difference ((b) - (a)).

depending on the voxel grid resolution. Figure 3(c) suggests that DGI subtracts slightly too much energy in all lit areas, while the reverse is true for shadowed parts of the scene. This error is due to a general overestimation and aliasing present in voxelized structures. In our diffuse case this error however spreads out evenly and is therefore only noticeable in direct comparison with a ground truth result.

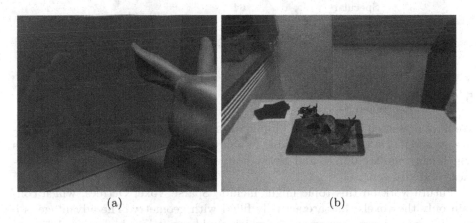

(a)   (b)

Fig. 4. Results. (a) Direct shadow vs reflected shadow. (b) The reflection of the virtual dragon is successfully modeled with DGI.

In some scenes additional artifacts can occur with the shadows, especially if shadows are visible in the specular reflections. The shadows created with the Voxel Cone Tracing are very smooth, the shadows seen in the reflection on the other hand are very sharp and blocky. That is because the latter ones are created by reading from the voxel grid with the very sharp specular cone and thus are not blurred with the mipmapping. An example for that can be seen in Fig. 4(a).

In Fig. 4(b) a result is shown. An XYZRGB dragon is reflected on a mirroring iPad surface while casting a shadow onto it. Glossy reflections are handled well with VCT, however highly specular surfaces easily reveal the voxelized nature of the reflection. This problem can be circumvented with either filtering mechanisms or higher voxel resolution, albeit at much higher memory cost.

The average computational cost for the algorithm are shown in Table 1. Noteworthy is the long time for the specular cone tracing. That time however can be drastically reduced by a wider cone aperture angle and therefore more blurred highlights.

Table 1. This table shows the duration of the single pipeline steps of the DGI. Note the high value for the specular cone.

Task	Average duration (in ms)
Voxelization	5
Reflective Shadow Map	0.2
Light Inject	3
Mipmap generation	8
Voxel Cone Tracing	
Diffuse	6
Specular	64
Shadow	4

5   Conclusion

We have presented Delta Global Illumination, a combination of Differential Rendering and Voxel Cone Tracing able to shade and relight Mixed Reality scenes which can simulate diffuse and glossy bounces of real geometry on virtual surfaces and vice versa.

Future work on this topic might include Sparse Voxel Octrees, which contain only the voxels that are actually filled with geometry. The advantage is a possibly much lower memory usage which could result in a higher resolution of the voxel grid. The drawback is that reading from that structure comes with a higher computational cost. Furthermore, the mipmap levels have to be calculated manually, which is presumably slower than the native mipmapping functions.

References

1. Ettl, A.S., Kuijper, A.: Text and image area classification in mobile scanned digitized documents. Int. J. Appl. Pattern Recogn. **1**(2), 173–198 (2014)

2. Engelke, T., Becker, M., Wuest, H., Keil, J., Kuijper, A.: MobileAR browser - a generic architecture for rapid AR-multi-level development. Expert Syst. Appl. **40**(7), 2704–2714 (2013)
3. Wientapper, F., Wuest, H., Kuijper, A.: Reconstruction and accurate alignment of feature maps for augmented reality. In: 3DIMPVT 2011: The First Joint 3DIM/3DPVT Conference (Hangzhou, China, May 16–19, 2011), pp. 140–147. IEEE (2011)
4. Wientapper, F., Wuest, H., Kuijper, A.: Composing the feature map retrieval process for robust and ready-to-use monocular tracking. Comput. Graph. **35**(4), 778–788 (2011)
5. Schwenk, K., Voss, G., Behr, J., Jung, Y., Limper, M., Herzig, P., Kuijper, A.: Extending a distributed virtual reality system with exchangeable rendering backends: techniques, applications, experiences. Vis. Comput. **29**(10), 1039–1049 (2013)
6. Olbrich, M., Graf, H., Kahn, S., Engelke, T., Keil, J., Riess, P., Webel, S., Bockholt, U., Picinbono, G.: Augmented reality supporting user-centric building information management. Vis. Comput. **29**(10), 1093–1105 (2013)
7. Debevec, P.: Rendering synthetic objects into real scenes: bridging traditional and image-based graphics with global illumination and high dynamic range photography. In: Proceedings of the 25th Annual Conference on Computer Graphics and Interactive Techniques, SIGGRAPH 1998, pp. 189–198 (1998)
8. Crassin, C., Neyret, F., Sainz, M., Green, S., Eisemann, E.: Interactive indirect illumination using voxel cone tracing. Comput. Graph. Forum (Proceedings of Pacific Graphics 2011) **30**(7), 1921–1930 (2011)
9. de Sorbier, F., Saito, H.: Stereoscopic augmented reality with pseudo-realistic global illumination effects. In: Proceedings of the SPIE 9011, Stereoscopic Displays and Applications XXV, pp. 90111W–90111W-14 (2014)
10. Viriyothai, K., Debevec, P.: Variance minimization light probe sampling. In: SIGGRAPH 2009: Posters. SIGGRAPH 2009, pp. 92:1–92:1 (2009)
11. Izadi, S., Kim, D., Hilliges, O., Molyneaux, D., Newcombe, R., Kohli, P., Shotton, J., Hodges, S., Freeman, D., Davison, A., Fitzgibbon, A.: Kinectfusion: real-time 3d reconstruction and interaction using a moving depth camera. In: Proceedings of the 24th Annual ACM Symposium on User Interface Software and Technology, UIST 2011, pp. 559–568 (2011)
12. Chatterjee, A., Jain, S., Govindu, V.M.: A pipeline for building 3d models using depth cameras. In: Proceedings of the Eighth Indian Conference on Computer Vision, Graphics and Image Processing, ICVGIP 2012, pp. 38:1–38:8 (2012)
13. Karsch, K., Sunkavalli, K., Hadap, S., Carr, N., Jin, H., Fonte, R., Sittig, M., Forsyth, D.: Automatic scene inference for 3d object compositing. ACM Trans. Graph. **33**(3), 32:1–32:15 (2014)
14. Keller, A.: Instant radiosity. In: Proceedings of the 24th annual conference on Computer graphics and interactive techniques, SIGGRAPH 1997, pp. 49–56 (1997)
15. Dachsbacher, C., Stamminger, M.: Reflective shadow maps. In: Proceedings of the 2005 Symposium on Interactive 3D Graphics and Games, I3D 2005, pp. 203–231(2005)
16. Ritschel, T., Dachsbacher, C., Grosch, T., Kautz, J.: The state of the art in interactive global illumination. Comput. Graph. Forum **31**(1), 160–188 (2012)
17. Knecht, M., Traxler, C., Mattausch, O., Purgathofer, W., Wimmer, M.: Differential instant radiosity for mixed reality. In: Proceedings of the 2010 IEEE International Symposium on Mixed and Augmented Reality, ISMAR 2010, pp. 99–107 (2010)

18. Lensing, P., Broll, W.: Instant indirect illumination for dynamic mixed reality scenes. In: Proceedings of the 2012 IEEE International Symposium on Mixed and Augmented Reality, ISMAR 2012, pp. 109–118 (2012)
19. Franke, T.A., Jung, Y.: Real-time mixed reality with gpu techniques. In: GRAPP 2008: Proceedings of the Third International Conference on Computer Vision Theory and Applications, pp. 249–252 (2008)
20. Franke, T.A.: Delta voxel cone tracing. In: IEEE International Symposium on Mixed and Augmented Reality, ISMAR 2014, pp. 39–44 (2014)
21. Kaplanyan, A., Dachsbacher, C.: Cascaded light propagation volumes for real-time indirect illumination. In: Proceedings of the 2010 ACM SIGGRAPH Symposium on Interactive 3D Graphics and Games, I3D 2010, pp. 99–107 (2010)
22. Franke, T.A.: Delta light propagation volumes for mixed reality. In: 2013 IEEE International Symposium on Mixed and Augmented Reality, ISMAR 2013, pp. 125–132 (2013)
23. Kato, H., Billinghurst, M.: Marker tracking and hmd calibration for a video-based augmented reality conferencing system. In: Proceedings of the 2nd IEEE and ACM International Workshop on Augmented Reality, IWAR 1999, pp. 85–94 (1999)
24. Jakob, W.: Mitsuba renderer (2010). http://www.mitsuba-renderer.org

Registration System Errors Perception in Augmented Reality Based on RGB-D Cameras

Daniel M. Tokunaga[1], Cléber G. Corrêa[1(✉)], Fernanda M. Bernardo[2],
João Bernardes[2], Edith Ranzini[3], Fátima L. S. Nunes[2], and Romero Tori[1]

[1] Escola Politécnica da Universidade de São Paulo, Sao Paulo, Brazil
{dmtokunaga,cleber.gimenez,tori}@usp.br
[2] School of Arts, Sciences and Humanities, University of Sao Paulo,
Sao Paulo, Brazil
{fernanda.bernardo,jlbernardes,fatima.nunes}@usp.br
[3] Pontifícia Universidade Católica de São Paulo, Sao Paulo, Brazil
edith.ranzini@pucsp.br

Abstract. One of the main objectives in augmented reality (AR) is to totally merge virtual information into the real world. However, different problems in computational processes can directly affect the user perception. Although several works investigate how rendering or interaction issues are perceived by the user, little has been studied of how spatial registration problems can affect the user perception in AR systems, even that registration being one of the central problems of AR. In this work, we study how system errors of three-points RANSAC pose estimation algorithm based on RGB-D cameras can affect the user perception, by applying psychophysical tests. With these user tests, we address how depth map and feature matching noises, among other issues, can affect the perception of object registration.

Keywords: 3D registering error · Augmented reality · Pose estimation · User perception

1 Introduction

Augmented reality (AR) systems became popular in recent years, with application in several areas such as education [1,2], health [3], industry [4] and entertainment [5]. The main idea behind AR is to combine virtual and real information in real-time, registering 3D information [6]. This idea seems to be simple in theory, however it involves several aspects such as rendering the virtual objects and capturing real environment data in order to combine both pieces of information. Azuma [6] defines three characteristics of AR, such as:

- three-dimensional (3D) space composed of real and virtual elements, with predominance of the real over the virtual;

R. Shumaker and S. Lackey (Eds.): VAMR 2015, LNCS 9179, pp. 119–129, 2015.
DOI: 10.1007/978-3-319-21067-4_14

– real-time human-computer interaction;
– 3D registering, with alignment among real and virtual elements.

Due to problems in rendering and capturing, commonly caused by technological limitations, such as resolution, processing power and noise of input devices; and aspects from real environment, such as lighting and real objects and camera motion, different errors may be generated by the system during the human-computer interaction. These system errors can differently affect the user perception of whether the virtual information is real or not.

Several works examined how rendering errors affect the user perception [7–10]. Sanches *et al.* [11] studied the system error perception in video based avatar rendering issues. Also, [12–14] studied perception in Virtual Reality systems with haptic interaction.

However, little has been investigated about how the 3D registering errors affect the user perception of virtual objects placed over real surfaces. We addressed this problem, studying different types of common errors inside RGB-D registering based on three-point RANSAC pose estimation method [15], which enables fast registration of rigid object and is widely used.

Our main objective is to analyze system errors of 3D registering according to users perception, through subjective tests. Our contribution is the analysis of how system errors are perceived by users and which errors more or less affect the perception. Therefore, analyzing how high or low the different AR system errors should be in order to achieve a better user perception, even with these errors, which would help in the development of these interactive systems.

2   Related Work

User perception of virtual information realism is a central focus in several works. Gkioulekas *et al.* [7] presented a user perception study on the role of the phase function in translucent objects. Also, Jarabo *et al.* [8] and Křivánek et al. [10] studied realism in global illumination rendering, Jarabo *et al.* [8] investigated the perception of complex dynamic scenes, such as crowd movements, and Křivánek *et al.* [10], the effect of global illumination approximation impact on perception.

MacDonnell *et al.* [9], Gelasca and Ebrahimi [16] and Sanches *et al.* [11] studied user perception related with human avatars, synthesized and captured. MacDonnell *et al.* [9] studied the effects of human avatars and realism perception, and pointed out the uncanny valley effect [17] in avatar rendering. Gelasca and Ebrahimi [16] and Sanches *et al.* [11], in turn, studied the artifacts of background segmentation of user videos. Where, Sanches *et al.* [11] focused on AR and its impacts on user perception.

Several works in haptic interaction research also use objective evaluations with psychophysical models to determine user perception when a user is submitted to tactile stimuli [12–14], analyzing the tolerance in the occurrence of certain noise or errors in haptic signals.

As spotted by the works presented above, several aspects related with perception in AR [6] were studied isolatedly, such as rendering or interactions. However, little has been studied about another central aspect of AR, the registration of real and virtual objects. Sanches *et al.* [11] directly studied perception in AR systems, yet, their work relied on rendering aspects. Our work addresses this gap, investigating perception in AR registering focusing on common system errors that can happen, analyzing how these errors affect the perception in AR.

3   Registering Method and User Test Stimuli

Registration of view in AR systems can be achieved by several approaches [18–20], and recently RGB-D cameras have become widely available. These cameras enable faster and easier methods of pose estimation. One pose estimation method based on these cameras are the three-points based RANSAC based methods [21], used in several works, such as Henry *et al.* [15]. These methods pose estimate known scene or objects based on correlation of known feature points with observed feature points, extracted using feature point extraction methods such as SIFT [19] or SURF [20]. In this work, we will use this three-points based RANSAC pose estimation with SURF feature points in order to analyze the method performance through system error based on user perception.

Two common system errors in this method are the noise present in RGB-D depth map, caused by the capturing system, and 2D (two-dimensional) position error of detected feature points in the image, caused by mismatches or position error of the feature matching algorithm. Also, clustering of the detected feature points, generated by occlusions of the object or because of the original object texture, is another error. This clustering (Fig. 1(a)) can cause pose estimation errors, since the points are not spread all over the object surface, small errors in captured data can thus affect the pose error more.

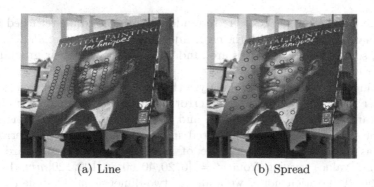

(a) Line   (b) Spread

Fig. 1. Feature point clustering.

In order to analyze the user perception, two controlled experiments were conducted. Here, 150 different ground truth images were pre-rendered with different plane image poses, in order to decrease pose related perception bias. For each

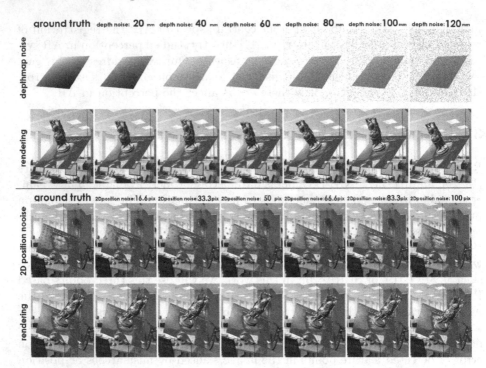

Fig. 2. Experiment 1 - images and error examples. First row: depth map noise; second row: pose estimation result using the noise added depth map; third row: 2D position noise; fourth row: pose estimation result. First column: the ground truth values and poses. Second to seventh column: the increase in noise values and their resulting poses, 20 to 120 mm of noise for depth map and 16.67 to 100 pixels for 2D position noise.

error value, all the 150 images were re-rendered with the result returned by our pose estimation algorithm with the error injected, as in Lepetit *et al.* [22]. In the user test, some of the 150 images are randomly shown with their ground truth images for each error value.

Experiment 1 was executed to analyze the effect of two types of errors themselves over the registration, without error combination. Two tests were preformed, varying the depth (DEPTH) and 2D position (POS_2D) noises with 7 different values for each, as presented in Fig. 2. The depth map errors are injected as a Gaussian random noise of mean $\mu = 0$ and standard variation with 7 values varying from $\sigma = [0, 20, 40, 60, 80, 100, 120]mm$. In order to add the 2D position noise, we added a two-dimensional Gaussian random noise of mean $\mu = 0$ and standard variation with 7 values varying from $\sigma = [0, 16.6, 33.3, 50, 66.6, 83.3, 100]pix$, similarly to depth noise. This experiment indicated how these two errors are perceived by users, and how they differ from computed absolute errors.

In Experiment 2, 4 variables were chosen: depth (DEPTH), 2D position (POS_2D), clustering type (CLUSTER) and object rendered over the plane

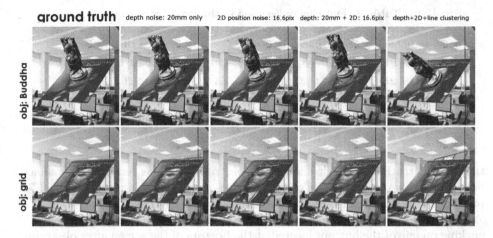

Fig. 3. Experiment 2 - images example. First row: Buddha as object, second row: red grid as object. First column: ground truth pose; second column: depth map noise only; third column: 2D position noise only; fourth column: combined depth and position noise; fifth column: noise combined with line clustering (Fig. 1(a)).

(OBJ). We varied the object, since one hypothesis was that the object can affect error perception, providing guides and clues t to the error. Figure 3 shows some examples of pose estimation results with these combined errors.

In this test, we varied the depth map noise variance with three different values $\sigma = [0, 20, 60]mm$. Also, the 2D position noise was modified with three different variances of $\sigma = [0, 16.6, 50]pix$. For the clustering, we used two different types, the spread and in line clustering as shown in Fig. 1. And, lastly, we chose two different objects to be rendered, the Happy Buddha object from the "Stanford 3D Scanning Repository"[1], as an object that is taller but does not occupy all the space of the pose estimated plane object; and a red grid that perfectly fits around the plane object, as shown in Fig. 6.

In Table 1, we show the user test stimuli used in the two user tests. It is worth pointing out that our objective here is to evaluate system errors and characteristics, not effects caused by environment setting. Therefore, screen, lighting conditions and other physical environment are not chosen as stimuli.

4   User Test Setup

The experiments were conducted in controlled physical environments, using common video monitors and an automated system to collect users opinions. A simple yes-no psychophysical task was used to compare two images. These two images were presented side by side on one screen, being an image to represent the ground truth and other with noise or equal to ground truth. The comparison of

---

[1] http://graphics.stanford.edu/data/3Dscanrep/.

Table 1. Full stimuli list used in the two experiments.

Variable	Experiment 1	Experiment 2
DEPTH	{0, 20, 40, 60, 80, 100, 120}	{0, 20, 60}
POS_2D	{0, 16.6, 33.3, 50, 66.6, 83.3, 100}	{0, 16.6, 50}
CLUSTER	Spread	{Spread, Line}
OBJ	Buddha	{Buddha, Grid}

the ground truth with itself allows to avoid response bias, ensuring a balance between the two answers. The pairs of images were shown in random order (70 pairs in the first experiment and 114 in the second experiment).

To each user was asked to select the option "Equal" or the option "Different", clicking on one of the buttons located at the bottom of the screen after observing the two images. A time for response was not specified; however, users should answer quickly. Figure 4 presents an example of the virtual environment used in the tests with the screen and the two images, as well as the buttons to register the user opinion. In each experiment, 17 subjects participated, the major part composed of students and professors.

Fig. 4. Test environment example.

In order to test statistically significant differences in answers to different scenarios, we chose one-way ANOVA (Analysis of Variance) for first experiment, aiming to analyze the effects of two variables separately (DEPTH and POS_2D); and four-way ANOVA for the second experiment, which allows analyzing the effect of one of the four variables (DEPTH, POS_2D, CLUSTER and OBJ), independently of the other variables (called *Main Effects*); as well as the effect of one variable when there is dependence on the level or levels of the other variables (one or more variables, with analysis of two, three and four variables), called *Interaction Effects*. After finding the effects (main and interaction), Tukey post-hoc test was selected to compare pairs of means and to determine the causes of these effects in both experiments.

5   Results

Figure 5 shows the results from the first user experiment. Here, the mean values of the percentage of times in which users perceived the errors inserted in the images are shown, as well as the ground truth and the computed pose errors. These data were processed with one-way ANOVA and Tukey post-hoc test, where null hypotheses were false in both cases, depth ($F = 30.97$, $p = 0.0224e^{-30}$) and 2D ($F = 26.75$, $p = 0.0311e^{-26}$).

From these graphs, it is possible to observe how the decrease of registration perception is different from the absolute computed error increase. The depth errors values are perceived almost as an inverse exponential function, from graph (Fig. 5(a)), where the computational error increases almost linearly. We could deduct that depth map noises are easily perceived by the user in this setup, once it creates rotation errors at the object pose estimation.

Two-dimensional position errors are also perceived differently from the computed errors (Fig. 5(c)). However, differently from depth map errors, the position noise decreases more slowly and the computed absolute error increases almost exponentially. This could be due to the nature of the pose error returned by this noise. Since only the position is varied and the depth map is clean in this test, the resulting error appears as a slide of the virtual object over the plane object, as seen in Fig. 5. With this, small errors are weakly perceived by the user.

Results of the second test, in which four different variables were chosen as stimuli, were processed with four-way ANOVA and Tukey post-hoc test. The full table of rejected null hypothesis, with their F and p-values, and returned

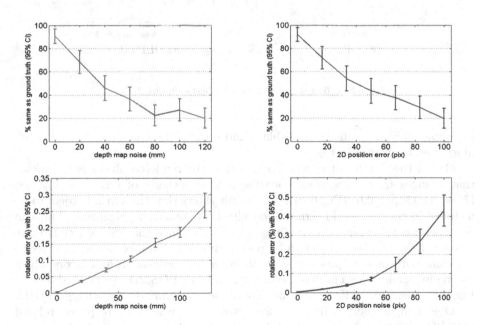

Fig. 5. User perception for Experiment 1 and computed errors.

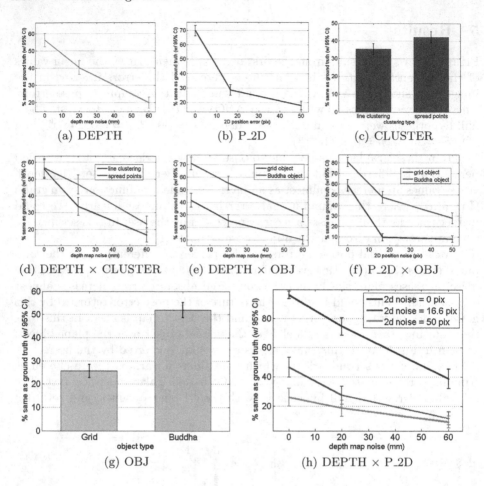

Fig. 6. User perception for experiment 2.

post-hoc analysis are listed in Table 2, and part of these significant results are illustrated by graphs in Fig. 6.

One of the significant effects found is that the rendered object is one factor that changes user perception, once the null hypothesis of OBJ was rejected ($F = 211.17$, $p \approx 0.0$) (Fig. 6(g)). This result shows that the virtual object to be included in the real world significantly affects registration perception. This can be explained by comparing the images in Fig. 3. Once the grid object is more aligned with the plane object to be pose estimated, the user has more clues to correlate both objects poses, making it easier for the user to find errors which the registration. This effect is clearer specially in POS_2D errors as shown in Fig. 6(f), where the difference in perception across errors decays with grid OBJ.

One change observed from the first experiment was the perceptions related with POS_2D error. In Experiment 1, POS_2D errors are less perceived by users;

Table 2. Significant results from experiment 2.

Effect	F,P-Values	Tuckey Post-Hoc Test
Main Effects		
DEPTH	$F = 148.89$, $p \approx 0$	Perception deteriorates almost lineally, all values are statistically different from each other
POS_2D	$F = 337.25$, $p \approx 0$	Perception deteriorates almost exponentially; all values are statistically different from each other
CLUSTER	$F = 15.41$, $p = 0.0001$	Spread points CLUSTER are better perceived than line CLUSTER
OBJ	$F = 234.82$, $p \approx 0$	OBJ Buddha is significantly better perceived then OBJ grid
Two-way interaction		
DEPTH*P_2D	$F = 16.62$, $p \approx 0$	P_2D noise without depth noises better than in most cases, only in (P_2D = 0, DEPTH = 60) == (P_2D = 16.6, DEPTH= 0) and (P_2D = 16.6, DEPTH = 20)
DEPTH*CLUSTER	$F = 4.35$, $p = 0.0131$	Difference between CLUSTER with DEPTH = 20
DEPTH*OBJ	$F = 3.87$, $p = 0.0211$	OBJ Buddha better perceived than grid in almost all cases, only (OBJ = Buddha, DEPTH = 60) =(OBJ = grid, DEPTH = 20)
POS_2D*OBJ	$F = 10.78$, $p \approx 0$	Grid OBJ has a strong decay, compared with the Buddha OBJ, with P_2D error increase
Three-way interaction		
DEPTH*POS_2D*OBJ	$F = 14.66$, $p \approx 0$	Perception has a strong decay in cases of grid OBJ with P_2D errors
POS_2D*CLUSTER*OBJ	$F = 4.41$, $p = 0.0123$	Perception has a strong decay in cases of grid OBJ with P_2D errors

however, in Experiment 2, POS_2D perception has a strong decrease with error increase (Fig. 5(b)). This can be explained by the point that POS_2D error perception could be strongly increased when combined with other types of errors, as in Figs. 6(f) and 6(h). Figure 6(h) allows observing that DEPTH errors are strongly affected by the POS_2D errors, meaning that combinations of both errors can generate worse perceptions.

Finally, one interesting issue is that CLUSTER related errors did not strongly affect user perception, although the null hypothesis was rejected. In Fig. 6(c), it is possible to observe that the change in perception is not strong with our clustering types, and from Fig. 6(d), the CLUSTER type was significant only for middle values of depth errors. Even the null hypothesis of the interaction effect of POS_2D and CLUSTER was not rejected, showing that clustering does not play a strong role in registration perception, with the level of clustering we applied to this work (illustrated in Fig. 1).

6   Conclusion

We discussed how system errors in the registration method applied to AR systems based on RGB-D cameras can affect users perception. Although, this registration process is one of the central aspects in AR systems, little about its perception has been studied. Based on yes-no psychophysical tests and ANOVA analysis, we spotted several traces of perception in AR, such as the role of relation between rendered object and real object, which directly affect perception.

Also, we address how some system errors appear in the object pose and how this affects the user perception. Effects such as depth map errors alone are more perceived than feature points position errors; however, when combined with other errors, position errors cause a huge decrease in perception. Another issue is that user perception is not identically related with the absolute computed error, having sudden decrease with even small changes in some errors.

Although our tests cover the major system errors in the RGB-D registration method, more tests need to be applied in future works, in order to fully explore registration related perception issues in AR. For example, how and why this real-virtual objects relationship affects perception, or effects of the test environment, such as screen resolution and illumination issues.

Acknowledgments. The authors would like to acknowledge the National Council for the Improvement of Higher Education Personnel (CAPES) for scholarships, and the Engineering Technology Development Foundation (FDTE) for funding of the project.

References

1. Santos, M., Chen, A., Taketomi, T., Yamamoto, G., Miyazaki, J., Kato, H.: Augmented reality learning experiences: survey of prototype design and evaluation. IEEE Trans. Learn. Technol. **7**(1), 38–56 (2014)
2. Lee, K.: Augmented reality in education and training. TechTrends **56**(2), 13–21 (2012)
3. Sielhorst, T., Feuerstein, M., Navab, N.: Advanced medical displays: a literature review of augmented reality. J. Disp. Technol. **4**(4), 451–467 (2008)

4. Ong, S.K., Yuan, M.L., Nee, A.Y.C.: Augmented reality applications in manufacturing: a survey. Int. J. Prod. Res. **46**, 2707–2742 (2008)
5. Thomas, B.H.: A survey of visual, mixed, and augmented reality gaming. Comput. Entertainment **10**(3), 3:1–3:33 (2012)
6. Azuma, R.T.: A survey of augmented reality. Presence Teleoperators Virtual Environ. **6**(4), 355–385 (1997)
7. Gkioulekas, I., Xiao, B., Zhao, S., Adelson, E.H., Zickler, T., Bala, K.: Understanding the role of phase function in translucent appearance. ACM Trans. Graph. **32**(5), 147:1–147:19 (2013)
8. Jarabo, A., Eyck, T.V., Sundstedt, V., Bala, K., Gutierrez, D., O'Sullivan, C.: Crowd light: evaluating the perceived fidelity of illuminated dynamic scenes. Comput. Graph. Forum **31**(2), 565–574 (2012)
9. McDonnell, R., Breidt, M., Bülthoff, H.H.: Render me real?: investigating the effect of render style on the perception of animated virtual humans. ACM Trans. Graph. **31**(4), 91:1–91:11 (2012)
10. Křivánek, J., Ferwerda, J.A., Bala, K.: Effects of global illumination approximations on material appearance. ACM Trans. Graph. **29**(4), 112:1–112:10 (2010)
11. Sanches, S., Silva, V., Nakamura, R., Tori, R.: Objective assessment of video segmentation quality for augmented reality. In: IEEE International Conference on Multimedia and Expo., pp. 1–6, July 2013
12. Steinbach, E., Hirche, S., Ernst, M., Brandi, F., Chaudhari, R., Kammerl, J., Vittorias, I.: Haptic communications. Proc. IEEE **100**(4), 937–956 (2012)
13. Chaudhari, R., Steinbach, E., Hirche, S.: Towards an objective quality evaluation framework for haptic data reduction. In: IEEE World Haptics Conference, pp. 539–544 (2011)
14. Sakr, N., Georganas, N., Zhao, J.: A perceptual quality metric for haptic signals. In: Proceedings of the IEEE International Workshop on Haptic, Audio and Visual Environments and Games, pp. 27–32, Ottawa, Ontario, Canada (2007)
15. Henry, P., Krainin, M., Herbst, E., Ren, X., Fox, D.: RGB-D mapping: using kinect-style depth cameras for dense 3D modeling of indoor environments. Int. J. Robot. Res. **31**(5), 647–663 (2012)
16. Gelasca, E.D., Ebrahimi, T.: On evaluating video object segmentation quality: a perceptually driven objective metric. IEEE J. Sel. Top. Sig. Proc. **3**(2), 319–335 (2009)
17. MacDorman, K.F., Green, R.D., Ho, C.C., Koch, C.T.: Too real for comfort? uncanny responses to computer generated faces. Comput. Hum. Behav. **25**(3), 695–710 (2009). Including the Special Issue: Enabling elderly users to create
18. Lima, J., Uchiyama, H., Teichrieb, V., Marchand, E.: Texture-less planar object detection and pose estimation using depth-assisted rectification of contours. In: 2012 IEEE International Symposium on Mixed and Augmented Reality, ISMAR 2012, pp. 297–298, Novmber 2012
19. Lowe, D.: Object recognition from local scale-invariant features. In: The Proceedings of the Seventh IEEE International Conference on Computer Vision, 1999, vol. 2, pp. 1150–1157 (1999)
20. Bay, H., Ess, A., Tuytelaars, T., Van Gool, L.: Speeded-up robust features (surf). Comput. Vis. Image Underst. **110**(3), 346–359 (2008)
21. Fischler, M.A., Bolles, R.C.: Random sample consensus: a paradigm for model fitting with applications to image analysis and automated cartography. Commun. ACM **24**(6), 381–395 (1981)
22. Lepetit, V., Moreno-Noguer, F., Fua, P.: EPnP: an accurate O(N) solution to the PnP problem. Int. J. Comput. Vision **81**(2), 155–166 (2009)

Local 3D Pose Estimation of Feature Points Based on RGB-D Information for Object Based Augmented Reality

Daniel M. Tokunaga[1]([✉]), Ricado Nakamura[1], João Bernardes[2],
Edith Ranzini[1,3], and Romero Tori[1]

[1] Escola Politécnica da Universidade de São Paulo, Sao Paulo, Brazil
dmtokunaga@acm.org
[2] School of Arts, Sciences and Humanities, University of São Paulo,
Sao Paulo, Brazil
[3] Pontifícia Universidade Católica de São Paulo, Sao Paulo, Brazil

Abstract. We here describe a novel approach for locally obtaining pose estimation of match feature points, observed using RGB-D cameras, in order to apply to locally planar object pose estimation with RANSAC method for augmented reality systems. Conventionally, object pose estimation based on RGB-D cameras are achieved by the correlation between observed 3D points captured by feature point matching and known 3D points of the object. However, in such methods, features are simplified as single 3D points, losing information of the feature and its neighborhood surface. This approach based on local 3D pose estimation of locally planar feature points, brings richer information for 3D pose estimation of planar, 3D rigid or deformable objects. This information enables more stable pose estimation across RANSAC settings than conventional three-points RANSAC methods.

Keywords: Computer vision · Pose estimation · Feature points

1 Introduction

Several systems in augmented reality (AR) use known markers inside the scene to register the view position and render virtual objects on the real scene. These markers can be a special pattern, such as fiducial markers, or textured objects [1]. In order to classify and to register these textured objects, conventional methods use feature points [2,3], generated by surface texture, and pose estimation methods, such as three-points RANSAC with RGB-D frames [4] or PnP solving methods [5].

These textured markers can be different classes of objects. Most AR systems use pose estimation of planar [2] and three-dimensional(3D) rigid objects [1]. Another class of objects, used as markers, are deformable objects. These objects, which change their shape over-time, can be pose estimated by methods such as [6]. However, in all of these presented pose estimation methods, detected feature

© Springer International Publishing Switzerland 2015
R. Shumaker and S. Lackey (Eds.): VAMR 2015, LNCS 9179, pp. 130–141, 2015.
DOI: 10.1007/978-3-319-21067-4_15

Fig. 1. Camera registration and rendering results, using planar and 3D rigid object makers.

points are simplified as a single point. As [7] shows, more information can be extracted from the captured information, as normal in case of RGB-D frames.

In this work, we introduce a novel approach of 3D pose estimation for several classes of markers, based on local 3D pose of locally planar feature points and RGB-D information. For each match feature of the RGB-D frame, we estimate its three-dimensional pose and, based on these feature point poses, the global pose of the object is estimated. This approach has the advantage of extracting more information from each matched feature point, giving richer information for the global pose estimation process, unlike previous works. Our local pose based registration and rendering results for rigid objects are shown in Fig. 1.

Our contributions in this paper are the local pose based pose estimation approach, the method to locally pose estimate each match feature point, as well as, the method for global pose estimation based on our approach combined with the RANSAC method [8], in order to achieve near real-time performance. With obtained results from Sect. 4, we show that is possible to achieve camera registration for AR systems with different classes of textured markers, and, that our method is more robust through different RANSAC settings as compared to conventional three-points based RANSAC methods in our evaluation settings. Furthermore, if better precision or different object models are required, our local pose information could be combined with more complex methods, since it only extract more information from the captured frames, and thus do not conflict with other solutions.

2   Related Works

Pose estimation of known objects, such as markers, based on their surface texture feature points is a well known problem in the literature. Several works pose estimate known objects,rigid or deformable, using images and video steam input such as Lepetit et al. [5], Lowe [2], Xiang et al. [9]. On the other hand, devices that can capture RGB-D information haves become widely available. These devices return depth information in real-time, making the capture of 3D poses of different objects more accurate or easier.

Lima et al. [1] and Lee et al. [10] achieve the pose estimation based on 3D positions of extracted object feature points using RGB-D frames. Marcon et al. [7] and Choi et al. [11] also pose estimate rigid objects based on RGB-D information and feature points, however, similarly to our work, they also extract normal information from the surface in order to be used in the pose estimation, using primary component analysis (PCA)[7] or vector products [11] of the surface around the feature point.

Also, Jordt et al. [12] and Pritchard et al. [6] fully estimates the pose of deformable objects based on the 3D points captured by RGB-D data and deformation models. In these works, pose estimation does not consider that objects has fixed positional relationship to each other feature point.

Besides object pose estimation, works of camera registration for environment location and mapping such as SLAM [13] also have similar approaches to our method, once it need to register a set of known point in the space to new observed ones. Works as Park et al. [14] achieve the camera registration based on ICP methods. On the other hand, Henry et al. [4], Taguchi et al. [15] and Lee et al. [13] proceeds the camera registration based on RGB-D information and point correlation. Furthermore, these works also implement the RANSAC method in order to achieve near real-time process time, as our work.

However, none of the presented works in this section explicitly extracts the local pose of detected feature point. Our work out-stands in this aspect, as we explicitly extract more information from each match feature point, in order to pose estimate different class of objects such as AR markers.

3   Method

In this section we will describe the method applied to obtain the object 3D pose. Here we separate the estimation method in 3 parts, the pre-process of object feature points, local pose estimation, and global pose estimation of rigid objects based on the local information. As explained in Sect. 1, our pose estimation approach is based on the local pose estimation of each feature point, giving us a rough estimation of the global pose.

Our assumptions are that, the feature points over the object surface are locally planar, and feature points orientations are generated by the local surface texture gradient, and not by the shape of the object. We also consider that camera projection matrix $\mathbf{K}_c$ of the RGB-D camera, the image I_{tex}, which contains the information of the surface texture of the object to be estimated, are known. As well as, its mapping function $f_{pos}(x_i, y_i)$, that maps the 2D coordinates at image plane coordinates to 3D position over the object surface at global coordinates, and $f_{vec}(x_i, y_i)$, that returns the normal vector of the surface from the image coordinates position, are also known.

3.1 Pre-process of Object Feature Points

The objective of this pre-process part is to extract robust features of the object F_{obj} and process three-dimensional information of each feature point in order to used them at local pose estimation, described in Sect. 3.2. The extraction of robust features is done by applying approaches similar to ASIFT [16], extracting features that are robust to background changes and affine transformations. Initially, the object is rendered with different camera positions, with transformation $\mathbf{E}_{cam}$, as [16]. Since we expect the features to be locally planar in this approach, the object is simplified as an image plane that contains the surface texture I_{tex} of the object. With this, even features of 3D objects or deformable objects are pre-processed in the same way as planar objects.

Then, for each camera position, we extract its feature points F_{view}. Also, the 3D information of each extracted feature point is calculated. First the 3D position of point $\mathbf{p}_{fts}$ is calculated using plane line intersection method between the rendered object plane with the line that crosses the camera position $\mathbf{p}_{cam}$ and the feature point 3D position $\mathbf{p}^{3D}$ detected at 2D position p^{img} of the rendered image plane. This 3D position related to the feature point is calculated as

$$\mathbf{p}^{3D} = \mathbf{E}_{cam}^{-1} \cdot (z_{img} \cdot (\mathbf{K}_c^{-1} p^{img})), \tag{1}$$

where z_{img} is some distance defined as distance of the image plane to the camera position, and E_{cam} is the rendered camera transformation matrix.

After calculating the 3D position, a 3D vector o_{fts} over the texture image plane that points toward the feature 2D orientation is calculated. This is done by calculating the three-dimensional position of point $\mathbf{p}_o$ in a similar way of calculating $\mathbf{p}_{fts}$, but instead of calculating using the rendered image position p^{img} of the feature, we use the 2D position

$$p_o^{img} = p^{img} + s v_{ori}, \tag{2}$$

where s is the size of the feature patch that was used to extract the feature point descriptor, and v_{ori} is the two-dimensional orientation vector of the feature. Then, o_{fts} is calculated as

$$o_{fts} = (\mathbf{p}_o - \mathbf{p}_{fts})/\|(\mathbf{p}_o - \mathbf{p}_{fts})\| \tag{3}$$

Finally, the normal of the feature n_{fts} is calculated. Once the object is converted into a planar image, the feature point normal is the same as that of the plane normal, $n_{fts} = n_{plane}$.

At this point, for each camera position $\mathbf{p}_{cam^i}$, feature point collection $F_{view^i} = \{F^0_{view^i}, \dots, F^n_{view^i}\}$ is listed with its 3D information. After listing all the collections in all the views, differently from [16], each listed feature points collection F_{view^i} at view position i is compared with other feature point collections F_{view^j} in different views j using feature matching methods, and only features that appear in more than n_v views are picked up. With this, feature points F_{obj} that are robust across views and backgrounds are filtered in order to be used at the pose estimation. Each feature point, $F^i_{obj} = \{\mathbf{p}^i_{fts}, \boldsymbol{n}^i_{fts}, \boldsymbol{o}^i_{fts}, dsc^i_{fts}\}$, contains three-dimensional information of position $\mathbf{p}^i_{fts}$, normal $\boldsymbol{n}^i_{fts}$, orientation vector $\boldsymbol{o}^i_{fts}$ and its descriptor dsc^i_{fts}. Figure 2 illustrates these information.

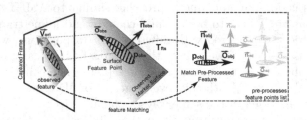

Fig. 2. Local pose estimation method. T_{fts} is calculated to match p, $\boldsymbol{n}$ and $\boldsymbol{o}$ of the pre-processed feature with the observed feature.

As a last task of this pre-process, all the calculated 3D information are reconverted to match the original object using functions $f_{pos}(x_i, y_i)$ and $f_{vec}(x_i, y_i)$. In case of planar objects, these information do not change, but for 3D rigid objects, these information are reconverted so they lie over the object surface. In case of the pose estimation in Fig. 1, they are converted into a cylindrical object with

$$f_{pos}(x_i, y_i) = [r\sin(\pi x_i/W), \ y_i, \ r\cos(\pi x_i/W)]^\mathsf{T}$$
$$f_{vec}(x_i, y_i) = [\sin(\pi x_i/W), \ 0, \ \cos(\pi x_i/W)]^\mathsf{T}$$
(4)

where, r is the radius of the object and W the total width of the texture image plane.

3.2 Local Pose Estimation

In order to estimate the local pose of the feature point using RGB-D information, initially, feature points are extracted from the newly captured RGB frame and compared with F_{obj}, extracted at the pre-process part, using the conventional feature match method. For each match feature point, the three-dimensional position $\mathbf{p}_{obs}$ at the surface of the object that generated the feature is calculated from its two-dimensional position p_f and depth d, obtained from the depth map.

Then, similarly to (2), using the size of patch s and two-dimensional orientation vector $\boldsymbol{v}_{ori}$ returned from the feature extraction, three-dimensional position

p_o of the object seen by the RGB frame at 2D position

$$p_o^{img} = p_f + s v_{ori} \tag{5}$$

is calculated. From p_o, obtained by p_o^{img} and its depth value, the vector that points toward the feature orientation over the object surface

$$o_{obs} = (\mathbf{p}_o - \mathbf{p}_{obs})/\|\mathbf{p}_o - \mathbf{p}_{obs}\| \tag{6}$$

is calculated.

Once the feature is considered to be locally planar, the cross product of any two non-collinear vectors that belong to the feature patch gives us the normal of the feature point n_{obs}. Thus, we calculate the feature normal by the cross product of o_{obs} with another vector over the observed surface. In order to guarantee that both vectors are not collinear, a 3D point $\mathbf{p}_{ort}$ over the surface is calculated similarly to (5) by the 2D point of the RGB frame at position $p_{ort}^{img} = p_f + s v_{ort}$, where v_{ort} is a vector in the RGB frame coordinates, orthogonal to v_{ori}. Then, we calculate n_{obs} as

$$n_{obs} = o_{obs} \times (\mathbf{p}_{ort} - \mathbf{p}_{obs}/\|\mathbf{p}_{ort} - \mathbf{p}_{obs}\|) \tag{7}$$

where $\mathbf{p}_{ort}$ is the point over the object surface calculated by p_{ort}^{img} and its depth value.

With $\mathbf{p}_{obs}$, o_{obs} and n_{obs}, it is possible to calculate the pose of the feature point $\mathbf{T}_f$ similarly to [11,17]. Here, we calculate this transformation as a combination of 3 transform matrices $\mathbf{T}_{r1}$, $\mathbf{T}_{r2}$ and $\mathbf{T}_t$. First, $\mathbf{T}_{r1}$ rotates the original feature normal n_{fts} to match with n_{obs}. This is done by a transformation that rotates around axis r_{a1} and angle a_1 as

$$\begin{aligned} r_{a1} &= n_{obs} \times n_{fts} \\ a_1 &= \arccos(n_{obs} \cdot n_{fts}) \end{aligned} \tag{8}$$

Then $\mathbf{T}_{r2}$ rotates the new coordinate system to match $\mathbf{T}_{r1} o_{fts}$ and o_{obs}. As (8), $\mathbf{T}_{r2}$ is calculated as a rotation transformation with axis r_{a2}, and angle a_2 as: $r_{a2} = o_{obs} \times (\mathbf{T}_{r1} \cdot o_{fts})$ and $a_2 = \arccos(o_{obs} \cdot (\mathbf{T}_{r1} \cdot o_{fts}))$. Finally $\mathbf{T}_t$ is a translation of the coordinate system to the observed point $\mathbf{p}_{obs}$, calculated as $t = \mathbf{p}_{obs} - \mathbf{T}_{r2} \cdot \mathbf{T}_{r1} \cdot \mathbf{p}_{fts}$.

The final transformation matrix of the feature pose $\mathbf{T}_f$ is given by $\mathbf{T}_f = (\mathbf{T}_t \cdot \mathbf{T}_{r2} \cdot \mathbf{T}_{r1})$. Figure 2 illustrates this pose estimation and Fig. 3 shows the pose obtained by each feature in a planar object.

3.3   Global Pose Estimation

In this approach, the global pose of a 3D rigid object is estimated based on local pose of the match features $\mathbf{T}_{fc} = \{\mathbf{T}_f^0, \ldots, \mathbf{T}_f^n\}$. Each pose returned by

Fig. 3. Estimated local poses of match features returned by our local pose estimation process. The coordinate system returned by each feature point is drawn over its position.

the feature point provides an estimation of the global pose. In order to achieve process time near real-time systems, we also applied a variant of RANSAC approach [8] to our global pose estimation. As in [8], initially a randomly selected subset $S1$ of the found feature points is selected by a percentage p_{subset}. Then, pose transformation matrices $\mathbf{T}_f^r$ within $\mathbf{T}_{fc}$ are randomly selected.

For each point within $S1$, the quadratic error of $\mathbf{T}_f^r$, $\epsilon^i = \|\mathbf{T}_f^r \cdot \mathbf{p}_{fts}^i - \mathbf{p}_{obs}^i\|^2$ is calculated as the distance between the observed positions of the feature in $S1$ and its pose estimated position based on $\mathbf{T}_f^r$, where $\mathbf{p}_{fts}^i$ is the original position of observed feature point at $\mathbf{p}_{obs}^i$. Then, the number of points n_τ that have distance error less than a threshold τ_{error} is counted.

However, unlike [8], we do not stop the search after any $\mathbf{T}_f$ that has n_τ larger then a percentage p_{found} of $S1$. Instead, we keep the search until we find n_{mean} transformations $\mathbf{T}_{RANSAC} = \{\mathbf{T}_0, \dots, \mathbf{T}_{n_{mean}}\}$ that satisfy ($n_\tau > p_{found} \cdot p_{subset} \cdot n$). Then, these transformations are converted to a set of vectors of translation t_f^i and quaternions q_f^i [17]. Finally, the object global position $\mathbf{T}_{obj}$ is calculated as the transformation matrix obtained by the transform resulting from the mean of the translations vectors t_f and quaternions q_f.

This change is due to the nature of error returned by our approach. Since o_{fts} and o_{obs} are both calculated by the projection of the object surface texture at the captured image, small projection errors at the image of the feature point orientation vector can happen, as can be seen in Fig. 3.

In case the RANSAC method can not find n_{mean} samples of valid transformations in N_{trial} trials, our global pose detection method returns the transformations $\mathbf{T}_{obj}$ that have the minimal error within the sampled transformation of the N_{trial}. This transformation is the one that minimizes the sum of the quadratic errors, calculated by

$$\mathbf{T}_{obj} = \underset{\mathbf{T}_f}{\operatorname{argmin}} \sum_{i=1}^{n} (\|\mathbf{T}_f \cdot \mathbf{p}_{fts}^i - \mathbf{p}_{obj}^i\|^2) \tag{9}$$

4   Experimental Results

In this section we show the results from our local pose estimation for object based augmented reality, as well as the experimental evaluation of the approach.

All the pose detection method was implemented in MATLAB code. The variables of our approach and method used for these tests, unless explicitly written in the subsection, are $n_v = 3$, $n_{mean} = 8$, RANSAC error threshold $\tau_{error} = 225\ mm^2 = (15mm)^2$ for our global pose method and $\tau_{error} = 25\ mm^2 = (5mm)^2$ for the three-point RANSAC, RANSAC percentage of subset $p_{subset} = 70\,\%$ and found $p_{found} = 70\,\%$. Also, all the process time values in this paper is calculated including the extraction and matching of feature points processes.

Figure 1 shows the rendering results of the object register based on planar and rigid object using real captured data. On these images, red lines show the estimated pose of the object. Note that our pose estimation decrease its accuracy for planar objects as the object becomes more orthogonal to the camera view. This is due to a decrease in the detected feature number and feature area used to estimate the normal. Since it has less area to estimate the local normal, the estimated vector o_{obs} and its 2D orthogonal vector, at equation (7), have less length, being more easily affected by noises.

Also, from Fig. 1, it is possible to observe that our local pose estimation algorithm can be used to pose estimate rigid 3D objects, due to the locally planar feature points hypothesis. Showing that even rounded objects can be estimated if their feature points are locally planar. More over, in these 3D object cases, some feature points will not be visible due to self occlusion, still, our local pose estimation based approach can estimate the marker pose.

4.1   Synthesized Data Evaluation

In order to evaluate our approach for the planar objects, we compared our approach to conventional RANSAC approach based on plane calculation from triangles formed by each three observed points, as in [4]. For the test setup, we generated several 1280×960 images and its corresponding depth map with the planar object placed in different poses, using a virtual calibrated camera. The object was placed in front of the camera with random translation and rotation.

Similarly to [5], the rotation error is measured as $E_{rot}(\%) = \|q_{true} - q\|/\|q\|$, and translation error as $E_{trans}(\%) = \|t_{true} - t\|/\|t\|$, where q_{true} and t_{true} are the ground truth quaternion rotation and translation values of the object in each frame. We present the translation and rotation error in Fig. 4 with a box plot representation, across different depth map noises and 2D position noises.

Here, depth map noise is added using Gaussian noise, with mean equal to 0 and standard deviation varying from $[0, \dots, 75]$ in millimeters, and a low pass filter, 3×3 frame mean convolution, is applied to simulate a AR system with noise and its filter. Similarly, 2D noise is added at the detected feature position at the image space as a Gaussian noise with mean 0 and deviation varying from $[0, \dots, 30]$ in pixels.

From these graphs, observe that our method has lower accuracy and higher variation with depth map noise, compared to conventional three-point RANSAC method. This is due to the fact that our method is based on local information, where small depth noises can generate big errors in the global pose, specially in rotation. However, when the noise increases, our method has better accuracy, as

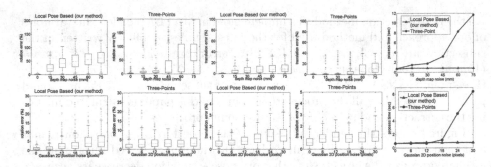

Fig. 4. Box plot evaluation and process time of our method and conventional three-points based RANSAC pose. Upper row: results across different depth map noise. Lower row: results across 2D noise of feature point detected position.

well as, lower variance in comparison to conventional method. For 2D noise case, our approach is more accurate for small 2D errors compared with three-points based RANSAC, since the surface around the feature point itself is not changing.

Furthermore, from the process time plots in the last column of Fig. 4, it is possible to observe that our method has a slow increase in process time across both type of noise values. However, the process time of the conventional three-point detection method rapidly increases with both types of noises. This is due to the failure of the RANSAC method.

In this setup, the RANSAC error thresholds are fixed with values empirically found to return good pose estimation across different poses. As the error increases, the tests rejection cases of RANSAC also increase, leading to more trials. Since our method is based on the local information of each feature point found, the total number of trials is equal to the total points found number n_f and induced errors only affect each point. On the other hand, the three-points method uses a combination of each 3 points, meaning that has $\binom{n_f}{3}$ of total trials, also, each noisy point affects a large number of trials. If m points are affected by noise, only $\binom{n_f-m}{3}$ are correct. Leading to a large number of failures, and thus to a larger process time.

In order to analyze the effect of the RANSAC error threshold, we evaluated the mean rotation error response across different depth map noises, varying from $[0, \ldots, 75]$ millimeters (mm), and RANSAC error thresholds, varying from $[5^2, \ldots, 85^2]$ in mm^2. We present these results and the process times in Fig. 5.

From this result, it is possible to observe that the three-points based RANSAC has a sudden increase in process time with the RANSAC error threshold decrease. However, from the mean error, it is possible to observe that it also has a sudden error increase with noise or RANSAC error threshold increase. This property allows observing that the three-points based RANSAC is sensitive to settings. In contrast, our local pose based approach does not present this characteristic, showing almost constant process time increase through RANSAC

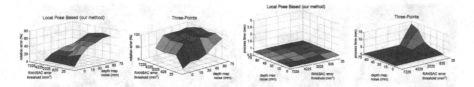

Fig. 5. Evaluation of our method and three-points based RANSAC, across RANSAC error threshold and depth map noise. Left two: rotation error. Right two: process time.

error decrease and noise increase, as well as, slow error increase through noise and RANSAC error threshold increase.

4.2 Other Results

This section shows other results obtained by our local pose approach, using it in a different way as described at Subsect. 3.3. Figures 6 and 7 show those results.

Fig. 6. Pose estimation based on a single feature point matching.

Figure 6 shows our pose estimation based on a single pre-processed feature point matching. The detected feature point pose is shown in the image by the rendered coordinate system using red, blue and green lines, over the detected feature point position. This result shows that, even with a single feature point to be matched, it is possible to retrieve the pose when this feature point is observed. Such a result is impossible to obtain using conventional three-points, or multiple-points, based pose estimation. This pose estimation could be used in markers with small surface area or in cases that are hard to observe multiple feature points of the marker due to occlusions.

Figure 7 shows our registration of deformable object as marker. In order to obtain these results, we do not fully detect the pose of the object as in [18]; instead, we use the local pose to obtain rough registration. This rough registration is obtained by finding the nearest match original feature point position to the position where the object should be rendered, and based on the pose of this

Fig. 7. Deformable marker rough registration.

feature point the object is rendered. In case of the result showed in Fig. 7, it is obtained by rendering a 3D model over each local pose found. Full deformable pose could be achieved by combining our results with more complex deformable models such as [6] or [18], since our method only extracts more information from the captured data. Moreover, the combination of our approach with other solutions in the literature would also be relatively easy due to this characteristic.

5   Conclusion

In this paper, we presented an approach, and methods that implements this approach, of pose estimation of objects, based on local poses of each match feature points in order to achieve the camera registration for AR systems. Based on this local pose estimation, we showed that several classes of objects, planar, 3D rigid or deformable, can be used as markers for camera registration. Also, the results show that our approach is more robust through RANSAC settings than conventional three-point based RANSAC.

Furthermore, our local pose-based approach is generic and not conflicting with other solutions, once it is only extracting more information from captured data. Therefore, could easily be combined with other solutions, allowing new ways for AR registration, similar to [6,12], or interaction, such as [19]. Future works lies on this characteristic, combining our approach with more complex tracking methods, or deformable object models [18].

Acknowledgments. The authors would like to acknowledge the National Council for the Improvement of Higher Education Personnel (CAPES) for scholarships, and the Engineering Technology Development Foundation (FDTE) for funding of the project.

References

1. Lima, J., Uchiyama, H., Teichrieb, V., Marchand, E.: Texture-less planar object detection and pose estimation using depth-assisted rectification of contours. In: 2012 IEEE International Symposium on Mixed and Augmented Reality, ISMAR, pp. 297–298, November 2012

2. Lowe, D.: Object recognition from local scale-invariant features. In: The Proceedings of the Seventh IEEE International Conference on Computer Vision, vol. 2, pp. 1150–1157 (1999)
3. Bay, H., Ess, A., Tuytelaars, T., Van Gool, L.: Speeded-up robust features (surf). Comput. Vis. Image Underst. 110(3), 346–359 (2008)
4. Henry, P., Krainin, M., Herbst, E., Ren, X., Fox, D.: Rgb-d mapping: using kinect-style depth cameras for dense 3d modeling of indoor environments. Int. J. Rob. Res. 31(5), 647–663 (2012)
5. Lepetit, V., Moreno-Noguer, F., Fua, P.: Epnp: an accurate o(n) solution to the pnp problem. Int. J. Comput. Vision 81(2), 155–166 (2009)
6. Pritchard, D., Heidrich, W.: Cloth motion capture. Comput. Graph. Forum 22(3), 263–271 (2003)
7. Marcon, M., Frigerio, E., Sarti, A., Tubaro, S.: 3D correspondences in textured depth-maps through planar similarity transform. In: 2012 IEEE International Conference on Emerging Signal Processing Applications, ESPA, pp. 17–20 January 2012
8. Fischler, M.A., Bolles, R.C.: Random sample consensus: a paradigm for model fitting with applications to image analysis and automated cartography. Commun. ACM 24(6), 381–395 (1981)
9. Xiang, Y., Mottaghi, R., Savarese, S.: Beyond pascal: a benchmark for 3d object detection in the wild. In: IEEE Winter Conference on Applications of Computer Vision, WACV (2014)
10. Lee, W., Park, N., Woo, W.: Depth-assisted real-time 3d object detection for augmented reality. In: International Conference on Artificial Reality and Telexistence, ICAT (2011)
11. Choi, C., Christensen, H.: 3D pose estimation of daily objects using an rgb-d camera. In: 2012 IEEE/RSJ International Conference on Intelligent Robots and Systems, IROS, pp. 3342–3349, October 2012
12. Jordt, A., Koch, R.: Direct model-based tracking of 3d object deformations in depth and color video. Int. J. Comput. Vision 102(1–3), 239–255 (2013)
13. Lee, K.R., Nguyen, T.: Robust tracking and mapping with a handheld rgb-d camera. In: 2014 IEEE Winter Conference on Applications of Computer Vision, WACV, pp. 1120–1127, March 2014
14. Park, Y., Lepetit, V., Woo, W.: Texture-less object tracking with online training using an rgb-d camera. In: 2011 10th IEEE International Symposium on Mixed and Augmented Reality, ISMAR, pp. 121–126, October 2011
15. Taguchi, Y., Jian, Y.D., Ramalingam, S., Feng, C.: Point-plane slam for hand-held 3d sensors. In: 2013 IEEE International Conference on Robotics and Automation, ICRA, pp. 5182–5189, May 2013
16. Morel, J.M., Yu, G.: Asift: a new framework for fully affine invariant image comparison. SIAM J. Img. Sci. 2(2), 438–469 (2009)
17. Horn, B.K.P.: Closed-form solution of absolute orientation using unit quaternions. J. Opt. Soc. Am. A 4(4), 629–642 (1987)
18. Pilet, J., Lepetit, V., Fua, P.: Fast non-rigid surface detection, registration and realistic augmentation. Int. J. Comput. Vision 76(2), 109–122 (2008)
19. Rendl, C., Kim, D., Fanello, S., Parzer, P., Rhemann, C., Taylor, J., Zirkl, M., Scheipl, G., Rothländer, T., Haller, M., Izadi, S.: Flexsense: a transparent self-sensing deformable surface. In: Proceedings of the 27th Annual ACM Symposium on User Interface Software and Technology. UIST 2014, pp. 129–138. ACM, New York, NY, USA (2014)

Towards a Structured Selection of Game Engines for Virtual Environments

Martin Westhoven[(✉)] and Thomas Alexander

Fraunhofer Institute for Communication, Information Processing
and Ergonomics FKIE, Human Factors, Wachtberg, Germany
{martin.westhoven,thomas.alexander}@fkie.fraunhofer.de

Abstract. Development and maintenance of virtual reality engines are coupled with large effort. It is therefore common today, to use existing solutions originating from the entertainment sector. This is often a compromise, since they fulfill individual requirements only in parts, due to their different background. The decision for a specific engine can have a large effect on the effort required to implement own functionality. The number of existing engines further complicates decision making. To enable a comprehensible and replicable decision making, we propose a structured selection process. In a multi-step approach, first the requirements and criteria for comparison are identified and analyzed. A pre-filtering is then used to select a feasible number of engines which are then compared in detail.

Keywords: Game engines · Virtual environments · Serious gaming

1 Introduction

Virtual Reality (VR) is usually associated with realistic computer-generated worlds and natural interaction with them. It is characterized by close, often multimodal, sensory contact with the artificial environment. When consistent, this allows for experiencing so-called presence. The basic idea is nothing new and numerous studies were published since the 90's. VR was often connected to complex and cost-intensive technologies, e.g. head-mounted displays or projection rooms, as well as custom software. During the last decade, the availability of low-cost commercial components changed the field, so that today even professional simulation systems use them for generating virtual environments. Often, games optimized for realistic rendering or their underlying engines are employed. Compared to custom in-house solutions, the rendering quality can thus be raised while simultaneously lowering the development cost.

Of the many genres of video games, those from a first person view are especially suited, as they often already aim for realism in the depiction of and interaction with virtual environments. Of those, 3D-action games focus on fighting and highly dynamic-sometimes even emotionally demanding-missions. Games such as Quake,[1] America's Army,[2] Operation Flashpoint,[3] Unreal[4] and FarCry[5] revealed the potential for professional

---

[1] © id Software, Mesquite, TX, USA.
[2] © US Army, MOVES Institute, Monterey, CA, USA.
[3] © Codemasters, Warwickshire, UK.
[4] © Epic Games, Raleigh, NC, USA.
[5] © CryTek GmbH, Frankfurt a.M., GER.

© Springer International Publishing Switzerland 2015
R. Shumaker and S. Lackey (Eds.): VAMR 2015, LNCS 9179, pp. 142–152, 2015.
DOI: 10.1007/978-3-319-21067-4_16

applications, as the development and maintenance cost of state-of-the-art in-house solutions was continually growing [1, 2].

The integration into professional simulator systems is sometimes also called Serious Gaming. Serious Gaming stands for the use of technologies and concepts originating from the entertainment sector for serious purposes. Playful aspects can, but in most cases do not have priority [3].

At first, such software was and is unsuited to be employed for professional and "serious" purposes. Empirical studies demand objectivity, validity, reliability and practicability. Furthermore, there exist several other, more technical requirements, such as controllability, reproducibility and the ability to protocol events. Aiming primarily at entertaining its users, game software often does not take these into account. They therefore require modifications which are coupled with additional effort. This has to be considered when performing respective studies, leading to high demands regarding the software to be chosen.

A requirements-oriented choice for an engine can reduce the effort required to accommodate for missing features and can therefore also result in a more preferable cost-benefit ratio. However, due to the large number of existing engines, this is again coupled with a large effort. Lewis and Jacobsen reported over 600 commercial engines in 2002 [4], while the database of devmaster.net[6] currently counts 370 engines, 283 of whom are actively developed and maintained. An exhaustive comparison of every engine for some intended purpose is thus normally not possible. Solutions which were successfully used in previous projects are often used instead. This is not always optimal and especially not possible for novices to the field. To lower the effort for a comparison to a feasible amount, the number of engines has to be reduced previous to a detailed consideration. Methodologies for selecting an engine can help making appropriate decisions. To maximize the benefit, the requirements of the field of application should also be taken into consideration.

This work focuses on the criteria on which a selection can be based and the measure for comparison. The selection criteria are closely scrutinized to identify those, which can be used in a pre-filtering step with low effort. The selection criteria are evaluated by a measure for the effort required for modifications [5]. First, relevant work is shown to locate this work in the field of research. Second, the approach is presented and finally an example is given to illustrate and discuss it.

2   Relevant Work

Previous work already tried to identify criteria for comparison of game engines: One approach is to divide engines into so-called functional blocks, which comprise of rendering, audio, physics and AI [6]. The number of existing engines is recognized as a problem and addressed by leaving out engines still in early development or engines missing essential features like e.g. audio support. Also, the availability of editors and their quality is considered. Finally though, direct monetary cost and popularity are used

---

[6] http://www.devmaster.net/devdb/engines, last accessed February 9th, 2015.

to decide which engines to compare. The detailed comparison focuses on modifiability, content and gameplay of the engines.

The selection of engines for displaying content in a first-person view is described in [7]. Criteria for initial filtering are actuality and popularity, especially in scientific work. The selected engines are compared in the topics of rendering, APIs, documentation and support.

When generating dynamic 3D-environments, the underlying engine is an important factor [8]. The selection criteria for an open-source engine are therefore discussed. Community support, documentation and licensing are of primary concern, whereas modifiability aspects form a secondary criterion.

The comparison of engines regarding their suitability for architectural design is discussed in [9]. Code accessibility is informally used to evaluate the engines from a developer's view and the editing tools to evaluate from an end user's view.

A framework for comparison of engines is presented by [10]. It identifies criteria for comparing game engines for use in serious games. Technical elements are distinguished from non-technical ones. Also, requirements from a gaming perspective are considered, e.g. support for creating a narrative. The respective elements are compared in free text and the results are visualized in tables showing the supported features.

Another work focuses on support for consumer VR technologies in game engines [5]. They argue, that with enough effort every feature can be implemented in any engine and that therefore support for single features is not very meaningful on its own. A so-called Level of Support is determined to assess the amount of effort required to modify an engine respectively. Qualitative and general properties are also considered if they allow for better estimating the suitability of an engine.

The aim of this work is to combine the different approaches for selecting game engines to enable a methodic procedure. The results of a requirements analysis are used as a starting point. The Level of Support notion is then used for technical detail comparison on basis of the collected filter and selection criteria.

3   Selection Criteria and Requirements

The identification of important criteria is essential for the selection of a suitable engine. Expanding [10] 's distinction of technical and non-technical elements, the criteria are divided into software-related, development-related and acquisition-related criteria. Table 1 gives an exemplary overview of possible criteria. Software-related criteria are those features the engine provides. They encompass development-related criteria as a whole or part-wise. The latter describe all those criteria, which have an influence on the development with the engine and therefore on the effort to modify it as well.

An example for a criterion which is development-related, but not software-related, is the experience of one's own developers. Finally, acquisition-related criteria are those criteria which are directly coupled with the availability of the engine. As a basis for identifying the most important criteria, the framework of [10] is extended by relevant criteria from [6] and [9].

Since criteria for comparison are defined directly through the requirements of the intended application, they cannot entirely be specified a forehand. The presented

Table 1. Classification of relevant example criteria for engine selection

Software	Development	Acquisition
Audiovisual display	Accessibility	Accessibility
Rendering	Documentation	Licensing
Animation	Support	Cost
Sound	Code Access	System Requirements
Streaming	Introduction Effort	
Functional display		
Scripting		
Supported AI		
Physics engine		
Event handling		
Combinability		
Component export/import		
Development tools		
Networking		
Client-Server		
Peer-to-Peer		
Heterogeneity		
Multi-platform support		

criteria can be used as a starting point for requirements analysis, but also during the analysis can new criteria for comparing the engines be found. Analogous it can be found, that specific criteria do not have to be considered in regard to the intended application. As an overarching requirement stands the goal to minimize the effort to satisfy the other requirements. An important aspect is therefore the possibly existent experience of a development team with the respective engines, the used programming languages and the useable development kits, as this can significantly influence the modification effort.

4   Pre-filtering

Exclusion criteria can offer a fast way for an initial filtering. They are therefore denoted as filter criteria. Especially easily examinable criteria such as the acquisition cost are suited for this use. To the contrary, a detailed comparison of rendering techniques would be ill-suited. It is furthermore favorable to examine such criteria, which cannot be addressed by modification or if so, only with difficulties.

Through this procedure, mainly accessibility-related criteria are considered, acquisition-related criteria in particular. Obviously, only those engines should be examined, which can be obtained after all.

The relevance of development-related criteria stems from their influence on the modifiability of an engine. Requirements of software-related criteria can be met with sufficient modification effort, the latter strongly depending on the development-related criteria, such as editor tools, documentation and support.

Previous work often uses fuzzy filtering criteria like breadth of use, innovative features, modularity and actuality. The breadth of use or popularity typically relates to the suitability of the application fields of the engine. This can be a signifier for the fulfillment of general requirements and can be checked quickly. Modularity can also be checked quickly, at least on the surface. It can yield insights on the effort required for modifications, making it a possible filter criterion. Modularity can also be extended afterwards, as is the case with e.g. the CryENGINE[7]'s community-developed plugin system.[8] The implementation of innovative features however depends on their respective complexity and is as such not generally suitable. Actuality on its own does not provide much information, since there are still hundreds of actively developed engines. Answering the question if an engine uses recent technology or how difficult it is to implement the technology into less recent engines requires a thorough examination and should therefore be performed only after a first filtering step.

Rarely mentioned is the possible experience of developers as a filter criterion. It can be checked quickly and be used as a supporting filter criterion.

How many engines should be compared in detail is dependent of the resources available and the requirements given. Other work compares between three to six engines [5–7, 9, 10], which also to our own experience amounts to a manageable effort.

5   Detail Comparison

Having gathered the requirements and chosen the engines to compare, the final step is to determine which engine fulfills most of the former. This can be measured by the approximate effort for modifying the engine towards satisfying the requirements. The examination of the support of graphics engines for VR technologies in [5] uses the following scale of effort:

1. Re-Engineering
2. Source-code modification
3. In-engine programming (scripting, plugins)
4. Graphical in-engine programming (e.g. Node graphs)
5. Natively supported

The respective items describe entry points for modifying an engine. A higher score is achieved when an engine fulfills the requirements or is easily modifiable to do so. It is obvious though, that the step from modifying source code to reverse engineering an engine is a huge leap. The scale can be used with software- and development-related criteria. Acquisition-related criteria, like e.g. the licensing cost, could also be measured with the modification effort, but the details of this measurement will likely be located in jurists' and business economists' areas of expertise. They will therefore not be considered in this work.

---

[7] © CryTek GmbH, Frankfurt a.M., GER.

[8] http://hendrikp.github.io/Plugin_SDK/, last accessed: January 30th, 2015.

6 Case Example: Requirements

A short example illustrates the method's usage: The background is the selection of a game engine for a laboratory environment. Apart from a setup with a treadmill and a large screen projection (see Fig. 1), the engine is to be used for immersive VR with head-mounted displays (HMD) with a large field of view (FOV) as well.

Fig. 1. Laboratory setup with treadmill and a large screen projection

The most common approach to create a large FOV as of now is to use optical lenses, which require the software to compensate for induced distortion. An example is the well-known Oculus Rift.[9] To avoid breaking the immersion, the presentation should be as close to reality as possible. As this is a rather imprecise requirement, this is broken down to the support for rendering techniques. The techniques of Tesselation [11], Screen Space Sub-Surface Scattering (SSSSS) [12] as well as Screen Space Directional Occlusion (SSDO) [13] are used exemplarily, since a full examination of rendering techniques would be well beyond the scope of this work. As further requirements, a high modifiability to include experimental components and networking capabilities to allow for cooperative scenarios are given.

Until now, the CryENGINE has been used and it is to be checked if this is really the best choice for this application. The development team therefore already has experience with the engine and the development tools. To determine the suitability of other engines, documentation, support and the learning curve of the engines are thus essential criteria.

7 Case Example: Filtering

To reduce the effort required for the filtering step, the criterion of popularity was used. Popularity is easy to assess by querying so-called modding websites, centered on everything needed to modify existing games, but also encompassing the means to build

---

[9] Oculus VR, Inc., Irvine, CA, USA.

entirely new games. We used the site Mod DB,[10] which listed the Unity[11] engine as the top engine at that time. The detail comparison was therefore between CryENGINE and Unity. There exist several other sites which list engines in a more or less detailed manner. Especially for novices to the field, these can give a good overview of existing engines.

8 Case Example: Detail Comparison

The support for immersive VR-HMDs is examined first. To non-natively compensate for the previously mentioned distortions often caused by the incorporated optics, an access point to the rendering pipeline is most helpful. CryENGINE offers this in combination with a rather expensive license variant and else restricts access. In the latter case, there is no possibility to include custom-built shaders and the rendering engine cannot be accessed directly. A computationally expensive approach is to modify the backbuffer after the engine finishes the rendering step. This is a source-code modification (2), whereas Unity offers native support (5) for most common devices.

Both CryENGINE and Unity implement Tessellation, the division of complex polygons into primitive surfaces, as triangulations. Also, both support the roughly approximated and normal-based Phong Tesselation [14]. In conclusion, both natively implement this feature (5).

The rendering of the diffusion of light in semi-transparent bodies, like skin or gems, can be computed in screen-space for real-time applications and is known as Screen-Space Sub-Surface Scattering. CryENGINE natively supports it (5), whereas in Unity a custom shader has to be implemented or bought (3).

Screen-Space Directional Occlusion extends the technique known as Screen-Space Ambient Occlusion (SSAO) [15], which allows to approximate light spread on non-reflexive surfaces. SSDO offers the possibility to include all light sources into the computation of Ambient Occlusion for generating shadows. Again CryENGINE natively supports the feature, while for Unity a shader has to be implemented (3).

Both engines offer ways to use third-party software libraries programmatically, thus making it easy to modify the engines. CryENGINE requires a source-code modification (2) and Unity allows adding libraries via the editor and using accessing them with scripts (3).

Networking support is offered by both engines natively for up to 32 clients (5).

Table 2 sums up the scores for the software-related criteria.

Documentation and support of the CryENGINE are organized together with tutorials and a support forum on a community website.[12] In addition there exist many unofficial video tutorials on both novice and expert topics. The documentation encompasses the development tools as well as tips on generating content like textures

---

[10] http://www.moddb.com/engines/top, last accessed: October 21st, 2014.

[11] © Unity Technologies, San Francisco, CA, USA.

[12] http://www.crydev.net, last accessed February 5th, 2015.

Table 2. Summary of the scores for software-related criteria

Criterion	CryENGINE	Unity
VR-HMD Support	2	5
Tesselation	5	5
Screen Space Sub-Surface Scattering	5	3
Screen Space Directional Occlusion	5	3
Modifiability	5	5
Networking	5	5
Sum	24	24

or 3D-models with external software. Against additional payment, licensees can also book courses and can contract the support team for development work.

Unity offers textual and video-based tutorials on their site,[13] organized both using keywords and topics. There is a separate documentation on scripting and unofficial books and tutorials exist as well. Technical support is generally free and the free version of the engine attracted a relatively large community which can be reached through a forum in addition. Sample projects help getting started quickly and the used components are available for free use.

To assess the learning curves, two simple scenarios were generated without prior knowledge on any of the two engines by a new colleague (see Fig. 2).

Fig. 2. Scenes in CryENGINE (left) and Unity (right)

Getting started with Unity is easy. Modelling terrain with satellite images and height maps only takes several minutes and adjusting height and textures or adding vegetation is intuitive. Placing objects is equally easy and imported assets are problematic only in occasions where e.g. automatic texturing fails due to non-standardized texture files. Since animations and scripts can be added to objects via drag and drop and

---

[13] http://unity3d.com, last accessed February 5th, 2015.

the parameters are added in editor, the learning curve only gets steeper when more complex custom scripts or shaders have to be implemented.

Terrain generation is equally easy in CryENGINE. Only importing satellite images is more complicated, since textures for different levels of detail have to be generated which requires a manual rasterization of the original image beforehand. Customizing height and texture as well as adding vegetation is also easy. The placement of objects is comparable to Unity, but importing requires native CryENGINE formats which always results in a detour via external modelling tools. Analogous to Unity, adding existing scripts or animations is rather easy and the learning curve steepens only when implementation work for custom scripts or source-code is required.

9   Case Example: Summary

Software-related criteria can be assessed easily. Both engines have the same score for the chosen criteria, since CryENGINE fulfills more requirements, but in Unity the respective modifications can be achieved more easily with in-engine tools. Concerning documentation, there exist comparable resources. The free support and more active community of Unity however are a notable advantage.

Taking the examined criteria into account, Unity would thus be suitable for a fresh start. Existing experience with CryENGINE however influences the ability to modify the engine as well as the ability to help new colleagues becoming acquainted with it. Switching the engine from CryENGINE to Unity would therefore rather result in more cost than benefit.

10   Discussion and Future Work

To enable a more structured and comprehensible process for selecting game engines, a multi-step approach was presented. It consists of identification of criteria for comparison and requirements, a pre-filtering step and a detail comparison.

The identification of comparison criteria is based on other work and is only exemplary, since requirements analysis for the specific application is always needed. Nevertheless it is a starting point which can be verified or modified by a follow-up requirements analysis. Categorizing the criteria helps in the decision which criteria can be used to filter the initial set of engines and which should be used in detail comparison. The class of development-related criteria overlaps with software-related criteria. It is planned to further examine this class to differentiate which of the criteria can actually be modified by software means.

Deciding which criteria to use for filtering depends on the requirements. It is thus difficult to offer more than general hints for their selection. Several criteria from other work are summarized which are mostly rather imprecise, but can be checked quickly. An example would be the popularity of engines. When time-wise possible, more precise criteria should be used to avoid dismissing e.g. less popular but perfectly suitable engines at this stage.

For detail comparison, we propose extending the score system for modification effort from [5] to all criteria which are software-dependent. This would allow for comprehensible scores for feature support. Some criteria however are ill-suited for these scores. This encompasses part of the development-related criteria as well as the acquisition. It would be desirable to also use a score system here, but for all practical purposes this will probably not be practicable. For example, the question arises as to how one could compare the documentations of engines. It is possible that work regarding document analysis can help in this case, which should be further investigated. Until then, a qualitative assessment remains the most practical solution, even if the results are somewhat diffuse.

The example illustrates the desirability of score systems throughout the comparison, since it would allow for weighting single criteria or even entire engines. Single criteria could be those of special importance for the intended application, while weighting an entire engine could be used to take the experience of developers with it into account. It would also be possible to use the weighting a posteriori, e.g. to examine which engine would be most suitable when leaving one or more aspects out.

References

1. Robillard, G., Bouchard, S., Fournier, T., Renaud, P.: Anxiety and presence during VR immersion: a comparative study of the reactions of phobic and non-phobic participants in therapeutic virtual environments derived from computer games. CyberPsychol. Behav. **6**(5), 467–476 (2003)
2. Lepouras, G., Vassilakis, C.: Virtual museums for all: employing game technology for edutainment. Virtual Reality **8**(2), 96–106 (2004)
3. Susi, T., Johannesson, M., Backlund, P.: Serious Games: an Overview. IKI Technical reports, HS-IKI-TR07-001, p. 28. Institutionen för Kommunikation och Information, Skövde, Sweden (2007)
4. Lewis, M., Jacobson, J.: Game engines. Commun. ACM **45**(1), 27 (2002)
5. Peek, E., Wünsche, B., Lutteroth, C.: Virtual reality capabilities of graphics engines. In: Skala, V. (ed.) WCSG 2013: Communication Papers Proceedings: 21st International Conference in Central Europe on Computer Graphics, Visualization and Computer Vision in co-operation with EUROGRAPHICS Association, pp. 40–48. Václav Skala – Union Agency, Pilsen (2013)
6. Marks, S., Windsor, J., Wünsche, B.: Evaluation of Game Engines for Simulated Surgical Training. In: Proceedings of the 5th International Conference of Computer Graphics and Interactive Techniques in Australia and Southeast Asia, pp. 273–280. ACM, New York (2007)
7. Trenholme, D., Smith, S.P.: Computer game engines for developing 1st-person virtual environments. Virtual Reality **12**(3), 181–187 (2008)
8. Catanese, S.A., Ferrara, E., Fiumara, G., Pagano, F.: Rendering of 3D dynamic virtual environments. In: Proceedings of the 4th International ICST Conference on Simulation Tools and Techniques, SIMUTools 2011, pp. 351–358, ICST, Brussels, Belgium (2011)
9. Sarhan, A.: The Utilisation of Games Technology for Environmental Design Education. Ph.D. thesis, University of Nottingham, UK (2012)

10. Petridis, P., Dunwell, I., Panzoli, D., Arnab, S., Protopsaltis, A., Hendrix, M., de Freitas, S.: Game engines selection framework for high-fidelity serious applications. Int. J. Interact. Worlds **2012**, 1–19 (2012)
11. Rockwood, A.: A generalized scanning technique for display of parametrically defined surfaces. Comput. Graph. Appl. IEEE **7**(8), 15–26 (1987)
12. Jimenez, J., Sundstedt, V., Gutierrez, D.: Screen-space perceptual rendering of human skin. ACM Trans. Appl. Percept. (TAP) **6**(4), 23 (2009)
13. Ritschel, T., Grosch, T., Seidel, H.-P.: Approximating dynamic global illumination in image space. In: Proceedings of the 2009 Symposium on Interactive 3D Graphics and Games, pp. 75–82, ACM, New York (2009)
14. Boubekeur, T., Alexa, M.: Phong tessellation. In: ACM SIGGRAPH Asia 2008 Papers, p. 141. ACM, New York (2008)
15. Bavoil, L., Sainz, M., Dimitrov, R.: Image-space Horizon-based ambient occlusion. In: ACM SIGGRAPH 2008 talks, p. 22. ACM, New York (2008)

Evaluation and Fair Comparison of Human Tracking Methods with PTZ Cameras

Alparslan Yildiz[1], Noriko Takemura[1], Yoshio Iwai[2]([⊠]), and Kosuke Sato[1]

[1] Osaka University, 1-3 Machikaneyamacho,
Toyonaka-shi Osaka 560-8531, Japan
[2] Tottori University, 4-101 Koyamacho-minami,
Tottori-shi Tottori 680-0945, Japan
iwai@ike.tottori-u.ac.jp

Abstract. Evaluation and comparison of methods, repeatability of experiments, and availability of data are the dynamics driving science forward. In computer vision, a database with ground-truth information enables fair comparison and facilitates rapid improvement of methods in a particular topic. Being a high-level discipline, Human-Computer Interaction (HCI) systems rises on numerous computer vision building blocks, including eye-gaze localization, human localization, action recognition, behavior analysis etc. using mostly active systems employing lasers, projectors, infrared scanners, pan-tilt-zoom cameras and other various active sensors.

In this research, we focus on fair comparison of human tracking methods with active (PTZ) cameras. Although there are databases on human tracking, no specific database is available for active (pan-tilt-zoom) camera human tracking. This is because active camera experiments are not repeatable, as camera views depend on previous decisions made by the system. Here, we address the above problem of systematical evaluation of active camera tracking methods and present a survey of their performances.

1 Introduction

Considering the large number of human tracking methods in the literature, there is a clear need for comparative evaluation of similar methods. A database of natural human movements with ground truth information makes it possible to compare methods and allows researchers to improve the performance of their algorithms more rapidly [4,5,9]. For fair comparison, all methods should be evaluated on the same data and the experiments should be repeatable. In human tracking methods, this requirement is highly dependent on the imaging hardware. Based on hardware specialization, we can divide the human tracking methods into two sub categories: *static camera tracking* and *PTZ camera tracking*. Static cameras, in our context, have a fixed position and orientation throughout the experiments. PTZ cameras, on the other hand, adaptively alter their orientations to capture more targets while their positions remain fixed.

© Springer International Publishing Switzerland 2015
R. Shumaker and S. Lackey (Eds.): VAMR 2015, LNCS 9179, pp. 153–161, 2015.
DOI: 10.1007/978-3-319-21067-4_17

In the case of static cameras, it is relatively easy to evaluate competing methods using a benchmark database such as those in [4, 5, 9] These databases usually consist of recorded camera view images and manually or automatically marked locations of humans on all or a subset of frames. During evaluation, the same camera images are fed into the evaluated methods and the outputs are compared with the ground truth data. The Human-Eva database [9] contains videos of articulated human motion and provides a comparative basis for accurate human pose estimation and motion tracking. The POM Pedestrian dataset [5] includes multiple camera recordings of pedestrians. Human locations in some of the videos in this database are manually marked to provide a basis for comparison of human tracking methods. Similarly, the PETS-2006 database [4] contains more natural movements of people in real environments.

The evaluation of competing methods for PTZ camera tracking problems, on the other hand, is not a trivial task. PTZ camera tracking methods consist of both camera reconfiguration and human tracking. The main problem with the former is repeatability. With PTZ cameras, the camera view image at any time-step depends on the actions of the PTZ cameras on all previous time-steps. Simply recording camera images is not sufficient for evaluation purposes. To the best of our knowledge, there is no publicly available database for evaluating PTZ camera reconfiguration methods. In this research, we present a method for generating repeatable PTZ camera reconfiguration experiments using real data. Our method takes static camera images and generates geometrically consistent virtual views of the PTZ cameras for any pan/tilt/zoom (PTZ) configuration. This is achieved with minimum calibration of the cameras; only the rectifying homography of the ground plane is necessary. The rectifying homography is also required in evaluations with static cameras, so it is usually available. Without requiring any additional user input, we can produce consistent PTZ camera views from static images, and evaluate competing PTZ camera reconfiguration methods on the same data. Synthetic PTZ cameras produced this way will have the camera center same as the original static cameras. This is actually desirable, because static cameras used to create human tracking databases would be located in a way that they would capture large areas and general views of the scene.

We convert a human tracking evaluation database that is captured with static cameras into an evaluation database for PTZ camera reconfiguration. The input to our system is the static camera images and the rectifying homography for the ground plane of each camera, which is readily available for the original static camera databases. The evaluation database is generated online with negligible computational cost. Our method, in a sense, simulate PTZ cameras given the recordings of wide angle static cameras. Camera positions and scene setup is naturally limited to the static camera positions. We do not see this as a limitation since our main objective here is to make repeatable experiments for PTZ camera reconfiguration methods. For all competing methods, our method provides the same camera images and diversity in camera views and camera positions can be achieved by using different static camera tracking databases.

Our method generates virtual PTZ cameras on desired pan/tilt speed or ranges. We do not have any limiting requirements for the static camera database as well.

However, one desirable property of static cameras of the input database would be that the camera views should not have very small field-of-views. In order to generate *meaningful* outputs, static camera views should be able to view at least a few people at the same time, so that we can generate virtual views using small portions of that view to track individuals with virtual PTZ cameras. Human tracking databases such as PETS-2006 [4] and POM [5] already satisfy this simple requirement. Other properties of the static camera databases such as image resolution, frame-rate, color quality, lighting quality, exact value of the field-of-view etc. are not major interests of this research, since all evaluated algorithms on these databases will use the same virtual views generated by our method. These properties may affect individual algorithms that are evaluated, however this is outside the scope of this research. We mainly aim to provide repeatable and fair experiments for PTZ camera reconfiguration methods.

For experimental evaluation in this research, we use well-known human tracking databases such as PETS-2006 and POM to generate the PTZ camera views. In this way, the natural movements of humans are reflected in the PTZ camera experiments, and the ground truth human locations on static camera images are translated to PTZ camera frames for evaluation.

2   PTZ Camera Reconfiguration Methods

We generated PTZ camera evaluation databases from POM and PETS-2006 videos, and compared several PTZ camera reconfiguration methods with out method in terms of performance. These methods, together with a brief explanation of their underlying algorithms, are listed below. The bold headings are our chosen abbreviations for future references to these methods in this paper.

Bidding. In a recent study, Li *et al.* [8] presented a tracking system for multiple PTZ cameras. They formulated PTZ camera reconfiguration as an assignment problem, where each target in the scene is assigned to a camera. The assignment problem is solved by an *auction* approach. For each target, each camera provides a *bid* on how well the camera can track the target. Once the bids have been collected, each target is assigned to a camera in such a way as to maximize the total bid.

Earliest. Costello *et al.* [3] formulated PTZ camera reconfiguration as a scheduling problem and utilized well-known scheduling policies to schedule the PTZ cameras. They reported the *earliest deadline* policy as the most successful one. This policy tries to maximize target coverage by scheduling the PTZ cameras to track those targets that are expected to leave the scene the soonest. In this way, more tracking time can be allocated to future targets.

MI. Sommerlade *et al.* [10] presented a probabilistic surveillance method for multiple PTZ cameras. In their method, the pan/tilt configuration of each camera is optimized to maximize mutual information. Multiple PTZ cameras are considered and optimized simultaneously.

Motion. Konda et al. [7] formulated coverage of targets as an assignment problem. Each camera is assigned either as *global* or *target* camera. While *global* cameras ensure the general coverage of the scene, *target* cameras are assigned to individual targets.

CFA. Munishwar et al. [1] presented a series of algorithms for multi-camera object coverage. In their study, they define a *force* between each target and possible pan configurations of each camera as the fitness for camera-target assignment. Finally, given the attraction of the computed forces, each camera is assigned to a pan configuration in a greedy fashion.

Occupancy. In the previous work [11] we devised a PTZ camera reconfiguration system that does not require the detection of targets in camera views. By registering each PTZ camera, we compute the ground occupancy maps for PTZ cameras and optimize camera configurations directly on the occupancy map. We also utilize multiple time-step estimations for better camera configuration decisions.

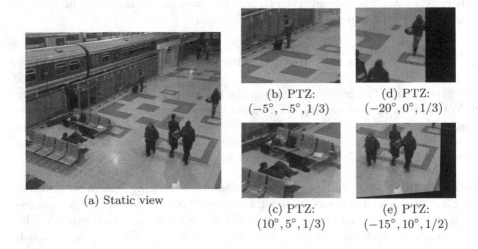

(a) Static view

(b) PTZ: $(-5°, -5°, 1/3)$

(c) PTZ: $(10°, 5°, 1/3)$

(d) PTZ: $(-20°, 0°, 1/3)$

(e) PTZ: $(-15°, 10°, 1/2)$

Fig. 1. Sample virtual views for a synthesized PTZ camera: (b), (c), (d), and (e) show the view of the virtual PTZ camera with varying (*pan,tilt, zoom*) configurations. The unit for pan and tilt options is degrees, and the unit for the zoom option is scaling relative to the original field-of-view in (a).

3   Calibration of Camera Time-Step

Using PTZ cameras, we are bound to make decisions in advance, because a PTZ camera will issue a pan/tilt command not instantly but by spending a short amount of time. The natural assumption is that, the time spent by the camera to perform an action is not random and can be modeled. First, let us consider the case where we have modeled the camera latency properly and we know how much milliseconds it would take to issue a given amount of pan/tilt operation. In this case, all our formulations using future time-steps would imply this calibrated latency value. Depending on the environment and scenario, a pan/tilt step may simply mean 5-10 degrees of movement around the camera center. Let us say, a pan step is 5 degrees of movement and 5 degrees of pan movement would take 100 ms for the camera to perform. Then in this case, the *next time-step* is simply 100 ms ahead of current time.

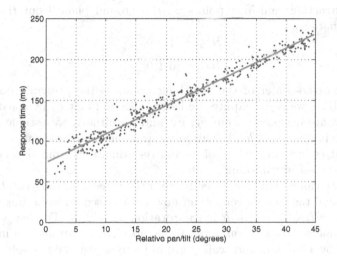

Fig. 2. Camera latency data

It is relatively easy to calibrate a PTZ camera for its latency and normalize time-steps using the latency information. For our Sony D-100 [2] cameras, we have measured pan/tilt latencies for various amount of rotations and the scatter data in Fig. 2 is gathered. The relationship is clearly modeled by a linear function.

For the rest of this work, the calibration of camera time-step is implicit and future time-steps are discretized by intervals of pan/tilt steps. For instance, next time-step is when the camera can complete a single pan/tilt step. Similarly, two time-steps into the future is when the camera can complete two pan/tilt steps. The length of pan/tilt step in angles is usually 5 or 10 degrees depending on the experimental environment.

4   PTZ Camera Synthesis

In this section, we describe our method for generating consistent views for PTZ cameras from static camera views. Fig. 1 demonstrates this process.

Initially we only require the rectifying homography H for the static camera view. This homography maps image coordinates to ground plane coordinates. For human tracking databases, such as PETS-2006, H is usually available because tracking methods depend heavily on it. Otherwise, it can be computed by manually providing four point correspondences. Although we describe our method for a single camera, it can readily be applied to multiple cameras.

PTZ camera views are simply rotated/zoomed views of the static camera with a smaller field-of-view. The rotation is around the camera center, and thus, can be performed with a linear image transformation once the camera matrix K is computed. Zoom and viewpoint alterations are possible by similarly utilizing the camera matrix. With some care, we can compute K directly from H. We begin by extracting vanishing points on the ground plane from H using the following equations:

$$Hv_x = [1\ 0\ 0]^T, \tag{1}$$

$$Hv_y = [0\ 1\ 0]^T. \tag{2}$$

Because the ortho-center of the vanishing points is the principle point, c, on the image plane, we can compute the last vanishing point v_z by constructing a triangle of vanishing points from v_x, v_y, and c. Initially, we estimate c as the center of the image, $(w/2, h/2)$. This gives us a very good estimate of v_z. Next, we collect edges in the direction of v_z and re-estimate v_z from these edges and c from the new set of vanishing points.

Finally, we can compute K directly from the three vanishing points [6]. Any rotation around the camera center can now be represented as an image homography, $H_r = KRK^{-1}$, where R is the rotation matrix in 3D. New views from the static camera view are computed by perspectively warping the image with H_r followed by a clipping and scaling around c to adjust the field-of-view. If we represent the clipping by homography H_{fov}, the rectifying homography for the new view can be given as $H_{new} = HH_r^{-1}H_{fov}^{-1}$.

Given a static camera view and the corresponding H, we compute PTZ camera views by applying the perspective warp $T = H_{fov}H_r$ to the static camera view. In practice, we precompute and store T and H_{new} matrices for each PTZ camera configuration.

Fig. 1 illustrates sample outputs of our PTZ camera view synthesis. See the figure caption for details.

4.1   PTZ Camera Synthesis Discussion

Main input to our view synthesis method is a human tracking database recorded with static cameras. We also require the ground rectifying homographies for each view. Generally these homographies are readily present for tracking databases, however they can easily be computed by manually marking 4 points on the view of the ground plane. Given recorded video of a static camera and its ground rectifying homography, our method synthesizes views of a virtual PTZ camera for any given pan, tilt and zoom configuration. New view generation consists of a planar image warping and is performed online with virtually free of computational cost. Thus, we do not need to store any external files for the newly generated database as new views are generated on demand with high consistency and speed.

Necessary delay is applied automatically consistent with the simulated PTZ camera. Computing the amount of delay is discussed in Sect. 3. During benchmarking, our system computes the required delay for a pan/tilt/zoom command and provides new images for PTZ camera reconfiguration methods only after the required delay has elapsed.

5   Experiments

We implemented the PTZ camera methods described in Sect. 2 using the information available in respective papers. We manually optimized the necessary parameters of the methods to obtain the best accuracy for our implementations and compared their performance on our synthetic PTZ camera databases created from the PETS-2006 and POM databases. Although the PETS-2006 database has a relatively low human density in the videos, the human movements in this database are quite natural. Conversely, the POM database includes unnatural human movements with a higher human density than in the PETS-2006 database. We chose these two databases because of the contrast in their density and motion properties.

While the POM database provides ground truth locations of humans for some intervals, the PETS-2006 database does not have any ground truth information. Thus, we marked the intermediate frames of the POM database and all the frames of the PETS-2006 database to provide a basis for fair comparison of the PTZ camera reconfiguration methods.

In all our experiments, we compared the competing methods in terms of accuracy and execution times. The unit of accuracy is *coverage*, which is defined as the ratio of the number of targets in the camera view(s) to the total number of targets in the scene. The unit of execution time is milliseconds per frame. We computed accuracy and execution times for all frames and report the mean values.

Table 1. Accuracy of different methods on PETS-2006

N-cams	Bidding [8]	Earliest [3]	MI [10]	Motion [7]	CFA [1]	Occp. [11]
1	0.5483	0.4922	0.4521	0.5268	0.5501	0.7347
2	0.5944	0.4879	0.4665	0.5532	0.6227	0.7792
3	0.7214	0.7693	0.5187	0.7069	0.7519	0.8493

Tables 1 and 2 give the accuracy of the PTZ camera methods on the PETS-2006 and POM databases, respectively. It is evident that the POM database is a more complex database for multiple PTZ cameras because the human density is relatively high. In contrast, the PETS-2006 database includes videos with low human density and PTZ cameras can capture these people with relatively high accuracy. In Fig. 3 the results are shown as graph plot. It is more evident on the graph that the method we devised outperforms other competing methods.

Table 2. Accuracy of different methods on POM

N-cams	Bidding [8]	Earliest [3]	MI [10]	Motion [7]	CFA [1]	Occp. [11]
1	0.2411	0.2958	0.3167	0.2547	0.3023	0.3549
2	0.2737	0.2521	0.3022	0.2711	0.3528	0.3627
3	0.4312	0.4456	0.4467	0.3914	0.5153	0.6842

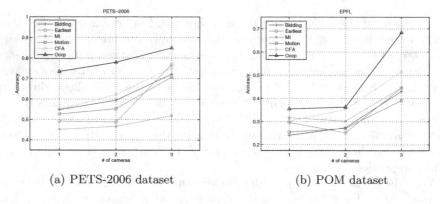

(a) PETS-2006 dataset   (b) POM dataset

Fig. 3. Accuracy of different methods on PETS-2006 and POM datasets

The results in Tables 1 and 2 give a fair comparison of the competing PTZ camera methods. Thus, we can safely conclude that, while in relatively low density scenarios with natural human movements (PETS-2006 database) our *Occupancy* method outperforms other methods, in a more dense scenario with unnatural human movements (POM database) all methods perform similarly.

Table 3. Execution times of different methods (ms/frame)

N-cams	Bidding [8]	Earliest [3]	MI [10]	Motion [7]	CFA [1]	Occp. [11]
1	108.01	108.78	125.55	122.06	98.06	10.64
2	180.27	171.08	265.10	218.92	175.62	17.72
3	250.34	210.56	630.22	341.77	223.67	32.76

Table 3 gives the execution times of the evaluated methods in milliseconds per frame. Note that different methods utilize different types of optimizations. For instance the *Bidding* method makes decisions for all cameras at the same time, whereas the *Earliest* method makes independent decisions for each camera, thus running faster. In such cases, making more accurate decisions appears to be vital, however, making faster decisions allows the methods to make faster acquisitions. A very slow running PTZ camera method can receive new information only at larger intervals, thus reducing its awareness of the environment.

6   Conclusions

There are publicly available databases for the evaluation of various vision tasks, such as stereo, optical flow, human tracking, and so on. These databases make it possible for fair comparison of competing methods, which encourages research and allows algorithms to evolve faster with increasing accuracy and speed. However, no evaluation database is available for PTZ camera reconfiguration. The reason for this is that PTZ camera experiments are not repeatable in a straightforward manner.

In this study, we devised a simple method for generating PTZ camera views from static camera views on demand to evaluate PTZ camera reconfiguration methods. The original databases included both natural and controlled human motion, which is desirable for the evaluation of competing methods. We tested several methods from the PTZ camera tracking literature and compared with our PTZ camera reconfiguration method [11].

References

1. Abu-Ghazaleh, V.M.N.: Coverage algorithms for visual sensor networks. ACM Trans. Sens. Netw. **9**(4), 1–31 (2013)
2. Camera, S.E.D.P.: http://pro.sony.com/bbsc/ssr/cat-industrialcameras/catrobo tic/product-EVID100/
3. Costello, C.J., Diehl, C.P., Banerjee, A., Fisher, H.: Scheduling an active camera to observe people. In: Proceedings of the ACM 2nd International Workshop on Video Surveillance and Sensor Networks. pp. 39–45 (2004)
4. Data, P.B.: http://www.cvg.rdg.ac.uk/~pets2006/data.html
5. Fleure, F., Berclaz, J., Lengagne, R., Fua, P.: Multicamera people tracking with a probabilistic occupancy map. IEEE Trans. Pattern Anal. Mach. Intell. **36**(8), 1614–1627 (2008)
6. Hartley, R., Zisserman, A.: Multiple View Geometry in Computer Vision. Cambridge University Press, Cambidge (2004)
7. Konda, K.R., Conci, N.: Real-time reconfiguration of ptz camera networks using motion field entropy and visual coverage. In: Proceedings of the International Conference on Distributed Smart Cameras (2014)
8. Li, Y., Bhanu, B.: Camera pan/tilt control with multiple trackers. In: International Conference on Pattern Recognition (2012)
9. Sigal, L., Balan, A.O., Black, M.J.: Humaneva: synchronized video and motion capture dataset and baseline algorithm for evaluation of articulated human motion. Int. J. Comput. Vis. **87**(1–2), 4–27 (2010)
10. Sommerlade, E., Reid, I.D.: Probabilistic surveillance with multiple active cameras. In: Proceedings of the IEEE International Conference on Robotics and Automation May 2010
11. Yildiz, A., Takemura, N., Hori, M., Iwai, Y., Sato, K.: Tracking people with active cameras using variable time-step decisions. IEICE Trans. Inform.Sys. **E97**(8), 1952–2216 (2014)

Agents and Robots
in Virtual Environments

Experimental Environments for Dismounted Human-Robot Multimodal Communications

Julian Abich IV(✉), Daniel J. Barber, and Lauren Reinerman-Jones

University of Central Florida (UCF), Institute for Simulation and Training (IST),
3100 Technology Parkway, Orlando, FL 32826, USA
{jabich,dbarber,lreinerm}@ist.ucf.edu

Abstract. The goal for multimodal communication (MMC) is to facilitate the conveyance of information through various modalities, such as auditory, visual, and tactile. MMC has become a major focus for enabling human-robot teaming, but it is often the case that the technological-state of robot capabilities is limited for research and development. Currently, robots often serve a single role, not equipped to interact dynamically with human team members. However, before that functionality is developed, it is important to understand what robot capability is needed for effective collaboration. Through the use of simulations, controlled systematic evaluation of MMC input and output devices can be evaluated to garner a better understanding of how to apply MMC with respect to user's abilities and preferences, as well as assess the communication hardware and software functionality. An experiment will be presented and discussed to illustrate this approach.

Keywords: Interactive simulation · Multimodal communication · Human-robot interaction · Dismounted soldiers

1 Introduction

The goal for multimodal communication (MMC) is to facilitate the conveyance of information through various modalities, such as auditory, visual, and tactile [1]. MMC has become a research focus within the domain of human-robot interaction (HRI) over the past few decades [2–4]. The appeal of MMC in robotics is largely due to the natural, intuitive, and flexible modes in which humans can communicate with robots. Dumas, Lalanne, and Oviatt [5] identified two main objectives for multimodal designs:

1. "support and accommodate users' perceptual and communicative capabilities"
2. "integrate computational skills of computers in the real world, by offering more natural ways of interactions to humans"

For these reasons, MMC is employed to facilitate more efficient human-robot teaming, but the current technological-state of robots must be expanded to support a more fluid and dynamic interaction. Therefore, systematic evaluation of robot hardware and software capabilities is essential to direct functional requirements. However, prior to development, a clear understanding of what robot capabilities are needed is essential to enable efficient human-robot team (HRT) interaction. In other words, the end-user's

© Springer International Publishing Switzerland 2015
R. Shumaker and S. Lackey (Eds.): VAMR 2015, LNCS 9179, pp. 165–173, 2015.
DOI: 10.1007/978-3-319-21067-4_18

abilities and preferences must be analyzed to suggest how the future of robot functionality should meet those demands and limitations. The ideal experimental environment for such evaluations is within an interactive simulated context to allow controlled investigation within an applicable setting.

It is often the case in robotics that the current state-of-the-art limits the evaluation of collaborative mixed-initiative teams. However, interactive simulations overcome this limitation to enable research in areas closely related to desired applications, especially in regards to HRI [6]. Being that the results of such investigations will drive the technological requirements of future robots, it is imperative that this line of research be conducted early within the design life-cycle to provide developers with end-user recommendations and avoid the costs associated with negligible prototypes [7]. The use of interactive simulation environments is a fitting solution for early MMC within HRT exploration and experimentation for a number of reasons.

2   MMC Interactive Simulation

Laboratory studies are conducted in controlled settings with little to no variation introduced that is irrelevant to the independent variables of interest. On the contrary, field studies are conducted in natural settings, usually in the setting of applicable interest, and careful effort is made to ensure only the independent variables of interest are manipulated wherever possible. It is quite indisputable that both approaches are unique and necessary to fully understand the impact of the independent variables on dependent variables of interest, but pure laboratory experiments tend to reduce the ecological and external validity while field studies reduce the level of internal validity. The bridge between laboratory and field experiments is simulation-based approaches.

Interactive simulations combine the stringent control of laboratory experiments with the reflected settings of field experiments to create an environment in which more detailed measurements can be utilized to better investigate underlying concepts of real-world tasks. This is important for MMC research within dismounted HRTs because it is not only pertinent that the hardware performs accurately and reliably, but it is also critical to determine the best MMC methods for enhancing HRTs. Unlike other forms of simulation, interactive simulations instill a greater sense of significant consequences in regards to successful performance, increases the level of physical interaction with robots, can potentially introduce intermittent variables that are perceived as unexpected, but are fully controlled, and expands the field-of-view and situation awareness of the user beyond the focus on a single computer monitor. Moreover, interactive simulations can also control details like weather and time, and ensure safety while still maintaining contextual validity to provide the best outlet for consistent tasking.

Another major benefit to using interactive simulations to evaluate HRI components of HRTs is that the robot does not actually have to possess full functionality. In other words, through what is referred to as the "Wizard of Oz (WoZ)" method [8, 9], unbeknownst to participants the robot is actually controlled by a second- or third-party, usually the researcher [for a review see 7]. Steinfeld et al. [9] have development a framework for such a method in which both human-centered, robot-centered, or a mix approach can be implemented to research HRI, with the focus presented here on human-centered approaches. This method has been shown to be effective to evaluate both individual [10] and group HRI [11]. Often for the human-centered approach, the robot's behavior is preprogrammed and only activated when the researcher observes that participants have correctly conveyed the communication sequence intended for an appropriate robot response. The researcher simply can trigger the robot to respond accordingly, while the participants believe they are controlling or directing the robot's behavior. Through this approach, concepts of usability and preference can be evaluated for current and future human-robot MMC technologies as well as assess the functionally of MMC hardware and software to capture and interpret the user's responses [6, 9].

3 Defining the Operational Environment

One area in which MMC for HRTs is most relevant is within the military domain, specifically regarding dismounted Soldiers. The U.S. Army has shifted its focus from developing platforms to investing more in the technology for dismounted Soldiers. It seems that the most effort has been allocated to developing expensive artillery and less on front-line combatants [12]. The recognition of this limitation by Army officials has helped direct resources back to the Soldiers with the solution of spawning robot teammates [12]. These robots will relieve Soldiers in ways such as carrying heavy gear, storing supplies for extensive mission durations, and will also assist in conducting intelligent, surveillance, and reconnaissance (ISR) tasks. However, before these capabilities and scenarios are delivered, an important HRI aspect must be resolved first – effective human-robot communication. MMC is the prescribed solution for HRTs, but less in known about the most effective means for communication under varying operational conditions. Prior to deploying robot teammates, extensive and rigorous tests on both input and output devices, as well as user preferences and abilities must be conducted. Generating interactive simulations for HRI will allow varying MMC methods to be tested under a multitude of contexts, exposing the optimal combination of communication modalities for HRTs in the operational environment of interest.

In 2010, the U.S. Army Research Laboratory (ARL) established the Robotics Collaborative Technology Alliance (RCTA) with the prospective vison that "… advanced autonomy-enabled technologies will play an even greater role in keeping our Soldiers safe" [13]. Within that program, one of the major focus areas is HRI, but even more so on the communication between Soldiers and robot teammates. Adopting the philosophy "from tools to teammates" [14], the Army's goal is to equip squads with autonomous robot capable of carrying out orders without the need of a dedicated technician to teleoperate them. In fact, robots may eventually out number Soldiers [15] making teleoperation nearly an impossible task and emphasizing the inherent need to develop an efficient and effective means of human-robot communication among single and multi-robot teammates.

Additionally, the Man Transportable Robotic System (MTRS) is a U.S. Army program in charge of converting the assortment of unmanned ground vehicles (UGVs) to a single configuration [16]. Part of that transition will involve a common communication architecture. Therefore, similar to the way humans are able to communicate with other humans, the same metaphoric principle will apply to Soldiers and robot teammates, especially when they all use the same language. This indicates, a positive transfer of training will occur in regards to HRI when Soldiers learn how to communicate with their robot teammates. The question remains: how should a Soldier communicate with a robot teammate? The answer: it depends.

Dismounted soldiers are taxed with a myriad of tasking conditions that can constantly fluctuate within the continuum of military operations. Often, soldiers are exposed to environments that inhibit clear communication, deprive sensory perception, or reduce mobility. Factors such as noise from air- and ground strikes, limited visibility due to time of day or air quality, and physical restrictions within confined areas all deteriorate the quality of communication. Further, Soldiers wear extensive amounts of gear including camouflage fatigues, about 40 pounds (18 kg) of body armor, an additional 80 pounds (36 kg) of supplies, and usually hold a personal weapon for protection [12], which all effect the types of MMC that Soldiers are physically capable of producing and receiving.

It is also necessary to assess those same factors on the performance of the MMC hardware and software. Speech recognition systems convert human verbal responses into a translatable signal for a robot to understand, and cameras or inertial measurement-units (IMUs) capturing arm and hand signals. In a controlled environment, these systems may perform accurately and reliably, but when exposed to the conditions typical of the Soldier's operational environment they may not. Since interactive simulation experimentation is the leading option available for research and training before Soldiers enter real-world environments, it is important to consider how each factor hinders clear communication between a Solider and a robot, and the best way to assess the effects on HRT performance.

4 Experimental Approach and Overview

A series of experiments has been proposed for investigation of MMC for dismounted HRTs, one of which is presented here. In order to successfully implement bidirectional MMC for dismounted HRTs, an understanding of both unidirectional interactions must be evaluated. Meaning, a clear understanding of both transmitting a message to a robot and receiving information from a robot should be investigated separately prior to experimentation of the full transaction in order to accurately identify the psychological, cognitive, and physical impact MMC has on dismounted HRTs. The modalities of interest for the present experiment were auditory and visual, specifically speech and gesture communication from a human to a robot.

Additionally, the same approach must be followed to test the hardware and software capabilities of MMC input and output devices to ensure system functionality meets set criteria [17]. Basically, if a speech recognition system is unable to correctly classify the audible response of the human teammate while performing a task within a quiet laboratory, then fielded applications of the hardware will likely fail. Similarly for gesture recognition systems, if they cannot classify the gesture response a human transmits while solely performing that task alone, then the system is sure to fail when the human must perform more than one task simultaneously.

This experiment simulated a surveillance operation, in which a novice population communicated commands using speech, gestures, and a combination thereof to a robot teammate. The goal for the task was three fold: 1) command a robot to report obstacles occluding the robot's navigation path (the orange cones), 2) travel to a specified location (WoZ controlled), and 3) screen the targeted location until further notice. Table 1 describes the options available for each type of command and Fig. 1 shows the controlled experimental tasking environment.

Table 1. The commands the human communicated to the robot using speech, gestures, and a combination thereof.

Type	Command
Report	"Report obstacles to the {West, East, North, South} side of the {West, East} building"
Move	"Move to the {West, East, North, South} side of the {West, East} building"
Screen	"Screen"

*For all commands, options with braces, {and}, are options for participants to choose based on the scenario presented to them

Fig. 1. (Left) This image represents the command sequence the human communicated to the robot. (Right) This image depicts the simulated experimental setup with the command sequence displayed on the screen. The same screen also presented robot responses.

Depending on the modality used for the task, participants were given a description of the scenario to justify the use of each modality and to provide an operational context. Table 2 illustrates the scenario description for each modality.

It is important to note that the use of the WoZ method was extensively controlled and warranted for this specific stage in the progression of MMC for dismounted HRTs. It also adheres to the recommendations for WoZ experiments described by Green, Hüttenrauch, and Eklundh [18]. In this experiment, the role of the participant was simply to send a command to a robot. The command was basically a simple navigation task. There was no task that required the participants to intervene if the robot was inaccurately performing the commanded task. Therefore, to ensure the robot successfully navigated to the desired locations, the WoZ approach was used to preprogram the

Table 2. The description of the scenarios presented to participants for each modality

Modality	Scenario Description
Speech	"In this scenario you will command the robot using speech only. Stealth is not a requirement and the robot is well within range to hear you."
Gesture	"In this scenario you will command the robot using gestures only. Stealth is a requirement in this case, and therefore silence is important."
Speech & Gesture	"In this scenario you will command the robot using both speech and gestures. Stealth is not a requirement, however it is possible that noise within the environment may interfere with your commands, therefore both speech & gestures must be used to ensure commands are received."

navigation routes the robots followed and to ensure the robot's behavior was consistent. The role of the researcher was merely to observe whether participants had correctly conveyed the right command and to initiate the robot's movement through a wireless device that solely progressed the robots navigation to preprogrammed waypoints using an indoor tracking system. During training, participants were told that if they did not correctly convey the correct command to the robot, then the robot would simply not respond at all (i.e. the researcher would not initiate robot movement and no text response on the screen). It was up to the participants to inquire if they were making a communication error. Since social interaction was not a concern for this experiment, the argument that a WoZ controlled robot can actually be considered a proxy through which humans interact with other humans is dismissed [19]. Additionally, the level of deception was minimal, if at all, implying the users' perceived usability and preferences were not affected by this approach.

Assessment was conducted in a pre- and post-test manner to capture the impact each communication modality had on participants and HRT performance before and after exposure to each modality type. To better understand the individual differences among participants they first completed a spatial orientation test, an attentional control assessment, and rated their expectations and perceived importance in regards to a robot's behavior. Spatial orientation ability is crucial when communicating with a non-collocated teammate to scout and patrol specific locations. Attentional control begins to take into account the effect the environment and individual differences in attention could have on MMC by assessing how easily distracted participants are when exposed to certain attentional grabbing factors, such as music, other people, or even internal feelings such as hunger. Expectation ratings are also important to assess prior to experimentation because participants can carry preconceived notions about how their interactions will take place, which may bias their behavior and post-task ratings. Preference for modality type was assessed using a system usability scale after being exposed to each modality and once again after completion of all scenarios to see if their perceptions changed by the end of the experiment. It is also important to gather data on the levels of perceived workload each modality elicits from each participant. The NASA-Task load Index (TLX) was used to determine how much workload was elicited by each modality and what type of workload was contributing the most (e.g. mental, temporal, or physical).

The speech and gesture recognition hardware were assessed by their ability to recognize the participants verbal and hand signals, respectively, and correctly classify them based on their pre-programmed lexicon. By using the WoZ approach, the scenario completion was not dependent on the hardware and software performance because the researcher determined if participants were correctly communicating the information to their robot teammate and controlled the robot's responses accordingly. In this manner, the human-centered approach allowed assessment of the user to be conducted separate from MMC input and output devices, which meant various devices could be tested as a between subjects factor without effecting the user's ratings of their interaction or even being aware that hardware tests were being conducted.

5 Discussion and Future Direction

This experiment lays foundational work for understanding the best methods for MMC within dismounted HRTs. Human behavior can be affected by the environment where tasks are being performed, therefore utilizing interactive simulations can provide a host of benefits from both the laboratory and field approaches that support more natural tasking environments, but employ laboratory control for more accurate and precise assessment. Interactive simulations are an ideal solution to investigate MMC within dismounted HRTs. These controlled and consistent environments allow detailed assessment to be attained while still reaching a level of task and environmental complexity only achievable in real-world scenarios. The research presented illustrates first steps in utilizing interactive simulations to understand best practices for MMC.

The approach taken for this experiment was to employ WoZ techniques to assess the usability and preference of various MMC methods while simultaneously evaluating the functional capabilities of MMC hardware and software devices. By assessing each modality separately and then combined, each communication method was analyzed individually to see if either mode, or combination, was preferred and more effective for HRT performance. This also allowed the hardware and software for each modality to be assessed in a separate manner to determine the baseline performance within a controlled environment.

The theoretical contributions of this line of research sheds light on the cognitive implications of MMC within HRTs. This work also expands upon current theoretical frameworks of human information-processing by providing use cases in which to apply and assess the concepts of resource allocation and time-sharing efficiency. Practical applications of this research informs MMC developers and robot designers about the limitations and preferences of end-users interacting in HRTs. It also provides an experimental approach for assessing the optimal combination of MMC within dismounted Soldier-Robot teams.

Future research should begin to incorporate more factors that will increase the fidelity of the simulations. This simulation experiment is not intended to be the final stage of investigation before recommendations are generated for MMC designers, but a step in a systematic and iterative process of slowly removing researcher control of the robot and employing more robot autonomy as technology progresses. Tests under varying noise, lighting conditions, and with secondary tasks will allow for a better representation of the operational environment and ideally more generalization of the results to support a positive transfer of training for communication across all HRT tasks. Additionally, methods of MMC should be investigated for communicating with more than a single robot teammate. Even more so, investigations should be expanded to assess how varying characteristics of the robots (e.g. gender of voice) and returning modes of communication (e.g. auditory vs visual feedback) effect the efficiency of HRTs. The more reflective the experimental setting is of the operational environment, the better suited and more effective HRTs will be when deployed.

Acknowledgements. This research was sponsored by the Army Research Laboratory (ARL) and was accomplished under Cooperative Agreement Number W911NF-10-2-0016. The views and conclusions contained in this document are those of the authors and should not be interpreted as representing the official policies, either expressed or implied, of ARL or the U.S. Government. The U.S. Government is authorized to reproduce and distribute reprints for Government purposes notwithstanding any copyright notation hereon.

References

1. Lackey, S., Barber, D., Reinerman, L., Badler, N.I., Hudson, I.: Defining next-generation multi-modal communication in human-robot interaction. In: Proceeding of the Human Factors and Ergonomics Society 55th Annual Meeting, vol. 55, pp. 461–464 (2011)
2. Oviatt, S.: Advances in robust multimodal interface design. IEEE Comput. Graphics Appl. **23**(5), 62–68 (2003)
3. Oviatt, S.L., Cohen, P.R., Fong, M., Frank, M.: A rapid semi-automatic simulation technique for investigating interactive speech and handwriting. In: Proceedings from International Conference on Spoken Language Processing pp. 1351–1354 (1992)
4. Jaimes, A., Sebe, N.: Multimodal human–computer interaction: a survey. Comput. Vis. Image Underst. **108**(1), 116–134 (2007)
5. Dumas, B., Lalanne, D., Oviatt, S.: Multimodal interfaces: a survey of principles, models and frameworks. In: Lalanne, D., Kohlas, J. (eds.) Human Machine Interaction: Lecture Notes in Computer Science, pp. 3–26. Springer, Heidelberg (2009)
6. Lackey, S., Barber, D., Reinerman-Jones, L.E., Ortiz, E., Fanfarelli, J.: Human robot communication. In: Hale, K., Staney, K. (eds.) Handbook of Virtual Environments, 2nd edn, pp. 959–1026. CRC Press, Boca Raton (2014). ISBN: 9781466511842
7. Riek, L.D.: Wizard of Oz studies in HRI: a systematic review and new reporting guidelines. J. Hum. Robot Interact. **1**(1), 119–136 (2012)
8. Kelley, J.F.: An iterative design methodology for user-friendly natural language office information applications. ACM Trans. Inform. Sys. (TOIS) **2**(1), 26–41 (1984)
9. Steinfeld, A., Jenkins, O.C., Scassellati, B.: The Oz of Wizard: Simulating the human for interaction research. In: 4th ACM/IEEE International Conference on Proceeding from the Human-Robot Interaction (HRI), pp. 101–107 (2009)
10. Viswanathan, P., Bell, J.L., Wang, R.H., Adhikari, B., Mackworth, A.K., Mihailidis, A., Miller, W.C., Mitchellb, I.M.: A wizard-of-Oz intelligent wheelchair study with cognitively-impaired older adults: attitudes toward user control. In: Proceedings from IEEE/RSJ International Conference on Intelligent Robots and Systems (IROS) Workshop on Assistive Robotics for Individuals with Disabilities: HRI Issues and Beyond, p. 1 (2014)
11. Shiomi, M., Kanda, T., Koizumi, S., Ishiguro, H., Hagita, N.: Group attention control for communication robots with wizard of OZ approach. In: Proceeding from Human-Robot Interaction (HRI), 2007 2nd ACM/IEEE International Conference pp. 121–128 (2007)

12. Beidel, E.: Army shift focus to dismounted Soldiers. (2011). Accessed 14 January 2015 from NationalDefenseMagazine.org: http://www.nationaldefensemagazine.org/archive/2011/April/Pages/ArmyShiftsFocustoDismountedSoldiers.aspx

13. U.S. Army.: Army researchers envision future robots (2014). Accessed 20 November 2014 from RoboticsTomorrow.com: http://www.roboticstomorrow.com/news/2014/11/04/army-researchers-envision-future-robots/5043/

14. Phillips, E., Ososky, S., Grove, J., Jenstch, F.: From tools to teammates: toward the development of appropriate mental models for intelligent robots. In: Proceedings from the Human Factors and Ergonomics Society 55th Annual Meeting, pp. 1491–1495 (2011)

15. Gaudin, S.: U.S. military may have 10 robots per soldier by 2023: Military expects to soon be using autonomous robots to carry soldiers' gear and scan for enemy combatants (2013). Accessed 18 November 2013 from ComputerWorld.com: http://www.computerworld.com/s/article/9244060/U.S._military_may_have_10_robots_per_soldier_by_2023

16. Gould, J.: US Army works toward single ground robot (2014). Accessed on 20 November 2014 from DefenseNews.com: http://www.defensenews.com/article/20141115/DEFREG02/311150033/US-Army-Works

17. Harris, J. Barber, D.: Speech and gesture interfaces for squad level human robot teaming. In: Proceedings from SPIE 9084: Unmanned Systems Technology XVI, 90840B, Baltimore (2014)

18. Green, A., Hüttenrauch, H., Eklundh, K.S.: Applying the Wizard-of-Oz framework to cooperative service discovery and configuration. In 13th IEEE International Workshop on Robot and Human Interactive Communication, pp. 575–580. IEEE (2004)

19. Weiss, A.: Validation of an evaluation framework for human-robot interaction. The impact of usability, social acceptance, user experience, and societal impact on collaboration with humanoid robots. [Doctoral dissertation]. University of Salzburg, Austria (2010)

Displays for Effective Human-Agent Teaming: The Role of Information Availability and Attention Management

Maia B. Cook[✉], Cory A. Rieth, and Mary K. Ngo

Pacific Science and Engineering Group, San Diego, USA
MaiaCook@pacific-science.com

Abstract. In military and industrial systems, visual displays form a critical link between humans and agents. Through visual displays, human operators monitor indications of agent status to detect issues and proactively manage emerging problems. As operators manage increasingly more agents, conveying status becomes an especially complex visualization challenge. To effectively manage operator attention and support proactivity, careful consideration must be given to *what information to provide access to* and *how best to assign visual salience* to that information. Here, we systematically analyze and empirically evaluate the effectiveness of standard and novel status indicator formats in supporting proactive monitoring of multiple agents. The results reveal shortfalls of standard formats fielded in today's control systems, inadequacies of those formats for future multi-agent monitoring, and benefits of novel formats. For application, we provide guidance for status format design and use, mitigations for improving inadequate formats, and inspiration for creating novel formats for improved monitoring.

Keywords: Evaluation methods and techniques · Information visualization · Intelligent and agent systems

1 Introduction

Effective communication is critical to the success of human-agent teams. Agents—embodied or software entities capable of independent action—and humans can communicate through a range of voice, visual, haptic, and other modalities. In this paper, we focus on human-agent communication that is *visual display-mediated*. In a variety of work domains involving unmanned and automated systems, visual displays are ubiquitous, and are often the human operator's primary means for maintaining awareness about system and agent status, detecting problems, and investigating, diagnosing, and correcting problems. The focus of the current paper and a companion paper [1] is on improving how agent status is expressed and represented in status displays to support task and cognitive needs of the operators responsible for managing the agents. In particular, we focus on the needs of operators faced with managing greater numbers of processes, agents, vehicles, and systems [2] across different work domains.

© Springer International Publishing Switzerland 2015
R. Shumaker and S. Lackey (Eds.): VAMR 2015, LNCS 9179, pp. 174–185, 2015.
DOI: 10.1007/978-3-319-21067-4_19

Operators in human-agent teams engage in *supervisory control tasks* [3]. In supervisory control, monitoring occurs on a frequent and often intermittent basis, as operators concurrently engage in several other critical activities [4, 5]. As operator workload continues to grow, it is becoming increasingly important for operators to monitor *proactively* to detect and resolve emerging issues *before* they worsen [4, 6, 7, 8].

To proactively monitor the status of multiple agents through visual displays, operators must search through status indicators to detect signs of current *and* emerging problems that warrant further investigation. To understand how to support effective search through status indicators, we can draw from the extensive literature on visual search, human attention, and the factors that control the distribution of attention in a scene (see [9, 10], for reviews). Existing design guidance informed by this research underscores the importance of making task-relevant information *accessible* through displays [11], and cueing operator attention to the highest priority information through *salient* visual cues [12, 13]. The challenge lies in appropriately applying this guidance, and in balancing information access and attention management. As Simon [14] noted over forty years ago *"...in an information-rich world, the wealth of information... creates a poverty of attention and a need to allocate that attention efficiently among the overabundance of information sources that might consume it..."*. In visual displays, providing access to too much information reduces the relative salience of information due to competition and clutter; conversely, de-cluttering can enhance relative salience but hinder access to the de-cluttered information [15].

To explore these issues in applied designs, we considered how information access and visual salience in standard formats in today's systems relate to proactively monitoring multiple agents. In terms of information access, we noted that many standard formats promote *"value* monitoring" as opposed to *"trend* monitoring." In terms of visual salience, we noted that if standard formats use salient cues at all, they direct attention to *current* problems as opposed to *future* problems. Motivated by these observations, we developed a novel trend-icon hybrid indicator format (*Trendicon*, patent pending, Fisher Rosemount Systems, Inc.) that provides access to information about worsening trend, and makes indicators with more extreme worsening trends more salient. In a recent experiment [7], Trendicons were contrasted with a standard "value monitoring" format (Numeric Values) and Trend Graphs as a baseline "trend monitoring" format. Participants attempted to proactively detect problems while monitoring displays with varying numbers of status indicators. Using Trendicons, the majority of problem detections were *proactive*; however, using Numeric Values and Trend Graphs, problem detections were largely *reactive*, occurring after an event became critical. Further, Trendicons led to a roughly fivefold increase in the estimated number of indicators that participants could proactively oversee, compared to Numeric Values and Trend Graphs. Trendicons' performance advantages were hypothesized to stem from improved access to worsening trends and more salient cues for more extreme worsening trends. Although Trend Graphs provide access to trend information, we hypothesized that their lack of direct access to, and undifferentiated coding and salience of, worsening trend were responsible for their associated reactive problem detections.

To investigate these hypotheses more deeply and extend them more broadly to other status formats, we conducted an analysis of information access and salience mapping across a range of status formats. The magnitude of this analysis is quite large, and therefore is split across two papers, with the focus of the current paper primarily on information accessibility and the focus of a companion paper [1] on assessing the assignment of visual salience to information. Across both papers, our goal is to provide an objective basis for pairing status indicator formats to operators' tasks, to improve task support and performance.

1.1 Status Indicator Formats Considered

Figure 1 presents a qualitative analysis of information accessibility across a range of standard, novel, and alternative indicator formats. Exemplars are illustrated for each format. Our analysis was limited to formats depicting the status of single agents (vs. multivariate status). The top of Fig. 1 shows an agent's indicator value plotted over time relative to a desired normal value (50), caution thresholds above (≥ 75) and below (≤ 25) normal, and warning thresholds further from normal (≥ 80 and ≤ 20). In the example, value and status gradually worsen, extend beyond caution and warning thresholds, and then resolve back into normal status. Key points along the time course are shown in each indicator format, for comparison. Considering how the formats appear at each time point through normal, worsening, and resolving status reveals strengths and weaknesses of using the formats to monitor current and future status. We consider the first seven formats first; each is described next.

Numeric Values show a digital representation of the agent's current value. In *Gauges*, a needle points to the agent's current value along a circular dial marked with ticks, numeric labels, and yellow caution and red warning regions. In *Bullet Graphs* [16], a filled bar conveys current value on a linear scale with yellow caution and red warning regions (see [17] for other variations). *Stoplight Coding* codes threshold-based categorical caution (yellow) and warning (red) states. Rather than applying Stoplight Coding to each format in Fig. 1, we treated it as an independent status format to separately assess its properties from the properties of other formats. *Trend Signature Plots* represent recent trend behavior with one of seven standard first and second order trend patterns, as described in [18]: steady state, ramping up or down, increasing or decreasing at an increasing rate, and increasing or decreasing at a decreasing rate. *Trend Graphs* continuously plot values along a trend line relative to a black centerline and yellow caution and red warning threshold lines. *Trendicons* represent current deviation from normal with an analog indicator bar extending from a centerline, and present trend information including recent trend (directional shape), rate of change (number of jet trails), and worsening trend (bold for worsening); see [7] for a detailed design description. Key findings from a systematic analysis of the information accessibility of these seven formats are reported next. This analysis motivated the design of three alternative status formats shown at the bottom of Fig. 1 and discussed below.

Formats cluster into three main categories of information accessibility: each format provides access primarily to *current value* (Numeric Values, Gauges, Bullet Graphs), ***current deviation*** (Stoplight Coding), or ***trend information*** (Trend Signature Plots, Trend Graphs, Trendicons). These groupings are shown in Fig. 1. Some current value-based and trend-based formats also provide less direct access to current deviation and current value. For example, Gauges require operators to compare needle position to normal (vertical) to obtain a rough estimate of current deviation.

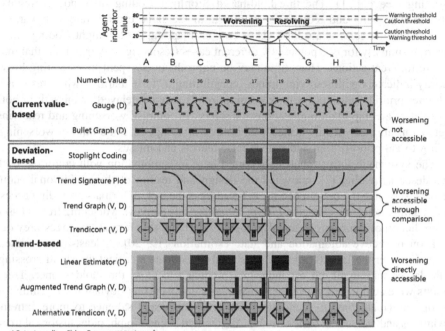

Fig. 1. Information access across status indicator formats as an agent's indicator value and status change over time. Formats mainly provide access to *current value*, *current deviation*, or *trend*; less direct access to current value (V) and deviation (D) across formats is noted. Formats provide no access, indirect access, or direct access to worsening trend, and identical, variable, or unique coding for worsening vs. resolving trend.

No standard format provides direct access to *worsening* trend, the key attribute needed for proactive monitoring. For some formats, information about worsening trend can be *derived* by combining multiple components or sequencing information over time to detect a pattern. However, it is difficult to engage in an efficient search for features that are not diagnostic, and for multiple features that must be compared, combined, or held in memory (vs. diagnostic, simple, and explicitly represented task-relevant features). For example, in the search for worsening trend in Trend Graphs, orientation alone is not a diagnostic cue; it must be combined with the direction/position of trending information relative to normal to assess if values are worsening by heading away from normal or resolving by returning to normal. As another example, the direction and rate of change of the Gauge's needle must be assessed over time to detect values heading away from normal. In contrast, a simple search strategy for worsening trends of "search for bold-outlined Trendicons" can be executed easily and effectively.

There is insufficient information access (and salience variation) to differentiate worsening vs. resolving status in standard formats. Current value-based formats appear similar for similar current values even when one is worsening and the other is resolving (see Fig. 1). The threshold-based Stoplight Coding does not distinguish between worsening and recovering states within the same caution range or warning range. Although color is a salient visual cue, its mapping for Stoplight Coding draws attention similarly for two potentially different cases (resolving vs. worsening) that may require different actions. Thus, time may be unproductively spent investigating lower priority indicators with resolving trends (constituting a "false alarm"), while responses to higher priority indicators with worsening trends may be delayed or missed; in both cases, there are important implications for safety. In contrast, worsening and resolving Trendicons are easily distinguished with bold (worsening) vs. not bold (not worsening) coding to aid prioritization and reduce false alarms and misses.

The systematic format analysis reported here in combination with empirical findings described earlier [7] motivated the design and testing of three additional status formats, shown at the bottom of Fig. 1. To address the lack of formats providing access to worsening trend, we created a *Linear Estimator* that conveys worsening trends based on prediction of future problems. The logic underlying this format leverages previous work on predictive automation and state estimation [19, 20]. A least-squared linear regression over the last 10 time points is used to estimate a critical threshold crossing, with darker achromatic fill for indicators predicted to cross threshold sooner. Trend Graphs were augmented with Linear Estimators and a current deviation bar (similar to the one in Trendicons) to facilitate access and map visual salience to more extreme deviations and worsening trends. In this Augmented Trend Graph, older historical trend information was also faded to de-clutter past events. Finally, the Linear Estimator was applied to the border of the Trendicon's directional shape to create an *Alternative Trendicon* intended to improve access to worsening trends and aid in prioritizing multiple worsening indicators.

2 Empirical Validation of Design Concepts

An empirical study was conducted to investigate the impact of the visual features intended to improve information access and attention management in the bottom three formats in Fig. 1. Since status displays are often consulted only occasionally during monitoring, the ability to easily detect and prioritize current and future problems is paramount. The current study tested the effectiveness of four status indicator formats (three new formats in Fig. 1 vs. Trend Graphs) in tasks that simulated intermittent monitoring under varying time pressure: quickly identifying the worst current indicator, quickly identifying the next indicator expected to go critical ("next-critical"), and thoughtfully prioritizing the three next-critical indicators. To test the robustness of the formats for monitoring multiple agents, the number of emerging problems was varied.

The goals of the experiment were to (1) validate the expected performance enhancements from improved information access and salience assignment in the novel and alternative formats compared to Trend Graphs, (2) determine the extent to which the strong Trendicon advantage found in a dynamic monitoring task [7] extends to intermittent monitoring, and (3) assess whether the available time for monitoring leads to performance tradeoffs for formats. Specifically, are formats that provide more detailed information access superior when more vs. less time is available for monitoring (and vice versa)? We hypothesized that more detailed trend information would improve accuracy on the less time-pressured ranking task for the Augmented Trend Graphs vs. Alternative Trendicons, and the reduced information in the Alternative Trendicons would support the more time-pressured next-critical task.

2.1   Methods

Participants. Twenty-four students (15 male; mean age = 21 years) recruited from local universities were paid for their participation. All reported normal or corrected-to-normal vision, gave informed consent, and were naïve to the intent of the study. The experiment was approved by a Federally-approved Institutional Review Board.

Stimuli. Each trial consisted of 24 status indicators shown in one of the four formats, Trend Graphs, Trendicons, Augmented Trend Graphs, or Alternative Trendicons (see Fig. 1), presented in a 4 by 6 array. Each indicator subtended roughly 1.9 degrees of visual angle. Both Trend Graph formats showed historical indicator values plotted over 60 time points. Both Trendicon formats used the previous 10 values to calculate recent changes. The historical data driving each indicator was randomly generated and identical across formats; indicator positions were shuffled within trials. Indicator values could range from 0 to 100, with a normal value of 50. Indicators with emerging problems were created by inserting a constant sloped deviation into the time course at a random time. These emerging problem indicators were constrained to be outside a normal range, but not yet in a critical state. Current deviations from normal for emerging problem indicators ranged from 12 to 45 units. Within a trial, the current values of indicators with emerging problems were roughly equally spaced in this range. All other indicators had current deviations from normal that were 10 units or less (values between 40 and 60). Stimuli were constrained so that on half the trials, the indicator with the current worst value was also the next to cross critical threshold, randomly ordered. Correct responses for identification or ranking of indicators projected to cross critical threshold were obtained by fitting a linear regression line for each indicator starting from the deviation onset and calculating the time until critical.

Design and Procedure. Four indicator formats (Trend Graphs, Trendicons, Augmented Trend Graphs, and Alternative Trendicons) and three numbers of emerging problems (3, 6, and 9) were tested in a within-subjects design. The order of indicator formats was blocked and counterbalanced between participants. Within each format block, task was blocked in sequential order (current worst, next-critical, ranking). The number of emerging problems (3, 6, or 9) was randomized over trials. There were 30 trials within each experimental format block. Each experimental block was preceded by a practice block with 12 practice trials. Participants' reaction times and indicator selections were recorded. To engage participants and discourage errors, performance feedback was given at the end of each trial.

Participants were asked to role-play a supervisor whose job was to monitor a team of autonomous robot vacuums as they cleaned houses. Participants were told that they would remotely view the energy use of robots through an array of 24 indicators, each showing the status of one robot. The participant's goal was to identify robots in danger of crossing into critical energy use ranges, either too high (≥ 95) or too low (≤ 5), so that a fictitious technician could prioritize robots in need of fixing. This proxy task for monitoring agent status was used to allow naïve participants to quickly learn and perform the task. Participants performed three tasks that involved monitoring current status and anticipating future status in arrays of static indicators: (1) quickly identify the indicator currently closest to a critical threshold (current worst task), (2) quickly identify the next indicator to cross a critical threshold (next-critical task), and (3) carefully rank the three next-critical indicators in order of anticipated threshold crossing (ranking task). Participants clicked on indicators to indicate their responses.

After participants gave their informed consent, the proctor provided instructions on the indicator formats and tasks, and demonstrated the task in detail. After participants successfully demonstrated comprehension of the task and formats, they completed the practice and experimental trials, followed by an experiment debrief and payment for participation. The entire procedure lasted about 90 min.

3   Results

Dependent variables were analyzed with repeated measures ANOVAs including within-subject factors of format and number of emerging problems. In cases where Mauchly's test for sphericity was significant, reported p values are Greenhouse-Geisser corrected. Reported effect sizes are generalized η^2 statistics. Each dependent variable and task, including each ranking response, was analyzed separately.

Participants' average accuracy and response times are plotted in Figs. 2 and 3. We investigated the results statistically through planned comparisons between targeted format pairs corresponding to the three goals of the experiment described in Sect. 2. Main effects of the number of emerging problems in the comparisons below do not relate to the hypotheses and are not reported.

(1) The expected performance enhancements from improving information access and salience assignment were found. Augmented Trend Graphs significantly improved performance relative to baseline Trend Graphs, resulting in faster and more accurate performance in all tasks (current worst, $F(1,23) = 4.43$, $p = .046$, $\eta^2 = 0.04$; all other tasks $F(1,23) \geq 13.00$, $p \leq .001$, $\eta^2 \geq 0.11$).

Performance with Augmented Trend Graphs matched and in some cases surpassed performance with Trendicons. Responses for the second and third rankings were faster and more accurate with Augmented Trend Graphs (all $F(1,23) \geq 8.40$, $p \leq .008$, $\eta^2 \geq 0.06$). Augmented Trend Graphs were also less impacted by the number of emerging problems than Trendicons in the current worst task ($F(2,46) = 4.13$, $p = .022$, $\eta^2 = 0.02$), and the second ($F(2,46) = 5.75$, $p = .006$, $\eta^2 = 0.04$) and third ($F(2,46) = 15.31$, $p < .001$, $\eta^2 = 0.13$) rank responses. Although response times with Trendicons were generally slower overall, they were *less* impacted by number of emerging problems in the next-critical (F(2,46) = 6.77, p = .003, η^2 = 0.01) and the first ranking tasks (F(2,46) = 7.40, p = .002, η^2 = 0.03).

The addition of the Linear Estimator enhanced performance with the Alternative Trendicons vs. the original Trendicons. Other than response times for the current worst task, performance was significantly better across the board for Alternative Trendicons (all F(1,23) ≥ 4.52, p ≤ .044, η^2 ≥ 0.04). The effect of more emerging problems was also less pronounced for Alternative Trendicons on the accuracy of the third ranking task (F(1,23) = 9.73, p < .001, η^2 = 0.09).

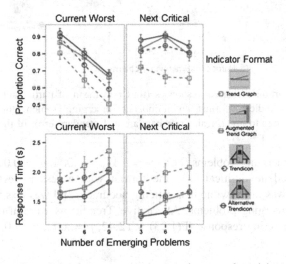

Fig. 2. Mean proportion of correct responses (top) and mean of participant median response times (bottom) across indicator formats and number of emerging problems for speeded identification of the current worst indicator (left) and the next indicator to go critical (right). Error bars are ± 1 standard error of the mean.

(2) The strong benefits of Trendicons over Trend Graphs observed in a dynamic monitoring task [7] generally extended to the static task paradigm in the current experiment. Performance was significantly more accurate for Trendicons vs. Trend Graphs for the current worst, next-critical, and ranking tasks (F(1,23) ≥ 5.86, p ≤ .024, η^2 ≥ 0.05), and responses were significantly faster for the ranking tasks (F(1,23) ≥ 4.40, p ≤ .047, η^2 ≥ 0.02) and marginally faster for the next-critical task (F(2,46) = 3.94, p = .059, η^2 = 0.05).

(3) Although the Augmented Trend Graphs and Alternative Trendicons resulted in similar performance on most measures, some of the expected time availability tradeoffs in formats were found. While accuracy for the (speeded) next-critical task did not differ significantly, response times to the next-critical task were faster for Alternative Trendicons vs. Augmented Trend Graphs (F(1,23) = 4.53, p = .044, η^2 = 0.04). Alternative Trendicons were also less impacted by the

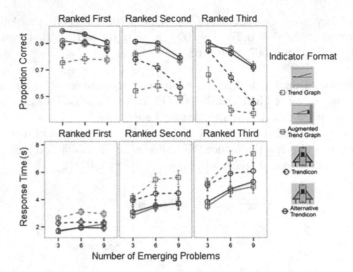

Fig. 3. Mean proportion of correct responses (top) and mean of participant median response times (bottom) across indicator formats and numbers of emerging problems for carefully ranking the next three indicators to go critical. Error bars are ± 1 standard error of the mean.

number of emerging problems ($F(2,46) = 5.42$, $p = .008$, $\eta^2 = 0.01$). Thus, for the time-pressured next-critical task, the format with access to *less* detailed trend information was faster without sacrificing accuracy, and was less impacted by the number of emerging problems. Alternative Trendicons were also more accurate for the first ranking response ($F(1,23) = 12.42$, $p = .002$, $\eta^2 = 0.11$).

4   Discussion

The design and use of status formats is often based on the convenience of using legacy formats already implemented in systems, the tradition of using the same formats over many years, and the familiarity of the formats to operators and system designers. This tendency to retain legacy formats can result in inadequate support when operator task needs change and evolve. To provide an objective basis for the design and use of status indicator formats that match operator task needs, we conducted a systematic analysis of a range of status indicator formats to assess their viability for supporting proactive monitoring of multiple agents.

This analysis revealed that many formats commonly used in today's control systems are not well-suited to support proactive monitoring, *and* are not poised to support the task needs of future operators who will need to proactively monitor multiple agents in densely populated visual displays. No standard formats directly code or cue attention to worsening trend, a key attribute needed to proactively monitor multiple agents. Noting these shortfalls, we focused our design guidance and decisions on what information to make accessible, how to map information importance to visual salience in formats, and how to maintain salience of the most important features in densely populated multi-agent displays to effectively manage attention. Based on the results of our analyses, we created novel formats and augmented existing formats and demonstrated their performance advantages through an empirical study.

Recognizing resistance to accepting new formats due to cost and biases toward familiar formats, we have proposed possible augmentations (i.e., the Linear Estimator) for sub-optimal standard formats to improve performance, as demonstrated with the Augmented Trend Graph. Specifically, the Augmented Trend Graphs improved accessibility and cueing of task-relevant information (worsening trend) missing from Trend Graphs. We also demonstrated performance gains from augmenting an already-improved format (Trendicon) with the Linear Estimator coding, which improved salience assignment and access to information needed to prioritize *multiple* worsening indicators. The Alternative Trendicons' speed advantage and robustness to number of emerging problems compared to the Augmented Trend Graphs suggests that the icon format may remain more robust when larger numbers of emerging problems must be searched through and prioritized.

Beyond the point designs discussed here, our analysis can be extended to assess the effectiveness of other formats (e.g., configural displays representing multivariate status, [21]) in different tasks. It can also identify features that can be applied to existing sub-optimal formats when changes to systems are limited, complement other design approaches (e.g., Ecological Interface Design, [22]), and inspire novel designs through combinations of features and development of new representations.

In related work, we are exploring computational modeling approaches to assess attention management and predict performance across formats to complement our behavioral data and inform the design of alternative formats [1]. Follow-on research will extend these modeling approaches to assess and validate the information access estimates reported here.

5 Conclusion

In the current paper, we analyzed and manipulated core properties of visual status indicator formats impacting human monitoring performance. This analysis revealed limitations of applying certain standard formats to multi-agent monitoring tasks, provided design mitigations to improve format effectiveness, and motivated the design and empirical testing of novel improved formats. Human-computer interaction researchers and system designers must ensure that information displays support the changing roles and task needs of human operators. This requires a principled and deliberate approach to design that considers the task needs and cognitive attributes of human operators, and that recognizes when formats require redesign, augmentation, or replacement.

Acknowledgements. This work was sponsored by the Office of Naval Research, Human & Bioengineered Systems (ONR 341), program officers Dr. Julie L. Marble and Dr. Jeffrey G. Morrison under contract N00014-12-C-0244. The authors thank Mr. Dan Manes and Mrs. Heather Kobus of Pacific Science & Engineering for technical assistance, and Dr. Harvey Smallman for helpful comments. The views expressed are those of the authors and do not reflect the official policy or position of the Office of Naval Research, Department of Defense, or US Government.

References

1. Rieth, C.A., Cook, M.B., Ngo, M.K.: Displays for effective human-agent teaming: evaluating attention management with computational models.In: Paper to be presented at the HCII 2015 Conference, invited session on Human-Agent Teaming and Agent Transparency, Los Angeles (in press)
2. U.S. Department of Defense (DoD). FY2013–2038 Unmanned Systems Integrated Roadmap. U.S. Department of Defense, Washington (2013)
3. Sheridan, T.B., Parasuraman, R.: Hum Autom. Interact. Rev. Hum. Fac. Ergon. **1**, 89–129 (2005)
4. Mumaw, R.J., Roth, E.M., Vicente, K.J., Burns, C.M.: There is more to monitoring a nuclear power plant than meets the eye. Hum. Factors **42**, 36–55 (2000)
5. St. John, M.F., King, M.A.: The four-second supervisor: multitasking supervision and its support. In: Proceedings of the Human Factors Ergonomics. Society 54th Annual Meeting, pp. 468–472 (2010)
6. Burns, C.M.: Towards proactive monitoring in the petrochemical industry. Safety Sci. **44**, 27–36 (2006)
7. Cook, M.B., Smallman, H.S., Rieth, C.A.: Increasing the effective span of control: advanced graphics for proactive, trend-based monitoring. IIE Trans. Occup. Ergon. Hum. Factors **2**, 137–151 (2014)
8. Smallman, H.S., Cook, M.B.: Proactive supervisory decision support from trend-based monitoring of autonomous and automated systems: a tale of two domains. In: Shumaker, Randall (ed.) VAMR 2013, Part II. LNCS, vol. 8022, pp. 320–329. Springer, Heidelberg (2013)
9. Eckstein, M.P.: Visual search: a retrospective. J. Vis. **11**, 14 (2011)
10. Wolfe, J., Horowitz, T.: What attributes guide the deployment of visual attention and how do they do it? Nat. Rev. Neurosci. **5**, 495–501 (2004)
11. Wickens, C.D., Hollands, J.G.: Attention, time-sharing, and workload. Eng. Psychol. Hum. Perform **3**, 439–479 (2000)
12. St. John, M.F., Smallman, H.S.: Staying up to speed: four design principles for maintaining and recovering situation awareness. J. Cognitive Eng. Decis. Making **2**, 118–139 (2008)
13. Wickens, C.D., McCarley, J.: Applied Attention Theory. Taylor & Francis, Boca Raton (2008)
14. Simon, H.A.: Designing organizations for an information-rich world. In: Greenberger, M. (ed.) Computers, Communications, and The Public Interest, pp. 37–72. The Johns Hopkins Press, Baltimore, MD (1971)
15. Yeh, M., Wickens, C.D.: Attentional filtering in the design of electronic map displays: a comparison of color coding, intensity coding, and decluttering techniques. Hum. Factors **43**, 543–562 (2001)
16. Few, S.: Information Dashboard Design. O'Reilly, Sebastopol (2006)
17. Reising, D.V.C., Bullemer, P.T.: A direct perception, span-of-control overview display to support a process control operator's situation awareness: a practice-oriented design process. In: Proceedings of the Human Factors Ergonomics Society 52nd Annual Meeting, pp. 267–271 (2008)
18. Guerlain, S., Jamieson, G.A., Bullemer, P., Blair, R.: The MPC elucidator: a case study in the design for human automation interaction. IEEE Trans. Syst. Man Cybern Syst. Hum. **32**, 25–40 (2002)
19. Sorkin, R.D., Kantowitz, B.H., Kantowitz, S.C.: Likelihood alarm displays. Hum. Factors **30**, 445–459 (1988)

20. Yin, S., Wickens, C.D., Helander, M., Laberge, J.C.: Predictive displays for a process-control schematic interface. Hum. Factors **57**, 110–124 (2015)
21. Bennett, K.B., Flach, J.M.: Graphical displays: implications for divided attention, focused attention, and problem solving. Hum. Factors **34**, 513–533 (1992)
22. Vicente, K.J., Rasmussen, J.: Ecological interface design: theoretical foundations. IEEE Trans. Syst. Man Cybern. **32**, 589–606 (1992)

Exploring the Implications of Virtual Human Research for Human-Robot Teams

Jonathan Gratch[1]([⊠]), Susan Hill[2], Louis-Philippe Morency[3],
David Pynadath[1], and David Traum[1]

[1] University of Southern California Institute for Creative Technologies,
Los Angeles, USA
{gratch,pynadath,traum}@ict.usc.edu
[2] Army Research Laboratory, Adelphi, USA
susan.g.hill.civ@mail.mil
[3] Carnegie Mellon University, Pittsburgh, USA
morency@cs.cmu.edu

Abstract. This article briefly explores potential synergies between the fields of virtual human and human-robot interaction research. We consider challenges in advancing the effectiveness of human-robot teams makes recommendations for enhancing this by facilitating synergies between robotics and virtual human research.

1 Introduction

Advances in autonomy raise the potential for rich partnerships between humans and machines. Human-robot teams are emerging across a range of high-stakes situations including military operations, first-responders and caring for vulnerable populations. To date, the preponderance of robotics research addresses the challenge of individual robots interacting with the physical environment, yet teamwork involves navigating a social environment. To address this gap, research on human-machine teams is increasingly turning to the social sciences to inform the design of automation. For example, the research into how to get users to trust automation increasingly builds on theories of how trust arises between people [1, 2]. Similarly, research into human-computer communication builds on theories of human verbal and nonverbal communication, often incorporating into automation analogs of facial expressions or bodily gestures [3, 4].

Whereas the robotics community is beginning to explore the role of social science theory and anthropomorphic techniques, these elements are the *raison d'être* for the field of virtual human research (e.g., see [5, 6] and the Intelligent Virtual Agent's conference series). Virtual humans are software artifacts that look like, act like and interact with humans but exist in virtual environments. To achieve this, the virtual humans must provide a sufficient illusion of human-like behavior that human users interpret, respond, and learn from such virtual interactions much as they would react in real-world social interactions. To this end, virtual humans must be responsive; that is, they must respond to the human user and to the events surrounding them. They must be

© Springer International Publishing Switzerland 2015
R. Shumaker and S. Lackey (Eds.): VAMR 2015, LNCS 9179, pp. 186–196, 2015.
DOI: 10.1007/978-3-319-21067-4_20

interpretable; the user must be able to interpret their response to situations, including their dynamic cognitive and emotional state, using the same verbal and non-verbal cues that people use to understand one another. Finally, they must evoke similar social effects as are expected to occur in face-to-face interactions (e.g., social anxiety, impression management, emotional contagion). Thus, the virtual humans cannot simply create an illusion of life through cleverly designed randomness in their behavior; they are successful to the extent that they evoke responses from humans indistinguishable from how people would respond to another person.

In this article, we highlight the need for greater collaboration between robotics and virtual human research. Virtual human research has placed a premium on how to understand, model and simulate spoken language, how to recognize and utilize nonverbal communication, and how to model and utilize social cognitive processes such as intention recognition, collaborative decision-making, and even the role of emotion in teams. Many of these capabilities are of relevance in human-robot interaction. Yet collaboration is required to translate these findings to the domain of robotics. Virtual human research is usually explored in "pristine" simulated or laboratory settings that finesse many of the challenges of operating in complex real-world environments. More fundamentally, the goal of much virtual human research is to literally replicate human appearance and behavior, yet this is less possible, and potentially less desired within the context of physical robots. Rather, a collaboration is required to understand which approaches are relevant and which are relevant in an analogous, if not literal form.

Here, we recommend several potentially fruitful points of interaction between virtual human and robotics research as it relates to the challenge of mixed human-machine teams. These include 1) research into the potential benefits but also pitfalls of incorporating anthropomorphic elements into robotic systems; 2) research aimed at transitioning natural language and 3) nonverbal communication techniques developed within the virtual human community into settings that involve human-machine teams; and 4) research into technology for enhancing trust in human-machine teams, including methods for automatically generating explanations of machine decisions and establishing shared mental models. Each of these recommendations are presented in the following sections of this article and are discussed in much greater detail in a technical report [7].

2   Cost/Benefit of Anthropomorphism in Human-Robot Teams

A growing trend within robotics has focused on endowing robots with more human-like characteristics, including human-like form, natural language and even emotions. This interest is fueled by the assumption that human-robot and human-computer interactions can be enhanced by bringing how we interact with machines closer to how we interact with other people, thereby leveraging the vast experience we have with human-human interaction. This assumption needs to be rigorously examined.

It is important to note that machines can be made more capable without necessarily making them more "natural" or human-like. Interaction with robots could be explicitly unnatural as naturalness might get in the way of efficiency (for example, communication with air-traffic controllers is highly scripted to be efficient while avoiding ambiguity). Research on natural interfaces demonstrates that machines can be made more human-like, but less research has considered if this benefits or harms human-machine team performance. Indeed, a review of the literature illustrates several examples where incorporating human-like qualities results in unintended and disruptive consequences. Attempts to merely replicate human characteristics overlooks an opportunity to improve on human-human interaction: might machines be designed to interact in different but complementary ways that make them better than "natural" teammates?

Some research has emphasized the potential benefits of anthropomorphism. For example, Gratch and colleagues have shown that a computer agent that incorporates rapport-building behaviors can enhance feelings of engagement and lead to greater self-disclosure in spoken interviews [8]. People favor human-like machines in economic settings when they incorporate human-like features, such as offering more money in a variety of economic games [9], and donating more money when asked by a human-like robot [10]. People are more persuaded by machines that incorporate human-like gestures [11] or humor [12]. Students have been shown to learn better when automated tutors incorporate emotional feedback [13]. Other research has shown that adding that adding human-like mental capabilities, like theory of mind, can improve joint outcomes in social games [14]. Many of these findings have been replicated within the context of human-robot interaction (e.g., [2, 15]).

Yet, other research has emphasized the potential harms of anthropomorphism. People lie to human-like machines, they get emotional, they make "irrational" decisions, and they evoke moral principles that get in the way of maximizing material rewards. For example, in medicine, it is important for healthcare providers to solicit honest information from their patients. Yet patients are more honest when being interviewed by a computer compared with being interviewed by a person [16]. Anthropomorphism can undermine this benefit by evoking the social mechanism of socially-desirable responding. Lucas, et al., showed a depression screening agent elicited more truthful and more diagnostic information when its "computerness" was made salient compared with an agent that emphasized its "humanness" [17]. In economic settings, people often make financially disadvantageous decision with human teammates [18] or human-like computers [9] when compared to decisions with a machine. More generally, people engage in more emotion, moral and reactive decision-making with other people compared to their interactions with computers, leading to a host of negative outcomes, especially in conflict situations [19, 20].

Opportunities for Research: Incorporating natural and anthropomorphic characteristics into robotic systems can have a strong impact on human-robot team effectiveness. Unfortunately, these effects can be both beneficial and harmful depending on a variety of task, contextual and individual factors. More research is needed regarding when and how anthropomorphism benefits human-machine systems. Specifically, we recommend research directed at selectively evoking social effects: In that human-like traits unconsciously evoke human-like responses, and that some responses have benefits but others harms, research is needed in how to distinguish and differentially evoke specific social effects that lead to benefits, while avoiding the evocation of disruptive social effects.

3 NLP for Virtual Humans and Robots

Virtual humans and robots are both artificial, automated agents that can engage in complex behavior and complex interaction with humans. Natural language is one of the main ways that humans communicate with each other, particularly for abstract concepts, processes, or objects that are not immediately visible or manipulable. By engaging in natural language dialogue, automated agents can make it easier to communicate with people by making use of this same communication method. There is a large degree of overlap in the kinds of tasks that robots and virtual humans can talk to people about.

Many issues make natural language processing difficult for automation, including noisy input, vagueness, and the contextual meaning of utterances. For most tasks, there has been more progress with virtual humans than robots in overcoming these challenges – both because less effort must be spent in creating the basic interactive capability with animations rather than robots with complex physical components, and because language generation in the virtual world finesses challenges with real world-perception, using instead meta-data or virtual world databases for perceptual information.

Much of the work on virtual human natural language dialogue can be adapted for improving human-robot natural language dialogue. For example a key problem for both domains is navigating through a complex environment and giving and understanding directions. Some examples of virtual human work include virtual characters on a mobile device who gives tours of a museum exhibit [21], and the GRUVE challenge on generating instructions in an urban environment [22]. Another shared problem is the Grounding problem, which involves coordination of interlocutors using multi-modal dialogue interaction to increase confidence of shared understanding. The computational models developed in [23] have been implemented and used within a number of virtual human systems (e.g., [24]). Another point of intersection is runtime and support software tools, authoring tools, and the development process that can be applied across domains. For example, speech recognizers, parsers, statistical classifiers [25], dialogue managers [26], language generators [27], and speech synthesizers [28], many freely available through the virtual human toolkit [29].

Finally, the development process itself is an area where robotics can exploit work pioneered in Virtual Human efforts. Natural language components need considerable training data to achieve high performance, but gathering this data is challenging for dialogue interaction, where the things people say to an artificial agent are determined by what the agent says and does. Thus, in order to gather the appropriate data, one already needs the system. The way out of this conundrum is a phased approach to data collection: beginning with purely human interaction, next moving to "wizard of oz" collection (where an agent is controlled by a human behind the curtain). Finally, versions of an automated system can be deployed and improved. A number of virtual human projects have followed this development path (e.g., [30, 31]).

Several challenges confront the use of virtual human technology in robotic systems. One of the greatest strengths for natural language processing for virtual humans in the virtual world is the ability to simplify the non-linguistic issues, such as perception, locomotion and manipulation. However, this simplification can also become a limitation, since it may not be straightforward to adapt algorithms tuned to the simplified environment to work in the real environment. Another challenge is that the roles for virtual humans and robots may tend to diverge, which, in turn, may tend to cause a divergence in the kinds of language used, and thus the best algorithms and tools. Virtual humans are generally meant to take the place of a real human in a social interaction, so communication is generally using the "agent as human" metaphor for communication. In cases where a robot is very non-human in appearance, perception and manipulation capabilities, and purpose, this metaphor may tend to break down when communication with some robots may be more like communication with animals than like people.

Opportunities for Research: From this review, we identify a number of opportunities to enhance the effectiveness of human-robot teams by adapting research capabilities already developed within the context of virtual human systems. This includes 1) adapting virtual human dialogue authoring and run-time tools for use with robotics applications; 2) using empirical methods for data collection and training of natural language processing components; 3) incorporating advanced dialogue management techniques, and 4) adapting virtual world efforts on object and route descriptions, particularly from the direction-giving challenges.

4 Nonverbal Communication

Face-to-face communication is a highly interactive process where participants mutually exchange and interpret linguistic and gestural signals. Communication dynamics represent the temporal relationship between these signals. Even when only one person speaks at a time, other participants exchange information continuously amongst themselves and with the speaker through gesture, gaze, posture and facial expressions. The transactional view of human communication shows an important dynamic between communicative behaviors where each person serves simultaneously as speaker and listener [32]. At the same time you send a message, you also receive messages from your own communications (individual dynamics) as well as from the reactions of the other person(s) (interpersonal dynamics).

Individual and interpersonal dynamics play a key role when a teacher automatically adjusts his/her explanations based on the student nonverbal behaviors, when a doctor diagnoses a disorder such as autism, or when a negotiator detects deception. An important challenge for artificial intelligence researchers is creating socially intelligent robots and computers, able to recognize, predict and analyze verbal and nonverbal dynamics during face-to-face communication. This will not only open up new avenues for human-computer interactions but create new computational tools for social and behavior researchers–software able to automatically analyze human social and nonverbal behaviors, and extract important interaction patterns.

Nonverbal communicative behavior analysis is a growing field with a large number of applications and especially within the field of virtual human research, where sensing is often simplified through the interaction of a seated person in a well-lit room where all interesting characters and environmental events exist with a fixed computer screen (e.g., see [33]). Over the past two decades, a first generation of multimodal approaches have been applied in many areas, including audio-visual speech recognition, multimodal object tracking, biometrics, human-computer interaction and multimedia analysis. Also related to this line of research is the research done on audio-visual emotion analysis. Several researchers used prosody (i.e., pitch, speaking rate, etc.) for speech based emotion recognition [34]. Some studies analyzed visual cues, such as facial expressions and body movements [35].

More recently, challenges have been organized focusing on the recognition of emotions using audio and visual cues (e.g., [36]) and drew the participation of many teams from around the world. Note however that all the previous work on audio-visual emotion analysis and multimodal perception was performed on dataset recorded in the laboratory. Also, most of these analyses focus on a generalization of behaviors over a large population, ignoring the idiosyncratic and cultural-specific behaviors of the participants.

Several challenges confront the immediate adoption of this technology to human-robot teams. A robot needs to not only understand the facial expression, body gestures and voice patterns, but it needs to put them in the context of the interactions in the external world, taking into account the multiple human participants, their individuality in expressing personality and emotions and events in the real world. Much of the virtual human research has also focused on dyadic interactions with a very abstract environment (such as a game or simple computer tasks). Rather, human-machine teams demand a focus on more complex interactions involving possibly multiple parties and complex relationships between these entities and environmental events. This will likely require extensions to standardized perception frameworks developed within the multimodal perception community.

Opportunities for Research: From this review, we identify a number of opportunities to enhance the effectiveness of human-robot teams by adapting research capabilities already developed within the context of virtual human systems. This includes (1) learning from readily available data from online website such YouTube, Twitter and Facebook where people are posting a large array of videos with multimodal behaviors and emotions; (2) multimodal deep learning, building on recent achievements in deep neural network modeling to learn the complementarity and synchrony between communicative modalities, and (3) context-based multimodal dialogue, that explicitly models nonverbal behaviors in the shared environment.

5   Trust and Theory of Mind

The increasing capability of autonomous systems has rarely translated into a similar increase in the capability of the human-machine team unit [37]. Studies have identified many causes underlying this phenomenon, but have also shown that simply increasing the capability of the automation in isolation will not suffice [38]. We must instead improve the quality of the interaction between automation and its human operators.

A critical aspect of this interaction is trust [1]. If an autonomous system is better than the human operator at a certain task, then we want the operator to trust the system, but if the system is worse, we want the operator to distrust it and perform the task manually. Failure to do so results in disuse of automation in the former case and misuse in the latter. Real-world case studies and laboratory experiments show that failures in both cases are common. To achieve proper use of automation, we must better understand why these trust failures occur and what steps we can take to avoid them.

An operator may be willing to trust an autonomous system that has never made a mistake, but it is also important that the operator not overreact to the mistakes that the system will inevitably make. Errors by an autonomous system often have a greater impact on trust than those made by human assistants [39]. Researcher has shown that human operators will more accurately trust an autonomous system if they have a more accurate understanding of its decision-making process and that explaining possible causes of errors can allow an autonomous system to maintain users' trust in the face of such errors [40].

It is thus clear that the transparency of the autonomous system is an important factor in earning appropriate trust. The need for such transparency has motivated researchers in artificial intelligence to develop autonomous agents capable of automatically explaining their decisions [41]. While such transparency certainly increases trust, it also generates a cost to human users in that they must divert attention to communication with an autonomous system. To best manage this cost/benefit tradeoff, the agent literature has framed the problem in terms of the impact of communication on team performance. Teammates communicate so that they can achieve a shared mental model that allows them to perform joint tasks in a coordinated fashion [42]. By weighing the cost of communication against its positive impact in achieving such shared models, agents can optimize their communication strategies to maximize team performance [43].

Transparency through team-oriented communication can help foster trust, but what an autonomous system says may not have as big an impact as what it does. It is thus also important that such systems make good decisions not just in communication, but also in choosing which tasks they do themselves, and which are better left to their teammates. Human-machine teams rely on this adjustable autonomy to flexibly assign different tasks to the most appropriate members, based on capability and situation [44]. Agent researchers have developed algorithms that can optimize the transfers of control that dynamically assign tasks among team members, both human and machine [45]. Combining these existing frameworks for both communication and adjustable autonomy allows researchers to model mixed teams of people, agents, and robots. More recently, we have extended this teamwork model into an agent-based representation of Theory of Mind reasoning [46], allowing agents to model the impact of their decisions on the mental models of their human teammates.

Like human-agent teams, human-robot teams also exhibit a need for trust, shared mental models, and adjustable autonomy. Unfortunately, there remains a sizeable gap between the human-subject studies that quantify human-robot team performance and existing agent-based coordination mechanisms. While the cited agent-based systems all derived better coordination with human users from their communication capability, there has been little quantitative evaluation of the effect (if any) this new capability had on their trust relationship with users. Furthermore, while there has been preliminary work on measuring this effect in virtual simulations of human-robot interaction [47], none of these agent coordination algorithms have been evaluated in a mixed team combining both human users with physical robots. It thus remains an open question as to the degree that existing human-agent algorithms can benefit human-robot teams.

Opportunities for Research: We see a large opportunity for enhancing the effectiveness of robot-human teams through the use of technology that enhances trust. We have also identified a number of gaps between existing algorithms and HRI needs, as well as algorithmic refinement to close that the gaps found. Such a cycle can support the adaptation of existing agent algorithms to the specific needs of human-robot teams. Specifically, we recommend basic and applied research that addresses (1) automatic explanation algorithms for human-robot trust; (2) domain-independent frameworks for establishing shared mental models in human-robot teams; (3) transfer-of-control strategies for adjustable autonomy for robots to maximize the capabilities of both their human teammates and themselves, and (4) Theory of Mind for robots to adapt to the individual differences across their human teammates.

6 Summary

To conclude, this article identified several points of profitable interaction between research on virtual humans and research on human-robot interaction. These include a focus on core technology shared by both domains – i.e., natural language processing, nonverbal communication – as well as research on how to replicate human interpersonal processes – such as interpersonal trust – within the context of human-machine teams. Finally, we suggest the importance of not blindly assuming that more human-like machines will necessarily yield better teammates, and research is required on which set of interpersonal processes benefit, as opposed to undermine, effective human-machine teams. These recommendations are explained in greater detail in the following technical report: [7].

Acknowledgements. This work is supported by the Army Research Laboratory. Statements and opinions expressed do not necessarily reflect the position or the policy of the United States Government, and no official endorsement should be inferred.

References

1. Lee, J.D., See, K.A.: Trust in automation: designing for appropriate reliance. Hum. Factors J. Hum. Factors Ergon. Soc. **46**(1), 50–80 (2004)
2. DeSteno, D., Breazeal, C., Frank, R.H., Pizarro, D., Baumann, J., Dickens, L., Lee, J.J.: Detecting the trustworthiness of novel partners in economic exchange. Psychol. Sci. **23**(12), 1549–1556 (2012)
3. Breazeal, C., Aryananda, L.: Recognition of affective communicative intent in robot-directed speech. Auton. Rob. **12**, 83–104 (2002)
4. Eyssel, F., et al.: If you sound like me, you must be more human: on the interplay of robot and user features on human-robot acceptance and anthropomorphism. In: Proceedings of the seventh annual ACM/IEEE international conference on Human-Robot Interaction, ACM (2012)

5. Cassell, J., et al.: Embodiment in conversational interfaces: rea. In: Conference on Human Factors in Computing Systems, Pittsburgh, PA (1999)
6. Gratch, J., et al.: Creating interactive virtual humans: some assembly required In: IEEE Intelligent Systems, pp. 54-61 (2002)
7. Gratch, J., et al.: Exploring the implications of virtual human research for human-robot teams. University of Southern California Institute for Creative Technologies (2014)
8. Gratch, J., Kang, S.-H., Wang, N.: Using social agents to explore theories of rapport and emotional resonance. In: Gratch, J., Marsella, S. (eds.) Social Emotions in Nature and Artifact. Oxford University Press, Cambridge (2014)
9. de Melo, C., Carnevale, P.J., Gratch, J.: Humans vs. Computers: The Effect of Perceived Agency on People's Decision Making. University of Southern California (2013)
10. Siegel, M.: Persuasive robotics: how robots change our minds. In: Media Arts and Sciences. MIT, Cambridge, MA (2009)
11. Koda, T., Mori, Y.: Effects of an agent's displaying self-adaptors during a serious conversation. In: Bickmore, T., Marsella, S., Sidner, C. (eds.) IVA 2014. LNCS, vol. 8637, pp. 240–249. Springer, Heidelberg (2014)
12. Morkes, J., Kernal, H.K., Nass, C.: Effects of humor in task-oriented human-computer interaction and computer-mediated communication: a direct test of SRCT theory. Hum. Comput. Interact. 14(4), 395–435 (1999)
13. Lester, J.C., Towns, S.G., FitzGerald, P.J.: Achieving affective impact: visual emotive communication in lifelike pedagogical agents. Int. J. Artif. Intell. Educ. 10(3–4), 278–291 (1999)
14. Yoshida, W., et al.: Neural mechanisms of belief inference during cooperative games. J. Neurosci. 30(32), 10744–10751 (2010)
15. Chidambaram, V., Chiang, Y.-H., Mutlu. B.: Designing persuasive robots: how robots might persuade people using vocal and nonverbal cues. In: Proceedings of the Seventh Annual ACM/IEEE International Conference on Human-Robot Interaction. ACM (2012)
16. Weisband, S., Kiesler, S.: Self disclosure on computer forms: meta-analysis and implcations. In: CHI (1996)
17. Lucas, G.M., et al.: It's only a computer: virtual humans increase willingness to disclose. Comput. Hum. Behav. 37, 94–100 (2014)
18. Sanfey, A.G., et al.: The neural basis of economic decision-making in the ultimatum game. Science 300(5626), 1755–1758 (2003)
19. Lytle, A.L., Brett, J.M., Shapiro, D.L.: The strategic use of interests, rights, and power to resolve disputes. Negot. J. 15(1), 31–51 (1999)
20. Dehghani, M., et al.: Sacred values and conflict over Iran's nuclear program. Judgment Decis. Making 5(7), 540–546 (2010)
21. Damiano, R., et al.: A stroll with Carletto: adaptation in drama-based tours with virtual characters. User Model. User-Adap. Inter. 18(5), 417–453 (2008)
22. Janarthanam, S., Lemon. O.: The GRUVE challenge: generating routes under uncertainty in virtual environments. In: Proceedings of the 13th European Workshop on Natural Language Generation. Association for Computational Linguistics (2011)
23. Traum, D.: A computational theory of grouding in natural language conversation. In: Computer Science Ph.D. thesis. University of Rochester, Rochester, NY (1994)
24. Traum, D., et al.: Negotiation over tasks in hybrid human-agent teams for simulation-based training. In: International Conference on Autonomous Agents and Multiagent Systems. Melbourne, Australia (2003)

25. Sagae, K., et al.: Towards natural language understanding of partial speech recognition results in dialogue systems. In: Proceedings of Human Language Technologies: The 2009 Annual Conference of the North American Chapter of the Association for Computational Linguistics, Companion Volume: Short Papers. Association for Computational Linguistics (2009)
26. Morbini, F., et al.: FLoReS: a forward looking, reward seeking, dialogue manager. In: Mariani, J., Rosset, S., Garnier-Rizet, M., Devillers, L. (eds.) Natural Interaction with Robots, Knowbots and Smartphones, pp. 313–325. Springer, New York (2014)
27. DeVault, D., Traum, D., Artstein, R.: Making grammar-based generation easier to deploy in dialogue systems. In: Proceedings of the 9th SIGdial Workshop on Discourse and Dialogue. Association for Computational Linguistics (2008)
28. Georgila, K., et al.: Practical evaluation of human and synthesized speech for virtual human dialogue systems. In: LREC (2012)
29. Hartholt, A., Traum, D., Marsella, S.C., Shapiro, A., Stratou, G., Leuski, A., Morency, L.-P., Gratch, J.: All together now. In: Aylett, R., Krenn, B., Pelachaud, C., Shimodaira, H. (eds.) IVA 2013. LNCS, vol. 8108, pp. 368–381. Springer, Heidelberg (2013)
30. Traum, D., Marsella, S.C., Gratch, J., Lee, J., Hartholt, A.: Multi-party, multi-issue, multi-strategy negotiation for multi-modal virtual agents. In: Prendinger, H., Lester, J., Ishizuka, M. (eds.) IVA 2008. LNCS (LNAI), vol. 5208, pp. 117–130. Springer, Heidelberg (2008)
31. DeVault, D., Mell, J., Gratch, J.: Toward natural turn-taking in a virtual human negotiation agent. In: AAAI Spring Symposium on Turn-taking and Coordination in Human-Machine Interaction. AAAI Press, Stanford, CA (2015)
32. Watzlawick, P., et al.: Pragmatics of Human Communication. A Study of Interactional Patterns, Pathologies, and Paradoxes, Paul Watzlawick, Janet Helmick Beavin, Don D. Jackson. WW Norton. (1967)
33. Vinciarelli, A., et al.: Social signals, their function, and automatic analysis: a survey. In: Proceedings of the 10th International Conference on Multimodal Interfaces, pp. 61-68. ACM, Chania, Crete, Greece (2008)
34. Tato, R., et al.: Emotional space improves emotion recognition. In: INTERSPEECH (2002)
35. Calder, A.J., et al.: Reading the mind from eye gaze. Neuropsychologia 40(8), 1129–1138 (2002)
36. Schuller, B., Valstar, M., Eyben, F., McKeown, G., Cowie, R., Pantic, M.: AVEC 2011–the first international audio/visual emotion challenge. In: D'Mello, S., Graesser, A., Schuller, B., Martin, J.-C. (eds.) ACII 2011, Part II. LNCS, vol. 6975, pp. 415–424. Springer, Heidelberg (2011)
37. Parasuraman, R., Riley, V.: Humans and automation: use, misuse, disuse, abuse. Hum. Factors J. Hum. Factors Ergon. Soc. 39(2), 230–253 (1997)
38. Sorkin, R.D., Woods, D.D.: Systems with human monitors: a signal detection analysis. Hum. Comput. Interact. 1(1), 49–75 (1985)
39. Dzindolet, M.T., et al.: The perceived utility of human and automated aids in a visual detection task. Hum. Factors J. Hum. Factors Ergon. Soc. 44(1), 79–94 (2002)
40. Dzindolet, M.T., et al.: The role of trust in automation reliance. Int. J. Hum Comput Stud. 58(6), 697–718 (2003)
41. Myers, K., et al.: An intelligent personal assistant for task and time management. AI Mag. 28(2), 47 (2007)
42. Grosz, B., Kraus, S.: Collaborative plans for complex group action. Artif. Intell. 86(2), 269–357 (1996)

43. Pynadath, D.V., Tambe. M.: Multiagent teamwork: analyzing the optimality and complexity of key theories and models. In: Proceedings of the First International Joint Conference on Autonomous Agents and Multiagent Systems: Part 2. ACM (2002)
44. Dorais, G., et al.: Adjustable autonomy for human-centered autonomous systems. In: Working notes of the Sixteenth International Joint Conference on Artificial Intelligence Workshop on Adjustable Autonomy Systems (1999)
45. Tambe, M., Scerri, P., Pynadath, D.V.: Adjustable autonomy for the real world. J. Artif. Intell. Res. 17(1), 171–228 (2002)
46. Pynadath, D.V., Marsella, S.C.: PsychSim: modeling theory of mind with decision-theoretic agents. In: IJCAI (2005)

Animation Guidelines for Believable Embodied Conversational Agent Gestures

Ivan Gris, Diego A. Rivera, and David Novick(✉)

Department of Computer Science, The University of Texas at El Paso,
500 West University Avenue, El Paso, TX 79968-0518, USA
ivangris4@gmail.com, darivera2@miners.utep.edu,
novick@utep.edu

Abstract. In animating embodied conversational agents (ECAs), run-time blending of animations can provide a large library of movements that increases the appearance of naturalness while decreasing the number of animations to be developed. This approach avoids the need to develop a costly full library of possible animations in advance of use. Our principal scientific contribution is the development of a model for gesture constraints that enables blended animations to represent naturalistic movement. Rather than creating over-detailed, fine-grained procedural animations or hundreds of motion-captured animation files, animators can include sets of their own animations for agents, blend them, and easily reuse animations, while constraining the ECA to use motions that would occur and transition naturally.

Keywords: Embodied conversational agents · Animation · Usability

1 Introduction

Animation of embodied conversational agents (ECAs) too often seem stilted or unnatural, despite animation's history as an art that has been practiced for over a century. In the movies and television, animation grew from a novelty to a major form of artistic expression, with major influence beyond the confines of the animation frame. Actors use principles and techniques from animation during their performances, and artists borrow elements from those performances to make their characters realistic. Cinematography, through the use of visual tricks, camera movements, actor training, and special effects, has created intricate visual storytelling elements that are usually not present in ECA systems. Perhaps ECAs do not feature realistic animation because there is little need for naturalistic animation in most computer applications. Most commercial computer applications are metaphor-driven, where users interpret an icon's image and associate it with its function without requiring a highly realistic animation. For example, users do not see or need a hyper-realistic 3D model of animated scissors every time they click on the "cut" function in common office applications. Likewise, users do not expect realistic animations for characters, when interpretation alone can suffice. Instead, users have come to expect non-realistic characters with limited functionality for whose actions users have the responsibility to interpret.

R. Shumaker and S. Lackey (Eds.): VAMR 2015, LNCS 9179, pp. 197–205, 2015.
DOI: 10.1007/978-3-319-21067-4_21

Ironically, as agents become more realistic, the unnaturalness of their animations can become more evident. Consequently, for human-ECA interactions to become more natural, agents will have to be more successful in interpreting users' gestures and the agents themselves will have to be more realistic in their selection and performance of gestures.

While some animation systems produce realistic and smooth movement for ECAs, research and development of the agents typically focus on the appropriateness or categorization of gestures in taxonomies that define what should be displayed in response to different user behaviors. The responsibility for animation quality is often delegated to an artist, who is limited by the requirements of the particular agent and who has little creative freedom to improve the expressiveness of gestures. As a practical matter, this approach produces rough-and-ready results but does not provide specific guidelines or replicable techniques for producing ECA animations that are appropriately realistic. What is needed, then, is a systematic approach to realistically natural gesture animations for ECAs that can be applied by developers who are not experts in animation.

To respond to this need, we developed an automated animation system that can create a wide range of realistic animations based on a small set of states that can be blended, combined, layered, and transitioned. Our approach is based on an adaptation of principles of lifelike animation and is implemented via an animation graph in Unity's Mecanim system. Our approach contrasts with that of other ways of specifying ECAs and their interactions. Systems such as BEAT (Cassell, et al. 2004) and SPARK (Vilhjálmsson 2005) provided a remarkable amount of detail for gesture based on discourse analysis, but unfortunately these approaches require large sets of micro-animations. And trying to save effort by generating these animations procedurally causes the animations to appear robotic and unnatural.

We seek to help developers and researchers with little background in 3-D modeling or animation to create more natural movement for their agents without requiring fine-grained motion capture. In this paper, accordingly, we review the principles of animation and adapt them to ECAs, describe the mechanism of our approach to producing natural animations based on these principles, describe the collection of a gesture corpus and the development of animations based on this corpus, and conclude with a brief discussion of future work.

2   Animation Principles

Traditional animation theory has suggested twelve principles for creating "the illusion of life" (Thomas & Johnston, 1981). In order of importance, the twelve principles are squash and stretch, anticipation, staging, pose to pose, follow-through or overlapping action, slow in and slow out, arcs, secondary action, timing, exaggeration, solid action and appeal. Although these guidelines were meant for artists, applying the principles to ECAs highlights flaws in standard approaches to animating agents. Accordingly, we describe in detail each animation principle and how it can be applied to ECAs.

Squash and Stretch. This principle provides the illusion of weight and volume. It is particularly useful in animating dialogue and facial expressions. In artistic terms, this is the most important factor, as it ensures that the character does not change shape and represents the character's weight. For ECAs, it is often preferable to simulate real-world physics so that users can better relate to the agent by acknowledging that the same real-world rules apply for both human and ECA. This principle might not apply to agents that are not human-like.

Anticipation. This principle involves the character's movement in preparation for major actions that they are about to perform. Common examples include running, jumping, or even a change of expression. Almost all real action has major or minor anticipation, yet this is one of the most overlooked animation principles in ECA development. Agents often need to react in real time to users' actions, often involving both speech and gesture. So by the time a system recognizes the user's communicative behaviors and formulates an appropriate response, the system is likely to have to perform immediately the agent's main gesture motion response, leaving no time to perform the anticipation animation. This is a key cause of agent actions appearing to be robotic, as it creates a move instantaneously with seemingly no previous thought or intent. To overcome this obstacle the system has to have a set of anticipation animations that can be used flexibly by predicting the animation that will be required; even as a broad guess can provide a more realistic animation through anticipation than omitting the anticipation animation.

Staging. This principle states that a pose or action should clearly communicate to the audience the mood, reaction, or idea of the character as it relates to the story and its continuity. Staging, in other words, directs the audience's attention to the story or the idea being told. This represents a problem for ECAs because cinematography often uses camera angles and close-ups to make certain story elements salient for the audience. In addition, care must be taken when building scenery and backgrounds so that they do not compete with the animation for the audience's attention. The main problem with staging, though, is that ECAs often do not have a proper stage on which to perform. This is a design issue that should be addressed early in development. In experiments (Gris et al. 2014), we have used staging techniques by providing our agents with a virtual environment. This approach has led to decreased memory loads and higher attention rates (Gris et al. 2014).

Straight Ahead and Pose-to-Pose Animation. Due to the nature of 3-D animation software, we use pose-to-pose animation via key frames. But this does not mean that that animations should be planned simply by creating an initial pose and a final pose, and then letting the 3D software interpolate the sequence automatically. Planning of animations should include transition between poses in the most natural way possible. To achieve this seamless effect, animations should be designed with the proper length, looping poses, and interruption segments so that animations can be combined or transitioned at any time.

Follow-Through and Overlapping Action. In simple terms, this principle means that nothing stops all at once. When an agent is moving and the animation ends, the agent cannot simply go to a static pose. Rather, it should blend with a weight shift or another appropriate motion that provides the illusion of continuous realistic movement, even though the main underlying action has stopped. Following this principle can eliminate unnatural movements such stopping in the middle of a step while walking.

Slow in and Slow Out. This is one of the most important principles for agents who do conversational turn-taking. This principle enables animators to soften the animation and make it more lifelike. Similar to anticipation, attention is drawn at the beginning of the animation and at the end of the animation, as these are often indicators of turn-taking. At the beginning of the motion, people will usually try to guess what the reaction will be, and at the end people need an indication to know that the agent is about to finish and that the users will able to jump into the interaction again.

Arcs. In 3D modeling all organic characters, including humans and animals, are made of curves. In contrast, robots are made of sharp edges. Animating organic characters follow arcs or slightly circular paths because of the nature of our joints. This principle applies to almost all physical movement, including turns, eye motion, wand walking paths. Accordingly, movements performed in a straight line will seem robotic or unnatural.

Secondary Action. The principle of secondary action applies to actions that enrich the main action. Secondary action adds character. For example, envision a male character about to invite a female character on a date. If it approaches the female character slowly often changing direction, it gives the impression of a shy and unsure character. However envision that same character with many concurrent secondary actions, such as fidgeting and frequent gaze movement away from the target character. These actions may not be necessary, but they enhance the animation by making it more obvious, clear, and natural (Lasseter 1987).

Timing. This is a highly subjective principle for animations that establish mood, emotion, and character reaction to the situation. For example, a pointing animation displayed in a faster timing can indicate a sense of urgency, while a slow pointing animation can indicate laziness or lack of interest. Most animation systems for ECAs permit developers to specify the time the animation should be running, but it is harder to find systems that can accelerate the animation, which is equally important.

Exaggeration. In a play, actors do not behave like normal human beings. Instead, they exaggerate their gestures to make them observable by the audience. While developers of agents commonly to try to make the animations as humanlike as possible, there is a potential benefit in exaggerating animations to make them more noticeable. Of course, one must be careful not to over-exaggerate; the risk is that of becoming too theatrical or excessively animated. Although some research has examined how big animations should be, based on the introversion or extraversion of the subjects (Neff et al. 2010; Hostetter et al. 2012), the field still lacks detailed guidelines for gesture amplitude. Artists' suggestions to use good taste and common sense are not very helpful in this regard. Moreover, perceived gesture amplitude depends on the distance from the display, the type of media, and the screen size (Detenber et al. 1996; Loomis et al. 2003).

Solid Drawing. In the 1930 s, animators used this approach to create a three-dimensional space from the two dimensions of drawings on paper. In the case of animated agents, though, this principle is redundant because agents' 3-D models already include solid drawing.

Appeal. This principle usually refers to visual attractiveness, but it can also be used as part of the character design to provide an agent with clear intentions. This is another highly subjective trait that should not be underestimated. In one of our pilot studies, users perceived an agent who was supposed to help users in a game scenario as being actually a potential enemy. Our intention was, of course, to convey a helpful, friendly character. But due to our lack of attention to the agent's visual appearance, our animated agent conveyed the opposite impression. In general, this is a trait that combines visual representation, dialog, context, and gestures, and it is difficult to achieve when any of these elements is missing.

Although all twelve principles were developed originally for traditional animation and to design characters for passive audiences that do not interact with agents, they can still help in developing agents that are more relatable, believable, and accurately representing what we want our agents to convey.

3 Animation Blend Tree

To enable developers of ECAs to use the twelve principles of animation, as adapted for agents as described in Sect. 2, we developed an animation design approach implemented as a tree of blendable animations. Our system, based on Unity's Mecanim, creates an autonomous animation workflow. We describe the principles of our animation tree and how its animations can be blended to create a very large number of naturalistic movements.

In Mecanim, the animation tree is a state machine where each state contains an animation and a weight. The weights of the animations are used to transition between them or blend animations that affect the same body parts. When there is a single animation being executed, its weight is equal to one. Every animation that is not being executed has a weight of zero. Each state transition transfers the weight of the current state towards the next intended state, until the new state has a weight of one and the previous state has a weight of zero. This means that at the midpoint of the transition each animation is being displayed with half the strength, containing properties of both animation states simultaneously. These transitions are not themselves states but rather the equivalent of a cross-fade between animations.

Using Mecanim's animation tree, we created, analyzed, and weighted a set of animations so that each state transition enforces adherence to the animation guidelines. That is, the structure and design of our implementation of the animation tree enables end users to link animations together while limiting the linking of unnatural animations (e.g., going from the running state to the crouching state), taking care to make transitions realistically gradual. Each state can include movements from any or all of the body-part layers listed at the top left of the figure. The blend tree can be expanded to include more movements.

In addition, our tree contains a set of layers that provide additional control for running animations procedurally in real time by enabling users to specify animations for fingers and hands, facial expressions, and upper and lower body separately. This effectively enables us to combine a happy facial expression while pointing with the left hand and walking, where otherwise it would require a specially designed animation that

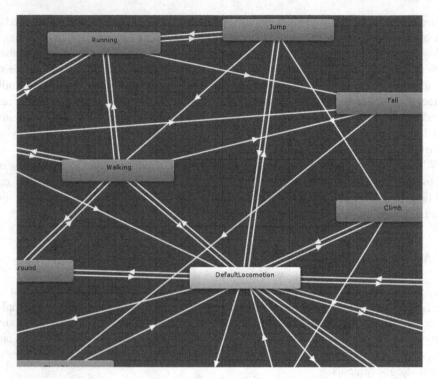

Fig. 1. A section of the animation tree detailing the permitted locomotion transitions for lower body movement. The labels of the animations differ in style (e.g., "Running" vs. "Jump") because some animations are continuous loops (e.g., running, walking), and others are one-time movements (e.g., jump, stumble).

would be useful only in this particular situation. Although it can be argued that crafting specific animations for each situation produces a more accurate representation of the intended movement, creating all of an agent's possible animations in this way be impossible because the combinatorial explosion of the movements of the different parts of the body. In our approach, the goal of the layers is to enable a maximum number of combinations from a small subset of independent general animations, while maintaining the naturalness and movement flow described in the twelve guidelines.

Figure 1 presents a subset of our animation tree. (We note that animation tree is the official name for Unity Mecanim structures, but our modifications effectively turn this "tree" into a graph.)

4   Methodology and Corpus

Given Mecanim's basic architecture, the twelve animation principles, and our proposed solution to the combinatorial explosion, we developed our particular animation tree for ECAs based on a series of observations of natural conversations. Our corpus contained twelve dyadic conversations. Each conversant was recorded in an otherwise empty

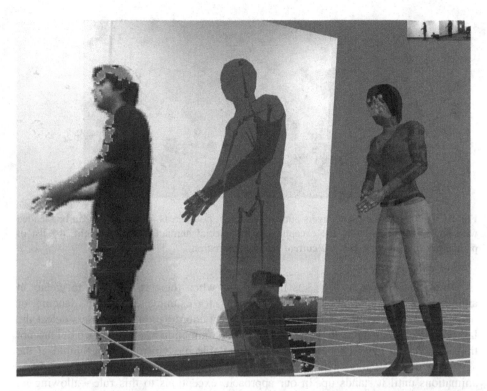

Fig. 2. From left to right, video and depth noise from the participant, motion capture data, and agent with animation data incorporated. The top right displays a thumbnail view of the raw front and side video as processed with iPi Soft.

room using two Kinect sensors that recorded side and front views for each participant, who stood facing each other. Each recording contained video and depth information, and this information was interpreted by motion capture software and translated to one of our agents, a full-body virtual 3D character. Each animated file was then empirically analyzed and categorized based on movement similarity. Figure 2 shows the stages of motion capture.

Because we sought to preserve naturalness of movement, we focused on the mechanics of the gesture rather than the gesture itself. That is, we studied the movements preceding the main gesture. For example, before performing an action such as pointing, leaning, or explaining, participants often prepared for several seconds before performing the intended gesture. Based on these observations, we classified the possible transition points between gestures, eliminating many possible but unnatural combinations that violated the animation principles. We also layered the captured animations by dividing the virtual character's body into lower body (locomotion), upper body, head, face, and hands. Additional layers were created for lip-sync and blinking controls; these, however, did not come from the motion capture analysis. Figure 3 presents the animation layers corresponding to the agent's body regions.

Fig. 3. To the left, the list of layers affecting different body areas. These layers can be blended with any or all others with the exception of the special animation. To the right, the list of parameters that characterizes the current running animation.

The *Special* layer in Fig. 3 is reserved for when there is the need to create an animation that is superimposed over all others—for example, a backflip, dancing, or other activity that requires simultaneous full-body coordination. Parameters detect the last pose into which animations are blended. If an animation has taken place but has not transitioned to a new state, the tree limits available movements. For example, if the agent sat down, it must remain sitting and cannot perform any other lower body animations until it stands up. In our approach, exceptions to this rule—allowing an agent to sit while pointing or explaining, for example—must be explicitly identified via connections in the tree.

5 Conclusion

While our animation tree is based on subjective principles, these principles reflect characteristics of movement that are consistently present in everyday interaction. By examining motion capture data from people engaged in dyadic conversation, we can observe, classify, layer, and replicate these animations. We can then infer a set of rules, based on the adaptation of the twelve animation principles as they apply to ECAs, and enforce them through our animation controller structure. The animation tree serves as a starting point for more elaborate animation patterns by helping developers with little animation knowledge set up realistic full-body animations, while retaining the potential to expand the solution to fit more unusual or additional cases.

We are currently using this system to create our next generation of ECA applications, which require real-time reactions to speech and gesture input, mimicry of gestures, and natural-looking movements. Future work includes creating a public animation library. We are also working on releasing the core version of our animation tree, which would enable non-animators to develop realistic movement for human-ECA interaction with minimal coding and no knowledge of animation.

References

Bates, J.: The role of emotion in believable agents. Commun. ACM **37**(7), 122–125 (1994)

Cassell, J., Vilhjálmsson, H.H., Bickmore, T.: BEAT: the behavior expression animation toolkit. In: Cassell, J., Högni, H., Bickmore, T. (eds.) Life-Like Characters, pp. 163–185. Springer, Berlin Heidelberg (2004)

Detenber, B.H., Reeves, B.: A bio-informational theory of emotion: Motion and image size effects on viewers. J. Communi. **46**(3), 66–84 (1996)

Gris, I., Novick, D., Camacho, A., Rivera, D.A., Gutierrez, M., Rayon, A.: Recorded speech, virtual environments, and the effectiveness of embodied conversational agents. In: Bickmore, T., Marsella, S., Sidner, C. (eds.) IVA 2014. LNCS, vol. 8637, pp. 182–185. Springer, Heidelberg (2014)

Hostetter, A.B., Potthoff, A.L.: Effects of personality and social situation on representational gesture production. Gesture **12**(1), 62–83 (2012)

Lasseter, J.: Principles of traditional animation applied to 3D computer animation. ACM Siggraph Comput. Graphics **21**(4), 35–44 (1987)

Loomis, J.M., Knapp, J.M.: Visual perception of egocentric distance in real and virtual environments. Virtual Adapt. Environ. **11**, 21–46 (2003)

Neff, M., Wang, Y., Abbott, R., Walker, M.: Evaluating the effect of gesture and language on personality perception in conversational agents. In: Safonova, A. (ed.) IVA 2010. LNCS, vol. 6356, pp. 222–235. Springer, Heidelberg (2010)

Thomas, F., Johnston, O., Frank, T.: The Illusion of life: Disney Animation, pp. 306–312. Hyperion, New York (1995)

Vilhjálmsson, H.H.: Augmenting online conversation through automated discourse tagging. In: Proceedings of the 38th Annual Hawaii International Conference on Systems Science System Sciences, HICSS 2005, pp. 109a-109a. IEEE, January 2005

A Mark-Up Language and Interpreter for Interactive Scenes for Embodied Conversational Agents

David Novick[✉], Mario Gutierrez, Ivan Gris, and Diego A. Rivera

Department of Computer Science, The University of Texas at El Paso,
500 West University Avenue, El Paso, TX 79968-0518, USA
novick@utep.edu,
{mgutierrez19,darivera2}@miners.utep.edu,
ivangris4@gmail.com

Abstract. Our research seeks to provide embodied conversational agents (ECAs) with behaviors that enable them to build and maintain rapport with human users. To conduct this research, we need to build agents and systems that can maintain high levels of engagement with humans over multiple interaction sessions. These sessions can potentially extend to longer periods of time to examine long-term effects of the virtual agent's behaviors. Our current ECA interacts with humans in a game called "Survival on Jungle Island." Throughout this game, users interact with our agent across several scenes. Each scene is composed of a collection of speech input, speech output, gesture input, gesture output, scenery, triggers, and decision points. Our prior system was developed with procedural code, which did not lend itself to rapid extension to new game scenes. So to enable effective authoring of the scenes for the "Jungle" game, we adopted a declarative approach. We developed ECA middleware that parses, interprets, and executes XML files that define the scenes. This paper presents the XML coding scheme and its implementation and describes the functional back-end enabled by the scene scripts.

Keywords: Embodied conversational agents · Scene · Interpreter · Parser

1 Introduction

Authoring of scenes in which embodied conversational (ECAs) agents interact with humans currently has limited technological support. Scenes tend to be written directly as a computer program that specifies procedurally how the ECA should behave. As the number and complexity of scenes increases, writing the scenes becomes correspondingly more difficult and more prone to the sorts of problems associated with unstructured code. Scene developers could write better scenes, more quickly, if they had a way to write scenes less like a writing a computer program and more like writing a script for a play.

Writing scenes for ECAs, however, is much more complicated than writing a play because the scenes have to account for the technical details of the agents' inputs and outputs through speech and gesture and the technical details of the agent's virtual world. Ideally, ECAs can interact with human beings in such a way that they require

© Springer International Publishing Switzerland 2015
R. Shumaker and S. Lackey (Eds.): VAMR 2015, LNCS 9179, pp. 206–215, 2015.
DOI: 10.1007/978-3-319-21067-4_22

little to no human intervention to complete tasks and or to navigate conversations. But writing scenes for this is a daunting task, especially when the interaction space involves shared reality, where the virtual side of the interaction contains with which both agent and human can interact). High-functionality ECA systems have to include gesture recognition for task-based processes, gesture recognition for general annotation, branching, 3D movement in virtual space, speech, and other sophisticated features.

The research program of UTEP's Advanced aGEnt eNgagement Team (AGENT) seeks to provide ECAs with behaviors that enable them to build and maintain rapport with human users. To conduct this research, we need to build agents and systems that can maintain high levels of engagement with humans over multiple interaction sessions. These multiple sessions can potentially run over longer periods of time to examine long-term effects of the virtual agent's behaviors, so our research team has to write and implement many scenes.

Our team's most recent system, "Escape from the Castle of the Vampire King" (Gris et al. 2014), had a human and ECA play a game over two sessions. The program, though, was essentially a text-based game, such as Colossal Cave (Crowther et al. 1976) and Zork (Anderson and Galley 1985), realized with an ECA serving as narrator and with game-appropriate scenery. Dialog management could be handled by a relatively simple command interpretation loop. Although development of the "Vampire King" game involved writing a program complex enough to require eventual refactoring, the system was still simple enough that it could be developed with traditional software engineering techniques.

Our current system, "Survival on Jungle Island," is much more complex, though. It has already has eight scenes, and we expect it to have at least eight more, so that the game can provide extended interaction between human and ECA. Consequently, development of "Jungle Island" using the procedural representations and traditional software engineering techniques we used for the "Vampire King" game would have made writing the game's many scenes unreasonably complicated and burdensome. This meant finding a much more efficient way of developing scenes for ECA systems, a way that would enable us to write dozens of scenes with only modest technical effort beyond imagining the scenes' substantive content.

The requirements of developing systems like "Jungle Island" led us to adopt a declarative approach to authoring scenes for human-ECA interaction. In our approach, developers write scenes as scripts, using a mark-up language represented as XML tags, and these scripts are interpreted by middleware to drive the real-time system. In this paper we present our XML-based mark-up language for scripting human-ECA interactions, describe its implementation in middleware, describe the functional back-end enabled by the scene scripts, contrast our approach with existing standards such as SAIBA, FML, and BML, present an excerpt of a representative scene script, discuss the advantages and limitations of our approach, and outline related future work.

2   Scene Mark-Up Language

In this section we review the functionality of our mark-up language and its interpreter. We discuss each tag and its function.

Scripts using the mark-up language rely on twelve XML tags to identify agent behaviors and scene flow. A scene is a session of interaction, typically designed to take four to five minutes, that includes multiple human-ECA exchanges. Each exchange is called an episode, and the flow of the dialog within a scene is managed by choosing different episodes as a function of users' responses.

In developing our ECA system, we aimed for a design that promoted the sensation of immersion in the virtual world and the naturalness of the interaction between human and ECA. This led us to adopt a robust approach that would provide scene developers with control of scene progression by adaptively enabling or disabling speech-recogntion grammars for specific dialogs, gesture recognition libraries for specific gesture event, and control of what happens in the 3D scenes.

Authors specify scenes declaratively with XML tags such as *scene* (a collection of episodes), *episode* (a spoken and/or gestural interaction concluding with a control-flow decision), *do* (a gesture), *speak* (an utterance, specified via a string that can be output through a voice synthesizer, with an optional file name for a recorded version of the utterance), *pause* (for some number of seconds or fractions of seconds), *decide* (a conditional construct based on speech or gesture input from the human, go (to an episode), and *nextscene*. Table 1 presents the tags, their parameters, and their functions.

Table 1. Name, parameters, and functions of the tags

Tag	Parameters	Function
scene	scene name	Name of the file. Corresponds to a 3D environment in Unity with the same name
episode	episode name	Name of the episode. Episode tags can contain any tag except scene
do	emotion, hands, locomotion and upper body	These tags specify the agent's animations. You can specify an animation for the face (emotion), hands, lower body (locomotion) and upper body
speak	wav file and speech string	Contains either a.wav file name as a string, and/or the text of what the character will say
decide	speech id or gesture id	Makes a dialog branching decision based on user's speech or gesture input
go	target episode	jumps to a new episode upon the conclusion of the current one or after a decide tag conditions have been met
pause	seconds	Pauses the interaction. Useful to avoid further input while the agent performs a lengthy animation.
createrule	grammar rule name	Sets the name of a grammar rule.
tag	grammar tag	Serves as the name of a grammar slot to which several items are mapped to. Each grammar rule can have any number of tags
items	grammar items	Items are the words users
ruleCall	grammar rule name	Calls a previously defined grammar. After tags and items were provided, grammars can be reused in any section through rule calls
nextscene	scene name	The name of the new scene to be loaded

(There are also memory tags, such as store and recall, that connect to an SWI-Prolog back-end so that enables the ECA to maintain a dynamic dialog model.)

The scene interpreter, implemented in C# for convenient integration with other modules of the ECA system, parses the XML script, creates scene, episode, and action objects corresponding to the script's tagged elements, and sends the objects to the ECA's run-time system for execution.

Our approach contrasts with that of some other standards for specifying ECAs and their interactions. In particular, our system differs from the SAIBA framework (Zwiers et al. 2011) so that our ECAs can more easily integrate cognitive functions across what would be separate modules in a SAIBA-compliant system. SAIBA's strong modularity may not be appropriate for interaction that is fine-grained or requires rich contextual information (Lee et al. 2008). Similarly, the strong theoretical frameworks of BML (Kopp et al. 2006) and FML (Heylen et al. 2008) tend to impose cognitive and operational models that may be over-detailed and limiting for ECAs intended to explore the frontiers of human-agent interaction in practical terms. In a sense, architectures such as BML and FML handle the interaction from the agent's point of view. In our case, we need additional control over the environment and its navigation for actions by both the user and the agent.

Each scene is contained in a file. Inside each scene there can be any number of episodes. Each episode can contain tags that enable the agent to speak, listen, decide, act, and then jump to other episodes. In addition, each scene corresponds to a physical, navigable 3D representation of the environment. By changing scenes, one can change the scenery—and even the agent, if required.

Inputs from humans to the ECA system come through speech and gesture. The author's parameters for decide tag determine how the system processes these inputs and chooses the next episode in the scene. In Sects. 3 and 4, respectively, we discuss the handling of speech output and input, and gesture output.

3 Speech Handling

In this section we focus on the speech modules, and in particular on the *speak* and *decide* speech tags. We begin with the *speak* tag, which specifies the ECA's spoken language output. To illustrate the scripting language's handling of speech, Fig. 1 presents an abridged episode from an early scene in the "Survival on Jungle Island" game. In this episode, as in all others, *speak* tags contain both a written and optionally an audio version of the dialog specified; for example, in the script below the file decideu1.wav is a recorded version of the utterance. Because authors can use text strings without speech files, they can quickly prototype and test scenes using synthetic speech before committing to recordings. When executing behaviors indicated with a *speak* tag, the system uses the audio file name to find the audio for playback and has the agent lip-sync to the audio through a dialog tree, implemented as a separate module.

The *decide* tag signals a branching condition, which determines which will be the next episode. The agent asks a question and provides two or more possible answers. When the speech-recognition module recognizes one of the answers with high confidence, the system branches to a named episode, which is a parameter for the *go* tag.

```
<episode "splitpaths5">
    <do emotion "Neutral" hands "Idle" Locomotion "Default" upperBody "Thinking"
        isSpecial "false" special "none">
    <speak "splitpaths5u1.wav" "So, where to now? Should we take the grassy path
        which leads to the jungle or take the rocky path which leads to the
        mountains?">
    <pause "1">
    <decide speech>
        <createRule "paths">
            <go "grassy"> </go>
                <tag "grass">
                    <items "grassy path" "grassy" "lets take the grassy path"
                        "lets take the path no one has been to" "the grassy
                        path" "the jungle" "the grassy path, i am afraid of
                        the mountains" "the grassy path is safer" "the safest
                        path" "the left one" "to the left" the one on the
                        left">
                </tag>
            <go "rocky"> </go>
                <tag "rock">
                    <items "rocky path" "rocky" "mountains" "the mountain
                        path" "the rocky road" "the right one" "the one on the
                        right" "let's seek altitude" "let's go to the moun-
                        tains" "we should take the rocky path" "the rocky path
                        to the mountain">
                </tag>
        </rule>
    </decide>
```

Fig. 1. A scene section using our markup-language. This script causes the agent to look thoughtful while asking a question (through a predefined audio file). It then pauses for a second to prevent the speech recognizer from listening to the playing audio file. Finally, a grammar is created inside a *decide* tag, which enables users to progress to the next episode or scene depending on their verbal expressions.

In the example in Fig. 1, "grassy" and "rocky" refer to other episodes of the scene, to which control will pass depending on the human's answer to the ECA's question.

To improve reusability, the *decide* tag can transfer control to any episode in the scene, enabling authors to create dialogs that loop until certain criteria are met. The grammar itself contains every word or phrase that can be recognized by the system and is not affected by the current state of the conversations. A speech-recognition grammar is in turn composed of rules. Each rule defines what words or phrases should be recognized during a particular dialog state, which is what we define as episode. As the control flow swaps the episode, the rule changes as well to enable a different set of available words for recognition. The idea behind this rule-based grammar, in which the rules act as speech-recognition separators for episodes, is to enable only a small subset of the whole grammar to be active at any given time. This in turn helps improve the recognition by not engaging in grammar over-coverage.

By creating a rule, an author can refer to a speech-recognition grammar in future episodes without the need to declare the grammar again. In other words, if a rule has been declared, it can be called and reused again from the script by just specifying the name. If the rule is being used for the first time, its name, tags, and items must be declared. The only requirement is that the grammar has been used at least once before being reused. This is the function of the *createrule* tag. Figure 2 shows a rule initialized from the script and a demonstration of how to reuse it, and Fig. 3 presents the standard grammar xml file that is created based on the script declaration.

```
<<scene "beach2">
    <episode "beach2c">
        <do emotion "Neutral" hands "Idle" Locomotion "StandUp" upperBody
            "Pointing" isSpecial "false" special "none">
        <speak "beach2au2.wav" "Here, let me help you up. Grab my hand.">
        <decide gesture>
            <go "trapped"> "Grab Hand" </go>
        </decide>
    </episode>
    <episode "trapped">
    . . .
    </episode>
</scene>
```

Fig. 2. In this scene the agent uses a combination of animations to extend its hand to the user. The agent then prompts the user to grab her hand through a decide tag. With only one option, it is a required gesture to progress through the interaction. After the user performs a "Grab Hand" the control flow decides on the next episode to execute. At the end, the scene changes. On the virtual side, a new environment is loaded.

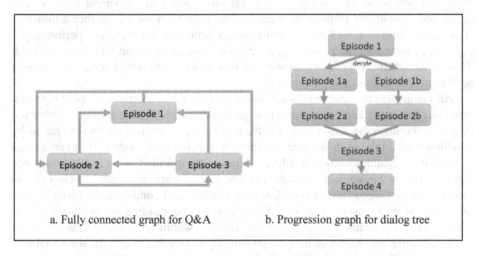

a. Fully connected graph for Q&A   b. Progression graph for dialog tree

Fig. 3. Graphs of episodes and transitions showing different styles of dialog paths

4 Gesture Handling

In this section we explain the implementation of the tags for performing and recognizing actions. In the example presented in Fig. 2, the interaction begins in scene "beach2" with the episode "start." The *do* tag accesses the animation tree to produce a blend of animations to produce the intended motion for the agent (Gris, Rivera & Novick 2015). The system uses a layered approach to animation that enables developers to specify the agent's actions with enough control to represent the desired situation and emotion but with enough abstraction as to avoid getting lost in detailed descriptions of animations. Movements of the body are specified in layers for loco-motion, emotion, upper-body, and hands.

The episode in Fig. 2 uses a *locomotion* layer, which enables the agent to walk around, move to the next waypoint, sit, crouch, crawl, or do any other movement that requires character displacement across the scene or lower body animations that change the current stance. In the example, the agent starts the scene by moving to a standing position, which is a valid transition because the default starting point for this particular scene was specified as crouching, even though agents generally start scenes in a standing position.

The *emotion* layer controls the configuration of the agent's face. All transitions are weighted and transitioned gradually between emotions; the transitions are handled by the system's additional animation-tree modules.

The *hands* parameter indicates the position or shape of the fingers. This is used for special circumstances such as pointing or making representational hand gestures.

Finally, the *upperBody* parameter specifies the action of the torso and arms. In the design of our ECA system and the mark-up language, we sought to avoid unnecessary or overspecialized animations. In the case of the scene in Fig. 2, the agent is extending its hand towards the user to help him or her cross a gap in the virtual scenery. The upper-body parameter is pointing because this enables reuse of another animation. A pointing animation includes an outstretched arm; without the hand performing a pointing gesture, too, the pointing gesture is just an extended arm with an open hand. This is one of the ways in which work is reused to create new interactions without additional low-level development work.

All parameters from these tags are parsed and stored to handle new agent gestures, providing flexibility and expandability of gesture libraries without having to delve too deeply in the implementation to access them. These animation libraries are created by combining multiple exchangeable parameters for separate body-part layers. After parsing, these gestures become available as they were specified, in an ordered sequence when called by the episode in control of the dialog state, however, developers can incorporate (outside of the markup language declaration) conditions or variables that affect the agent's gesture behavior depending on the runtime observations of the interaction. For example, a developer can specify within an episode a gesture con-taining surprise for the upper body animation layer, and happiness for the facial ani-mation layer. If, however, this normally happy moment is obscured by a series of user transgressions that the developer kept track of throughout the interaction, the "do" tag queue can be accessed at runtime and animations can be overwritten. This provides additional control over the otherwise static declaration, although it requires an addi-tional abstraction layer between the rendering application and the xml interpreter that we do not provide.

For gestures, the *decide* tag connects to the ECA system's gesture-recognition module. In episode in Fig. 2, the agent waits for the user to extend his or her hand towards the screen. The gesture is then captured and processed by a Kinect and our gesture-recognition software. Similar to the way the decide tag works for speech, this list can contain several gestures leading to different episodes, depending on the gesture performed by the human. Depending on the gesture that the user performs, the *decide* tag will transfer control to the appropriate episode. This is also useful to create activities that require a gesture response to progress. Gestures are specific to the application; in the case of our most recent ongoing project, they represent survival activities, such as lighting a fire, spear fishing, and signaling for help.

5 Conclusion

We developed an XML-based scene markup language that supports a variety of features for speech, gesture, memory, and scene handling in human-ECA interaction. Our approach limits detail of gesture animation in favor of abstraction and reusability. We focused on making the markup language extendable and adaptable for use as mid-layer software for agents using different architectures.

The scene markup language enables authors of scripts to develop dialog paths that can vary depending on the nature of the application. In a Q&A application, the dialog path will revisit states multiple times and in any order, as shown in Fig. 3a, as a fully connected graph. In a storytelling application, the dialog path will follow a decision-based progression, as shown in Fig. 3b, as a dialog tree. The markup language enables both forms to be created by adjusting parameters and rearranging the episode order.

In the markup language, tags are flexible and new tags can be added; however, changes made to the structure will require the users to update their scripts. Our language enforces consistency but does not provide it automatically.

We have successfully tested our mark-up language in two different projects. First, we wrote scripts for eight scenes that take advantage of scene transition, episode transition, gesture management, and dialog management. Second, we updated our previous agents to our new architecture. Where our previous agents took months to develop, the updated versions were recreated from scratch in a few hours, including additional animation, gesture and lip-sync features.

A major advantage of this approach is the relative ease of authoring scenes. Rather than having to write procedural code, which is typically hard to understand, modify, and debug, scene authors can create scenes declaratively and more easily reuse or adapt episodes. Undergraduate computer science students in a course on innovation in technology were able write scripts efficiently, producing a dozen scenes in which they were able to express creativity in the human-agent interaction rather than be concerned with implementation.

Our approach has limitations of design and implementation. In terms of design, our approach is fundamentally limited by its orientation toward scene-driven interaction. For human-ECA systems that are more about spontaneous, less-constrained interaction than episodic storytelling, an FML/BML approach might be more appropriate. In terms of implementation, we found that rewriting scripts to conform to updates in the specification of the markup language or changes to our file-naming conventions turned out to be tedious. Improvements to the system would include a tool for automatic updating of scripts to conform to changes in the scripting specification and a tool to update filename changes when you update the script. For example, if the naming convention for audio files changes, the tool would spare the author from having to update manually all names for both the scripts and the files. As another example, we plan to update the tags associated with the grammar rules so that the tag names are createRule and callRule (instead of ruleCall) and so that these tags close with/createRule and/callRule (instead of/rule, which is an artifact from system's iterative development).

A second implementation improvement involves extending the availability of gesture interpretation. In addition to detecting gestures specified in the decide tags, our system also tracks the human's conversational gestures throughout the interaction session outside the decide tags. These include gestures such as crossed arms, normal stance, hand(s) on hip, hand(s) on face, and many others. Currently, these gestures are recognized through a background process that produces a gesture-annotation file for research of human-ECA interaction. It might be helpful to authors to integrate this annotation functionality to the markup language declarations so that they could access the human's gestures in real time.

A third implementation improvement would provide a higher-level authoring tool. Currently, authors create scene scripts by writing XML code directly, producing files similar to those in Figs. 1 and 2. Our plans for future work include developing a WYSWYG authoring system for the scripts that would generate the XML files automatically. This would enable non-technical authors to develop new scene scripts. As it is, we use the current version of the system for generating new scenes for the "Survival on Jungle Island" game and will be using the system to create our next-generation applications.

References

Anderson, T., Galley, S.: The History of Zork. The New Zork Times, New York (1985)

Crowther, W., Woods, D., Black, K.: Colossal cave adventure. Computer Game. Intellect Books, Bristol (1976)

Rayon, A., Gris, I., Novick, D., Camacho, A., Rivera, D.A., Gutierrez, M.: Recorded speech, virtual environments, and the effectiveness of embodied conversational agents. In: Bickmore, T., Marsella, S., Sidner, C. (eds.) IVA 2014. LNCS, vol. 8637, pp. 182–185. Springer, Heidelberg (2014)

Gris, I., Novick, D., Rivera, D.A., and Gutierrez, M.: UTEP's AGENT architecture. In: IVA 2014 Workshop on Architectures and Standards for IVAs, Intelligent Virtual Agents (2014), Boston, August 2014

Gris, I., Rivera, D.A., Novick, D.: Animation guidelines for believable embodied conversational agent gestures In: HCII 2015, Seattle, 2–7 August 2015 (in press)

Heylen, D., Kopp, S., Marsella, S.C., Pelachaud, C., Vilhjálmsson, H.H.: The next step towards a function markup language. In: Prendinger, H., Lester, J.C., Ishizuka, M. (eds.) IVA 2008. LNCS (LNAI), vol. 5208, pp. 270–280. Springer, Heidelberg (2008)

Kopp, S., Krenn, B., Marsella, S.C., Marshall, A.N., Pelachaud, C., Pirker, H., Thórisson, K.R., Vilhjálmsson, H.H.: Towards a common framework for multimodal generation: the behavior markup language. In: Gratch, J., Young, M., Aylett, R.S., Ballin, D., Olivier, P. (eds.) IVA 2006. LNCS (LNAI), vol. 4133, pp. 205–217. Springer, Heidelberg (2006)

Lee, J., DeVault, D., Marsella, S., Traum, D.: Thoughts on FML: behavior generation in the virtual human communication architecture. In: AAMAS (2008)

Novick, D., Gris, I.: Building rapport between human and eca: a pilot study. In: Kurosu, M. (ed.) HCI 2014, Part II. LNCS, vol. 8511, pp. 472–480. Springer, Heidelberg (2014)

Zwiers, J., van Welbergen, H., Reidsma, D.: Continuous interaction within the SAIBA framework. In: Vilhjálmsson, H.H., Kopp, S., Marsella, S., Thórisson, K.R. (eds.) IVA 2011. LNCS, vol. 6895, pp. 324–330. Springer, Heidelberg (2011)

Displays for Effective Human-Agent Teaming: Evaluating Attention Management with Computational Models

Cory A. Rieth[✉], Maia B. Cook, and Mary K. Ngo

Pacific Science and Engineering Group, San Diego, USA
CoryRieth@pacific-science.com

Abstract. In information-dense work domains, the effectiveness of display formats in drawing attention to task-relevant information is critical. In this paper, we demonstrate a method to evaluate this capability for on-screen indicators used to proactively monitor multiple automated agents. To estimate the effectiveness of indicator formats in drawing attention to emerging problems, we compared the visual salience of indicators, as measured by computational models, to task-relevant attributes needed during proactive monitoring. The results revealed that standard formats generally do not draw attention to the information needed to identify emerging problems in multi-indicator displays, and validated the success of formats designed to more closely map task-relevant information to visual salience. We additionally report an extended saliency-based monitoring model to predict task performance from saliency and discuss implications for broader design and application.

Keywords: Information visualization · Intelligent and agent systems · Evaluation methods and techniques

1 Introduction

Across many work domains, humans must maintain awareness of multiple dynamic information sources relating to complex processes, automation, autonomous vehicles, information networks, or multi-agent teams. Human-computer interface (HCI) designers are faced with difficult and important decisions regarding what information to convey and in what format to convey it. While more information is often regarded as beneficial, the amount of information presented must be measured against the limitations of human attention. Basic research has characterized the limitations of human attention and motivated consideration of attention management in HCI design [1, 2]. Our goal is to provide a scientific basis for the design and pairing of indicator formats with task needs to reduce the load placed on human attention by multiple parameters that must be monitored. In the companion to this work [3], we provide a qualitative analysis and experimental evaluation of several standard indicator formats, as well as novel formats. In this paper, we bring a new rigor to the study of attention management by applying computational models of human attention to illustrate and objectively evaluate how well different indicator formats highlight task-relevant information and support task performance.

© Springer International Publishing Switzerland 2015
R. Shumaker and S. Lackey (Eds.): VAMR 2015, LNCS 9179, pp. 216–227, 2015.
DOI: 10.1007/978-3-319-21067-4_23

Information-dense displays can be more effectively managed if task-relevant information is more salient, and perceptually "pops out" from the background. We refer to the relationship between the importance of information and how well it automatically draws human attention as *salience mapping*. Improving and evaluating salience mapping requires both knowing what information is important for a task (and when it is important), and applying or creating indicator formats with features that draw attention to important information. One common example is stoplight coding, which typically highlights information as yellow or red when a threshold is crossed. However, mapping salience to threshold categories does not discriminate between worsening and resolving trends, and does not help users prioritize within caution or warning categories. The mapping of salience is key to making it useful for the task at hand; this example raises the question how salience can be more effectively mapped to draw attention to different aspects of status for different task needs.

Finding information needed for specific tasks requires a search through available information. An established body of research on visual search [4, 5] has experimentally identified many visual features that facilitate efficient searches for targets surrounded by large numbers of distractors. These efficient searches occur when targets are clearly differentiated by basic features such as color, intensity, orientation, size, shape, motion, and luminance onset/change [6, 7]. Contrast in these basic features between an item and surround make the item salient. Salience in this sense describes the attention-drawing properties resulting from visual features independent of a particular task, referred to more formally as bottom-up salience.

Study and evaluation of salience mapping requires an objective measurement of salience. One method is to use existing computational models of image salience developed by attention researchers, e.g. [8–12]. These models are evaluated by their ability to predict where humans will look in images. Evaluating salience through computational models is faster and less costly than repeated eye movement studies and is additionally robust to top-down task strategies involving covert shifts of attention. These models compute the salience at each pixel in an input image to predict eye-fixations from visual features in the input. We applied these models to measure the salience of indicator formats displaying information varying in priority, and assess salience mapping as the relationship between priority and measured salience. Applying these models also served to hone our own understanding of how effectively indicator formats map salience. We have explored and applied several models (Graph-Based Visual Salience [11], SUN [10], and CovSal [9]) to indicator formats in custom displays and to display stimuli from our previous experiments [3, 13].

We focus on the task of monitoring a large team of automated agents through multiple continuously-valued variables presented in a bank of visual indicators. The ultimate goal of this task is to identify emerging problems before they manifest, termed proactive monitoring [14–16]. Proactive monitoring becomes increasingly important with larger teams and more information. Two attributes required for successful proactive monitoring of a single variable are: the current deviation from steady state value (current deviation), and trending away from steady state (worsening trends) [15]. Applying the above research on salience and visual search, proactive monitoring should be facilitated by making higher current deviations and faster worsening trends more salient. In the rest of this paper we demonstrate the application of salience modeling to measure how effectively indicator formats direct attention to these attributes. Section 2 describes a broad analysis of salience mapping in ten indicator formats, and Sect. 3 applies the approach in more detail to stimuli from human performance experiments, and extends it to capture task performance.

2 Applying Salience Modeling to Evaluate Salience Mapping

Here we give a brief overview of Fig. 1, followed by discussion of the relative priority of the key time points depicted in the figure, an introduction of the formats tested, salience modeling details, and further discussion. Figure 1 compares several formats (as rows) over multiple points in time (as columns) as a problem emerges and recovers. The top of Fig. 1 depicts an illustrative trajectory for a single agent plotted over time relative to the desired normal value (50), caution thresholds (≥ 75 and ≤ 25), and warning thresholds (≥ 80 and ≤ 20). The agent's trajectory starts at a normal state, worsens, and then recovers. Key time points labeled with capital letters were chosen to illustrate different degrees of task importance. Below, the input images for each format

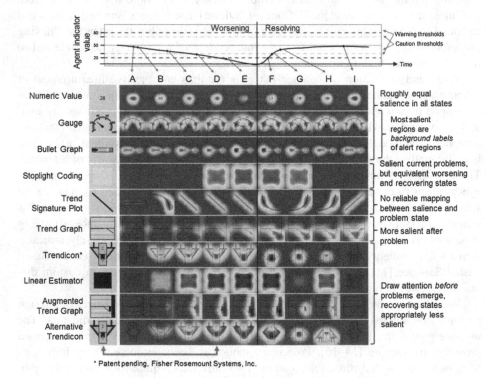

* Patent pending, Fisher Rosemount Systems, Inc.

Fig. 1. Salience of different indicator formats at time points along an illustrative trajectory. The graph at the top illustrates the trajectory over time and the time points used. The depiction of each format was run through the GBVS model [11] surrounded by normal state indicators of the same format, and the output salience map is depicted overlaid with the input. The far left column left shows the raw image input corresponding to column D.

and time point are shown overlaid with the measured salience maps (see Fig. 1 in [3] for the raw images). Formats with a strong positive relationship between priority and measured salience have higher salience at time points with emerging worsening trends or high current deviations. A lack of relationship between salience and these attributes indicates poor salience mapping and suggests that search through a large array of indicators will be difficult.

In Fig. 1, the time point labeled A has a normal current value, is relatively steady, and therefore does not merit concern. Points B-E are all worsening and have increasing deviations from normal, reaching a caution state by D and a warning state by E. Accordingly, these time points are increasingly concerning, in order from B to E. At point F, the value is starting to return to normal, but is still in a warning state. At point G the agent is in a caution state, but is headed back to normal. Points H and I show the value resolving. Note that point H is resolving very quickly, and depending on agent characteristics, may be in danger of overshooting normal. Overall, we consider the rough order in decreasing concern to be E, F, D, C, H, G, B, I, and finally A; depending on assumptions about agent dynamics, slight variations in this ordering are sensible, particularly positions H and G.

The indicator formats analyzed included standard formats used widely across domains (Numeric Values, Gauges, Bullet Graphs [17], Stoplight Coding, and Trend Graphs), formats proposed in the literature (Trend Signature Plots, [18]), and novel formats we have designed specifically to include trend information and to map critical information to salience (Trendicons, patent pending, Fisher Rosemount Systems, Inc., Linear Estimators, Predictive Trendicons, and Augmented Trend Graphs – see [3] for more detailed descriptions of all formats). Note that although Stoplight Coding is often combined with other formats for attention management, we evaluated it separately to cleanly assess the properties inherent to each format. Each of these different formats provides access to different types of information, at differing levels of fidelity, and using different features, to support proactive monitoring to varying degrees, as discussed elsewhere [3].

The details of computational models of salience differ, but most operate in a broadly similar fashion, given that they are all rooted in a common understanding of low-level visual processing. First, the input image is decomposed into a feature-based representation, for example Gabor filters of varying spatial scales and orientations, and/or hue in a normalized color space. Then contrast with surrounding features is calculated, normalized, and combined into an overall "salience map". In general, the output was similar between models we tested, with some explainable discrepancies (e.g. CovSal [9] rarely found the lines in graphs salient, because it has very coarse orientation resolution). For brevity, in this paper we only show output from the Graph-Based Visual Salience (GBVS) model [11]. We used the default parameters of GBVS, with the exception of increasing the processing resolution and number of orientation channels. Additionally, to allow meaningful comparisons between different salience maps, we modified it to output raw as opposed to normalized salience maps. To obtain a relative measure of saliency, each indicator format at each key point in time was run through the GBVS model surrounded by eight normal indicators of the same format (identical to time point A). Overall salience readings were normalized within each format type for presentation. The GBVS output is overlaid on the indicator format image as heatmaps, with hotter colors representing greater salience.

The analysis of salience mapping across formats revealed several important find-ings, discussed next. In particular, many formats fail to relate current deviations or worsening trends to salience. Only a few formats successfully map current deviations and worsening trends to salience. Throughout this review we highlight specific features that draw attention and how they do or do not relate to the key information attributes.

Failures of Relating Current Deviations to Salience. Current deviation is not related to salience for most of the formats reviewed, including Numeric Values, Gauges, Bullet Graphs, Trend Signature Plots, and Trend Graphs. While there seems to be some increased salience for the most deviant current values in the Gauges and Bullet Graphs, salience is driven even more strongly by the colored regions and dark bars. While color-coded critical regions are initially helpful as an intuitive label, they distract from dynamic task needs. The Trend Graph does increase in salience leading up to the problem, but it remains salient after the problem as resolved. Although these formats are often combined with Stoplight Coding, which is notably salient once the caution or warning threshold is crossed, Stoplight Coding effectively only provides a binary indicator of deviation through saliency.

Failures of Relating Worsening Trends to Salience. Worsening trend was unrelated to salience for Numeric Values, Gauges, Bullet Graphs, Stoplight Coding, Trend Signature Plots, or Trend Graphs. The salience of Stoplight Coding does not dis-criminate the newly emerging problem at time points D and E from the resolving one at F and G. Trend Signature Plots do draw attention based on trend characteristics, as do Trend Graphs with orientation or alignment. However, similar to Stoplight Coding, they do not distinguish worsening from resolving trends. In fact, Trend Graphs are more salient *after* the problem has peaked, when the event is in the graphs history.

Successes in Salience Mapping. The bottom four formats in Fig. 1 (Trendicons, Linear Estimator, Alternative Trendicons, and Augmented Trend Graphs) were all designed to relate current deviation and worsening trends to salience and generally balance saliency between the two. However there are some interesting differences in the design strategies used, which we will review in turn. Both Trendicon formats incorporate separate features to map to different task-relevant attributes. The contrast of the center deviation bar in Trendicons directly draws attention for more deviant values. The shape coding of the direction arrow creates different orientations, and especially draws attention when the Trendicon border thickens as it is worsening (or darkened in the Alternative Trendicon, see below). The salience model shows that the steady state Trendicon at time point A draws little attention. However for the worsening indicator of time point B, the thick outline and jet trials are much more salient. The more deviant indicators at time points C through E also draw attention, increasingly with the more extreme current values. Deviant indicators that have stopped worsening, and started to return to normal at time points F through I are comparatively less salient (although still more salient than a steady normal state Trendicon).

The Linear Estimator, like the Stoplight Coding, is not in and of itself a format, but intended as an augmentation. The Linear Estimator and its underlying automation integrates task-relevant features and maps them directly to more salient intensities. However, while Stoplight Coding maps color to a few discrete current states based on current deviation, the Linear Estimator maps intensity to graded predictions of future state, incorporating both current deviation and trend information. This has a number of effects. The choice of intensity rather than color is non-consequential, except that it helps avoid overusing the color, reserving it for critical situations. Using a graded coding helps prioritize multiple indicators. More critically for proactive monitoring is that the Linear Estimator maps intensities to predictions of future state. To the extent these predictions are accurate, the Linear Estimator preemptively warns users about likely problems through salience (here the model driving those predictions is rather simple, but analogous schemes could be used for more complex models). The salience predicted by GBVS [11] roughly matches intensity, and is generally higher for the indicators in a problematic current state (time points E and F), followed by those leading up to a problematic current state (B through D, in order), those resolving (G through H), and those in a steady normal state (A and I). Note the increased salience at time point H is caused by a prediction (in this case incorrect) that the indicator will overshoot normal. The Alternative Trendicon and Augmented Trend Graph are combinations of the Linear Estimator with Trendicons (replacing the thickness-coding of worsening with the intensity from the Linear Estimator) and Trend Graphs (augmenting the Trend Graph with a Linear Estimator bar to the right, a current deviation bar, and faded history). Like their parent formats, the Alternative Trendicon and Augmented Trend Graph map current deviation and worsening trends to salience.

3   Applying Salience Modeling to Experimental Data

In a recent study [13] we empirically assessed human monitoring performance for a subset of the formats in Fig. 1. We compared the effectiveness of Numeric Values, Trend Graphs, and Trendicons in supporting proactive problem detections in 4, 12 and 24 simultaneously-monitored dynamic indicators. The results demonstrated significant performance improvements in the form of earlier and more accurate detections of emerging problems for Trendicon over the standard Numeric Values and Trend Graphs. We hypothesized that the performance improvements were due to the reliable mapping of visual salience to important attributes for proactive monitoring in Trendicons. Here, we present application of the GBVS [11] model to demonstrate quantitatively that Trendicons do indeed map salience to the core task properties of proactive monitoring more effectively than the other formats. We also present a new salience-based monitoring (SBM) model that relates salience to human performance.

3.1   Detailed Salience Mapping Evaluation

We ran each frame of the experiment stimuli [13] through the GBVS [11] model to obtain a measurement of salience over time for each indicator and format, and related the salience to the depicted information over time. We used the median salience over the entire indicator region as a measure of indicator salience.

Figure 2 illustrates changes in saliency over time for the tested formats. The figure shows an indicator value from an experiment trial containing a critical event

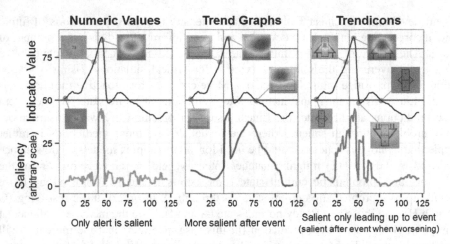

Fig. 2. Relationship between an identical indicator trajectory (top) and measured salience (bottom) for Numeric Value (left), Trend Graphs (middle) and Trendicon (right) formats. The trajectory consists of normal behavior, with an inserted anomalous event and recovery. Callouts show the model output overlaid on the input at various key time points. The vertical gray line indicates the onset of the critical event and associated stoplight alert.

(top) plotted against the time course of measured salience for the Numeric Value, Trend Graph, and Trendicon formats (bottom). The salience model output is overlaid on the indicator display image at key points in time. All formats start with roughly equivalent salience, and show a sharp increase in salience due to stoplight alerts that appeared when a critical threshold was crossed. The saliency of the Numeric Value format is variable, but gives no indication of the impending problem. For the Trend Graph format, there is an increase in salience leading up to the alert event. However, the salience increases after the alert as the event moves into the graphs history. While this would not be a problem for a single indicator, with many indicators this would now serve as a distraction. In contrast, Trendicons jump in salience earlier, more definitively, and continue increasing in salience up through the onset of the alert. After the indicator recovers, salience goes back down to baseline (increasing for short periods of time as the indicator worsens again).

Figure 3 shows how the salience model output relates to deviation from normal value and trend over the entire experiment. The figure shows scatterplots of the salience of indicators at a 1,764 sampled points from indicators used in the experiment (spacing samples in time and excluding time points with alerts present) between the measured salience and the actual deviation from normal (top) and a measure of worsening (the slope from a linear regression over the past 10 time steps, with sign set to be positive for slopes heading toward normal, and to be negative for slopes heading away from normal, shown at the bottom). The inset numbers are Spearman rank correlation statistics and associated p values. Although significant for current deviation, Numeric Values and Trend Graphs showed very weak correlations with current deviation and worsening trends (in terms of ρ) compared to those found with Trendicons.

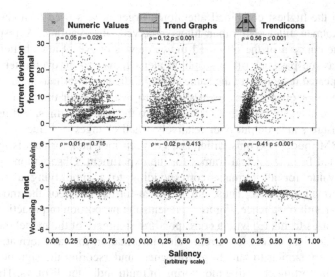

Fig. 3. Scatter plots of measured indicator format salience at non-alert times versus current deviation (top) and trend (bottom). Regression lines are plotted in the background and inset values are Spearman's rank correlation statistics and associated p-values.

3.2 Salience-Based Monitoring (SBM) Model

Above, we showed how the salience modeling can be used to assess the mapping of salience to task-relevant information. While the use of salience models can help inform predictions about the effectiveness of different formats, they do not make a connection between salience and actual monitoring performance. For example, they do not explain variations in performance with different numbers of indicators ("span of control" effects) [13]. To explain behavior, a computational model of how people use the salience information to make responses is needed. We developed a salience-based monitoring (SBM) model that uses the salience model output to decide what indicators to observe. The SBM model assumes equal information access across formats, but differential salience, measured by running GBVS [11] on actual frames from the experiment. This allows us to test how well differential salience alone explains our experimental results [13]. We do not claim that the SBM model captures the process by which humans complete this task, but that it is a computational demonstration of the rational consequences of differential salience on performance.

The SBM model maintains internal beliefs about each indicator in the task through a Kalman filter that estimates the indicator's value, velocity, and acceleration given intermittent value observations. Kalman model parameters were trained with fully observed practice trials. As a measure of the model's "concern", its internal beliefs were used to calculate the probability that each indicator would cross threshold in the next second. Every 250 ms (the time between updates of the experiment, but also close to the average human inter-saccade time), the salience of each indicator and the model's concern were combined as a measure of attentional urgency. At each time step, a veridical observation of current value (but not velocity or acceleration) of the indicator with the highest combined attentional urgency was used to update the corresponding Kalman filter. No other filters received observations. A response was recorded if the concern of the observed indicator was above .9 after belief updating. The model was run passively, thus stoplight alerts remained on even after responses. To prevent repeated responses to the same critical indicator, after making a response no further responses or observations were allowed to that indicator until after 1 s. These parameters were coarsely set with consideration to the task dynamics, and investigated by hand to ensure stable output over relatively small changes in value.

To the SBM model, the only difference between indicator formats is the salience values computed from the actual frames for the experiment. Observations yielded the true current value for all formats, corresponding to a simplifying assumption of complete information access. Thus, any between-format effect of the model can be explained as a result of salience. Figure 4 presents the proportion of proactive, reactive, and miss responses from [13] with a corresponding summary of the model output. Even with full and identical access to current value information for each format, the model behavior was very similar to human performance, underscoring the significant impact of salience in supporting proactive monitoring of multi-indicator displays. These results fall out of the calculated salience of indicators in the experiment combined with the belief update and response components of the model.

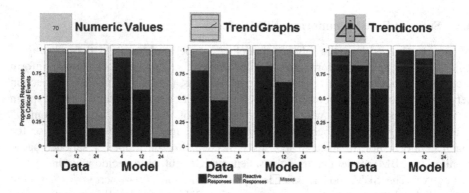

Fig. 4. Proportion of proactive responses as measured behaviorally [13] and from the SBM model. *Proactive detections* were responses for the next-critical indicator that occurred before it crossed critical threshold; *reactive responses* were responses for an indicator after it crossed threshold.

4   Discussion

In this work we have explored the effectiveness of visual indicator formats to manage human attention in information-dense environments by relating the importance of individual indicators to perceptual salience. We have demonstrated how computational models can be used to quickly and objectively evaluate salience mapping and also capture the impacts of indicator formats on human performance. Additionally, this work has highlighted several important considerations for designers of indicator formats, both for visual displays mediating communication between humans and agents, visual displays more broadly, and communication through other sensory modalities.

There are a variety of potential further applications of these computational models. They can easily be applied to whole displays to highlight how background and organization affects the relative salience of individual indicators. In addition to the results presented here, we have used the salience and SBM models to make predictions about task variations (e.g., speeding up or slowing down the pace of the task, prioritization in intermittent monitoring as in [3]), the contributions of specific attributes to overall salience (e.g. the worsening feature of Trendicons), and performance with other indicator formats. The models could also be extended to monitor and adapt salience in real time to enable different prioritization schemes for different situations (e.g. lowering the contrast of lower priority alerts so higher priority alerts stand out). However, we caution against designing "to the model" by iteratively adjusting designs to maximize a model-derived measure. The models should be considered as an evaluation tool and used in conjunction with other evaluation methods.

The above analysis and modeling work has led us to a greater appreciation for the power of intentionally mapping salience to task-relevant information through format design. In practice, this is unfortunately more difficult than it sounds. The foundational design step for making relevant information salient is identifying the relevant information for the task or tasks being performed. This task context is important since even subtle changes in the task or how the task is performed can alter the importance of information, or how much salience is needed to direct attention. For example, with displays used intermittently or peripherally, small changes in salience, such as those in the Linear Estimator described here, will go unnoticed longer than coarse ones, such as those in the Trendicons or Stoplight Coding.

Once task-relevant attributes have been identified, designers can depict these attributes using visual elements that relate priority to salience, exploiting the basic features identified by attention researchers [19] (color, intensity, orientation, size, shape, motion, luminance change, etc.). The designs considered here illustrate two strategies for doing so. In the Trendicons, a configural strategy [20] is used, maintaining separable features that contribute to overall salience, making the format more flexible to multiple overlapping tasks requiring component information access. The Linear Estimator takes a more integrative approach by combining raw current deviation and trend into a composite measure of importance for a specific task (although it is intended to be combined with other formats providing separable information access, as in the Alternative Trendicon and Augmented Trend Graph).

The salience mapping of individual formats must also be considered in the context of the salience within an entire display. Salient features are salient only because they stand out from the background. Consequently, indicators can more effectively and more precisely draw attention when background elements are less salient. In our observations of model salience maps, even subtle attributes like excessive outlines noticeably reduce the salience of orientation. Removing these elements when possible, as also encouraged by information rich display design [21], can increase opportunities for useful salience mapping using more subtle features like orientation and alignment.

Finally, while we have motivated this work in the context of visual displays as a method of communication, the concepts of salience and salience mapping, as well as our general approach, can be applied to other communication methods (e.g. verbal or auditory cues). Carefully and sparingly using salient auditory, tactile, or multimodal features to draw attention to important task information against a potentially noisy background, is analogous to the approach we have outlined for visual indicators.

5 Conclusion

As humans are expected to work with more information, the effectiveness of indicator formats in directing attention becomes increasingly important. In this paper, drawing from decades of research on attention, we showed how computational models can help evaluate the extent to which indicator formats draw attention to task-relevant information, and can be used to predict the performance impact of different formats. Our results are broadly applicable to the monitoring of multiple information sources and our approach can help reveal the strengths and weaknesses of existing displays, guide the design of new formats, and can even be extended to other sensory modalities. With increases in available information and operator responsibility, HCI designers must balance access to information with the limitations of human attention. We hope that this work provides examples and tools to help achieve that balance.

Acknowledgements. This work was sponsored by the Office of Naval Research, Human & Bioengineered Systems (ONR 341), program officers Dr. Julie L. Marble and Dr. Jeffrey G. Morrison under contract N00014-12-C-0244. The authors thank Mr. Dan Manes and Mrs. Heather Kobus of Pacific Science & Engineering for technical assistance, and Dr. Harvey Smallman for helpful comments. The views expressed are those of the authors and do not reflect the official policy or position of the Office of Naval Research, Department of Defense, or the US Government.

References

1. Wickens, C.D., Hollands, J.G.: Engineering Psychology and Human Performance. Prentice Hall, New Jersey (2000)
2. St. John, M.F., Smallman, H.S.: Staying up to speed: four design principles for maintaining and recovering situation awareness. J. Cogn. Eng. Decis. Making **2**, 118–139 (2008)
3. Cook, M.B., Rieth, C.A., Ngo, M.K.: Displays for effective human-agent teaming: the role of information availability and attention management. In: Shumaker, R., Lackey, S. (eds.) VAMR 2015. LNCS, vol. 9179. Springer, Heidelberg (2015)
4. Treisman, A., Gelade, G.: A feature-integration theory of attention. Cogn. Psychol. **12**, 97–136 (1980)
5. Eckstein, M.P.: Visual search: a retrospective. J. Vis. **11**, 14 (2011)
6. Duncan, J., Humphreys, G.W.: Visual search and stimulus similarity. Psychol. Rev. **96**, 433–458 (1989)
7. Wolfe, J.M.: The rules of guidance in visual search. In: Kundu, M.K., Mitra, S., Mazumdar, D., Pal, S.K. (eds.) PerMIn 2012. LNCS, vol. 7143, pp. 1–10. Springer, Heidelberg (2012)

8. Itti, L., Koch, C., Niebur, E.: A model of saliency-based visual attention for rapid scene analysis. IEEE Trans. Pattern Anal. Mach. Intell. **20**, 1254–1259 (1998)
9. Erdem, E., Erdem, A.: Visual saliency estimation by nonlinearly integrating features using region covariances. J. Vis. **13**, 1–20 (2013)
10. Zhang, L., Tong, M.H., Marks, T.K., Shan, H., Cottrell, G.W.: SUN: a bayesian framework for saliency using natural statistics. J. Vis. **8**, 1–20 (2008)
11. Harel, J., Koch, C., Perona, P.: Graph-based visual saliency. Adv. Neural Inf. Process. Syst. 545–552 (2006)
12. Judd, T., Durand, F., Torralba, A.: A Benchmark of Computational Models of Saliency to Predict Human Fixations (2012). http://saliency.mit.edu/
13. Cook, M.B., Smallman, H.S., Rieth, C.A.: Increasing the effective span of control: advanced graphics for proactive, trend-based monitoring. IIE Trans. Occup. Ergon. Hum. Factors **2**, 137–151 (2014)
14. Burns, C.M.: Towards proactive monitoring in the petrochemical industry. Saf. Sci. **44**, 27–36 (2006)
15. Smallman, H.S., Cook, M.B.: Proactive supervisory decision support from trend-based monitoring of autonomous and automated systems: a tale of two domains. In: Shumaker, R. (ed.) VAMR 2013, Part II. LNCS, vol. 8022, pp. 320–329. Springer, Heidelberg (2013)
16. Mumaw, R.J., Roth, E.M., Vicente, K.J., Burns, C.M.: There is more to monitoring a nuclear power plan than meets the eye. Hum. Factors **42**, 36–55 (2000)
17. Few, S.: Information Dashboard Design. O'Reilly, Sebastopol (2006)
18. Guerlain, S., Jamieson, G.A., Bullemer, P., Blair, R.: The MPC elucidator: a case study in the design for human-automation interaction. IEEE Trans. Syst. Man Cybern. A Syst. Hum. **32**, 25–40 (2004)
19. Wolfe, J., Horowitz, T.: What attributes guide the deployment of visual attention and how do they do it? Nat. Rev. Neurosci. **5**, 495–501 (2004)
20. Bennett, K.B., Flach, J.M.: Graphical displays: implications for divided attention, focused attention, and problem solving. Hum. **34**, 513–533 (1992)
21. Braseth, A.O., Veland, Ø., Welch, R.: Information rich display design. In: 4th American Nuclear Society International Topical Meeting on NPIC&HMIT (2004)

Intelligent Agents for Virtual Simulation of Human-Robot Interaction

Ning Wang[1]([⊠]), David V. Pynadath[1], K.V. Unnikrishnan[1],
Santosh Shankar[2], and Chirag Merchant[1]

[1] Institute for Creative Technologies, University of Southern California,
12015 Waterfront Drive, Playa Vista, CA 90094-2536, USA
nwang@ict.usc.edu
http://people.ict.usc.edu/~nwang/
[2] Apple, Inc., Cupertino, CA 95014, USA

Abstract. To study how robots can work better with humans as a team, we have designed an agent-based online testbed that supports virtual simulation of domain-independent human-robot interaction. The simulation is implemented as an online game where humans and virtual robots work together in simulated scenarios. This testbed allows researchers to carry out human-robot interaction studies and gain better understanding of, for example, how a robot's communication can improve human-robot team performance by fostering better trust relationships among humans and their robot teammates. In this paper, we discuss the requirements, challenges and the design of such human-robot simulation. We illustrate its operation with an example human-robot joint reconnaissance task.

Keywords: Human robot interaction · Intelligent virtual agent · Social simulation

1 Introduction

Robots have become increasingly prevalent and no doubt will become an integral part of future human society. From factory robotic arms, to expressive humanoids, robots have evolved from machines operated by humans to autonomous intelligent entities that operate with humans. As robots gain complexity and autonomy, it is important yet increasingly challenging for humans to understand their decision process. Research has shown that people will more accurately trust an autonomous system, such as a robot, if they have a more accurate understanding of its decision-making process [21]. Trust is a critical element to how humans and robots perform together [22]. For example, if robots are more suited than humans for a certain task, then we want the humans to trust the robots to perform that task. If the robots are less suited, then we want the humans to appropriately gauge the robots' ability and have people perform the task manually. Failure to do so results in disuse of robots in the former case and misuse in the latter [28]. Real-world case studies and laboratory experiments show that failures in both cases are common [22].

© Springer International Publishing Switzerland 2015
R. Shumaker and S. Lackey (Eds.): VAMR 2015, LNCS 9179, pp. 228–239, 2015.
DOI: 10.1007/978-3-319-21067-4_24

Successful human-robot interaction (HRI) therefore relies on the robot's ability to make its decision-making process transparent to the people it works with. However, while hand-crafted explanations have been effective in providing such transparency [10], we are interested here in pursuing a more general approach to explanation that can be reused across domains. As a first step toward that goal, we need an experimental testbed that will allow us to quantify the effectiveness of different explanation algorithms in terms of their ability to make a robot's decision-making process transparent to humans.

There are several challenges and requirements in the design and implementation of such a testbed. The first challenge is how to model a HRI scenario that facilitates the research of robot communication. Section 2 surveys the literature on HRI simulations, and Sect. 3 presents the requirements that we extracted from that survey with respect to studying human-robot trust relationships. A second challenge for such a simulation is the generation of the autonomous behaviors of the robots within that scenario. The robot's decision-making must account for the complex planning, noisy sensors, faulty effectors, etc. that complicate even single-robot execution and that are often the root of trust failures in HRI. Section 4 describes how we use a multiagent social simulation framework, PsychSim [24,31], as the agent-based platform for our testbed. Importantly for our purposes, PsychSim includes sensitivity analysis algorithms for explanations [30] that are based in a general decision-theoretic agent framework [16].

The resulting virtual simulation thus provides an experimental testbed that allows researchers to carry out online human-subject studies and gain better understanding of how a robot's communication can improve human-robot team performance by fostering better trust relationships among humans and their robot teammates. In this paper, we discuss the design decisions in the implementation of the agent-based online testbed that supports virtual simulation of domain-independent HRI.

2 Related Work

There is a large body of work on simulating HRI. In the review presented here, we take the perspective of the needs of a testbed specifically for studying human-robot trust. Many HRI simulations seek a high-fidelity re-creation of the physical capabilities of a robot and the physical environment it operates in. For example, Gazebo Player is a 3D simulation framework that contains several models of real robots with a variety of sensors (e.g., camera, laser scanner) [19]. Although this framework supports various kinds of dynamic interaction, dynamic objects (especially humans) are not integrated in the framework. Another high-fidelity simulation environment, USARSim, models urban search-and-rescue robots to provide a research tool for the study of HRI and multirobot coordination [23]. USARSim includes realistic simulations of the physical environment and the physical robots, focusing on tasks like maneuvering through rubble, fallen buildings, etc.

While simulation of physical interaction is important for HRI, the emphasis of our human-robot trust testbed is more on the social interaction. Thus for the time being, we instead focus on simulations that use lower-fidelity models of the physical environment, and use an agent-based simulation to highlight the robot's decision-making challenges (e.g., planning, coordination). For example, Military Operations in Urban Terrain (MOUT) have been modeled within multiagent simulations that capture both team coordination and HRI [11]. However, these particular agents generate the behavior for both the robots and the humans. While such a simulation can provide useful insight into the impact of different coordination strategies on team performance, we instead need an *interactive* simulation to gather behavior data from human participants.

A variety of interactive simulations have modeled scenarios in which people work with a simulated robot subordinate. One environment used the ADAPT framework [37] to build a simulated marketplace, which a semi-autonomous robot navigates based on multimodal directions from human soldiers [6]. The Mixed Initiative eXperimental (MIX) testbed [1] supported a simulation of a generic military crew station to study the differential impact of autonomous systems that are teleoperated, semi-autonomous, or adaptive between the two [8]. Human operators worked with unmanned vehicles under their direction to perform reconnaissance tasks in a hostile environment. This testbed has been successful in measuring the impact of the level of the robot's autonomy on the cognitive load and, in turn, task performance of those operators.

The cooperative nature of this joint reconnaissance task and the complementary responsibilities of humans and robots represent two critical features for our human-robot trust scenario. However, we first need to adapt the task to move the robots away from being directly supervised by a human operator and instead give them full autonomy. In other words, we wish to elevate the robot to the status of teammate, rather than subordinate. By removing the human from the supervisory role, we allow for the possibility for both misuse and disuse of the robot, which is critical in being able to induce trust failures.

Fully autonomous robots have shared a simulated space with people in scenarios like emergency response [34], assisted living [3], and joint cooking tasks [39]. The platforms used for these scenarios, like SIGVerse [39] and the HRI extension of SimVis3D [14], do provide an environment for creating simulations of joint tasks between people and autonomous robots where we could induce the needed trust failures. However, to systematically vary the robot's domain-level and communication-level capabilities, we also require an underlying agent platform on which we can explore general-purpose algorithms for both decision-making and explanation generation.

3   HRI Design

The examination of relevant HRI simulations with respect to the needs of trust exercises leads to the following list of requirements for our testbed:

1. The simulation should encourage the human and the robot to work together as a team (as in [6, 8, 11]). The mission should require joint effort, so that neither

the person nor the robot can achieve the objective by working in isolation. We thus design a joint reconnaissance mission, where the robot scouts out potential dangers to its human teammates, who are responsible for conducting a detailed search to locate a hostage and gather other important intelligence. Thus, the robot cannot achieve the search objective itself, while the human teammates run the risk of being harmed if they ignore the robot's scouting reports.

2. The simulation should encourage people to work along-side the robot, instead of just being its tele-operators (as in real-world scenarios like bomb disposal or disaster response, or in simulated scenarios [6,8]). This means that, in the scenario, the robot should be able to complete its tasks fully autonomously without the human teammate's input. The human teammate is not required to monitor the robot's progress and give commands to the robot on what to do next at every step.

3. With the robot's being capable of acting without supervision, we must also assign the humans their own tasks; otherwise, they may revert to passively monitoring the robot's actions. Thus, we designed the simulation so that the human is also moving through the simulated environment, instead of being a stationary observer/operator of the robot. Surveys have shown that one role that robot teammates might be expected to play is that of a reconnaissance scout, on the lookout for potential threats to their human teammates [38]. We therefore designed our task so that the robot serves as exactly such an advanced scout to sniff out danger, as its human teammates follow up with their own reconnaissance tasks (e.g., searching buildings to locate a hostage). By placing a time limit on completing the joint mission, we incentivize the human (and the robot) to continually pursue their own tasks in parallel.

4. The simulation should encourage communication between humans and the robot, so that the robot can take an active role in establishing trust. To achieve this goal, we took away the interface elements that would provide users with constant situational awareness about the environment and the robots. For example, after the robot scouts a building, we could simply mark the building on the map as red or green to signal whether it is safe or unsafe for human teammates to enter. However, this would take away the opportunity for the robot to directly communicate with its teammates. Similarly, we could directly show the human team members the robot's "raw" sensor readings, but again, this would take away an opportunity for the robot to explain its decisions based on those readings (not to mention potentially creating cognitive overload for the humans). Instead, the human teammates receive information (e.g., assessments, explanations) from the robot only when it actively communicates to them.

5. The task performed by the human and the robot in the simulation should introduce sources of distrust (e.g. robot malfunction, uncertainty in the environment, etc.). While people may occasionally distrust even a robot that never makes a mistake, we would rather ensure the occurrence of mistakes that threaten the trust relationship. Controlling these potential trust failures gives us a better opportunity to research ways to use explanation to

(re)establish trust. We therefore design the robot so that it will not have perfect knowledge of the environment and add variable limitations to the robot's sensors (e.g., varying error rates in its detection of dangerous chemicals). Studies have shown that the frequency and significance of errors can greatly impact user trust in an online system (e.g., a series of small mistakes is worse than one big one [7]). We therefore expect that controlling the error dimensions will be essential in isolating these trust failures and identifying the best explanation algorithms for repairing them.

6. While surveys can provide insight into the human-robot trust relationship, we also want more objective measures of trust in the form of behavioral data. Prior studies have used the "take-over" and "hand-over" behavior a human supervisor does to a robot worker (e.g. takes over a task the robot is currently performing and does it by himself instead) as a measure of the trust or distrust he had in the robot [41]. We follow a similar model in constructing our scenario to include behavioral indicators of disuse and misuse deriving from lack of trust and too much trust, respectively, in the robot. For example, if the human teammate follows the robot's recommendation (e.g., avoids going into a building that the robot said was unsafe), this behavior would be an objective indicator of trust. In contrast, we might infer a lack of trust if the human asks the robot to re-search an area that the robot has already searched. Additionally, our user interface allows the human to choose to directly view the camera feed of the robot. Using this function can be an indication that the human teammates wishes to oversee the robot's behavior and thus, a lack of trust.

7. To ensure that the human teammate's behavior can be indicative of his trust in the robot (e.g., following the robot's recommendation), the robot's mistakes (e.g., incorrectly identifying a building as safe) should have an inherent cost to its human teammates. Otherwise, there will be no reason for the human teammates to *not* act based on the robot's communication. Studies have shown that people will follow the requests of even an incompetent robot if the negative consequences are somewhat trivial [36]. We therefore design our game so that inappropriate trust of the robot can potentially lead to failure to complete the mission and to even "death" of the player.

4   Agent-Based Simulation of HRI

To meet these requirements, we have implemented an agent-based online testbed that supports virtual simulation of domain-independent HRI. Our agent framework, PsychSim [24, 31], combines two established agent technologies—decision-theoretic planning [16] and recursive modeling [12]. Decision-theoretic planning provides an agent with quantitative utility calculations that allow agents to assess tradeoffs between alternative decisions under uncertainty. Recursive modeling gives the agents a *theory of mind* [40], allowing them to form beliefs about the human users' preferences, factor those preferences into the agent's own decisions, and update its beliefs in response to observations of the user's decisions.

The combination of decision theory and theory of mind within a PsychSim agent has proven to be very rich for modeling human decision-making across a wide variety of social and psychological phenomena [32]. This modeling richness has in turn enabled PsychSim agents to operate in a variety of human-agent interaction scenarios [15, 17, 18, 26, 27].

PsychSim agents generate their beliefs and behaviors by solving partially observable Markov decision problems (POMDPs) [9, 16]. The POMDP model's quantitative transition probabilities, observation probabilities, and reward functions are a natural fit for our application domain, and they have proven successful in both robot navigation [4, 20] and HRI [29]. In our own work, we have used POMDPs to implement agents that acted as 24/7 personal assistants that teamed with researchers to handle a variety of their daily tasks [5, 33]. In precise terms, a POMDP is a tuple, $\langle S, A, T, \Omega, O, R \rangle$, that we describe in terms of our human-robot team.

The *state*, S, consists of objective facts about the world, some of which may be hidden from the robot itself. By using a *factored* state representation [2, 13], the model maintains separate labels and values of each feature of the state, such as the separate locations of the robot, its human teammate, the hostage, and the dangerous chemicals. The state also includes feature-value pairs that represent the respective health levels of the teammate and hostage, any current commands from the teammate, and the accumulated time cost so far. Again, while this state represents the true value of all of these features, the robot cannot directly access this true state.

The robot's available *actions*, A, correspond to the possible decisions it can make. Given its search mission, the robot's primary decision is where to move to next. We divide the environment into a set of discrete waypoints, so the robot's action set includes potentially moving to any of them. The robot also makes a decision as to whether to declare a location as safe or unsafe for its human teammate. For example, if the robot believes that dangerous chemicals are at its current location, then it will want its teammate to take adequate preparations before entering. Because there is a time cost to such preparations, the robot may instead decide to declare the location safe, so that its teammates can more quickly complete their own reconnaissance tasks in the building.

The state of the world changes in response to the actions performed by the robot. We model these dynamics using a *transition probability*, T function that captures the possibly uncertain effects of these actions on the subsequent state. We simplify the robot's navigation task by assuming that a decision to move to a specific waypoint succeeds deterministically. However, we could relax this assumption to decrease the robot's movement ability, as is done in more realistic robot navigation models [4, 20]. The robot's recommendation decision affects the health of its teammate and the hostage, although only stochastically, as there is no guarantee that the teammate will follow the recommendation. Instead, a recommendation that a building is safe (unsafe) has a high (low) probability of decreasing the teammate's health if there are, in fact, chemicals present.

As already mentioned, the robot and human teammate have only indirect information about the true state of the world. Within the POMDP model, this information comes through a subset of possible *observations*, Ω, that are probabilistically dependent (through the *observation function*, O) on the true values of the corresponding state features. We make some simplifying assumptions, namely that the robot can observe the location of itself and its teammate with no error (e.g., via GPS).

However, it cannot directly observe the locations of the hostage or dangerous chemicals. Instead, it receives a local reading about their presence (or absence) at its current location. For example, if dangerous chemicals are present, then the robot's chemical sensor will detect them with a high probability. However, there is also a lower, but nonzero, probability that the sensor will *not* detect them. In addition to such a false negative, there is also a potential false positive reading, where there is a low, but nonzero, probability that it will detect chemicals even if there are none present.

Partial observability gives the robot only a subjective view of the world, where it forms beliefs about what it *thinks* is the state of the world, computed via standard POMDP *state estimation* algorithms. For example, the robot's beliefs include its subjective view on the location of the hostage, potentially capturing statements like: "There is an 80 % probability that the hostage is being held at my current location." or "If you visit this waypoint, there is a 60 % chance that you will be exposed to dangerous chemicals." By varying the accuracy of the robot's observation models, we will decrease the accuracy of its beliefs and, subsequently, its recommendations to its human teammates.

On the other hand, the structured dependency structure of the observation function gives the robot explicit knowledge of the uncertainty in its own observations. It can thus communicate its noisy sensor model to its human teammates, potentially making statements like, "My chemical sensor has a 20 % chance of generating a false negative." Therefore, even though a less capable robot's recommendations may be less reliable to its teammate, the robot will be able to explicitly explain that inaccuracy in a way that mitigates the impact to the trust relationship.

PsychSim's POMDP framework instantiates the human-robot team's mission objectives as a *reward*, R, that maps the state of the world into a real-valued evaluation of benefit for the agent. The highest reward is earned in states where the hostage is rescued and all buildings have been explored by the human teammate. This reward component incentivizes the robot to pursue the overall mission objective. There is also an increasingly positive reward associated with level of the human teammate's health. This reward component punishes the robot if it fails to warn its teammate of dangerous buildings. Finally, there is a negative reward that increases with the time cost of the current state. This motivates the robot to complete the mission as quickly as possible. By providing different weights to these goals, we can change the priorities that the robot assigns to them. For example, by lowering the weight of the teammate's health reward, the robot may allow its teammate to search waypoints that are potentially dangerous, in the hope of finding the hostage sooner. Alternatively, lowering the weight on the time cost reward might motivate the robot to wait until being almost certain of a building's threat level (e.g., by repeated observations) before recommending that its teammate visit anywhere.

The robot can arrive at such policies based on its POMDP model of the world by determining the optimal action based on its current beliefs about the state of the world [16]. Rather than perform an offline computation of a complete optimal policy over all possible beliefs, we instead take an online approach so that the robot makes optimal decisions with respect to only its current beliefs [35]. The robot uses a bounded lookahead procedure that seeks to maximize expected reward by simulating the dynamics of the world from its current belief state. In particular, the robot first uses the transition function to project the immediate effect of a candidate action, and then projects a finite number of steps into the future, weighing each state against its reward function. Following such an online algorithm, the robot can thus choose the optimal action with respect to its current beliefs.

On top of this POMDP layer, PsychSim provides a suite of algorithms that are useful for studying domain-independent explanation. By exploring variations of these algorithms within PsychSim's scenario-independent language, we ensure that the results can be re-used by other researchers studying other HRI domains, especially those using POMDP-based agents or robots. To begin with, Psych-Sim agents provide support for transparent reasoning that is a requirement for our testbed. PsychSim's original purpose was human-in-the-loop social simulation. To identify and repair errors in a social-simulation model, the human user must be able to understand the POMDP reasoning process that the agents went through in generating their simulation behavior. In other words, the agents' reasoning must be transparent to the user. To this end, PsychSim's interface made the agent's reasoning process available to the user, in the form of a branching tree representing its expected value calculation. The user could expand branches as needed to drill down into the agent's considerations across possible decisions and outcomes.

This tree provided a maximum amount of transparency, but it also provided a high volume of data, often obscuring the most salient features from the analyst. Therefore, PsychSim imposes a *piecewise* linear structure on the underlying agent models that allows it to quantify the degree to which state features, observations, and goals are salient to a given decision [30]. PsychSim exploits this capability to augment the agent's reasoning trace by highlighting points of possible interest to the user. For example, the interface can identify the belief that the decision is most sensitive to (e.g., quantifying how saving time along a particular route outweighs the increased threat level). We have some anecdotal evidence that the identification of such critical points was useful in previous applications like human-in-the-loop modeling and tutor recommendations.

In this work, we apply this capability to the robot's explanations to its human teammate. In explaining its recommendation that a certain building is safe, the robot can use this sensitivity analysis to decide whether the most salient reward component is the minimization of time cost or the maximization of teammate health. It can then easily map the identified motivation into natural-language expression. Similarly, it can use its lookahead process to generate a natural-language expression of the anticipated consequences to its teammates who violate its recommendation—e.g., "If you visit this location, you will be exposed to the toxic chemicals that are here, and your health will suffer." By implementing robots that use different explanations of its decision-making process, we can quantify the differential impact that they have on human-robot trust and team performance.

5 Discussion

During the design process of an interactive simulation, there is a delicate balance between simulation and game. We learned to maintain this balance to make sure that the simulation serves our purpose of a testbed for studying human-robot trust. For example, we leave out common game elements like scoring, using mission success/failure as a performance indicator. This encourages the human teammate to focus on the mission with the robot, instead of trying to maximize a score that's indicative of his personal performance. We also omitted the usual game elements that help game players' situational awareness, but discourage communication between players and robot, as we observed in our early playtesting.

Our immediate next step is to use the testbed to gather data on how a robot's explanations of its decision process impact human-robot trust and team performance. The explanations are currently provided by the robot during the mission. We are planning to extend the robot's explanation to continue after the mission is completed. This offers the robot an opportunity to "repair" the trust relationship with its teammate, particularly when the mission ends in failure.

The current robot only interacts with people who are its teammates. However, robots in the real world will often have to interact with people who do not share its same mission objective. A future variation of our scenario can include, for example, civilian bystanders in the town where the mission is carried out. The relationships between the robot and people in these different roles will call for different explanation strategies used by the robot. For example, the robot may not want to offer explanations of its decisions to civilians in order to maintain social distance and relative power. The need to maintain social distance will likely engender additional considerations of communication tactics like politeness.

Finally, we are exploring the transition of the scenario from a simulated robot to a physical one. Compared to virtual simulations, teaming up with a physical robot that operates in the same space as a human can potentially increase the stakes of trusting the robot. Additionally, we expect this physical testbed to elevate certain dimensions (e.g., robot embodiment) in importance, as well as providing a higher-fidelity testbed for studying the factors that impact human-robot trust.

References

1. Barber, D., Davis, L., Nicholson, D., Finkelstein, N., Chen, J.Y.: The mixed initiative experimental (MIX) testbed for human robot interactions with varied levels of automation. Technical report, DTIC Document (2008)

2. Boutilier, C., Dearden, R., Goldszmidt, M.: Stochastic dynamic programming with factored representations. Artif. Intell. **121**(1), 49–107 (2000)
3. Braun, T., Wettach, J., Berns, K.: A customizable, multi-host simulation and visualization framework for robot applications. In: Lee, S., Suh II, H., Kim, M.S. (eds.) Recent Progress in Robotics: Viable Robotic Service to Human, pp. 357–369. Springer, Heidelberg (2008)
4. Cassandra, A.R., Kaelbling, L.P., Kurien, J.A.: Acting under uncertainty: Discrete Bayesian models for mobile-robot navigation. In: Proceedings of the IEEE/RSJ International Conference on Intelligent Robots and Systems, vol. 2, pp. 963–972 (1996)
5. Chalupsky, H., Gil, Y., Knoblock, C.A., Lerman, K., Oh, J., Pynadath, D.V., Russ, T.A., Tambe, M.: Electric elves: agent technology for supporting human organizations. AI Mag. **23**(2), 11–24 (2002)
6. Cockburn, J., Solomon, Y., Kapadia, M., Badler, N.: Multi-modal human robot interaction in a simulation environment. Technical report, University of Pennsylvania (2013)
7. Corritore, C.L., Kracher, B., Wiedenbeck, S.: On-line trust: concepts, evolving themes, a model. Int. J. Hum. Comput. Stud. **58**(6), 737–758 (2003)
8. Cosenzo, K., Chen, J., Reinerman-Jones, L., Barnes, M., Nicholson, D.: Adaptive automation effects on operator performance during a reconnaissance mission with an unmanned ground vehicle. In: Proceedings of the Human Factors and Ergonomics Society Annual Meeting, vol. 54, pp. 2135–2139. SAGE Publications (2010)
9. Doshi, P., Perez, D.: Generalized point based value iteration for interactive POMDPs. In: Proceedings of the Conference on Artificial Intelligence, pp. 63–68 (2008)
10. Dzindolet, M.T., Peterson, S.A., Pomranky, R.A., Pierce, L.G., Beck, H.P.: The role of trust in automation reliance. Int. J. Hum. Comput. Stud. **58**, 697–718 (2003)
11. Giachetti, R.E., Marcelli, V., Cifuentes, J., Rojas, J.A.: An agent-based simulation model of human-robot team performance in military environments. Syst. Eng. **16**(1), 15–28 (2013)
12. Gmytrasiewicz, P.J., Durfee, E.H.: A rigorous, operational formalization of recursive modeling. In: Proceedings of the International Conference on Multi-Agent Systems, pp. 125–132 (1995)
13. Guestrin, C., Koller, D., Parr, R., Venkataraman, S.: Efficient solution algorithms for factored mdps. J. Artif. Intell. Res. **19**, 399–468 (2003)
14. Hirth, J., Mehdi, S.A., Schmitz, N., Berns, K.: Development of a simulated environment for human-robot interaction. TELKOMNIKA (Telecommun. Comput. Electron. Control) **9**(3), 465–472 (2011)
15. Johnson, W.L., Valente, A.: Tactical language and culture training systems: using AI to teach foreign languages and cultures. Artif. Intell. Mag. **30**(2), 72–84 (2009)
16. Kaelbling, L.P., Littman, M.L., Cassandra, A.R.: Planning and acting in partially observable stochastic domains. Artif. Intell. **101**, 99–134 (1998)
17. Kim, J.M., Hill, J.R.W., Durlach, P.J., Lane, H.C., Forbell, E., Core, M., Marsella, S., Pynadath, D., Hart, J.: BiLAT: a game-based environment for practicing negotiation in a cultural context. Int. J. Artif. Intell. Educ. Special Issue on Ill-Defined Domains **19**(3), 289–308 (2009)
18. Klatt, J., Marsella, S., Krämer, N.C.: Negotiations in the context of AIDS prevention: an agent-based model using theory of mind. In: Vilhjálmsson, H.H., Kopp, S., Marsella, S., Thórisson, K.R. (eds.) IVA 2011. LNCS, vol. 6895, pp. 209–215. Springer, Heidelberg (2011)

19. Koenig, N., Howard, A.: Design and use paradigms for gazebo, an open-source multi-robot simulator. In: Proceedings of the IEEE/RSJ International Conference on Intelligent Robots and Systems, vol. 3, pp. 2149–2154. IEEE (2004)

20. Koenig, S., Simmons, R.: Xavier: a robot navigation architecture based on partially observable Markov decision process models. In: Kortenkamp, D., Bonasso, R.P., Murphy, R.R. (eds.) Artificial Intelligence Based Mobile Robotics: Case Studies of Successful Robot Systems, pp. 91–122. MIT Press, Cambridge (1998)

21. Lee, J., Moray, N.: Trust, control strategies and allocation of function in human-machine systems. Ergonomics 35(10), 1243–1270 (1992)

22. Lee, J.D., See, K.A.: Trust in automation: designing for appropriate reliance. Hum. Factors J. Hum. Factors Ergonomics Soc. 46(1), 50–80 (2004)

23. Lewis, M., Wang, J., Hughes, S.: USARSim: simulation for the study of human-robot interaction. J. Cogn. Eng. Decis. Mak. 1(1), 98–120 (2007)

24. Marsella, S.C., Pynadath, D.V., Read, S.J.: PsychSim: agent-based modeling of social interactions and influence. In: Proceedings of the International Conference on Cognitive Modeling, pp. 243–248 (2004)

25. Mayer, R.C., Davis, J.H., Schoorman, F.D.: An integrative model of organizational trust. Acad. Manag. Rev. 20(3), 709–734 (1995)

26. McAlinden, R., Gordon, A., Lane, H.C., Pynadath, D.: UrbanSim: a game-based simulation for counterinsurgency and stability-focused operations. In: Proceedings of the AIED Workshop on Intelligent Educational Games (2009)

27. Miller, L.C., Marsella, S., Dey, T., Appleby, P.R., Christensen, J.L., Klatt, J., Read, S.J.: Socially optimized learning in virtual environments (SOLVE). In: Si, M., Thue, D., André, E., Lester, J., Tanenbaum, J., Zammitto, V. (eds.) ICIDS 2011. LNCS, vol. 7069, pp. 182–192. Springer, Heidelberg (2011)

28. Parasuraman, R., Riley, V.: Humans and automation: use, misuse, disuse, abuse. Hum. Factors 39(2), 230–253 (1997)

29. Pineau, J., Montemerlo, M., Pollack, M., Roy, N., Thrun, S.: Towards robotic assistants in nursing homes: challenges and results. Robot. Autonomous Syst. 42(3), 271–281 (2003)

30. Pynadath, D.V., Marsella, S.C.: Fitting and compilation of multiagent models through piecewise linear functions. In: Proceedings of the International Conference on Autonomous Agents and Multi Agent Systems, pp. 1197–1204 (2004)

31. Pynadath, D.V., Marsella, S.C.: PsychSim: Modeling theory of mind with decision-theoretic agents. In: Proceedings of the International Joint Conference on Artificial Intelligence, pp. 1181–1186 (2005)

32. Pynadath, D.V., Si, M., Marsella, S.C.: Modeling theory of mind and cognitive appraisal with decision-theoretic agents. In: Gratch, J., Marsella, S. (eds.) Social Emotions in Nature and Artifact: Emotions in Human and Human-Computer Interaction, pp. 70–87. Oxford University Press, Oxford (2014)

33. Pynadath, D.V., Tambe, M.: Electric elves: adjustable autonomy in real-world multi-agent environments. In: Dautenhahn, K., Bond, A., Canamero, D., Edmonds, B. (eds.) Socially Intelligent Agents: Creating Relationships with Computers and Robots, Chap. 12, pp. 101–108. Kluwer, Dordrecht (2002)

34. Robinette, P., Howard, A.M.: Trust in emergency evacuation robots.In: Proceedings of the IEEE International Symposium on Safety, Security, and Rescue Robotics, pp. 1–6. IEEE (2012)

35. Ross, S., Pineau, J., Paquet, S., Chaib-Draa, B.: Online planning algorithms for POMDPs. J. Artif. Intell. Res. 32, 663–704 (2008)

36. Salem, M., Lakatos, G., Amirabdollahian, F., Dautenhahn, K.: Would you trust a (faulty) robot?: Effects of error, task type and personality on human-robot cooperation and trust. In: Proceedings of the Tenth Annual ACM/IEEE International Conference on Human-Robot Interaction, HRI 2015, pp. 141–148. ACM, New York (2015)
37. Shoulson, A., Marshak, N., Kapadia, M., Badler, N.I.: Adapt: the agent developmentand prototyping testbed. IEEE Trans. Vis. Comput. Graph. **20**(7), 1035–1047 (2014)
38. Swiecicki, C.C., Elliott, L.R., Wooldridge, R.: Squad-level soldier-robot dynamics: Exploring future concepts involving intelligent autonomous robots. Technical report ARL-TR-7215, Army Research Laboratory (2015)
39. Tan, J.T.C., Inamura, T.: Sigverse: a cloud computing architecture simulation platform for social human-robot interaction. In: Proceedings of the International Conference on Robotics and Automation, pp. 1310–1315. IEEE (2012)
40. Whiten, A. (ed.): Natural Theories of Mind. Basil Blackwell, Oxford (1991)
41. Xu, A., Dudek, G.: Optimo: online probabilistic trust inference model for asymmetric human-robot collaborations. In: Proceedings of the Tenth Annual ACM/IEEE International Conference on Human-Robot Interaction, HRI 2015, pp. 221–228. ACM, New York (2015)

VR for Learning and Training

GlassClass: Exploring the Design, Implementation, and Acceptance of Google Glass in the Classroom

Dave A. Berque[✉] and James T. Newman

Computer Science Department, DePauw University,
Greencastle, IN 46135, USA
{dberque,jamesnewman_2015}@depauw.edu

Abstract. Google Glass is worn like a pair of eye-glasses and is controlled with a small screen, touchpad, and microphone. A variety of Augmented Reality and Mixed Reality Glassware applications are available for Glass. However, due to the size and position of the screen, it is hard for onlookers to discern what the user is doing while using these applications. Additionally, the user can surreptitiously take pictures and record videos of nearby people and things, resulting in privacy concerns. We hypothesized that use of Glassware in a specific domain, where onlookers were apprised of the use of the Glassware, would be better accepted than the more generic use of Glassware. This paper reports on our design, implementation and evaluation of several Glass applications to enhance communication between teachers and students in the classroom and presents results from a study that suggests that students accept the use of Glassware in this environment.

Keywords: Augmented reality · Google glass · Glassware · Educational applications of glassware · Wearable computing

1 Introduction and Motivation

Human Computer Interaction has been defined by the Association for Computing Machinery Special Interest Group on Computer Human Interaction (ACM SIGCHI) as being "concerned with the design, evaluation, and implementation of interactive computing systems for human use and with the study of major phenomena surrounding them." [4] Wearable computing, a subfield of Human Computer Interaction, studies the integration of technology with clothing and other fashion accessories. Some examples of wearable computers that are currently being explored include watches, fitness trackers, and perhaps most controversial, the Google Glass.

Glass, which has not yet proven itself to be as useful as other forms of wearable computing, is worn like a pair of eye-glasses and is controlled with a small screen, touchpad, and microphone. Figure 1 shows how Glass appears when worn by a user. A variety of Augmented Reality and Mixed Reality Glassware applications are available for Glass. However, due to the size and position of the Google Glass screen, it is hard for onlookers to discern what the user is doing while using these applications. Additionally, the user can surreptitiously take pictures and record videos of nearby

© Springer International Publishing Switzerland 2015
R. Shumaker and S. Lackey (Eds.): VAMR 2015, LNCS 9179, pp. 243–250, 2015.
DOI: 10.1007/978-3-319-21067-4_25

people and things, raising privacy concerns. The term "glassholes" has even been coined to describe public users of Glass (see, for example, [5]).

Fig. 1. Google Glass on a user

We hypothesized that Glass would be better accepted, and more useful, when it was applied to a specific domain instead of being worn in more general settings. There are other examples of wearable computers that are both useful and accepted in specific domains, although they are not fit for more general use. A classic example are the headsets that are used by fast-food workers to process drive-through orders. Because everyone understands why the headsets are being worn, and everyone understands the value of the headsets in this particular context, they do not seem out of place or intrusive.

We believe that use of Glassware in specific domains, where onlookers understand the value of the Glassware, would result in the pushback than we have seen with more public, and possibly invasive, uses of Glassware. To test this hypothesis in an educational setting, we designed and implemented several Glass applications to enhance communication between teachers and students in the classroom and conducted a pilot study to measure student acceptance of Glass in the classroom.

2 System Design

We designed and implemented three software systems for use in a classroom or laboratory environment in which each student is doing work on a standard laptop or desktop computer. For example, the students may be using the computers to take notes, to solve problems using discipline specific software, to write computer programs, etc. Each of our systems is comprised of a student component that runs on each student's desktop or laptop computer as well as a teacher component that runs on Google Glass. Each of the three teacher components is written in Java and uses Google's GDK (Glass Development Kit [1]) which is an add-on to the Android Development Kit [2]. Two of the student components are written using standard web technologies (HTML, CSS, JavaScript) and the third is written as a C#.NET application. In each case, the teacher component interoperates with the corresponding student component through a backend that uses parse.com [3] as a database to permit information to be exchanged between the teacher and students.

2.1 Glass Gauge

The first application, called *Glass Gauge*, is designed to be used while the teacher is presenting new material to the students. At the start of the class period the teacher starts the *Glass Gauge* application. The *Glass Gauge* application signals to parse.com that the class is in progress. Students can then login to the web site that comprises the student component of *Glass Gauge*. By entering a code provided by the teacher, each student can connect to the teacher's class. Once logged in and connected, each student can set and/or reset his or her level of understanding to indicate if he or she "understands", "mostly understands" or "does not understand" the topic the teacher is presenting. The students set these statuses using a drop-down menu. The teacher, wearing Glass, sees an aggregate of the students' statuses in real-time on the eye display. This allows the teacher to naturally adjust the pace of his or her presentation based on the aggregated level of understanding of the class.

2.2 Glass Screen Share

The second application, called *Glass Screen Share*, also has a student component and a teacher component. In this case, the student component is written in C# .NET and runs in the background on each student's computer. The student component of *Glass Screen Share* takes a screen shot of the student's display every fifteen seconds. A thumbnail version of each screen shot is uploaded silently to parse.com. The thumbnails are retrieved by the teacher version of *Glass Screen Share* every fifteen seconds and are automatically presented on Glass as a list of thumbnails that the teacher can scroll through. Each thumbnail is labeled with the name of the corresponding student, which allows the teacher to see which students are on task. If a student is not on task, the teacher can approach the student to help refocus the student or to offer help. This dissuades students from becoming distracted with applications such as Facebook while using computers in the classroom.

2.3 Glass Request

The final application is called *Glass Request* and is designed for use in a laboratory or other active-learning environment. At the start of the class period, the teacher starts the *Glass Request* application, which signals to parse.com that the class is in progress.

Students can then login to the web site that comprises the student component of *Glass Request*. By entering a code provided by the teacher, each student can connect to the teacher's class. Once logged in and connected, each student can use a menu to indicate when she or he needs attention from the teacher. The student can either indicate that she or he needs assistance in completing a step of the assignment, or that she or he has completed the assignment and is ready to be checked off. Using Glass, the teacher sees a summary of the number of students who requested attention either because they have a question about a step of the assignment or because they have completed the assignment and are ready to be checked off. The summary that the teacher sees is shown in Fig. 2.

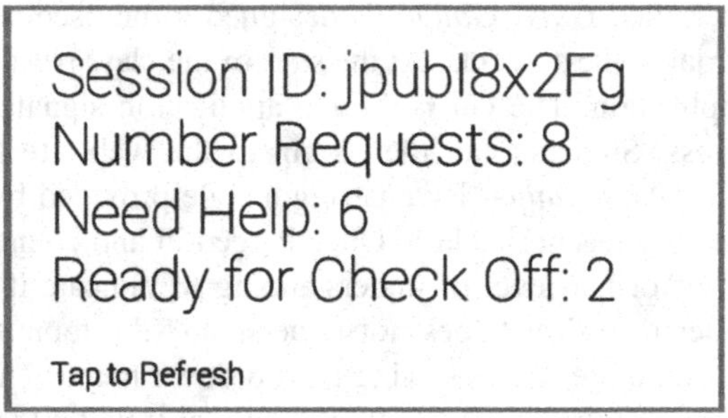

Session ID: jpubI8x2Fg
Number Requests: 8
Need Help: 6
Ready for Check Off: 2

Tap to Refresh

Fig. 2. Initial display of the teacher's *Glass Request* application. The teacher can tap to refresh the display or can scroll to see list of the individual students who have requested attention.

The teacher can scroll from the summary card through a list that represents the specific students who have completed the assignment and are ready to be checked off. This list is ordered by the length of time each student has been waiting. One entry from this list is shown in Fig. 3. The list of students who are ready to be checked off is followed by a list of students who need assistance with one of the steps of the assignment. Again, this list is ordered by the length of time each student has been waiting. An example entry from this part of the list is shown in Fig. 4.

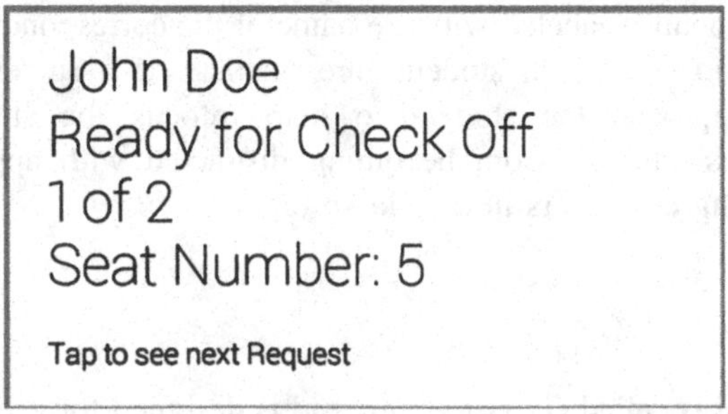

John Doe
Ready for Check Off
1 of 2
Seat Number: 5

Tap to see next Request

Fig. 3. Teacher's Glass Request application, showing a student who is ready to be checked off. The teacher can scroll to see additional students who have requested attention.

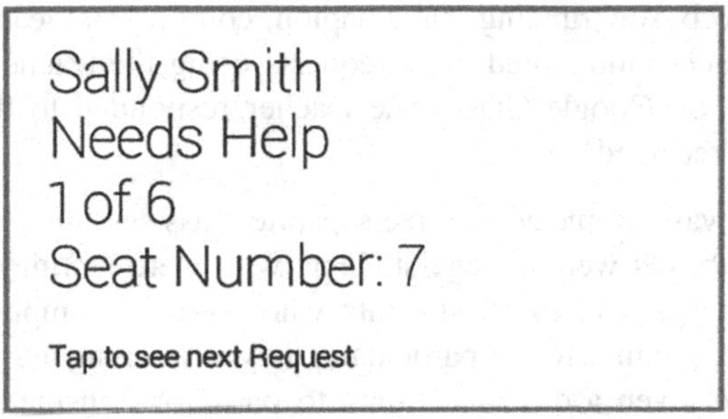

```
Sally Smith
Needs Help
1 of 6
Seat Number: 7

Tap to see next Request
```

Fig. 4. Teacher's Glass Request application, showing the first student out of six students who need assistance with the assignment. This student is seated in location 7 in the room. The teacher can scroll to see additional students who have requested attention.

3   Laboratory Study

3.1   Study Design

In order to test student acceptance of a teacher's use of Glass in a classroom, we received Institutional Review Board approval to conduct a user study related to the *Glass Request* application that was described in the previous section. As a proxy for a real classroom activity, students who participated in the study were asked to read sample GRE and SAT passages and they were next asked to answer objective questions about those passages on a paper answer sheet. After completing certain parts of the activity, students were told to ask the experimenter (who was acting as the classroom teacher) to check their work before they moved on to answer questions about a new set of passages. In order to ask the teacher to check their work, students had to get the teacher's attention. We varied the technique that was used by the students to get the teacher's attention.

For the purpose of this study, we built a version of the teacher component of *Glass Request* that runs on a standard Android phone, in addition to the version that runs on Glass as previously described. The phone version of the system displays the list of students who need attention on the phone interface instead of on Glass, but is otherwise similar to the Glass version. This allowed us to compare student acceptance across three conditions:

- In the **no-technology (hand raising) condition,** students requested attention from the teacher by raising their hands and waiting for the teacher to notice them. The teacher did his best to respond to requests in the order received.
- In the **cellphone condition** students requested attention from the teacher by making a request through the student component of *Glass Request*, which was running on a web site on a laptop computer at each student's desk. The teacher monitored these requests using the teacher version of *Glass Request* running on a cellphone. The teacher responded to the requests in the order they were received.
- In the **Glass condition** students still requested assistance from the experimenter by making a request through the student component of *Glass Request*, which was

running on a web site running on a laptop computer at each student's desk. However, the teacher monitored these requests using the teacher version of *Glass Request* running on Google Glass. The teacher responded to the requests in the order they were received.

The pilot study was completed as three separate class sessions, one for each of the three conditions. Subjects were college students who were recruited primarily via an email message that was sent to all students who were on-campus working for the summer. As subjects volunteered to participate, they were assigned to one of the three conditions and were given a day and a time to participate in the study. In total, 25 students participated in the study.

Regardless of the condition, the study procedure consisted of five parts, as described below. Taken in total, the five parts took just under an hour to complete.

In **part one** each student completed an Informed Consent form. The form presented the presented with an overview of the experimental procedure for the condition the student had been assigned to.

In **part two** of the study the teacher oriented the classroom of students to the task they would be asked to complete. Specifically, the teacher explained to the class that they would be reading passages taking from publically available SAT and GRE practice exams, and would be answering objective questions about those passages. For the cellphone condition and the Glass condition the teacher also showed the class how to request attention from the experimenter using software running in their web browser. However, for the no-technology condition the teacher told the class that they could request attention by raising their hands.

In **part three** of the study each student was given a handout that contained two sample GRE/SAT reading comprehension passages. Each passage had between three and ten objective questions associated with it. The students were asked to read the passages and to record their answers to the questions on the paper, which also served as an answer sheet. When a student completed all of the questions for the set of passages, they requested assistance from the teacher (by raising their hands if they were in the no-technology condition, or by using the web browser if they were in the other conditions).

When a teacher assisted a student, the teacher used an answer key to check the student's work and wrote a check or an X next to each answer. If there were any mistakes, the student was asked to review the reading, correct the work, and ask for attention again. When a student eventually answered all of the questions correctly, the teacher collected the handout and then asked the student to repeat the process with a second handout with two additional passages and associated questions. This process was repeated with a third and final handout as well.

In **part four** of the study, after each student had correctly answered questions for all three handouts, the teacher administered an exit survey. In addition to basic demographic information, students were asked questions about their satisfaction with waiting for help from the teacher and about their satisfaction with their experience. Subjects were also asked to provide any additional information they wished to share.

In the **fifth and final part** of the study, each subject was debriefed, thanked and paid $10.00 in cash as compensation for his or her time.

3.2   Study Results

In total, 25 students participated in the study. The students ranged in age from 18 to 22 and 8 of the students were female while 17 were male. There were 8 students in the Glass condition, 9 in the cell phone condition and 8 in the no technology (hand raising) condition.

At the end of the study each student completed an exit survey indicating her or her satisfaction with various aspects of the experience. Each student responded to the satisfaction questions by indicating his or her level of agreement with statements using a Likert Scale where 1 = Strongly Disagree, 2 = Disagree, 3 = Neutral, 4 = Agree, 5 = Strongly Agree. The mean response for subjects in each of the three conditions is shown in Table 1 for several of the key questions on the exit survey.

Table 1. Summary of key survey questions

Question	Google Glass	Cell phone	Hand raising
The process that was used for the teacher to see that I needed to have my work checked made me uncomfortable.	1.6	2.3	2.0
The process that was used for the teacher to see that I needed to have my work checked interfered with my experience today.	1.6	1.8	1.4
The process that was used for the teacher to see that I needed to have my work checked enhanced my experience today.	3.5	3.7	3.0

Students in the Google Glass condition made open-ended comments including:

- "Didn't enhance [my experience] obviously, but it in no way interfered with my experience"
- "The process that was used enhanced my experience. I liked it a lot better than, say raising my hand to indicated I needed my answers to be checked."
- "It made it easier for me to interact with the teacher, and my arm didn't get tired from being stuck in the air for minutes at a time."
- "The method the teacher used to check my work had no influence on my experience."
- "The instructor was grading my work within seconds of my signaling of assistance."
- "When there were numerous people ready to have their answers checked it could take a few minutes to be acknowledged, which is to be expected with one teacher."

4   Conclusion

Students in this study did not feel uncomfortable by the teacher's use of Google Glass to monitor requests for assistance. The students also did not believe that the teacher's use of Google Glass interfered with their experience. However, the students were neutral when asked if their teacher's use of Google Glass enhanced their experience.

These results are limited by the small sample size and relatively homogeneous group of subjects who participated. However, it appears that the concerns that are sometimes raised when Google Glass is used in a general setting may not carry over to the use of Google Glass in more focused environments such as classrooms.

5 Future Work

Potential future work includes conducting a larger user study that evaluates student acceptance of the other applications in the suite. In addition, we would like to study the use of our applications in a real classroom environment to see how students and teachers respond to the applications in this context. We are also interested in extending the teacher's side of the applications, for example by adding functionality that allows teachers to track and analyze various data such as the number of times a student requested help and time intervals between requests. Finally, we would like to build and test domain-specific Google Glass applications for environments other than the classroom and user populations other than students. This would help us to determine the extent to which our results generalize to other domains and to other types of users.

Acknowledgement. This work was supported by NSF grant number CNS-1156893.

References

1. Google Glass Development Kit. https://developers.google.com/glass/develop/gdk/index
2. Google Android Development Kit. http://developer.android.com/sdk/index.html
3. Parse Development Kit. https://www.parse.com/
4. ACM SIGCHI Curricula for Human-Computer Interaction. http://old.sigchi.org/cdg/cdg2.html#2_1
5. Gross, D.: Google: How not to be a Glasshole. www.cnn.com/2014/02/19/tech/mobile/google-glasshole/index.html

Augmented Reality Training of Military Tasks: Reactions from Subject Matter Experts

Roberto Champney[1(✉)], Stephanie J. Lackey[2(✉)], Kay Stanney[1],
and Stephanie Quinn[1]

[1] Design Interactive, Inc., Orlando, FL, USA
{roberto, kay, stephanie.quinn}@designinteractive.net
[2] Institute for Simulation and Training, Orlando, FL, USA
slackey@ist.ucf.edu

Abstract. The purpose of this research effort was to understand the training utility of augmented reality and simulation-based training capabilities in an outdoor field environment. Specifically, this research focused on evaluating the training efficacy of the Augmented Immersive Team Training (AITT) system, a portable augmented reality training solution that targets Forward Observer (FO) tasks associated with a Call for Fire (CFF) mission. The assessment focused on evaluating training utility, satisfaction, usability, simulator sickness, presence, immersion and appropriateness of the fidelity cues provided by the AITT system. Data were gathered via questionnaires. The results of this study provided insight for formative evolution of the AITT system design and may have implications to other similar technologies.

Keywords: Augmented reality · Training · Learning · Immersive virtual reality · Wearable technology · Mixed reality · Training systems

1 Introduction

Augmented Reality (AR), an emerging interactive technology that merges elements of the physical real-world environment with virtual computer generated imagery, promises to be a viable pedagogical venue for the training of a variety of domains. Kamarainen et al. (2013) demonstrated that the "authentic" participatory experience provided by AR training systems can increase the effectiveness of instruction, while improving trainee attention, engagement, and motivation. As the technology matures, AR is thus poised to quickly expand from a focus on information presentation and entertainment to applications for learning and exploring (Johnson, Smith, Willis, Levine, & Haywood, 2011). It is not uncommon, however, for new and innovative training technology such as AR to simply be incorporated into the latest educational applications without regard to how best the technology supports learning. Before AR receives widespread adoption into educational applications, it is thus necessary to understand what makes AR a promising technology for training. Bitter and Corral (2014) suggest the training effectiveness of AR will be highest in situations where the technology is aligned with solid educational theories. In this regard, Dunleavy and Dede (2014) have suggested that AR is particularly well suited to situated and

© Springer International Publishing Switzerland 2015
R. Shumaker and S. Lackey (Eds.): VAMR 2015, LNCS 9179, pp. 251–262, 2015.
DOI: 10.1007/978-3-319-21067-4_26

constructivist learning theories that involve authentic inquiry and active observation, which is supported by probes and scaffolding. This is important to understand because some past studies have failed to demonstrate the training value of AR Zhu et al., (2014). The current study examined the potential of AR to support learning of complex skills in an outdoor context.

2 Background

This study consisted of a formative evaluation of the Augmented Immersive Team Trainer (AITT) system. AITT is an AR training capability designed to support Forward Observers (FO) in conducting CFF tasks. AITT's innovation, as compared to other immersive virtual reality or PC based trainers, lies in its portable-outdoor capability. In contrast to most simulation based training systems that rely on an indoor lighting environment, the AITT allows training on-site – whether indoor our outside – via a wearable AR system. This allows the training to take place at the operational site or at relevant environments (e.g., live fire range).

Call for Fire. US Marines and other Services' ground Warfighters often employ artillery or mortars in support of their missions. To employ these weapons Warfighters need to coordinate with other teams to ensure the successful and safe use of these tools. A CFF is a message that contains specific information that is used to effectively conduct an attack on a particular target (U.S. Army, 1991). This message is created and communicated by an FO and contains the appropriate method of fire, which is determined by factors such as target type and location, potential friendly and civilian presence, and FO distance to target (Strensrud, Fragomeni, & Garrity, 2013). The Fire Direction Center (FDC) receives this message and initiates fire commands to a Firing Unit after the requested fire support is verified or modified. The FO conducts a CFF request in three transmissions in order to communicate detailed information that is necessary for the FDC to execute the mission. Each of the transmissions requires the FO to be highly observant and to utilize effective decision making skills in a high-risk environment. The first transmission consists of the FO identifying himself and declaring a warning order. A warning order contains the method of target location (e.g., shift from known point), type of mission (e.g., fire for effect), and size of requested fire (e.g., battalion). The second transmission consists of the target's location and the location accuracy, the latter of which is critical for the mission to be effective. The third transmission consists of a detailed target description, method of engagement, and method of fire and control. Once the FDC receives the information provided in the three transmissions, the fire commands are reviewed, approved and disseminated to the Firing Unit, which executes the specific methods at the target location. The FO must then observe and report height of round bursts, as well as communicate requests for fire adjustments on the target and the effect of the rounds on the target. These complex and coordinated tasks involve affective skills associated with listening, acknowledging, and responding to the information from the FDC, psychomotor skills associated with perceiving, calibrating, adapting to, and reacting to the current state of the environment, and cognitive skills associated with evaluating, comparing, and predicting the fire adjustments needed.

Augmented Reality Training. Conventional classroom instruction of the affective, psychomotor, and cognitive skills associated with a CFF mission requires far-transfer: applying knowledge learned in the classroom situation to a far different outdoor context (Champney, Surpris, Carroll, & Cohn, 2014). The potential advantage of the AITT AR-solution for situated learning (Bossard and Kermarrec 2006; Lave & Wenger, 1990) of CFF mission is its ability to simulate real-world contexts that allow trainees to master authentic FO tasks in meaningful and realistic outdoor environments, which means that trainees must attain only near-transfer to achieve preparation for the operational (outdoor) environment. Beyond embedded learning within relevant environments, from a constructivist learning theory perspective, (Dunleavy & Dede, 2014) the AITT provides the following conditions that are likely to enhance learning: (1) allows for social negotiation between the FDC and FO, (2) allows for multiple perspectives (i.e., views of a limitless number of outdoor environments), (3) provides self-directed and active learning opportunities of FO tasks, and (4) supports and facilitates metacognitive strategies within the experience when coupled with an after action review that provides feedback. Within the armed forces domain, AR is also valuable for its ability to repeatedly provide opportunities to train otherwise hazardous or expensive tasks and thus have a high return on training investment.

3 Participants

A total of five (5) U.S. Marines participated in this study. All participants were male, had normal or corrected to normal vision, and ranged in age from 24 to 38 ($M = 31$, $SD = 6.8$). The average number of years of military service was 8.15 ($SD = 2.36$) and participants reported their current role as Forward Observer (FO), Expeditionary Warfare School (EWS) Student, or Joint Terminal Attack Controller (JTAC). The prior experience of CFF missions completed by the participants ranged from 30 to 400 ($M = 132$, $SD = 152$) missions. All participants reported they had trained others to perform CFF mission tasks.

4 Materials

The following tools were used to gather data during the study.

Training Utility Questionnaire (Task Execution): Participants answered 9 questions regarding the system's ability to support the execution and thus practice of CFF tasks. These questions were targeted at understanding the perceived utility of the AITT system for CFF training. Participants answered using a five-item Likert scale anchored by 1-Strongly Disagree and 5-Strongly Agree.

Satisfaction Questionnaire: The Net Promoter Score (NPS; Reichheld, 2003) method was used as a measure of satisfaction with the AITT system for use in CFF training.

The scale has defined cut-offs to indicate the likelihood of an individual to promote a product being assessed. Participants answered the following question: *"How likely is it that you would recommend the AITT for use as a CFF trainer?"*

System Usability Scale (SUS): The AITT's global usability was evaluated using the SUS (Brooke, 1996), a 10-item Likert scale anchored by 1-Strongly Disagree and 5-Strongly Agree (provides a total score ranging from 0-1-00).

AITT Fidelity Questionnaire: This questionnaire sought participants' impressions regarding the realism of the AITT system with regards to the multimodal (sensory) experience. Participants used a five-item Likert scale mentioned above (1-Strongly Disagree and 5-Strongly Agree) to assess the fidelity of the system. The responses for each individual question were averaged.

Simulator Sickness Questionnaire (SSQ): The SSQ (Kennedy et al., 1993) was used to assess any adverse symptoms associated with using the AITT system. The SSQ consists of a checklist of 26 symptoms, each of which is related in terms of degree of severity (none, slight, moderate, severe), with the highest possible total score (most severe) being 300. A weighted scoring procedure is used to obtain a global score reflecting the overall discomfort level known as the Total Severity (TS) score, along with three subscales representing separable but somewhat correlated dimensions of simulator sickness (i.e., Nausea [N], Oculomotor Disturbances [O], and Disorientation [D]).

Presence Questionnaire: Presence, the sense of "being" in a different place than where a user is physically located (Witmer & Singer, 1998), was reported on four subscales. The Involvement/Control subscale reflects a user's psychological state resulting from focusing attention on stimuli and is comprised of control, realism, and sensory factors. The Natural Interaction subscale addresses control and realism factors affecting the match between virtual and real objects and environments. The Resolution subscale solely focuses on sensory factors. The Interface Quality subscale accounts for distraction and control factors. Participants answered all subscales using a seven-item Likert scale anchored by 1-Strongly Disagree and 7-Strongly Agree.

Immersion Questionnaire: A relevant subset of questions from Jennett et al. (2008) was used in this study, which evaluates a user's feelings of cognitive absorption and flow. Participants answered using a five-item Likert scale anchored by 1-Strongly Disagree and 5-Strongly Agree.

5 Method

Kirkpatrick's (1994) first of four levels of evaluation (i.e., 1. trainee reactions, versus 2. learning, 3. transfer and 4. impact), served as the basis for a formative evaluation of the AITT system. Specifically, the present evaluation sought to evaluate reactions from Subject Matter Experts (SMEs) regarding the constructs of training utility, satisfaction, usability, fidelity, simulator sickness, presence, and immersion via questionnaires, as well as evaluate task execution via observation (including notes taken by the

Experimenter while he/she observed participants interacting with the AITT system). The evaluation took place in a large, open field in Quantico, VA. The field was lined with trees and a building and parking lot were at the North end of the field.

Upon arrival to the field, the participant was asked to read and sign an informed consent form, which described the tasks involved in the study and notified him that his participation was completely voluntary. The participant was then asked to fill out the Simulator Sickness Questionnaire (SSQ) Kennedy et al., (1993). Next, the participant was fitted with a portable AITT setup and was allowed to familiarize himself with the system.

The participant was then asked to execute three (3) CFF missions in the following order: (1) Grid method, (2) Polar method, and (3) Shift from Known Point method. The Grid method consisted of a scenario in which the CFF was to be conducted on one squad of enemy dismounts. The Polar method consisted of a scenario in which the CFF was to be conducted on an enemy vehicle in the parking lot next to the field. The Shift from Known Point method used the location of the enemy vehicle from the Polar method in order to execute the CFF on an additional enemy vehicle. All scenarios had targets that were Danger Close, and thus participants were told to ignore Danger Close procedures for purposes of the testing. All three CFF missions allowed the participant to use a simulated VECTOR 21 (for coordinates and range finding, as well as real-world tools including a), map, protractor, notepad and pencil. In addition, all CFF missions were self-paced and self-directed. Figure. 1(a) and (b) show participants interacting with the AITT system. The time immersed in the AITT system ranged from 29 to 46 min ($M = 39.4$ min., $SD = 7.0$).

Upon completion of the three CFF missions, the participant immediately filled out the training utility, satisfaction, usability, fidelity, simulator sickness, presence, and immersion questionnaires, The experimenter was present while the participant filled out the questionnaires in order to answer any questions and to take notes of comments the participant provided. The duration of the entire experiment was approximately 1.5 h per participant.

(a) Kneeling   (b) Prone Position

Fig. 1. Participant interacting with AITT system

6 Results and Discussion

The sections below detail the findings from the study.

Training Capability. With regard to training utility, questionnaire responses ranged from 3.6 to 4.7 (M = 4.19, SD = 0.68), with these scores indicating that most participants agreed (4) that the AITT has the ability to support execution and practice of the tasks necessary to correctly and accurately conduct a CFF, with the exception of one aspect. The average response to the statement, *"The system allowed me to properly utilize all the tools necessary for a CFF mission (e.g., map, compass, Binos/VECTOR 21, radio)"* resulted in an average score of 3.6 (SD = 1.52), which was a neutral score. It should be noted that the only simulated tool utilized by the participants was the VECTOR 21; all other tools (i.e., map, protractor, notepad and pencil) were real-world tools. Further review of comments and notes highlighted the possible cause of this rating as being the interference caused by the Head Mounted Display (HMD) with these real-world tools. While the participant transitioned from observing the AR environment and utilizing the real-world CFF tools, participants needed to 'flip' the HMD up to utilize these tools or find other workarounds (e.g., raise head while looking down under the HMD), which made it hard to make use of those other tools. This indicates a need to better merge the elements of the physical real-world environment that are to be coordinated with virtual computer generated imagery.

Satisfaction. With regard to satisfaction, the AITT's NPS was 40 % (percentage of Promoters [60 %] minus percentage of Detractors [20 %]), reflecting relatively high support for the AITT's training capability. This NPS is higher than the average NPS of 20 % for popular products, including Microsoft Word, Google Calendar, Dropbox and Adobe Photoshop (Sauro, 2014). The results of the NPS indicate that although the majority of the participants were promoters of the AITT system, there was one detractor and one passive participant. A review of these individuals' comments and reported perceptions may indicate what elements of the AITT may be driving their dissatisfaction or hesitation to promote the system. Specifically, the detractor was concerned with the physical aspects of the AITT system, stating that the prototype appeared fragile and cumbersome ("Marines would break it"). At the same time, this participant also had positive feelings regarding the system and its use for training CFF. While it is understood that the version of the AITT system evaluated is a prototype, participants had a difficult time understanding what would be the quality and ruggedness of the final operational version. As such, their comments regarding the durability of the system were based on what they observed and experienced. The takeaway from this feedback is that the system must be very ruggedized before fielding. The passive participant also had positive feelings, stating that the system seems like a great tool for teaching basic CFF. He gave several recommendations for improvement, such as making the displays more adjustable and blocking ambient light. These comments point to the need to more adjustable and immersive AR headset.

Usability. With regard to usability, the AITT's SUS score was a 54, which would correspond with an adjective measure of "OK" usability (Bangor, Kortum, & Miller, 2009); scores above 68 correlate with systems having high usability. Based on the responses, it was clear that while participants were motivated to use the system, they were hesitant about their ability to use the system unaided (e.g.,: "I think I would need the support of a technical person to be able to use this system" and "I need to learn a lot of things before I could get going with this system" were the highest rated negative statements in the SUS). It must be noted that the version of the AITT evaluated was a prototype and requires additional refinement to ensure a high level of usability.

Simulator Fidelity. Overall, participants agreed that the AITT scenarios were believable and the visual detail of simulated objects was presented realistically, with the exception of Ordnance Damage. Participants tended to be neutral with regard to the degree of realism of the sounds and behaviors of simulated objects. While participants agreed that the Binos looked, felt and behaved as expected in the real world, the VECTOR 21 functionality was rated neutral. Additionally, participants rated the visual simulation update-rate when turning their head as adequate (see Table 1).

Table 1. Degree of realism of AITT and specific objects

Question	Average Response (SD)					
	Ground Vehicles	People	Ordnance (e.g., smoke, explosion, etc.)	Ordnance Damage	Binos	Vector 21
1. The visual detail of the simulated objects was presented realistically in the system	4 (0)	4.2 (0.45)	4.2 (0.84)	3.4 (1.52)	–	–
2. The sounds of the simulated objects were presented realistically in the system	3 (1.79)	–	3.2 (0.45)	–	–	–
3. The behavior of the simulated objects is realistic (e.g., how they moved, reacted, etc.)	2.4 (0.55)	3.5 (0.58)	3.8 (0.84)	3.4 (0.89)	–	–
4. The simulated tools looked, felt and behaved as expected in the real world	–	–	–	–	4 (0)	3.4 (0.89)

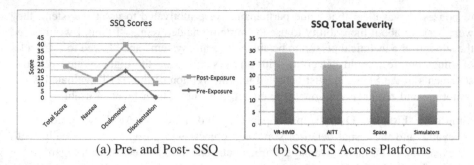

(a) Pre- and Post- SSQ   (b) SSQ TS Across Platforms

Fig. 2. Simulator sickness results

Simulator Sickness. Figure 2a below shows the average pre- and post- exposure SSQ scores. Exposure to the AITT system resulted in higher total severity (TS), as well as nausea (N), oculomotor (O), and disorientation (D) scores for 3 of the 5 participants. It is interesting to note that the SSQ profile for AITT is O > N>D, which is the same as the typical profile for simulators and different from that of virtual reality systems, which is D > N>O profile (Stanney et al., 1998). The significance of this finding is unclear and requires further study. Figure 2b shows that the sickness associated with the AITT AR-technology is a bit lower than that experienced with VR systems but higher than space and simulator sickness (Stanney et al., 1998).

Presence. The subscale means for Involvement/Control and Resolution indicate positive participant perceptions on average compared to the maximum score possible (see Table 2). However, the means of the Natural Interaction and Interface Quality subscales require further study due to the bimodal nature of the results shown in Figs. 3 and 4. Recent efforts investigating the impact of wearable interfaces upon Presence generally report higher levels of Presence than was found in this AITT study (Taylor & Barnett, 2013). The awkward merging of the virtual and real-world discussed in the Training Capability section above, the AR headset adjustability and ambient light issues noted in the Satisfaction section above, and the sickness symptoms reported in the Simulator Sickness section above may be collectively driving down presence. These results point to the need to enhance the naturalness of interaction (the bridging of real and virtual) and

Table 2. Presence subscale ratings

Results				
Presence subscale ratings				
Descriptive statistics	Involvement/control	Natural interaction	Resolution	Interface quality
Mean (*M*)	54.2	12.2	9.6	12.8
Standard Deviation (*SD*)	9.83	4.48	1.67	4.21
Maximum Score Possible	84	21	14	21

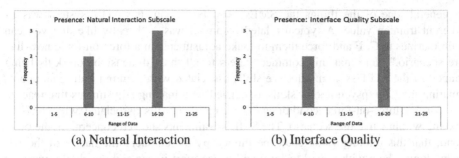

(a) Natural Interaction   (b) Interface Quality

Fig. 3. Immersion subscale frequency charts

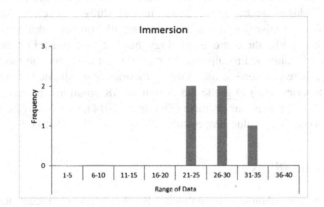

Fig. 4. Immersion frequency chart

interface quality (the AR headset adjustability and ambient lighting conditions) of future AR training solutions.

Italics indicate average rating of Neutral or below.

Immersion. Figure 4 shows the number of participants whose average immersion scores fell within the range categories provided. The full data range is included on the horizontal axis to aid the reader's understanding of responses relative to the range of possible outcomes. An average immersion score of 27.2 ($SD = 2.86$) out of a maximum of 40 was reported on the modified Immersion questionnaire, which equates to a 68 % immersion rating on the full survey. Previous results (Jennett, et al., 2008) based upon the full survey showed a comparable percentage (58-75 %), which indicated a relatively strong level of cognitive absorption and flow in the AITT system.

Observations and Notes. Based on the observations and notes that were taken during the study, the value of AR training for CFF was evaluated. As aforementioned, past research has suggested that AR provides a rich contextual learning environment to aid in acquiring complex task skills, such as decision making and asset allocation, while providing learners with a more personalized (self-direct /self-paced) and engaging learning experience. These findings continued to hold true in the present study.

In general, one of the things the SMEs liked best about the AITT system was its inherent training value. A typical related comment was – "I really like that you can train marines to CFF and force them to make adjustments in a force-on-force now live fire scenario." Note that this comment refers to all three dimensions of skills being trained in the AITT system: affective skills associated with communicating and coordinating the CFF, psychomotor skills associated with making adjustments that react to the current force-on-force conditions, and cognitive skills associated with decision making within a live fire scenario. The SME's comments showed concern, on the other hand, that this training value could be limited by the cumbersome nature of the AR technology – both with regard to form and fit /comfort issues and the clunky merging of the virtual with the real-world tools. A typical comment in this regard was a SME that indicated what he liked least about the AITT system was "the comfort and gear accountability." Based on the observations in this study it is clear that while AR technology holds promise for enhancing training of complex skills such as those associated with a CFF, there are technology hurdles that must first be overcome. Further, this study continued to support the premise that to derive the most benefit out of AR training, there is a need to use learning theories (e.g., situated learning theories, constructivist theories, etc.) to guide the design of AR solutions, as some past efforts have failed to show tremendous promise (Zhu et al., 2014), which may be why AR has yet to have a compelling value proposition (Nguyen & Blau, 2014).

7 Recommendations

Based on the results obtained from this study, the following recommendations for improving AR training systems are proposed.

1. *Tool Utility*: Participants consistently rated the utility of the AITT as high for its ability to support execution and training of CFF tasks. Nevertheless, the AR system's equipment affected the participant's ability to interact with the real world CFF tools necessary for task execution (e.g., map, compass, etc.). During the evaluation, it was noticed that participants were often frustrated with the need to "flip" the headset up in order to use the CFF tools. *As such, there is a need to identify ways to seamlessly transition between virtual and real-world views in AR training applications to reduce user frustration.*
2. *Satisfaction*: Participants were frustrated with the lack of adjustability of the headset and the ambient light in the outdoor environment. *It is recommended that AR displays be designed with adjustability in mind, i.e., provide an appropriate eye relief and lock in angle to make the display easier to see; provide a shield to block ambient light above the display to help with viewing the display on bright days.*
3. *Usability*: Participants indicated feeling intimidated by the highly technical setup required for use of the AITT system and feared it would be cumbersome in its current form to cost effectively support AR training, as technical support would be needed to keep the system up and running. *It is recommended that an AR training solution be coupled with a training management system that can walk instructors and trainees through how to easily set-up and use the system.*

4. *Fidelity*: Participants provided high ratings for the visual realism of ground vehicles, people, and the Binos look, feel, and function. Yet participants provided neutral responses to the visual realism of ordnance damage. Battle damage assessment (BDA) is crucial in determining CFF mission effectiveness. BDA involves evaluating the type, quantity, and location of damage. Thus, BDA tasks involve psychomotor and cognitive skills, such as using sensory cues from the environment to comprehend the battle scene, then estimating the battle damage and interpreting what the impact is to mission effectiveness. *While high fidelity for all cues in an AR training system is not necessary, it is important to identify the set of tasks similar to ordnance damage, which rely on sensorial discrimination and other such skills that require high fidelity to support task performance.*

5. *Simulator Sickness*: The amount of time an individual is immersed in an interactive training system has been found to be directly related to symptoms of simulator sickness (Nelson, Roe, Bolia, & Morley, 2000). After an average of 39.4 min of being immersed in the AITT system, symptoms of simulator sickness were higher than baseline levels, space sickness, and simulator sickness (see Figs. 2a and 2b), particularly with regard to oculomotor disruption (e.g., eyestrain, inability to focus). Until the visual discomfort associated with AR displays can be resolved, *it is recommended that the amount of time in an AR headset be limited (< 30 min) and regular break schedules be imposed in order to reduce the adverse effects related to protracted AR immersion.*

Acknowledgements. This material is based upon work supported in part by the Office of Naval Research (ONR) under contract N00014-12-C-0216. Any opinions, findings and conclusions or recommendations expressed in this material are those of the authors and do not necessarily reflect the views or the endorsement of ONR.

References

Bangor, A., Kortum, P., Miller, J.: Determining what individual sus scores mean: adding an adjective rating scale. J. Usability 4(3), 114–123 (2009)

Bitter, G., Corral, A.: The pedagogical potential of augmented reality apps. Int. J. Eng. Sci. Invention 3(10), 13–17 (2014)

Bossard, C., Kermarrec, G.: Conditions that facilitate transfer of learning in virtual environments. J. Inf. Commun. Technol., ICTTA 2006 1, 604–609 (2006)

Brooke, J.: SUS: a quick and dirty usability scale. In: Jordan, P.W., Thomas, B., Weerdmeester, B.A., McClelland, A.L. (eds.) Usability Evaluation in Industry. Taylor and Francis, London (1996)

Champney, R.K., Surpris, G., Carroll, M., Cohn, J.: Conducting training transfer studies in virtual environments. In: Hale, K.S., Stanney, K. (eds.) Handbook of Virtual Environments: Design, Implementation, and Applications, 2nd edn, pp. 781–795. CRC Press, Boca Raton, FL (2014)

Dunleavy, M., Dede, C.: Augmented reality teaching and learning. In: Spector, J.M., Merrill, M.D., Elen, J., Bishop, M.J. (eds.) The Handbook of Research for Educational Communications and Technology, 4th edn, pp. 735–745. Springer, New York (2014)

Hale, K.S., Stanney, K.: Effects of low stereo acuity on performance, presence and sickness within a virtual environment. Appl. Ergonomics **37**, 329–339 (2004)

Jennett, C., Cox, A.L., Cairns, P., Dhoparee, S., Epps, A., Tijs, T., Walton, A.: Measuring and defining the experience of immersion in games. Int. J. Hum Comput Stud. **66**(9), 641–661 (2008)

Johnson, L., Smith, R., Willis, H., Levine, A., Haywood, K.: The 2011 Horizon Report. The New Media Consortium, Austin, TX (2011)

Kamarainen, A.M., et al.: EcoMOBILE: Integrating augmented reality and probeware with environmental education field trips. Comput. Educ. **68**, 545–556 (2013)

Kennedy, R.S., Lane, N.E., Berbaum, K.S., Lilienthal, M.G.: Simulator sickness questionnaire: an enhanced method for quantifying simulator sickness. Int. J. Aviat. Psychol. **3**(3), 203–220 (1993)

Kirkpatrick, D.L.: Evaluating Training Programs: The Four Levels. Berrett-Koehler, San Francisco, CA (1994)

Lave, J., Wenger, E.: Situated Learning: Legitimate Peripheral Participation. Cambridge University Press, Cambridge, UK (1990)

Nelson, W.T., Roe, M.M., Bolia, R.S., Morley, R.M.: Assessing Simulator Sickness in a See-Through HMD: Effects of Time Delay, Time on Task, and Task Complexity (ADA: 430344). Air Force Research Laboratory, Wright-Patterson Air Force Base, OH (2000)

Nguyen, T.H., Blau, B.: Market guide to augmented reality. Gartner report No: G00268639. Gartner, Inc (2014)

Reichheld, F.F.: The one number you need to grow. Harvard Bus. Rev. **81**(12), 46–55 (2003)

Sauro, J.: Software usability and net promoter benchmarks for (2014). 14 October 2014. www.measuringucom/blog/softwar-benchmarks14.php. Accessed 8 November 2014

Stanney, K.M., et al.: Aftereffects and sense of presence in virtual environments: formulation of a research and development agenda. report sponsored by the life sciences division at NASA headquarters. Int. J. Hum.-Comput. Interact. **10**(2), 135–187 (1998)

Strensrud, B.S., Fragomeni, G., Garrity, P.: Autonomy requirements for virtual JFO training. In: Proceedings of the Interservice/Industry Training, Simulation, and Education Conference (I/ITSEC). NTSA. Arlington, VA (2013)

Taylor, G.S., Barnett, J.S.: Evaluation of wearable simulation interface for military training. Hum. Factors **55**(3), 672–690 (2013)

Army, U.S.: FM 6-30: Tactics, Techniques, and Procedures for Observed Fire. Department of the Army, Washington, DC (1991)

Witmer, B.G., Singer, M.J.: Measuring presence in virtual environments: A presence questionnaire. Presence **7**(3), 225–240 (1998)

Zhu, E., Hadadgar, A., Masiello, I., Zary, N.: Augmented reality in healthcare education: an integrative review. PeerJ 2:e469; doi:10.7717/peerj.469 (2014)

Training Effectiveness Evaluation: Call for Fire Trainer – Augmented Virtuality (CFFT-AV)

Gino Fragomeni[1(✉)], Stephanie J. Lackey[2], Roberto Champney[3],
Julie Nanette Salcedo[2], and Stephen Serge[2]

[1] U.S. Army Research Laboratory, Orlando, FL, USA
gino.f.fragomeni.civ@mail.mil
[2] University of Central Florida, Institute for Simulation and Training,
Orlando, FL, USA
{slackey,jsalcedo,sserge}@ist.ucf.edu
[3] Design Interactive, Inc., Orlando, FL, USA
roberto@designinteractive.net

Abstract. As emerging technologies continue to modernize battlefield systems, the use of Mixed Reality (MR) training has been increasingly proposed as a lower cost and more time-effective alternative to live training. However, there has been minimal empirical data to demonstrate the effectiveness of MR type training which leaders require to make informed decisions about training device acquisition. In an effort to assist in the decision making process of future training system acquisition a Training Effectiveness Evaluation (TEE) is being conducted by U.S. Army Research Laboratory (ARL) Human Research and Engineering Directorate (HRED), Simulation and Training Technology Center (STTC) on the Call for Fire Trainer – Augmented Virtuality (CFFT-AV). This paper describes the methodology of the TEE with regard to the effectiveness of AV as a platform within the Call for Fire (CFF) task domain and how AV technologies and methods can impact CFF training.

Keywords: Augmented virtuality · Simulation-Based training · Joint forward observer

1 Introduction

The Army Learning Concept for 2015 [1] calls for implementing technology-enabled training for demanding tasks within the operational environment. One such role is that of the Joint Fires Observers (JFO), who serve as the link between dismounted units and supporting fires elements. The JFO task domain, roles, and responsibilities require complex decision-making in high-risk environments. Existing Simulation-Based Training (SBT) systems offer increased opportunities for training and certification, and have demonstrated training efficacy, but fail to fully resolve throughput issues. Furthermore, fielded JFO SBT systems lack portability and their associated costs (e.g., hardware, role players) can be prohibitive. One way of reducing cost is to leverage Augmented Virtuality (AV), which theoretically provides comparable cognitive fidelity

R. Shumaker and S. Lackey (Eds.): VAMR 2015, LNCS 9179, pp. 263–272, 2015.
DOI: 10.1007/978-3-319-21067-4_27

to augmented reality with less cost. A key element of designing SBT systems is the need to identify what elements of the operational task experience need to be replicated in the simulation environment (i.e., simulator fidelity). Too much fidelity may result in overly expensive systems that do not necessarily provide better training. Too little or the wrong kind of fidelity may result in systems that do not support the required training. Thus, a careful balance is needed to achieve the best Return on Investment (ROI). In order to more fully understand how AV technologies and methods impact Call for Fire (CFF) training effectiveness and compare to existing systems, an empirical evaluation is required. ARL-HRED-STTC is conducting a Training Effectiveness Evaluation (TEE) to evaluate the role of an AV training systems for effectively training CFF as well as inform the academic and applied training literature with regard to the effectiveness of AV as a platform. The goal of the CFFT-AV evaluation is to blend live and virtual worlds to provide individual and team training. The objective of this research is to assess the training effectiveness of AV within the CFF task domain. Specifically, this effort will address four research questions:

1. How much more or less effectiveness does the AV technology, device, or method provide compared to the existing CFFT II system?
2. How much more or less does the AV technology, device, or method of training costs compared to the existing CFFT II system?
3. Does the AV technology provide the appropriate level of fidelity to enable accomplishment of both individual and team learning objectives?
4. What is the ROI of the AV technology, device, or method for CFF training?

   This paper describes the TEE CFF to inform how AV technologies and methods impact CFF training.

2   Background

2.1   The Operational Domain

A CFF is a request to execute an attack on a selected target using a specified method of fire [2, 3]. Requests are initiated by a JFO who serves as the communication link between dismounted and fire support units [3]. During a CFF mission, the JFO takes an observation post usually located some distance from the fight, but positioned to enable him to visually locate and identify targets and clearly spot fire rounds [2, 3]. From his post, the JFO identifies the target location and determines an appropriate method of fire. The JFO operational setting is a high-risk and dynamic environment that requires complex decision-making abilities. When selecting the method of fire, JFOs must consider the threat composition and location, position of friendly and neutral elements, potential terrain effects, and direction of incoming fires [3]. Once the firing method is selected, the JFO transmits the CFF request to a Fire Direction Center (FDC) that determines the availability of the requested fire support and disseminates the fire commands to a Firing Unit. Due to the criticality and complexity of the CFF domain, CFF training is highly involved, requiring a JFO trainee to demonstrate proficiency in three specific duty areas. First, essential training and classroom academics include a demonstrated understanding of the individual tasks and information necessary to perform a CFF. Specifically, this portion of the training cycle facilitates a trainee's ability to evaluate current tactical situations, capabilities of fixed and rotary wing aircraft, effects of weather and terrain, and nuances of radio communications. Next, mission preparation provides familiarization with equipment and effective communication with fire support units. Finally, CFF execution requires a sound understanding of the task domain and demonstrating so through live or simulated execution of the CFF task [4].

2.2 Joint Fires Observer Course

The Army established the Joint Fires Observer Course (JFOC) to train and certify Soldiers in the Tactics, Techniques and Procedures (TTP) learned during combat operations in Afghanistan and Iraq. The course integrates simulation systems in order to enhance the capabilities of Soldiers attending the JFOC and/or Soldiers conducting semi-annual currency requirements. Training Soldiers in a VE has been effective, but falls short of actual training in the field or while deployed. However, virtual training increases the proficiency of the Soldier prior to live training and, ultimately, combat operations. These simulations evaluate a student's ability to conduct several of the hardest simulation examinations during the JFOC that have a historically high failure rate. These include conducting a Type 2 Close Air Support (CAS) mission with a Joint Terminal Attack Controller (JTAC), estimating distance to a known (or unknown) point, utilizing a laser designation device such as the Special Operations Forces Laser Rangefinder Designator (SOFLAM) or the Lightweight Laser Designator Rangefinder (LLDR) and calling for and adjusting Naval Gunfire (NGF). The Army JFO program is designed to help fill the void that currently exists between the number of JTACs the Army says it needs to conduct operations and what the Air Force can currently provide. The program focuses on training the "Company Fire Support Officers/NCOs, Platoon Forward Observers, Combat Observation Lasing Teams and members of scout/reconnaissance organizations. These individuals will be taught the skill sets necessary to assist JTACs in conducting Type II and Type III CAS. The Army's goal is to have one JFO per maneuver platoon. The JFO Memorandum of Agreement (MOA), that has been signed between the Departments of Army and Air Force and the United States Special Operations Command, defines the JFO as: "A trained service member who can request, adjust, and control surface-to-surface fires, provide targeting information in support of Type II and III CAS terminal attack controls, and perform autonomous Terminal Guidance Operations (TGO).

2.3 Development of the Call for Fire Trainer

Beginning in the mid 1990's call for fire system trainers were evolved for various user groups and agencies. The earliest system which has been fielded for the United States Army and is still operational is the Call for Fire Trainer (CFFT) which is currently supported by The Program Executive Office for Simulation, Training and Instrumentation (PEO-STRI). CFFT/CFFT II is an initial call for fire system primarily designed for a classroom environment. The CFFT is fielded around the world in various configurations utilizing an instructor station, one or more enhanced student stations, and a number of additional stations where a student can sit and observe the battlefield view in the front of the classroom. The CFFT is an individual and/or collective training system that provides a simulated battlefield environment for training Forward Observers (FOs) at the institutional and unit level. The system is designed to be transportable and provide advanced distributed learning, Simulated Military Equipment (SME), virtual environments, and computer-generated forces using One Semi-Automated Forces (OneSAF). The CFFT II is a technology upgrade of the guard unit armory device full-crew interactive simulation trainer II (GUARDFIST II). In addition to the 19 basic fire support tasks trained on the GUARDFIST II, the CFFT II can be used to train CAS, NGF, mortar registration, and suppression of enemy air defense tasks. The importability of terrain databases, combined with the inherent flexibility of the OneSAF Test Bed (OTB) scenario, also enhances the realism of the training environment. The CFFT II consists of instructor and student stations. There are two variations of the student station, standard and enhanced. The standard student station is composed of a map and a set of binoculars. The enhanced student station is composed of SME such as the simulated LLDR, virtual military equipment such as virtual Night Vision Goggles (NVGs), and a student control computer. The CFFT II can be configured to accommodate 4, 12, or 30 student stations (1:4, 1:12, and 1:30 configurations). Regardless of the configuration, each CFFT II has at least one enhanced student station and one instructor station; the remainder of the students use standard student stations.

2.4   Joint Fires Effects Training System (JFETS)

The Joint Fires Effects Training System (JFETS) is an evolutionary development of the approved CFFT. It was developed as a test bed at the Fires Battle Lab, Ft. Sill to test new concepts of inserting higher fidelity into the fire support training environment. JFETS is an immersive trainer consisting of tailored modules for Open Terrain (OTM), Urban Terrain (UTM), and close air support (CASM). Two additional modules for After Action Reviews (AAR) and Fires Effects Coordination (FECM) comprise the entire developmental JFETS system. The open terrain, urban terrain, and close air support modules are characterized by a robust visual system embedded in a training space designed to emulate geographical or cultural aspects of the southwest Asia operational area. However, there is a lack of empirical data available to assess the impact of the "immersive" aspects of the developmental JFETS upon trainee performance. Anecdotal data indicate the current configuration may facilitate performance by improving user "buy-in." As with the CFFT-AV, no empirical data have been collected to support interview responses on this issue. The data provide evidence to conclude that very high fidelity visual systems and realistically modeled (for form, fit, and function) SME produce improved training transfer. The developmental JFETS has been anecdotally reported by the users as an effective training system. There is a desire to advance the training system and more fully integrate it within existing Field Artillery School core curricula. One challenge hindering full integration is throughput due to current configuration parameters and a lack of design recommendations to move integration forward.

2.5   Immersive Dome Technologies

The military training enterprise has explored alternative dome projection technologies for JTAC and JFO training domains. An example of such a dome is shown in (Fig. 1) that is in use at the JTAC School at Nellis, AFB. Domes have been attractive for JTAC/JFO training because of the immersive nature of the dome environment.

Fig. 1. JTAC dome

There are two primary approaches to dome architecture, rear projection and front projection. The two main advantages of rear projection are, no projectors are visible to the student, and the student can use tactical night vision goggles to enhance the light projected from the rear. However, there are several disadvantages of the dome architecture. Traditionally, domes have a very large footprint to accommodate the projector throw which hampers point of need training device availability. Additionally, the light level inside domes is diminished by the light attenuation of the screen material and the curved shape of screens present problems in edge blending and projector alignment with the multiple projectors. The geometry in domes also presents various problems. There is a discontinuity where the flat top meets the curved sides and sides tend to have a slight hour-glass shape, which impact visual requirements such as arc and pixel. There are a number of commercially available front projection domes that could be used to meet training requirements and have much smaller footprint, a brighter display, and would present far fewer problems with edge blending and alignment. Regardless, the dome approach is primarily regarded as an option due to the immersive nature that engages the trainee better than traditional projection found in a CFFT type device.

2.6   Call for Fire Trainer – Augmented Virtuality

The Call For Fire Trainer – Augmented Virtuality (CFFT-AV) is a prototype training device designed within the context of the Reality-Virtuality (RV) continuum, specifically for the Joint Forward Observers (JFOs) use case. Augmented Virtuality (AV), the augmentation of a virtual setting with real objects provides a means to merge a richly layered, multi-modal, 3D real experience into a Virtual Environment (VE). The essence of this approach is to provide students with a mixed reality experience by means of an optical see-through head-mounted display (HMD). With this kind of interface, it is possible to create voids in the rendered scene graph of a virtual environment allowing the real-world, physical environment surrounding the student to be viewed normally. With a high-resolution tracking solution, the real-world objects produce scene-graph voids created on-the-fly to match the object's size, position and orientation relative to the student. This capability eliminates the need in current technology for students to remove HMDs to view real-world objects. In addition to the use of real-world objects, the CFFT-AV incorporates a novel approach to the design of surrogates to simulate additional equipment needed for training in the CFF task domain. This approach utilizes tracked, inert objects with the general shape and heft of devices like M22 and Vector 21 Binoculars, Lensatic Compass, Defense Advanced GPS Receiver (DAGR), Infrared Zoom Laser Illuminator Designator (IZLID), LLDR, and the M4 weapon. These surrogates include knobs, buttons and switches that provide USB inputs to the system. As they are tracked, the objects appear as corresponding virtual models in the student's field of view. For devices that have a reticle view, the HMD's view switches to a rendered frustum of the near-eye device view when brought in proximity to the student's eyes (Fig. 2). Fabricated from inexpensive material, these surrogates offer a significant cost advantage over the SME commonly employed in existing SBT systems. This mix of real-world and surrogate objects mitigates a principal criticism of current virtual reality CFF training systems that require a student to transition between real-world and virtual world interfaces. Such use cases are generally viewed as awkward and distracting, significantly decrementing the immersive qualities of the simulation and the student's suspension of disbelief.

Fig. 2. Example of an M22 binocular rendered frustum

2.7   Mixed Reality – Virtuality Continuum

Milgram [5, 6] describes a taxonomy that identifies how augmented reality and virtual reality are related. He defines the Reality-Virtuality continuum shown in Fig. 3.

The real world and a totally virtual environment are at the two ends of this continuum with the middle region called Mixed Reality (MR). Augmented Reality (AR) lies near the real-world end of the spectrum with the predominate perception being the real-world augmented by computer generated data. AV is a term created by Milgram to identify systems that are mostly synthetic with some real world added, such as the CFFT-AV. AV, the augmentation of a virtual setting with real objects provides a means to merge a richly layered, multi-modal, 3D real experience into a VE [7]. Design industry paves the road for more innovations in AV [9], a more expansive form of VR. Despite its potential, AV has not received as much attention as VR and AR. AV has only been applied in very limited domains: as displays on unmanned air vehicles [10], 3D video-conferencing systems [11] and a scientific center [12]. Recognized research effort towards AV applications in the military training domain is fairly limited.

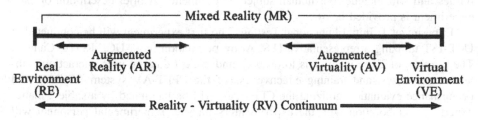

Fig. 3. Simplified representation of reality-virtuality continuum

3   Training Effectiveness Evaluation

3.1   Problem Statement

Existing JFO SBT systems offer increased opportunities for training and certification, and have demonstrated training efficacy, but often do not provide an immersive learning environment. Furthermore, fielded JFO SBT systems have fallen short at addressing the "point of need" training gap and their associated costs (e.g., hardware, support personnel) can be prohibitive. One possible way of reducing cost and increasing immersion is to leverage AV, which theoretically provides comparable cognitive fidelity to AR with less cost. While certain technical challenges persist, a necessary step remains: evaluating the value and effectiveness of AV simulation by identifying what elements of the JFO training experience need to be replicated in the simulation environment (i.e., simulator fidelity). Excessive fidelity may result in a cost prohibitive system that does not provide a measurable improvement in training, while too little or the wrong kind of fidelity may result in a system that does not support the required training requirements. Thus, a careful balance is required to achieve the best ROI for the training acquisition community. In order to more fully understand how AV technologies and methods impact JFO training effectiveness and compare to existing SBT systems, an empirical evaluation is required. This assessment needs to take into account the acquisition and retention of procedural knowledge and cognitive decision-making capability. Practical AR is viewed by many in the military enterprise as the objective end-state for the future of U.S. ground forces training. The goal of this evaluation is to assist the U.S. Army decision making process of future training system acquisition with respect to the JFO use case, combining the flexibility and lower cost of simulation with the fidelity of live training by incorporating mixed reality technologies.

3.2 Methodology

The purpose of this research is to understand and explore the application of AV technologies, devices, and methods aimed at small unit leader and individual Soldier tasks. The objective of the present research effort is to evaluate the training effectiveness of AV within the CFF task domain. The CFFT-AV system includes a head-mounted display (HMD), game-engine software, motion tracking, a compass, binoculars, and a terrain map. The evaluation will focus on the system's operational and training capabilities and will include four human subject experiments. A brief description of each experiment is provided below.

Experiment 1: Initial Functional Testing. The first experiment will be conducted at UCF-IST utilizing a representative U.S. Army population (e.g., UCF ROTC Cadets). The purpose of Experiment 1 is to observe and collect data on user interaction, subjective responses, and training effectiveness of the CFFT-AV system. Training and performance evaluation utilizing the CFFT-AV will be facilitated by a subject matter expert in collaboration with the experimenters on site. Experimental personnel will collect performance evaluation data and will administer subjective questionnaires related to the participants' experiences during training within the CFFT-AV system.

Experiment 2: Baseline Data Collection. The second experiment will be conducted at a representative U.S. Army facility (e.g., Ft. Sill, OK) and utilize active duty U.S. Army personnel as participants. The purpose of Experiment 2 is to obtain baseline performance data on the use and effectiveness of the traditional CFFT II training system. The CFFT-II system uses a projected display with accompanying tools to project augmented reality information on the screen to aid in training of the Call for Fire task. Operation of and interaction with the traditional training system will be facilitated by U.S. Army and contracted instructors on site. Experimental personnel will collect instructors' performance evaluation data and will administer subjective questionnaires related to the Soldiers' experiences during training within the CFFT II system.

Experiment 3: AV Evaluation (Phase 1). The third experiment will be conducted at a representative U.S. Army facility (e.g., Ft. Sill, OK) and utilize active duty U.S. Army personnel as participants. The purpose of Experiment 3 is to evaluate the training effectiveness metrics of the CFFT-AV system and compare those results to the traditional CFFT II system results obtained during Experiment 2. The task scope for the metrics evaluated will focus on basic CFF skills. Soldier training and performance evaluation utilizing the CFFT-AV will be facilitated by active duty or reserve U.S. Army instructors on site. Experimental personnel will collect instructors' performance evaluation data and will administer subjective questionnaires related to the Soldiers' experiences during training within the CFFT-AV system.

Experiment 4: AV Evaluation (Phase 2). The fourth experiment will be conducted at a representative U.S. Army facility (e.g., Ft. Sill, OK) and utilize active duty U.S.

Army personnel as participants. The purpose of Experiment 4 is to evaluate the training effectiveness metrics of the CFFT-AV system and compare those results to the traditional CFFT II system results obtained during Experiment 2. The task scope for the metrics evaluated will include advanced CFF skills. Soldier training and performance evaluation utilizing the CFFT-AV will be facilitated by active duty or reserve U.S. Army instructors on site. Experimental personnel will collect instructors' performance evaluation data and will administer subjective questionnaires related to the Soldiers' experiences during training within the CFFT-AV system.

Advancements in technology in the recent past have led to immersive 3D, 360 simulations being used successfully to train both civilian and military aviators. The level of this success has led those in the military to seek ways in which to incorporate this technology in other areas of military training. It is hoped that by using immersive VEs a Soldier may be provided training opportunities not afforded in the traditional classroom or in field exercises and can do so without the risk of injury. Moreover, supplemental training in a simulator can greatly reduce the costs associated with using live ammunition during field exercises. Studies designed to ascertain just how humans acquire new concepts and knowledge through the use of immersive and virtual environments lag behind the development and utilization of such sophisticated technology. People often attest that learning in an immersive environment is enjoyable, engaging, and beneficial; however, actual empirical data supporting improved performance is less available.

4 Conclusion

This TEE will provide empirical data to assess the effectiveness of MR, specifically in the area of AV. Undoubtedly, more research will be required to determine if training in immersive environments transfers to live training environments more readily than training in traditional technical training environments. This effort is intended to assess if there are measurable performance and perception differences between Soldiers trained in an AV environment and those trained in a traditional classroom environment. Furthermore, this investigation will inform future research assessing the impact of immersive technologies on the transfer to tactical environments and Warfighter skill sustainment. At a minimum, the CFFT-AV TEE will assist in promoting effective implementation of technology-enabled training for JFO tasks in CFF operations and assist the U.S. Army decision making process of future training system acquisition with respect to the JFO use case.

References

1. U.S. Army: The U.S. Army Learning Concept for 2015, U.S. Army (2011)
2. U.S. Army: FM 6–30: Tactics, Techniques, and Procedures for Observed Fire, U.S. Army, Washington (1991)
3. Stensrund, B., Fragomeni, G., Garrity, P.: Autonomy requirements for virtual JFO training. In: Proceedings of Interservice/Industry Training, Simulation and Education Conference, Orlando (2013)

4. U.S. Army: JCAS Memorandum of Agreement: Joint Fires Observer. U.S. Army, Washington (2013)
5. Milgram, P., Kishino, F.: A taxonomy of mixed reality visual displays. IEICE Trans. Inf. Syst. **E77-D**(12), 1321–1329 (1994)
6. Milgram, P., Takemura, H., Utsumi, A., Kishino, F.: Augmented reality: a class of displays on the reality-virtuality continuum. In: SPIE 2351 Telemanipulator and Telepresence Technologies, p. 282 (1994)
7. Milgram, P., Colquhoun, H.: A taxonomy of real and virtual world display ingeration. In: Mixed Reality-Merging Real and Virtual Worlds, pp. 1–16 (1999)
8. Oxman, R.E.: Design media for the cognitive designer. Autom. Constr. **9**(4), 337–346 (2000)
9. Rackliffe, N.: An Augmented Virtuality Display for Improving UAV Usability, Bedford (2005)
10. Regenbrecht, H., Lum, T., Kohler, P., Ott, C., Wagner, M., Wilke, W., Mueller, E.: Using augmented virtuality for remote collaboration. Presence: Teleoperators and Virtual Environ.-Spec. Issue: Adv. Collaborative Virtual Environ. **13**(3), 338–354 (2005)
11. Clarke, J., Vines, J., Mark, E.: An Augmented Virtuality Scientific Data Center. Army Research Laboratory, Aberdeen Proving Ground (2004)

Design and Analysis of the Learning Process Management System

Songfeng Gao[✉] and Ziqi Wang

School of Industry Engineering,
Beijing University of Civil Engineering and Architecture, Beijing 100044, China
gaosongfeng@bucea.edu.cn, lj230405@sina.com

Abstract. In this paper, we put forward a set of learning process management system. This system, integrating the monitoring and feedback functions which are widely ignored in other current teaching platforms, focus on the students' learning process, and digitizing the users' daily learning. From login this platform, to recording the user's learning habits and learning methods, at the same time, this system shows users' learning situation in the form of graphs showing and provides the objective effective data for the "teaching" and "learning". The learning process management system aims at helping students to establish the purpose of good study habits and learning methods.

Keywords: Learning process · Teaching platform · Process management · Process feedback · .net platform

1 Introduction

With the development and the mature of Internet technology, the teaching mode is changing from the traditional classroom to teaching system. However, the student lack of autonomy in the process of using teaching system, and, at present, some of the teaching system without effective learning regulatory mechanisms, which leads to the loose learning environment relatively, and the teaching quality cannot reach the effect desired. According to the survey, that 46.2 % of people hold that the main factor of the influence on teaching learning system is lack of the monitoring mechanism of learning process, while only 28.2 % of people consider that the reason is the design of the teaching system itself [1]. So, now, a method of learning process management should be applied into the process of the student daily learning.

The learning process management feedbacks and manages the whole process that involved the kinds of elements, links and methods of the study. It has been widely used and formed a complete set of management system in European and American countries. When the management method applied into the teaching system, it will not only real-time monitoring the process of learning, at the same time, feedback the learning stat to students objectively, but, more important, improve the quality of teaching, and the teachers could carry out targeted teaching according to each student's specific learning situation.

2   The Implementation of the Main Functions

In order to make up for other teaching systems could not monitor and feedback the learning process of the students, learning management system arises at the historic moment. Guided by the learning process management method, it mode of C/S framework, based on. Net platform, uses C # programming language implementation, and equips SQL Server 2005 database to complete the actual demand of data processing and storage.

In terms of functional design, according to the result of requirement analysis phase, the system, in the functional design, include the login management, the teaching management and the online discussion three parent functions. And the teaching management is divided into three child functions, that is the learning time management, progress management and operation management (Fig. 1).

2.1   The Design Principles

The design Principles of the learning process management system integrates the basic design methods of the process management in general, in order to flexible utilize the real learning, teaching and manage the process effectively in the actual work. Each functional module of the system independent of each other, development respectively, that reduces the data coupling, improves robustness, and it's convenience for the system maintainability and expansion of the subsequent function. (System data flow

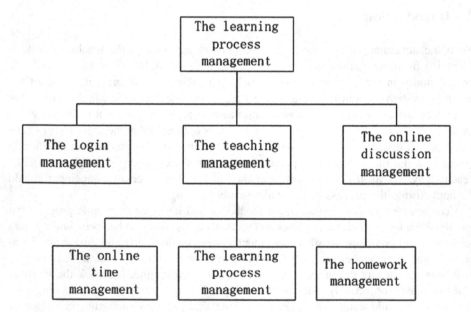

Fig. 1. The functional configuration chart of the learning process management

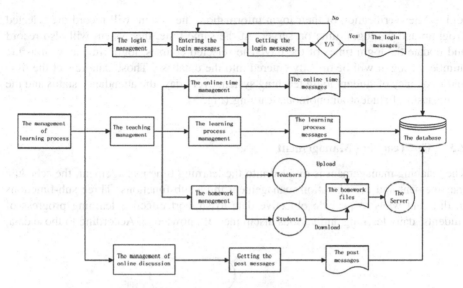

Fig. 2. The data flow chart of the learning process management

diagram in Fig. 2) While, during development process of the system, we give full consideration to the actual needs of teachers and students, and based on the following principles to create an efficient and practical learning process system for them .

Clearly Orientation. By adhering to the manage and feedback the users' learning process, the principle of the guide students to cultivate a good study habit, the system make efficiently complete the task of learning and form their own learning methods come true.

Friendly UI. Fully considering the demands and experience of the user groups at using this system, to build a good environment for household work and study more convenient.

A closed-Loop Feedback. Closed loop management allows users, according to the feedback data, to summarize their own learning habits, learning ways, learning progress, the implementation of learning goals and some other relates. At the same time, the teachers also assess the performance of students reasonably and scientifically.

Flexible Learning. On the basis of the closed loop management, the flexible learning will come true. According to the feedback data, users will real-time adjust the focus on "teaching" and "learning".

2.2 The Login Management

The login module complete simulation the attendance functions of the actual teaching and, reflecting students' study habits by the specific time and the numbers of students log on the system in the daily. Students need to course selection at teaching platform login. After verification of their login information, the system will record the selected program and the logon time on server. At the same time, the system will also record and update the login times of the day. The selected courses, login time as well as the number of logon will be directly entered into the database. Those data reflect the time and frequency of student login teaching system every day, the attendance status and the enthusiasm of student autonomous learning (Fig. 3).

2.3   The Teaching Management

The teaching management is divided into the learning time management, the schedule management and the operation management three sub-functions. Three sub-functions in different ways to provide objective data to support effective learning progress of students' daily learning and various disciplines of knowledge. According to those data,

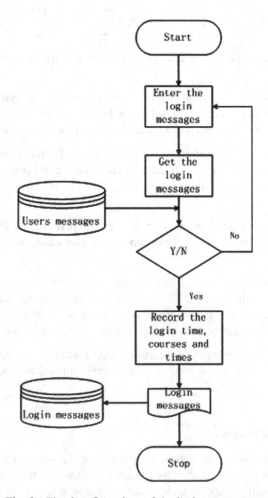

Fig. 3. The data flow chart of the login management

students can more clearly to know the level of their own understanding on different disciplines, reasonable arrange the learning time, strengthen their weakness. During the process of teaching, at the same time, it's easy for teachers more intuitive to find the problems of each student in the course of study, timely to adjust the focus of the work, and to arrange reasonable and effective teaching task according to the actual the situation.

2.4 The Online Time Management

The long learning management module is used to record the length of time students in the system. The data reflects the continuity of their learning process, and has the appropriate oversight mechanisms. The calculation of the learning time is the different between the time of starting learning content and the time of exiting. Theoretically speaking, the longer a student learn discipline, on the one hand, the more thorough understanding, the more firmly grasp, from the other hand, it also reflects the attitudes of students and the degree of the teachers' task [2]. Of course, in order to prevent students from speculative psychology, when the user does not operate the system in a period of time, the system will be appropriate message. The interval time, from the message appears to it be closed, will not be include in the learning time. As for the so-called interval time, in order to avoid the conventional teaching time and recess time are included in the learning time, the each interval time generated within a random integer (30, 45).

2.5 The Learning Process Management

The learning process management module's function is to prompt the user last study progress, and update the new one. The implementation process is that, when student end of the current subject learning, system will update their new courseware currently knowledge nodes and the number of the new courseware page into the database. If the student login this system in the next time, the system will extract the latest data from the database and displayed in the form of a dialog to them. While the teacher can also view this feature to adjust the teaching schedule, and carry out more targeted teaching.

2.6 The Homework Management

The homework management simulates the actual homework of the teaching process, the content covers the main knowledge of the each chapter, that makes students better understand the application of the relevant knowledge. After studying the each chapter's knowledge, students need to complete the corresponding chapter exercises. The teachers will published the homework files to the server, and the students download those files from their teaching platform client. Students should upload their files after they finish the homework, and teachers will download those to marking. For late homework marking and correction are also in this form.

2.7 The Online Discussion Management

Online discussion management will record the stat of students' posts and replies in the forum of the system. In the forum, teachers regularly publish some information or a related study and discussion of learning content, which assists students to better understand the relevant knowledge and builds up a platform to communication with the teacher after class for them. System will record each student's posting, if one's selected as essence, it will be in the students' grades. Through this form of network brainstorming, it established a relaxed and pleasant atmosphere for learning and discussion but a good relationship between teachers and students.

3 The Analysis of System Innovation

The biggest innovation of this system is the feedback mechanism. By the help with recording their daily learning, students and teachers will find the problems during the learning process, and development of response measures timely, so that to achieve real-time effective teaching purposes. Based on the reflection situation of the above managements, teachers score for students' grade. So pay attention to the evaluation process of daily learning process is more objective truth. The students' grades in addition to the above results, it will also include the daily test scores, eventually in the form of a graph showing. And the students, on the one hand, also can be more intuitive to see the trend of learning state of their own, in order to summarize and reflect the individual learning situation conveniently. On the other hand, teachers can find the students' problems in those data, seek teaching focus and achieve the best result of teach students in accordance with their aptitude.

The learning process in the form of graphs to present to the user is another major innovation system, it is taking into account the effect produced by the Graphic Organizers on process management. Generally speaking, graphic organization is to use visual way to represent knowledge, concepts, or graphical structure view, order or process. It can be used for a variety of learning activities, such as brainstorming, idea generation, analysis of information, organization of information and expression discovery, etc. It also helps learners to enhance interest in learning, stimulate the motivation, reduce or release boredom, improve recall rate, clarify information, organizational thinking and promote understanding [3]. Graphic organizer of a recognized feature is that it can show learners thinking process "logic" and "integrity", clear the extent of the understanding and insufficient [4].

4 Conclusion

The learning process management system is originally designed to manage learning process of the students, to guide students to effective learning and foster a good learning ability. Based on this new way of weakening the evaluation of traditional examination, enhance the fairness and scientific. The difference between this system and the current teaching system is that, it focuses on the process of the whole learning management, and always accompanied by the students. On the one hand, it makes the learning process digitized, objectively feedback student learning, and more effectively assess their learning status. On the other hand, it provides an accurate and effective feedback information and guidance on the relevance and effectiveness for teachers. Not only to share the tasks of teachers, but also allow them to carry out selective teaching, the maximum meet the actual needs of students. In the subsequent version of the system, we will further expand the system monitoring mechanism, besides, rich the way of interaction with the user and the evaluation methods of the system, so that to meet the needs of the market and users.

References

1. Minghua, T., Bin, W.: Research on monitoring strategies and implement methods in the online learning process. Distance Educ. Chaina 3 (2010)
2. Handa, M.: Design and realization of the online learning process monitoring system. J. Exp. Technol. Manag. 5(28), 93–95 (2011)
3. On learning process management for the distance learner. J. Distance Educ. 3 63–66 (2009)
4. Reference: Graphic Organizers[DB/OL][2008-04-08]

Applying Research in the Cognitive Sciences to the Design and Delivery of Instruction in Virtual Reality Learning Environments

Martin S. Goodwin[✉], Travis Wiltshire, and Stephen M. Fiore

Institute for Simulation and Training, University of Central Florida,
Orlando, FL, USA
{mgoodwin, twiltshi, sfiore}@ist.ucf.edu

Abstract. Current approaches to the design and delivery of instruction in virtual reality learning environments (VRLEs) draw heavily from traditional instructional strategies and design practices. This is problematic given that these strategies and practices were developed for learning contexts lacking the dynamic nature and capabilities of technology-rich, immersive learning environments. This directly affects the instructional efficacy of VRLEs by creating a dichotomy between the learning interface, which emphasizes knowledge as object, and the learning environment, which can emphasize knowledge as action. Drawing from theory and research in the cognitive sciences on embodied and enactive cognition, we present an instructional strategy that addresses this dichotomy by incorporating techniques and design practices that are better aligned with the learning dynamics provided by VRLEs.

Keywords: Virtual reality learning environments · Simulation-based training · Instructional design · Embodied cognition · Enactive cognition

1 Introduction

Virtual reality learning environments (VRLEs) provide dynamic experiences that can positively influence instructional outcomes. However, current approaches to the design and delivery of instruction within these environments are largely based on traditional methods that tend to emphasize technological capabilities at the expense of the actual learning experience [1]. Emerging technologies are providing for higher degrees of physical and psychological immersion within VRLEs, resulting in greater levels of fidelity and providing opportunities for more profound and meaningful learner experiences, and hence, better instructional outcomes.

A review of the current literature reveals mixed results of the instructional efficacy of VRLEs. While some studies have demonstrated the instructional benefits of these environments, particularly with respect to learner control [2], and the ability of learners to leverage existing knowledge to create new concepts [3, 4], other studies have indicated that the use of these environments provide either marginal or negative effects on learning outcomes. The factors influencing these undesirable effects stem from an over-reliance on learning technologies, a lack of focus on the manner in which those technologies affect the critical factors that facilitate learning, and/or the absence of

© Springer International Publishing Switzerland 2015
R. Shumaker and S. Lackey (Eds.): VAMR 2015, LNCS 9179, pp. 280–291, 2015.
DOI: 10.1007/978-3-319-21067-4_29

comprehensive instructional strategies and supporting design practices to guide the learning experience. These marginal or negative effects on learning outcomes are most prominent when these environments are used to teach conceptual knowledge [5–7].

The aim of this paper is to examine how research in the cognitive sciences can be applied to address current issues surrounding the instructional efficacy of VRLEs. While the strategies we provide are relevant to all types of learning in these environments, we are particularly focused on how VRLEs can positively mediate the development of conceptual knowledge. There are unique challenges to developing strategies for teaching this type of knowledge in VRLEs, and these challenges have typically been addressed by increasing the technological capabilities of these environments, with minimal positive results [1, 5]. Our approach to addressing these challenges relies not on technology, but on the use of the human body as an instrument to optimize learning and comprehension. Central to our approach is a distinction between the opposing concepts of knowledge-as-object and knowledge-as-action. The former treats knowledge as a separate reality that is external to, and must be obtained by, the learner, while the latter treats knowledge as the integrated result of a learner engaging with her environment through bodily action. Our approach emphasizes the treatment of knowledge as action by applying cognitive science research on embodied and enactive cognition (hereafter EEC) to conceptualize an instructional strategy that capitalizes on the dynamics and interactive nature of VRLEs.

More specifically, we make a distinction between two forms of EEC instructional design for VRLEs. The first can be construed of as a superior way to teach psychomotor knowledge and skills. It is superior because the VRLE helps the learner use her body for a task that requires the body. For example, an instructional objective could be to learn complex psychomotor skills such as performing a surgical procedure. In traditional learning contexts, a student would read about this and see diagrams with arrows indicating areas for cutting. In computer-based learning, a student could view an animation to see how the surgery is performed (e.g., observe it in real time). With a joystick, a student could manipulate certain parameters in a simulation to change a simulated scalpel. But, within a VRLE, a student can actually use her body by holding a wand that simulates a scalpel and can enact the kind of cutting that is necessary and "feel" the skin under the wand (with force-feedback, etc.). So this is, essentially, a high-fidelity simulation mimicking a complex task environment that draws from EEC, often implicitly, to make it better. We recognize the value of VRLEs for this type of learning, but we suggest pushing our thinking further. So we propose a more unique way to teach conceptual knowledge. It is unique specifically because it makes use of the body as a way to understand complex concepts that are actually abstract and difficult to comprehend/imagine (e.g., gravity). For example, an instructional objective could be to learn concepts from physics related to force, trajectory, velocity, and gravity. In traditional learning contexts, a student would read about this and see diagrams. In computer-based learning, a student could view an animation. With a joystick, a student could manipulate certain parameters (e.g., trajectory) and see a change. But within a VRLE, a student can use her body to apply force (e.g., a kick), and study trajectory (e.g., aim the kick), and see how velocity is altered when it nears a large or small celestial body [8, 9]. Recent work has specifically examined manipulations of forms of embodiment and enaction and their relationship to learning [10–13]. We build upon this work to formulate an instructional strategy that we call Structured Enactive Engagement in Learning (SEEL). The SEEL strategy codifies and formalizes a set of testable instructional design approaches to guide learning experiences in VRLEs.

2   Embodied and Enactive Cognition (EEC)

Recent developments in the cognitive and neural sciences view the mind, not as a symbolic logic processor passively operating upon inputs and generating outputs but, rather, as a mind embodied through which cognition is tightly coupled with the body's sensory and motor systems [14–16]. This perspective is in stark contrast to information processing theories of cognition (also known as "cognitivist" theorizing [17]). The theoretical starting point of this embodied view of cognition is that brains are control systems for biological bodies and that these bodies are immersed in, and interact with, rich real-world surroundings [18–20]. Notions of embodied cognition, coupled with the perspective of interacting with, and being reciprocally influenced by, the environment (i.e., enactive cognition), is a theoretical perspective that seeks to overcome limitations of information processing theory, which, essentially, disengaged the brain from both the body and the environment in which they are situated [20, 21]. In this way, cognition is integrated with, and influenced by, the body's adaptivity to its environment and a form of sensorimotor integration with the world. Extensive review of theory and research in the tradition of embodied and enactive cognition is beyond the scope of this paper and can be found elsewhere [15, 20, 22, 23].

We suggest that embodied and enactive cognition (EEC) provides an important stepping off point from which to conceptualize instructional approaches better able to leverage the dynamic, enactive nature of VRLEs. EEC reconceptualizes interaction in the VRLE in such a way that the use of brain and body forms a fundamental basis for learning. Deeper learning can emerge through a continuous process of interaction between the learner, the learning content, and the environment in which they are immersed [24, 25]. As such, EEC provides an important scaffold for considering interaction within VRLEs, as it focuses on the complex relationship between cognition, mind, and body-centric experience within a contextual learning space [26–28].

A growing number of experimental studies support EEC theorizing by documenting the interaction between the body and the environment in service of learning and performance [29, 30]. In this section, we provide an example of human performance that illustrates how theorizing based upon cognitivist views versus EEC would yield different instructional approaches. Specifically, the "outfielder problem" has been used to distinguish between cognitivist theorizing and the deeper aspects of EEC [31, 32].

The outfielder problem concerns itself with how a baseball outfielder knows where to position himself to catch a fly ball. In this scenario, the outfielder can use either predictive or prospective control methods to catch the ball. On the one hand, predictive methods are based on a cognitivistic approach and suggest that the outfielder attempts to determine where the ball is headed based on the development of a mental model using such factors as ball speed, angle, and trajectory. Once the prediction is made, the outfielder moves to the predicted position and attempts to catch the ball. If the prediction is flawed, the ball will not be caught. On the other hand, prospective control methods draw from EEC theory to suggest that the outfielder uses perception-action coupling and runs to align himself with the general trajectory of the ball. This negates its directional offset, and the outfielder moves either forward or backward to match the acceleration of the ball in order to be positioned in the right place at the right time to make the catch.

Importantly, the prospective control method makes no use of mental representations to predict the best position to intercept the ball. Instead, the solution to catching the ball evolves through an interaction of the outfielder with his movements and his dynamic perceptions of the changing environment as the solution is implemented [33]. In essence, the outfielder and his environment become structurally coupled, and, through their interaction, they co-emerge to achieve a successful outcome [24]. To test these predictions, Fink, Foo, and Warren [31] used their Virtual Environment Navigation Laboratory, which allowed for whole-body displacement in an experimental setting. Specifically, by varying trajectories of the ball in the virtual environment, they were able to test whether participants relied upon predictive or prospective control. Their results suggest that participants tracked the ball based upon apparent acceleration, thus supporting EEC-based prospective control theory.

The implications of these results to the design and delivery of instruction in VRLEs are profound, yet thoroughly underexplored. Specifically, studies like this show how embodiment and enaction are used to develop solutions to problems through one's interaction with the environment; solutions co-emerging as the body moves through the environment. This is critical given that such solutions were previously assumed to be solved purely internally by the brain, essentially, acting independent of the body. With respect to instructional strategies used in VRLEs, this concept of co-emergence precludes the use of the prescriptive, linear processes upon which traditional instructional approaches are based. Our argument is that the capabilities of VRLEs need to be better leveraged through the application of holistic instructional strategies that optimize the interaction between brain, body, and environment. Thus, EEC can be used to develop learning techniques that carefully balance the structural constraints of the learning experience with the ability of the learner to freely interact within the learning space. It is this type of embodied, enactive engagement that recent work has shown to have the most direct impact on the development of a more robust and effective learning experience [34]. It is from this perspective that we have developed the SEEL instructional strategy.

3   Structured Enactive Engagement in Learning (SEEL)

The SEEL strategy represents an important step in modifying the design and delivery of instruction in VRLEs and the incorporation of the underlying theories that better support instructional practices within these environments. It is not intended to completely replace current instructional design principles. Instead, it is meant to inform and guide the next generation of instructional design and development for VRLEs by providing the conceptual framework from which new research and practice may emerge. It provides a holistic perspective for the development of learning experiences that integrate the findings of cognitive science research with established, complementary design practices to optimize the means by which instruction is designed and delivered in dynamic, enactive environments.

The SEEL strategy provides an iterative approach to enactive learning engagement based upon theory and empirical research. It consists of five distinct phases that provide a comprehensive approach to enactive instructional design, development, and application. We next describe these in turn.

3.1   Analyze/Determine Instructional Context

The initial phase of the SEEL strategy involves the analysis and determination of the instructional context of the learning experience. Since learning and performance are not prescribed within the EEC paradigm, the intent of this phase is not to develop precise instructional interactions. Rather, it is to identify the overall instructional context and the underlying strategies within which a set of learning outcomes can be facilitated [35].

Foundational to this phase of the SEEL strategy is the concept that separation between the learner and what is to be learned should not exist. In other words, in line with situated theories of learning, cognition is shaped by the learner's interactive experience, both mental and physical, within specific contexts [24–26]. The focus is on enactive engagement and the embodied nature of the learning experience and how these can establish the overall structure of the instructional approach. This phase involves a thorough analysis and identification of the learning objectives that can be enacted and embodied. This includes using learners as active models to demonstrate an underlying concept or theory, as opposed to presenting that same concept or theory statically (e.g., as text or as an unchanging diagram). This phase repurposes traditional task, learner, and instructional analyses by extending their application toward more enactive, embodied instructional techniques.

The goal, then, is to identify what learning objectives can be implemented in the VRLE such that the learner is able to interact with that content. For example, if the learner needs to understand physical principles or formulas, we explore how those can be made concrete in the VRLE, such that the learner is not passively taking in that information and is, rather, actively engaged with content to understand the underlying principles. Consider that computer-based learning provides approaches such as interactive algebra. These allow learners to sketch graphs and see how formulas changed or modify formula inputs to see how graphs changed [12]. We suggest that VRLEs can leverage such approaches and make them more engaging through full body interaction to foster deeper learning.

3.2   Analyze/Identify Instructional Resources

The analysis and identification of instructional resources focuses on the tools, technologies, and settings used to create the learning experience. The specific efforts pursued during this phase focus on the acquisition or development of the artifacts used to facilitate learning. These artifacts may include objects, models, interfaces, systems, or the environment itself relevant to the instructional context. Key efforts during this phase include the identification of context-relevant artifacts to support the learning outcomes identified in the previous phase. Artifacts should be used to embody learning objectives, instead of merely being used as tools or props to demonstrate concepts or procedures. In this sense, artifacts are not just things that support the learning experience, they are intimately wedded to the learning experience.

A number of studies have demonstrated the distinct advantages of employing techniques that emphasize embodied, enactive engagement with instructional artifacts. As examples, studies focused on situated and simulation-based learning [36], model progression schemas and inquiry learning [37], and enaction within the context of mathematics education [10, 13], have each documented the interaction between learner and artifact in support of knowledge acquisition. Learning is embodied in experience, and, through embodied engagement, in practice. Through the use of material artifacts, new experiences are made and additional skills are acquired. This, in turn, transforms future experiences and the responses afforded by such situations [38]. As such, the tools, technologies, and settings used to facilitate learning should focus on the instructional experiences of the learner. Recent work has specifically examined manipulations of forms of embodiment and their relation to learning. Johnson-Glenberg, et al. [11] varied instructional artifacts in embodied, enactive learning contexts to enable learners to map abstract concepts to their bodily movements. This study included an experiment in which the concept of chemical titration was taught by allowing learners to manipulate virtual molecules on a floor projection with a hand-held tracking wand. The objective here was to create a fully titrated virtual solution, as indicated by visual and aural cues within the learning environment. Two groups of participants were subjected to a sequence of regular and embodied instructional strategies with the order of the sequence counterbalanced among the groups. Learning outcomes were measured using a pretest, midtest, and posttest. Learning gains were significantly higher using embodied instruction. Lindgren, et al. [9] developed a room-sized mixed reality simulation that enabled learners to explore the concepts of gravitational forces in space by using their bodies to guide the path of an asteroid as it interacted with the gravitational effects of celestial objects. In an experiment in which participants compared their whole-body experience in the simulated environment with a desktop version of the same simulation, the whole-body experience rated significantly higher in facilitating learning and learner enjoyment. Both of these examples illustrate how instructional artifacts, from hand-held wands to learners' own bodies, can be used to ground abstract concepts in embodied actions and facilitate better learning outcomes.

3.3   Establish/Revise Learning Environment

This phase is concerned with the initial development and subsequent revision of the learning environment, which encompasses the physical setting in which learning will occur as well as the instructional, physical, and virtual interfaces with which the learner will engage.

Co-emergence is a key component in this phase since it focuses on the recursive changes that occur between the learner and the learning environment based on their interactions [39]. Indeed, one of the foundational premises of enactive learning is that cognition and environment are inter-connected and that the interaction dynamics of learners, technologies, interfaces, and the instruction itself, facilitates mutual learning [40]. Following on naturally from our prior phases, here the emphasis is on 'how' interaction with the artifacts can be instantiated. Phase 1 identified what learning objectives could be targets for enaction and Phase 2 helped determine what could be made concrete by leveraging EEC theory. This phase is meant to explicate how co-emergence can occur; that is, how the learner's interaction with artifacts and the environment can make the learning content more apparent. The goal, then, is to ensure VRLEs create and reinforce *instructional interactions*.

Our concept of instructional interactions and the co-emergence they provide is exemplified by the Mathematics Image Trainer for Proportion (MIT-P) [34]. This device consists of a vertically oriented computer monitor and motion tracking devices to track the positions of a learner's hands. Learners are seated at a desk in front of the monitor and are able to change the screen color by manipulating the relative positions of their hands. Learners interact with the device to embody the concepts of proportionality and ratios, with a specific focus on multiplicative scaling (i.e., a proportional progression, such as 1:2 = 2:4). The device measures the relative positions of the learner's hands, calculates the ratio of these measures, and compares it to a preset value. The color of the screen is green if the ratio matches the present value. If it doesn't match, the screen is red. The learner attempts to maintain the green screen color while increasing the distance between her hands. The objective of this experience is to explore the complex concept of proportional progression through interaction with a changing environment. The dynamics of the learner's actions and the changing environment that results from those actions are the co-emergent properties that facilitate learning.

3.4   Implement/Guide Learning

This phase involves the actual *performance* of instruction. Building on the concept of co-emergence, the performance of instruction focuses on an ongoing exploration of enactive experiences. Here the concept of knowledge as action is instantiated. Within this activity, the roles of the learner and instructor become less distinct than in traditional instructional approaches. The role of the instructor is now to help facilitate the learning experience by guiding the learner's attention through questions, practice, highlights, or other such strategies [35].

Central to the facilitation of learning in this phase is the concept of sense-making. In this context, sense-making characterizes knowledge as a domain of possibilities created by the meaning a learner ascribes to the experience gained through embodied interaction with the environment [38, 39]. VRLEs, thus, enable a large repertoire of action possibilities the learner must navigate and, through this navigation, come to understand how the learner's movements are related to learning objectives. Through the rich virtual experience (e.g., complex interactions, improved perceptual capacities), the learner engages with the learning content, acting and reacting with the changing environment through the principle of co-emergence. This engagement affords predictions about the learning content that can be tested through additional movement within the VRLE and with the material artifacts [39, 41]. In this way, VRLEs provide an ideal opportunity for sense-making as they allow learners to apply the knowledge and skills they are acquiring through full-bodied interactions with material artifacts used to embody the learning experience. Within the context of the structured engagement, this may facilitate sense-making as a function of the degree to which learners are able to diagnose flaws in their current understanding and receive feedback that allows them to improve their understanding [42–44].

3.5 Analyze/Assess/Revise Learning Outcomes

This phase highlights the adaptable, iterative nature of the SEEL strategy by providing a means for analyzing, assessing, and revising learning outcomes based on changing situational or learner requirements. Analysis and assessment activities may involve qualitatively or quantitatively derived evaluations of the instructional efficacy of the implemented strategy. Results from these analyses can be used to modify any aspect of the instructional approach to address learning issues or meet changing needs. Activities performed during this phase can be accomplished through formative and summative evaluation efforts. Formative evaluations would be used to improve instructional approaches in the VRLE through design feedback and other types of validation efforts and this would typically occur during the development process. After the instructional approaches have been implemented, summative evaluation techniques would be used to determine the quality of the instruction and its role within the overall learning paradigm. The main objective of this phase is to focus on the learning experience itself and the efficacy of instructional approaches.

4   Conclusion

Current approaches to the design and delivery of instruction in VRLEs draw heavily from traditional instructional design practices. This is problematic given that many of these practices were developed for learning and training contexts lacking the fidelity provided by modern simulation and training environments. This directly affects the instructional efficacy of VRLEs by creating a dichotomy between the learning interface, which emphasizes knowledge as object, and the learning environment, which provides an opportunity for knowledge as action. In this paper, we have addressed this dichotomy using the concept of embodied and enactive cognition to conceptualize an instructional strategy more in line with the dynamic, immersive nature of VRLEs. In this context, embodied and enactive cognition help to reconceptualize the interaction between the learner and the learning environment and strongly influences instructional approaches and applied practices that facilitate increased instructional efficacy within these environments. It is from this perspective that the SEEL strategy was developed. Table 1 provides a summary of the key elements of this strategy.

As noted, we conceive of the SEEL approach as a method of leveraging theory in cognitive science as well as developing concepts in the learning sciences. Granted,

Table 1. Key Elements of the SEEL Strategy

Phase	Focus/Goal	References
Analyze/Determine Instructional Context	• Establish the instructional context of the learning experience. • Identify the learning objectives that can be enacted and embodied.	[24–26, 35]
Analyze/Identify Instructional Resources	• Determine the tools, technologies, and settings used to create the learning experience. • Identify instructional artifacts that ground target concepts in embodied action.	[9, 11, 34]
Establish/Revise the Learning Environment	• Design the learning experience through the integration of the environment, context, and instructional artifacts. • Establish and instantiate how the learner's interaction with artifacts and the environment can make the learning content more apparent.	[34, 39, 40]
Implement/Guide Learning	• Facilitate ongoing exploration of enactive experiences. • Promote sense-making through the use and expansion of action possibilities within the learning space.	[38, 39, 41–44]
Analyze/Assess/Revise Learning Outcomes	• Establish qualitatively or quantitatively derived evaluations to assess the instructional efficacy of implemented approaches. • Modify the instructional approach as required to address learning issues or meet changing needs.	[34, 35]

VRLEs naturally lend themselves to teaching psychomotor knowledge and skills because they afford the opportunity to teach a task where the learner uses her body in a task that requires the body. But what we propose is that VRLEs can do much more. That is, they can provide a unique context where the learner uses her body in a task not requiring the body. The key element is the amount of immersion into an experience the VRLE provides and the degree to which the body is used to alter the learning content and target the learning objectives. The focus is on teaching conceptual knowledge; that is, teaching an abstraction that is difficult to experience through something like text or diagrams alone. An enactive VRLE makes it more concrete by putting the body into the experience and allowing the body to feel the abstraction and alter the abstraction, thus adding a new modality to the learning experience.

In sum, supported by the congruence between embodied cognition and the enactive, immersive nature of VRLEs, the SEEL strategy represents a shift in the development and use of instructional approaches and the underlying theories that support those approaches. It provides a holistic perspective for the application of learning strategies that integrate the findings of cognitive science research with established, complementary practices to optimize the learning experience in VRLEs. Overall, the SEEL strategy establishes a foundation for the development of an instructional approach more suited for virtual environments, while also providing a basis from which a new generation of instructional research and practice may emerge.

References

1. Van Buskirk, W., Cornejo, J., Astwood, R., Russell, S., Dorsey, D., Dalton, J.: A theoretical framework for developing systematic instructional guidance for virtual environment training. In: Schmorrow, D., Cohn, J.V., Nicholson, D. (Eds.) The PSI Handbook of Virtual Environments for Training and Education: Developments for The Military and Beyond, vol. 1. Learning, Requirements, and Metrics, pp. 97–113. Praeger Security International, Wesport (2009)
2. Kraiger, K., Jerden, E.: A meta-analytic investigation of learner control: Old findings and new directions. In: Fiore, S.M., Salas, E. (Eds.) Toward a Science of Distributed Learning, pp. 65–90. APA, Washington, DC (2007)
3. Reid, D.J., Zhang, J., Chen, Q.: Supporting scientific discovery learning in a simulation environment. J. Comput. Ass. Learning 19, 9–20 (2003)
4. Zantow, K., Knowlton, D.S., Sharp, D.C.: More than fun and games: Reconsidering the virtues of strategic management simulations. Acad. Manag. Learn. Edu. 4, 451–458 (2005)
5. Bell, B.S., Kanar, A.M., Kozlowski, S.W.J.: Current Issues and Future Directions in Simulation-Based Training. Cornell University, Center for Advanced Human Resource Studies (2008)
6. Cannon-Bowers, J.A., Bowers, C.A.: Synthetic learning environments: On developing a science of simulation, games and virtual worlds for training. In: Kozlowski, S.W.J., Salas, E. (eds.) Learning, Training, and Development in Organizations. Erlbaum, Mahwah (2009)
7. Fraser, K., Ma, I., Teteris, E., Baxter, H., Wright, B., McLaughlin, K.: Emotion, cognitive load and learning outcomes during simulation training. Med. Edu. 46(11), 1055–1062 (2012)
8. Johnson-Glenberg, M.: What is learning in a mixed reality environment and what does an "embodied lesson" mean. Embodied Games for Learning Laboratory, Arizona State University (2012)
9. Lindgren, R., Tscholl, M., Moshell, J.: MEteor: developing physics concepts through body-based interaction with a mixed reality simulation. Paper Presented at Physics Education Research Conference 2013, 17–18 July 2013, Portland, OR (2013)
10. Nunez, R.E., Edwards, L.D., Matos, J.F.: Embodied cognition as grounding for situatedness and context in mathematics education. Edu. Stud. Math. 39(3), 45–65 (1999)
11. Johnson-Glenberg, M.C., Birchfield, D.A., Tolentino, L., Koziupa, T.: Collaborative embodied learning in mixed reality motion-capture environments: Two science studies. J. Edu. Psychol. 106(1), 86–104 (2014)
12. Kang, B., LaViola, J.: "LogicPad: a pen-based application for visualization and verification of boolean algebra". In: Proceedings of the 2012 International Conference on Intelligent User Interfaces, pp. 265–268 (2012)
13. Abrahamson, D., Howison, M.:. Embodied artifacts: coordinated action as an object-to-think-with. In: Holton, D.L., Gee, J.P.(eds.) Embodied and Enactive Approaches to Instruction: Implications and Innovations. Paper Presented at the Annual Meeting of the American Educational Research Association, April 30–May 4 (2010)
14. Gallese, V., Lakoff, G.: The Brains Concepts: The Role of the Sensory-Motor System in Conceptual Knowledge. Cogn. Neuropsychol. 22(3), 455–479 (2005)
15. Gibbs, R.W.: Embodiment and Cognitive Science. Cambridge University Press, New York (2006)
16. Varela, F.J., Thompson, E., Rosch, E.: The Embodied Mind: Cognitive Science and Human Experience. MIT Press, Cambridge (1991)
17. Newell, A., Simon, H.A.: Human Problem Solving. Prentice-Hall, Englewood Cliffs (1972)

18. Clark, A.: Embodied, situated, and distributed cognition. In: Bechtel, W., Graham, G. (eds.) A Companion to Cognitive Science, pp. 506–517. Blackwell, Malden (1998)
19. Gallagher, S.: How the Body Shapes the Mind. Oxford University Press, Oxford (2005)
20. Wilson, M.: Six views of embodied cognition. Psychon. Bull. Rev. **9**, 625–636 (2002)
21. Varela, F.J., Thompson, E., Rosch, E.: The Embodied Mind: Cognitive Science and Human Experience. MIT Press, Cambridge (1991)
22. Barsalou, L.W.: Grounded Cognition. Ann. Rev. Psychol. **59**, 617–645 (2009)
23. Clark, A.: Supersizing the Mind: Embodiment, Action, and Cognitive Extension. Oxford University Press, New York (2008)
24. Mondada, L.: Understanding as an embodied, situated and sequential achievement in interaction. J. Pragmatics **43**(2011), 542–552 (2011)
25. Winn, W.: Learning in artificial environments: Embodiment, embeddedness, and dynamic adaptation. Technol., Instr., Cogn. Learn. **1**(1), 87–114 (2003)
26. Rambusch, J., Ziemke, T.: The role of embodiment in situated learning. In: Bara, B.G., Barsalou, L., Bucciarelli, M. (Eds.) Proceedings of the 27th Annual Conference of the Cognitive Science Society, pp. 1803–1808 (2005)
27. Kazan, T.: Teaching the student body: Towards an embodied pedagogy. Doctoral Thesis: University of Illinois at Chicago (2001)
28. de Koning, B.B., Tabbers, H.K.: Facilitating understanding of movements in dynamic visualizations: An embodied perspective. Edu. Psychol. Rev. **23**(4), 501–521 (2011)
29. Eerland, A., Guadalupe, T.M., Zwaan, R.A.: Which way you lean-physically-affects your decision-making. Psychol. Psychiatry J. **2011**(11), 65 (2011)
30. Miles, L., Lind, L., Macrae, C.: Moving Through Time. Psychol. Sci. **21**(2), 222–223 (2010)
31. Fink, P.W., Foo, P.S., Warren, W.H.: Catching fly balls in virtual reality: A critical test of the outfielder problem. J. Vis. **9**(13), 1–8 (2009)
32. McBeath, M.K., Shaffer, D.M., Kaiser, M.K.: How baseball outfielders determine where to run to catch fly balls. Science **268**(5210), 569–573 (1995)
33. Wilson, A.D., Golonka, S.: Embodied cognition is not what you think it is. Front. Psychol. **4**(58), 1–13 (2013)
34. Abrahamson, D., Lindgren, R.: Embodiment and embodied design. Cambridge Handbook of the Learning Sciences. Cambridge University Press, Cambridge (2014)
35. Li, Q., Clark, B., Winchester, I.: Instructional design and technology grounded in enactivism: A paradigm shift? Br. J. Edu. Technol. **41**(3), 403–419 (2009)
36. Zheng, R.: Effects of situated learning on students' knowledge acquisition: An individual differences perspective. J. Edu. Comput. Res. **43**(4), 467–487 (2010)
37. Mulder, Y.G., Lazonder, A.W., de Jong, T., Anjewierden, A., Bollen, L.: Validating and optimizing the effects of model progression in simulation-based inquiry learning. J. Sci. Edu. Technol. **21**(6), 722–729 (2012)
38. Di Paolo, E.A., Rohde, M., De Jaegher, H.: Horizons for the enactive mind: Values, social interaction, and play. In: Stewart, J., Gapenne, O., Di Paolo, E.A. (eds.) Enaction: Towards a New Paradigm for Cognitive Science, pp. 33–87. MIT Press, Cambridge (2010)
39. Vernon, D.: Enaction as a conceptual framework for developmental cognitive robotics. Paladyn **1**(2), 89–98 (2010)
40. Steenbeek, H., van Geert, P.: The emergence of learning-teaching trajectories in education: a complex dynamic systems approach. Nonlinear Dyn., Psychol., Life Sci. **17**(2), 233–267 (2013)
41. Klein, G., Phillips, J.K., Rall, E.L., Peluso, D.A.: A data/frame theory of sensemaking. In: Hoffman, R.R. (ed.) Expertise out of context: Proceedings of the 6th International Conference on Naturalistic Decision Making, pp. 113–155. Lawrence Erlbaum & Associates, Mahwah (2006)

42. Bransford, J.D., Schwartz, D.L.: It takes expertise to make expertise: Some thoughts about why and how and reflections on the themes in Chapters 15-18. In: Development of Professional Expertise: Toward Measurement of Expert Performance and Design of Optimal Learning Environments, pp. 432–438. Cambridge University Press, Cambridge (2009)

43. Klein, G., Baxter, H.C.: Cognitive transformation theory: Contrasting cognitive and behavioral learning. In: Cohn, J.V., Schmorrow, D., Nicholson, D. (eds.) The PSI Handbook of Virtual Environments for Training and Education: Developments for the Military and Beyond. vol. 1. Learning, Requirements, and Metrics, pp. 50–64. Praeger Security International, Wesport (2009)

44. Wiltshire, T.J., Neville, K., Lauth, M., Rinkinen, C., Ramirez, L.: Applications of cognitive transformation theory: examining the role of sensemaking in the instruction of air traffic control students. J. Cogn. Eng. Decis. Making 8(3), 219–247 (2014)

Virtual Approach to Psychomotor Skills Training: Manipulating the Appearance of Avatars to Influence Learning

Irwin Hudson[1](✉) and Karla Badillo-Urquiola[2]

[1] U.S. Army Research Laboratory, Orlando, FL, USA
irwin.hudson@us.army.mil
[2] Institute for Simulation and Training, University of Central Florida,
Orlando, FL, USA
kbadillo@ist.ucf.edu

Abstract. Using avatars as virtual instructors is becoming increasingly popular in the military domain due to the emerging advances in distributive technologies (e.g., internet, virtual worlds, etc.). The use of virtual environments and avatars are viable means for achieving enhancements in the area of psychomotor skill development. Although prior research has focused on investigating the benefits of implementing virtual agents into learning environments, there is limited research on examining the impact an avatar's physical appearance has on training. The purpose of this paper is to examine the fundamental applications of three types of virtual avatars (i.e., generic, highly recognizable subject matter expert (SME), and doppelganger) and provide recommendations for future psychomotor skills training. A case study assesses the benefits of applying this virtual approach to physical therapy. Finally, this research seeks to expand the knowledge base of several training domains, such as the military, rehabilitation, high performance athletic training, etc.

Keywords: Agent · Avatar · Doppelganger · Physical therapy · Psychomotor learning · Virtual environments · Virtual reality

1 Introduction

Today's technologies are rapidly advancing, causing a revolution in the nature of warfare. These dramatic changes demand quicker and more accessible training methods for preparing our military forces for combat. As a result, Virtual Environments (VEs) have been implemented as a supplement for traditional training methods. According to Schroeder [1, 2], VEs are "computer-generated display[s] that allow or compel the user (or users) to have a sense of being present in an environment other than the one they are actually in, and to interact with that environment" (p. 25). These environments can accommodate individual and team training through transportable and cost-effective means [3]. While there has been much progress in developing training that prepares warfighters for their military operations, there is an urgency to explore the benefits of VEs for Soldiers transitioning from military to civilian life. As of September 1, 2014 the total number of major limb amputations due to battle injuries, between the

© Springer International Publishing Switzerland 2015
R. Shumaker and S. Lackey (Eds.): VAMR 2015, LNCS 9179, pp. 292–299, 2015.
DOI: 10.1007/978-3-319-21067-4_30

years 2000 and 2014, is 1,573 [4]. These individuals are returning home with new disabilities that involve embracing many changes (i.e., physical, psychological, and emotional). Fortunately, emerging technologies in the area of Clinical Virtual Reality are being researched in hopes of addressing the challenges these Veterans and their families face in their daily lives.

Past research suggests that virtual environments and avatars are viable means for clinical assessment and intervention [5–8], especially for achieving enhancements in the area of psychomotor skill development [9]. In addition, research findings indicate that the manner in which the virtual representation, or avatar, of an individual is presented can change his or her behaviors and beliefs [10]. This leads to the question, "Does an avatar's appearance effect an individual's ability to learn?" According to Baylor [11], the ability to blend our real physical characteristics with a virtual avatar has potential for motivational and affective impacts. This paper aims to address this question by providing an overview of three types of virtual avatars (i.e., generic, highly recognizable subject matter expert (SME), and doppelganger) and current research conducted on their applications. In addition, a use-case scenario is provided to illustrate the benefits of applying this virtual approach to physical therapy. The findings of this research will be used as a theoretical foundation for further investigation on the effects of an avatar's appearance on a learner. Finally, this research will expand the knowledge base of several training domains, such as the military, rehabilitation, high performance athletic training, etc.

2   Avatars

An avatar is any entity that becomes a representation of its user; an icon, a pawn in a game board, or a computer animation are examples of avatars even though they do not necessarily resemble or behave like their user [12]. A 2-dimensional (2D) or 3-dimensional (3D) computer animation that represents a human in a VE is referred to as a virtual human or agent [13]. Agents differ from avatars in the manner in which they are controlled; an avatar is typically controlled by a human, while an agent is controlled by computer algorithms [13–15].

Recent research efforts have outlined the importance of accurately modeling human behavior cues onto 2D and 3D models in VEs [16–18]. Baylor [11] argues that the appearance of an avatar is a vital element for promoting motivation for learning. In addition, research conducted by Jeremy Bailenson and colleagues at Stanford University suggests that individuals change their behaviors according to the appearance of their avatar [10, 12]. Appearance for the purposes of this paper will be operationally defined as the physical attributes of an avatar represented in the VE. The subsequent sections will provide an overview on the three different avatars of interest. Images were developed and customized in house for use in this paper.

2.1   Virtual Human

As previously stated, a virtual human is a computer-generated model that appears as a human in a VE. It is a generic representation that does not represent any specific user.

Fig. 1. Example of a virtual human

These entities are typically customizable; a user can change certain features of the avatar (e.g., hair color, eye color, clothing, etc.). Figure 1 provides an example of a virtual human. Research indicates that a virtual human that is the same sex, race, or similar behaviors as their users provoke learning [19, 20].

2.2 Subject Matter Expert

SME, also known as a domain expert, is an individual that is highly knowledgeable in a specific topic area. For example, a SME on the topic of American football can be a coach, a football player, or an athletic trainer. These individuals are authorities in their field of study. Figure 2 displays an example of an American football SME avatar. Limited research is found on the effects a SME avatar has on an individual's learning outcomes.

Fig. 2. Example of an American football SME Avatar

2.3   Doppelganger

The word doppelganger is German for "double" or "look-alike" [21]. For the purposes of this paper, a doppelganger is defined as a virtual representation of the self [21–23]. Often times in video games, a player can design his or her avatar to resemble themselves. For example, the Nintendo Wii allows individuals to design their "mii," an avatar, to look like them. These avatars are typically controlled by the player. Once an avatar resembles its user, but it is not controlled directly by the user (meaning it is controlled by a different user or computer algorithms), then it is consider a doppelganger. Figure 3 displays an example of an individual (right) and his doppelganger (left). Figure 4 is an addition example of an individual (left) and his doppelganger (right). Research has shown that individuals that watched their doppelganger exercise expressed and acted upon their intention to exercise as well [22]. This suggests that doppelgangers may invoke a sense of motivation in their users.

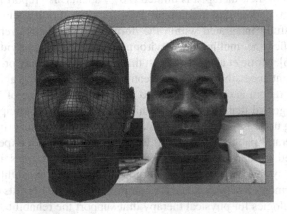

Fig. 3. Example of a doppelganger and the represented individual (Authorization and consent to use the photograph in this figure were obtained from the live model)

Fig. 4. Example of an individual and his doppelganger (Authorization and consent to use the photograph in this figure were obtained from the live model)

3 Application Domain

Physical therapy or physiotherapy, often referred to by its abbreviated acronym PT, is a health care profession that seeks to bring about positive changes or enhancements to physical impairments. Physical therapists are licensed professionals that provide intervention strategies that teach their patients various techniques to reduce pain, restore function, and prevent disability [24]. They operate in a variety of settings, including hospitals, private practices, schools, nursing homes, as well as sports and fitness facilities.

Improving the quality of life for motor rehabilitation patients depends mostly on three factors, which are intervention, task oriented training, and repetition [26]. However, several issues in regards to traditional PT have emerged, including time and accessibility. To take full advantage of their treatment options, patients must travel to a clinic or medical office. This implies that once a patient returns home the ability to access the support of their therapist is limited [26]. Patients also report feeling boredom and fatigue when undergoing traditional PT [25, 27]. Fortunately, virtual reality (VR) has successfully integrated within the domains of medicine, rehabilitation, and psychology to offer the multimodal environment needed to individualize patients' treatments [25, 26]. Morie et al. [27] suggest that virtual worlds may provide the patient the desired constant accessibility to their treatments, as well as the ability to visualize their progress. Boredom and fatigue seem to mitigate with the use of VR for therapy; Research has suggested that VRs provide enjoyment from the participant [25].

The following use-case scenario depicts a fictional scene for the primary user group (i.e., physical therapy patients), capturing how the end-users are expected to interact with the proposed virtual approach to PT. The scenario provides insights on key elements of the system, including its purpose, functional capabilities, and safety measures. Furthermore, it sets the stage for comprehending the benefits of using avatars and virtual technologies for physical therapy that support the rehabilitation of Soldiers, athletes and others.

3.1 Use-Case Scenario

Fred is a 36 year-old former U.S. Coast Guard Soldier. He is the husband of Chloe and a father of 4 (Jack, Isabella, Christian, and Desiree). After 16 years of military service he was injured in battle and recently underwent total Anterior Cruciate Ligament (ACL) reconstruction surgery. Although the doctors feel that the surgery went exceptionally well, Fred is experiencing severe pain and discomfort when attempting to straighten the knee out 90 degrees.

After receiving daily 1 h sessions of traditional PT for three weeks, Fred seems to be making little, if any, progress on getting his knee beyond 45 degrees. His physical therapist believes it is Fred's lack of motivation and unwillingness to complete the exercises that are preventing him to progress.

After examining the x-rays and magnetic resonance imaging (MRI) results of Fred's surgically repaired knee, the doctors and therapists agree that there is nothing physically impeding Fred's ability to straighten out his knee. Therefore, they recommended that Fred undergo a series of Virtual Physical Therapy (VPT) sessions, with the intention to alter Fred's state of mind and provide him with the necessary motivation to improve the movement of his knee.

During the VPT sessions, Fred interacts with his doppelganger. The doppelganger highly resembles Fred's physical persona and has undergone the same surgery as Fred. It illustrates to Fred the different exercises needed to straighten his knee. The avatar takes Fred through the before, during, and after phases of the surgery in hopes of eliciting motivation and guiding Fred to improvement. Fred enjoys the VPT sessions because it incorporates his three P's (i.e., portable, personal, and practical). Fred is able to access this training at home and at the therapist's office. The software also captures his progress and allows Fred to review it. The therapist is also alerted when Fred has completed assigned exercises.

3.2 Limitations

Several limitations were identified throughout this investigation. As the aesthetics of avatars becomes more human-like, the theory of the uncanny valley should be explored. This theory, coined by robotics professor Masahiro Mori [28], posits that our affinity towards human-like avatars increases to a degree and then a sense of revulsion appears. Although it has been widely cited, there is still much to explore. Current research is being conducted on producing a set of heuristics for avoiding the uncanny valley [28, 29].

Another limitation found in the research is accurately modeling behavior using virtual avatars. The mobility of an agent is directly connected to believability [18] and believability is important for training transfer. Research focusing on the appearance of avatars will need to take into considerations the limitations in the mobility of the avatars chosen. Future investigation should look into determining the best suited platform for incorporating virtual avatars for the purposes of physical therapy.

4 Conclusion

Clinical Virtual Reality, specifically in the area of rehabilitation, is a relatively new area of research and development. Many researchers have focused on incorporating VEs or VR into healthcare professions, however, there is still limited research on the area of utilizing virtual avatars for therapy. Future research should focus on investigating the impacts of virtual therapists and the effect an avatar's appearance can have on the patient. Ultimately, this use-case scenario provided in this paper conveys the need for examining how the manipulation of an avatar's appearance affects the psychomotor learning obtained by the patient.

Acknowledgements. This research was sponsored by the U.S. Army Research Laboratory – Human Research Engineering Directorate Simulation and Training Center (ARL HRED STTC), in collaboration with the Institute for Simulation and Training at the University of Central Florida. The views and conclusions contained in this document are those of the authors and should not be interpreted as representing the official policies, either expressed or implied, of

ARL HRED STTC or the U.S. Government. The U.S. Government is authorized to reproduce and distribute reprints for Government purposes notwithstanding any copyright notation hereon.

References

1. Schroeder, R.: Possible Worlds: The Social Dynamic of Virtual Reality Technologies. Westview Press, Boulder (1996)
2. Schroeder, R.: Defining virtual worlds and virtual environments. JVWR 1(1) (2008)
3. Wilson, C.: Avatars, Virtual Reality Technology, and the U.S. Military: Emerging Policy Issues. CRS Report for Congress (2008)
4. Fischer, H.A.: Guide to U.S. Military Casuality Statistics: Operation Inherent Resolve, Operation New Dawn, Operation Iraqi Freedom, and Operation Enduring Freedom. Congressional Research Service Report (2014). http://fas.org/sgp/crs/natsec/RS22452.pdf
5. Difede, J., Cukor, J., Jayasinghe, N., Patt, I., Jedel, S., Spielman, L., Giosan, C., Hoffman, H.G.: Virtual reality exposure therapy for the treatment of posttraumatic stress disorder following September 11, 2001. J. Clin. Psychiatry 68, 1639–1647 (2007)
6. Difede, J., Hoffman, H.G.: Virtual reality exposure therapy for world trade center post-traumatic stress disorder: a case report. CyberPsychol Behav. 5, 529–535 (2002)
7. Holden, M.K.: Virtual environments for motor rehabilitation: review. CyberPsychol Behav. 8, 187–211 (2005)
8. Rizzo, A., Parsons, T.D., Lange, B., Kenney, P., Buckwalter, J.G., Rothbaum, B., Difede, J., Frazier, J., Newman, B., Williams, J., Reger, G.: Virtual reality goes to war: a brief review of the future of military behavioral healthcare. J. Clin. Psychol. Med. Settings 18, 176–187 (2011)
9. Seymour, N.E., Gallagher, A.G., Roman, S.A., O'Brien, M.K., Bansal, V.K., Andersen, D.K., Satava, R.M.: Virtual reality training improves operating room performance. Ann. Surg. 236, 458–464 (2002)
10. Yee, N., Bailenson, J.N.: The proteus effect: self transformations in virtual reality. Hum Commun Res. 33, 271–290 (2007)
11. Baylor, A.L.: Review: promoting motivation with virtual agents and avatars: role of visual presence and appearance. Phil. Trans. R. Soc. B. 364, 2559–2565 (2009)
12. Bailenson, J.N., Yee, N., Blascovich, J., Guadagno, R.E.: Transformed social interaction in mediated interpersonal communication. In: Konijn, E., Tanis, M., Utz, S., Linden, A. (eds.) Mediated Interpersonal Communication, pp. 77–99. Routledge, New York (2008)
13. Fox, J., Ahn, S.J., Janssen, J., Yeykelis, L., Segovia, K., Bailenson, J.N.: Avatars Versus Agents: A Meta-Analysis Quantifying the Effect of Agency. Human-Computer Interaction (in Press)
14. Bailenson, J.N., Blascovich, J.: Avatars. In: Bainbridge, W.S. Berkshire (ed.) Encyclopedia of Human-Computer Interaction, Great Barrington, MA, pp.64–68 (2004)
15. Ahn, S.J., Fox, J., Bailenson, J.N.: Avatars. In: Bainbridge, W.S. (ed.) Leadership in Science and Technology: A Reference Handbook. SAGE Publications (2012)
16. Lackey, S.J., Badillo-Urquiola, K.A., Ortiz, E.C.: Research-driven recommendations for implementing biometric cues in virtual environments. In: MODSIM World Conference (2014)
17. Lackey, S.J., Badillo-Urquiola, K.A., Ortiz, E.C., Hudson, I.L.: A process for developing accurate kinesic cues in virtual environments. In: 24th Conference on Behavior Representation in Modeling and Simulation Conference (2015)
18. Maraj, C.S., Lackey, S.J., Badillo-Urquiola, K.A., Ortiz, E.C., Hudson, I.L.: Modeling proxemic cues for simulation-based training in virtual environments. In: MODSIM World Conference (2015)

19. Andsager, J.L., Bemker, V., Choi, H.L., Torwel, V.: Perceived Similarity of Exemplar Traits and Behavior: Effects on Message Evaluation. Commun. Res. **33**, 3–18 (2006)
20. Ito, K.E., Kalyanaraman, S., Brown, J.D., Miller, W.C.: Factors Affecting Avatar Use in a STI Prevention CD-ROM. J. Adolescent Health **42**, S19 (2008)
21. Bailenson, J.N., Segovia, K.Y.: Virtual doppelgangers: psychological effects of avatars who ignore their owners. In: Bainbridge, W.S. (ed.) Online Worlds: Covergence of the Real and the Virtual Human-Computer Interaction Series, pp. 175–186. Springer, London (2010)
22. Bailenson, J.N.: Doppelgangers: a new form of self? The Psychologist **25**(1), 36–39 (2012)
23. Aymerich-Franch, L., Bailenson, J.N.: The use of doppelgangers in virtual reality to treat public speaking anxiety: a gender comparison. In: Proceedings of the International Society for Presence Research Annual Conference, 17–19 March, Vienna, Austria (2014)
24. American Physical Therapy Association. http://www.apta.org/AboutPTs/
25. Sveistrup, H.: Review: Motor Rehabilitation Using Virtual Reality. JNER **1**, 10 (2004)
26. Morie, J.F., Lathan, C.E., Skinner, A., Chance, E., Rajpurohit, D., Haynes, K.: Using Virtual World Activities for Amputee Rehabilitation. In: Jaume-I-Capo, A., Mesejo-Chiong, A. (eds) Proceedings of AIRtech (2011)
27. Johnson, D.A., Rose, F.D., Ruston, S., Pentland, B., Atree, E.A.: Virtual reality: a new prosthesis for brain injury rehabilitation. Scot. Med. J. **43**, 81–83 (1998)
28. Mori, M., MacDorman, K.F.: The uncanny valley robotics & automation magazine. IEEE **19** (2), 98–100 (2012)
29. Brenton, H., Gillies, M., Ballin, D., Chatting, D.: The uncanny valley: does it exist. In: Proceedings of Conference of Human Computer Interaction, Workshop on Human Animated Character Interaction (2005)

Squad Overmatch: Using Virtual Technology to Enhance Live Training Environments

Patrick M. Ogden[1(✉)], Terry N. Wollert[2], Paul Butler[1],
and Julie N. Salcedo[3]

[1] MITRE, Orlando, FL, USA
pmollb@gmail.com, pvbutler@mitre.org
[2] FLETC, Glynco, GA, USA
terry.wollert@dhs.gov
[3] Institute for Simulation and Training,
University of Central Florida, Orlando, FL, USA
jsalcedo@ist.ucf.edu

Abstract. The application of virtual augmentation to the U.S. Army's training continuum may reduce Post-Traumatic Stress (PTS) and suicides by increasing Soldiers' resilience and cognitive skills at the squad level pre-deployment. This may be accomplished through current programs of record with technological injections, thereby enhancing the training experience improving involvement and retention. Virtual platforms also invite more skill and task repetitions at a much lower cost and reduced risk of injury.

In support of the squad as a decisive force, MG Brown, 2011 Commander at the Maneuver Center of Excellence, conducted a study to identify the critical aspects of U.S. Army training support needed to prepare squads to see first and act first. Focusing on the training devices utilized at the squad level, the concept was to build an enhanced training environment that would make our squads more resilient, efficient, and effective through improvements in human performance. This was demonstrated through virtual insertions into current programs of record spanning the gaming, virtual, and live continuums.

Using data from Walter Reed Medical Center and the Federal Law Enforcement Training Center on stressors and stress exposure training, the study assessed where such exposures could be inserted during the current U.S. Army training cycle. Leveraging standard U.S. Army battle drills, a series of scenarios were developed incorporating the most detrimental of stressors including; loss of a comrade, defensive and unintentional civilian casualties, and witnessing of a death. Soldiers experienced a gradual increase of knowledge and stress through a base scenario in the gaming environment and two subsequent scenarios in the virtual and live environments. Each scenario built upon the previous and was driven by a standard U.S. Army mission planning at the platoon level and intelligence injects. The live scenarios used virtual targets and interactive avatars, live actors, and battlefield effects to enhance the training environment.

1 Introduction

Post-Traumatic Stress (PTS) is a problem that has persisted for decades, but has only garnered significant attention in recent years. One need only to review the PTS and suicide rate statistics published monthly on the Army G-1 portal to realize that this has

© Springer International Publishing Switzerland 2015
R. Shumaker and S. Lackey (Eds.): VAMR 2015, LNCS 9179, pp. 300–308, 2015.
DOI: 10.1007/978-3-319-21067-4_31

and continues to be a serious problem for our country. Since 2006, mental disorders account for more hospitalizations of U.S. service members than any other major diagnostic category [1]. For three years, the Chief of Staff of the Army (G-8) has funded the Squad Overmatch Study to evaluate training methodologies and technologies that could potentially reduce the magnitude of PTS and PTS-related suicides, and improve Soldier performance, resilience, and readiness.

This paper presents the motivation and justification of virtual immersive experiences for stress exposure and resilience training, which led to the Squad Overmatch Study. Additionally, this paper describes the method used to incorporate realistic combat stressors during training and the initial Soldier reactions. Feedback obtained via the Squad Overmatch Study Soldier demonstration served to detail the state of the technology and advances enabling realistic training, to inform how these advances may be employed in a program of instruction, and how virtual training can enhance cognitive and combat skills for the improvement of resilience, mental performance, and situational awareness. It also addresses the hesitancy of law enforcement and military to embrace fully the power of virtual immersion.

The Squad Overmatch Study Team was a result of the expertise in the community collaborating to seek solutions to support virtual immersive training requirements. For example, ballistic accuracy was formulated and applied to virtual models to evoke a realistic visual for participants. Additionally, haptic and olfactory stimuli were applied to further enhance the live experience.

Battlefield effects and live actors completed the blending of the environments to provide total suspension of actual exercise location and intent. Ultimately, an intense training experience enabling Soldiers to see, smell, feel, communicate and react with players they encountered in the gaming and virtual exercises was developed. Interaction with previously encountered players provided an opportunity to further develop cognitive perception and resilience on a more personal level as the Soldiers were finally forced to decide and act when faced with the familiar characters.

1.1 Stressors

The stressors incorporated in the Squad Overmatch Study were selected from a list of 54 stressors vetted by the Walter Reed Army Institute of Research (WRAIR). Table 1 the stressors selected based on knowledge gathered from subject matter experts in the field of Combat Actions [2].

1.2 Training

Presently, there is a considerable lack of virtual training applications for sectors that must engage and eliminate enemy combatants or criminals. The value and validity of virtual training are often considered insufficient compared to live training. Resistance to adopt virtual training methods may result from inexperience and unfamiliarity with virtual capabilities, or budgetary restrictions that limit investment in virtual training.

The military and the Federal Law Enforcement Training Centers (FLETC) have spent large amounts of money building live training facilities that support traditional

Table 1. Combat stressors and potential implications

Stressor	Potential implications
Death of a squad member	Impact the performance and psyche of the unit
Death of an enemy combatant.	Impact Soldier's performance during combat engagement.
Death of an innocent civilian.	Impact sense of control over a combat situation.
Direct fire with the enemy.	Potentially life changing event, with long term effects on the psyche.
Clearing buildings and searching homes.	Highest stress mission with the highest risk of casualties.
Seeing injured women and children you could not help.	Impact sense of control over a combat situation and feelings of cultural or moral unacceptance.
Squad member wounded in action.	Interrupt the unit's ability to continue operations for a period of time.
Attack on a Forward Operating Base.	Impact sense of control over own safety or security.

methods that rely on paper and plastic targets. While this traditional method builds rote muscle memory of the skills required to engage a stationary target with a weapon, it does not provide effective training for development of cognitive skills under stress to enhance human performance. It also fails to add contextual reality to the engagement that replicates anything close to the graphic trauma of the ballistic impact of a bullet on a human.

In combat, Soldiers may hesitate or freeze when faced with the ultimate test of fighting or dying because training continues to use non-contextual environments that cannot adequately prepare Soldiers for the realities of combat. Is it any wonder that the rate of PTS diagnoses are among the highest for service men and women?

Through virtual training, there is now the ability to produce targets for both laser and live fire engagements which replicate accurate ballistic damage in wounding and death. They can produce the sounds, sights, and smells needed to expose men and women, who will face these traumatic events, prior to its occurring in the line of duty. This applies to our men and women in uniform and law enforcement agencies. There must be an investment in a robust continuum that applies cognitive performance enhancement builds resilience. It cannot be single dimensional training environment if we are to be successful. The results, shown in Squad Overmatch, call for the need of technological enhancements of the training.

1.3 Resilience Training

The Comprehensive Soldier and Family Fitness (CSF2) program is a training concept that teaches actions required to deliver resilience and performance enhancement training benefits to U.S. Army members. The purpose of resilience training for the Squad Overmatch study was to show the need for a change in the continuum for Military and Law Enforcement; as both have seen increases in suicide related deaths and individuals experiencing PTS symptoms. It has become an issue at all levels of military and law enforcement from local to federal agencies.

2   Method

As mentioned earlier, the Squad Overmatch Study team conducted four two-day events that demonstrated a cognitive focused training curriculum to four combat-experienced infantry squads stationed at Fort Benning, Georgia. The demonstration implemented stressors and realistic events using various virtual technologies. The virtual technologies are classified into two broad areas: gaming and immersive. The gaming technology used was the Virtual BattleSpace 3 (VBS3) platform. The immersive technology used was the U.S. Army's Dismounted Soldier Training System (DSTS) running VBS3. The situations and characters represented in the gaming and immersive training environments displayed cues that could evoke cognitive skills in the training audience via virtual and auditory stimulation cues. All reactions were measured against the baseline technologies used as current programs of record by the U.S. Army.

2.1   Participants

Participants included four squads, eight Soldiers per squad, (n = 32) from the 3rd Infantry Division, 3rd Brigade Combat Team at Fort Benning, Georgia. Participants' ages ranged from 19 to 28. Participants were all male.

2.2   Testbed

Procedures followed the U.S. Army's "Crawl-Walk-Run" model for training exercises and preparing for high risk training events. The gaming condition served as the Crawl phase, virtual immersive condition served as the Walk phase, and live training served as the Run phase. Use of this model was to display the virtues of using gaming and virtual to aid in risk reduction for live and build the robust immersion required to enhance cognitive performance of Small Unit members.

Gaming (Crawl). The gaming session of the demonstration consisted of using stress-based scenarios implemented in VBS3. The demonstration included two scenarios: a platoon operation involving a cordon and search for a high-value target that culminated in a direct fire engagement, and an operation in which a squad entered a marketplace to conduct tactical questioning of a suspect individual. The setting for these scenarios was an urban village. The study team coordinated with the U.S. Army's Training and Doctrine Command's (TRADOC) Training Brain Operations Center (TBOC) to obtain a realistic, to-scale VBS3 model of the Fort Benning Phase II CACTF. The platoon leaders of two squads joined the demonstration and performed their roles. After Action Reviews (AAR) were led by Sergeants Major (SGM) who guided open discussions focused on tactical actions and decisions.

The study team incorporated eight of the WRAIR stressors into the gaming scenarios. The team used the VBS3 scenario editor to create the sequence of events and developed specific scripts to model desired behaviors defined in the scenarios. The wounding model of VBS3 enabled the team to accurately represent the casualties resulting from the one-on-one engagements with enemy combatants in search-and-clear and mass casualties caused by an improvised explosive device (IED) missions. Integration of external audio files enabled the team to insert realistic sounds of the marketplace and the wounded characters.

The team also used the VBS3 game engine to develop non-interactive animated videos to deliver the Operations Order (OPORD) and a prologue video to present a background context for the scenarios. The OPORD video enabled the team to produce and deliver a concise and consistent OPORD message to each squad audience. The prologue video provided an "up close and personal" glimpse into the lives of the family that the Soldiers would ultimately encounter during the scenarios.

Further, the study team created specific "cut scenes," particularly in tactical questioning situations, in which a key player (such as the squad leader) was required to remain in a fixed position and listen to recorded dialogue. The cut scenes differed from the non-interactive animated videos. In the non-interactive animated videos, all players (i.e., participants) were prohibited from touching the VBS workstations, whereas, in the cut scenes, only the squad leader was prohibited from interacting with his workstation, while other players were free to interact with the game. Although the ability to interact directly with a character in the game is desirable, the study team wanted to constrain the player in some circumstances to create a specific situation about which the team sought feedback through tactical questioning.

The Fort Benning training laboratory was well equipped to support the demonstration, and utilized the VBS3 Communication Net Radio Simulator (CNR-Sim) to support communications among the squad members, between the squad leader and platoon leader, and for role players. During the demonstration, the study team discovered the need to establish a more rigorous process for communicating how to use CNR-Sim and a regimented process for performing communications checks. Another valuable lesson learned was that squads should be provided VBS3 familiarization training prior to interaction with the platform. The study team attempted to deliver such training, however, scheduling challenges prevented this in some cases.

For comparison, the study team also implemented the tactical questioning segment of the IED scenario in a commercial game engine, utilizing the same dialogue used in VBS3, but rendering the scene using the terrain and urban models provided by the commercial product. The Squad Overmatch Study team chose the commercial product based on prior research that indicated considerable fidelity, particularly for its support of highly detailed facial features, lifelike movement, and urban and rural settings. The scenario was non-interactive.

The motivation for recreating the tactical questioning scenario was to elicit feedback from the Soldiers on the technology's ability to support cognitive skills training. Soldier feedback on the Advanced Situational Awareness (ASA) aspects of the implementation was overwhelmingly positive. The detailed facial expressions enabled Soldiers to observe ASA cues to identify when a character was being truthful, evasive, or lying. Additionally, the richness of the urban environment provided more complex features and shadowing, forcing the Soldiers to stay more focused versus an environment where structures and characters are represented as simple polygonal entities.

One squad leader, who was a former graphic artist, commented that the "attention to detail was…in depth…and this helped with the situational awareness [and] atmospherics."

Virtual (Walk). The virtual session of the demonstration used the DSTS. Each squad experienced a stress-based scenario in the DSTS environment as part of the progression from gaming to virtual and eventually to live. The virtual session consisted of completing a "clearing and searching home" scenario nearly identical to the one used in gaming. Unlike the gaming condition, the current version of DSTS requires scenarios to be developed in VBS2. The study team confirmed that the squads were familiar with the context and the mission, therefore, no prologue was presented. As with gaming, the platoon leaders for two of the squads participated in their roles in the demonstration, and the AARs were led by a SGM who guided an open discussion focused on tactical actions and decisions.

DSTS employs the same CNR-Sim communications system as VBS3, and no communications issues were experienced. As in the gaming sessions, the study team served as role players, representing civilians and platoon leaders for two squads (as before, the actual platoon leaders of the other two squads participated in their roles). The study team had investigated providing scents and haptic feedback to the Soldiers wearing the DSTS, but the demonstration did not include this feature. The team has identified this as an area of possible future enhancement.

The more immersive DSTS environment elicited many positive comments from the squads. The immersion provided by DSTS offered more realism and the mission was more challenging, even though it was similar to the gaming scenario. One team leader noted the realism of the tactical questioning of a captured enemy combatant. A squad leader commented how his heart began racing as he and his team "stacked" and prepared to enter a safe house and how viewing the scenario through the helmet-mounted display (HMD), which blocks out the peripheral vision, provided more immersion than the scenarios presented on a VBS workstation. A second squad leader described another benefit of the DSTS system—the weight and distribution of the equipment was similar to the squad's go-to-war gear and caused physical fatigue similar to what they would experience when on patrol. Several Soldiers reported being "hot and sweaty." A third squad leader stated that while live training provides the most realistic experience, the ability to use virtual systems, such as DSTS, enables squads to train patrols with kinetics (contact) without actually being in the field. Several other comments centered on the intensity and decision making that induced stress. No Soldiers reported incidents of simulation sickness.

While the DSTS feedback was generally positive, Soldiers suggested a number of improvements. Some focused on the lack of familiarity with the controls (e.g., most issues could have been effectively managed by more familiarization training), whereas others focused on the scenario commenting that it would have been useful if they could have interacted with the townspeople. Soldiers generally considered the audible cues provided by role players as effective. One squad leader was so distracted by a screaming female role player, who represented the daughter of a noncombatant woman who was accidentally killed in a search-and-clear operation, that he directed his team lead to "go tell that girl to shut the < expletive > up." This type of reaction is not unexpected, because having to manage the death of a civilian and the reactions of a grieving relative added to the stress of the situation. The study team's research indicates that if the Soldier had received an integrated curriculum of cognitive training as part of his warrior skills training he might have applied self-regulation and coping techniques to manage his composure, remain alert, and be more effective.

Live (Run). Using the same scenario based events the Squads had experienced in the gaming and virtual environment the Combined Arms Training Facility (CATF) at Selby Hill in Fort Benning, Ga was the site for the culminating event in the live environment.

As in the previous parts of the demonstration, the live environment was augmented with new technologies to the CATF for the expansion of cognitive performance and stress exposure. The Squads were exposed to audible cues, indirect fire, IED explosions, artificially intelligent targets, human sounds of distress, and live role players.

The Squads were given an OPORD by a SGM and then conducted a test fire of their Multiple Integrated Laser Engagement System (MILES) gear in a secluded area just outside the enhanced live demonstration area. Upon completion they were given instructions from their platoon leader via radio on what actions to execute and report.

The Squad was exposed to increasing levels of stress and cues as they executed the tasks directed by the platoon leader. These cues were audible, visual, olfactory and physical taxation through load and environmental stress.

As the Squads progressed through the CATF their actions were noted by a team of observers from the areas of operational, situation awareness, and resilience expertise. The interactions with live and virtual were recorded for use in an Enhanced After Action Review (EAAR) upon completion of the exercise.

The array of reactions varied as the Squads had a mix of both combat and non-combat Soldiers. The reactions to the various stimulations was evidenced in comments and actions noted by the observers for the EAAR. Of note was the continual variance of reaction to the layering of stress and decisions made due to proper or improper cognitive performance by leaders and Soldiers. Evidence of not properly adhering to the required task when exposed to technologies that were stimulating occurred with each Squad.

The infusion of virtual interaction and virtual targets combined with a small amount of live actor stimulation and battlefield effects enabled a continued, layered training continuum to invoke cognitive performance and stress overload forcing the Soldiers to employ resilience and coping techniques as taught in the foundation training and reinforced through gaming, virtual and culminating in the live exercise.

3   Study Implications

With each exposure to a traumatic event we accept, adapt, or reject the experience. Military and law enforcement personnel are often exposed to stressful and traumatic encounters and, therefore, need resilience and cognitive capability to select and execute the right decisions. Ineffective or inappropriate decisions may result in catastrophic outcomes such as accidental death of innocent civilians or loss of a comrade.

There is a means to forge a path, to correct the current training continuum, issues through immersion into graphic, interactive training environments that force decision making and constant evaluation during stressful combat situations.

The layering of stress inducing events invoked a loss of the ability to function during the exercises for several individuals, as evidenced by comments such as, "I went blank" and "It put me back in Iraq" This type of environment will bring causation to the learning methods they are placed into and force realistic reactions under stress to build resilience and levels of efficient thought processes based on the degree of overload applied during any given scenario. Thereby, the building of resilience has begun to enhance overall human performance and expansion of the human dimension in durability and cognition.

Altogether, anecdotal evidence indicated four implications of the study:

1. Validation for the proposed training continuum aligns with the current U.S. Army training model.
2. Current U.S. Army programs of record may be enhanced with low cost technological insertions
3. The resilience and cognitive performance of our Soldiers may be enhanced by creating a progression of immersive events in gaming, virtual and live environments.
4. Participating Soldiers recognized the value of each portion of the proposed training continuum.

4 Limitations

A predominate issue with the military and law enforcement is budget. A large portion of training dollars are allocated to live environments that are not producing the contextual realism we need. Many technologies are still too expensive and lack the throughput to outfit the U.S. Army or the FLETC.

Time to develop skill sets through repetition is a major constraint as well. From scenario design to execution the environment required to make these exercises accessible, repeatable and affordable is considerable. To address this limitation, an equitable balance of virtual versus live training needs to be established.

Development of resilience and stress exposure training to enhance human performance will require investment in the necessary education and technology. Failure to support such training may negatively impact military and law enforcement preparedness and, subsequently, perpetuate the rise of PTS and PTS-related suicides.

5 Conclusion

There is a steady rise in terroristic and criminal activity in modern conflicts capable of inducing PTS in military and law enforcement personnel, which further emphasizes the need for stress exposure and resilience type training. The Squad Overmatch Study sought to assess Soldier reactions to a layered approach to stress exposure and resilience training that incorporated gaming, virtual immersive, and live environments. Based on anecdotal evidence, the participating Soldiers recognized the value of stress exposure and resilience training and reported a high degree of realism during the technology demonstration.

This study and follow-up studies like it will serve as the foundation to promote enhancement of U.S. Army training with a layered approach. Research efforts in this area will benefit from interaction among Academia, Industry, the Department of Defense, the Department of Homeland Security, and the Department of Justice. Successful collaboration must include open agendas to address shortcomings, needs, and opportunities to support the continued evolution of training and technology.

References

1. Army G1 Portal (2011). www.usarmy.mil
2. LTC McGurk, D., Melissa Waitsman, M.D.: Walter Reed Army Research Institute (2012)

Leveraging Stress and Intrinsic Motivation to Assess Scaffolding During Simulation-Based Training

Julie Nanette Salcedo[(✉)], Stephanie J. Lackey,
and Karla A. Badillo-Urquiola

Institute for Simulation and Training, University of Central Florida,
Orlando, FL, USA
{jsalcedo,slackey,kbadillo}@ist.ucf.edu

Abstract. Instructional designers in the Simulation-Based Training (SBT) community are becoming increasingly interested in incorporating scaffolding strategies into the SBT pedagogical paradigm. Scaffolding models of instruction involve the adaptation of instructional delivery methods or content so that the learner may gradually acquire the knowledge or skill until mastery and independence are achieved [1, 2]. One goal for incorporating scaffolding models into SBT is to bridge the gap between trainees' immediate knowledge and skill with their potential level of understanding when provided with scaffolded support. This gap represents an optimal level of learning often referred to as the Zone of Proximal Development (ZPD). ZPD may be maintained dynamically through the adjustment of instructional support and challenge levels [3]. Theoretically, for ZPD to be achieved, the training experience should be neither too easy nor too difficult. A challenge in implementing scaffolding in SBT and assessing its effectiveness is the lack of metrics to measure a trainee's ZPD. Therefore, this study investigates the use of stress and intrinsic motivation metrics using the Dundee Stress State Questionnaire (DSSQ) and the Intrinsic Motivation Inventory (IMI) to assess the level of challenge elicited by selected instructional strategies in SBT for behavior cue analysis. Participants completed pre-test, training, practice, and post-test scenarios in one of three conditions including a Control and two instructional strategy conditions, Massed Exposure and Highlighting. Participants reported their stress using the DSSQ after each training and practice scenario and overall intrinsic motivation using the IMI at the end of all scenarios. Results compared stress and intrinsic motivation levels between conditions. Ultimately, the results indicate that Massed Exposure strategy may be preferable to maintain ZPD during SBT for behavior cue analysis.

Keywords: Simulation-based training · Instructional strategies · Instructional design · Scaffolding · Stress · Motivation

1 Introduction

1.1 Behavior Cue Analysis

Behavior cue analysis techniques provide the perceptual skills necessary for Warfighters to maintain their situation awareness in a combat environment and mitigate the

© Springer International Publishing Switzerland 2015
R. Shumaker and S. Lackey (Eds.): VAMR 2015, LNCS 9179, pp. 309–320, 2015.
DOI: 10.1007/978-3-319-21067-4_32

occurrence of a critical incident [4]. Training in behavior cue analysis prepares War-fighters to proactively detect threats among the human terrain along various axioms of human behavior such as physiological indicators, body language, and socio-cultural behavior patterns [5]. The scope of the behavior cue analysis tasks in this experiment included the detection and classification of non-verbal behaviors. The process of behavior cue analysis begins with establishing an environmental baseline, identifying anomalies, and then selecting a course of action [6].

Traditionally, behavior cue analysis and related strategies are trained in classroom-based and live training settings. Currently, instructional design efforts are progressing towards Simulation-Based Training (SBT) of behavior cue analysis type tasks in virtual settings. However, SBT lacking in constructive pedagogy is both ineffective and inefficient, and has shown to elicit negative training [7]. Behavior cue analysis is a largely perceptual task, therefore, selected SBT strategies should improve perceptual ability.

1.2 Instructional Strategies

Literature on training and education provides evidence to support the idea that implementing instructional strategies into SBT can effectively improve the perceptual skills of military personnel [8]. In this experiment, two strategies were chosen for further investigation due to their relevance to improve perceptual skills–Massed Exposure and Highlighting. Massed Exposure, also referred to as massed practice, consists of presenting a high volume of stimuli within a reduced time period [8]. Highlighting refers to directing the attention of the learner to significant training content utilizing a non-related content element [9, 10]. Previous empirical research suggests that utilization of the Massed Exposure or Highlighting strategies during virtual behavior cue analysis training may improve trainees' response time for the detection of target behaviors [4, 11]. Although performance outcomes are a critical consideration in the design of effective SBT, considering the trainee experience may improve SBT efficiency. There is increasing interest among the instructional design community to incorporate SBT strategies that support a scaffolding model of instruction through the maintenance of a trainee's Zone of Proximal Development (ZPD).

1.3 Zone of Proximal Development

Scaffolding involves the adaptation of instructional delivery methods or content to guide the learner through a gradual acquisition of the knowledge or skill until mastery and independence are achieved [1, 2]. In SBT, scaffolding models may bridge the gap between trainees' immediate knowledge and skill and their potential level of understanding when scaffolded support is provided. This gap represents the optimal level of learning referred to as ZPD. The goal of ZPD is to provide learning opportunities that encourage and advance the ability to accomplish a task or conduct a skill independently [12]. During instruction, ZPD may be maintained dynamically through the adjustment of instructional support and challenge levels [3]. Theoretically, the optimal level of learning in the ZPD range may be achieved through pedagogical methods that offer enough challenge to extend and develop a learner's knowledge and proficiency without overwhelming them [2]. Constructs that relate to ZPD are stress state and intrinsic motivation. High levels of stress during a task may indicate that an individual's processing of cognitive information is being overloaded due to the delivery method of instruction. In addition, the task at hand may be too demanding, which inhibits skill acquisition. In contrast, task engagement and motivation may decrease if the challenge level is too low, therefore, underutilizing the learner's cognitive resources.

1.4   Stress

Within the stress state construct, task demands are classified into three dimensions: task engagement, distress, and worry [13, 14]. Task engagement includes feelings of arousal, interest, motivation, and concentration, while distress is characterized by an unpleasant state of tension indicative of low confidence and low perceived control. Worry refers to feelings of low self-esteem, cognitive interference, and feelings of task-induced self-consciousness.

1.5   Intrinsic Motivation

Intrinsic motivation is herein defined as the internal desire to perform well on an external task as is influenced by the perceived level of effort, improvement, competence, pressure, tension, interest, and enjoyment during a task [15]. Evidence suggests that intrinsic motivation positively impacts performance outcomes [16], and low levels of intrinsic motivation have been correlated with indifference [17, 18].

1.6   Research Objective

The objective of this study was to assess the effect of the instructional strategies on stress and intrinsic motivation experienced during training as well as the relationships between these constructs in a SBT context for the behavior cue analysis task. Ultimately, the goal of this investigation was to take the initial steps towards exploring the efficacy of leveraging stress state and intrinsic motivation to measure ZPD during SBT and monitor the effectiveness of scaffolding strategies.

2   Method

2.1   Participants

A total of 123 participants from the University of Central Florida and the surrounding community were used for this experiment. The following inclusion and exclusion criteria were used to recruit participants: between 18 and 40 years of age, U.S. citizenship, and normal or corrected to normal vision. In addition, to adhere to the U.S. Army vision requirements and previous experimentation, full color vision according to the Ishihara's Tests for Colour Deficiency was also a requirement [19]. A total of eight participants were omitted, due to technical difficulties, voluntary discontinuation of participation, and failure to meet the proficiency requirements. Data from 115 participants, 56 female and 59 male, were analyzed. The ages ranged from 18 to 33 years (M = 22.05, SD = 3.02). Monetary payment or class credit was provided as compensation.

2.2   Experimental Testbed

Virtual Battlespace 2 (VBS2) version 2.0 software was used to develop the virtual environment scenarios in this experiment. The scenario terrains were Middle Eastern and Culturally Agnostic. Culturally Agnostic is a non-geotypical environment. Twelve distinct virtual 3D models of four skin tones (i.e., fair, light, medium, and dark) were used to display a total of eight human behavior cues, four target and four non-target. The virtual models were arranged in groups of four alternated between the left and right sides of the route.

2.3   Experimental Design

This experiment assessed the effectiveness of two instructional strategies (i.e., Massed Exposure and Highlighting) against a Control condition by conducting a between groups design.

2.4   Measures

The Dundee Stress State Questionnaire (DSSQ) is a validated measure that was used to measure task related stress by three 0-32 point scales that comprise task engagement, distress, and worry [13, 14].

The Intrinsic Motivation Inventory (IMI) consists of individually validated scales selected for their relevance with the experimental task domain. The selected scales contain statements related to four aspects of intrinsic motivation including: Effort and Improvement, Pressure and Tension, Perceived Competence, and Interest and Enjoyment [15]. Participants rated their agreement with each statement along a 1-7 point Likert scale with "not at all true" and "very true" as the minimum and maximum scale anchors, respectively.

2.5   Procedure

Each participant was given the Informed Consent document to read and sign. The document provided the experiment's purpose, tasks, minimal risks, and benefits, as well as the participant's rights as a volunteer. To verify whether the participant fulfilled the study restrictions, the pre-experimental questionnaire and color deficiency test were then administered by the researcher. Afterward, the participant filled-out a paper-based demographics questionnaire and was randomly assigned to one of the following conditions: control, massed exposure, and highlighting.

To acquaint the participant with the virtual environment and experimental task of monitoring the virtual UGS, selecting the classification button, and clicking on the detected target, an interface training presentation was then provided. Following the presentation, the participant practiced the target detection and classification task by completing an interface training scenario. To avoid priming effects, the targets used were yellow and red colored barrels which were unrelated to the stimuli in the succeeding scenarios. To continue the experiment, the participant must have received at least 75 % detection accuracy at the end of the scenario. All participants were provided up to two opportunities to obtain the proficiency score.

Then, a slide presentation explaining the task for the pre-test scenario was given. The participant was asked to monitor the virtual UGS display, as well as detect and classify targets that appeared to be exhibiting aggressiveness or nervousness according to the participant's personal experience. After completing the pre-test scenario, the participant was given a five minute break.

Next, another slide presentation was provided to present the training content. This gave an overview of behavior cue analysis and the Kinesics domain, as well as described each target behavior cue and the corresponding classification. Examples of each target behavior cue were supplied in the form of photographs. If the participant was assigned to the highlighting or massed exposure conditions, content on the instructional strategy as it applied to the training scenario was also included. Then the participant completed two training scenarios. After each training scenario, the participant completed a computer-based DSSQ.

Following the training phase, an additional presentation was provided on the practice scenarios that followed. Once again, the participant completed the computer-based DSSQ after each practice scenario. After finishing the scenarios, a five minute break was offered. After the break, a final slide presentation was given introducing the post-test followed by the post-test scenario. Upon completion of the post-test scenario, the participant completed the computer-based IMI. Finally, the participant was debriefed and dismissed.

3   Results

Two-way mixed ANOVAs with scenario type (training 1, training 2, practice 1, and practice 2) as the within-subjects factor and instructional strategy (Control, Massed Exposure, and Highlighting) as the between-subjects factor were conducted to assess the main effects and interaction effects for the Distress, Engagement, and Worry scales of the DSSQ. All reported degrees of freedom for the interaction effects and main effects of scenario type reflect the Greenhouse-Geisser correction for sphericity in SPSS.

There was a significant main effect of scenario type for the Distress scale, F (2.49, 279.27) = 6.83, $p < .001$, $\eta_P^2 = .057$, with decreases in distress from the first to the second training scenario followed by an increase in distress for the first and second practice scenarios (Fig. 1). This was qualified by a significant interaction effect between scenario type and instructional strategy for the Distress scale, F (4.99, 279.27) = 2.95, $p = .013$, $\eta_P^2 = .050$.

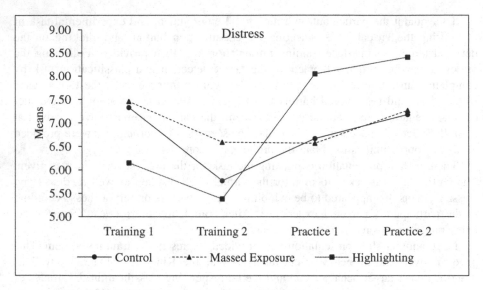

Fig. 1. Individual group means for the DSSQ Distress scale per scenario

There was also a significant main effect of scenario type for the Engagement scale, $F\ (2.54,\ 284.23) = 16.09$, $p < .001$, $\eta_P^2 = .126$, with a trend toward decreasing task engagement over time in the Control and Massed Exposure conditions (Fig. 2). The Highlighting condition had a decrease in task engagement from the first to the second training scenario, an increase in task engagement for the first practice scenario, and another decrease in task engagement by the second practice scenario. There was also a significant interaction effect between scenario type and instructional strategy for the Engagement scale, $F\ (5.08,\ 284.23) = 6.76$, $p < .001$, $\eta_P^2 = .108$.

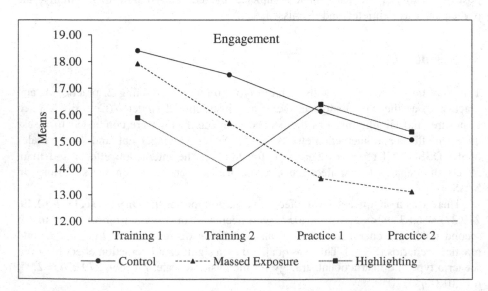

Fig. 2. Individual group means for the DSSQ Engagement scale per scenario

For the Worry scale, there was a significant main effect of instructional strategy, F (2, 112) = 2.95, p = .040, η_P^2 = .056. This was qualified by a significant interaction effect between scenario type and instructional strategy for the Worry scale, F (4.80, 268. 56) = 2.78, p = .020, η_P^2 = .047. There was trend toward increased worry in the Massed Exposure condition. Although the Worry scores were significantly lower in the Control compared to the Highlighting group, both conditions had relatively stable levels of worry across scenarios (Fig. 3).

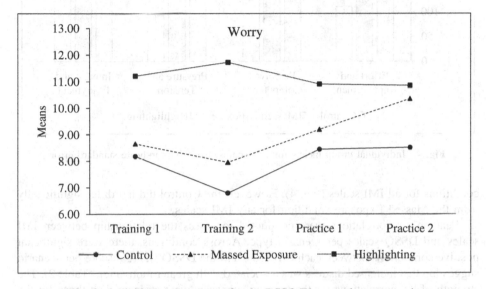

Fig. 3. Individual group means for the DSSQ Worry scale per scenario

One-way between groups ANOVAs revealed a significant effect of instructional strategy for each IMI scale including: Effort and Improvement, Perceived Competence, Pressure and Tension, and Interest and Enjoyment (Table 1).

Table 1. Between groups ANOVAs results for the IMI scales.

	Control M (SD)	Massed Exposure M (SD)	Highlighting M (SD)	$F_{2,\ 112}$	p
Effort and Improvement	198.1 (79.07)	185.38 (98.55)	110.54 (98.87)	10.15	<.001
Perceived Competence	230.55 (83.35)	233.97 (100.43)	139.35 (97.02)	12.65	<.001
Pressure and Tension	160.02 (69.46)	173.73 (88.16)	93.41 (91.40)	10.19	<.001
Interest and Enjoyment	268.45 (108.84)	280.91 (124.30)	163.65 (118.61)	11.62	<.001

Post hoc analyses using Bonferroni correction revealed significantly lower scores ($p < .01$) in the Highlighting condition compared to the Control and Massed Exposure

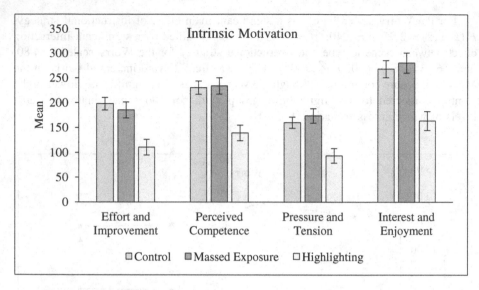

Fig. 4. Individual group means for IMI scales. Error bars indicate standard error

conditions for all IMI scales (Fig. 4). However, the Control did not differ significantly from the Massed Exposure condition for any IMI scales.

Pearson's r correlations were conducted to assess the relationship between IMI scales and DSSQ scales per scenario type. Across conditions, there were significant positive correlations between each IMI scale and the DSSQ Distress score per scenario suggesting that increased distress was associated with greater motivation (Table 2). The strength of the correlations for the training scenarios were stronger than those for the practice scenarios.

Table 2. Correlations between DSSQ distress and IMI scales across conditions

	Effort and improvement	Perceived competence	Pressure and tension	Interest and enjoyment
Training 1 Distress	.487**	.547**	.446**	.517**
Training 2 Distress	.499**	.548**	.493**	.468**
Practice 1 Distress	.285**	.335**	.243**	.242**
Practice 2 Distress	.283**	.361**	.241**	.258**

$*p < .05$; $**p < .01$; Note: Reported correlations represent results across conditions (n = 115), yet these overall results were also relatively consistent with between group results.

Between groups, only the Massed Exposure and Highlighting conditions revealed significant correlations between worry and intrinsic motivation (Table 3). In the Massed Exposure condition, the Effort and Improvement, Perceived Competence, and Interest and Enjoyment scales of the IMI were positively correlated with the DSSQ Worry scale in the first training scenario only. In the Highlighting condition, the Effort and Improvement and Interest and Enjoyment scales were positively correlated with the DSSQ Worry scale in the first and second training scenarios. Additionally, the Perceived Competence scale was positively correlated with DSSQ Worry in training scenario two. The Pressure and Tension scale of the IMI did not correlate significantly with the DSSQ Worry scale. Further, the DSSQ Engagement scale did not significantly correlate with any IMI scales.

Table 3. Correlations between DSSQ worry and IMI scales for the massed exposure and highlighting groups.

		Effort and improvement	Perceived competence	Pressure and tension	Interest and enjoyment
Massed Exposure	Training 1 Worry	.353*	.437*	.175	.337*
	Training 2 Worry	.231	.305	.093	.179
High-lighting	Training 1 Worry	.470**	.304	.212	.340*
	Training 2 Worry	.438**	.329*	.239	.364*

*p < .05; **p < .01

4 Discussion

In all three conditions, the level of distress decreased by the second training scenario indicating that repeated exposure to a task during training may gradually reduce trainee distress overtime, regardless of the type of instructional support provided. However, while the level of distress in the Control and Massed Exposure conditions remained relatively stable through the practice phase, the Highlighting condition revealed a nearly three point increase in distress from the second training scenario to the second practice scenario. This considerable increase in the Highlighting condition suggests that the removal of explicit, highly indicative instructional support, such as the non-content feature used to signal targets, may increase trainee distress when completing the task independently. Due to the target detection assistance provided by the non-content feature in the Highlighting training scenarios, participants in this group were ultimately required to only *classify* the target behavior cues. The Highlighting participants may not have employed perceptual skills for target detection, such as pattern recognition [8], during training scenarios, and thus, the amount of distress may have increased because the participants expended greater effort to conduct the entire behavior cue analysis procedure (i.e., detection and classification) during practice scenarios. The correlations between distress and the level of effort and improvement reinforce this phenomenon.

Participants in both the Control and Massed Exposure conditions experienced a gradual decrease in the level of task engagement from one training or practice scenario to the next. The decrease in task engagement in the Control and Massed Exposure groups may be attributed to boredom or disinterest in the task due to the similarities in the presentation of content between the training and practice scenarios. The Highlighting group indicated more fluctuation in task engagement between scenarios. Perhaps the novelty of the non-content feature peaked the participants' engagement in the task during the initial exposure, but their engagement waned by the end of the training phase. Likewise, the initial absence of the non-content feature in the first practice scenario may have prompted participants to re-engage in the task, yet, the level of engagement dropped once again by the end of the practice phase, possibly due to disinterest.

Per condition, the level of worry remained fairly stable with approximately a one to two point fluctuation from one scenario to the next. The Highlighting group revealed the highest level of worry overall. During training scenarios, perhaps participants receiving the Highlighting strategy were concerned that they were not familiar with the detection aspect of the task because targets were indicated for them. Conversely, perhaps during the practice scenarios when target detection assistance was not provided, the participants were worried that they may have missed some targets. Additionally, although the change was not significant, the increase in worry during the practice scenarios in the Massed Exposure condition may indicate that participants were worried that they were missing targets because the task may have seemed simpler due to the reduced target probability compared to the training scenarios.

Intrinsic motivation was lowest in the Highlighting condition, while the higher levels in the Control and Massed Exposure conditions were similar. The positive correlations of distress and worry with the IMI subscales suggest that participants' level of stress may have impacted their intrinsic motivation, regardless of condition. Combined with the two-way ANOVA results, it is possible that the level of challenge elicited by each instructional strategy affected participants' perception of their own ability to conduct the task successfully as well as their motivation to remain engaged in the task. Perhaps the training scenarios applying the Highlighting strategy were too easy. Interestingly, distress was low and worry was high during the Highlighting training scenarios. Distress is more closely related to the task experience, while worry is more aligned with external influences [13, 14]. Therefore, low distress may be an indicator that the instructional support did not provide enough challenge and high worry may relate to a lower level of intrinsic motivation. Conversely, the greater distress and lower worry in the Massed Exposure condition may indicate that the Massed Exposure strategy offered a preferred level of challenge during training, and, consequently, greater intrinsic motivation. However, the IMI was administered only once upon the conclusion of all scenarios. The single instance of the measure may have reduced its sensitivity to adequately assess intrinsic motivation. In order to further delineate the impact of intrinsic motivation on stress state and vice versa, future experimental designs should administer the IMI in the same manner as the DSSQ after each scenario.

5   Conclusion

Ultimately, the intention of this effort was to expand the body of instructional design research related to the measurement and monitoring of ZPD and the effectiveness of scaffolding methods in SBT. Clearly, it is evident from the results of this experiment that the Highlighting strategy provided the lowest level of challenge and reduced intrinsic motivation, while the Massed Exposure strategy provided a greater level of challenge and increased intrinsic motivation. From a scaffolding perspective, incorporating the Highlighting strategy into SBT may diminish the capability of the training platform to maintain a trainee's ZPD. Although further empirical research is necessary, according to the results herein, the Massed Exposure strategy may be the preferred option to maintain a trainee's ZPD during SBT.

Acknowledgement. This research was sponsored by the U.S. Army Research Laboratory–Human Research Engineering Directorate Simulation and Training Center (ARL HRED STTC), in collaboration with the Institute for Simulation and Training at the University of Central Florida. This work is supported in part by ARL HRED STTC contract W91CRB08D0015. The views and conclusions contained in this document are those of the authors and should not be interpreted as representing the official policies, either expressed or implied, of ARL HRED STTC or the U.S. Government. The U.S. Government is authorized to reproduce and distribute reprints for Government purposes notwithstanding any copyright notation hereon.

References

1. Puntambekar, S., Hubscher, R.: Tools for scaffolding students in a complex learning environment: what have we gained and what have we missed? Edu. Psychol. **40**(1), 1–12 (2005)
2. Van de Pol, J., Volman, M., Beishuizen, J.: Scaffolding in teacher-student interaction: a decade of research. Edu. Psychol. Rev. **22**(3), 271–296 (2010)
3. Hirumi, A., Appelman, B., Van Eck, R.: Preparing instructional designers for game-based learning: part 1. TechTrends **54**(3), 27–37 (2010)
4. Lackey, S.J., Salcedo, J.N.: Assessing instructional strategies for training robot-aided isr tasks in simulated environments. In: 2014 Annual Simulation Symposium. No. 2. Society for Computer Simulation International, San Diego (2014)
5. Gideons, C.D., Padilla, F.M., Lethin, C.R.: Combat Hunter: The Training Continues. Marine Corp Gazette **92**(9), 79–84 (2008)
6. Fautua, D., Schatz, S.: Border Hunter Research Technical Report. U.S. Joint Forces Command, Norfolk (2010)
7. Oser, R.L., Gualtieri, J.W., Cannon-Bowers, J.A., Salas, E.: Training team problem solving skills: an event-based approach. Comput. Hum. Behav. **15**, 441–462 (1999)
8. Carrol, M., Milham, L., Champney, R.: Military observations: perceptual skills training strategies. In: 2009 Interservice/Industry Training, Simulation, and Education Conference. No. 9287. National Training and Simulation Association, Arlington (2009)
9. De Koning, B.B., Tabbers, H.K., Rikers, R.M., Paas, F.: Attention guidance in learning from a complex animation: seeing is understanding? Lear. Instr. **20**(2), 111–122 (2010)
10. Underwood, G.: Visual attention and the transition from novice to advanced driver. Ergonomics **50**(8), 1235–1249 (2007)

11. Salcedo, J.N.: Instructional Strategies for Scenario-Based Training in Human Behavior Cue Analysis with Robot-Aided Intelligence, Surveillance, Reconnaissance. Unpublished Doctoral Dissertation. University of Central Florida, Orlando (2014)
12. Vygotsky, L.S.: Mind in society: the development of higher psychological processes. Harvard University Press, Cambridge (1978)
13. Matthews, G., Szalma, J., Panganiban, A.R., Neubauer, C., Warm, J.S.: Profiling task stress with the dundee stress state questionnaire. In: Cavalcanti, L., Azevedo, S. (Eds.) Psychology of Stress: New Research, Nova Science, Hauppauge, pp. 49–90 (2013)
14. Matthews, G., Campbell, S.E., Falconer, S., Joyner, L.A., Huggins, J., Gilliland, K., Grier, R., Warm, J.S.: Fundamental dimensions of subjective state in performance settings: task engagement, distress, and worry. Emotion **2**, 315–340 (2002)
15. McAuley, E., Duncan, T., Tammen, V.V.: Psychometric Properties of the Intrinsic Motivation Inventory in a Competitive Sport Setting: A Confirmatory Factor Analysis Research Quarterly for Exercise and Sport. Res. Q. Exerc. Sport **60**, 48–58 (1989)
16. Oskarsson, P.A., Nählinder, S., Svensson, E.: A meta study of transfer of training. In: 54th Annual Meeting of the Human Factors and Ergonomics Society. Sage, San Diego (2010)
17. Carroll, M., Kokini, C., Champney, R., Sottilare, R., Goldberg, B.: Modeling trainee affective and cognitive state using low cost sensors. In: Interservice/Industry Training, Simulation, and Education Conference. No. 11215. National Training and Simulation Association, Arlington (2011)
18. Craig, S., Graesser, A.C., Sullins, J., Gholson, B.: Affect and learning: an exploratory look into the role of affect in learning. J. Edu. Media **29**, 241–250 (2004)
19. Ishihara, S.: Ishihara's Tests for Colour Deficiency. Kanehara Trading, Tokyo (2013)

Working the Modes: Understanding the Value of Multiple Modalities of Technologies for Learning and Training Success

Eileen Smith[1(✉)], Ron Tarr[1], Cali Fidopiastis[1], and Michael Carney[2]

[1] Institute for Simulation and Training,
University of Central Florida, Orlando, FL, USA
{esmith, rtarr}@ist.ucf.edu, cfidopia@gmail.com
[2] Canon USA, Inc, Melville, NY, USA
mcarney@cusa.canon.com

Abstract. Technology for learning has a great potential to decrease training time, as well as impart complex knowledge to the learner. However, one technology may not provide the complete learning experience. We discuss this issue using a fielded fire rescue incident command simulation-based training. Of first importance is properly defining the training material, and then assessing the efficacy of the training through scenario-based critique. The immersive nature of the incident command simulation allowed learners of all ages and backgrounds to experience the realism of a fire command post. Newer immersive technologies are discussed that will support transfer of training, as well as provide seamless integration into real world settings. Finally, we advocate for the development of direct brain measures of the learning process within operational environments. In this way, instructional design becomes a true brain-based approach and selecting the supporting technology for learning delivery is more exact for the learning purpose.

Keywords: Learning · Training · Modeling and simulation · Education · Virtual reality · Psychophysiological metrics · Transfer · Mastery · Systems design · Immersion · Mixed reality · Assessment

1 Introduction

"Simulation will help learning" is a popular mantra these days among many decision-makers; many times their action, unfortunately, is to run to purchase the latest technological toy with the hopes that learning will occur better. In reality, learning is a journey toward understanding the processes, procedures, backgrounds, culture, nuances, etc. of the particular topic under study, and is best accomplished with a spectrum of technological tools. In this paper, we discuss the basis for understanding how well designed simulations utilize multiple modalities as they support the learner on their journey, from the specific standpoint of learning purpose, training success, use of immersive technologies and confirming impact models.

© Springer International Publishing Switzerland 2015
R. Shumaker and S. Lackey (Eds.): VAMR 2015, LNCS 9179, pp. 321–328, 2015.
DOI: 10.1007/978-3-319-21067-4_33

The learner's journey today and into the future has the opportunity to be supported by robust tools for creating and delivering interactive learning experiences, where dynamic simulations drive engaging scenarios. These experiences, when designed well, allow the learner to set parameters and drive events through decision-making so that the learner can scaffold experiences toward deeper understanding. Quality experience design uses multiple types of technology; with each doing what it does best for learning impact. From reading established text, to live discussions, to data-driven computer training exercises, to immersive simulation to test transfer to the operational environment, all work together so that each learner is successful in today's complex workplace; a workplace that is increasingly interdisciplinary, telepresence-based, and intergenerational. That last element has promise to help illuminate foundations for personalizing learning.

Today's learner has global connections readily available, and learning in today's connected society means that the notion of intergenerational teaming is being tested regularly. We no longer always know the age/race/gender of the people we are interacting with online. We do not actually care; we care about the quality of their interaction with us, and the contextual quality of the value exchanged between us. Online, you would never know that "Tom", the paleontologist that has been helping you understand Jurassic sea creatures, is 12 years old. How many of us would have even read Tom's answer if we had known in advance his age? That simple example parallels thousands of transactions between humans and technology every day. Simulation allows the learner to explore based on the level of those exploring with them, or test ideas and concepts with those on a more advanced level. The psychographics of the people we interact with take priority over the demographics; the value is in the shared island of expertise. This holistic view begins to illuminate how we might support each learner, what prerequisites, additional challenges, even remediation, will uniquely help them progress toward mastery. What is their ability to handle workload? What motivates them to keep working through the difficult moments? How can they best be rewarded?

As that journey progresses the ability of a system to capture data on the learner's behavior begins to build a personal learning library, based on unique choices by learners. As time progresses, the library can be analyzed to see progression toward performance metrics, or topic mastery, or situational awareness if targeting soft skills.

In 2012, a training project for the Orange County Fire Rescue Department looked at improving individual mastery of fire command for every lieutenant in the county fire division. Success in the training was the demonstration of mastery by each trainee. As will be described in another section of this paper, the training curriculum completely redesigned based upon an enhanced understanding of the necessary performance metrics for success. The final segment of the training was a series of sessions in an immersive simulator, mirroring a live fire scene in one of seven environments found in Orange County, Florida [1]. The training chiefs set up scenario parameters, and events unfolded as the trainee made and communicated decisions to the virtual firefighters on the scene. The system design provided the capability to capture decisions made or not made by the trainee, establishing a data file on their emerging command mastery of a complex multi-layered experience.

As the fire command project unfolded in development, visitors to the research facility from all different ages and backgrounds were given the opportunity to become fire professionals and try the simulation. It quickly became apparent that both adult and adolescent learners responded to the immersive simulation, and were quickly motivated to make decisions and change them based on the results. These observations led researchers to discuss a concept for a virtual world to host learning activities that focus on critical thinking and problem-solving, using performance-based design scaffolding from naïve to advanced understanding in real world environments. Researchers believe this initiative will have important information for the experience design field on using technology to help learner empowerment at all levels of competence, and build quality learning and training systems for all learners that leads to the ability to demonstrate mastery. In the next section, we discuss performance metric development as a precursor to technology choices.

2   Performance and Their Metrics as Foundation of Impact

The focus and the reason for training, especially when using advanced learning technology like simulation, are really to improve human performance. Whether this is to prepare a soldier for combat or a surgeon to perform surgery, training should always focus on enhancing the abilities of a human to perform some behaviors directed toward their job, home, or recreational pursuits. However, recent years shows a shift in focus from improving performance to understanding content and classroom presentation. This shift is partially due to remnants of the efficiency and the process improvement ideas of the industrial revolution, as well as the incomplete transition from traditional journeyman/apprentice training that relied on subject matter experts for content development.

The very issue is that technology is not the sole solution to improved performance outcomes after training. The learning content must accurately reflect the analysis of expert performance, which then can translate into a delivery system that improves the learner's ability to process that information. The result of which is a positive change in behavior leading to successful execution of tasks. Thus, the role of the media delivery tool is to enhance the learning or training material for effective and efficient transfer of that information to the learner/trainee.

Human behavior, especially expert behavior, is both complex and hard to elicit. There are behavioral measures and methods for modeling expertise: however, it takes much more time to capture and translate this information to appropriate learner material and activities. Introducing technology simply adds a new method to an old and most often incomplete process.

In the next section, we describe an example of how to elicit expertise by using methods of ethnographic reporting followed by a breakdown of candidate behaviors into their sub-components and associated assessment measures of success in achieving those behaviors. These behaviors and measures translate into organized learning components for the training/learning material. This translation represents the Design phase of the Instructional System Design process. The model combines expert testimony and behavioral measures that account for several types and levels of learning, which requires different instruction design methods to meet the learner's needs [2].

We demonstrate the use of technology as an enhancement to the training material in the Orange County Fire Rescue Department Incident Fire Command simulation-based training system. The training was targeted for new Company Officers (CO) who needed to lead a team to determine how best to put out a fire under different environmental and material conditions. To target gap areas in the current training, designers performed "ride-alongs" to acquire an ethnographic report of context, tools, interactions, communications, and others behaviors necessary for successful Incident Command (IC) performance.

The intent of the ethnographic report is to objectively describe the activities, personnel, tools, and behaviors across a series of different incidences. The designer organizes and analyzes the detailed activities and presents that information to an IC expert. The IC expert assists in capturing key cues and decisions, along with metrics of success at the more detailed levels. This process identifies gaps in performance between the senior IC personnel and the incoming CO.

The next aspect of this design process raises the level of IC contextual information by interviewing other firefighters and simulating other types of field related fire activities. Flow charts described steps in the IC process from arrival reports, to diagnosing the type of fire based on "reading smoke" and the type of building construction, to selection of different tactics and how to communicate tactics to the fire fighters. Comparisons between the current training content and the new training model identified gaps among successful outcome performance, trainee's prior knowledge and current training methods.

The result of this approach was a detailed blueprint of IC training that began with 11 h of pre-training via the web. Desktop training provided guided lecture using case study incidents that demonstrated application and practice with feedback of successful IC resolution. Once the CO reached a level of competence, he or she was brought into an immersive simulation that required the CO to perform their job in a Fire Scene situation in which they had to be the IC and command the avatar firefighters in properly engaging the fire. IC experts critiqued the CO's performance based upon criterion identified as critical in the initial phases of the design.

The success of this training implementation did not depend on a single training delivery platform. Each level of successful performance outcomes necessitated the correct technology that matched the purpose of the training. The mapping or transfer of the performance outcomes to the appropriate technology depended upon the accurately and systematically defined, detailed description of successful performance delineated through the ethnographic report, behavior deconstruction, along with subject matter expert input. By focusing on the performance outcomes and then choosing the types of technologies that best delivered that content, we achieved a high level of success in training a very complex and dangerous task. The ultimate test of training and learning is transfer from the training environment to the operational environment, and it is at this stage in the learning journey that emerging immersive technologies can efficiently and effectively assess transfer into application.

3 Value of Immersive Technology

As discussed, successful learning and training should use a range of technologies best suited for success toward a measurable training or learning goal. Just the way the abacus allowed a visual representation of numbers for merchants and students, so do computer graphics and virtual worlds allow learners today to visualize learning environments, people and events. Simulations allow us to interact in real-time within the context of learning environments. The actions and reactions are real; the movements, procedures, tactics and strategies are directly applicable to real world circumstances, with the benefit that simulations can collect rich data.

By designing learning environments with clear performance metrics and learning objectives as the foundation, the interactivity becomes seamless and intuitive, leaving only learners and mentors working toward a common goal. Along with individual content knowledge gathering, group discussions both face-to-face and online, and even computer-based small scale simulations, we now have rich emerging technologies with high levels of immersion, that allow us to more intuitively navigate the virtual worlds that we create. As the way we interface with the technology begins to mimic our natural impulses and motions, the complexity and types of learning environments we can achieve become more applicable to the diversity and complexity seen in everyday life.

To demonstrate application of training or learning as an outcome metric to the journey, we move to using the tools of the real world environment rather than the trappings of the training environment. Immersive simulations allow us to proceduralize tasks. Research has shown greater engagement with immersive VR and MR technologies because the training environment seems real to the trainees. Head mounted displays allow us to use our natural senses to experience virtual content. We move our heads and eyes to experience a virtual space as we would in reality. Tracking devices allow us to interface spatial information between the physical space and the virtual elements.

Mixed Reality (MR) engages the learner in direct, first person interaction with a real-time environment containing both physical and virtual assets and agents. Because one attains the highest level of realism and immersion, MR spaces can reduce costs and increase productivity. One cost saving aspect of MR is that the design no longer necessitates a large number of physical prototypes of learning environments. Engineers can now review their data in 3d physical space the same way they could review a costly physical mockup. Using MR they can walk around an object, and intuitively move it with their hands. Interacting with a life-size representation of the object allows one to understand the total system and how complex parts with their forces work together or in opposition. In a time when our virtual worlds are melding with the physical world on many levels, training and learning need to move effortlessly between the two realities.

This information exchange between the physical world and the learner, whether through technology or real world experience, must account for the active learning process of the human brain. The change to the individual during learning is an internal process demonstrated through external action. As we establish best practices of how to design learning experiences with these emerging technologies, we need to understand the impact of the technology and the learning models on the learning process itself. We explore this opportunity in the next section.

4 Effectiveness Measures in Training and Education

The previous sections discuss the journey of the learner through their lifespan and across different learning spaces (e.g., college courses or specific training). Each of these learning spaces has the potential to enhance the learning experience and the applicable knowledge outcomes of that experience using technology. From a neurobiological perspective, learning by definition is the process that constructs memories, while memory is the outcome of learning [3]. This operational definition of learning provides a foundation to: (1) determine effectiveness measures that can predict human performance and (2) define gaps and solutions for directly measuring the learning process. Currently, we determine the success or failure of learning by assessing an indirect measure of the outcome of the learning process: behavior or the memory guided appropriate action to accomplish a set of tasks. However, what a person actually knows may not be observable in behavior. Is this behavioral approach enough to determine the effectiveness or how well the learning transfers to the real world?

The contention of this section is that along the history of defining best practices in instructional design, we have also run parallel in defining how the brain learns across the life cycle. Many instructional design strategies are abstractions of common knowledge of how the brain functions. For example, cognitive load theory derives from the assumption that working memory is a short-term brain store for material the brain is currently processing and suffers from overloading. Thus, the appropriate delivery of learning content is one that does not burden this brain processor [4]. While researchers search for a means to validate this brain-based instructional design approach (ex. [5]), there is still a reliance on assumptions about how the brain integrates information across sensory modalities to facilitate the learning process. These assumptions are yet another abstraction of the models, and more often metaphors we use to understand the brain. Technology affords the opportunity to apply the close-enough external learning strategies and cues, while stimulating the internal learning processes without knowing all the details.

This "close enough" combined approach of learner appropriate content and compatible technology delivery systems is an intermediary step to better understanding how the brain learns in context, naturalistically during the process of learning. Investigations within military-relevant training suggest that electroencephalography (EEG) can validly assess signatures of attention, memory and workload during the learning process [6, 7]. These EEG measures also offer a reliable means to quantify accurately key aspects of information processing [8].

The field of virtual rehabilitation shows successful examples of choosing the right technology to deliver effective re-training or treatment to the patient [9]. The user-centered design of the therapy environment takes into account the separate and integrated contributions of the technology and therapy content. The use of psychophysiological measures provides a means to evaluate objectively the brain state changes of the patient and to monitor those changes that relate to positive retraining.

More importantly, brain monitoring can occur in real world settings under conditions that reflect the learner's true environment. We extended this method of user-centered assessment of learning content and technology delivery system to serious games for training [10]. Results from this work suggest that brain based instructional design theories are not completely accurate or generalizable across learning spaces.

The current and future challenge then is to understand the learning process within the context of the learning space (e.g., classroom or in the field). To accomplish this, we must go beyond our abstractions of how we think the brain learns and really understand the biological process of learning. In so doing, we can stop adding incomplete theories and assumptions to the decision of what content and what technology are best suited for the learning space.

5 Conclusion

In this paper, we explore the impact of technology and instructional design on the learner. Preliminary results from the Orange County Fire Rescue Department Incident Fire Command simulation-based training system show that this type of immersive simulation allowed any person experiencing the training to build bridges in their knowledge such that they could transfer their experience to the real world, sometimes in novel ways. However, the preliminary web-based training was necessary to build the knowledge base for the Fire Command Officers to improve their job performance in the simulation and the real world. Thus, multiple modalities of technology were needed to achieve successful outcomes. The future question is why and how does this technology coupled with the training context affect the learning process. For this, final step the use of unobtrusive psychophysiological measures is the key. This combined approach will take us from brain-based learning theory to application with true measurable success.

References

1. Tarr, R., Smith, E., Totten, E., Carney, M., Wajda, M.: Utilizing simulation and game-based learning to enhance incident commander training. In: Inter-service/Industry Training, Simulation, and Education Conference (I/ITSEC), Orlando, Florida (2014)
2. Gagne, R.: Military training and principles of learning. Am. Psychol. **17**, 263–276 (1962)
3. Squire, L.R.: Memory and Brain. Oxford University Press, New York (1987)
4. Sweller, J., van Merriënboer, J.J.G., Paas, F.: Cognitive architecture and instructional design. Educ. Psychol. Rev. **10**, 251–296 (1998)
5. Brünken, R., Plass, J.L., Leutner, D.: Direct measurement of cognitive load in multimedia learning. Educ. Psychol. **38**, 53–62 (2003)
6. Berka, C., Levendowski, D., Lumicao, M., Yau, A., Davis, G., Zivkovic, V.: EEG correlates of task engagement and mental workload in vigilance, learning and memory tasks. Aviat. Space Envir. Md. **78**(5), B231–B244 (2007)
7. Berka, C., Levendowski, D.J., Cvetinovic, M., Petrovic, M.M., Davis, G.F., Lumicao, M.N., Popovic, M.V., Zivkovic, V.T., Olmstead, R.E., Westbrook, P.: Real-time analysis of EEG indices of alertness, cognition and memory acquired with a wireless EEG headset. Special Issue Int. J. Hum-Comput. Augmented Cogn. **17**(2), 151–170 (2004)

8. Poythress, M., Russell, C., Siegel, S., Tremoulet, P., Craven, P., Berka, C., Levendowski, D., Chang, D., Baskin, A., Champney, R., Hale, K.: Correlation between expected workload and EEG Indices of cognitive workload and task engagement. In: Schmorrow, D., Stanney, K., Reeves, L. (eds.) Augmented Cognition: Past, Present and Future, pp. 32–44. Strategic Analysis Inc, Arlington, VA (2006)
9. Fidopiastis, C.M., Rizzo, A.A., Rolland, J.P.: User-centered virtual environment design for cognitive rehabilitation. J. of Neuroengin. Rehabil. **7**, 11 (2010). http://www.jneuroengrehab.com/content/7/1/11
10. Oskorus, A.L., Andre, T.S., Ripley, T.R., Meyer, R.E., Fidopiastis, C.M., Andrews, D.H., Fitzgerald, P.C.: An approach to accelerated learning and psychophysiological measures of engagement. In: The Interservice/Industry Training, Simulation & Education Conference (I/ITSEC), Orlando, FL (2011)

Augmenting Reality in Sensor Based Training Games

Peter A. Smith[✉]

University of Central Florida, Orlando, FL, USA
Peter.smith@ucf.edu

Abstract. Building an Augmented Reality experience has traditionally been limited by the use of physical markers, and GPS capabilities that are hampered indoors. Physical markers are intrusive in an environment that is dual use between an AR and more traditional experience, making them a less than popular choice for physical locations. GPS solves many of these problems outdoors. Unfortunately, this cannot be capitalized on in an indoor setting where interference from the building cannot guarantee the fidelity of the location data. A recent technology is a low energy Bluetooth transmitter that allows devices to determine their proximity to the transmitter. These devices can be configured and installed discretely in a physical location and power AR experiences and also open up new opportunities to augment, extend, push, and track a user's experience.

Keywords: iBeacon · BLE · Augmented reality · Location based training

1 Introduction

Building an Augmented Reality (AR) experience has traditionally been powered by the use of physical markers and GPS. Unfortunately these technologies have various limitations that keep them from breaking into the main stream. Physical markers are intrusive in an environment that is dual use between an AR and more traditional experience making them a less than popular choice for physical locations. GPS can be useful in many of these outdoor location based games like Google's Ingress [1]. Unfortunately, this cannot be capitalized on in an indoor setting where interference from the building cannot guarantee high enough fidelity of the location data.

A recent technology pioneered by Apple, the iBeacon, has created a solution to this problem [2]. While pioneered by Apple, the iBeacon can interact with any Bluetooth enabled phone including Android devices. Using new technologies such as iBeacon the precise location of an AR device such as a phone or head mount display (HMD) can be determined through triangulation in any room with three or more beacons [6]. This information can be leveraged to generate a similar experience to traditional AR. This could include interacting with real and virtual objects and people.

The iBeacon is a Bluetooth Low Energy (BLE) transmitter that allows devices to determine their proximity to the transmitter, without causing a large battery drain on the user's device. These iBeacons can be configured and installed discretely in a physical location and power AR experiences and also open up new opportunities to interact in

© Springer International Publishing Switzerland 2015
R. Shumaker and S. Lackey (Eds.): VAMR 2015, LNCS 9179, pp. 329–336, 2015.
DOI: 10.1007/978-3-319-21067-4_34

physical environments not previously possible. They can be used to augment, extend, push, and track a user's experience.

2 Sensor Enabled Augmented Reality Technologies

Using sensors to enable augmented reality experiences is not a new idea. The main type of this is paper based markers viewed by a devices camera. These include custom markers viewed by a camera, Near Field Communication (NFC), and BLE devices like iBeacon.

2.1 Camera Based Paper Markers

Camera Based Paper Markers are the most common type of AR experience. They often use custom markers that can be identified and interacted with. A good example of this is the AR games included with the Nintendo 3DS [3]. Each 3DS comes packed with a pack of cards representing various characters in Nintendo's games. They can be viewed with the cameras in the device and games can be played in the real world, as 3D characters appear on the video being displayed on screen. The paper markers provide context for the games to place the objects. The unfortunate side effect is that the markers are needed for the device to orient itself. In the end, they can easily clutter a physical space.

Also, most markers do not contain any information not already associated with the companion app. One solution to this is the Quick Response (QR) Code. QR Codes provide links or other textual information imbedded in the system. This information, however, cannot be directly changed by the app.

2.2 Near Field Communication

Near Field Communication (NFC) can be used in similar ways to QR Codes for augmented reality applications. While its strength is not in creating 3D overlays of information, they can still be used to augment the user's view of a world. NFC uses a standard for sending data over short distances through radio waves. They require devices to be close to them, and enable two devices to transmit information between them in a peer to peer fashion. They allow the user to both read the data out of them as well as write new data to the NFC chip.

NFC has grown rapidly in popularity as it is the technology powering the Skylanders and Disney Infinity games [4]. In these games when a player puts a toy on a reader the player can now play as that toy. Further they can save their characters stats from the game as they change.

The drawback of NFC is the range is not far. Devices often need to be within a few inches to work. So while AR information can be sent to a device they lose the ability to interact from afar. The main solution to this is combining NFC with camera based markers [5].

2.3   BLE Devices

Bluetooth Low Energy is the standard behind the iBeacon. The iBeacon can be placed in a location and will communicate out to devices. There is no need for line of site, like you have with cameras, and they can reach across long distances (roughly 250 feet). This may initially make them seem to be an obvious solution to augmented reality, but unlike other technologies it is more difficult to get extremely accurate location data without multiple iBeacons present in the space, because there is no directional data in relation to distance from an iBeacon. Knowing your distance from 3, however, allow for triangulation.

Knowing a device's distance from one iBeacon is still useful information. It is easy to tell if a device is in a general location, like standing in front of an exhibit, or in a restaurant. This can be used to augment reality in a multitude of ways.

2.4   A Comparison of Available Technologies

It can easily become confusing to determine which technology is right for a given application. While each technology has its strengths they all have their weaknesses as well. It is not easy enough to just say iBeacon is the right solution all the time, but it does solve many of the problems that current solutions have. The following table should help weigh the options available when making a technology decision about sensors in AR (Table 1).

3   Augmented Reality and IBeacons

The recent technological advances made possible through iBeacon are empowering sensor based AR implementations in a far more seamless way than ever before. By wirelessly providing location data to devices without the need for GPS or paper markers, AR experiences can work indoors without polluting the space with markers. The iBeacon technology can interact in AR environments in four primary ways, by augmenting the user experience, extending the use experience, pushing the user to new experiences, or track the user as they interact normally.

3.1   Augment

These experiences can be extremely accurate and depend upon a Head Mount Display (HMD) technology that can track an individual's location within a space and present them with virtual objects or an overlay of a space, the use of beacons allows an individual's position in a space to be accurately determined, allowing the physical space to respond to a user's location. For example, a traditional AR might allow a surgeon to see an overlay on a patient's abdomen that represents where specific organs are within the body using a head mount display. That overlay might be present within the head mount display throughout an experience.

Table 1. Comparison of available AR sensor tech, modified from [7]

Technology	iBeacon	NFC	Markers
Hardware Requirements	Requires a handheld device that supports Bluetooth Low Energy.	Requires a handheld device that supports Near Field Communication (Not iOS)	Requires a device that has a camera installed.
Range	Up to 250 feet away and as close as a few inches.	A few inches away at most. The ability to touch handheld preferred.	Needs a direct line of sight, but could work across varied distances depending upon camera resolution.
App Requirements	Apps must know about specific beacons in advance and know what to do when those beacons are detected	App does not need to know about specific NFC chips though they can. Information can be stored and shared directly from the chip.	Apps may know about specific markers, but some standard format markers can contain information (QR Codes) and could use general purpose apps.
Setup Required by User	The user only needs to install the app and possibly enable Bluetooth through the phones settings. This can be done through the app as well.	The user needs to install the app and enable NFC on their phones. They will also need to physically touch sensors.	The user may have a general purpose app or might need to install a specific app. No other functions need to be modified.
Setup Required by app developer	iBeacons need to be placed in specific locations by the developer. Finding the best location can be difficult.	NFC tags are placed in specific places. Generally easier to place than iBeacons, but may require specific information written to them.	Unique markers must be developed with visual variation.
Benefit	Can determine locations in and around buildings with high accuracy and no physical connection from the user. Can be used for long and short distances.	Can contain information.	Low cost solution Supports most devices

(*Continued*)

Table 1. (*Continued*)

Technology	iBeacon	NFC	Markers
Technology	Can be completely hidden	Can record information for user. Inexpensive Easily Hidden from view	
Issues	Higher cost than other solutions Proximity is directionless Requires Bluetooth on the device	Needs magnetic shielding on metal Short Range No iOS support	Needs line of sight Cannot be hidden Often considered unsightly

Although, when leveraging iBeacon technology, a user might instead be prompted via their device, such as a phone or a tablet to view the same overlay only when they approach the patient's side, the power of Bring Your Own Device (BYOD) AR is present in this. Imagine, for example a factory employee who needs to repair a faulty part in a large machine. Using iBeacon like technology, that user might be prompted to access the repair manual for a specific machine when he/she arrives at the machine itself. This repair manual might include all of the necessary media including 3D models of the parts that need to be fixed, diagnostic information, videos, and step by step instructions.

3.2 Extend

The iBeacons can also be used to extend an experience. Used in informal educational settings, like museums, interactions could result in an additional experiences being provided to the user. For example, if a user was visiting an exhibit about earthquakes at their local science museum, they might have access to games, simulations, videos and various other supplementary information and media related to earthquakes on their phones. This information could be unlocked as they explore different parts of the exhibit and extend the experience for the user. They might decide to spend a few minutes playing these while they are viewing the exhibit, or they might choose to delve deeper into the content when they get home.

Similarly, a student strolling through a park might notice a statue with little information on the small plate installed at its base. Using a technology like iBeacon, that student might have access to relevant websites, information, and other media that surround the statue. This information could be saved, and even tracked via new informal learning management systems. But most importantly, it would be available in an easy to access format on a user's own device.

3.3 Push

The most common use of iBeacons is their ability to push information to a user. By determining proximity of the user to a particular beacon, the system can be used to push notices, information, media or any targeted messages. These messages can be used to provide contextual information about the current location or guide the user to the next one.

A user who visits a store in the mall for the first time, for example, might receive a push notification welcoming them to that store and asking them if they would like to join a loyalty program or receive any coupons or sales that are happening. The same user might be rewarded for multiple visits to the store, and pushed information about items they typically purchase being highlighted.

Health applications could push messages guiding users to take the stairs when they are near the elevator. Integration with other technologies might allow users to receive suggestions of what to order at a restaurant based on the number of calories they had previously logged that day and their weight related goals. This same technology can be used to push a user further through the physical world by suggesting the go somewhere else, similarly to the hotter/colder game children play.

3.4 Track

One of the biggest advantages of iBeacon over traditional AR technologies is the ability to track the users as they interact with the iBeacons. The experience is based on users connecting to the iBeacons and sharing that data with a server. So, while the iBeacon powers the experience the infrastructure is also designed around tracking how they are used. This tracking does not need to be explicitly shared with the user. It is possible to track that a user is taking the stairs vs the elevator, or turns right compared to left when entering a space. This information can be used to optimize the use of a space.

In retail it would be possible to determine a customer's shopping habits, and use that data to direct coupons to the customer. In a school it could be used to determine if a student showed up to class, or if a Hall Pass ever made it to the bathroom or Principles office. Of course, this information can be logged and used to customize pushing and extending, it can exist on its own.

4 Limitations

One significant limitation of technologies like iBeacon is their reliance on a user provided device. While some organizations and educational institution might provide devices to learners, such as tablets or computers; these technologies have been designed to capture your attention outside of formal learning during regular life experiences, necessitating in some cases that the user leverage their personal device. While the concept of using a personal device is certainly not uncommon (termed BYOD for bring your own device), significant portions of the world at large do not

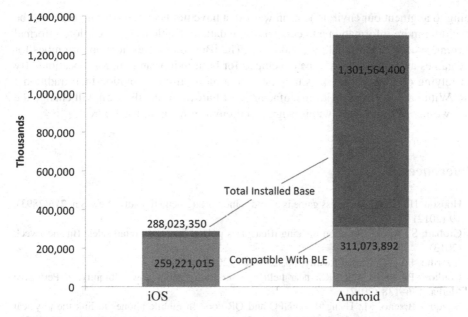

Fig. 1. Global active smartphones compatible with BLE (Source: BI Intelligence) [8]

have the technology that would be necessary to take full advantage of the features that technologies like iBeacon would require (Fig. 1).

Additionally, many individuals might be hesitant to use their personal devices as certainly tracking occurs, and individual privacy might be perceived as being at risk. While getting a message that a product was left in a virtual shopping cart online is interesting, getting a message that says you might have left a tangible object in an actual shopping cart might border on creepy. Honoring user's privacy is becoming more and more of an issue. The role of COPA is also at question here. AR implementations that leverage technologies such as iBeacon that work most efficiently when consumed on personal devices would have to innovatively create value propositions for individual users that would entice them to use the technology and not to opt out of receiving information and notifications.

This could present additional problems for those who pay for data usage or by text message. While Bluetooth is free, it is generally used to prompt internet traffic through the device. If this traffic is not wanted or valuable and has the user incur cost, these apps will soon find themselves uninstalled. Providing value for sharing data is also an important issue.

5 Conclusions

The use of iBeacon technology is increasing at a dramatic rate. The major industry driving this forward is retail, but as it becomes ubiquitous there, the technology is going to become an important driver in other experiences as well. The technology is going to augment our environments in ways that have not been thought of yet. It will be providing more information and context to the data available as users explore informal learning spaces, art installations, and more. The iBeacon creates new opportunities for AR games and applications to be developed for both indoor and outdoor locations. By not relying on physical markers they provide a more discreet solution than traditional AR. With backing from major manufacturers of hardware, the iBeacon will change the way we interact and learn within augmented environments in the future.

References

1. Hodson, H.: Google's ingress game is a gold mine for augmented reality. New Sci. **216**(2893), 19 (2012)
2. Grobart, S.: Apple's location-tracking iBeacon is poised for use in retail sales. Businessweek (2013)
3. Inzerillo, L.: Augmented Reality, pp. 250–257 (2011)
4. Coulton, P.: SKYLANDERS: near field in your living room now. Ubiquity: J. Pervasive Media, 136–138 (2012)
5. Vazquez-Brseno, M.: Using RFID/NFC and QR-code in mobile phones to link the physical and the digital world. In: Deliyannis, I. (ed.) Interactive Multimedia. InTech, pp. 219–242 (2012)
6. Gasser, M.: In-network aggregation techniques in wireless sensor networks. Internet Economics VIII, p. 7 (2014)
7. Scramboo. iBeacons, NFC, Augmented Realty, QR Codes – What's best for engaging users? Part 3. Scramboo Blog. http://www.scramboo.com/ibeacons-nfc-augmented-reality-qr-codes-what-is-best-for-engaging-mobile-users-part-3
8. Smith, C.: More Than Half A Billion Smartphones Are Ready For The Coming Beacon Retail Revolution BI Insider. http://www.alltrinidadtobago.com/2014/06/chart-more-than-half-billion.html

A Serious-Game Framework to Improve Physician/Nurse Communication

Marjorie Zielke[1(✉)], Susan Houston[2], Mary Elizabeth Mancini[3],
Gary Hardee[1], Louann Cole[4], Djakhangir Zakhidov[1], Ute Fischer[5],
and Timothy Lewis[1]

[1] Arts and Technology, University of Texas at Dallas, Richardson, TX, USA
{margez,ghardee,dxz021000,timothy.lewis}@utdallas.edu
[2] Nursing Research, Baylor Scott and White Health, Dallas, TX, USA
susan.houston@baylorhealth.edu
[3] College of Nursing and Health Innovation, University of Texas at Arlington,
Arlington, TX, USA
mancini@uta.edu
[4] Center of Clinical Effectiveness, Baylor Scott and White Health,
Dallas, TX, USA
louannc@baylorhealth.edu
[5] School of Lit., Media and Comm., Georgia Institute of Technology,
Atlanta, GA, USA
ute.fischer@gatech.edu

Abstract. This paper focuses on a serious-game framework for a dialogue-driven game called GLIMPSE (A Game to Learn Important Communications Methods for Patient Safety Enhancement). The eight essential components of the framework include: recommended communication behavior; accurate translation; narrative-driven, role-playing episodes that allow practice in different challenging situations; perspective sharing mechanisms; a design paradigm that accommodates time challenges of participants; motivational gameplay rewards; feedback/assessment mechanisms; and curriculum. The paper explores how the framework was developed as well as implementation challenges, lessons learned and opportunities for future research.

Keywords: Dashboards · Interprofessional communication · Narrative systems · Patient safety · Perspective sharing · Persuasive technology · Physician/nurse communication · Role-playing · SBAR · Serious games · Serious game framework · Team-based communication · Learning portals

1 Introduction

This paper focuses on a serious-game framework for a dialogue-driven serious game called GLIMPSE (A Game to Learn Important Communications Methods for Patient Safety Enhancement). GLIMPSE was a research project completed in March 2015 sponsored by the Agency for Healthcare Research and Quality (AHRQ). The research was done in collaboration with the Virtual Humans and Synthetic Societies Lab within the Modeling and Simulation Center at the University of Texas at Dallas, The College

© Springer International Publishing Switzerland 2015
R. Shumaker and S. Lackey (Eds.): VAMR 2015, LNCS 9179, pp. 337–348, 2015.
DOI: 10.1007/978-3-319-21067-4_35

of Nursing at the University of Texas at Arlington and Baylor Scott & White Health. The game's purpose is to increase perspective sharing and role empathy among physicians and nurses as a way to improve communication and ultimately patient safety. The project focuses on a critical topic in medical practice today. "Current research indicates that ineffective communication among healthcare professionals is one of the leading causes of medical errors and patient harm" [1]. To this end, communication improvement and interprofessional teamwork is a major theme of healthcare professional education, and new interface strategies for learning and practicing effective communication are an important research area.

2 Characteristics of the Design Challenge

Several distinct design challenges and opportunities exist with the physician-nurse audience that is the target of GLIMPSE. Physicians and nurses have limited time for work place education. Changing schedules, expected turnover and similar issues add to the basic availability of the target users. This schedule variability lends itself to the need for asynchronous time paradigms where participants can work independently at their own pace, and yet, at other times synchronous learning opportunities may be desired. Another characteristic of communications-based education is that it inherently requires role-playing and perspective sharing. This requirement is difficult to portray realistically without virtual characterization which a gaming paradigm can provide. A game provides a setting where physicians and nurses can practice sensitive or potentially inflammatory situations within a safe environment. A serious game construct includes the ability to represent complex relationships, nuance and levels and the flexibility to represent individual and team dynamics. Just-in-Time training and expandability is another characteristic that game-based frameworks can provide. Users can review the game content at will. Growth in computer-based, mobile and tablet paradigms encourages research in serious-game frameworks. An episodic game provides chunked story-based narrative content that fits the periodic training timeframes of working medical professionals. A game-based format allows for ongoing onboarding of new staff on organizational culture. A game paradigm can provide motivation, feedback and assessment opportunities. A serious game framework provides a persuasive technology paradigm that encourages behavioral change. Finally, communication fits well into a serious game construct.

3 Communication Is a Game

The daily interactions of healthcare professionals often resemble an intricate and challenging game. In real life, physicians and nurses daily gain and lose relationship points because of communication. Stress, lack of sleep, cultural and social barriers, emergencies, and professional rank and status are just some of the variables that may cause communication breakdowns and ensuing negative patient outcomes. When healthcare professionals do not address problems, voice concerns, or show respect, patients can suffer. Just as in real life, in GLIMPSE, a player wins interaction points, or iPoints, by being courteous and showing respect, by taking opportunities to repair relationships, and by using the recommended communication techniques. A player can lose iPoints by showing anger, letting their ego guide their communication decisions, or by failing to use recommended communication techniques. In GLIMPSE players have the opportunity to step out of their usual professional role and explore other perspectives. This perspective-sharing capability allows players to experience how cultural differences, professional responsibilities, and perceived social status along with personality conflicts and workplace distractions affect communication.

4 Similar Research

"Serious games applications related to health and healthcare are becoming more common, and today there exists a large number of them" [2]. Furthermore, "high-fidelity medical simulations are educationally effective and simulation-based education complements medical education in patient care settings" [3]. Yet research into the effectiveness of virtual reality, game-based simulations for medical education and healthcare workforce training has been limited. Most validation studies of virtual simulation and training-type games focus on a narrow set of surgical skills such as laparoscopic and endoscopic training [4]. Very little has been published on how to implement fuller, organization-wide curriculum characteristics such as interprofessional team-based communication, perspective sharing, patient-centered "just culture" which balances safety and accountability [5], and behavioral/attitudinal changes that lead to improved outcomes, into a serious game experience. One study in the defense sector proposes a design framework called the "simulation experience design method" which focuses on "designing user supports for cross-cultural discovery by way of interactions, narratives, how communication defines a place, and how user co-created emergent culture could result in more intrinsically motivating virtual environments that in turn engender more equitable intercultural communication" [6]. Another healthcare game design study [7] concludes "designing healthcare games based on behavioral models can increase the usability of the game in order to improve the effectiveness of the game's desired healthcare outcomes." These studies suggest a need for research on how educational designers can create rich systems of experiences for healthcare simulation and training.

5 Gamification, Serious Games and Persuasive Technology

The terms gamification and serious games are often used interchangeably, but they are not synonymous. A clarification of these terms is helpful for defining the framework. Further, a discussion of the characteristics of persuasive technology is also helpful for framework conceptualization.

Gamification is the use of game design elements and game mechanics such as badges and leaderboards in non-game contexts [8]. For example, Dominguez and colleagues explored the value of gamifying an online course on "Qualification for Users of ICT (Information and Communications Technology)" [8]. In contrast, serious games are complete original games for non-entertainment purposes [9]. Clearly, the GLIMPSE research is a serious game.

Interestingly, the research of B.J. Fogg on persuasive technology directly parallels the framework findings, and in particular the research process to create GLIMPSE. Fogg defines persuasive technology as "an interactive product designed to change attitudes or behaviors or both by making a desired outcome easier to achieve" [10]. Fogg identifies seven types of persuasive technology tools that relate to the components of the framework described here including *reduction* or simplifying, *tailoring* or "computer products relevant to individuals to change attitudes or behaviors," and *suggestion technology* or "an interactive product that suggests a behavior at the most opportune moment" [10].

6 A Serious-Game Framework to Improve Physician/Nurse Communication

Given the game parameters and requirements, the following eight key elements of A Serious-Game Framework to Improve Physician/Nurse Communication are proposed. These eight essential components include: recommended communication behavior; accurate translation; narrative-driven, role-playing episodes that allow practice in different challenging situations; perspective-sharing mechanisms; a design paradigm that accommodates time challenges of participants; motivational gameplay rewards; feedback/assessment mechanisms; and curriculum. These are discussed below.

6.1 Recommended Communications Behavior

Within the GLIMPSE game, two goal behavior paradigms were presented: Situation, Background, Assessment, Recommendation (SBAR), and Team-based Communication (TBC). Each of these are discussed below.

Situation Background Assessment Recommendation (SBAR). Mnemonic tools such as SBAR, AIDET (acknowledge, introduce, duration, explanation, thank you) and PACE (patient problem, assessment, continuing changes, evaluation) are used in healthcare environments to facilitate interprofessional and patient/provider communication [11, 12]. SBAR was created by the military and adopted in healthcare to promote effective and consistent communication among providers. The tool's effectiveness has been evaluated from a quality improvement and research perspective with results suggesting that the tool improves handoffs, rounding, interdisciplinary communication and patient safety [13, 14]. The Institute for Health Improvement endorsed SBAR [15] because its use promotes standardization of communication. GLIMPSE includes interactive episodes to teach SBAR and how it might be adapted for different communications situations in order to reduce errors and promote quality patient care.

Team-Based Communication (TBC). As teams bring together individuals with different social status, communication patterns likely reflect these differences and can reinforce a hierarchical team structure [16]. For instance, surveys of critical care physicians and nurses revealed differences in their understanding of teamwork consistent with their status [17, 18]. Physician responses suggest they perceived themselves as the ones who give orders to nurses, whereas nurses reported difficulties in expressing concerns or criticism. Research on pilot communication shows that such status-based communication may undermine effective teamwork [19–21] and can generate complacency. High-status team members might discourage subordinates from speaking up and might misunderstand the intentions of subordinates or dismiss their suggestions.

An alternative to status-based communication is "team-centered communication," which was presented in GLIMPSE as "team-based communication" to avoid confusion with other types of team training. Fischer [22] uses the "team-centered communications" term to characterize strategies that emphasize team members' shared responsibilities for solving a problem. Team-centered communication does not deny differences in status, experience and expertise among team members, but these differences are not used to elevate the views of an individual or to curtail communication between team members. Team-centered communication is grounded in the team members' understanding that they are jointly responsible for accomplishing a task. Team-centered communication is a generic model. Although it was developed for and tested with cockpit crews [19], its underlying assumptions are applicable to other domains. Game design incorporated the model's concepts into dialog and gameplay.

6.2 Accurate Translation

A game designed to affect face-to-face behavior must translate to the workplace. Translation includes physical environment, gameplay, narrative and dialog authenticity and realism, rewards and assessments. For example, research revealed that administration, physicians, nurses and patients occasionally send thank you notes as illustrated by A(1) and B(1) in Fig. 1. This reward system is integrated into GLIMPSE.

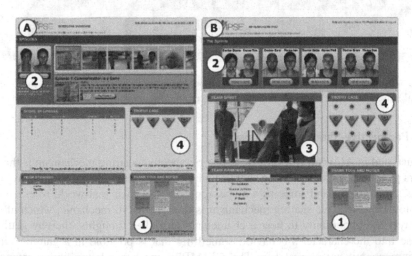

Fig. 1. GLIMPSE included personal (A) and team (B) dashboards to track progress

6.3 Narrative-Driven, Role-Playing Episodes that Allow Practice in Different Challenging Situations

GLIMPSE is a dialog-driven narrative game. The issues that the simulation addresses are the communication barriers that arise during conversations between physicians and nurses as they care for patients. Conversation choices presented to participants and the resulting dialog from characters reflect the commonplace, and sometimes cultural, communication conflicts that can occur in hospital environments. In the GLIMPSE storyline, an elderly patient presents to the Emergency Department with a hip fracture. The story emerges throughout the episodes from new complications in the patient's condition. The story timeline as presented in Fig. 2 below introduces new conflicts in interactive episodes. The overarching narrative, the dialog and the feedback mechanisms are designed to reflect the patient's perspective of how well her care team works together and to reinforce the two communications strategies, SBAR and TBC. Dialog was written specifically with a four-prong, "4P" strategy. (1) Patient: to always return the focus on patient safety; (2) Perspective sharing: to reflect the differences in how physicians and nurses might communicate. (3) Plausibility: to accurately reflect real-world hospital experiences as well as the teaching objectives. (4) Plot: to quickly move busy, work-distracted professionals along branching narrative paths to accomplish teaching moments in each episode. This "4P" strategy led to the design of dialog game features such as Thought Bubbles, which allow participants to pause and reflect on how their own emotions might affect what is said, and therefore, how the plot might branch as a result. Thought Bubbles reinforce perspective sharing and keep the story focused on the patient.

Fig. 2. The story timeline is divided into 12 short episodes that follow a patient through her hospital stay. Interactive episodes engage the player in communications conflicts that arise.

6.4 Perspective-Sharing Mechanisms

As illustrated in A(2) and B(2) in Fig. 1, one perspective-sharing mechanism is that the players pick both doctor and nurse characters before beginning the game and play some episodes as a doctor and some as a nurse, regardless of their real-world roles.

Another perspective-sharing mechanism is the GLIMPSE mechanic, which affords the player the opportunity to hear a character's unspoken thoughts, thereby getting a glimpse into the character's behavior, something that is possible in a gaming virtual environment, but not in real life. The GLIMPSE mechanic helps with perspective sharing, allowing insight into a virtual colleague's behavior and making players aware of unspoken, underlying emotions. Players also get points for taking the time in the game to get a GLIMPSE. This design is illustrated in E in Fig. 3.

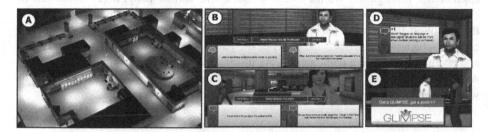

Fig. 3. GLIMPSE simulates a hospital unit (A) and the ability to converse with characters (B, C). The game offers participants immediate feedback on their decisions (D) and perspective sharing through gameplay features like the GLIMPSE mechanic (E).

6.5   A Design Paradigm that Accommodates Time Challenges of Participants

As outlined above, physicians and nurses in general are time challenged, and the nature of their workdays requires design consideration. Further, physicians and nurses do not work the same schedules all the time and may be off work for several days and then return. Synchronous gameplay presents challenges because physicians and nurses would have difficulty collaborating to play the game. While nurses might have an easier time coordinating, that was not the research focus. Therefore an "implied" team paradigm was created where physicians and nurses were assigned to teams and had the opportunity to collaborate and compete with other teams, but actual coordination was not required to progress in the game. Further, as illustrated in B(3) in Fig. 1, a team puzzle which reinforced the goal of a positive patient outcome could be unlocked across episodes by the team. Puzzle pieces were awarded to the first member of the team who completed an episode.

Further accommodating the users, the project was web-based, organized around episodic content and built in the Unity game engine. The purpose of these delivery mechanisms was to allow participants to log in and log out and be able to play a few episodes at a time, at home or at work, as time permitted within approximately a two-week period. Episodes were never more than 10 minute long and were accompanied by transition videos to create lesson and story continuity in the event large gaps of time elapsed before the physicians and nurses continued in the process.

In addition, as illustrated in Fig. 1, a simple dashboard schema was adopted that clearly showed what character selections the physicians and nurses had chosen, what episode the participant was experiencing, number of episodes completed, points earned, badges and thank you notes earned. As shown in Fig. 1, players had both a personal (A) and a team (B) dashboard available.

6.6 Motivational Gameplay Rewards

Several motivational gameplay awards were developed. These include earning interaction points (iPoints) based on choices that reflected the SBAR or TBC recommended approaches, mini-games within some episodes and earned badges. As illustrated in Fig. 1, participants could see their own progress and that of their team and other teams in the cohort through the personal (A) and team (B) dashboards. Players could earn badges, which both rewarded the goals of the game – such as using SBAR and TBC – and encouraged ongoing participation. As illustrated in A(4) and B(4) in Fig. 1, badges were awarded at both the individual player and team level. Continuing education credit was offered to the physicians since the game included ethics content.

6.7 Feedback/Assessment Mechanisms

Feedback was achieved holistically through the dashboard as outlined above and also through step-by-step dialog and Thought Bubble choices, as illustrated in Fig. 3 (B) and (D). All of the data were collected by player and team and are available for analysis. Participants also completed pre- and post-participation knowledge and satisfaction surveys that were part of the game dashboard.

6.8 Curriculum

The curriculum for interprofessional communication was developed based on a literature review, semi-structured interviews with nurses and physicians, and one nurse focus group. The curriculum was presented to participants through all of the mechanisms described above. The interviewees and focus group participants were asked open-ended questions that were sub-grouped into scenarios, strategies used to improve communication and communication challenges. Interviews and the focus group were one to two hours in duration, were audio recorded and transcribed verbatim. The transcripts were then analyzed for descriptive and prescriptive themes, which were then used to inform curriculum development.

The curriculum's key learning objectives were: (a) demonstrate understanding of the consequences of lack of positive communication and collaboration between physicians and nurses, (b) identify common causes of poor physician-nurse communication, and (c) develop approaches to enhancing physician-nurse communication, such as SBAR and TBC, for patient-centered care using a shared-perspective approach. The narrative, episode dialog and gaming components reflected the curriculum and communication challenges identified. Episode scripts and dialog were vetted for accuracy and authenticity by nurses and physicians. The SBAR and TBC recommended communication strategies were also a major part of the implemented curriculum.

7 Implementation Challenges, Lessons Learned and Opportunities for Further Research

GLIMPSE is successful complex research, but was not without implementation challenges, lessons learned and opportunities for further research, as discussed below.

7.1 Implementation Challenges

Implementation challenges were encountered due to the game subject matter, nature of healthcare environments, and technical implementation. Each of these are discussed below.

As mentioned in the framework, it is critical that the narrative represent real-life situations. This requirement created unexpected delays during script development, as editing for authenticity required additional nurse/physician interviews.

Further, during the research timeframe, preparation for regulatory reviews and an increased workload due to holiday and staffing shortages contributed to nursing time constraints. Physicians experienced similar time demands due to scheduling conflicts. Competing priorities including Joint Commission review, Magnet appraiser audit, and visiting regulatory agencies disrupted the continuity of the intervention. These distractions made it difficult to fully engage participants in the activity. The intervention was implemented during the holiday season, causing disruptions in study team site visits and the availability of participants to obtain additional instruction for game completion. Inconsistent use of email by participants made follow-up by study staff problematic. Facility reorganization and employee turnover was distracting to participants and impacted gameplay. Sample size varied among nurses and physicians which made team play challenging. Participants had inconsistent levels of computer literacy, which made it difficult to provide standardized instructions.

The intervention facility was found to have some insufficient computer hardware, software and informatics to support the intervention. Computers varied on individual units. Additional computers were requested and installed at a central location on each unit, requiring additional time and coordination between tech support, nursing and study staff. Web browser changes were required for most computers. The study team was able to provide only limited tech support to participants.

A synchronous gameplay intervention would have been helpful to add to the research to compare response levels, but the research timeline did not permit this added activity. An unanticipated lack of interest in gaming was exhibited by some members of the target audience. Although identified by physicians as a desired component for game design in pre-development research, the competitive aspect of the game did not seem as important in the actual gameplay for some participants. Finally, as illustrated below in Fig. 4, more challenging and unique episodes were sometimes confusing to users and seemed to not always function as designed; this could be due to personal computer age and compatibility. Action items within the research timeline for more interim usability tests with the exact target audience would have been helpful.

Fig. 4. In episode 6 participants were asked to search the environment and click on GLIMPSE icons to unlock audio posters with key game lessons and messages. The episode was studied extensively in the VHSS Lab and refined for ease of use. Despite this testing, this episode was overly challenging to some participants and appeared to not work well on some intervention site computers. Finding the correct level of complexity in interfaces like GLIMPSE is a research challenge.

7.2 Lessons Learned

The use of serious gaming as a strategy for changing behaviors of health professionals is in its infancy. The lessons learned from this project are derived from its most significant challenges. These include:

- Need to identify and focus on a limited number of key learning objectives.
- Typical professional development activities for health professionals tend to be broad and have numerous learning objectives. By nature of the game experience, the number of learning objectives needed to be limited and clearly stated in terms that the developers could understand. When developing a game for health professionals, including a process for curriculum design is essential.
- Importance of knowing the audience. What may seem artistically appropriate or engaging for "gamers" may not be clinically accurate or engaging for health professionals. Although the project plan included time for review, need for extensive dialog between content experts and developers was more than anticipated.
- Knowing the limitations of the technical requirements in advance. For health professionals, use of the game for professional development while on duty is important. When developing games for health professionals, consideration needs to be given to the game technical requirements versus robust firewalls and other technical constraints that may exist in healthcare settings.

7.3 Opportunities for Future Research

This project provides a solid foundation for further research on the use of serious gaming for healthcare professionals. Further research opportunities include: Is serious gaming an efficient and effective learning strategy to change behaviors (beyond acquiring knowledge) of healthcare professionals? What are the characteristics of learners most likely to achieve desired educational outcomes using a gaming strategy? What are the most and least desirable characteristics of a game for this population?

8   Summary

This paper discusses innovative research into interface designs that can take advantage of serious games and other emerging frameworks to enhance physician/nurse communication and improve patient safety. Presented is an eight-point framework that includes: recommended communication behavior; accurate translation; narrative-driven, role-playing episodes that allow practice in different challenging situations; perspective sharing mechanisms; a design paradigm that accommodates time-challenges of participants; motivational gameplay rewards; feedback/assessment mechanisms; and curriculum.

Lessons learned include the need to identify and focus on a limited number of key learning objectives; the importance of knowing the audience; and knowing the limitations of the technical requirements in advance. Opportunities for future research include: Is serious gaming an efficient and effective learning strategy to change behaviors (beyond acquiring knowledge) of health professionals? What are the characteristics of learners most likely to achieve desired educational outcomes using a gaming strategy? What are the most and least desirable characteristics of a game for this population? While GLIMPSE certainly uncovered a variety of unique implementation challenges, the framework presented here provides a solid foundation for further research to develop the promise of serious game for interprofessional communication enhancement for physicians and nurses and other healthcare professionals.

Acknowledgements. This project was sponsored by the Agency for Healthcare Research and Quality (AHRQ) with the Title - Improving Physician and Nurse Communication with Serious Gaming – award number R18HS020416. We would also like to thank the physicians and nurses of Baylor Scott & White Health for their participation as subject matter experts. We also thank all members of the Virtual Humans and Synthetic Societies Lab at the University of Texas at Dallas. We would like to acknowledge Dr. Mary Lou Bond for her development of the curriculum research. We would like to acknowledge Dr. Yan Xiao for his guidance and inspiration.

References

1. Dingley, C., Daughterty, K., Derieg, M., Persing, R.: Improving patient safety through provider communication strategy enhancements. In: Henriksen, K., Battles, J.B., Keyes, M.A., Grady, M.L. (eds.) Advances in Patient Safety: New Directions and Alternative Approaches, vol. 3. Agency for Healthcare Research and Quality, Rockville (2008)
2. Susi, T., Johannesson, M., Backlund, P.: Serious Games: An Overview. Institutionen för kommunikation och information, Skövde (2007)
3. Barry Issenberg, S., Mcgaghie, W., Petrusa, E., Lee Gordon, D., Scalese, R.: Features and uses of high-fidelity medical simulations that lead to effective learning: a BEME systematic review. Med. Teach. **27**(1), 10–28 (2005). doi:10.1080/01421590500046924
4. Graafland, M., Schraagen, J., Schijven, M.: Systematic review of serious games for medical education and surgical skills training. Br. J. Surg. **99**(10), 1322–1330 (2012). doi:10.1002/bjs.8819

5. Dekker, Sidney. Just culture: Balancing safety and accountability. Ashgate Publishing, Ltd., 2012

6. Raybourn, E.: designing intercultural agents for multicultural interactions. In: Payr, S., Trappl, R. (eds.) Agent Culture: Human-Agent Interaction in A Multicultural World, 1st edn, pp. 267–285. Lawrence Erlbaum, Mahwah (2008)

7. Kharrazi, H., Faiola, A., Defazio, J.: Healthcare game design: behavioral modeling of serious gaming design for children with chronic diseases. In: Jacko, J.A. (ed.) HCI International 2009, Part IV. LNCS, vol. 5613, pp. 335–344. Springer, Heidelberg (2009)

8. Domínguez, A., de-Navarrete, J.S., de-Marcos, L., Fernández-Sanz, L., Pagés, C., Martínez-Herráiz, J.: Gamifying learning experiences: practical implications and outcomes. Computers & Education, 63, pp. 380–392 (2013). doi:10.1016/j.compedu.2012.12.020

9. Deterding, S., Dixon, D., Khaled, R., Nacke, L.: From game design elements to gamefulness. In: Proceedings of the 15th International Academic MindTrek Conference on Envisioning Future Media Environments - MindTrek 2011 (2011). doi:10.1145/2181037.2181040

10. Fogg, B.: Persuasive Technology. Morgan Kaufmann, Boston (2003)

11. Riesenberg, L., Leitzsch, J., Little, B.: Systematic review of handoff mnemonics literature. Am. J. Med. Qual. 24(3), 196–204 (2009). doi:10.1177/1062860609332512

12. Staggers, N., Blaz, J.: Research on nursing handoffs for medical and surgical settings: an integrative review. J. Adv. Nurs. 69(2), 247–262 (2012). doi:10.1111/j.1365-2648.2012.06087.x

13. Randmaa, M., Martensson, G., Swenne, C.L., Engstrom, M.: SBAR improves communication and safety climate and decreases incident reports due to communication errors in an anaesthetic clinic: a prospective intervention study. BMJ Open 4(1), e004268–e004268 (2014). doi:10.1136/bmjopen-2013-004268

14. Cornell, P., Gervis, M.G., Yates, L., Vardaman, J.M.: Impact of SBAR on nurse shift reports and staff rounding. MEDSURG Nursing 23(5), 334–342 (2014)

15. Institute for Health Improvement (2011). SBAR Technique for Communicating: A Situational briefing Model. http://www.ihi.org/knowledge/Pages/Tools/SBARTechniqueforCommunicationASituationalBriefingModel.aspx. Accessed 4 March 2015

16. Brown, P., Levinson, S.: Politeness. Cambridge University Press, Cambridge (1987)

17. Pronovost, P.: Acute decompensation after removing a central line: practical approaches to increasing safety in the intensive care unit. Ann. Intern. Med. 140(12), 1025–1033 (2004). doi:10.7326/0003-4819-140-12-200406150-00013

18. Thomas, E., Sexton, J., Helmreich, R.: Discrepant attitudes about teamwork among critical care nurses and physicians*. Crit. Care Med. 31(3), 956–959 (2003). doi:10.1097/01.ccm.0000056183.89175.76

19. Fischer, U., Orasanu, J.: Error-Challenging Strategies: Their Role in Preventing and Correcting Errors. Proc. Hum. Factors Ergon. Soc. Ann. Meet. 44(1), 30–33 (2000). doi:10.1177/154193120004400109

20. Linde, C.: The quantitative study of communicative success: politeness and accidents in aviation discourse. Lang. Soc. 17(03), 375 (1988). doi:10.1017/s0047404500012951

21. Orasanu, J., Fischer, U., McDonnell, L., et al.: How do flight crews detect and prevent errors? findings from a flight simulation study. Proc. Hum. Factors Ergon. Soc. Ann. Meet. 42(3), 191–195 (1998). doi:10.1177/154193129804200302

22. Fischer, U.: Cultural Variability In Crew Discourse. Georgia Institute of Technology, Atlanta (2000)

VR in Health and Culture

Low Cost Hand-Tracking Devices to Design Customized Medical Devices

Giorgio Colombo[1], Giancarlo Facoetti[2], Caterina Rizzi[2],
and Andrea Vitali[2(✉)]

[1] Department of Mechanical Engineering, Polytechnic of Milan, Milan, Italy
giorgio.colombo@polimi.it
[2] Department of Management, Information and Production Engineering,
University of Bergamo (BG), Dalmine, Italy
{giancarlo.facoetti,caterina.rizzi,
andrea.vitalil}@unibg.it

Abstract. This paper concerns the development of a Natural User Interface (NUI) for lower limb prosthesis design. The proposed solution exploits the Leap Motion device to emulate traditional design tasks manually performed by the prosthetist. We first illustrate why hand-tracking devices can be adopted to design socket of lower limb prosthesis using virtual prototyping tools. Then, we introduce the developed NUI and its features mainly with regards to ergonomics and ease of use. Finally, preliminary tests are illustrated as well as results reached so far.

Keywords: Augmented interaction · Hand-tracking devices · SMA

1 Introduction

During last years, low-cost hand-tracking devices have attracted the attention of many researchers who try to make more natural the interaction with application emulating real procedure, such as training in surgery, design of custom-fit products and clothing [1, 15]. The main idea is to find alternative solutions to recreate professional virtual environments to allow the end-user to do his/her work with no particular skills about IT. In fact, the use of hand-tracking devices becomes very interesting when we try to emulate traditional workflows mainly done using either hands/fingers or objects held in hand.

Among different commercial hand-tracking devices, we consider the Leap motion device [14] as best choice for our research activity. The underlying idea is to include this interaction style within a knowledge-based CAD system, named Socket Modelling Assistant (SMA) [3], specifically developed to design lower limb socket. SMA permits to create the virtual model of a prosthetic socket according to the patient's anthropometric measurements and his/her digital model. SMA emulates traditional process manufacturing to create socket shape, which is the most critical part of whole prosthesis. During traditional process, the technician continuously uses her/his hands to shape the socket. Initially, s/he makes an evaluation of the amputee and creates a negative cast manipulating plaster patches directly on patient's residual limb. Then,

R. Shumaker and S. Lackey (Eds.): VAMR 2015, LNCS 9179, pp. 351–360, 2015.
DOI: 10.1007/978-3-319-21067-4_36

Fig. 1. Some traditional steps of socket manufacturing process.

s/he realizes the positive model that is manually modified by adding and removing chalk in specific zones and according to stump measurements and morphology (Fig. 1).

Our aim is to emulate manual operations directly using both hand-tracking and haptic devices. In this paper, we focus the attention on the development of the software interface to create a Natural User Interface (NUI) for hand-tracking devices. To this end, we have developed a NUI mainly based on the use of Leap Motion device to interact with the 3D models of the residual limb and the socket. Many research works have been done to study and improve the quality of this type of NUI, in particular, we paid attention to different aspects mainly related to ergonomics and ease of use, which are the most important features to recreate a better user's experience with augmented interaction.

2 Scientific Background

Virtual reality is the emulation of environment in which human being can perform a series of actions in order to interact with 3D objects We focus our attention on virtual reality that permits to recreate sensory experience through the emulation of tactile sense [12]. The emulation of tactile sense is possible using computer devices that are now available at low cost and, thus, we can exploit them in different research works to understand real potentialities for using new solutions in real contexts, such as lower limb prosthesis design and clothing [10]. In this section, we describe different IT devices to recreate virtual reality as well as different issues relative to the software development of natural user interface for hand-tracking devices.

2.1 Haptic Devices and Hand/Tracking Devices

Emulation of tactile sense considers two types of devices, i.e., haptic and hand-tracking devices. Haptic devices recreate force-feedback to emulate sense of touch according to shapes and material associated to 3D objects in a virtual environment. There are several haptic devices, such as single contact-point haptic devices with different degrees of freedom and haptic gloves. Among different available solutions, we have exploited both low cost haptic devices (i.e., Novint Falcon) and developed in house haptic-mouse) to emulate some operation during socket design with SMA [9].

a)   b)   c)   d)

Fig. 2. Low cost hand-tracking devices: Leap Motion device (a), Intel Gesture Camera (b), Duo3D device (c) and Microsoft Kinect V2.

Hand-tracking devices are able to detect motion of hands/fingers and object held in hand [11, 17, 21]. There are different hand-tracking devices on the market, among which Leap Motion device, Intel Gesture Camera, Duo3D and Microsoft Kinect 2.0 (Fig. 2).

The Leap motion device exploits two IR cameras to determine position and orientation of hands/fingers with high precision. Tracking is very accurate and it can be calibrated to map fingertip positions on the screen. Leap motion device has been used in several research works in order to try a new type of interaction with applications [4, 11]. Furthermore, this hand-tracking device can be used with Oculus Rift to increase the quality of user experience into a virtual system. Figure 3 shows how Leap Motion device is used with Oculus Rift device. This solution is able to track hands/fingers according to natural motion of head.

Intel Gesture Camera includes RGB and depth camera as well as microphones. It is able to detect simple gestures, such as waving, swiping and circling with hand. Intel gesture camera permits also face analysis and speech recognition.

Duo3D is very small and ultra-compact and it's an ideal solution for mobile projects. Duo3D offers different technologies on its board, i.e., an accelerometer, a gyroscope, a temperature sensor as well as two IR cameras.

Microsoft Kinect v2 offers an HD-RGB camera and a powerful IR sensor as well. A large field of view allows this sensor to track object and people closer to the cameras. Just simple gesturers can be tracked by it, such as open and closed hands.

Furthermore, they make available software development kits (SDKs), which permit to create software interfaces with other applications. In this research work, we pay attention on Leap Motion device and its SDK because it allows us to simply define a set of gestures as well as basic hands/fingers tracking.

Fig. 3. Leap Motion device and Oculus Rift.

2.2 Natural User Interface

NUI is an emerging concept in Human/Computer Interaction that refers to an interface that becomes invisible to its user with successive learned interactions related to natural human behavior. As stated in [16] *"The word natural is used because most computer interfaces use artificial control devices whose operation has to be learned. A NUI relies on a user being able to carry out relatively natural motions, movements or gestures that they quickly discover control the computer application or manipulate the digital content"*. In other words, designed NUI has to be able to make user experience very simple and comfortable. Preliminary research works have been carried out in order to understand and consequently solve matters related to NUIs for hand-tracking devices [7, 8, 13, 22].

Developed software interfaces have to implement a set of features to create the most comfortable user interface to interact which chosen hand-tracking device. The aim of this research work is the NUI design between Leap Motion device and a virtual system, which permits to design prosthetic socket. In the next section, we describe the features of the application for prosthetic modelling as well as software architecture to which the developed NUI is linked.

3 Prosthetic Socket Modelling

Socket modelling assistant is a CAD application that allows designing socket of lower limb prosthesis starting from the digital model of the patient (Fig. 4.a). It is based on a knowledge guided approach and makes available a virtual environment where the user can emulate actions made by orthopedic technicians during traditional manufacturing process. Starting from MRI images, SMA is able to automatically reconstruct the 3D model of the residual limb by exploiting NURBS surfaces [6]. Then, a set of virtual tools allows user to mold virtual socket shape according to patient's data (Fig. 4.b).

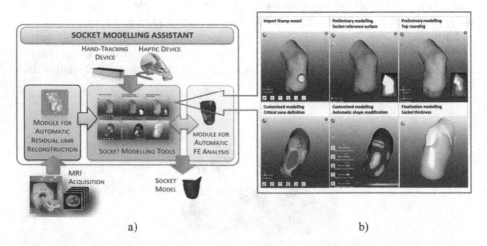

a)   b)

Fig. 4. (a) SMA main modules and (b) modelling virtual tools.

Virtual tools are subdivided in three main groups according to type of modeling tasks:

1. *Preliminary modeling.* Generation of a preliminary geometric model of the socket onto which other specific modifications will be applied to achieve the functional shape. The main operations during this phase are carried out almost completely in automatic way according to patient characteristics and traditional process.
2. *Customized modeling.* Customization of socket model according to the residual limb morphology. The user can proceed in two different ways: automatic or interactive shape manipulation. Indeed, an ad hoc modeling tool permits to modify the shape according to the stump tonicity.
3. *Completing the socket geometric model.* The designer shapes the upper edge in an automatic or semi-automatic way, and the system automatically trims the model along defined upper edge and applies the socket thickness to obtain the final socket model.

As described above, the virtual tools of SMA emulate the operation usually made by technicians who continuously use his/her hands to modify the chalk of residuum positive model to define the socket and used to create the thermoformed socket. This feature has been possible through the development of a software interface, which permits to interact with the 3D environment using either traditional interaction devices (e.g., mouse and keyboard) or hand-tracking and haptic devices.

Finally, an external module exploits a FEA commercial system (i.e., Abaqus) to study the residuum socket interaction [2]. The designed socket can be exported in different formats (e.g., STL and IGES) that may be used to create real model using 3D printer or emulating gait analysis using virtual bio-mechanicals models.

3.1 Software Architecture

The whole system has been completely developed in C ++ using open source SDKs, such as Qt [18], VTK [20] and OpenCascade [19]. Qt allowed us to create the user interface in very simple way using a graphic editor. The Visualization Tool Kit permits to manage advanced modelling techniques, such as implicit modelling, mesh reduction and Delaunay triangulation as well. VTK exploits OpenGL or DirectX in automatic way and thus, the developer can realize his/her applications in very simple way. OpenCascade is a software library, which permits to develop complex CAD, CAM and CAE system. We used OpenCascade mainly for its exporting modules, which allow us to save socket model in either STL or IGES format. Furthermore, a developed in house software library, named SimplyNURBS, has been used to manage NURBS surface. SimplyNURBS permits to recreate 3D model of residuum from MRI volume through the use of modules that hide every complex aspect relative to NURBS models, such as mathematical models and operation applied to them [5].

The modularity of software architecture allows us to add a new module, which exploits Leap Motion device in order to interact with SMA using hands/fingers. In the next section we describe different steps to design NUI to achieve our aim.

4   NUI Design for Hand-Tracking Devices in SMA

NUI design for hand-tracking devices has to be based on definition of rules that are useful to design an intuitive interaction for a generic application. Leap motion developers subdivided these rules as follows [14]:

- *Ergonomics, Posture and Environment.* We have to consider how much fatigue the interaction creates at arms and shoulders.
- *Virtual Space Mapping and Interaction Resolution.* Every gesture has to be mapped according to 2D screen resolution and 3D virtual environment of the application.
- *Dynamic Feedback and Gestalt Intermediates.* The interface has to give user the best feedback in order to understand what happened using a particular gesture.
- *Interaction Space: Separation, States and Transitions.* User has to be able to understand which type of action is activated during interaction.

These rules are implemented into every software interface that exploits hand-tracking devices. In the last year, we aimed at creating a NUI to make more natural the interaction with SMA using Leap Motion device. Preliminary experimentation has been executed to design a good NUI, but many problems came to light with regards to ease of use and ergonomics during long lasting interaction. In fact, testers were not able to learn how to interact with SMA in correct way, because they didn't understand which gesture was activated and thus, they couldn't execute the correct action to model 3D socket shape. Furthermore, a long lasting interaction using Leap Motion device created fatigue to arms and shoulders making users' experience very tiring and useless.

4.1   Gestures Definition

Before starting to develop the software interface, we have defined a set of gestures according to different actions that are executed to design the socket with SMA. They are the following ones:

- *Horizontal motion of single finger to move* from one modeling tool to another one.
- *Free motions of a single finger to* move the selection cursor.
- *Palm rotation of right hand to rotate the* stump and socket models during the use of the modeling tools.
- *Vertical motions of the palms* to zoom–in and out of 3D models.
- *Movement of thin object hold in hand* (e.g., a pencil) to geometrically modify the 3D geometric model. This can be used, for example, to mark with pencil of different colors critical zones as done traditionally by the prosthetist (Fig. 8.a).
- Action of pinch to select a point of surface in order to modify socket shape according to the residuum virtual model (Fig. 8.b and c) and create the socket upper edge.

Other gestures have been added in order to give a better feedback to the user during interaction with SMA. In particular, there are two available interaction styles;

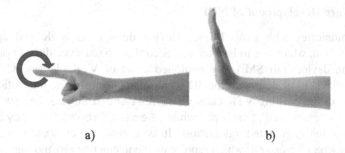

a)   b)

Fig. 5. Gestures used to switch between the Camera and Modification modalities.

Camera and Modification. Camera style rotates 3D model following the orientation of a palm. In this modality, other gestures are disabled. Modification style permits to execute actions relative to socket design according to the gestures previously described.

To switch between the two modalities, one has to put a hand above the sensor with thumb and index finger extended and, then, trace a circle in the air (Fig. 5.a).

To move the hand without interacting, the user has to face the palm to the screen. In this way you can find a more comfortable position or rest your hand without compromising the current state of the application (Fig. 5.b).

The user can always check the confidence of data coming from the Leap Motion device. This percentage is displayed at the bottom of the software interface. This percentage permits to understand which is the state of the detected action. Indeed, if percentage is under 20 % the detected gestures is considered NOT_DETECTED; while percentage is between 20 % and 65 % a warning icon appears on left lower corner of screen. If confidence is over 65 % user can interact with high precision.

In order to provide additional feedback there is an icon at the right bottom corner of the screen showing which hand gesture has been detected (Fig. 6).

The gestures are few because the user has to learn how to interact with SMA in a very simple way. The difference among gestures allows user to distinguish each action from the other ones and thus, the use of augmented interaction appears simple and intuitive during user's experience.

Fig. 6. Icon and progress bar into SMA to show state of interaction using Leap Motion device.

4.2   Software Development of NUI

SMA communicates with Leap Motion device through its SDK and applies the appropriate action, which has to be executed according to retrieved data. In order to use Leap Motion device into SMA, we exploited a set of VTK classes, which makes available methods to interact with the 3D scene of application. The interaction handler is a subclass of the existing VTK class vtkInteractorStyle, i.e., vtkInteractorStyleTrackballcamera; while SensorInteractorStyle is an abstract class for augmented interaction. It is a subclass of vtkInteractorStyleTrackballcamera, which represents the interactions by moving the camera. In our class some methods are over-ridden and some abstract methods are introduced (Fig. 7).

Some of the most important fields and methods are described in the following:

- enableSensor() and disableSensor(): abstract methods that enable/disable the interaction when user is using an hand-tracking device.
- transformVector(double* vector): method for transforming a vector from the sensor coordinate system to the VTK scene coordinate system.
- OnTimer(): abstract method redefined in this class and implemented in the specialized class. This method is executed every 50 ms in order to query hand-tracking device and execute the correct action according to detected gesture.

This class has been extended with another class in order to use Leap Motion device. LeapInteractorStyle contains a set of methods and instructions to exploit Leap motion SDK. Some of the most important fields and methods are described in the following:

- State: its value may be either CAMERA or MODIFICATION, which depends by the current interaction mode.
- NextMode(): method that switches between interaction modes.
- leapController: Leap Motion instance that communicates with the device. From this object we get all information about hands and movements through software instructions of Leap Motion SDK.

In these methods, there are the instructions, which permit to give information to the user in order to understand what happens during the interaction, such as quality of interaction, interaction mode and state of each action.

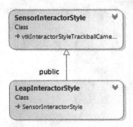

Fig. 7. UML class diagram of software interface for exploiting Leap Motion device within SMA.

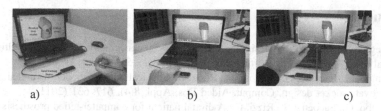

Fig. 8. Marking critical zones of residual limb (a), pinch action to model socket shape (b and c).

5 Preliminary Tests and Results

The system has been tested with ten volunteers to evaluate system performances especially with regards ergonomics, ease of use and precision. The testers were six male and four female with different levels of experience (i.e., beginners and experts) regarding the use of hand-tracking device. First a demo was carried out to show how to execute modeling operations by means of the Leap Motion device. Then, each tester performed the three main basic operations until s/he was able to interact in natural way without the help of technical staff. The modeling operations were: basic interactions with 3D environment (e.g., zoom in and out), marking critical zones (Fig. 8a) and trim-line definition (Fig. 8.b–c).

Testers with a low level of experience found very useful the icons showing the detected gestures but the gestures should be repeated from 5 to 8 times to be properly executed by the user and detected by the system especially for tasks involving 3D geometry modifications. Experts were able to correctly perform the modeling tasks with no more than 2–3 trials.

Regarding ergonomics issues, the new version of the NUI and related gestures allows an adequate and long lasting interaction without fatigue at the arms.

The icons permit to simply learn how to interact with SMA and have been considered helpful mainly by beginners. On the other hand, experts have appreciated the progress bar while beginners were more concentrated on gesture execution and detection.

6 Conclusion

This paper presents the use of Leap Motion device to design the socket for lower limb prosthesis. We have implemented a new NUI starting from a set of rules related to ergonomics and ease of use. The NUI has been tested by volunteers who provided a positive feedback. We have planned to introduce other technologies in order to make more natural and realistic the interaction with SMA system, such as Oculus Rift and last version of Microsoft Kinect.

Finally, tests have been planned with a set of orthopedic technicians who will use our system to design a wearable socket as well as to experiment this new development approach in other contexts, such as consumer products design and clothing.

References

1. Bordegoni, M., Ferrise, F.: Designing interaction with consumer products in a multisensory virtual reality environment. Virtual Phy. Prototyp. **8**(1), 51–64 (2013)
2. Colombo, G., Facoetti, G., Morotti, R., Rizzi, C.: Physically based modelling and simulation to innovate socket design. Comput. Aided Des. Appl. **8**(4), 617–631 (2011)
3. Colombo, G., Facoetti, G., Rizzi, C.: A digital patient for computer-aided prosthesis design. Interface Focus **3**(2), 20120082 (2013)
4. Colombo, G., Facoetti, G., Rizzi, C., Vitali, A.: Socket virtual design based on low cost hand tracking and haptic devices. In: Proceedings of the 12th ACM SIGGRAPH International Conference on Virtual-Reality Continuum and Its Applications in Industry, pp. 63–70. ACM (2013)
5. Colombo, G., Facoetti, G., Rizzi, C., Vitali, A.: SimplyNURBS: a software library to model nurbs for medical applications. In: CAD 2014: International CAD Conference and Exhibition, Hong Kong (China), 23–26 June 2014. CAD Solution (2014)
6. Colombo, G., Facoetti, G., Rizzi, C., Vitali, A., Zanello, A.: Automatic 3D reconstruction of transfemoral residual limb from MRI images. In: Duffy, V.G. (ed.) HCII 2013 and DHM 2013, Part II. LNCS, vol. 8026, pp. 324–332. Springer, Heidelberg (2013)
7. Colombo, G., Rizzi, C., Facoetti, G., Vitali, A.: A preliminary study of new interaction devices to enhance virtual socket design. In: ASME 2014 International Design Engineering Technical Conferences and Computers and Information in Engineering Conference, p. V01BT02A036. American Society of Mechanical Engineers (2014)
8. Delimarschi, D., Swartzendruber, G., Kagdi, H.H.: Enabling integrated development environments with natural user interface interactions. In: ICPC, pp. 126–129 (2014)
9. Facoetti, G., Vitali, A., Colombo, G., Rizzi, C.: A low cost haptic mouse for prosthetic socket modeling. In: Duffy, V.G. (ed.) DHM 2014. LNCS, vol. 8529, pp. 508–515. Springer, Heidelberg (2014)
10. Fontana, M., Carubelli, A., Rizzi, C., Cugini, U.: Cloth assembler: a cad module for feature-based garment pattern assembly. Comput. Aided Des. Appl. **2**(6), 795–804 (2005)
11. Hodson, H.: Leap motion hacks show potential of new gesture tech. New Sci. **218**(2911), 21 (2013)
12. Kaltenborn, K.F., Rienhoff, O.: Virtual reality in medicine. Methods Inf. Med. **32**(5), 407–417 (1993)
13. Kaushik, M., Jain, R., et al.: Natural user interfaces: trend in virtual interaction. arXiv: 1405.0101 (2014)
14. Leap Motion Devices. https://www.leapmotion.com/
15. Meier, U., López, O., Monserrat, C., Juan, M.C., Alcaniz, M.: Real-time deformable models for surgery simulation: a survey. Comput. Methods Programs Biomed. **77**(3), 183–197 (2005)
16. NuiGroup. http://nuigroup.com/go/lite
17. Oikonomidis, I., Kyriazis, N., Argyros, A.A.: Efficient model- based 3d tracking of hand articulations using kinect. In: BMVC, vol. 1, p. 3 (2011)
18. Qt Project (2013). http://qt-project.org/
19. OPEN CASCADE S.A.S. http://www.opencascade.org/
20. VTK. http://www.vtk.org/
21. Wang, R.Y.,Popović, J.: Real-time hand-tracking with a color glove. ACM Trans. Graph. (TOG) **28**(3), 63 (2009)
22. Wigdor, D., Wixon, D.: Brave NUI World: Designing Natural User Interfaces for Touch and Gesture. Elsevier, Amsterdam (2011)

Effect of 3D Projection Mapping Art: Digital Surrealism

Soyoung Jung[1(✉)], Frank Biocca[1,2], and Daeun Lee[2]

[1] S.I. Newhouse School of Public Communicatoin, Syracuse University,
201 University Ave., Syracuse, NY 13202, USA
sjung01@syr.edu
[2] Interaction Science, SungKyunKwan University,
Sungkyunkwan-Ro, Jongno-Gu, Seoul, Korea

Abstract. This study examines the superior effect of spatialized projection mapping, also known as spatialized augmented reality or three-dimensional projection mapping, compared to projection on the screen. Specifically, to examine the effect of this modality, other variables are limited, such as sound effects or any other contents. The stimuli have little representative meaning with moving geometric patterns. The results show that spatialized projection mapping has been positively evaluated and that it elicits greater spatial presence.

Keywords: Augmented reality · Spatialized projection mapping · Three dimensional projection mapping · Psychological effect · Spatial memory

1 Introduction

Physical three-dimensional projection mapping involved projecting images (light) and augmented objects in the physical environment with digital imagery. Typically the imagery conforms to the physical object. The image embodied visual information in the physical space. Then audiences perceive synesthetic information, the merging of virtual information and the 3D physical object without a head-mounted display (HMD) or smartphone display. According to Bimber and Rasker, this medium is defined as spatialized augmented reality or 3D projection mapping (2005). The key difference between this medium and a single-user augmented reality interface is the multiple-user experience since it projects an image on the physical object directly.

This study examines how virtual information and environments are perceived and evaluated when they are experienced on project conformed objects as opposed to the standard flat screen environment. Therefore, we examine the perceived psychological effect of this spatialized augmented reality.

2 Project Mapped Augmented Reality

2.1 Introduction Transforming the Perception of Space

The main difference between two stimuli (3D mixed reality and 2D surface) is the tangibility, which was allowed form real 3D object. This study examines the effect of a

© Springer International Publishing Switzerland 2015
R. Shumaker and S. Lackey (Eds.): VAMR 2015, LNCS 9179, pp. 361–367, 2015.
DOI: 10.1007/978-3-319-21067-4_37

form of augmented or mixed reality called projection mapping and its conceptualization a class of displays on reality-virtually continuum (Milgram and et al., 1995). Three-dimensional (3D) projection mapping. The technology projects a virtual image on real world surfaces which has potential tangibility (Jung, Lee, and Biocca, 2014). Figure 1 shows that the spatial 3D mapping is a form of augmented reality, especially when mapped to 3D objects and surfaces.

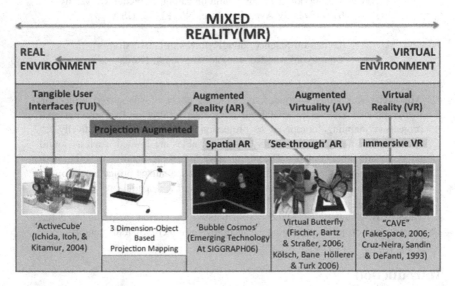

Fig. 1. Projection augmented or 3D projection mapping among milgram and kashion's "continuum of display" (1994).

The technology is frequently used in large scale and small-scale performance applications. However, the 3D mapping technology has not been well defined. There is a sense of that the projection mapping affects user experience and perception, but this has not been studied.

2.2   Production, Advertisement, and Art

At the level of performance spatialized projection mapping related technology has been widely used as stage design for musicals, concerts, promotion events, advertisements, media façade art, etc. For example, the Atlantis Resort and palm Island in Dubai held its grand opening with 3D hi-definition video projection (2011) mapping on buildings to animate and perceptually distort the buildings.

At the personal and interactive space, Microsoft Research has demonstrated the concept of "RoomAlive: Magical Experience Enabled by Scalable, Adaptive Projector-Camera Units" (2015). Figure 2 show the image of RoomAlive. In this demostration the virtual environment is distorted to conform to spatial configuration of room. This is then used to guide animated spaces, characters, and interactivity features.

By conforming the physical space of the room the virtual environment appears integrated and more tangible and "real." The very core concept of Room Alive and projection mapping in general is that the virtual appears to be more present in the physical space. In previous studies we have demonstrated an augmented reality information produces superior performance in users when attached and embedded in objects (Tang, Owen, Biocca, & Mou, 2003 and Jung et al. 2014). Virtual objects appear to be embodied.

Fig. 2. RoomAlive: magical experiences enabled by scalable, adaptive projector-camera units. Users can experience immersive, augmented reality in the real room without a head mounted display so that realistic visual information is perceived.

2.3 Spatial Presence

Without any screens or lenses, the projection mapping presents the virtual layer directly onto the physical object. Spatialized projection-mapped objects provide viewers with a greater sense of spatial presence (Tang, Owen, Biocca, & Mou, 2003 and Tang, Biocca, & Lim, 2004).

The unique trait of projection mapping is that the virtual representation is perceived to be part of the physical object and environment. Jung and et al. mentioned that "the sense of 'thingness' may be stronger than that created by the ghostly overlays of some head-mounted augmented reality and hologram technology." Compared to spatialized projection mapping, the low fidelity of hologram images reduces the sense of realism (Satoshi and et al. 1994). The virtual images in projection mapping are embodied by the real object, which has its own physical presence; therefore, projection mapping has provided spatial presence and perceived reality of environment.

Therefore, this study examines the effect of spatialized projection mapping (3D) comparing with 2-dimensional (2D) flat screens.

3   Method

The simulations of Fig. 3 show that the sizes of projected images are same and the distance from medium to audience are same as well for the experiment purpose. The images of Fig. 1 show that real image from experiment.

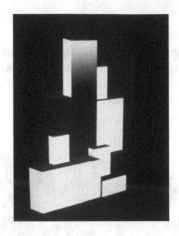

Fig. 3. Stimuli: (left) spatialized 3D augmented reality projection mapping onto physical object' surfaces; (right) the same augmented reality projection on a flat surface.

For the experimental purpose, this study compares same abstract content on same size of physical object or flat screens. The images of Fig. 4 shows how the two mediums are differently projected images on the physical object or on the flat screen.

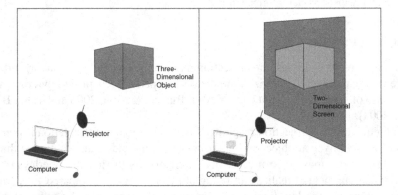

Fig. 4. Stimuli: (left) spatialized 3D augmented reality projection mapping onto mapped 3D surfaces; (right) standard 2D projection of patterns on a flat surface.

3.1 Procedure

Before the experiment, all participants (n = 24) were recruited by an online bulletin board at a university in Seoul, Korea. Upon arrival, all participants were introduced to the experiment, given the consent form, and guided to the experiment room by the experimenter. Randomly, half of the participants were assigned to watch spatialized projection mapping stimulus and the other half of the participants were assigned to watch projection mapping on the flat screen. After that, they were asked to fill out questionnaires of satisfaction, enjoyment, and presence. For the participation, they were compensated with 2000 Korean won (US $2).

First, all participants entered a dark and isolated room. After that, they were asked to watch video art work on 3D physical object or 2D screen. And then they were guided out of the dark room and asked to response to questionnaires of satisfaction, enjoyment, and presence on the PC.

Stimulus Material. For the stimulus material the objects were made with various white cubes. And its total size was approximately 97 cm x86 cm. To project the image we used Samsung SP-L300WG which has Cuboids-object with 3D projection video, flat screen with 3D modeling video.

3.2 Measurement

Presence. To measure perceived engagement, a presence questionnaire which was borrowed from Igroup Presence Questionnaire (IPQ) by Schubert et al. (2001) and Lessiter et al.'s scales (2001) and the questionnaire modified for this research was used. It was an index composed of six items. Participants answered how well the sentences, - for example, "I was completely captivated by the virtual world." - described their impression on the stimulus material, on ten-point Likert scales ranging from "Strongly Disagree" to "Strongly Agree."

Engagement, Satisfaction and Engagement. Participants indicated how well the word, "satisfied" &"enjoyable" described their impression on the stimulus material, on a ten-point Likert scale ranging from "Describes Very Poorly" to "Describes Very Well."

4 Results

Independent t-tests were carried out to measure two groups users' presence, engagement, satisfaction and enjoyment.   The results of t-test show that average scores of presence and engagement measurement were significantly higher from 3D than 2D $p < 0.1$.

Presence. There was significant difference in scores for 3D projection mapping $M = 7.66$, $SD = 2.01$ and 2D projection $M = 3.63$, $SD = 2.61$; $t(22) = 4.158$, $p = .01$ (two-tailed).

Engagement. The scores of engagement for 3D projection mapping $M = 6.91$, $SD = 2.87$ and 2D projection $M = 3.41$, $SD = 1.50$ have differences significantly t (22) = 3.73, $p = .01$ (two- tailed).

Satisfaction. There was marginally significant difference in satisfaction scores for 3D $M = 6.33$, $SD = 2.7$ and 2D projection $M = 6.91$, $SD = 1.31$; $t(22) = 1.85$, $p = .07$ (two-tailed).

Enjoyment. The scores of engagement for 3D projection mapping $M = 6.91$, $SD = 1.31$ and 2D projection $M = 4.9$, $SD = 2.31$ have differences significantly t (22) = 2.60, $p = .01$ (two- tailed).

5 Discussion

The results of presence measurement include how people immerse the mixed reality; it means that the 3D projection mapping bring them to different virtual reality however, they realize the real objects as well.

According to our study, experiencing 3D projection mapping elicits more spatial presence, enjoyment, and satisfaction than a standard 2D flat screen does. Therefore, the popularity of the projection mapping modality in various usages is not just a heuristic preference by developers or any decision makers, but it can also be explained with standardized measurements.

References

Anderson, R.E.: Social impacts of computing: codes of professional ethics. Soc. Sci. Comput. Rev. **10**(2), 453–469 (1992)

Bimber, O., Raskar, R.: Spatial augmented reality: Merging real and virtual worlds. A K Peters, Wellesley (2005)

Schuemie, Martijn J., et al.: Research on presence in virtual reality: a survey. Cyberpsychology Behav. **4**(2), 183–201 (2001). Mary Ann Liebert, Inc

Jung, S., Lee, D., Biocca, F.: Seeing augmented reality is more moving and memorable: comparing the psychological effects of 3- dimensional projection mapping versus 2-dimensional projection. In: Proceedings of PRESENCE 2014, ISPR 2014: The 15th International Conference on Presence. Vienna (2014)

Dalsgaard, P., Halskov, K.: 3D projection on physical objects: design insights from five real life cases. In: CHI (2011) • Session: Non-flat Displays

RoomAlive. (2015). Accessed 1 January 2015, from http://research.microsoft.com/en-us/projects/roomalive/

Schubert, T.W., Friedmann, F., Regenbrecht, H.T.: Decomposing the sense of presence: factor an- alytic insights. In: Presented at the 2nd International Work- shop on Presence, University of Essex, UK, 6–7 April 1999

"RoomAlive." RoomAlive – Microsoft Research. Micro soft Research, n.d. Web. 05 January 2015. http://research.microsoft.com/en-us/projects/roomalive/

Schubert, T.W., Friedmann, F., Regenbrecht, H.: The experience of presence: factor analytic insights. Presence Teleoperators virtual Environ. **10**, 266–281 (2001)

Usoh, M., Catena, E., Arman, S., Slater, M.: Using presence questionnaires in reality. presence, in press. augmented reality: a class of displays on the reality-virtuality continuum. In: Photonics for Industrial Applications . International Society for Optics and Photonics, pp. 282–292 (2000)

Lessiter, J., Freeman, J., Keogh, E., Davidoff, J.: A cross-media presence questionnaire: The ITC-sense of presence inventory. Presence **10**(3), 282–297 (2001)

Jung, S., Lee, DE., Biocca, F.: Seeing Augmented Reality is More Moving and Memorable: Comparing the Psychological Effects of 3-Dimensional Projection Mapping Versus 2-Dimensional Projection (2014)

Tang, A., Biocca, F., Lim, L.: Comparing differences in presence during social interaction in augmented reality versus virtual reality environments: an exploratory study. In: Raya, M.A., Solaz, B.R. (eds.) Proceedings of PRESENCE 2004, 7th Annual International Workshop on Presence, pp. 204–208. Valencia, Spain (2004)

Tang, A., Owen, C., Biocca, F., Mou, W.: Comparative effectiveness of augmented reality in object assembly. In: Proceedings of the Conference on Human Factors in Computing Systems (ACM CHI), pp. 73–80. ACM Press, New York (2003)

Satoshi Yamazaki et al : Multiply recorded hologram for security. US Patent. 5,319,476 (1994)

Sundar, S.S., Tamul, D.J., Wu, M.: Capturing cool: measures for assessing coolness of technological products. Int. J. Hum Comput Stud. **72**(2), 169–180 (2014)

The Most Amazing 3D Building Projection. YouTube. YouTube, 26 November 2011. Web. 05 January. (2015). https://www.youtube.com/watch?v=UG85VgLOdPA

Vorderer, P., Wirth, W., Gouveia, F.R., Biocca, F., Saari, T., Jäncke, F., Jäncke, P.: MEC spatial presence questionnaire (MEC-SPQ): Short documentation and instructions for application. report to the european community, Project Presence: MEC (IST-2001–37661) (2004)

Schubert, T.W.: The sense of presence in virtual environments. Zeitschrift für. Medienpsychologie **15**(2), 69–71 (2003)

Human Factors and Interaction Strategies in Three-Dimensional Virtual Environments to Support the Development of Digital Interactive Therapeutic Toy: A Systematic Review

Eunice P. dos Santos Nunes[1]([⊠]), Eduardo M. Lemos[1],
Cristiano Maciel[1], and Clodoaldo Nunes[2]

[1] Laboratório de Ambientes Virtuais Interativos (LAVI) – Instituto de
Computação, Universidade Federal de Mato Grosso (UFMT),
Cuiabá, MT, Brazil
{eunice.ufmt,emartinslemos,crismac}@gmail.com
[2] Departamento da Área de Informática (DAI) – Instituto Federal de Educação,
Ciência e Tecnologia de Mato Grosso (IFMT), Cuiabá, MT, Brazil
clodoaldo.nunes@cba.ifmt.edu.br

Abstract. Therapeutic Toy is applied in the hospital environment in order to explain to the child about the procedure he/she will go through. In order to this, the professionals of health usually use physical material, such as dolls and hospital accessories. However, there is a possibility of exploring Augmented and Virtual Reality systems to develop a therapeutic toy in a digital and interactive way. The main goal of this paper is to present results of a Systematic Review (SR), which seeks to identify if Three-Dimensional Virtual Environments (3D VEs) have been used focusing to assist the hospitalized children, which interaction strategies have been used and which human factors have been explored. The results allowed researchers to formulate hypotheses based on the human factors e strategies of interaction identified, to specify a Preliminary Reference Model for the development of Digital Interactive Therapeutic Toy.

Keywords: Three-dimensional virtual environments · Human factors · Interaction strategies · Hospitalized children

1 Introduction

In Brazil Therapeutic Toy (TT) is a tool used by health professionals with hospitalized children. In general, the Therapeutic Toy is applied in the hospital environment in order to explain to the child the procedure he/she will undergo and try to prepare him/her for it, as a way to minimize anxiety after the procedure or to contribute to the improvement of the medical treatment [4, 15].

This source aims to develop the reliability between the child and the health professional by stimulating recovery and performing as a physical and psychological

© Springer International Publishing Switzerland 2015
R. Shumaker and S. Lackey (Eds.): VAMR 2015, LNCS 9179, pp. 368–378, 2015.
DOI: 10.1007/978-3-319-21067-4_38

exercise. The professional usually uses physical materials, such as dolls and hospital accessories, for the child to expose his/her feelings.

However, in addition to physical materials, there is a possibility of exploring Virtual Reality (VR) and Augmented Reality (AR) systems to develop a therapeutic toy in a digital and interactive way, here named Digital Interactive Therapeutic Toy (DITT), that can be applied in different contexts in the health field in order to assist hospitalized children. The present work is part of a bigger context that focuses on establishing a reference model to develop the Digital Interactive Therapeutic Toy.

The main goal of this paper is to present results of a Systematic Review (SR), based on the specialized literature, which seeks to identify if Three-Dimensional Virtual Environments (3D VEs) have been employed with a focus on assisting the hospitalized child and which interaction strategies have been applied. In this context, interaction strategies are considered games, collaborations, avatars and virtual humans, intelligent agents and natural interfaces. The human factors that may influence the children's emotional and social aspects by exploring such environments are also investigated in the SR, given that interaction is composed of human factors.

In addition to this introduction, this article is structured into the following sections: Sect. 2 describes the methodology used in this research, Sect. 3 presents the state of the art with the results of the Systematic Review, and Sect. 4 discusses the results found, including the preliminary suggestion of a Reference Model for conceiving the Digital Interactive Therapeutic Toy. Finally, Sect. 5 details the final considerations of this research.

2 Methodology

The investigation methodology applied in this study was the process of a Systematic Review of the literature that was based on a searching strings combination, varying between database IEEE, ACM, ISI Web of Knowledge, Springer and Google Scholar by trying to answer the following research questions:

(1) What are the interaction strategies that have been applied in 3D VEs to assist the hospitalized children?

(2) What are the human factors that influence the emotional and social aspects of hospitalized children and how they can be exploited with the use of the conventional therapeutic toy or therapeutic toy supported by 3D VEs?

In the preliminary selection phase, the title and abstract of each article were analyzed. The works included and excluded by the Systematic Review in the final selection phase were defined according to the inclusion and exclusion criteria established in the protocol of the Systematic Review, which consisted of analyzing the full text of the articles included in the preliminary selection. After the final selection, the extraction results followed.

Initially, publications were sought from the last five years, aiming to identify new approaches. However, some previous publications, which were considered relevant, were included in the Systematic Review.

Figure 1 presents a flowchart of the different phases arising from the Systematic Review, based on PRISMA (Preferred Reporting Items for Systematic Reviews and

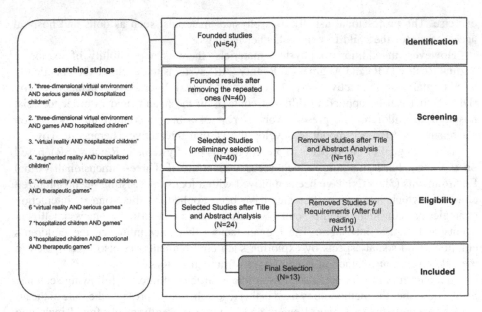

Founded studies
(N=54)

Identification

searching strings

1. "three-dimensional virtual environment AND serious games AND hospitalized children"

2. "three-dimensional virtual environment AND games AND hospitalized children"

3. "virtual reality AND hospitalized children"

4. "augmented reality AND hospitalized children"

5. "virtual reality AND hospitalized children AND therapeutic games"

6 "virtual reality AND serious games"

7 "hospitalized children AND games"

8 "hospitalized children AND emotional AND therapeutic games"

Founded results after removing the repeated ones (N=40)

Screening

Selected Studies (preliminary selection) (N=40)

Removed studies after Title and Abstract Analysis (N=16)

Selected Studies after Title and Abstract Analysis (N=24)

Removed Studies by Requirements (After full reading) (N=11)

Eligibility

Final Selection (N=13)

Included

Fig. 1. Distribution of studies included and excluded from Systematic Review

Meta-Analyses) [9]. This flowchart aims to present a quantitative SR process, from the initial identification of studies through database search to the final selection of articles included in the data analysis.

As observed in Fig. 1, 54 studies were found by applying search strings. In the preliminary selection phase, 24 articles were selected, out of which only 13 articles were included in the final SR selection. These articles sought to answer the research questions posed in the SR protocol.

The following attributes were selected from each study: application environment, interaction strategies and explored human factors. Subsequently, a relational analysis was conducted of the main interaction strategies and the identified human factors.

Considering the results obtained from the Systematic Review, a foundation was proposed for a preliminary version of the Reference Model for the development of the Digital Interactive Therapeutic Toy, which is presented in Sect. 4.

3   Results of the Systematic Review

The following paragraphs present a summary of the 13 articles that were analyzed. Each one of the articles was individually analyzed. It should be highlighted that, out of the 13 articles included in the final SR selection, three articles refer to the investigation of Therapeutic Toy application using physical objects, such as dolls and hospital accessories, in order to simulate real hospital procedure situations. These studies symbolize the first steps of the study, and also render a deeper understanding of the context of the investigation, since these aspects translate the motivation to develop Digital Interactive Therapeutic Toy.

In this perspective, a study by Kiche and Almeida [7] investigated the use of Therapeutic Toy before the process of changing surgical dressings in order to compare pain reactions uttered by children during the dressing change, both before and after emotional preparation with Therapeutic Toy. The authors observed that, based on the experiments that were conducted, employing TT before the hospital procedure significantly reduced the children's level of pain and muscle tension.

Another research by Fontes et al. [4] defends the application of Therapeutic Toy to relieve tension in children due to hospitalization. By employing dramatization, healthcare professionals prepared the child for a surgical procedure. The authors show evidence that playing interactively causes hospitalized children to interact with the hospital environment and express their feelings and emotions, and it also provides resources for humanized assistance.

The study by Silva et al. [12] analyzed a specific health field database published from 1998 to 2006 and verified that Therapeutic Toy has been applied in Brazil in different forms, including the waiting room of a children's outpatient department as well as in the assistance to children with cancer. The authors highlight that the hospital routine can incorporate the advantages of playing as a therapeutic resource since it allows the child to express their feelings and understand the procedures that are about to be conducted and it may lead to a closer bond between the child and the healthcare team.

Considering the studies above, we can say that the application of Therapeutic Toy has been widely investigated in the health field for many years with evidence that interactive play can, in addition to the aforementioned aspects, build a feeling of trust between the hospitalized child and the healthcare professional, stimulate recovery and act as physical and psychological exercise.

The remaining 10 articles included in the final SR seek to answer research questions and apply different interaction strategies in order to explore the physical and emotional aspects of children. Section 3.1 presents a summary of the article analysis.

3.1 3D VEs Applied as Therapeutic Toy

The study by Tarrin, Petit and Chêne [14] proposes the development of 3D network applications with the aim of improving the quality of life in hospitalized children who need to be isolated in sterilized rooms. Although this research was published more than five years ago, the proposal is still relevant to our research. The applications are built in a multimodal platform, which includes networked 3D graphics, sound and forced feedback, whose main aim is to provide physical interaction between children and other people who are outside their room, using tactile senses and thus offering entertainment to the hospitalized child. Another aim of the research is to elaborate a methodology of haptic design in which users are involved in the process of designing. The researchers suggest using 3D network applications with game-based 3D VEs. The idea is innovating; however, we did not find publications that show experiments conducted with hospitalized children.

In this context, Chan et al. [3] present a study that applies a game-based 3D VE, aiming to reduce pain during surgical dressing changes in children who suffered burns. The VE scenario occurs in an ice cream factory because the cold sensation may suggest pain relief considering the experience of having been burned [3] apud [16]. With the VR system intervention, even when children were not completely immersed in the game during their dressing change, their feelings and behavior were more controlled and manageable. Thus, results suggest that 3D VE can be useful in relieving pain and anxiety in anticipation associated with pediatric care for burns. Nonetheless, according to the authors, further studies are required with larger trials. Furthermore, when children were recruited for the study, they were already in the third or fifth round of dressing change and had likely developed fear in anticipation.

In a study by Bickmore, Pfeifer and Jack [2], the authors developed a VE with "Virtual Humans" in order to represent nurses in the hospital environment. The purpose of the research is to remove communication barriers between the health professional and the children. Thus, children talk to virtual nurses about many hospital situations, thus developing a communication ability. In addition, the child can interact with the nurse at any moment, thus minimizing the sensation of abandonment, considering that in low-income hospitals there is a shortage of healthcare professionals. The experiments conducted produced results that show "Virtual Humans" can contribute to communication ability and aid in the therapeutic treatment of hospitalized children.

Research developed by Schmitt et al. [13] investigates the effects of immersive Virtual Reality as an analgesic technique to help treat children who suffered burns. Through game-based SnowWorld immersive VE, the child, equipped with Oculus Rift, uses the mouse or keyboard to throw snowballs at penguins, igloos, mammoths, snowmen and other animals, entities or objects that remind them of very cold places. Experiments with 54 hospitalized children and teenagers aged six to nineteen, during five days, were monitored by a therapy specialist. The results suggest that immersive Virtual Reality is a non-pharmacologic technique that is effective to relieve pain in children with burns and minimize the need for strong medication, in addition to improving their mood.

In the study presented by Akabane et al. [1], the authors developed the collaborative game-based 3D VE "Puchi Planet". The environment simulates a "trip" around the world. In the VE, the child can be a photographer or a pilot, in addition to storing whichever data is considered relevant, such as the most interesting places visited. When the child remains hospitalized for long periods of time, there is a tendency towards reducing communication which, many times, restricts interaction to family members only. Furthermore, the child stops discovering new places, which can discourage curiosity and knowledge acquisition. This way, "Puchi Planet" seeks to stimulate the children's interaction with other people through a collaborative environment, besides allowing the child to explore new places.

González, Collazos and González [5] highlight that children who are hospitalized for long periods of time are susceptible to developing stress and anxiety caused by the discomfort resulting from treating the illness, fear of medical procedures, among other factors. Thus, a recommended solution to compensate the situation would be promoting activities with games and/or therapeutic toys. In this context, the authors developed a collaborative game as an alternative to interaction and entertainment. The game aims to create bonding activities with children who are constantly in hospital, as well as bring them closer to family members and colleagues who used to be part of their lives. In the game, the child needs to undergo individual and collective stages, in addition to accomplishing cooperative missions. Experiments were conducted with children in a hospital context and the results were generally satisfactory. In the negative side, factors of apprehension and/or frustration were found in the first moments of the game, but they were overcome by participants.

A study by Pykhtine et al. [10] investigates play therapy, which deals with a therapeutic approach currently used with children. Considering that digital technology is now a big part of children's lives, the authors state that game and Virtual Reality applications have succeeded when employed in psychotherapy for treating a wide range of anxiety, panic disorders and phobias. Thus, as part of a user-centered design process, researchers monitored, throughout one year, the application of non-directive therapeutic play with children. Based on this experience, the authors propose a set of design requisites to develop digital technologies that seek to act as toys within the play therapy context. In order to do so, the authors developed the Magic Land prototype based on the requisites raised. The first results were positive.

Tranquada, Chen and Chisik [15] present the development of a game-based VE called "Hospital Hero". The aim of the VE is to help the children deal with stress, anxiety and fear of visiting emergency rooms, by becoming familiar with the environment, tools and equipment, medical team, patients and medical procedures, thus rendering the experience less traumatic. Furthermore, VE allows the child to meet other hospitalized children in similar situations. Hospital Hero is a game that helps patients; for instance, in a situation in which patients who are lost and are supposed to collect hospital tools and supplies in a maize that simulates hospital hallways. Although the game has not yet been formally employed in a hospital, the prototype was tested on a tablet with university students in order to verify usability problems and interface design. The prototype was also tested in primary school children to gather preliminary results and evaluate the experimental project.

The study by Huerga, Lade and Mueller [6] proposes a game-based 3D VE that, along with the physical environment, involves physical play and stimulates the child's imagination. The system is divided into three stages: i) corporal games that occur in real physical spaces, where the child plays with a puppet that simulates an animal, ii) virtual games, in which the child explores body movements by means of a Kinect device using a 3D VE; and iii) corporal-virtual games, in which both former steps are combined in a 3D VE controlled by the child's glove and connected by movement sensors. The proposal of the spatial-corporal design aims to reformulate the corporal perception of the hospitalized child in order to improve self-confidence. Authors declare that the results obtained with children were positive and that work can help designers who display interest in developing digital play for sick children.

Lastly, a 3D imagery therapy game design, which explores image psychotherapy, is proposed by Sajjad et al. [11]. In this context, the 3Dimensional Graphical Imagery Therapy (3D GIT) meant for brain tumor children seeks to avoid psychological diseases that can be accentuated by anxiety, fear, anger and perception of inferiority. The theme of the game explores the child's "battle" against the disease, which in this case is cancer, using guns (white blood cells) to attempt to vanquish the enemy (brain tumor). Each dead enemy in the game increases the player's "lifespan". As the phases go by, the child finds some fruit and medication, which help the child improve his/her life condition. It is worth highlighting that enemies can vary in type, such as viruses and bacteria.

Experimental tests with users were conducted in three hospitals, analyzing different behaviors of a cancer patient, before and after applying the therapy with the proposed game design. The results showed significant improvement in behavior of children with brain tumors, especially decreased anger and anxiety and increased self-confidence. Therefore, the authors state that the proposed game design can be effective.

4 Discussion

Considering the results of the Systematic Review, we show how academic literature portrays the conception of the 3D VE applied to assist hospitalized children in different contexts. The main resources of interaction identified in the included studies are presented in Fig. 2, which answers to the first research question - 1) What are the interaction strategies that have been applied in 3D VEs to assist hospitalized children?

Figure 2 shows a percentage of the 13 studies according to interaction strategies. There is evidently large interest in games, since 90 % of studies conceive 3D VEs based on games. This interest can be related to the fact that games favor multiple interactions and stimulate participants to explore their limitations in a pro-active and exploratory manner.

Regarding the second question of the research – "2) What are the human factors that influence the emotional and social aspects of hospitalized children and how can they be explored with the use of the conventional therapeutic toy or therapeutic toy supported by 3D VEs?", literature shows that:

- There are many human factors explored in 3D VEs conceived in order to assist hospitalized children: agitation, anxiety, fear, feelings of isolation, learning deficit, pain, inferiority complex and stress. These factors represent negative psychological aspects of the child and are generally triggered by disease and hospitalization. Other human factors can be stimulated with the application of 3D VEs and were identified in the SR, such as: curiosity, confidence and familiarity with the healthcare team.

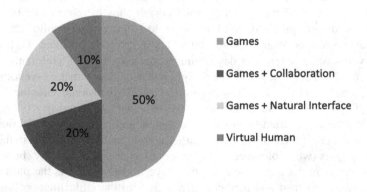

Fig. 2. Distribution of interaction strategies found in 3D VEs

- In order to avoid maintaining a linearity of events, the content addressed in 3D VEs conceived to assist hospitalized children relate the scenario and interaction strategies with human factors that are meant to be explored in the child.
- Initiatives of conception of 3D VEs are applied in specific situations, seeking to explore communication, creativity, socializing, entertainment, self-confidence, the reduction of pain or trauma during a medical procedure, exploring unknown places or as a stimulus to learning.
- The studies seek to maintain the focus of the child away from characteristics that can revert the positive evolution of medical treatment, considering that distress caused by the hospital environment, especially in cases of long periods of stay, can be harmful to the child, leading to psychological problems such as depression, anxiety, learning disorders, among others.

From the discussions held by the results of the systematic review it is possible to relate the most favorable interaction techniques for each type of human factor identified as limitations and characteristics of hospitalized children.

Thus, it should be highlighted that the results of the Systematic Review allowed researchers to formulate hypotheses from interaction strategies and human factors identified and to specify a preliminary Reference Model for the development of Digital Interactive Therapeutic Toy, as is illustrated by Fig. 3, which presents the components of the model.

The preliminary Reference Model includes **Human Factors** and the **Interaction Strategies** identified in SR, the **Development Requirements** and **Technical Support**. Note that the proposal is to develop Digital Interactive Therapeutic Toy that can be executed in mobile devices and the data should be accessed and sent to cloud storage.

It should be noted that the target audience includes hospitalized children, both literate and illiterate, as foresees the component **Target Audience** illustrated in Fig. 3. Regarding the component **Technical Support**, the model suggests an area of FAQ (frequently asked questions), Know Issues and Know-how, described below:

- FAQ – seeks to help users by displaying the most common doubts concerning situations of constant difficulties encountered by the user when employing the 3D VE.
- Known Issues – problems identified by users and reported for being considered in the next 3D VE update. Includes a contact area between the user and the developer.
- Know-how – destined to clarify different situations, including tutorials and tips that users can apply to improve their experience in using the 3D VE.

5 Final Considerations

The concept of 3D VEs, especially game-based 3D VEs, has been a research topic in the context of hospitalized children, as can be observed in the SR results. This interest is linked to the advances of technology and digital accessibility in different age ranges and social classes.

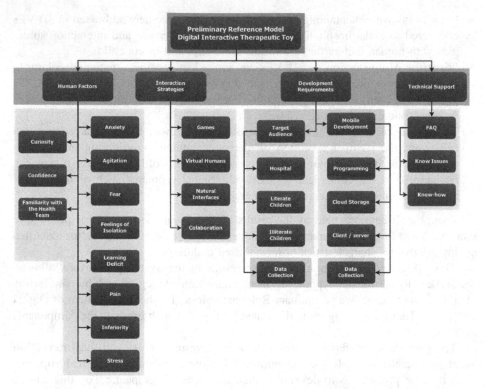

Fig. 3. Suggestion of preliminary reference model for the conception of digital interactive therapeutic toy.

The foundation of the scientific research serves as an incentive to the development of Therapeutic Toys, in digital format, in order to aid in the treatment of hospitalized children, with a focus on reducing distress developed by these children, learning disabilities, and lack of communication between patient and health professional.

In this sense, the study of human factors that influence the behavior of the children who will use the toys is crucial. It is up to researchers and developers of these artifacts to create strategies for considering these factors in the design of the applications. One of the challenges of these research studies is recording and measuring user behavior and how feelings are expressed, such as the need for choosing appropriate methods, the complexity of treatments which patients undergo, and the subjectivity concerning the human being.

Research studies with this approach, as the HCI field mandates, require an interdisciplinary development, which should involve, in addition to specialists in technology, therapists, psychologists, pedagogues, medical doctors, among others professionals in related fields.

Regarding the model, this preliminary version offers useful elements to projectors who intend to develop Digital Interactive Therapeutic Toy. The elements of the model consider human factors and interaction strategies that are relevant to the audience being targeted.

Finally, as future research, we suggest investigating methodologies regarding the development of Digital Interactive Therapeutic Toy that can allow the inclusion of users in conceiving tests and solutions, considering human factors. One of these include participatory design [8], which allows an interdisciplinary treatment of these matters. Another line of investigation concerns methods and parameters of usability assessment and knowledge acquisition in 3D VEs that develop the role of a Therapeutic Toy.

References

1. Akabane, S., Leu, J., Iwadate, H., Inakage, M., Nakayama, S., Chang, E., Furukawa, S.: Puchi Planet : A Tangible Interface Design for Hospitalized Children, 1345–1350 (2011)
2. Bickmore, T.W., Pfeifer, L.M., Jack, B.W.: Taking the Time to Care : Empowering Low Health Literacy Hospital Patients with Virtual Nurse Agents, 1265–1274 (2009)
3. Chan, E.A., Chung, J.W., Wong, T.K., Lien, A.S., Yang, J.Y.: Application of a virtual reality prototype for pain relief of pediatric burn in Taiwan. J. Clin. Nurs. **16**(4), 786–793 (2007). doi:10.1111/j.1365-2702.2006.01719.x
4. Fontes, C.M.B., da Mondini, C.C.S.D., Moraes, M.C.A.F., Bachega, M.I., Maximino, N.P.: Utilização do brinquedo terapêutico na assistência à criança hospitalizada. Revista Brasileira de Educação Especial **16**(1), 95–106 (2010). doi:10.1590/S1413-65382010000100008
5. González, C.S., Collazos, C., González, J.L.: The importance of human factors to enhance the user experience in videogames (2012)
6. Huerga, R.S., Lade, J., Mueller, F.F.: Three Themes for Designing Games That Aim to Promote a Positive Body Perception in Hospitalized Children, 198–203 (2013). Accessed http://link.springer.com/chapter/10.1007/978-3-642-37157-8_24
7. Kiche, M.T., de Almeida, F.A.: Brinquedo terapêutico estratégia de alívio da dor e tensão durante o curativo cirúrgico em crianças. Acta Paulista de Enfermagem **22**(2), 125–130 (2009). doi:10.1590/S0103-21002009000200002
8. Moffatt, K., McGrenere, J., Purves, B., Klawe, M.: The participatory design of a sound and image enhanced daily planner for people with aphasia. In: Proceedings of the SIGCHI Conference on Human Factors in Computing Systems, pp. 407–414. ACM, Vienna (2004)
9. Moher, D., Liberati, A., Tetzlaff, J., Altman, D.G.: Preferred reporting items for systematic reviews and meta-analyses the prisma statement. BMJ **339**, 332–336 (2009)
10. Pykhtine, O., Balaam, M., Wood, G., Pattison, S., Kharrufa, A., Olivier, P.: Magic land. In: Proceedings of the Designing Interactive Systems Conference on - DIS 2012, p. 136. ACM Press, New York (2012). doi:10.1145/2317956.2317978
11. Sajjad, S., Abdullah, A.H., Sharif, M., Mohsin, S.: Psychotherapy Through Video Game to Target Illness Related Prob-lematic Behaviors of Children with Brain Tumor, 62–72 (2014)
12. Silva, S.H., et al.: Humanização em pediatria: o brinquedo como recurso na assistência de enfermagem à criança hospitalizada. Pediatr. mod **46**(3), 101–104 (2010)
13. Schmitt, Y.S., Hoffman, H.G., Blough, D.K., Patterson, D.R., Jensen, M.P., Soltani, M., Sharar, S.R.: A randomized, controlled trial of immersive virtual reality analgesia, during physical therapy for pediatric burns. Burns J. Int. Soc. Burn Injuries **37**(1), 61–68 (2011). doi:10.1016/j.burns.2010.07.007
14. Tarrin, N., Petit, G., Chêne, D.: Network Force-Feedback Applications for Hospitalized Children in Sterile Room, 157–160 (2006)

15. Tranquada, S., Chen, M., Chisik, Y.: Hospital Hero : A Game for Reducing Stress and Anxiety of Hospitalized Children in Emergency Room, 638–641 (2013)
16. Hoffman, H., Patterson, D., Carrougher, G., Sharar, S.: The effectiveness of virtual reality based pain control with multiple treatments. Clin. J. Pain **17**, 229–235 (2001)

Development and Evaluation of an Easy-to-Use Stereoscopic Ability Test to Assess the Individual Ability to Process Stereoscopic Media

Daniel Pietschmann[✉], Benny Liebold[✉], Peter Ohler,
and Georg Valtin

Chemnitz University of Technology, Institute for Media Research,
Chemnitz, Germany
{daniel.pietschmann,benny.liebold,peter.ohler,
georg.valtin}@phil.tu-chemnitz.de

Abstract. With the rise of 3D cinema in recent years, 3D stereoscopic images have quickly conquered the entertainment industry. As a consequence, many scholars from different research disciplines study the effects of stereoscopy on user experience, task performance, or naturalism. However, parts of the population suffer from stereoblindness and are unable to process stereo images. For scientific studies, it is important to assess stereoblindness to avoid bias in the gathered data. Several clinical tests are available to measure deficiencies in stereo vision, but they often require special equipment and a trained investigator. We developed an easy to use and economic Stereoscopic Ability Test (SAT) that can be used directly within the intended experimental environment. Initial evaluation data for the test and guidelines for the test application are discussed.

Keywords: Stereoscopic vision · Psychology · Experimental · Diagnostics

1 Introduction

In recent years 3D technology has become publicly more and more accepted and by now almost every new TV-set is capable of 3D presentation. Research in stereoscopic virtual reality [1], video games [2, 3], and 3D-cinema [4] became more popular as well. On the other hand, not all users can enjoy the stereoscopic media: Some users are stereoblind, other users have healthy vision, but suffer from unacceptable side-effects such as nausea and headaches as part of motion- or cybersickness [2]. In this paper, we focus on users who suffer from stereoblindness. Reasons for not being able to process binocular depth information may stem from the loss of vision in one eye or medical disorder that prevent the eyes from processing binocular depth cues correctly (e.g. amblyopia, optic nerve hypoplasia, strabismus). While this group of users is still capable of perceiving monocular depth cues (e.g. relative size, motion parallax, accommodation, occlusion), they are incapable of directly perceiving an object's distance through eye convergence.

© Springer International Publishing Switzerland 2015
R. Shumaker and S. Lackey (Eds.): VAMR 2015, LNCS 9179, pp. 379–387, 2015.
DOI: 10.1007/978-3-319-21067-4_39

With reported numbers of the stereoblind population ranging from 2 to 12 percent [5, 6], this can have two serious effects on studies on stereoscopic media: First, stereoblind participants represent a strong bias in a study's sample. When stereoscopic 3D is manipulated in an experiment, they are unaffected by the manipulation, and whenever stereoscopic 3D is enabled in a virtual environment, they might be outperformed by the other participants due to a lack of spatial information. Second, using stereoscopic 3D can have benefits for user experience (UX). Thus, stereoblind participants might provide different UX ratings compared to participants with healthy vision. Most notably, participants may not be fully aware that their stereoscopic vision is impaired. Consequently, it is important to assess participants' ability to perceive stereoscopic images as part of a study. While there are many clinical tests for stereoblindness (e.g. cover tests, bagolini lenses, worth's four dots, measurement of accommodation and near point of convergence, etc.), they often require special equipment and a trained investigator to derive correct conclusions [7].

Additionally, while clinical tests assess general stereo vision for depth perception, stereoscopic media do not provide visual stimuli with real visual depth. Instead, the illusion of depth is created by introducing disparity between the images for both eyes on a fixed distance. Thus, the user has to adapt to the necessary convergence, while keeping accommodation constantly at the display. This is different from real depth perception, for which convergence and accommodation are highly correlated. Thus, to assess the ability to process depth cues in 3D media, the instrument should focus on the stereoscopic technology and its specific characteristics in addition to real stereo vision. Furthermore, from a methodological standpoint, assessing stereo vision within the same medium (i.e. display) that is used in a given study increases internal validity. Thus, our goal was to develop an easy-to-use test for stereoblindness that could be used with a wide range of stereoscopic displays.

2   Depth Perception and Stereoscopic Media

The function of human depth perception is the estimation of distances within our three-dimensional environment. Our eyes perceive two-dimensional images (one with each eye), but our cognitive system interprets all available stimuli to extract depth cues. The images on both retinas differ by the interpupilar distance (IPD) so that objects are perceived from two (slightly) different perspectives (i.e. disparity). Our cognitive system interprets both monocular and binocular spatial cues. Monocular cues include occlusion and relative sizes of objects, height in the visual field, linear and aerial perspective, texture gradients, and motion parallax [8]. Binocular cues encompass accommodation and vergence of muscles in the eyes and stereopsis [8].

Accommodation refers to the adaptation of the eye lenses to focus near or far objects. Vergence describes the rotation of the eyes towards each other (convergence) to focus near objects or away from each other (divergence) to focus far objects. Both processes are highly correlated and enable binocular vision. Due to physical constraints, binocular vision is usually limited to short distances of two to three meters, whereas we can interpret monocular depth information far beyond 30 meters and more [9].

2.1 Stereoscopic Media

Stereoscopy relies on the ability of the human perceptual apparatus to process separate images with each eye. Each eye is presented with a slightly different two-dimensional image, resulting in the illusion of binocular depth perception.

The first stereoscopic photographs were used in a Wheatstone's mirror stereoscope in the 19th century, and later in stereograms. The tradition of stereoscopic media is long, and features many different technologies to present stereo images [10], e.g. the color anaglyph system which was used in 3D movies in the early 20th century.

Stereoscopic images have been used in virtual reality systems since the early 1990s [11, 12]. In recent years, a new trend of stereoscopic media sparked in the movie industry with the release of movies like *Avatar* [13]. It quickly reached mainstream home entertainment like television and video games. Today, almost any new television set or video game console is capable of presenting stereoscopic media content. Currently, researchers are looking for new ways to minimize side effects caused by the technology [14, 15] and to maximize user experience with stereoscopic media, e.g. by including depth cues in cinematography [16] or video game design [17, 18]. In recent the past, new low-cost solutions (e.g. VR headsets such as Oculus Rift) were introduced to consumers, emphasizing the importance of further research on interaction design, positive and negative effects as well as future directions of stereoscopic media.

Currently, there are many different technologies to implement stereoscopy, divided into four main categories: (1) Active stereoscopic methods achieve the separation of both images through active shutters. These systems are usually glasses with built-in liquid crystal layers, which darken when voltage is applied, effectively blocking the view of an eye when an image is intended for the other eye and vice versa. (2) Passive systems do not use electrical components, and separate the images through color filters (e.g. anaglyph), prisms (e.g. chromadepth system) or polarization filters. (3) Head-mounted-displays do not require the separation of two superimposed images, as they can present two distinct images for each eye (e.g. on two small displays or side-by-side display). (4) Methods without special viewing aids are called autostereoscopic display technologies, as the stereo effect is achieved by viewing the images from a specific position (e.g. parallax barriers, volumetric displays, holography).

As stereoscopy relies on the illusion of depth cues, there are several key drawbacks like double images or simulation sickness [19]. When using HMDs, passive or active techniques, the images are presented on a flat surface with a simulated parallax. The parallax results in a convergence of the eyes behind the display pane. By manipulating this parallax, objects can be displayed in front or behind the display pane. This may result in a vergence-accommodation-conflict: When focusing objects with real binocular vision, accommodation and convergence are concordant with the estimation of the distance to the object. In stereoscopy, vergence and accommodation are different from each other, resulting in conflicting information about the distance estimation. This is especially true for scenes with very different fields of depth. Eye stain is induced by repeatedly changing focus from foreground to background objects. These problems can be minimized by limiting objects to only a small field of depth. If the display is farther away from the eyes, the distances between objects is also reduced, thus reducing the differences in the field of depth. Additionally, problems may occur if the images are computed with the wrong IPD or with a curvature of the visible field, e.g. by different fields of view.

In practice, this means that due to physical limitations, stereoscopy is limited to a smaller area of depth perception than real stereo vision [20]. For long-term interactions, applications should even limit the use of depth cues to only a small portion of this area (Percival's Zone of Comfort [21]).

3   Development of a Stereoscopic Ability Test

The development of a test for the stereoscopic ability during media exposure faces three major challenges. First, the test needs to assess stereoscopic ability by isolating binocular visual cues. As long as users are able to infer depth information from monocular visual cues, for example from object size or texture resolution, the test has no diagnostic value. Second, the test needs to be compatible with various technological setups, may it be VR-environments, such as CAVE or HMD, TV-sets, or simple PC-based presentations. As a result, the test has to ensure that it produces similar results across all platforms. Furthermore, the created stimuli need to be easily supported by every platform. Third, the measure needs to account both for stereo blindness and for interindividual differences in familiarity with stereoscopic display technology. Thus, stimuli with appropriate difficulty levels need to be created.

We decided to develop the stimulus materials in a 3D editor to ensure a convenient manipulation of object parameters. The stimuli can be exported as two images (one for each eye), which should be feasible for most use cases. The images can either be directly displayed on the respective eye (HMD) or implemented into a 3D-movie format, which allows displaying the stimuli easily on modern TV-sets. Another option is to directly implement the 3D-objects into a rendering engine (e.g. CAVE-setups). We chose the 3D-editor *Blender 2.68* (Blender Foundation), because it is freely available and allows other researchers to change parameters, if necessary. The stereoscopic rendering within Blender is carried out by the Blender-Plugin *Stereoscopic Rendering in Blender 2.7*[1], which is also freely available. The plugin provides support for eye-based camera positions and automatically sets the near and far plane as well as the focal plane for stereoscopic presentations to guide the developer during the positioning of 3D elements in the scene.

Our goal was to develop a pool of different stimuli with varying difficulty that would undergo a pretest to select the most appropriate for the final test. As a starting point we decided to include four tasks into the test both to cover different aspects of stereoscopic vision during media use and to avoid boredom and learning effects during the testing procedure. Within each task either one (task 1) or three (tasks 2-4) grey squares were presented. Regardless of their positioning in the screen, each square was individually sized so that every square had the same size on the screen. We also did not

---

[1] http://www.noeol.de/s3d/

Fig. 1. In this example item (side-by-side presentation) of the stereoscopic ability Test (SAT), participants had to sort the squares front to back.

apply a complex texture to the squares, but colored them in a solid grey. This way it was assured that all monocular depth cues were removed from the squares. Because this procedure made focusing the squares nearly impossible (after all, they had no texture), we added a letter (A, B, C) to each square. The implemented tasks were the following (see also Fig. 1):

Task 1: Focal Plane Comparison. During task 1 participants had to decide whether a single square was in front of the screen or behind it. The task contained 53 items with varying depth. We expected the items near the focal plane to have the highest difficulty.

Task 2: Deviation Detection. In task 2 participants saw three squares, which were either all on the same plane or not. Half of the 56 items depicted a group of squares with identical depth. The remaining items depicted squares, which had a fixed distance between them and a varying distance from the observer. We expected items far away from the observer to be the most difficult, as the relative distance between the squares becomes smaller with increasing distance from the observer.

Task 3: Oddity Detection. During task 3 participants had to indicate, which of the displayed squares was different from the others. While two random squares were always on the same plane, one square was either behind or in front of that plane with varying distance. This task included 52 items. We expected smaller distances between the items to result in higher item difficulty.

Task 4: Sorting Task. In task 4 participants had to sort the squares from front to back. While the mutual distance between the squares was identical for every item, all squares varied in their distance to the observer. We again expected items farther away from the observer to be the most difficult. The task contained 44 items.

4 Empirical Evaluation

The evaluation of the created stimuli included two small-scale studies aiming to assess first estimations of psychometric properties of the scale.

4.1 Apparatus and Task

The stimuli were exported from Blender as two separate images for each eye. We then combined both images into side-by-side images with a resolution of 1920 × 1080 pixel using image-processing software. The stimuli were presented using side-by-side 3D-conversion on a 55" Full-HD TV-set with passive stereoscopy. The seating distance was standardized according to THX distance recommendations (*diagonal display size divided by 0.84*). Apart from the illumination from the TV-set, the room was completely dark.

All stimuli were presented using the software *E-Prime 2.0* (Psychology Software Tools), which allowed recording of user button presses for each stimulus. Each task began with an instruction followed by example items. The actual items were presented in a randomized order. Further, we took two measures to minimize eye-strain and exhaustion. First, every item was followed by a two seconds black screen. Second, we implemented a non-interruptible one-minute pause after task 2.

4.2 Procedure

Participants•were recruited via mailing lists. After their arrival, they were explained that they were taking a test to assess their stereoscopic ability and their informed consent was gathered. We pointed out that the presentation of stereoscopic images could lead to symptoms of simulator sickness and that they could abort the experiment at any time, should they feel uncomfortable. They then took a seat in a comfortable cinema chair in front of the TV-set and put on the polarization glasses. We specifically instructed the participants, not to glimpse past the glasses.

4.3 Results of Study 1

In the first study, N = 8 participants (all normal sighted) answered all 215 stimuli. Our goal was to gather early estimates for the item characteristics of the developed stimuli. Thus, we conducted a preliminary item analysis to select suited stimuli. Most stimuli proved very easy and, thus, had only little diagnostic value for the developed test. As expected, item difficulty was highest, when the target stimulus was closest to the point of reference (i.e. the screen plane or other items). For each of the four tasks, we selected items of varying difficulty to cover a wide range of stereoscopic blindness and familiarity with stereoscopic displays. Because all items could be answered either correctly or wrong, an item difficulty approaching .50 in consecutive items from one task represents the threshold level at which, only half of the participants are able to provide the correct answer. Because this answering format also has a chance-level of

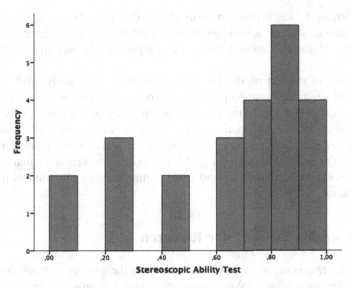

Fig. 2. Distribution of the raw values of the stereoscopic ability test

p = .50, items of this difficulty basically reflect that participants guessed the answer, because they were just about not able to give a definite answer. In most cases, these items only represented a small range of the manipulated parameters near the point of reference. We therefore created new items around these points, which were slightly more easy or difficult, to be able to select from a bigger pool of stimuli for the final test. The final sample consisted of 156 stimuli.

4.4   Results of Study 2

A sample of N = 26 student participants (mean age: 23 years; female: 16; 53.8% corrected to normal vision) had to complete all 156 stimuli to determine the final item selection for the Stereoscopic Ability Test (SAT). Items ranged from .38 to .88 regarding their difficulty. The final stimuli were selected according to their difficulty, variance, and variety of tasks in order to create a sensitive measure. From the initial set of items, 12 stimuli were selected to be included in the final test. The final scale had a mean score of $M = .66$ ($SD = .296$; see Fig. 2). Reliability analysis indicated a high internal consistency with $\alpha = .88$. An exploratory factor analysis supports the idea that the SAT has one underlying factor with $R^2 = .46$ and high factor loadings for every item. When only participants with scores higher than $M = .50$ are analyzed, the SAT sufficiently follows a normal distribution.

4.5   Discussion

Our goal was to develop an easy-to-use test to assess participants' stereo blindness and familiarity with stereoscopic display technology. The Stereoscopic Ability Test

(SAT) consists of 12 items that can be displayed on every stereoscopic display. The employed analyses suggest a high sensitivity to interindividual differences in stereoscopic ability and the high internal consistency suggests a reliable and one-dimensional measure.

The validity of the test needs to be addressed in a future study. Still, the current results give at least weak support for the discriminative power of the test, as few participants score rather low in the test with the majority of the participants achieving medium to high scores. An open question remains, why some participants scored significantly lower than chance level ($p = .50$). Even stereo blind participants should score values of $M = .50$. Although our goal is not to develop a measure that could serve clinical purposes, the test needs at least to be compared with one clinical measure of stereo blindness.

5   Implementing the SAT for Research

The developed test items are freely available from the project website (http://www.medkom.tu-chemnitz.de/sat/). We provide the blender project files necessary to implement the stimuli in rendering engines as well as ready to use side-by-side images for simple use cases such as TV-sets. The website also features statistics of the test evaluations (including future studies), explanations for stimulus implementation as well as guidelines for test usage.

Acknowledgements. The work presented has been partially funded by the German Research Foundation (DFG) as part of the research training group Connecting Virtual and Real Social Worlds (grant 1780). We thank Marius Paul and Anne Frey for their help in the creation of the stimuli. We would also like to express our gratitude to the Blender Foundation and the developer of the Blender-Plugin Stereoscopic Rendering in Blender 2.7 (http://www.noeol.de/s3d/).

References

1. Baños, R.M., Botella, C., Alcañiz, M., Liaño, B.A., Guerrero, B., Rey, B.: Immersion and emotion: Their impact on the sense of presence. CyberPsychology Behav. **7**, 734–741 (2004)
2. Häkkinen, J., Pölönen, M., Takatalo, J., Nyman, G.: Simulator sickness in virtual display gaming: a comparison of stereoscopic and non-stereoscopic situations. In: 8th International Conference on Human Computer Interaction with Mobile Devices and Services Helsinki (2006)
3. Takatalo, J., Kawai, T., Kaistinen, J., Nyman, G., Hakkinen, J.: User experience in 3D stereoscopic games. Media Psychol. **14**, 387–414 (2011)
4. Sobieraj, S., Krämer, N.C., Engler, M., Siebert, M.: The influence of 3D screenings on presence and perceived entertainment. In: International Society for Presence Research Annual Conference (ISPR 2011), Edinburgh (2011)
5. Richards, W.: Stereopsis and stereoblindness. Exp. Brain Res. **10**, 380–388 (1970)
6. van Mierlo, C.M., Brenner, E., Smeets, J.B.: Better performance with two eyes than with one in stereo-blind subjects judgments of motion in depth. Vis. Res. **51**, 1249–1253 (2011)

7. Lee, J., McIntyre, A.: Clin. tests binocular vis. Eye **10**(Pt 2), 282–285 (1996)
8. Coren, S., Ward, L.M., Enns, J.D.: Sensation and Perception. Harcourt Brace College Publishers, New York (1994)
9. Cutting, E., Vishton, P.M.: Perceiving layout and knowing distances: the interaction of relative potency, and contextual use of different information about depth. In: Epstein, W., Rogers, S. (eds.) Perception of Space and Motion. Academic Press, San Diego, CA (1995)
10. King, R.D.: A brief history of stereoscopy. Wiley Interdisc. Rev. Comput. Stat. **5**, 334–340 (2013)
11. Biocca, F.: virtual reality technology: a tutorial. J. Commun. **42**, 23–72 (1992)
12. Steuer, J.: Defining virtual reality: dimensions determining telepresence. J. of Commun. **42**, 73–93 (1992)
13. Cameron, J.: Avatar. pp. 162 min. Twentieth Century Fox (2009)
14. Woods, A.J., MacKenzie, K.J., Watt, S.J., Holliman, N.S., Dodgson, N.A.: Eliminating accommodation-convergence conflicts in stereoscopic displays: can multiple focal-plane displays elicit continuous and consistent vergence and accommodation responses? 7524, 752417-752417-752410 (2010)
15. Lambooij, M., Ijsselsteijn, W., Fortuin, M., Heynderickx, I.: Visual discomfort and visual fatigue of stereoscopic displays: a review. J. Imaging Sci. Technol. **53**, 1–14 (2009)
16. Liu, C.-W., Huang, T.-H., Chang, M.-H., Lee, K.-Y., Liang, C.-K., Chuang, Y.-Y.: 3D cinematography principles and their applications to stereoscopic media processing, 253 (2011)
17. Schild, J., LaViola, J.J., Masuch, M.: Altering gameplay behavior using stereoscopic 3D vision-based video game design. In: SIGCHI Conference on Human Factors in Computing Systems ACM CHI (2014)
18. Rivett, J., Holliman, N.S.: Stereoscopic game design and evaluation. In: Stereoscopic Displays and Applications XXIV. SPIE - The International Society for Optical Engineering (2013)
19. Kennedy, R.S., Lane, N.E., Berbaum, K.S., Lilienthal, M.G.: Simulator sickness questionnaire: an enhanced method for quantifying simulator sickness. Int. J. Aviat. Psychol. **3**, 203–220 (1993)
20. Ware, C., Gobrecht, C., Paton, M.: Dynamic adjustment of stereo display parameters. IEEE Trans. Sys. Man Cybernen. Part Sys. Hum. **28**, 56–65 (1998)
21. Hoffman, D.M., Girshick, A.R., Akeley, K., Banks, M.S.: Vergence-accommodation conflicts hinder visual performance and cause visual fatigue. J. Vis. **8**, 33:31–33:30 (2008)

The Virtual Meditative Walk: An Immersive Virtual Environment for Pain Self-modulation Through Mindfulness-Based Stress Reduction Meditation

Xin Tong[✉], Diane Gromala, Amber Choo, Ashfaq Amin,
and Chris Shaw

Simon Fraser University, Surrey, Canada
{tongxint, gromala, achoo,
ashfaq_mahmood_amin, shaw}@sfu.ca

Abstract. One in five people in North America experience chronic pain. The primary non-pharmacological approach to treat chronic pain is to 'manage' pain by practices like Mindfulness-based Stress Reduction (MBSR) Meditation. Previous research shows the potential of mindfulness meditation to help foster patients' emotional wellbeing and pain self-modulation. Thus, the Virtual Reality (VR) system named "Virtual Meditative Walk" (VMW) was developed to help patients direct their attention inward through mindfulness meditation, which incorporates biofeedback sensors, an immersive virtual environment, and stereoscopic sound. It was specifically designed to help patients to learn MBSR meditation by providing real-time feedback, and to provide further training reinforcement. VMW enables patients to manage their chronic pain by providing real-time immersive visual signals and sonic feedback, which are mapped to their physiological biofeedback data. In the proof-of-concept study, this combination of immersive VR and MBSR meditation pain self-modulation technique proved to be effective for managing chronic pain.

Keywords: Virtual reality · Chronic pain · Mindfulness-based stress reduction meditation · Immersive environment

1 Introduction

It is estimated that 20 % of people in North America [1] and 15-20 % in industrialized nations [2] suffer from chronic pain. Defined as pain that lasts more than 6 months and persists beyond the healing of its putative cause, chronic pain usually involves neurobiological, psychological and social dimensions [3]. Chronic pain also lasts much longer than acute pain, and is not be associated with any observable bodily damage and might persist for a lifetime.

Although pharmacological approaches are the most common treatment method, they cannot address all aspects of the condition. Furthermore, analgesics such as opioids can have serious side effects, such as both dependency and addictive tendencies [4, 5]. Hoffman et al. demonstrated that immersive Virtual Reality (VR) is an effective

© Springer International Publishing Switzerland 2015
R. Shumaker and S. Lackey (Eds.): VAMR 2015, LNCS 9179, pp. 388–397, 2015.
DOI: 10.1007/978-3-319-21067-4_40

way to manage attention in VR as a form of pain distraction for short-term, acute pain [7]. Therefore, VR can be used as a powerful pain control technique to manage and modulate pain [8]. However, it is not yet known if the immersive VR is helpful for managing chronic pain (CP) on a long-term scale.

For managing chronic or long-term pain, one of the standard supplementary or adjuvant approaches is mindfulness-based stress reduction (MBSR). MBSR meditation has been used for a long time to help CP patients to reduce their stress and improve their health via improvements in the maintenance of their psychological states [6], which is particularly important for chronic pain patients as the persistence of pain itself is stress-inducing and is known to have attendant emotional components. Therefore, the MBSR component and biofeedback mechanism were combined and incorporated when developing the virtual environment (VE).

The research described in this paper is our first phase towards studying how effective and efficient the immersive VR MBSR approach may be when combined with biofeedback for CP patients. Our prior research strongly suggested that it was effective in reducing stress among 411 healthy users, particularly among those who had never meditated before [14]. Subsequently, as preparation for building a VE specific to patients' needs and requirements, we studied numerous aspects of CP patients: Quality of Life (QoL), habits using technology, specific/variable problems and sequelae, sonic preferences and sensitivities [14], attitudes toward meditation practices, and what they imagined when they try to meditate or visualize to reduce their pain levels.

2 Related Work

While treatment of severe chronic pain solely by pharmacological approaches is limited and problematic [9], there are alternatives and adjuvant approaches that help patients better manage their long-term pain and reduce its intensity.

Medical VR has emerged over the past two decades, including rehabilitation, surgical simulators, and telepresence surgery [10]. Researchers in 2003 [10] designed the Meditation Chamber, an immersive virtual environment to train participants to reduce their stress. Biofeedback sensors were adopted to monitor arousal, and this data in turn affected the VE's visual assets. The results indicated a positive influence of their VE: participants successfully managed their stress levels while observing the VE's continuously changing visual feedback, which was more effective than biofeedback alone in the control group.

VR has also proven to be an effective method to reduce acute pain resulting from wound care in burn patients [12]. Hoffman et al. designed a distraction-based VR study; the results showed up to a 50 % reduction in patients' perceived pain. Several other VR applications not built upon pain distraction were also developed to mitigate pain. Shiri et al. developed a VR system to treat pediatric headaches with biofeedback sensors [12]. In patients who had chronic headaches, galvanic skin response (GSR) levels were obtained over ten sessions, each lasting 30 min. The biofeedback data was then used to affect the environment that the participants were immersed in. After the participants were instructed to perform relaxation techniques (the more they relaxed, the happier their picture appeared in the VE), it was found that patients with migraines experienced a significant decrease in headache pain in the experiment [13].

Prior VR work offers 15 years of compelling evidence that VR is an "effective non-pharmacological analgesic" — for acute pain. Although the mechanism is not well understood, it is believed that VR is an especially strong instantiation of pain distraction because it involves numerous perceptual and motor senses. Though the length of those studies varied, most were 10-20 min in duration. In our earlier studies [10] for chronic pain, however, it was clear that many patients are not able to either sit or stand for more than 20 min. What is important here is that unlike traditional meditation training engaged in by healthy people, these patients' limitations require modification, not in the MBSR training content, but in their configuration via the length of time.

These works indicate that VR has been effective for treating acute pain; however, such VEs present limitations for managing chronic pain. Thus, our research focuses on utilizing immersive VR as an intervention to teach MBSR, a well-established pain management technique, which in turn may enable patients to more easily develop and adhere to an effective long-term pain management tool.

3   Virtual Meditative Walk

3.1   Environment Design

The Virtual Meditative Walk (VMW) incorporates a unique virtual environment with biofeedback for MBSR meditation training, and thereby addresses chronic pain patients' specific needs. The system is designed to directly generate a feedback loop of chronic pain patients' specific embodied conditions, bodily awareness, and potentially the sense of agency that they may develop by better coping with or reducing their persistent pain. We employ VR technologies for pain mitigation and management by controlling changes in 3D visual & sonic elements based on mindfulness-based stress reduction (MBSR) and biofeedback data in real-time to support their learning of mindfulness meditation techniques. MBSR, a form of mindfulness meditation, is a technique that takes time and effort to learn. Initially, it requires a focus on one's internal states, rather than on the world. The VR scene and its path design was showed in Fig. 1 below. Over time, patients learn to use this awareness outside of the VR.

Fig. 1. Path design in VMW virtual environment

The design of the Virtual Meditative Walk (VMW) provides a peaceful, non-distracting and safe environment for users to immerse themselves in as they learn to intentionally control the physiological aspects that are necessary to achieve the positive effects of MBSR. The VMW is a VE where participants immersed in the virtual reality find themselves "walking" in a beautiful forest composed primarily of a deciduous forest and undergrowth with subtle ambient breezes. The surrounding area is relatively mountainous, reminiscent of the trails found along the northwest coast of North America. The camera slowly moves along a flat, worn dirt pathway, as if the user is walking. The GSR sensors continuously track the patient's changing arousal levels, and in turn modify the VMW's atmospheric weather. The light fog in the forest, for example, recedes as a patient's GSR levels start to stabilize, inferring a mindful state. Alternatively, the fog thickens and draws closer when the patient's arousal levels increase. This serves as seamless visual feedback for patients immersed in the VMW. The two images in Fig. 2 show how the VE changes according to variable changes in the patients' biofeedback data.

Fig. 2. As patients approach an inferred meditative state, the fog begins to dissipate (top to bottom), and sounds become more audible and spatial.

3.2 Focusing More Attention Inward with Outward VR Changes

During the system design process, we took into consideration patients' proprioceptive and interoceptive senses, which strongly shape human movement, interaction and experience, in order to bring embodied states—and how they are affected or trans-formed—into conscious awareness by mapping the changes in those embodied states (through biofeedback mechanisms such as galvanic skin response and heart rate variability) onto changes in visual and sonic qualities of VR environment.

It is important to note that pain distraction is NOT an appropriate strategy for long-term pain management; therefore, we developed a very different paradigm. Our new paradigm of "chronic pain self-modulation" builds on techniques known to be effective treatments for CP: MBSR and biofeedback. Pain doctors recommend them for self-managing CP, but they take significant effort to learn and to practice everyday. Our prior studies suggest that VR can help because it gives users immediate and immersive feedback. In this way, users can have a better sense of whether their efforts are actually producing any changes in stress levels.

4   User Proof-of-Concept Study

The study is a proof-of-concept designed to assess whether most CP patients are capable of 12-minute sessions, and if one session has measurable results that are comparable to prior studies with healthy people (i.e., are patients capable of focusing inward, and can they learn to change their GSR?).

4.1   Goals

A study was designed to test the minimal effectiveness of the Virtual Meditative Walk system. In the long term, the system is designed to be used over six sessions, which is an introduction parallel to learning MBSR in more traditional ways, such as FTF group lessons and recorded training sessions. For this VR approach, we wanted to determine if an immersive Virtual Environment, combined with MBSR training and biofeedback, helps pain patients better manage and self-modulate their pain by reducing perceived pain levels among chronic pain patients in the short term, using the minimal possible time period of one session.

4.2   Participants and Procedures

Thirteen patients ranging from 35 to 55 years of age (mean = 49, SD = 8.2) participated in the study in an established pain clinic. Each patient had a diagnosis of chronic pain. Six participants (3 male, 3 female) were randomly assigned to the control group, and the other seven (3 male, 4 female) were assigned to the VR group. Although 20 participants were originally recruited, 7 of them either chose not to complete the study because of pain, or failed to finish our questionnaires.

As for the patients' type of pain, it is crucial to understand that CP is considered to be a dysfunction of the pain response system. Therefore, categorization is often deemed to be counterproductive, since it draws researchers back into habitual ways of confusing the pain system dysfunction with acute pain; acute pain is the common understanding of pain that results from injury or infection, and functions in the short term as an alert to danger, injury or threat. While subcategories of pain type are used by a subset of health professionals and researchers who focus on CP, they are often categories of neuropathic, nociceptive and idiopathic pain. Also, while patients may cite the source of pain (such as in their lower back, legs, hips, neck, and shoulders), pain can be "referred". Moreover, chronic pain, as a systemic dysfunction, often leads to complex and distributed pain. For our readership, therefore, this complexity is beyond the scope of the paper (or page limits). More importantly, based on our prior publications in ACM fields, stating "which" category almost always derails the point of the research findings because readers return to habitual ways of thinking that CP is "just" acute pain, that it behaves in known ways, and that it can be cured.

4.3   Procedures

During meditation sessions, we monitored GSR levels of patients and used this data to drive the dynamics of the VE in real-time. This real-time biofeedback system allowed patients to become aware of their progress as they performed mindfulness and encouraged them to pursue the practice. During the session, the patient saw a foggy forest, with the fog representing the patient's GSR level. As patients intentionally reduced their stress level inferred from GSR data, the fog faded, and indicating that the patient was approaching or in a meditative state. The fog indicated the cause-and-effect mechanism of biofeedback in the VE. Based on early design tests and on one of our former studies [15], the fog animation was designed with abstraction in mind. The fog aimed to distribute the attention of the user while displaying the changes of GSR in real-time.

The participant was first informed of the whole study and procedures, and then the GSR sensors were attached to two fingers. In the control group, participants listened to the MBSR training audio. In the VR group, participants listened to the same MBSR training audio while immersed in the VMW environment. Both groups were given 12 min for the MBSR training (shown in Fig. 3).

4.4   Apparatus

The construction of the physical setup for the VMW required the use of a stereoscopic VR display. The display is mounted on a movable arm to ensure flexibility and to maximize patient comfort. The GSR sensors, which are small clips, were gently put onto two of the patient's fingertips; none of the participants reported discomfort from their use. GSR data was used to control the biofeedback system in VR, but it was not adopted to compare pain levels. The assumption is: to immerse patients in the VE so that their GSR data were not displayed as a 2D graph, but rather had a major influence

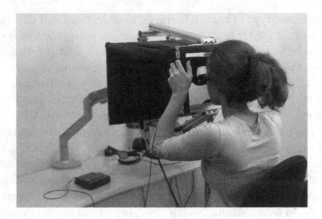

Fig. 3. The participant is learning MBSR in VMW

on the VE that is consistent with VR's immersive capabilities. Consequently, the raw GSR data was not used for comparing two groups.

A pain questionnaire was given to the patients both before and after the study session in order to compare perceived reported pain levels. The 11-point Numerical Rating Scale (NRS) was used as the instrument for patients to self-report their pain levels between the numerical values 0 and 10 (10 means the worst pain possible and 0 means no pain at all). The NRS instrument is standard in pain research in the health domain. For patients, NRS is simple in terms of understanding and ease of use; therefore, it was used to avoid distressing the pain patients with complex and lengthy questionnaires, which are commonly and repeatedly used in pain clinics.

4.5   Results and Analysis

A two-way mixed ANOVA was run to analyze the collected data. Time and condition were two independent variables. Time was the within-subjects factor, and the subjects design was between-subjects design – a participant either belonged to the VR group or to the control group.

We found a significant main effect of Time, $F(1, 11) = 10.44$, $p < .01$. The main effect of Condition was not significant, $F(1, 11) = 1.53$, $p > .05$. This indicated that when the time at which the NRS was measured is ignored, the initial pain level in the VR group was not significantly different than that in the control group. There was a significant Time x Condition interaction, $F(1, 11) = 8.16$, $p < .05$, indicating that the changes in the pain level in the VR group were significantly different compared to the change in the control group. Specifically, there was a significant drop in NRS ratings in the VR group, $t(6) = 2.86$, $p < .05$, but a very weak drop in the control group, $t(5) = 1.24$, $p > .05$. These findings indicate that the VMW (VR paired with bio-feedback for MBSR training) was significantly more effective than MBSR alone at reducing reported pain levels among participants.

4.6   Discussion

In the clinical pain clinic settings, we taught participants to learn a basic level of MSBR in the study with our VR system. We also imported VMW to mobile terminals as a software application for reinforcement for regular practice outside of the clinic, and to capture and track adherence to regular MBSR practice. Therefore, in our next phase, we plan to strengthen patients' self-care and management skills: (1) through VR therapy by providing six VR sessions in the doctors' clinic; and (2) providing mobile APP training so they can keep learning and practicing pain self-management in the same context.

Although the single trial outlined does not speak to the effectiveness of potential long-term capabilities for VR chronic pain self-management, the VMW enables chronic pain patients to consider that their pain experiences could be further managed through MBSR practiced over the long-term. By multiple training sessions and regularized practice, patients can learn to more easily situate the psychophysical mediation of their internal experiences into everyday life. The pain reduction reported by the NRS data is an early step in proving that VR and biofeedback systems may be an effective first step in promoting this behavioural change, and potentially to afford patients with a greater sense that they are able to self-manage their pain to some degree. This is an important factor since many CP patients report a sense of hopelessness [1].

For the past two decades, research on VR for pain has been focusing on interventions for acute pain. However, our focus is on how to utilize VR as a technology that could also benefit patients who live with long term chronic pain. By implementing an effective non-pharmacological analgesic approach—MBSR meditation—we believe the VR is more suitable for chronic pain patients and that such pain self-modulation may provide a more appropriate approach useful over the long term than short term pain distraction. Our immersive VR project, the Virtual Meditative Walk, and the study results demonstrate its potential positive effect.

Future studies with longer immersion times and a focus on how long the analgesic effect may linger after the meditative session is the natural next step in continuing this line of inquiry. The introduction of more detailed reporting methods of perceived pain, such as the use of the McGill Pain Questionnaire, could also yield new insights into the details surrounding perceived reported pain after the VR intervention. This will require greater effort put towards the understanding of chronic pain patient experience, studied within the context of the clinic to ensure that patients' comfort and stamina are not negatively impacted by the time and effort that would be required if patients needed to travel elsewhere, such as to a research lab.

5   Conclusion

In this paper, we briefly discussed how an immersive Virtual Environment, the Virtual Meditative Walk, could be designed for chronic pain patients to learn pain self-modulation. By designing a VR system that incorporates biofeedback mechanisms to support learning MSBR meditation, this technological intervention may be an effective and long term non-pharmacological approach, compared to traditional pain management. Further, by teaching MBSR to chronic pain patients in this context, we believe that their pain self-modulation ability can be improved and Potentionally sustained by long-term practice. Moreover, although this VR intervention is designed to address a difficult, complex and long-term condition of chronic pain, it is not limited to chronic pain patients; health practitioners, nurses, and patients suffering from acute pain symptoms can benefit from learning MBSR to foster psychophysiological attentiveness as well as pain, stress and anxiety-modulation capabilities.

References

1. Gatchel, R.J., Peng, Y.B., Peters, M.L., Fuchs, P.N., Turk, D.C.: The biopsychosocial approach to chronic pain: scientific advances and future directions. Psychol. Bull. **133**(4), 581–624 (2007)
2. Macfarlane, G.J., McBeth, J., Silman, A.J.: Widespread body pain and mortality: prospective population based study. BMJ **323**(7314), 662–665 (2001)
3. Fishbain, D.A., Cole, B., Lewis, J., Rosomoff, H.L., Rosomoff, R.S.: What percentage of chronic nonmalignant pain patients exposed to chronic opioid analgesic therapy develop abuse/addiction and/or aberrant drug-related behaviors? A structured evidence-based review. Pain Med. Malden Mass **9**(4), 444–459 (2008)
4. Jamison, R.N., Ross, E.L., Michna, E., Chen, L.Q., Holcomb, C., Wasan, A.D.: Substance misuse treatment for high-risk chronic pain patients on opioid therapy: a randomized trial. Pain **150**(3), 390–400 (2010)
5. Reibel, D.K., Greeson, J.M., Brainard, G.C., Rosenzweig, S.: Mindfulness-based stress reduction and health-related quality of life in a heterogeneous patient population. Gen. Hosp. Psychiatry **23**(4), 183–192 (2001)
6. Hoffman, H.G., Chambers, G.T., Meyer, W.J., Arceneaux, L.L., Russell, W.J., Seibel, E.J., Richards, T.L., Sharar, S.R., Patterson, D.R.: Virtual reality as an adjunctive non-pharmacologic analgesic for acute burn pain during medical procedures. Ann. Behav. Med. Publ. Soc. Behav. Med. **41**(2), 183–191 (2011)
7. Hoffman, H.G., Patterson, D.R., Carrougher, G.J., Sharar, S.R.: Effectiveness of virtual reality-based pain control with multiple treatments. Clin. J. Pain **17**(3), 229–235 (2001)
8. Baer, R.A.: Mindfulness training as a clinical intervention: a conceptual and empirical review. Clin. Psychol. Sci. Pract. **10**(2), 125–143 (2003)
9. Satava, R.M.: Surgical robotics: the early chronicles: a personal historical perspective. Surg. Laparosc. Endosc. Percutan. Tech. **12**(1), 6–16 (2002)
10. Shaw, C., Gromala, D., Song, M.: The meditation chamber: towards self-modulation. In: Proceedings of the. ENACTIVE 2007
11. Murray, C.D., Pettifer, S., Howard, T., Patchick, E.L., Caillette, F., Kulkarni, J., Bamford, C.: The treatment of phantom limb pain using immersive virtual reality: three case studies. Disabil. Rehabil. **29**(18), 1465–1469 (2007)
12. Shiri, S., Feintuch, U., Weiss, N., Pustilnik, A., Geffen, T., Kay, B., Meiner, Z., Berger, I.: A virtual reality system combined with biofeedback for treating pediatric chronic headache–a pilot study. Pain Med. Malden Mass **14**(5), 621–627 (2013)
13. Varni, J.W., Seid, M., Rode, C.A.: The PedsQL: measurement model for the pediatric quality of life inventory. Med. Care **37**(2), 126–139 (1999)

14. Nazemi, M., Mobini, M., Barnes, S.J., Gromala, D.: Gender difference in auditory stimulus sensitivity in patients with chronic pain. In: 8th Congress of the European Federation of IASP® Chapters, Florence (2013)
15. Gromala, D., Song, M., Yim, J., Fox, T., Barnes, S., Nazemi, M., Shaw, C., Squire, P.: Immersive VR: a non-pharmacological analgesic for chronic pain?. In: CHI 2011 Extended Abstracts, pp. 1171–1176

Digital Archiving of Takigi Noh Based on Reflectance Analysis

Wataru Wakita[1](✉), Shiro Tanaka[1], Kohei Furukawa[2],
Kozaburo Hachimura[1], and Hiromi T. Tanaka[1]

[1] Department of Human and Computer Intelligence, College of Information
Science and Engineering, Ritsumeikan University, Kusatsu, Japan
{wakita,stanaka,hiromi}@cv.ci.ritsumei.ac.jp,
hachimura@media.ritsumei.ac.jp
[2] Department of Image Arts and Sciences, College of Image Arts and Sciences,
Ritsumeikan University, Kyoto, Japan
kohei-f@im.ritsumei.ac.jp

Abstract. We propose a real-time bidirectional texture function (BTF) and image-based lighting (IBL) rendering of the Takigi Noh based on reflectance analysis. Firstly, we measured a sample of the Noh costume by omnidirectional anisotropic reflectance measurement system called Optical Gyro Measuring Machine (OGM), and we modeled the BTF of the Noh costume based on multi-illuminated High Dynamic Range (HDR) image analysis and modeled Noh stage in 3D based on archival records. Secondly, we captured motion data of Noh player, and modeled Noh player wearing a costume. To achieve the real-time rendering, we modeled the Noh costume by mass spring damper model. Finally, we modeled animated ambient map based on the Improving Noise to achieve the real-time dynamic lighting by fire of the Takigi, and we calculated the optical reflection by the IBL and deformation of the Noh costume.

Keywords: Real-time rendering · BTF · Takigi noh · Reflectance analysis · Digital museum

1 Introduction

Recently, research on the digital archive [1, 2] by various digital technologies have been attracted attention. In Japan, research on the digital museum [3] have been conducted. In this work, we attempt to archive the Takigi Noh digitally. The Noh (traditional masked dance-drama) is one of the traditional arts in Japan. Among this, there is one called Takigi (firewood) Noh which is performed by burning firewood around the stage after sunset. In Takigi Noh, Noh costumes of gold brocades shines beautifully with torches set around the Noh stage that provide the illumination (see Fig. 1).

The Noh costume is interlaced with gold threads and silk, and has fine 3D structure. Therefore, it has very complex anisotropic reflecting property. The hue of the Noh costume is changing according to the incident direction of light and the view direction.

© Springer International Publishing Switzerland 2015
R. Shumaker and S. Lackey (Eds.): VAMR 2015, LNCS 9179, pp. 398–408, 2015.
DOI: 10.1007/978-3-319-21067-4_41

Fig. 1. Takigi Noh [4]

Therefore, we model the Noh costume under the fabric structure and anisotropic reflectance, then we set the torches around Noh stage, and represent the anisotropic reflectance of the Noh costume fabric under dynamic lighting with torches.

In previous work, we modeled and represented the anisotropic reflection of the Noh costume based on the reflectance analysis [5], and we proposed a real-time anisotropic rendering method of the Noh costume which is lit by the firewood around the Noh stage [6]. In this work, we propose a real-time bidirectional texture function (BTF) and image-based lighting (IBL) rendering of the Takigi Noh based on reflectance analysis. Firstly, we measured a sample of the Noh costume by omnidirectional anisotropic reflectance measurement system called Optical Gyro Measuring Machine (OGM), and we modeled the BTF of the Noh costume based on multi-illuminated High Dynamic Range (HDR) image analysis and modeled Noh stage in 3D based on archival records. Secondly, we captured motion data of Noh player, and modeled Noh player wearing a costume. To achieve the real-time rendering, we modeled the Noh costume by mass spring damper model. Finally, we modeled animated ambient map based on the Improving Noise to achieve the real-time dynamic lighting by fire of the Takigi, and we calculated the optical reflection by the IBL and deformation of the Noh costume.

2   Related Work

The anisotropic reflectance of object surface can be characterized from the bidirectional reflectance distribution function (BRDF) which is the ratio of the irradiance from an arbitrary lighting direction to the radiance from any viewing direction at any point. Also, the permeable object surface can be characterized from the bidirectional transmittance distribution function (BTDF) which is the ratio of the transmitted light from an arbitrary lighting direction to the radiance from any viewing direction at any point [7]. Recently, some approaches which applied the BTDF [8], the bidirectional scattering distribution function (BSDF) [9], and the radiative transfer equation (RTE) [10] for the fabric are proposed. To achieve the realistic rendering of Noh costume, it is necessary to consider these properties because Noh costume is interlaced with permeable threads and gold brocades. In this work, we consider the BTF at the present stage.

About the lighting effect, for the rendering under real-world multiple light sources, image based lighting (IBL) rendering [11], which uses actual captured images (of the environmental map) as environment illumination information, is considered. IBL rendering considers the incidence light from all directions. However, it uses a large amount of calculation thus rendering in real-time is difficult. To reduce the computational cost, environment map sampling method [12–16], environment map and BRDF product method [17–20], and the direct calculation method from environment map [21–26] are proposed. In these methods, ambient light is constant and the environment will not change. Moreover, in the easy-to-use approach of BRDF [26], focused sampling is obtained from the incident direction. With fewer necessary pre-calculation, real-time rendering of BRDF is possible. However, this method is not applicable to BTF real-time rendering. On the other hand, to represent the bonfire, there are two methods: physically-based method [27] and a method by procedural texture [28]. However, the computational cost for lighting is a problem. Furthermore, it is difficult to use the procedural texture directly, which is easy-to-use for the dynamic light. Therefore, we represent the flame by procedural texture, which is easy-to-use, as the dynamic ambient map. It is expected to represent dynamic flame and ambient light in the same calculation as direct calculation method from environment map.

3 Reflectance Analysis of Noh Costume

Silk is primarily used in the Takigi Noh costume fabrics. The costume is interlaced with gold threads as shown in Fig. 2. Gold brocades, and colorful patterns such as flowers, leaves and branches, are woven into vermillion or red base.

The fabrics are generally woven using warp and weft patterns. The gold brocade can be interwoven using the warp-weft pattern with the red base. In Noh costumes, the aforementioned pattern is done throughout the whole fabric. However, arrangements that do not resemble the pattern of the silk threads are also present. The Noh costume fabric is made up of warp-weft patterns in an up-and-down arrangement. The weave of the underlying fabric is primarily composed of plain fabric, twill, and satin. These three

Fig. 2. Noh costume with gold brocades

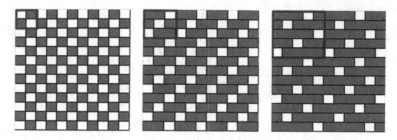

Fig. 3. Weave structure chart

types of weave are the most commonly produced. Figure 3 shows the three types of weave and their corresponding pattern representation. White area denotes warp, while gray denotes weft. The minimal recurring pattern in each weave is bounded by the red frame, which will be referred to as weave structure.

In this work, we modeled the BTF of the Noh costume based on multi-illuminated High Dynamic Range (HDR) image analysis. We don't consider the optical transmission for the costume in current work and use the surface model. Noh costume with gold brocade has 3D structures. Therefore, it is necessary to define the BRDF at each points of surface to portray the anisotropic reflectance faithfully.

The reflection characteristic at any point on the surface of the object, that is, the ratio of the reflected light from the incident light with respect to the incident direction in any viewing point can be described using BTF. Figure 4 shows the geometric representation of BTF (Fig. 5).

BTF $f_r(\theta_i, \varphi_i, \theta_r, \varphi_r, u, v)$ shown in Eq. 1 is defined in the spherical coordinate system as the ratio of the radiance $L_r(\theta_r, \varphi_r, u, v)$ from the incident direction $L(\theta_i, \varphi_i)$ taken from the viewing direction (θ_r, φ_r) for texel (u, v), which is any point on the object surface, to the irradiance $L_i(\theta_i, \varphi_i, u, v)$ taken from the incident direction. The minimum recurring pattern, shown in Fig. 3, in a Noh costume fabric is considered as the observed weave structure. We measured Noh costume with the OGM and estimated the diffuse reflection component, specular reflection component, normal vector, tangent vector, and standard deviations σ_x and σ_y which are based on the Ashikhmin model [29].

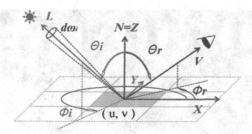

Fig. 4. Geometric representation of BTF

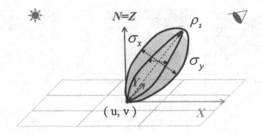

Fig. 5. Anisotropic BTF

4 Modeling of the Takigi Noh

4.1 Takigi Noh Stage

We modeled Noh stage in 3D based on archival records [30]. Figure 6 shows a restored 3D model of the Noh stage.

To portray the Takigi Noh, we disposed Takigi objects to around the Noh stage (see Fig. 7). We used the Perlin Fire [31] to generate fire animation.

Moreover, we calculate the IBL from animated ambient map of generated fire images directly. Figure 8 shows ambient map of the Noh stage.

Fig. 6. 3D model of Noh stage

Fig. 7. Takigi model based on the Perlin Fire

Fig. 8. Animated ambient map

4.2 Animation of the Noh Player

We captured a motion of the Noh player with the infrared tracking system, and measured 6 DOF data (3 directions of movement and 3 directions of rotation) of 19 markers. Figure 9 shows a part of motion capture data.

4.3 Noh Costume

From reflectance analysis, parameters of the BTF texture such as the diffuse reflection component ρ_d, specular reflection component ρ_s normal vector n, tangent vector t, and standard deviations σ_x and σ_y are estimated. Figure 10 shows a part of the BTF textures of the Noh costume.

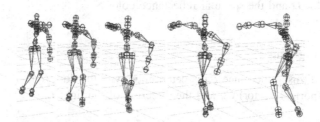

Fig. 9. Motion capture data of a Noh player.

Fig. 10. Part of the BTF textures of Noh costume. From left, diffuse map, normal map, specular map, σ_x map, and σ_y map.

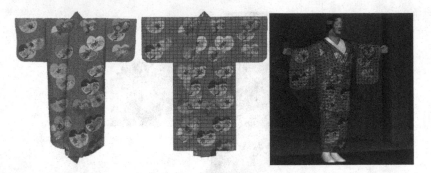

Fig. 11. 3D model of Noh costume and clothed player

Diffuse map represents the color, normal map represents the surface gradient, specular map represents the power of specular reflection, and σ_x map and σ_y map are represents the spread of anisotropic reflection. Then we created a 3D model of Noh costume and clothed player (see Fig. 11).

5 Rendering

We calculate the anisotropic reflectance of the Noh costume with IBL at per-fragment. To do the per-fragment lighting, it is necessary to program with the shader language. There are several shader languages such as the High Level Shader Language (HLSL), OpenGL Shading Language (GLSL), and C for graphics (Cg). In this work, we used GLSL that is compatible with OpenGL.

Final color of each pixel on the display is determined with sum of the diffuse reflectance color D and the specular reflectance color S.

5.1 Diffuse Lighting

The power of diffuse reflectance P_d is determined with the dot product of the gradient of the object (normal vector) C_n and the direction of the light L.

$$P_d = C_n \cdot L, \tag{1}$$

where, C_n is the 3D vector that converted from the color of the object that mapped the normal map, L is direction to the 4 Takigi objects that placed around the Noh stage. Then, diffuse reflectance color D is determined with product of the object color C_d that mapped the diffuse map and the color of fire C_l.

$$D = P_d C_l, \tag{2}$$

where, C_l is average color of the center of the fire, and it is inversely proportional to the square of distance from fire.

5.2   Specular Lighting

We used the Ashikhmin model to the Noh costume and used the Blinn-Phong model to other object. In Ashikhmin model, the power of specular reflectance P_s is calculated according to the following equation.

$$P_s = \frac{D(\theta_h \varphi_h)}{\cos \theta_i \cos \theta_r},$$

(3)

$$D(\theta_h \varphi_h) = \rho_s exp\left(-\tan^2\theta_h\left(\frac{\cos^2\varphi_h}{\sigma_x^2} + \frac{\sin^2\varphi_h}{\sigma_y^2}\right)\right),$$

(4)

where, $D(\theta_h, \varphi_h)$ is the small surface distribution function at each texel (u, v). The binormal vector $b = n \times t$ in which (θ_n, φ_n) is the direction of the normal vector n of the thread, and (θ_t, φ_t) i is the direction of the tangent vector t. The half vector H taken from the local Cartesian coordinate system is h, and its direction (θ_h, φ_h) is determined. θ_h is the angle between n and h, φ_h is the angle between the projected vector h in the XY-plane and t. ρ_s is the specular reflection component, σ_x is the standard deviation in the X-direction, and σ_y is the standard deviation in Y-direction.

ρ_s is obtained from the maximum value of specular reflection component $\rho_{bd,s}(\theta_i, \varphi_i, 0, 0)$ observed from BRDF data. t is the direction of the maximum dispersion of points of $\rho_{bd,s}(\theta_i, \varphi_i, 0, 0)$ projected on the XY-plane. Furthermore, σ_x and σ_y in Eqs. 3 and 4 are obtained.

In Blinn-Phong model, the power of specular reflectance P_s is calculated according to the following equation.

$$P_s = (H \cdot C_n)^{\rho_s}$$

(5)

Then, specular reflectance color S is determined with product of the P_s and the color of ambient map C_a that is reflected from view vector to the object.

$$S = P_s C_a$$

(6)

6   Results

Figure 12 shows rendering results of the Takigi Noh stage. It can see flickers of the bonfire and attenuation of the bonfire light.

Figure 13 shows rendering results of the Blinn-Phong model and Ashikhmin model. Ashikhmin model can see hexagonal pattern clearly because we considered the specular lobe.

Figure 14 shows rendering results of Noh animation This frame rate is 60 Hz.

Fig. 12. Rendering results of the Takigi Noh stage

(a)   Blinn-Phong model

(b)   Ashikhmin model

Fig. 13. Comparison of shading model, (a) Blinn-Phong model, (b) Ashikhmin model

Fig. 14. Results of Noh animation

7 Conclusion

We proposed a real-time BTF and IBL rendering of the Takigi Noh based on reflectance analysis. Firstly, we measured a sample of the Noh costume by omnidirectional anisotropic reflectance measurement system, and we modeled the BTF of the Noh costume based on multi-illuminated HDR image analysis and modeled Noh stage in 3D based on archival records. Secondly, we captured motion data of Noh player, and modeled Noh player wearing a costume. To achieve the real-time rendering, we modeled the Noh costume by mass spring damper model. Finally, we modeled animated ambient map based on the Improving Noise to achieve the real-time dynamic lighting by fire of the Takigi, and we calculated the optical reflection by the IBL and deformation of the Noh costume. As a result, we achieved a real-time BTF and IBL rendering in the dynamic lighting.

In future work, we consider the physically-based IBL lighting of Takigi and deformation of Noh costume, and the BSDF.

References

1. Styliani, S., Fotis, L., Kostas, K., Petros, P.: Virtual museums, a survey and some issues for consideration. J. Cult. Heritage **10**(4), 520–528 (2009)
2. Carrozzino, M., Bergamasco, M.: Beyond virtual museums: experiencing immersive virtual reality in real museums. J. Cult. Heritage **11**(4), 452–458 (2010)
3. Hirose, M., Tanikawa, T.: Overview of the digital museum project'. In: Proceedings of the 9th ACM SIGGRAPH Conference on Virtual-Reality Continuum and its Applications in Industry, pp.11–16 (2010)
4. Noh: Momiji-gari. http://www.pref.oita.jp/site/archive/200637.html
5. Takeda, Y., Tanaka, H.T.: Multi-resolution anisotropic BTF modeling of gold brocade fabrics based on multi-illuminated HDR image analysis'. IEICE Trans. Inf. Syst. (D) **J91-D**(12), 2729–2738 (2008)
6. Nishiwaki, Y., Wakita, W., Tanaka, H.T.: Real-time anisotropic reflectance rendering of noh-costume with bonfire flickering effect. ITE Trans. Media Technol. Appl. **2**(3), 217–224 (2014)
7. Bartell, F.O., Dereniak, E.L., Wolfe, W.L.: The theory and measurement of bidirectional reflectance distribution function (brdf) and bidirectional transmittance distribution function (BTDF). In: SPIE 0257, Radiation Scattering in Optical Systems, pp. 154–160 (1981)
8. Ishida, A., Ishigo, E., Aiba, E., Nagata, N.: Lace curtain: rendering animation of woven cloth using BRDF/BTDF - estimating physical characteristic from subjective impression. In: ACM SIGGRAPH 2012 Posters, vol. 6 (2012)
9. Sadeghi, I., Bisker, O., Deken, J.D., Jensen, H.W.: A practical microcylinder appearance model for cloth rendering. ACM Trans. Graph. **32**(2), 14:1–14:12 (2013)
10. Zhao, S., Hasan, M., Ramamoorthi, R., Bala, K.: Building volumetric appearance models of fabric using micro CT imaging. ACM Trans. Graph. **32**(4) (2013)
11. Debevec, P.: Rendering synthetic objects into real scenes: bridging traditional and image-based graphics with global illumination and high dynamic range photography. In: ACM SIGGRAPH 1998, pp. 189–198 (1998)

12. Arvo, J.: Stratified sampling of 2-manifolds. In: ACM SIGGRAPH 2001 Course Notes, 29, August 2001
13. Debevec, P.: A median cut algorithm for light probe sampling. In: Proceedings of the ACM SIGGRAPH 2005 Posters, p. 66 (2005)
14. Agarwal, S., Ramamoorthi, R., Belongie, S., Wann Jensen, H.: Structured importance sampling of environment maps. ACM Trans. Graph. **22**(3), 605–612 (2003)
15. Ostromoukhov, V., Donohue, C., Jodoin, P.-M.: Fast Hierarchical Importance Sampling with Blue Noise Properties. ACM Trans. Graph. **23**(3), 488–495 (2004)
16. Lawrence, J., Rusinkiewicz, S., Ramamoorthi, R.: Adaptive numerical cumulative distribution functions for efficient importance sampling. In: Proceedings the Sixteenth Eurographics conference on Rendering Techniques, pp. 1–20 (2005)
17. Burke, D., Ghosh, A., Heidrich, W.: Bidirectional importance sampling for direct illumination. In: Proceedings of the Sixteenth Eurographics Conference on Rendering Techniques, pp. 147–156 (2005)
18. Clarberg, P., Jarosz, W., Moller, T.A., Jensen, H.W.: Wavelet importance sampling: efficiently evaluating products of complex functions. ACM Trans. Graph. **24**(3), 1166–1175 (2005)
19. Huang, H.-D., Chen, Y., Tong, X., Wang, W.-C.: Incremental wavelet importance sampling for direct illumination In: Proceedings of the 2007 ACM Symposium on Virtual Reality Software and Technology, pp. 149–152 (2007)
20. Jarosz, W., Carr, N.A., Jensen, H.W.: Importance sampling spherical harmonics. Comput. Graph. Forum **28**(2), 577–586 (2009)
21. Kautz, J., McCool, M.D.: Approximation of glossy reflection with prefiltered environment maps. In: Graphics Interface, pp. 119–126 (2000)
22. Ramamoorthi, R., Hanrahan, P.: An Efficient representation for irradiance environment maps. In: Proceedings of the ACM SIGGRAPH 2001, pp. 497–500 (2001)
23. Ramamoorthi, R., Hanrahan, P.: Frequency space environment map rendering. ACM Trans. Graph. **21**(3), 517–526 (2002)
24. Sloan, P.-P., Kautz, J., Snyder, J.: Precomputed radiance transfer for real-time rendering in dynamic, low-frequency lighting environments. ACM Trans. Graph. **21**(3), 527–536 (2002)
25. Ng, R., Ramamoorthi, R., Hanrahan, P.: All-frequency shadows using non-linear wavelet lighting approximation. ACM Trans. Graph. **22**(3), 376–381 (2003)
26. Krivanek, J., Colbert, M.: Real-time shading with filtered importance sampling. Comput. Graph. Forum **27**(4), 1147–1154 (2008)
27. Nguyen, D.Q., Fedkiw, R., Jensen, H.W.: Physically based modeling and animation of fire. ACM Trans. Graph. **21**(3), 721–728 (2002)
28. Perlin, K.: Real-Time Shading. In: SIGGRAPH Course Notes, ch. 2, Noise Hardware (2001)
29. Ashikhmin, M., Premoze, S., Shirley, P.: A microfacet-based BRDF generator. In: ACM SIGGRAPH 2000, pp. 65–74 (2000)
30. Furukawa, K., Woong, C., Hachimura, K.: Digital restoration of the historical noh theater and its application. IPSJ Symp. Ser. **2005**(10), 131–134 (2005)
31. Fuller, A.R., Krishnan, H., Mahrous, K., Hamann, B., Joy, K. I.: Real-time procedural volumetric fire. In: Proceedings of the 2007 Symposium on Interactive 3D Graphics and Games, pp. 175–180 (2007)

Multimodal Digital Taste Experience
with D'Licious Vessel

Liangkun Yan$^{(\boxtimes)}$, Barry Chew, Jie Sun, Li-An Chiu,
Nimesha Ranasinghe, and Ellen Yi-Luen Do

Keio-NUS CUTE Center, National University of Singapore,
Singapore, Singapore
{idmyl,idmsunj,nimesha,ellendo}@nus.edu.sg,
{chew.barry,lian600058}@gmail.com

Abstract. Increasingly, people are replacing soft drinks with natural fruit juices, since soft drinks usually contain excessive sugar and little nutrition. This paper introduces a multimodal digital taste control system 'D'Licious Vessel' and the respective prototypes. The goal is to provide a digital solution to health concerns regarding overuse of sugar in our daily drinks by decreasing the natural sourness. The system applies gentle electrical signals to a person's tongue to trigger different taste sensations and improve the taste of drinks digitally without involving consumption of actual chemicals. We conducted user studies in a public setting to collect the experimental data and to find the system's effectiveness in improving the taste of lemon juice. During the study, participants were provided with lemon juice and asked to compare the taste difference while drinking with different settings of the taste stimulation prototype. Their opinions for different prototype designs are recorded and discussed.

Keywords: Flavor · Digital taste · Multimodal interaction · User interfaces · Virtual reality

1 Introduction

Taste is an important sensory perception for animals to judge the quality of food [1]. In addition, people enjoy taste sensations while consuming food and drinks. Condiments and artificial flavoring have been used to improve taste experience throughout human history [2]. But people today are seeking for healthier choices over food and drinks. More people are choosing natural fruit juices or water over soft drinks to avoid high sugar intake that causes obesity [3] and other health problems [4]. However, people seem to dislike sourness in many fruit juices [5] and prefer the sugar-sweetened soft drinks [3]. Our team aims to improve the taste of natural fruit juices, such as reducing the sourness or even create minor sweetness digitally without consumption of actual chemicals. Moreover, in recent years, more questions have been raised by the public on the safety and long term health effect regarding the type and amount of condiments usage. On the other hand, the elderly and particular patients after certain treatments may suffer from degrading taste reception. This paper introduces a multimodal digital

© Springer International Publishing Switzerland 2015
R. Shumaker and S. Lackey (Eds.): VAMR 2015, LNCS 9179, pp. 409–418, 2015.
DOI: 10.1007/978-3-319-21067-4_42

taste control system - D'Licious Vessel, to provide a digital solution to the health concerns above.

Taste sensation is commonly triggered by chemical reactions between food particles and taste receptor cells in taste buds [6]. Shown in recent studies, by applying a gentle electric signal to the tongue, it is also possible to stimulate different taste sensations digitally without any actual chemical involved [7]. Previously, the common belief that different taste sensations are actually located on different areas of the tongue, known as the 'tongue map', has been proven to be a wrong concept [8]. Every taste bud on the tongue are now found to contain all necessary taste receptor cells responsible for the 5 basic tastes, namely sweet, sour, bitter, salty and umami [9]. Thus, by applying gentle electric signal only to the tip of tongue, it is possible to trigger different taste sensations.

Tongue stimulation is not the only factor for taste perception. Many other factors like smell, temperature and chewing texture all have their effects on taste perception [10]. Moreover, many researches have proven that there is a strong association that the color of food and drinks influences our taste perceptions [11]. Before sending anything into mouth, we actually judge the taste with our eyes first, i.e. visual influence. When drinks present with same content but in different colors, people may have different taste perceptions [12]. For example, people perceive a sourer taste when yellow is present in the drinks. Thus in D'Licious Vessel, besides tongue stimulation, visual stimulation will also be used for digital taste perception [13].

This study aims to generate the taste sensations by controlling and manipulating taste perception factors in a digital way. D'Licious Vessel contains embedded electronic control modules to achieve taste sensations enhancement by two kinds of stimulations: electronic pulses stimulation on the tongue and visual stimulations using Light-Emitting Diodes (LED). D'Licious Vessel can enhances the sweetness, sourness, saltiness or bitterness in natural fruit juices by primarily applying gentle and adjustable electrical pulses on the human tongue as shown in Fig. 1. The multi-color light emitted by LED is used to change our perception of taste as well.

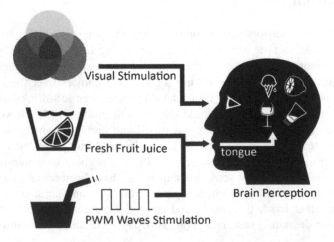

Fig. 1. Digital taste stimulation

2   System Description and Prototypes

2.1   Digital Taste Control System

By applying different electric signals, different taste sensation modes are able to be triggered [14]. The electronic signal used in the control system is Pulse-width modulation (PWM) waves. Pulse-width modulation (PWM) is a modulation technique generally used to contain information by controlling the width of the pulse (the pulse duration). The modes and their respective signal range are determined in the earlier research stage of this project [15]. The signal amplitude used in prototypes is 2 V, which means the waves contain only 2 values: 2 V (on) and 0 (off). Different taste modes are achieved by varying the duty cycle of the PWM waves, namely the respective duration of 'on' and 'off' in each period. Based on early stage research, three taste modes were categorized: salty, bitter and sour and they can be operated in a relatively lower frequency of 400-500 kHz. Thus the frequency of the system is fixed at 490 kHz (Arduino pro mini default frequency). The PWM duty cycle range for each mode is shown in Fig. 2.

The system is an embedded control module providing multimodal experience. The user interface allows users to perform mode selection by themselves using a rotary knob or push button. This mechanism also facilitates users to explore different settings of the system to find their own preferred taste sensations depending on the juice taste. D'Licious Vessel project aims to provide digital taste experience in different eating and drinking circumstances. Currently a bottle and a spoon prototype have been developed.

As shown in Fig. 3, both prototypes adopt this user interface design. Both have two outputs: (1) electrical pulses that are sent to the tongue through a pair of silver electrodes and (2) the multi-color LEDs. The two outputs are controlled by the user according to the mode selected.

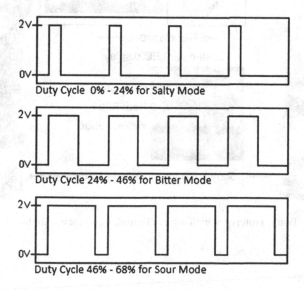

Fig. 2. PWM waves duty cycle range

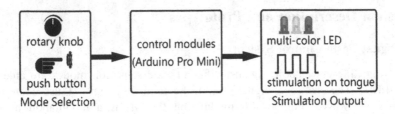

Fig. 3. User interface design

2.2 Prototypes

Bottle prototype is designed to function as a hydration vessel where it encourages people to drink via the bottle during their daily hydration. The bottle prototype has a rotary knob that corresponds to a varying intensity of the PWM waves supplied to the tongue when it is rotated. This enables the mode and its respective strength to be changed. It also allows users to find out the most suitable electric pulse strength for them to enjoy a specific taste.

Figure 4 shows the first and second version of the bottle prototypes. Both have a similar base design but different mouthpieces. For the first prototype, electrodes are (two silver rings) secured around a straw, while the second prototype uses a different design with silver electrodes attached on the rim of bottle. A rotary knob and a mode indicating scale is attached at the base for each prototype, allowing users to choose the electronic pulses according to their own preferences. LED lights are used to indicate and psychologically enhance different taste modes, blue for salty, red for bitter and

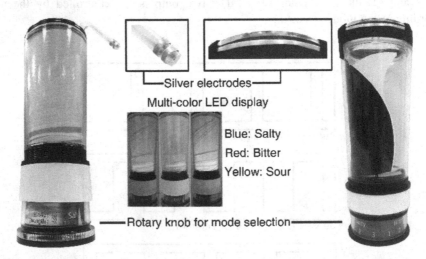

Fig. 4. Bottle prototypes with silver electrodes and rotary knob indication

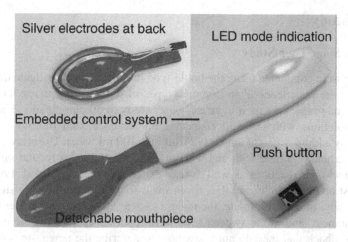

Fig. 5. Spoon type prototype

yellow for sour. The light intensity is directly linked with the electronic pulse strength for each mode.

We provided both bottle type prototypes for informal demo sessions and collected users' opinions on the design during the initial stage. Compared with the straw-type prototype, the majority stated that the second prototype provides a better user experience which is more user-friendly and has an easier cleaning procedure.

Spoon prototype is mainly designed to cater for individuals who suffer degradation in their taste sensation. It aims to enhance their taste sensations during their meal. Figure 5 shows the second version of the spoon. The first version (called Taste +) was designed by previous research team at Keio-NUS CUTE Center [16].

In both versions of spoon prototype, push button is used to toggle between three different preset modes. The preset modes correspond to three different discrete values of electronic pulse strength. This design minimizes the space required for the electronics, giving a comfortable grip for the users. The LED in the prototype serves as a mode indicator. The silver electrodes are 2 pieces follow the shape of spoon outline, attached at the back of the spoon where is usually licked by tongue. Although its appearance is greatly different from the bottle type, the internal electronic module is similar.

The main design improvement of second version compared with the first version is the detachable head part that can be replaced easily. It allows a throughout cleaning regarding hygiene concerns and can be changed into other cutlery easily if necessary. Currently, a replaceable fork mouthpiece is in production. It has an additional bitter mode besides the salty and sour mode in first version [17]. Also, the sliding cover design conceals the electric system more firmly in the handle. Besides bottle type and spoon type, other design applications also have been worked on. Lollipop and chopsticks are some of the other designs that are currently being developed.

3   User Study

3.1   Early Stage User Study

User studies were conducted using the bottle-type prototypes to investigate the effect of multimodal taste experience. Four common types of diluted fruit juices: lemon, pineapple, lime and grape were used in an early user study of 30 participants. There were a total of 3 solutions with different concentration for each kind of fruit juices. It is formulated by adding different amount of fruit into 100 ml water. Users are required to compare the change in taste with and without digital taste modes for the same diluted fruit juice, and their reactions as well as user experience were recorded. Lemon juice had the most obvious results and thus is our main focus in the following study. In the early user study, under salty mode, the majority (over 50 %) stated a better taste juice with less sourness, and minor sweeter taste were reported by 13 % of the users. Also, 6 % gave feedback that they do not know how to describe the new taste sensation but the juices tasted significantly better as compared to consuming lemon juice without digital stimulations.

3.2   User Study During the Public Exhibition

During our showcase at Singapore Art Science Museum, we conducted a larger user study with the 48 people who volunteered to try the new digital taste experience. We provided lemon juice to a particular user with same concentration: 3 g of lemon slices in 100 ml of water in our bottle type prototype. Although the bottle type provides a free and smooth mode and strength change, for better analysis purposes, we chose 6 fix mode and strength combinations for the participants. The six combinations are: weak salty, strong salty; weak bitter, strong bitter; weak sour and strong sour. Their respective duty cycles are stated below with the results. Participants were asked to provide feedback regarding the taste change of lemon juice compared with the original, as well as their opinions on the prototype design or the overall project.

Salty Mode. For weak salty mode, shown in Fig. 6, corresponding to a PWM wave with duty cycle about 10-12 %, we have identified that almost 60 % of the users registered no change in the taste of the lemon juice. Almost 25 % of the participants however did register a sourer taste in the lemon juice after drinking through the D'Licious Vessel in the experiment. Also 4 % of the users registered a taste difference but could not describe the taste. These unrecognized taste sensations are subsequently categorized under 'others'.

For strong salty mode, corresponding to a PWM wave with duty cycle about 20-22 %, we have identified that 13 % of the users responded that the lemon juice became saltier and the changes were significant. 29 % of the participants felt that the lemon juice was sourer, which was the result of the induced taste sensations when the current passed through the tongue.

Bitter Mode. For weak bitter mode, shown in Fig. 7, corresponding to PWM wave with duty cycle about 30-35 %, we have identified that there is a slight increase in the

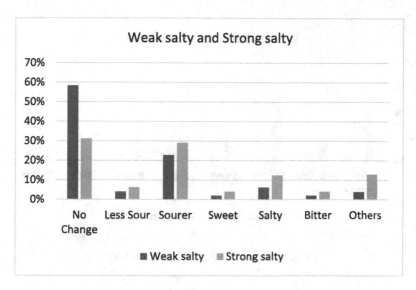

Fig. 6. Results analysis for salty modes

number of participants (10 %) who have detected bitterness in the lemon juice. However, 23 % of the participants still managed to register an increase in sourness of the lemon juice, where some participants labelling the lemon juice as more 'lemony'.

For strong bitter mode, corresponding to PWM wave with duty cycle 40-45 %, we have identified that almost 10 % of the participants responded a sweeter taste in their lemon juice. The slight sweetness was detected when the participants consume the lemon juice while touching the silver electrodes. 13 % of the participants' responded that the taste of the juice was awful.

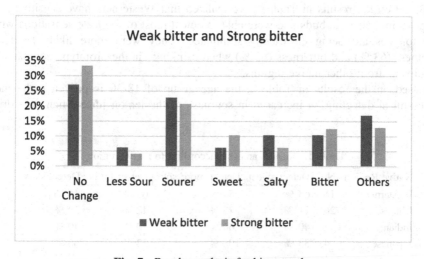

Fig. 7. Results analysis for bitter modes

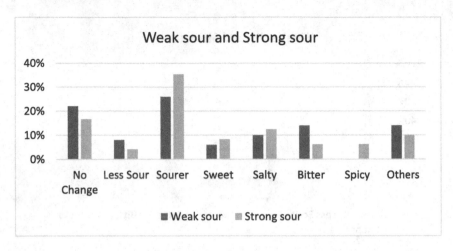

Fig. 8. Results analysis for sour modes

Sour Mode. For weak sour mode, shown in Fig. 8, corresponding to a PWM wave with duty cycle about 50-55 %, we have identified that 14 % of the participants registered a bitter taste. Another 8 % of the users detected a slightly less sour taste in the same cup of lemon juice.

For strong sour mode, corresponding to a PWM wave with duty cycle about 60-65 % there is a significant increase in the number of participants detecting an increase in sourness of the lemon juice. Some of the users found the sourness unbearable and described the juice as 'definitely more lemony'. 8 % of the participants found it amusing and delightful to detect a slight increase in sweetness while drinking the lemon juice in this mode.

Furthermore, we also categorized the results based on their native region (Table 1) and age group (Table 2) of the participants.

Based on the results in Table 1, we realized that Westerners have sensitive taste receptors in their taste buds and were able to detect most of the taste sensations when their tongues are being electrically stimulated. They were more likely to detect sweetness (63 %) and bitterness (63 %) when drinking via the prototype compared to participants from other native regions.

Based on the results in Table 2, the age group of 18-30 is proven to be most successful in detecting an increased in sourness of the lemon juice when they drink

Table 1. Results analysis according to native region

Native Region	No.	Detect sweet	Detect more sour	Detect bitter	Detect salty
Westerner	11	63 %	54 %	63 %	45 %
Chinese	26	11 %	73 %	42 %	38 %
Indian	5	40 %	60 %	40 %	40 %
Japanese	4	33 %	100 %	33 %	66 %

Table 2. Results analysis according to age group

Age Group	No.	Detect sweet	Detect more sour	Detect bitter	Detect salty
<18	16	25 %	63 %	38 %	19 %
18-30	16	13 %	94 %	25 %	38 %
31-50	12	25 %	83 %	50 %	50 %
>50	4	0	25 %	50 %	0

from the prototype. Another interesting result was that the participants from the age group between 31-50 have a higher tendency to detect a different taste as compared to the other age groups during the experiments.

4 Conclusions

Although the user study results are not highly consistent yet, from the overall user study results, we may conclude that the prototype is able to improve the drinking experience for a number of users.

Also, participants (regardless of their tasting results) all showed interests in this new digital sensation experience. They supported the idea of digitally stimulated taste sensation, as they will be able to enjoy food with less health concerns.

In order to provide a more consistent user experience for everyone, more user studies and further investigation is required. Prototype development is also worked on to provide users with a more divergent and more pleasant experiences.

Acknowledgments. This research is supported by the National Research Foundation, Prime Minister's Office, Singapore under its International Research Centre @ Singapore Funding Initiative and administered by the Interactive & Digital Media Programme Office. The first version of spoon prototype 'Taste+' is developed by Keio-NUS CUTE Center research team: staff members: Dr. Nimesha Ranasinghe, Ms. Kuan-Yi Lee, Mr. Suthokumar Gajan, and industrial design students: Mr. Hua Bin Kok, Ms. Tzu-Hsuan Yang, Ms. Gloria Huiyi Ngiam, mentored by Professor Ellen Yi-Luen Do. The Taste + spoon design won the second prize of Design Challenge at the inaugural Stanford Center on Longevity in April 2014 [18].

References

1. Huang, A.L., Chen, X., Hoon, M.A., Chandrashekar, J., Guo, W., Tränkner, D., Ryba, N.J. P., Zuker, C.S.: The cells and logic for mammalian sour taste detection. Nature **442**(7105), 934–938 (2006)
2. Farrell, K.T.: A brief look at the long history of spices. In Spices, Condiments and Seasonings, 2nd edn., pp. 5–6. Springer Science & Business Media (1998)
3. Vartanian, L.R., Brownell, K.D., Schwartz, M.B.: Effects of soft drink consumption on nutrition and health: A systematic review and meta-analysis. Am. J. Pub. Health **97**(4), 667–675 (2007)

4. Harnack, L., Stang, J., Story, M.: Soft drink consumption among US children and adolescents: nutritional consequences. J. Am. Diet. Assoc. **99**(4), 436–441 (1999)
5. Mela, D.J.: Why do we like what we like? J. Sci. Food Agric. **81**(1), 10–16 (2001)
6. Chiras, D.D.: The senses. In: Human Biology, 5th edn., p. 201. Jones & Bartlett Publishers, Sudbury (2005)
7. Ranasinghe, N., Nakatsu, R., Nii, H., Ponnampalam, G.: Tongue mounted interface for digitally actuating the sense of taste. In: 2012 16th International Symposium Wearable Computers (ISWC), pp. 80–87. IEEE Computer Society (2012)
8. Wanjek, C.: The Tongue Map: Tasteless Myth Debunked (2006). http://www.livescience.com/7113-tongue-map-tasteless-myth-debunked.html. Accessed 14 November 2014, from livescience
9. O'Connor, A.: The Claim: Tongue Is Mapped Into Four Areas of Taste (2008). http://www.nytimes.com/2008/11/11/health/11real.html?_r=2&. Accessed 10 November 2014, from The New York Times
10. Auvray, M., Spence, C.: The multisensory perception of flavor. Conscious. Cogn. **17**(3), 1016–1031 (2008)
11. Shankar, M.U., Levitan, C.A., Prescott, J., Spence, C.: The influence of color and label information on flavor. Chem. Percept. **2**, 53–58 (2009)
12. King, B., Duineveld, C.: Factors affecting the perception of naturalness and flavor strength in citrus drinks. Ann NY Acad. Sci. **855**, 847–853 (1998)
13. Zampini, M., Wantling, E., Phillips, N., Spence, C.: Multisensory flavor perception: Assessing the influence of fruit acids. Food Qual. Pref. **19**, 335–343 (2008)
14. Ranasinghe, N., Cheok, A.D., Fernando, O.N.N., Nii, H., Gopalakrishnakone, P.: Digital taste: electronic stimulation of taste sensations. In: Keyson, D.V., Maher, M.L., Streitz, N., Cheok, A., Augusto, J.C., Wichert, R., Englebienne, G., Aghajan, H., Kröse, B.J. (eds.) AmI 2011. LNCS, vol. 7040, pp. 345–349. Springer, Heidelberg (2011)
15. Ranasinghe, N., Lee, K., Do, E.Y.L.: FunRasa: an interactive drinking platform. In: Proceedings of the 8th International Conference on Tangible, Embedded and Embodied Interaction, pp. 133–136. ACM (2014)
16. National University of Singapore: Electronic spoon helps the elderly age tastefully (2014). http://news.nus.edu.sg/highlights/7686-electronic-spoon-helps-the-elderly-age-tastefully. Accessed 17 Feburary 2015
17. Ranasinghe, N., Lee, K.Y., Suthokumar, G., Do, E.Y.L.: Taste +: digitally enhancing taste sensations of food and beverages. In Proceedings of the ACM International Conference on Multimedia, pp. 737–738. ACM (2014)
18. Stanford Center on Longevity: Design Challeng Winners Announced (2014). http://longevity3.stanford.edu/design-challenge-winners-announced/. Accessed 17 Feburary 2015

Industrial and Military Applications

Assessing Performance Using Kinesic Behavior Cues in a Game-Based Training Environment

Karla A. Badillo-Urquiola[✉] and Crystal S. Maraj

Institute for Simulation and Training,
University of Central Florida, Orlando, USA
{kbadillo, cmaraj}@ist.ucf.edu

Abstract. Warfighters are trained in Behavior Cue Analysis to detect anomalies in their environment amongst several domains. This research highlights the Kinesics domain for Behavior Cue Analysis training. As efforts to transition from live, classroom-based training to distributed virtual environment training continue, investigating instructional gaming strategies that elicit improved performance and user perception becomes progressively important. Applying gaming strategies (e.g., goals, competition, feedback, etc.) to Simulation-Based Training, offers a novel approach to delivering the core curriculum for Behavior Cue Analysis. This paper examines two game-based strategies (i.e., excessive positive feedback and competition) to determine the difference in performance scores (i.e., detection and classification accuracy). The results showed no significant difference in performance; however, insight was gained on the significance of excessive positive feedback. Consequently, the paper considers the application of game-based strategies for training behavior cues, as well as discusses the limitations and alternatives for future research.

Keywords: Behavior cue detection · Game-based training · Gaming strategies · Kinesics · Performance

1 Introduction

According to the education literature, the concept of Edutainment refers to creating a learning activity that fosters excitement, engagement, and enjoyment [1, 2]. A form of Edutainment that encourages learning through the use of video games is Game-based Learning. Video games are web- or PC-based systems used often for entertainment purposes, but have applications that extend to a multitude of domains such as education, therapy, simulation, etc. The term "serious games" has evolved from Game-based Learning to describe video games for entertainment that promote learning and contain elements of instruction [3, 4]. The two instructional gaming elements of interest include excessive positive feedback and competition. Excessive positive feedback elicits a sense of power and control in the learner by providing the individual with specific information regarding their performance [5, 6]. In order for this strategy to be effective, it must not impede the learner's task objectives. On the other hand, competition provides the learner with an increasing desire to win. By utilizing a leaderboard, the individual is motivated to do well in the task which ultimately leads to learning. These

© Springer International Publishing Switzerland 2015
R. Shumaker and S. Lackey (Eds.): VAMR 2015, LNCS 9179, pp. 421–428, 2015.
DOI: 10.1007/978-3-319-21067-4_43

instructional elements can be applied to Simulation-Based Training (SBT), a method for providing structured practice and learning experiences. One area of application for SBT is the Military domain. Within the Military domain, there are increasing efforts to incorporate SBT as a supplement for classroom-based instruction and live-training on Behavior Cue Analysis. Behavior Cue Analysis is a decision-making procedure focused on training that provides the necessary preparation for strengthening Warfighters' perceptual skills. Warfighters are trained to proactively identify anomalies in an irregular and ambiguous environment by means of six domains of behavior cues (i.e., Biometrics, Kinesics, Proxemics, Geographics, Atmospherics, and Iconography/Symbolism) [7]. The procedure of Behavior Cue Analysis involves determining a baseline, detecting and classifying behavior cues, and deciding whether the behavior is an anomaly in the baseline. Figure 1 illustrate the process of Behavior Cue Analysis.

This research effort focuses on investigating personal cues (i.e., the behaviors of an individual), specifically cues in the Kinesics domain. Kinesics is the manner in which nonverbal messages are conveyed [9, 10]. Some examples of kinesic cues are gestures, facial expressions, body language, and body positioning. Past research has examined the effectiveness of kinesic cues for Behavior Cue Analysis training using SBT [11, 12]. For this research effort we examined four kinesic cues (i.e., check six, clenched fist, slap hands, and wring hands). Table 1 provides a description and classification for each cue.

This research augments previous efforts on the Kinesics domain by investigating instructional gaming strategies that elicit a motivation to learn. The three conditions

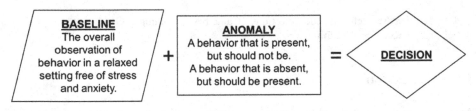

Fig. 1. Behavior Cue Detection [8]

Table 1. Kinesic Cue Descriptions and Classifications

Kinesic Cue	Description	Target State Classification
Check Six	The head turns to look over the shoulder or the body turns around 180°.	Nervous
Clenched Fist	Fingers are curled and squeezed into the palms.	Aggressive
Slap Hands	The back of one hand hits the palm of the other hand.	Aggressive
Wring Hands	Squeezing and twisting both hands together.	Nervous

(i.e., control, excessive positive feedback, and competition) were assessed using performance measures (e.g., detection and classification accuracy). The purpose of this study compared different Game-based Training (GBT) conditions to assess their effectiveness for Behavior Cue Analysis training. These findings can provide policy makers with empirical evidence for understanding the use of GBT as a method of instruction. Furthermore, the research and training communities can benefit from this line of research by utilizing GBT strategies for detecting Kinesic cues using a VE.

2 Method

2.1 Participants

A total of 91 participants were recruited from the University of Central Florida and the surrounding community. The sample included 44 females and 47 males, between the ages of 18 and 40 ($M = 21.47$, $SD = 3.71$). All participants were U.S. citizens and required to have normal or corrected to normal vision. To adhere to the U.S. Army vision requirements, participation in the experiment required full color vision according to the Ishihara's Tests for Colour Deficiency [13]. Previous participation in Behavior cue detection studies was restricted due to the similarities between the experimental tasks. Participants were compensated $10 per hour for a duration of 1.5 hours of participation.

2.2 Materials

Virtual Battlespace 2 (VBS2) Version 2.0 development software was used as the platform for this study, because of the flexibility to customize scenarios and its high quality display of kinesic cues.

2.3 Experimental Design

A between-subjects design was conducted using one independent variable (i.e., feedback) with two levels (i.e., excessive positive feedback and competition) and two dependent variables (i.e., detection accuracy and classification accuracy). A control condition was also added to compare the two levels of feedback and asses performance. For the control group, participants were asked to detect and classify targets as exhibiting aggressiveness or nervousness without any instructional support. In contrast, during the excessive positive feedback condition a small, green box appeared after every correct identification, stating "Correct Cue Identified Good Job-Keep Going!" For every three consecutive positive identifications, a larger notification box appeared stating "Three positive Identifications in a row Hit Streak Good Job, Keep Going!" Figure 2 displays the two forms of feedback. Thirdly, in the competition condition, participants were informed that a leaderboard (see Figure 3) will be shown at the beginning and the end of the experiment, as well as after each vignette. The leaderboard will show the participant's performance score. Finally, Detection accuracy

Fig. 2. Representation of the Excessive Positive Feedback Condition

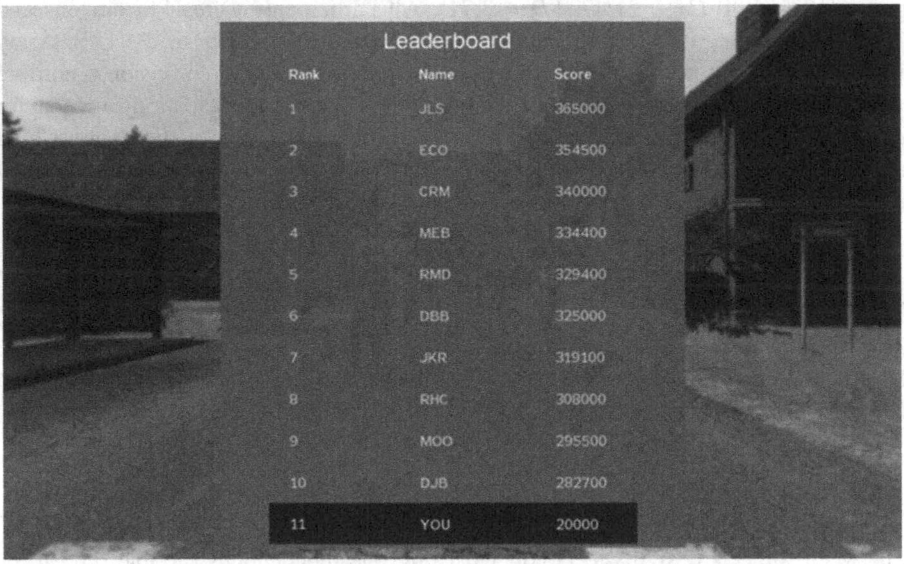

Fig. 3. Representation of the Leaderboard in the Competition Condition

measured the ratio between number of correctly identified kinesic cue targets and the total number of kinesic cue targets. Classification accuracy measured the ratio between the number of detected and classified kinesic cue targets and the total number of kinesic cue targets.

2.4 Procedure

Upon arrival, participants were asked a series of pre-experimental questions, in addition to taking the Ishihara Test for Colour Blindness [13], to verify that he or she fulfilled the study restrictions. After passing the requirements, the participant read and signed the Informed Consent document, describing the purpose, tasks, risks, and benefits to participating in the experiment. Then, a paper-based demographics questionnaire was given, asking for the participant's age, sex, highest level of education, military experience, current health state, proficiency using a computer, and video game proficiency. Next, the participant was randomly assigned to one of the three conditions: control, excessive positive feedback, and competition. The participant viewed a narrated slide presentation that familiarized him or her with the virtual environment interface and the experimental task (i.e., monitoring the virtual unmanned ground system (UGS), selecting the classification button, and clicking on the desired target). Following the interface training presentation, the participant completed a scenario, allowing him or her to practice the detection and classification experimental task. The stimuli of this scenario were colored barrels, unrelated to the additional tasks of the study, to avoid priming effects. Next, the participant viewed another set of presentation slides describing the pre-test scenario task. In the pre-test scenario, the participant was required to monitor the virtual UGS, as well as detect and classify virtual agents that exhibited aggressiveness or nervousness based on prior knowledge and experience. Following the pre-test scenario, a narrated presentation on behavior cue analysis training content was provided. The presentation covered the purpose of behavior cue analysis, the Kinesics domain, and described each target behavior cue with its associated classification. Example photographs demonstrating each target behavior were also included. Towards the end of the presentation, instructions on identifying and classifying the kinesic cues in the following scenario vignettes were provided. If the participant was assigned to the competition condition, then a three letter identifier (e.g., KAB) was requested. This was used as a way for the participant to identify his or her score at the end of the study. All initials and scores remained anonymous. A leaderboard listing past scores was shown. All participants completed four scenario vignettes. The scenarios were given in a randomized and counterbalanced order. At the end of the four scenarios, a second leaderboard with the participant's three letter identifier and score was shown to each participant in the competition condition. A final narrated presentation introducing the post-test scenario was then provided. The participant completed the post-test scenario. Finally, the participant was debriefed and dismissed.

3 Results

The normality of the distribution of scores was assessed for detection and classification accuracy, using the Kolmogorov-Smirnov statistic. Results showed a violation of the assumption of normality for both detection and classification accuracy. Due to the absence of a normally distributed curve and to better meet the assumptions of normality, the data for this experiment was transformed. The data showed signs of a negative distribution, therefore, a reflect and logarithm transformation formula was used.

A one-way between-groups analysis of variance (ANOVA) was conducted to examine the impact of game-based strategies on detection and classification accuracy. Participants were divided into three groups according to the applied instructional strategy: Group 1: control, Group 2: excessive positive feedback, and Group 3:

Table 2. Transformed Detection and Classification Accuracy Means

Condition	Detection Accuracy	Classification Accuracy
Group 1 – Control	.68	1.00
Group 2 – Excessive Positive Feedback	.67	.85
Group 3 – Leaderboard	.70	.91

Leaderboard. There was no significant difference between detection and classification scores. While the results are not statistically significant, the detection and classification accuracy means can be examined for practical significance. Table 2 displays the means for each group.

To interpret the transformed means, the lowest value becomes the highest reported value. On the other hand, the highest mean value is interpreted as the lowest score. As a result, the detection accuracy performance score for excessive positive feedback group was the highest ($M = .67$), followed by the control group ($M = .68$), then the leaderboard group ($M = .70$). The excessive positive feedback group also had the highest classification accuracy performance score ($M = .85$), however the leaderboard group ($M = .91$) performed better than the control group ($M = 1.00$).

Additionally, the influence of game-based strategies on the percent change in performance scores (i.e., detection accuracy and classification accuracy) from the pre-test scenario to the post-test scenario was assessed with a one-way between-groups ANOVAs. There was no significant difference in game-based strategies for detection and classification accuracy. However, the results support the previous findings for excessive positive feedback and its impact on performance. Overall, these results provide a foundation for investigating the role of excessive positive feedback.

4   Discussion

Although the results in this experiment are not significant, there are practical reasons to examine the means. As previously stated, the excessive positive feedback group had the best performance score. A possible explanation for this outcome could be the presentation of the feedback. Excessive positive feedback is descriptive, intended for the learner to know exactly how he or she is performing and what needs to be improved. The goal of this feedback is to improve a learner's performance without obtruding or detracting from the training task. Learners received immediate feedback during the excessive positive feedback condition, providing the opportunity to improve instantly. In contrast, the competition condition did not provide immediate feedback. The goal of the leaderboard is to measure the learner's performance with an overall score. It offers a summary of the learner's performance, but it does not guide the learner towards improvement. The learner has to wait until the end of the scenarios to receive a score. Finally, investigation into the role of excessive positive feedback and competition should examine the impact of psychological constructs (e.g., engagement and motivation) on performance. Specifically, how these measures would contribute to the previously stated research findings.

5 Limitations

An inconsistency between the training slides and the experimenter script was identified that may have contributed to the participants' performance scores. In the training slides, the instructions indicated that the leaderboard would be shown after each vignette, but it was only shown before the first vignette and after the last vignette. The participant received no feedback in between vignettes, therefore there was a limited capacity for improvement. Future research should incorporate the leaderboard after each vignette to examine whether there is an improvement in performance.

6 Conclusion

This paper incorporated instructional gaming strategies in a GBT environment to assess performance of kinesic behavior cues. Overall, this research effort provides insight and offers recommendations to the training and education community. One future recommendation involves the investigation into the rate of feedback (i.e., number of times feedback is presented) and its impact on performance. Another recommendation would be to explore areas of practical application (e.g., local and state law enforcement agencies, training and educational domains, etc.) to determine the effectiveness of the instructional strategies. Finally, despite the limitations confronted with the leaderboard, future recommendation into the full examination of the leaderboard as an instructional strategy is warranted to understand its application on Behavior Cue Analysis research.

Acknowledgements. This research was sponsored by the U.S. Army Research Laboratory–Human Research Engineering Directorate Simulation and Training Center (ARL HRED STTC), in collaboration with the Institute for Simulation and Training at the University of Central Florida. This work is supported in part by ARL HRED STTC contract W911NF-14-2-0021. The views and conclusions contained in this document are those of the authors and should not be interpreted as representing the official policies, either expressed or implied, of ARL HRED STTC or the U.S. Government. The U.S. Government is authorized to reproduce and distribute reprints for Government purposes notwithstanding any copyright notation hereon.

References

1. Okan, Z.: Edutainment and Learning. Encyclopedia of the Sciences of Learning, pp. 1080–1082. Springer, US (2012)
2. Okan, Z.: Edutainment: is learning at risk? Br. J. Edu. Technol. **34**, 255–264 (2003)
3. Erhel, S., Jamet, E.: Digital game-based learning: impact of instructions and feedback on motivation and learning effectiveness. Comput. Educ. **67**, 156–167 (2013)
4. Susi, T., Johannesson, M., Backlund, P.: Serious games- an overview. Technical report, University of Skovde, Sweden (2007)
5. Juul, J.: A Casual Revolution: Reinventing Video Games and Their Players. MIT Press, Cambridge (2010)

6. Vandewaetere, M., Cornillie, F., Clarebout, G., Desmet, P.: Adaptivity in educational games: including player and gameplay characteristics. Int. J. High. Edu. **2**(2), 106–114 (2013)
7. Gideons, C.D., Padilla, F.M., Lethin, C.: Combat hunter: the training continues. Marine Corps Gazette **92**(9), 79–84 (2008)
8. Badillo-Urquiola, K.A., Lackey, S.J., Ortiz, E.C.: Kinesic cues: how to effectively simulate body language in a virtual environment. Poster Session Presented at the Society for Advancement of Chicano and Native Americans in Science National Conference, San Antonio, TX, October 2013
9. Birdwhistell, R.L.: Kinesics and context. University of Pennsylvania Press, Philadelphia (1970)
10. Leathers, D.G.: Bodily communication. In: Leathers, D.G. (ed.) Successful Nonverbal Communication: Principles and Applications, 3rd edn, pp. 65–86. Allyn & Bacon, Boston (1997)
11. Lackey, S., Maraj, C., Salcedo, J., Ortiz, E., Hudson, I.: Assessing performance of kinesic cue analysis in simulation-based training environments. In: Proceedings of Interservice/Industry Training, Simulation, and Education Conference (2013)
12. Salcedo, J., Ortiz, E., Maraj, C., Lackey, S., Hudson, I.: Assessing engagement in simulation-based training systems for virtual kinesic cue detection training. In: Shumaker, R. (ed.) VAMR 2013, Part I. LNCS, vol. 8021, pp. 211–220. Springer, Heidelberg (2013)
13. Ishihara, S.: Ishihara's Tests for Colour Deficiency. Kanehara Trading, Tokyo (2013)

The Virtual Dressing Room: A Usability and User Experience Study

Michael B. Holte$^{(\boxtimes)}$, Yi Gao, and Eva Petersson Brooks

Department of Architecture, Design and Media Technology,
Aalborg University, Esbjerg, Denmark
{mbh,gao,ep}@create.aau.dk

Abstract. This paper presents the design and evaluation of a usability and user experience test of a virtual dressing room. First, we motivate and introduce our recent developed prototype of a virtual dressing room. Next, we present the research and test design grounded in related usability and user experience studies. We give a description of the experimental setup and the execution of the designed usability and user experience test. To this end, we report interesting results and discuss the results with respect to user-centered design and development of a virtual dressing room.

Keywords: Human-computer interaction · Usability · User experience · Virtual reality · Augmented reality · Computer graphics · Computer vision · Pose estimation · Gesture recognition · 3D imaging · 3D scanning and textile industry

1 Introduction

Online shopping has become popular, and today people are increasingly shopping online; most of them are satisfied buying certain types of goods online like books, electronics, tickets etc. But when it comes to buying clothes online, they are not entirely satisfied [1]. Many people choose not to shop online due to privacy (e.g., sharing body measurements) and security issues [2]. A report shows that there is 25 % return rate in the online clothing industry in Denmark alone. The reason for the returns at this moment can be speculated as, the clothes do not fit the customers properly or the customers simply dislike the cloth when they actually wear it. As a result there is an increase in the costs for the online retailers and dissatisfaction among the consumers. On the other hand manufactures and the retailers are striving to develop a solution that is more satisfying to their consumers with fewer returns. Apparently, the consumers are looking for more reliable solutions for buying clothes online. The industry is beginning to recognize that new technologies like virtual-reality and 3D camera-based systems have great potential to solve this problem. Hence, the virtual dressing room addresses this problem by enabling the consumers to try on the virtual version of the clothes on their virtual 3D avatar/profile before buying the real clothes.

An important aspect of designing and developing a virtual dressing room is its usability, and to this end, the user experience. Not much research has been conducted on design and development of a virtual dressing room or virtual trying-on of garments [3]. Some solutions to the problem have been developed, e.g. [4, 5]. However, these are

© Springer International Publishing Switzerland 2015
R. Shumaker and S. Lackey (Eds.): VAMR 2015, LNCS 9179, pp. 429–437, 2015.
DOI: 10.1007/978-3-319-21067-4_44

more commercial of nature, and do not address research related questions on usability and user experience.

This work presents a study on usability and user experience of a virtual dressing room. The objective of this work is to design a usability and user experience test for evaluation of a virtual dressing room. The purpose of the evaluation is to report valuable usability and user experience results, and discuss the results with respect to user-centered design and development of a virtual dressing room. Hence, the research is an attempt to answer the central question (with focus on usability and user experience): how can virtual-reality based systems benefit the online apparel shopping behavior of the consumers and enhance their shopping experience? The work is of interest for the human-computer interaction community, and in general for anyone with interest in usability, user experience, interaction design, virtual/augmented reality, computer graphics, computer vision etc.

The contributions of this work are threefold: (1) We introduce our recent developed prototype of a state-of-the-art virtual dressing room (Sect. 2). (2) We design a usability and user experience test for evaluation of a virtual dressing room, grounded in related usability and user experience studies (Sect. 3). (3) We give a description of the experimental setup and the execution of the designed usability and user experience test. To this end, we report interesting results, and discuss the outcome with respect to user-centered design and development of a virtual dressing room (Sect. 4). Finally, we give concluding remarks (Sect. 5).

2   The Virtual Dressing Room

In this section we introduce our prototype of a virtual dressing room. The virtual dressing room solution can be divided into two modules: the front-end module consisting of the avatar solution, where the avatar is a close representation of the person's size and shape, targeted customers buying cloth online, and the back-end module involving the 3D scanning of clothing to produce digital clothing for the virtual dressing room, targeted the cloth companies (see Fig. 1). This usability and user experience study is solely based on the front-end consumer interface.

Fig. 1. The virtual dressing room prototype including the front-end interactive user interface and the back-end 3D cloth scanner.

2.1   The Front-End Avatar Solution

The front-end avatar solution consists of a user interface, where first the user's body shape is measured using a Microsoft Kinect sensor. These measurements are used to morph (adjust) the body shape and size of a predefined human model in real-time according to the actual body measurements of the user, which will become the user's avatar. Hence, the user can see an avatar, with their size and shape, and through movements captured with a Microsoft Kinect, recognize and accept this avatar as a reflection of them self. Next, the user will be able to select and try on a number of different clothing using his/her avatar through a gesture-based natural user interface. Clothes are applied to the model and optimized to avoid compenetration while following the body deformations. Because the avatars size and shape will be a close representation of their own, they will be able to see how the clothes fit on them as a person.

2.2   The Back-End 3D Cloth Scanning

The clothes are made digital by scanning real clothes using a Microsoft Kinect sensor. While creating digital clothing using specialized programs, e.g. Marvelous Designer 2 [6], is a time consuming process, the 3D scanning process is relatively fast. The model is acquired via registration of different views while rotating on a platform; a complete rotation is performed approximately in 60 s, however, we have achieved satisfactory results even with rotations of 15 s. The surface is textured using the RGB images acquired during the scanning process, and the color of the occluded parts is approximated via K-Nearest Neighbors.

3   Usability and User Experience

To evaluate the usability and user experience of the developed prototype of a virtual dressing room, we present a test design including quantitative and qualitative measurements of usability and user experience. This involves measurement of utility, ease of use, efficiency, the user's motivation for using the solution, user similarity and identification with respect to the avatar, possible issues with recording and storing body measurements, and user demographics to investigate customer behavior patterns.

We adopt the System Usability Scale (SUS) [7, 8]. SUS is a scale based on a questionnaire designed to give a score of subjective usability of a digital system, and allows different systems to be compared. SUS consists of 10 questions with 5 or 7 response options for respondents, ranging from strongly agree to strongly disagree:

1. I think that I would like to use this system frequently.
2. I found the system unnecessarily complex.
3. I thought the system was easy to use.
4. I think that I would need the support of a technical person to be able to use this system.
5. I found the various functions in this system were well integrated.
6. I thought there was too much inconsistency in this system.
7. I would imagine that most people would learn to use this system very quickly.

8. I found the system very cumbersome to use.
9. I felt very confident using the system.
10. I needed to learn a lot of things before I could get going with this system.

SUS does not offer an exhaustive assessment, but a general comparable indication of the overall level of usability of a system, with low cost, and minimal strain on participants [7, 8]. SUS has become an industry standard, with references in over 1300 articles and publications. The noted benefits of using SUS include that it (1) is a very easy scale to administer to participants, (2) can be used on small sample sizes with reliable results, and (3) is valid; it can effectively differentiate between usable and unusable systems.

A large empirical evaluation of the SUS, found the scale to be a reliable and accurate for measuring usability, and to be useful for iterative design processes [9]. The evaluation was based on more than 2300 individual surveys from over 200 studies, and also introduced a set of acceptability ranges to help interpreting SUS scores. SUS scores range from 0 (negative) to 100 (positive). According to Bangor et al. [9], scores below 50 are "not acceptable", scores from 50 to 63 are "low marginal", scores from 64 to 69 are "high marginal" and scores above 70 are "acceptable".

Both Brooke [7, 8] and Bangor et al. [9] were against doing analysis on individual SUS questions, as they are very codependent. Furthermore, Banger et al. [9], recommend that SUS scores be regarded together with more specific observations and qualitative user statements. For this usability and user experience study, we combine SUS with the following demographic information, and usability and user experience questions specifically targeting the virtual dressing room:

11. Gender.
12. Age.
13. Average yearly income.
14. How frequent do you buy clothes online during a year?
15. Where would you prefer to use a virtual dressing room?
16. How do you feel about storing your user profile incl. body measurements in a private online profile?
17. Does the avatar look realistic?
18. Does the avatar move realistically according to your movements?
19. Does the avatar's body size and shape look similar to yours?
20. Can you identify yourself with the avatar?

For the 10 SUS questions and question 16 – 20 we use a Likert scale ranging from 1 to 7, where 7 is the best score and 4 is the average score. Furthermore, we use interviews for detailed qualitative user statements and video observations.

4   Experimental Results

The evaluation and data collection has been carried out in the mall "Kolding Storcenter" in Denmark. A total of 75 people took part in the experiment. The prototype was installed in a 4.5 m × 3 m black tent, which offers privacy and sufficient space for the user to move freely during virtual try-on of garments. The test setup can be seen in Figs. 1 and 2. The users where not restricted by time or number of virtual try-ons, but were given freedom to use and explore the system as they pleased while being video recorded. After, the users were asked to answer the questionnaire, and if interested, take part of a short interview.

Fig. 2. Test setup in the mall "Kolding Storcenter" in Denmark

55 % of the 75 test participants were women and 45 % men. The participants' age distribution is as follows: 1 % [1–10 years], 36 % [11–20 years], 32 % [21–30 years], 11 % [31–40 years], 8 % [41–50 years], 8 % [51–60 years] and 4 % [61–70 years]. Hence, 68 % of the participants were teenagers and young adults in the age range of 11–30 years. 43 % had an income below 100,000 DKK, 24 % [100,000–200,000 DKK], 25 % [200,000–500,000 DKK] and 3 % above 500,000 DKK. Note that the last 5 % of the participants did not answer this question. 22 % of the participants buy clothes online [0–5 times a year], 27 % [6 – 10 times a year], 8 % [11–15 times a year], 12 % [16 – 20 times a year] and 31 % more than 20 times a year. 48 % prefer to use a virtual dressing room at home, 13 % in retail stores and 39 % at both locations.

The individual SUS question results are shown in Fig. 3. The overall SUS score for the prototype is 68 ("high marginal"), which is an average usability score corresponding to 50 % percentile rank from usability testing of 500 selected studies (see Fig. 4) [10]. The score is calculated based on the SUS guidelines in [7, 8]. It should be noted that only 39 of the 75 participants answered the SUS questionnaire.

In Fig. 5 the results of question 16 to 20 are shown. The participants' feeling about storing their user profile including body measurements, scored a mean value of 3.39, hence, slight below average (average = 4.00). This indicates that the participants are not that confident about having an online body profile. The prototype is scoring mean values of 3.51, 4.36, 3.59 and 3.16 with respect to the four realism aspects: avatar appearance, movement, body size and shape, and self-identification. With a score of 4.36, the realism of the avatar movement according to the user is rated highest by the participants, while the VDR is rated slightly below average with respect to the other three realism aspects. This indicates that the Kinect-based skeleton tracker used for animating the movement of the avatar is an acceptable solution. In contrast, the appearance, body size and shape of the avatar are found less realistic. Although the

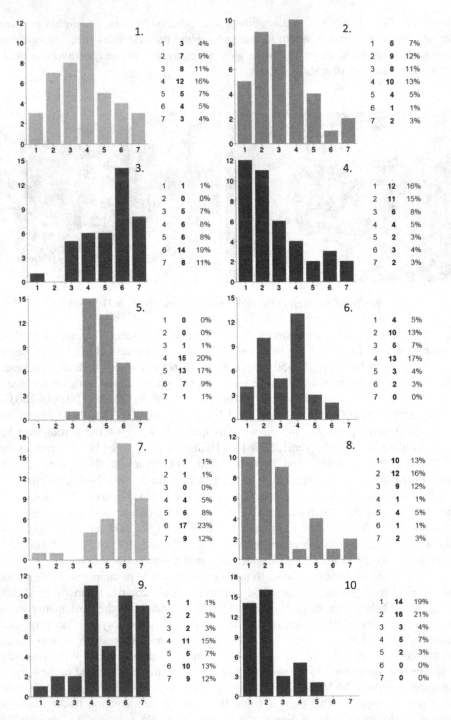

Fig. 3. Plots showing the distribution of the responses to each of the 10 SUS questions. Note that the respective SUS question number is shown at the top right of each plot.

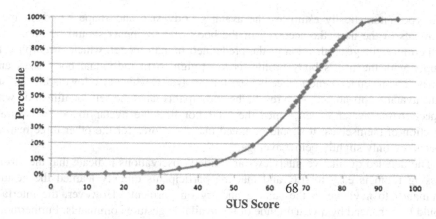

Fig. 4. The figure shows the percentile ranking of usability testing using SUS. The evaluated virtual dressing room prototype produce a SUS score of 68, which is an average usability score corresponding to 50 % percentile rank from usability testing of 500 selected studies [10].

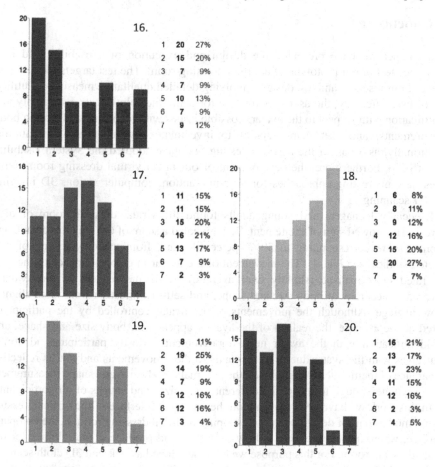

Fig. 5. Results of question 16 to 20 in form of plots of Likert scale scores from 1 to 7. Note that the respective question number is shown at the top right of each plot.

prototype automatically estimates the avatar's body size and shape based on measurements of the user, the accuracy of the body measurements should be improved. Furthermore, the generalization of the predefined human model, which is morphed to comply with the user's body profile, is too rough to fit individual body sizes and shapes. To this end, a generic face is used for the avatar, which also lowers the realism of the avatar's appearance. As a result, the participants rated the self-identification with respect to the avatar lowest, since they did not find the avatar to be an accurate reflection of themselves. It should be noted that the scores for the other three realism aspects are only slightly below average.

The detailed qualitative interviews and video observations indicate that the virtual dressing room is easy to use, and that the participants quickly learned the gesture commands to navigate in the catalog and try on garments. However, the interface should be enhanced by a visual guide of the available gesture commands. Furthermore, feedback on optimal size of garments and the possibility to try different sizes are desired improvements to the prototype.

5 Conclusion

In this paper we have presented the design and execution of a usability and user experience test of our prototype of a virtual dressing room. The test targets the different aspect of our research and test design, involving detailed qualitative measures of utility, ease of use, efficiency, the user's motivation for using the solution, user similarity and identification with respect to the avatar, possible issues with recording and storing body measurements, and user demographics to investigate customer behavior patterns. Additionally, as a part of the usability testing, we have adopted the System Usability Scale (SUS). Furthermore, the development of our novel virtual dressing room introduces new interesting approaches for user interaction, computer vision, 3D imaging and 3D scanning.

Especially teenagers and young adults found the virtual dressing room of high interest, and showed sign of excitement. SUS revealed a score of 68, which is an average usability score corresponding to 50 % percentile rank from usability testing of 500 selected studies (see Fig. 4). The movement of the avatar in correspondence to the user was rated most realistic (slightly over average), while the realism of the avatar's appearance, accuracy of body size and shape, and self-identification were rated slightly below average. Although the movements of the avatar controlled by the participants scored above average, the realism of the avatars appearance, body size and shape, and self-identification with the avatar need improvements. Mostly participants identified themselves with the avatar due to its responds to their movements and not its reflective appearance of themselves. Additionally, the automatic body size and shape measurement is not accurate enough to reflect the different body sizes and shapes of all participants.

In this work we have been focusing on the customer interface of the virtual dressing room. Another part of designing and developing a virtual dressing room is the company interface, where a major concern is how to design and produce digital clothes for the virtual dressing room. For this purpose we have developed a back-end 3D cloth scanner, which would be interesting to test in another usability and user experience study.

Acknowledgements. The research leading to these results has received funding from The Danish National Advanced Technology Foundation under the research project "Virtual Dressing Room".

References

1. Schaupp, L.C., Belanger, F.: A conjoint analysis of online consumer satisfaction. J Electron. Comm. Res. **6**(2), 95–111 (2005)
2. Hoffman, D.L., Novak, T.P., Peralta, M.: Building consumer trust online. Commun. ACM **42**(4), 80–85 (1999)
3. Holte, M.B.: The virtual dressing room: a perspective on recent developments. In: Shumaker, R. (ed.) VAMR 2013, Part II. LNCS, vol. 8022, pp. 241–250. Springer, Heidelberg (2013)
4. LazyLazy.com. http://lazylazy.com/en-DK/content/shoppingfeatures
5. Fitnect Interactive Kft., 2040 Budaörs, Hungary. http://www.fitnect.hu
6. Marvelous Designer. Product. http://www.marvelousdesigner.com/marvelous/Default.aspx
7. Brooke, J.: SUS - a quick and dirty usability scale. In: Jordan, P.W., Thomas, B., Weerdmeester, B.A., McClelland, A.L. (eds.) Usability Evaluation in Industry. Taylor and Francis, London (1996)
8. Brooke, J.: SUS: A Retrospective. A Retros. J. Usabil. Stud. **8**(2), 29–40 (2013)
9. Bangor, A., Kortum, P.T., Miller, J.T.: An empirical evaluation of the system usability scale. Int. J. Hum.-Comput. Inter. **24**(6), 574–594 (2008)
10. Sauro, J.: Measuring Usability with the System Usability Scale (SUS). http://www.measuringusability.com/sus.php

Occlusion Management in Augmented Reality Systems for Machine-Tools

Claudia Gheorghe$^{(\boxtimes)}$, Didier Rizzotti, François Tièche,
Francesco Carrino, Omar Abou Khaled, and Elena Mugellini

University of Applied Sciences and Arts Western Switzerland,
Delémont, Switzerland
{claudia.gheorghe,didier.rizzotti,
francois.tieche}@he-arc.ch, {francesco.carrino,
omar.abouKhaled,elena.mugellini}@hes-so.ch

Abstract. Nowadays, augmented reality systems must be as realistic as possible. A major issue of such a system is to present the augmentations as an integrated part of the environment. Sometimes the virtual parts must be placed and hidden partially or even totally behind a real object. This problem is known under the name of "occlusion problem". In this paper we present a pragmatic solution to manage the occlusion problem based on the prior knowledge of the position and shape of the real objects in two particular scenarios. Only the conception and the qualitative evaluation of the developed system are detailed down the line.

Keywords: Augmented reality · Occlusion · 3D tracking · 3D modeling

1 Introduction

Augmented reality systems enhance a real scene caught by a camera with virtual objects, in real time. The first augmented reality applications were based on marker tracking and consisted of only superposing basic augmentations on the real scene, like: text, images or simple 3D objects.

Further, more advanced technology has been developed using marker less tracking on 2D image or 3D objects. These technologies are usually based on computer vision or depth cameras, but they can also be combined with other devices like accelerometer, GPS, compass, and deployed on mobile devices. Nowadays, augmented reality is useful in many applications: military, industrial, medical but also gaming, commercial and entertaining.

The key measure of an AR system is how realistically it integrates augmentations with the real world. In the simplest systems, the augmentations are superposed to the image of real environments and they always appear in front of the real objects. In a more realistic approach the virtual and real objects are coexisting and real objects can also be placed in front of virtual ones. In this paper, we introduce a solution to manage the occlusion in augmented reality systems.

Our project proposes a solution tested in two specific cases:

- An application simulating the machining of a virtual piece on a real machine-tool.
- An application creating a "magical mirror" in which a patient can see his face reflection wearing a virtual dental prosthesis.

© Springer International Publishing Switzerland 2015
R. Shumaker and S. Lackey (Eds.): VAMR 2015, LNCS 9179, pp. 438–446, 2015.
DOI: 10.1007/978-3-319-21067-4_45

We focus our discussion on the first case because the methodology used and the solution tested is the same in the two cases. For the second case, only the differences and the results will be presented.

2 Background and Related Work

Realistic merging of virtual and real requires that the virtual objects behave in a physical manner in the created environment: they can be occluded or shadowed by the real objects around. Theoretically, this can be attained by comparing the depth of each object on the scene and place them accordingly. In practice, different teams proposed different solutions.

To the best of our knowledge, in 1997 Berger [1] published the first algorithm that managed this problem by tracking the objects that can cause occlusion in the 3D scene using image analysis. Since then, several improvements have been proposed: Tian et al. [2] 2010 and Sanches et al. [3] 2012 have used the same method, while Lepetit et al. [4] used stereovision-based approaches to improve the 3D tracking.

With a similar concept, Kamat et al. [5] used "Time of Flight" (TOF) cameras, achieving better results in terms of speed and robustness.

A team from the Tübingen University (Fischer et al. [6]) proposed an approach based on the prior knowledge of the shape and position of the objects that may cause occlusion. Although limited to a specific application, their method was capable of generating augmented images, in which virtual objects appeared correctly overlapped or occluded by the patient anatomy.

In 2012, Dong et al. [7] tried to combine a depth-sensing TOF camera with frame buffer algorithms. The depth information was processed in parallel using OpenGL shading language (GLSL) and render-to-texture (RTT) techniques.

A most recent work of Leal-Meléndrez et al. [8], from 2013, presented a strategy based on Kinect sensor. The distances between real and virtual objects are calculated and the occluded parts of the virtual object are removed from the scene.

The solution proposed by our project is a combination of the last two approaches: the prior knowledge of the environment with frame buffer algorithms ([6, 7]). This solution is tested in the two specific and complementary scenarios:

- A known environment with rigid and moving objects, where the position of the camera does not change.
- An unknown environment with deformable and moving objects, where the position of the camera changes.

3 First Use Case

3.1 Scenario

In the first scenario we choose to test our algorithm in a known environment, the inside of machine tool, where the objects, the piece and the tools, are rigid and the position of the camera doesn't change.

For this scenario we are simulating the machining of a virtual piece on a real machine-tool in real time. The machine is a single-spindle, automatic turning with CNC, EvoDeco 16a, produced by Tornos SA. EvoDeco is a high-end machine, designed to create small pieces with a diameter up to 16 mm (see Fig. 1). The machine has a Fanuc CNC system and an integrated computer. The CNC controls all the machine functionalities: the movements of the working piece and the displacement of the tools on each tool system.

Fig. 1. EvoDeco 16a

First of all, for a better understanding of the project a brief introduction of how the machine works is required. The machine has four *independent* tool systems (1 → yellow, 2 → orange, 3 → blue, 4 → green and brown as depicted in Fig. 2), consisting in 10 translations and 6 rotating axes. Each of these systems can hold several tools and they can have two or three degrees of freedom. Different tools can be used to shape the raw material into the wanted form. Within our project only the first system (with 2 degree of freedom) is used. The red part in the Fig. 2 is the spindle and it is used

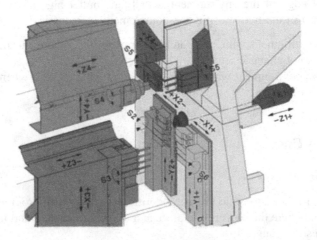

Fig. 2. EvoDeco tools system

to hold the raw material bar. The spindle has 2 axes: one for the rotation and one for the translation. This means the bar is continuously rotating and moving on a horizontal line (left-right on the Fig. 2) while the active tool can execute the cutting.

In a normal workflow process:

- The operator of the machine designs the piece.
- He/she chooses the appropriate raw material bar and puts it into the spindle part.
- He/she chooses the appropriate tools to cut the bar and fixes them onto the right support.
- He/she programs the machine, providing a sequence of movement instructions to follow on the different axes.

The innovative part of this project is to use the AR for machining the piece. The machine is a close and secure environment. Using AR the users can have an overview of what is happening inside the machine and how the raw bar is shaped in real time. AR application gives a more immersive perception of the whole experiment and it can be used as a sales or control tool.

Even if the piece is machined in a virtual environment, the normal workflow of the machine must be followed, and therefore the piece must be designed first. We choose to create a simple piece of 30 mm length and 12 mm diameter, made of brass. It is composed of three cylinders of the same length but with different diameters (see Fig. 3).

Fig. 3. Example of a final piece

The needed tools are: a cutting tool for the initial and final cut and a 90° burin for the rest of the form. A file containing a sequence of movements must also be provided to the machine. The only difference with a real machining is that the machine is working without any material bar, in a so called *matterless* state (Fig. 4).

As any normal AR system requires a camera, an IDS uEye 5250 is placed inside the machine oriented towards the spindle and the main tools that are used for machining the piece. The position of the camera was carefully chosen to avoid disturbing the normal flow of the machine. Finally, we attached the camera to the machine wall with a magnetic support. The near machine lamp lighted up the machine interior.

The simulation is working on a computer connected to the machine. The rendering can be seen on a screen nearby the machine (see Fig. 4).

3.2 Methods

The technical approach of the solution for the occlusion problem is described below.

3D Models and Animations. The real piece that we are simulating in AR is changing her shape continuously according to the machine program. The same behavior must be

Fig. 4. Working environment

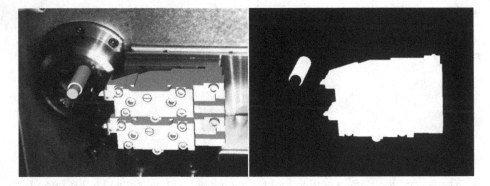

Fig. 5. Scene without occlusion algorithm (on the left) and occlusion mask (on the right)

reproduced on the virtual environment. The solution adopted is to create a 3D model of a cylinder of 30 mm length and 12 mm in diameter which represents the initial bar and to apply a deformation to this model for simulating the real machining. To achieve a good quality performance trade off the initial cylinder is modeled by using a lot of little stacked cylinder slices (more precisely, 30 slices). By knowing the exact movements of the machine from the machine program, we pre-calculated the deformation before the visualization is rendered on the scene. The deformation consists in changing the diameter of each little cylinder that collided with the active tool.

However, the piece is not the only 3D model used in the simulation. In order to implement our occlusion solution, we also created the 3D models for each object interacting with the piece on the real machine: in our case, the two tools used on the real machine to cut the piece and the spindle that holds the metallic bar. Because those parts are more complex than a simple cylinder, a modeling tool is used (3DS Max) and the result is imported into the simulation program. An animation sequence is created using the same machine program in order to apply the movements of the real tools to their virtual representation.

Occlusion Management. The most important part of this project is the management of the occlusion. The proposed solution is based on a prior knowledge about the sizes and the positions of the objects which will partially hide the augmentations. Having this information we create geometrical representation of those objects and we add them into the virtual world. The next step is to use frame buffer algorithms to replace the pixels of those objects with the pixels of the same object rendered in the video image. The resulting image is rendered to the screen.

A 3D model of each of these objects is created and added in the virtual world. Initially, the spindle is not moving however the piece is moving. Thus at the beginning only a little part of the piece is visible while in the end the whole piece will be exposed. As for the tools, they are continuously moving to shape the material into the final piece. In some frames they can be in front of the piece, hiding it either partially or totally. In the virtual world, those cases are managed by the 3D engine (OpenSceneGraph) by using occlusion culling algorithms that disable the rendering of objects when they are not currently seen by the camera. Using only the objects that generate occlusions we create a mask at each frame. The white pixels in the mask (Fig. 5, on the right) represent the position of this objects caught for one frame. Using this mask we replace them with the pixels found into the same location on the video image. The resulting image is shown at the screen and is creating the visual effect of the real tool cutting a virtual piece.

Fig. 6. Occlusion mask (left) and the scene as resulted from the occlusion algorithm

The Communication Between the Simulation and the Machine. The simulation is performed in real time. On the screen the user will see the machining of the virtual piece using the real tools. The two worlds must be synchronized to achieve this state. The machine is working due to the machine program. The same file is parsed and used to animate the virtual representation of machine parts. At the same time the two of them must move together. An IP connection was established to assure the communication between the machine and the simulation. This connection allows us to periodically require the current status of the machine. According to the state of the machine the pre-calculated piece animation is updated (paused or played).

4 Second Use Case

4.1 Scenario

In the second scenario, a more challenging environment was tested. This simulation shows to the user an augmented image of herself/himself wearing his new dental prosthesis. Therefore, the camera is moving and the objects are deformable. We chose to limit the final demo to a full dental prosthesis having the same color for each user. This case is much more complex from a technical point of view, because a tracking system must be developed in order to place the prosthesis at the right place on the user's image. A Kinect depth camera was replacing the simple IDS camera. Using Kinect allowed us to track the relative position of the user, and in particular her/his face, to the camera.

4.2 Methods

In this case, a virtual prosthesis was modeled using the same 3D modeling tool, 3DS Max. For a higher degree of freedom two models were used: one for the upper jaw and another for the lower jaw.

The real challenging part of this simulation was to place the prosthesis on the right position on the user image. The Kinect face tracking is used to determine the user position relative to the camera. The face tracking outputs the position of 100 points on the tracked face. The closer points to the interest zone are the tip of the nose and chin. Those points are used as the reference points to approximate the exact position of the prosthesis at each frame. An animation sequence is used to translate on the vertical axis the two models according to the mouth opening. The distance between the two reference points is computed each frame and is compared with the default distance which corresponds to the "mouth close" state.

In this second scenario the environment is not known and the interactions between the real parts and the virtual parts are very different. The virtual parts, the teeth, are visible only when the user smiles or opens the mouth. Using Kinect Face tracking, we could retrieve the mouth contour at each frame. This contour is used to create the replacement mask (Fig. 6, left). In this case all the pixels that are outside the mouth opening are replaced with the pixels on the video image caught by the Kinect RGB camera. The finale image is rendered to the screen and the result can be seen in the Fig. 6 (right).

5 Discussion

The preliminary tests we performed during this study showed a series of interesting points to be analyzed and developed in future works.

The simulation of the virtual piece is very realistic. The solutions chosen to solve the challenges of this application show very good results. The application is synchronized with the machine. The piece is shaped according to the movements of the

Fig. 7. Final scene with occlusion

machine and thanks to our occlusion management the real tools can be seen in front of the piece (Fig. 8).

For the next steps, it will be interesting to extend the system to a different piece with a more complex shape, or to another machine. Furthermore, we can imagine a system where more than one camera is used in order to have different angles of view or a system where the user can control the camera movements. Finally, in order to make the integration more realistic, it will be interesting to change the lights and shadows of the virtual world accordingly with the light conditions of the real world.

The second scenario was more complex to treat. Therefore, the results of the simulation were less stable compared to the first scenario. The management of the occlusion is working well but the tracking is not always so robust. In the present implementation we used the first version of Kinect for Windows which has some limitations: the user must be positioned at a minimum distance of 50 cm from the camera and he should remain in the field of vision of the camera (57.5° horizontal × 43.5° vertical). A good improvement of the developed system will be to use a more efficient device for tracking the user position, like Kinect version 2 or another device. Furthermore, we can imagine changing the dental prosthesis color to adapt to the user's features, or using partial prosthesis accordingly to the user's needs.

6 Conclusion

Occlusion management could be a big improvement for augmented reality in different fields of applications. It allows:

- Making the integration between real and virtual world seamless.
- Increasing the immersion offered by AR application.
- Opening the door to numerous applications otherwise impossible

In this work, we developed a system for managing the occlusion problem of augmented reality systems and we tested it on two concrete cases. We chose this particular approach for at least two reasons: the first one was to gather knowledge while starting with a controlled environment and then, to apply this experience to a more complex case to study the current limitations. The second reason was to ensure that our solution is reliable and adaptable to various situations.

Despite the limitations discussed in the previous section, most of them resulting from the limitations of the tracking device, this work has brought us one step closer to a realistic and easy way to use augmented reality applications out of the lab. The quick evolution of new devices available on the market might soon close the gap by providing a more accurate tracking.

For what concerns the use of augmented reality in the field of machines-tools, we think virtual machining is quite promising. We can imagine also other applications like machines-tools teaching, machines-tools maintenance, and marketing applications.

Finally, we have to continue to explore others technologies and approaches to apply them in other fields of application.

References

1. Berger, M.-O.: Resolving occlusion in augmented reality: a contour based approach without 3D reconstruction. In: 1997 IEEE Computer Society Conference
2. Tian, Y., Guan, T., Wang, C.: Real-time occlusion handling in augmented reality based on an object tracking approach In: Sensors (2010)
3. Sanches, S., Tokunaga, D.M., Silva, V.F., Sementille, A.C., Tori, R.: Mutual occlusion between real and virtual elements in augmented reality based on fiducial markers. In: 2012 IEEE Workshop on the Applications of Computer Vision (2012)
4. Lepetit, V., Berger, M.-O.: Handling occlusion in augmented reality systems: a semi-automatic method. In: IEEE and ACM International Symposium on Augmented Reality 2000 (2000)
5. Kamat, V.R., Dong, S.: Resolving incorrect visual occlusion in outdoor augmented reality usingtof camera and opengl frame buffer. In: Proceedings of 2011 NSF CMMI Engineering Research and Innovation Conference (2011)
6. Fischer, J., Bartz, D., Strasser, W.: Occlusion Handling for Medical Augmented Reality using a Volumetric Phantom Model. In: VRST 2004 (2004)
7. Dong, S., Feng, C., Kamat, V.: Real-time occlusion handling for dynamic augmented reality using geometric sensing and graphical shading. J. Comput. Civ. Eng. 27(6), 607–621 (2013)
8. Leal-Meléndrez, J.A., Altamirano-Robles, L., Gonzalez, J.A.: Occlusion handling in video-based augmented reality using the kinect sensor for indoor registration. In: Ruiz-Shulcloper, J., Sanniti di Baja, G. (eds.) CIARP 2013, Part II. LNCS, vol. 8259, pp. 447–454. Springer, Heidelberg (2013)

Human-Computer Collaboration in Adaptive Supervisory Control and Function Allocation of Autonomous System Teams

Robert S. Gutzwiller, Douglas S. Lange$^{(\boxtimes)}$, John Reeder,
Rob L. Morris, and Olinda Rodas

Space and Naval Warfare Systems Center Pacific, San Diego, CA, USA
{robert.s.gutzwiller1,doug.lange,john.reeder,
rob.morris,maria.rodas}@navy.mil

Abstract. The foundation for a collaborative, man-machine system for adaptive performance of tasks in a multiple, heterogeneous unmanned system teaming environment is discussed. An autonomics system is proposed to monitor missions and overall system attributes, including those of the operator, autonomy, states of the world, and the mission. These variables are compared within a model of the global system, and strategies that re-allocate tasks can be executed based on a mission-health perspective (such as relieving an overloaded user by taking over incoming tasks). Operators still have control over the allocation via a task manager, which also provides a function allocation interface, and accomplishes an initial attempt at transparency. We plan to learn about configurations of function allocation from human-in-the-loop experiments, using machine learning and operator feedback. Integrating autonomics, machine learning, and operator feedback is expected to improve collaboration, transparency, and human-machine performance.

Keywords: Autonomics · Autonomous systems · Supervisory control · Task models

1 Introduction

Human roles in unmanned vehicle command and control (C2) are in flux, transitioning between responsibility for one situated vehicle, to a supervisor responsible for many abstracted, automated vehicles [1, 2]. This supervisory role is very similar to military command and control in terms of providing commanders intent to agents, planning and monitoring their actions, intervening if necessary, and learning from feedback about how the mission is being performed [3, 4]. The rapid advance of technology and recent autonomous ship trials prove such role transitions are imminent for the warfighter [5].

Understanding and improving human-machine teaming is needed to aid future supervisors [6]. In the current paper, we provide the first steps for our adaptive function allocation methods. These help guide our ultimate goal of autonomics implementation for human-machine cooperation with teams of autonomous heterogeneous vehicles.

Many systems benefit from human-centered integration [7–9], although automating tasks occasionally has notable downsides, such as lowered situation awareness,

© Springer International Publishing Switzerland 2015
R. Shumaker and S. Lackey (Eds.): VAMR 2015, LNCS 9179, pp. 447–456, 2015.
DOI: 10.1007/978-3-319-21067-4_46

increased workload and increased operator complacency [10–13]. Costs of automation are sometimes a function of human attention allocation. A complacent operator allocates attention differently than an attentive one who is constantly checking up on automated systems or teams [13].

As a human supervisor, tasks require four general information processing phases; acquiring information, analyzing it, coming to a decision and executing it. Automation of a task within each phase may vary across a single automated system [14], but there usually are tradeoffs in performance and attention as a result. These tradeoffs are more favorable for higher degrees of automation of information acquisition and analysis, compared to the automation of decisions - but there are always tradeoffs ([15, 16]). In part, adaptive systems are an answer to this problem. However, an open question is about how to divide functions and tasks between automation and humans. In the unmanned system domain, especially, this is a pressing issue because automation is necessary but the demand to maintain awareness for the task, and transparency in the available automation, are both high.

2 Methods

We have chosen a "playbook" approach to the supervision of multiple unmanned vehicles [17–19] as one potential solution in a wide spectrum of control abstractions, in part because decision making is left to the operator (choosing plays), and because of the documented benefits of these systems in the literature [19–21]. These systems can be made to adapt to the environment, operator and the tasks at hand [20]. Adaptation in this sense represents updating "who does what" dynamically, in addition to determining task sequences and deadlines, and adapting information presentation [22]. These adaptive approaches typically outperform static levels-of-automation approaches [8, 21].

Function allocation schemes should reflect the contextual dynamics of real-world supervision. The lack of dynamics is exactly what is poorly addressed by static LOA perspectives [23, 24]. Therefore we focus on methods that allow for adaptation of task performance with automation, understanding that dynamics encompass a wide range of possibilities. Determining which are useful is something that machine learning may aid, but this is a long term goal not addressed in detail here. In order to implement an adaptive system in the context of multiple, heterogeneous vehicle command and control, we are also employing the use of autonomics to help achieve system goals.

Autonomic approaches manage complex systems such that they exhibit self-adaptation in response to demands on the system or degradation of performance. One such autonomics approach is the Rainbow autonomics framework (Fig. 1), developed at Carnegie Mellon University (CMU) [25]. Rainbow employs an architecture-based, self-adaptation approach that models the managed system through an architecture description language, receives information from the system through gauges from probes that read data from different points within the managed system, and then executes strategies. These strategies provide instruction on how the managed system should adapt to sensed changes in order to maintain "health" (which can be characterized with different metrics).

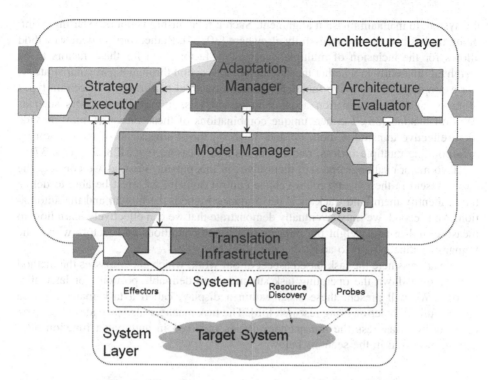

Fig. 1. The rainbow autonomics framework. [From 25]

In a system consisting of teams of unmanned vehicles under the supervisory control of a single operator, necessarily there must exist some level of autonomy for the vehicles to operate without the operator being responsible for remote operation [26]. As the number of vehicles, and teams of vehicles begins to proliferate, there also must be enough automation to assist the supervisor in managing a large complex situation, which rapidly overwhelms the limitations of memory, attention, and basic human performance (e.g., [27]). Adaptation becomes a question of whether autonomy should be in charge (and allocating tasks), and the relative level at which the autonomy should be operating within a range - from completely manual to largely automatic performance [20, 28, 29]. Movement along this range has been used to reduce workload for operators in demanding tasks.

The autonomics framework can play a central role in controlling such a "sliding scale" of autonomy, allowing for adaptive automation approaches in supervisory control. Because the primary role of Rainbow is to observe and maintain holistic system and mission health, autonomics can adjust the level of autonomy based upon multiple conditions within the system. These conditions may include operator workload [30] and attention allocation [31, 32], attention required for a task, risk associated with a task or with the autonomy, risk associated with failing to act, operator input on autonomy allowance [33], and other such determinable parameters.

For example, when autonomics detects an overloaded operator, it could set the autonomy level higher, potentially relieving the burden on the operator and allowing the system to maintain mission alignment. Such a relationship is not our starting point, though it has been done successfully elsewhere [30, 34]. Rather, our particular method allows for the inclusion of multiple, measurable factors, and for these factors to be weighted differently in whether the autonomy takes action through a particular strategy. For example, while adaptive function allocation may aid performance of certain types of tasks, such as information acquisition or analysis, it may harm others such as decision making [35]. Further, unique combinations of these measures may provide more effective transitions, both up and down on the sliding scale of automation by incorporating multiple factors, rather than a single measure (e.g., [28, 29], [36, 37]).

Two major challenges present themselves in this pursuit. First, as we consider the tasks present in the existing multi-vehicle control domain, we must be able to define them, identify them, and track their performance by both the human and the automation. And second, we must eventually demonstrate that we can effectively learn how to measure, utilize and weight the impacts of various conditions and factors within the human-machine system to adapt the allocation sets.

We address here the task-based aspect of our work, which encompasses the method used to breakdown the operating task structure into definable portions for later allocations. We will present these tasks within a display, called a task manager, used successfully in other ongoing research [38]. The task manager also provides us with an opportunity to address the transparency issues involved in automated function allocation, discussed in the sections below.

3   Task Model

3.1   Task Methods Hierarchy

Providing assistance to supervisors in managing and performing tasks requires assisting automation to have some model of the tasks involved. Task models have been well studied and reviewed. Our approach traces its roots to the task structures defined by Chandrasekaran et al. [39]. Chandrasekaran's task structure is a bipartite directed acyclic graph (DAG) of tasks, methods and subtasks. As in most DAG structures, these components may be applied recursively. The bipartite and recursive nature of this task structure results in tasks decomposed into methods, which in turn are composed of subtasks, which are simply tasks themselves.

Tasks represent elements that must be performed in order to execute the method. Methods are alternative approaches to completing a task. Therefore, the DAG has characteristics of decision trees as well (Fig. 2).

Task generation can occur either through user initiation, or agents that recognize particular properties within the system. When that happens, a task, defined in the structure above, gets created and then must be queued for a supervisor, or an autonomous agent assisting a supervisor. The systems first decisions are who will perform the task and by what method. Some methods may only be suitable for human efforts, and some for computer. Some tasks require collaborative efforts, where some of the sub-tasks are performed by human supervisors and others by automation.

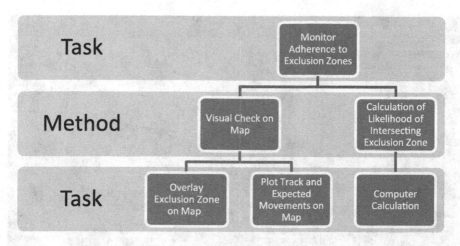

Fig. 2. Example structure: the bipartite nature creates alternating levels of tasks and methods

Algorithms can be used to make initial decisions or suggestions concerning tasking. With proper instrumentation this decision can be made by considering properties of the environment; the attention available from the supervisor with the history of the supervisor's performance for this type of task, other ongoing tasks, their current workload, authorizations; the user-automation working agreements which help define and constrain who can do what (and when they can do it); and the mission's goals.

These granular tasks and their associated methods represent a breakdown of the multiple vehicle task space. They will be unique to a specific platform or unmanned C2 system; yet the principles on which our measurements, and the autonomics system are based may have wider applicability. For example, Rainbow can sit "on top" of other systems, an does not interfere with their operations – therefore it can be integrated somewhat easily into existing systems, and the majority of the work is in developing the appropriate probes and gauges for the system to sample information through.

3.2 Task Manager Display

To provide visibility to the user and ultimate control over tasking, our initial task management system was developed. It will allow the user, as well as the autonomic controls, to reprioritize tasking for the human and autonomous assistant. The display itself provides information on the current tasking for both entities (Fig. 3).

While allowing the user to dictate allocation necessarily adds to the load for the operator, it allows the operator awareness of the tasks "to be done" in the scenario as well. Even if no tasks were to be performed by an automated agent, the task management interface provides an aid to the operator concerning tasks to be completed (reducing the demands on prospective memory; [40, 41]). The use of such an interface is a starting point for incorporating basic intent inference, as was done in prior programs, allowing us to facilitate tasks when they are selected by the operator to be completed, by pulling up the relevant task information for a given method. The instrumentation of the task

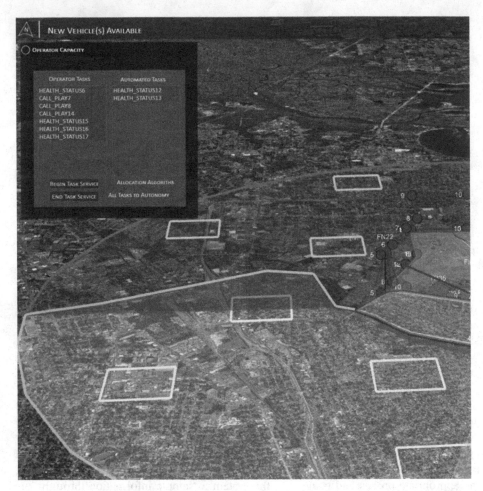

Fig. 3. Initial Prototype of Task Manager Displaying Simple User Interface with Task Queues

manager will also provide us, as researchers, the important data concerning task shedding and other task management behaviors including switching, and the effects of interruptions – both known issues in this domain.

Finally, the task manager also provides some insight into the operations of the autonomy. For example, if the autonomy senses operator overload and begins to task authorized tasks to the automation but the user is not actually overloaded, this will be self-evident by examining the automation's task queue. As we explore methods of prioritization within the queues themselves, potentially giving the automation authority to appropriately weight the importance of certain tasks for the human operator to aid in decision making, the interface will be expanded to incorporate and present information on how priority decisions were made. It may even be possible to allow the working agreement between the human and the automation to include an agreed-upon priority ranking to develop expectations between the two entities.

4 Risk-Attention Metric

Ultimately, if we are to choose between supervisor(s) and autonomous assistant(s) for performing tasks, we need to weigh the capabilities of each against current load, and utilize known human factors in the decision. The human factors utilized are meant to ensure that we maximize the collaborative decision making and performance ability of the human-computer team. One way to do that is to balance risk vs. attention. The fundamental idea is that if the most capable agent to do a particular action is available, i.e., the one that reduces risk in performance of the action, it would be the natural agent to select if all agents (human as well as autonomous) were completely available.

However, when available attention is not uniform or abundant, we need to balance taking on risk to manage attention. This is something humans naturally do, though they may not be optimal. This is further complicated by the risks posed by human performance factors, such as the need for situational awareness and understanding what the automation is doing.

If the workload is fairly light, we want the operator to pay attention to more tasks, despite the computer being able to help. This will help keep operator situational awareness up and prevent operators from becoming overly complacent concerning the remaining automation. If the workload is heavy enough to put operations at risk because of limited operator attention availability, then we want the computer (or other people) to perform more of the tasks. Therefore, we want to utilize scores concerning the ability of the computer to perform a task, relative to the ability of the human supervisors to perform the same task; however our approach differs in that it is also weighing contextual and adaptive factors, and that some operations will be limited by our incorporation of working agreements. The difference between which agents do what is essentially a measure of the risk in turning the task over to that agent. There is additional interest in using this metric to evaluate the teaming of humans and automation to perform certain tasks (e.g., a truly collaborative "method" for performance), which may rank lower on risk than either agent performing alone.

Measuring attention availability is more difficult. At its most straightforward, we can measure how far behind schedule the task queue has become. Every task will have some deadline (hard or soft), and tasks will have a distribution of predicted durations depending on who has been assigned the task. It becomes an easy matter to count the number of times that deadlines are missed over a particular time window as one fundamental attribute of performance: it is by no means the only one. More advanced methods that measure other actions by the operators, biometrics [32], and other characteristics of the tasks may be beneficial and could be incorporated when available.

As this is work in progress, we have not yet experimented to find the appropriate range of risk/attention values for maintaining situational awareness of both the automation, and the tasks themselves. This is the essence of the experimentation that we will begin with the prototype task manager in late 2015. As a final note, we have alluded to the use of machine learning to determine what an optimal configuration of function allocations may be, based on recent developments in measuring their efficacy [24]. These measures require user performance as well, but represent a further stage of development for this work, and one that holds great promise for helping to determine appropriate allocation schemas, and how to adapt them (yet has not been done before). It explores a range of potential solutions much more expansive than a typical analysis may uncover or engineering might suggest.

5 Summary

As C2 develops technologically, reliable methods for human interaction with an adaptive range of automation and autonomy must be established. Ultimately the attention allocation policy of a user plays a significant role in determining tradeoffs. As operators freely choose where to allocate attention, reduced workload provided by automated assistance leaves both negative and positive behaviors as possible outcomes.

We are of course wary of schemes which employ high degrees of automation, but, we also consider here that tradeoffs are a natural and persistent byproduct of function allocation [15]. By allowing an autonomics framework to aid in task management and providing an initial display of this aiding, we hope to provide adaptations and timely support for the system and the user that accurately reflect the state of both, in context of the mission. This method is sufficiently different from other methods of function allocation as to suggest it could be beneficial. It may allow for adaptation that is not opaque, and thus of great benefit.

Finally, we have touched on a relatively new concept of working agreements between what the autonomy can and can't do as set by the human [33]. This addresses the complexities of expectation-based faults, wherein the human expects the automation to perform (or does not). It also increases the collaboration of the human-system team. Overall, then, we are making progress toward more cooperation and more transparency in these types of systems.

Acknowledgements.   This work was supported by the Space and Naval Warfare Systems Center Pacific Naval Innovative Science and Engineering Program. This work was also supported by the US Department of Defense Autonomy Research Pilot Initiative under the project entitled "Realizing Autonomy via Intelligent Adaptive Hybrid Control".

References

1. Sheridan, T.B.: Humans and automation: Systems design and research issues. Human Factors and Ergnomics Society Wiley, Santa Monica/New York (2002)
2. Finn, A., Scheding, S.: Developments and Challenges for Autonomous Unmanned Systems, p. 237. Springer-Verlag, Berlin Heidelberg (2010)
3. Willard, R.: Rediscover the art of command and control. Proc. - United States Nav. Inst. **128** (10), 52–54 (2002)
4. Sheridan, T.B., Parasuraman, R.: Human-automation interaction. Rev. Hum. Factors Ergonomics **1**(41), 89–129 (2005)
5. Tucker, P.: Inside the Navy's secret swarm robot experiment. Defense One, 05 October 2014
6. Chen, J.Y.C., Barnes, M.J.: Human–agent teaming for multirobot control: a review of human factors issues. IEEE Trans. Hum.-Mach. Syst. **44**(1), 13–29 (2014)

7. Endsley, M.R., Kaber, D.B.: Level of automation effects on performance, situation awareness and workload in a dynamic control task. Ergonomics **42**(3), 462–492 (1999)

8. Kaber, D.B., Endsley, M.R.: The effects of level of automation and adaptive automation on human performance, situation awareness and workload in a dynamic control task. Theor. Issues Ergon. Sci. **5**(2), 113–153 (2004)

9. Cummings, M.L., How, J., Whitten, A., Toupet, O.: The impact of human-automation collaboration in decentralized multiple unmanned vehicle control. In: Proceedings IEEE (2011)

10. Bainbridge, L.: Ironies of automation. Automatica **19**(6), 775–779 (1983)

11. Endsley, M.R., Kiris, E.O.: The out-of-the-loop performance problem and level of control in automation. Hum. Factors **37**(2), 381–394 (1995)

12. Kirlik, A.: Modeling strategic behavior in human-automation interaction: why an 'aid' can (and should) go unused. Hum. Factors **35**(2), 221–242 (1993)

13. Parasuraman, R., Manzey, D.H.: Complacency and bias in human use of automation: An attentional integration. Hum. Factors **52**(3), 381–410 (2010)

14. Parasuraman, R., Sheridan, T.B., Wickens, C.D.: A model for types and levels of human interaction with automation. IEEE Trans. Syst. Man Cybern. Part A Syst. Hum. **30**(3), 286–297 (2000)

15. Onnasch, L., Wickens, C.D., Li, H., Manzey, D.: Human performance consequences of stages and levels of automation: an integrated meta-analysis. Hum. Factors **56**(3), 476–488 (2014)

16. Rovira, E., McGarry, K., Parasuraman, R.: Effects of imperfect automation on decision making in a simulated command and control task. Hum. Factors **49**(1), 76–87 (2007)

17. Miller, C.A., Parasuraman, R.: Designing for flexible interaction between humans and automation: delegation interfaces for supervisory control. Hum. Factors **49**(1), 57–75 (2007)

18. Parasuraman, R., Galster, S., Squire, P., Furukawa, H., Miller, C.: A Flexible Delegation-Type Interface Enhances System Performance in Human Supervision of Multiple Robots: Empirical Studies With RoboFlag. IEEE Trans. Syst. Man Cybern. Part A Syst. Hum. **35**(4), 481–493 (2005)

19. Squire, P.N., Parasuraman, R.: Effects of automation and task load on task switching during human supervision of multiple semi-autonomous robots in a dynamic environment. Ergonomics **53**(8), 951–961 (2010)

20. Scallen, S.F., Hancock, P.A.: Implementing adaptive function allocation. Int. J. Aviat. Psychol. **11**(2), 197–221 (2001)

21. Parasuraman, R., Mouloua, M., Molloy, R.: Effects of adaptive task allocation on monitoring automation. Hum. Factors **38**(4), 665–679 (1996)

22. Feigh, K., Dorneich, M.C., Hayes, C.C.: Toward a characterization of adaptive systems: a framework for researchers and system designers. Hum. Factors **54**(6), 1008–1024 (2012)

23. Kaber, D.B.: Adaptive Automation, In: Oxford Handbook of Cognitive Engineering, J. Lee and A. Kirlik, Eds. Oxford University Press, Oxford (2013)

24. Pritchett, A.R., Kim, S.Y., Feigh, K.M.: Measuring human-automation function allocation. J. Cogn. Eng. Decis. Mak. **8**(1), 52–77 (2013)

25. Garlan, D., Cheng, S., Huang, A., Schmerl, B., Steenkiste, P.: Rainbow: architecture-based self-adaptation with reusable infrastructure. IEEE Comput. **37**(10), 46–54 (2004)

26. Cummings, M.: Operator interaction with centralized versus decentralized UAV architectures. HAL Lab MIT Dep. Aeronaut. Astronaut., pp. 1–13, 2013

27. Cummings, M., Mastracchio, C., Thornburg, K., Mkrtchyan, A.: Boredom and Distraction in Multiple Unmanned Vehicle Superisory Control. Interact. Comput. **25**(1), 34–47 (2013)

28. Scerbo, M.W.: Theoretical perspectives on adaptive automation. In: Parasuraman, R., Mouloua, M. (eds.) Automation and Human Performance: Theory and Applications, pp. 37–63. Erlbaum, Mahwah, NJ (1996)

29. Johnson, A.W., Oman, C.M., Sheridan, T.B., Duda, K.R.: Dynamic task allocation in operational systems: Issues, gaps, and recommendations. In: 2014 IEEE Aerospace Conference, pp. 1–15 (2014)

30. Wilson, G., Russell, C.: Performance enhancement in an uninhabited air vehicle task using psychophysiologically determined adaptive aiding. Hum. Factors **49**(6), 1005–1018 (2007)

31. Ratwani, R., McCurry, J.M., Trafton, J.G.: Single operator, multiple robots: an eye movement based theoretic model of operator situation awareness. In: Present. 5th ACM/IEEE International Conference Human-Robot Interact, pp. 235–242 (2010)

32. Breslow, L., Gartenberg, D., McCurry, J.M., Trafton, J.: Dynamic operator overload: a model for predicting workload during supervisory control. IEEE Trans. Hum.-Mach. Syst. **44**(1), 30–40 (2014)

33. de Greef, T., Arciszewski, H., Neerincx, M.: Adaptive automation based on an object-oriented task model: implementation and evaluation in a realistic C2 environment. J. Cogn. Eng. Decis. Mak **4**(2), 152–182 (2010)

34. Bailey, N.R., Scerbo, M.W., Freeman, F.G., Mikulka, P.J., Scott, L.A.: Comparison of a brain-based adaptive system and a manual adaptable system for invoking automation. Hum. Factors **48**(4), 693–709 (2006)

35. Kaber, D., Wright, M., Prinzel, L., Clamann, M.: Adaptive automation of human-machine system information-processing functions. Hum. Factors **47**, 730–741 (2005)

36. Rouse, W.: Adaptive aiding for human/computer control. Hum. Factors **30**(4), 431–443 (1988)

37. Inagaki, T.: Adaptive automation: sharing and trading of control, In: Handbook of Cognitive Task Design, Hollnagel, E. (ed.), LEA, pp. 147–169 (2003)

38. Rodas, M., DiVita, J., Morris, R.: Introducing a task prioritization tool in a complex supervisory control environment. Cogn. Methods Situat. Aware. Decis. Support, pp. 79–82, 2014

39. Chandrasekaran, B., Johnson, T.R., Smith, J.W.: Task-structure analysis for knowledge modeling. Commun. ACM **33**(9), 124–136 (1992)

40. Dodhia, R., Dismukes, R.: Interruptions create prospective memory tasks. Appl. Cogn. Psychol. **89**, 73–89 (2009)

41. Dismukes, R., Nowinski, J.: Prospective memory, concurrent task management, and pilot error. In: Kramer, A., Wiegmann, D., Kirlik, A. (eds.) Attention: From theory to practice, pp. 225–236. Oxford University Press, New York (2007)

ARTiSt — An Augmented Reality Testbed for Intelligent Technical Systems

Bassem Hassan[1], Jörg Stöcklein[2]([⊠]), and Jan Berssenbrügge[2]

[1] Fraunhofer Institute for Production Technology IPT,
Aachen, Germany
`Bassem.Hassan@ipt.fraunhofer.de`
[2] Heinz Nixdorf Institute at University of Paderborn,
Paderborn, Germany
`{Joerg.Stoecklein,Jan.Berssenbruegge}@hni.upb.de`

Abstract. This paper describes a simulation and visualization environment called **ARTiSt** (**A**ugmented **R**eality **T**estbed for **i**ntelligent technical **S**ystems), which serves as a tool for developing extension modules for the miniature robot BeBot. It allows developers to simulate, visualize, analyze, and optimize new simulated components with existing, real system components. In ARTiSt real BeBots combined with virtual prototypes of a lifter- and a transporter-module, which are attached on top of the real BeBot. The simulation of the virtual components and the management of real BeBots are realized with MATLAB/Simulink. The determination of important parameters for the simulation of the real BeBots, such as real-world position and -rotation, is done using an Augmented Reality tracking system. A camera, installed on top of the testbed, continuously captures the testbed and determines the real-world transformation of the BeBots. The calculated transformations are the basis for further pathfinding within the simulation in MATLAB/Simulink.

1 Introduction

Virtual Prototyping is a technique, which applies *Virtual Reality*-based product development for the engineering of mechanical and mechatronic systems. Virtual prototyping is based on the modeling, design, and analysis of *Virtual Prototypes*, e.g. computer-internal models, which are executed and analyzed in a Virtual Environment.

Virtual Prototypes are typically developed prior to physical prototypes (or mock-ups), which are mainly profitable for relatively small subsystems. Compared to physical prototypes, the development of Virtual Prototypes is less expensive and time-consuming, and Virtual Prototypes provide a significantly higher flexibility for change requests and variant management. Moreover, due to the virtualization of the prototype and the environment, Virtual Prototypes facilitate the early evaluation of the final product. All experiments can be conducted under controlled conditions of a well structured *Virtual Test Bench* and, for instance, can easily be repeated for regression testing.

R. Shumaker and S. Lackey (Eds.): VAMR 2015, LNCS 9179, pp. 457–469, 2015.
DOI: 10.1007/978-3-319-21067-4_47

Fig. 1. Visualization of virtual modules on real BeBots using augmented reality.

Rapid prototyping in the product development process, uses Virtual Prototypes in conjunction with direct manufacturing methods, e.g. 3D printing, is successfully applicable nowadays. Products can thereby be virtually designed and tested and are manufactured to successful optimization and validation in the direct manufacturing process. Thus, a product component by component developed and virtual and real components are evaluated simultaneously with the help of *Augmented Reality.*

In our Project *ARTiSt* physical miniature robots BeBots work together with virtual prototypes of a lifter- and a transporter-module, which are attached on top of the real BeBot, in real-time. In order to evaluate both, the real miniature robots and the virtual extension modules, we use Augmented Reality to correctly combine both prototypes together. A simulation is used for calculating the optimal motion paths of the BeBots and the controlling commands for lifting and transporting the objects.

The visualization of the virtual advanced modules (lifter, transporter) attached to the top of the real BeBots is realized by means of an Augmented Reality application for mobile devices (see Fig. 1). This allows an intuitive visual analysis of the interaction of all the components using the magic lens metaphor. The Augmented Reality application is connected via wireless network to the simulation engine developed in MATLAB/Simulink. That enables the direct visualization of the calculated parameters of the simulation in the virtual model.

Objective of the simulation is to demonstrate cooperation of two BeBots, were one BeBot acts as a transporter, carrying collected objetcts to its destination, and cooperate with a lifter, collecting objects and puts them on the transporter. Both robots work efficiently in collecting and transporting virtual objects which were distributed interactively on the testbed. Therefore, the lifter and the transporter need to coordinate themselves autonomously. This process can be analyzed using the Augmented Reality application.

After the validation of the simulation, the optimized structure of advanced modules can be produced in the direct manufacturing process. This approach reduces the number of real samples and prototypes considerably.

2   Essentials

This paper combines technologies from the domains of *Virtual Reality*, *Virtual Prototyping*, and *Augmented Reality* with methods developed for mechatronic system. In the following paragraphs, the basic principles of these technologies as well as the test platform used will be described in short.

2.1   Virtual Reality, Augmented Reality and Virtual Prototype

Virtual Reality (VR) provides methods for the analysis and evaluation of test results. Using VR during the product development process is not unusual. For example, VR is applied in the field of mechanical engineering and plant engineering in order to plan and evaluate technical systems [11].

Augmented Reality (AR), in comparison to VR, is still a novel technology. AR is a human-computer-interface, which superimposes the perception of reality with computer-generated information. Today, most AR applications can be found in niches. Cutting-edge fields are automotive development and marketing. For instance, automotive development uses AR for the evaluation of new automotive prototypes and for the preparation of experiments [3,10]. In the marketing sector AR often used for product presentation. Recently, a manufacturer of toy building blocks tested AR, in order to present the final product on top of the package [5].

A *Virtual Prototype* (VP) is the computer-internal representation of a real prototype of a product [4]. The VP is based on the *Digital Mock-Up* (DMU). The DMU represents the shape and the structure of the product. The foundations of the DMU are composed of two types of models: 3D-CAD for shape and the logical structure of the product. The VP extends the DMU because further aspects are taken into account which are aspects like the kinematics, dynamics, strength, or information processing. A computer-internal model represents each of these aspects.

A *Virtual Environment* (VE) is a synthetic, computer generated environment, which presents a visual, haptic, and auditive simulation of a real world [1]. A VE for developing, analyzing, improving, and testing VPs is composed of one or multiple VPs integrated into the VE. A detailed explanation can be found in [8].

2.2   Specification of the Miniature Robot BeBot

The miniature robot *BeBot* (see Fig. 2) has a size of approximately 9 by 9 cm and a height of about 5 cm. Its chassis uses **MID** (Molded Interconnect Devices)

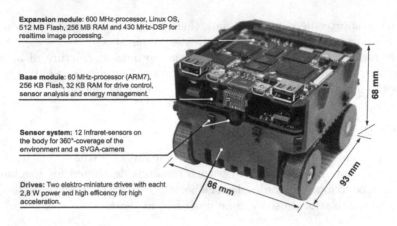

Expansion module: 600 MHz-processor, Linux OS, 512 MB Flash, 256 MB RAM and 430 MHz-DSP for realtime image processing.

Base module: 60 MHz-processor (ARM7), 256 KB Flash, 32 KB RAM for drive control, sensor analysis and energy management.

Sensor system: 12 Infraret-sensors on the body for 360°-coverage of the environment and a SVGA-camera

Drives: Two elektro-miniature drives with eacht 2,8 W power and high efficency for high acceleration.

68 mm

93 mm

86 mm

Fig. 2. BeBot with hardware components.

technology, where printed circuit board tracks directly applied on the body surface. MID offers new possibilities for the synergistic integration of mechanics and electronics [2]. This technology is used for mounting 12 infrared sensors, a micro controller, several transistors, and resistors for preprocessing directly on the robot chassis. The drive of the robot consists of a chain drive. Together with two 2.8 W DC gear motors with built-in encoders the robot offers robust motion even on slightly rough ground. The complete system is supplied by a 3.7 V/3900 mAh lithium-ion accumulator. The BeBot uses a modular concept of information processing with two board slots. The lower board implements basic functions like motor control and power supply. An *ARM 7* based micro controller provides enough computational power to implement low-level behavior. The module also contains a three axis acceleration sensor, a yaw rate gyroscope, and a sensor for battery monitoring. The upper slot provides more powerful information processing and wireless communication. It is equipped with a low power system-on-chip (SoC) with package-on-package memory and provides an *ARM Cortex-A8 600* MHz high performance processor, a TIC64x+ digital signal processor, 256 MB main and 512 MB flash memory. This allows the computation of complex algorithms and image processing direct-on the system. The integrated wireless communication standards Bluetooth and IEEE 802.11 wireless network offer communication with various bandwidth and power consumption. The board is equipped with a small camera and two microphones for a substantial perception of the environment. Different techniques for energy saving like dynamic frequency and voltage scaling as well as dynamic power-down of non-used hardware components including RF processing, combining powerful computation capability with long battery life time. Additional I2C, UART, USB, MMC/SDcard, camera and memory interfaces as well as a small module slot provides great expansion capabilities. An infrared communication interface allows the cordless equipment with mechanical extension modules. The software environment uses *OpenRobotix*, which is based on OpenEmbedded and allows the generation of a fully customize Linux operating system. It generates cross-compiled software packages and images for the embedded target. The existing software branch was extended to contain the robot-specific information, patches, and additional software like drivers for the robot hardware and the Player network server.

3   BeBot Application Scenario

The miniature robot BeBot was developed as a demonstration platform to evaluate different advanced algorithms and technologies such as: swarm intelligent algorithms, dynamic reconfiguration, multi agent systems, molded interconnected devices as well as self-optimization functionalities. In order to demonstrate, investigate, and evaluate these algorithms and technologies with the help of the miniature robot BeBot, application scenarios have to be designed and developed.

For ARTiSt we have developed an application scenario which focuses on two different parts in the development process: The product development of external modules attached to the BeBot in order to fulfill a specific task on the one hand. On the other hand the algorithmic development of strategies which enable two or more BeBots to work together on a global task but with different subtasks for each BeBot.

The ARTiSt application scenario is shown in Fig. 3. The objective is to collect three different-colored objects within the testbed and place them in their corresponding drop areas. The objects are randomly placed within the testbed at the beginning by the user. Then a group of BeBots (in our case two) should cooperatively collect these objects. Each BeBot has one of two pre-defined roles, though: one can act like a transporter, which collects all objects and transports

Fig. 3. Application scenario.

them to the drop zones. The other BeBot works as a lifter, which picks each objects and puts it into a free storage of the transporter. Both BeBots are working independently but in cooperation with the other group members.

3.1 Development of BeBots Extension Modules

In order to realize the two pre-defined roles of the BeBot (transporter and lifter) two extension modules have to be developed and attached with the existing main vehicle. The development of these extension modules has been done with the help of virtual prototyping and simulation.

Today, virtual prototyping is an integral part of the product development process. In virtual prototyping, a computer model of the product under development is generated and subsequently tested, just like a real prototype. This way, design errors can already be detected in the early phases of the product development process and alternative designs of a product can be virtually examined, without having to build a real prototype. This reduces time and costs in product development and raises product quality.

Each of the two extension modules has particular requirements according to the specific task in the application scenario. The requirements and are described as following:

Requirements of the Lifter Extension Module: The lifter extension module should be able to pick up and lift different object types from the ground and load them into the transporter extension module. Therefore, it should have a gripping unit to do the picking. The gripping unit should move in a vertical direction in order to lift the object from the ground and put it into the transporter extension module. Additionally, for sensing the dimensions of the picked object, the gripping unit should include an infrared sensor placed between the two gripping arms. This also ensures that the object is located correctly between the gripping arms. Moreover, the gripping unit should be equipped with a pressure sensor to measure the gripping power applied on the object. According to the modular concept of the BeBot, the lifter module should be controlled by a separate circuit board and should have its own power supply.

Requirements of the Transporter Extension Module: The transporter module should be able to carry and transport at least four different objects at once, each object on a separated cavity. The load operation should be done with the help of the lifter module, but the transporter module can independently transport and unload the objects in their drop areas. The unload process could be done for each object individually. According to the modular concept of the BeBot, the transporter module should be controlled by a separate circuit board and should have its own power supply.

3.2 Virtual Prototyping of the Extension Modules

In order to develop the extension modules for the BeBots virtual prototyping and simulation techniques have been used. Both extension modules are *mechatronic systems* and therefore consist of the three main components:

Mechanical Component: Each extension module includes mechanical parts, e.g. the lifting unit or the unload mechanic.

Electronic Components: Each extension module includes sensors and actuators, e.g. a infrared sensor in the lifter or a servo motor in the transporter, and a control circuit board.

Software Components: For each extension module a customized control software is developed to operate all functions.

To develop each of the three main components different approaches are used, which will be described below:

Mechanical Construction of the Extension Modules: Based on each extension module requirements, its mechanical construction has to be developed. Nevertheless, there are numerous designs of each extension module fulfilling the predefined requirements. Therefore, the innovation funnel model has been used in order to select the best mechanical construction of the extension modules.

The best mechanical construction selection process is consisting of the following four phases:

1. **Brainstorming:** In this phase, the involved design group has to generate many possible concepts of the extension modules' mechanical construction.
2. **Documentation:** In this phase, the generated mechanical constructions in the brainstorming phase have to be documented by means of their mechanisms and components.
3. **Evaluation:** In this phase, the documented mechanical constructions have to be evaluated with the help of the following criteria: cost, weight, needed space, dimensions, efficiency, and simplicity of control.
4. **Selection:** In this phase, a mechanical construction has to be selected based on the evaluation of the different mechanical constructions.

A 3D model of the selected mechanical construction of each extension module has been developed with help of a CAD tool. In this work, we used CATIA to construct the 3D models. extension module.

Additionally, a physical model of each module has to be modeled. The model of the extension module represents the mechanical construction as a multi body system, sensors, actuators and the control algorithm. In this work we, used Matlab/Simulink to build up the physical models of the extension modules.

Controlling Circuit Boards for the Extension Modules: The development of the two controlling circuit boards for the extension modules was done in three phases.

The first phase was the schematic design. In this phase, the electronic components have been selected and connected to each others. Moreover, the interaction between the different electronics components have been simulated and tested with the help of a schematic editor tool. In this work, we used the tool EAGLE for the development of the electronic circuit board.

The second phase was the layout design. In this phase, layouts of the circuit boards have been carried out. The layout design has been done by positing the electronic components within the predefined dimensions of the circuit board (5 by 7 cm).

The third phase was the conducting path design. In this phase, conducting paths of each copper connection as well as its thickness have to be created with the different layers of the circuit. Our circuit boards have a compact size. Therefore, each circuit board has 7 connection layers. Nowadays, electronic circuits design tools e.g. Eagle can create the routing plane automatically within the different layers of the electronic circuit board.

Controlling Software for the Extension Modules: In order to control the extension modules, a control algorithm has to be programmed for each module. The control algorithm should collect signals from the different sensors and calculates the control signal for each actuator. The control algorithm of each extension module will be executed with the help of a micro controller on the control circuit.

The controlling software program is written in ANSI-C programming language. It has the advantage testing the control algorithm virtually by embedding the code in the Matlab/Simulink environment by using s-functions.

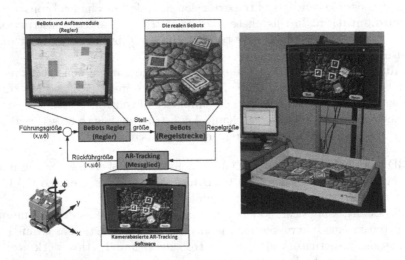

Fig. 4. Structure of the augmented reality testbed.

4   The Augmented Reality Testbed

In this section, we describe the structure of our augmented reality testbed ARTiSt by means of the specific scenario described in Sect. 3. However, ARTiSt can also be used in other scenarios, e.g. evaluating other extension modules for the BeBot or examine cooperative and competitive team strategies for other tasks. However, to be able to use ARTiSt in other scenarios, the structure of the testbed and the use of different components to set up an own scenario has to be understood.

To enable the virtual extension modules to interact with the physical BeBots we used the AR technology (see Fig. 4). AR is used for registering virtual objects with real-world objects, in this case the virtual extension modules with the real BeBots. For the user, who looks through an AR device, the virtual objects seem to exist in the real world. For an operable simulation, the computer must know the exact position and orientation of the real world and all its objects.

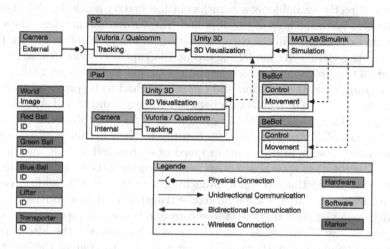

Fig. 5. Hardware and software structure of the ARTiSt-system.

Figure 5 illustrates the hardware and software structure of the ARTiSt system. A standard PC with an attached video camera serves as main component. With the help of the video system, all different markers are detected using a third-party tracking system. We use *Qualcomm Vuforia* [7] as an AR tracking system because of the easy usage and the possibility to track large images which can be partially occluded. The system has to track the following objects:

The BeBots: Two BeBots have to be tracked by the system to ensure that the virtual extension modules are properly registered in the visualization and to send the world coordinates to the simulation.

The Collectable Objects: The Marker representing the virtual objects, which will be picked up, must be tracked by the system. Each of the marker can be placed across the testbed by the user randomly before starting the simulation.

The World: The System has to know the origin of the world. This is vital for the calculation of the position of both BeBots and the user-placed objects. All objects and BeBots must be in world-space for proper simulation.

For the BeBots and for the objects, we used so-called ID-markers, as the tracking software is able to detect them even under bad light conditions. For tracking the origin of the world, we used an image marker, since ID-markers have the disadvantage that the tracker looses the detection, if parts of the marker are covered. Image markers can be partial occluded but will be still detected by the tracking system. Using an image marker, which covers the entire floor of the testbed, was sufficient to be able to detect the origin of the world in any situation.

The tracking system Vuforia was integrated as plugin in the 3D visualization system *Unity3D* [9]. Therefore, the position and orientation of the tracked markers is directly available as a transformation matrix inside the 3d visualization software. With the help of the supplied transformation matrices, the virtual objects can be registered in the correct position within the captured video frame. Overlaying the virtual 3D model on top of the captured video frame produces a correct 3D impression. As the simulation of the BeBots was realized with MATLAB/Simulink, the position and orientation had to be provided to it. This was done by a local UDP connection between Unity3D and MATLAB/Simulink, where Unity3D sends each tracked position. In MATLAB/Simulink the motion paths of each BeBot are calculated, according to their actual position and orientation, which results in the rotation speed of each individual DC motor of the BeBots. The rotation speeds are then sent as commands to the BeBots using a wireless lan connection. When approaching a virtual object, additional commands for lifting the objects are send to the transporter BeBot. But, as the lifter only exists as a virtual prototype, these commands are not executed on the real BeBot but in the 3D visualization system, which simulates the lifting process of objects. Therefore, the 3D visualization was able to control the lifter, grab the virtual objects, and drop it into an empty slot of the virtual transporter extension module.

The virtual objects can only be seen on a monitor attached to the testbed, as illustrated in Fig. 4, which restrict the viewing angle for the user. Therefore, we developed a 3D visualization for a mobile device, which is able to augment the real BeBots and the virtual objects as the 3D visualization running on the PC but can be used as a mobile 'window to the world' [6]. In fact, as we used Unity3D as the implementation platform, we can reuse the same project, we developed for the PC, also for the mobile device. This cuts the development of both version to the half. The mobile device uses its internal camera module to capture the real world environment and detects all markers inside. On the detected marker, the virtual 3D objects can be registered. As on the PC version of the visualization we use Vuforia as AR tracker. Nowadays, mobile devices are powerful enough to do the video capturing, the AR tracking, and the 3D visualization of the virtual 3D objects in real-time. Therefore, the mobile version of the visualization runs stand-alone. To enable a synchronous animation of the mobile application and the PC software, we synchronized both applications using a wireless network connection. Unity3D offers a suitable solution for this problem. Thereby, the commands sent by the MATLAB/Simulink simulation are only received by the

PC version of the visualization. The animations of the 3D objects are then synchronized, using the network synchronization option of Unity3D. We do not need to connect the mobile application to the MATLAB/Simulink simulation, thus saving network bandwidth, simulation execution time, and implementation effort.

All relationships between the different software applications we use in ARTiSt are illustrated in Fig. 5. Figure 5 illustrates how the PC and the mobile device is communicating, which channels for communication are used and what kind of markers are used for the different AR objects. As the MATLAB/Simulink simulation was part of a former project, we were able to build the 3D visualization and AR part of the testbed for both platforms in less then 2 weeks. This rapid development can only be achieved because of the use of a full-featured 3D visualization software platform like Unity3D.

5 Implementation of the Prototype Scenario

After starting the test scenario, the AR-Tracking software calculates the position (X, Y) and the orientation angle (ϕ) of each object regarding to the workspace coordinate system (origin point is on the top right corner). There are five objects marked by AR-Markers, as mentioned in section Sect. 4: both BeBots (lifter and transporter) and the three collectible objects. The AR-Tracking software send the detected position and orientation (X, Y, ϕ) of each object in tracked world coordinates to the scenario controller.

Based on the five object positions and orientations, the scenario controller calculates the object collection order depending on the pre-programmed strategy e.g. collect the objects as fast as possible or collect the objects with minimum energy consumption. The scenario controller sends the position and orientation of the next object to be collected to the lifter-BeBot controller.

Based on the current position and orientation of the lifter-BeBot and the next object position, the lifter-BeBot motion controller software calculates the shortest motion path reaching the next object. The motion path in this case contains the position (X, Y) of the target point as well as the target orientation (ϕ). The target angle is the desired lifter-BeBot orientation on the target point. The lifter-BeBot motion controller sends the path information to the lifter-Bebot collision avoidance controller.

Based on the Lifter motion path and the position and orientation of the others objects as well as the transporter-BeBot, the lifter collision avoidance has to ensure that there is no collision between the lifter-BeBot from one side and the other objects from the other side along the selected motion path. If a collision is detected, the collision avoidance controller has to define a maneuver in form of a new motion path in order to avoid the collision. The new motion path in this case contains more than one target position and orientation (typically three points) in order to achieve the collision avoidance maneuver. Therefore, the lifter-Bebot collision avoidance controller sends the new calculated motion path in the form of current point position and orientation and an array of target point positions and orientations to the motion controller. If no collision is detected, the originally calculated motion path in the form of current point position and orientation and target point position and orientation will be sent.

The lifter-BeBot motion controller is a fuzzy logic controller, which controls two parameters: the BeBot translation and the BeBot rotation by operating the two motors of the BeBot. As soon as the lifter-BeBot motion controller has reached the target point successfully, it sends a signal to the extension module controller to confirm that the target position and orientation has been reached. The lifter-BeBot extension module controller starts to operate the gripping mechanism in order to grip the object with help of the simulated infrared and gripping pressure sensors. As soon as the extension module controller successfully has gripped the object, it sends a confirmation signal to the scenario controller to confirm that the first object is in the gripper.

Based on the current position of the lifter-Bebot and the current position of the transporter-BeBot, the scenario controller calculates in which transporter-carriage the object has to be loaded and also calculates the target position and orientation for the transporter-BeBot. The transporter-BeBot controllers (motion and collision avoidance) control the motors until it reach the target position and orientation. It works with the same procedure like the lifter-BeBot controllers. As soon as the transporter-BeBot successfully reached the target point, it sends a confirmation signal to the scenario controller. The scenario controller sends a signal to the gripper to release the object into the transporter-BeBot carriage. The pervious steps are repeated until all the objects have been collected. As soon as all objects have been collected, the scenario controller calculates for the transporters the unload path in form of three target points: red drop-point, green drop-point and blue drop-point. The scenario controllers send the target position and orientation of the target drop points one by one.

The transporter-BeBot controllers (motion and collision avoidance) control the transporter-BeBot motors until they reach the drop-point position and the target orientation. As soon as the transporter-BeBot has reached the drop-point successfully, it sends a confirmation signal to the scenario controller. The scenario controller sends a signal to the transporter to unload a specific object regarding to the drop-point color. After unloading all objects, the scenario controllers end the simulation.

6   Conclusion

This paper described an augmented reality testbed for the development of intelligent technical systems. The presented approach has been implemented and applied successfully during the development of extension modules for the miniature robot BeBot. The presented approach showed the significant strength of integrated modeling, simulation, and AR techniques together in an environment, which support the development of an extension for an existing systems. This approach has been validated with the help of the presented application scenario 'extension modules development for BeBots' but it can be modified and used in other application scenarios, e.g. development of existing machines extensions.

References

1. Gutiérrez, M., Vexo, F., Thalmann, D.: Stepping into Virtual Reality. Springer, London (2008)
2. Kaiser, I., Kaulmann, T., Gausemeier, J., Witkowski, U.: Miniaturization of autonomous robot by the new technology molded interconnect devices (mid). In: Proceedings of the 4th International AMiRE Symposium, Buenos Aires (2007)
3. Klinker, G., Dutoit, A.H., Bauer, M., Bayer, J., Novak, V., Matzke, D.: Fata morgana a presentation system for product design. In: ISMAR 2002: Proceedings of the 1st International Symposium on Mixed and Augmented Reality. IEEE Computer Society, September 2002
4. Krause, F.-L., Jansen, H., Kind, C., Rothenburg, U.: Virtual product development as an engine for innovation. In: Krause, F.-L. (ed.) The Future of Product Development, pp. 703–713. Springer, Berlin (2007)
5. Metaio. The LEGO group to boost retail with metaio. Press release, December 2008
6. Milgram, P., Takemura, H., Utsumi, A., Kishino, F.: Augmented reality: a class of displays on the reality-virtuality continuum (1995)
7. Qualcomm Connected Experiences, Inc., Qualcomm Vuforia Developer Portal (2015). https://developer.vuforia.com
8. Radkowski, R., Waßmann, H.: Software-agent supported virtual experimental environment for virtual prototypes of mechatronic systems. In: Proceedings of the ASME 2010 World Conference on Innovative Virtual Reality WINVR2010, Ames, Iowa, USA, 12–14 May 2010
9. Unity Technologies. Unity - Game engine, tools and mulitplatform (2015). http://www.unity3d.com
10. Wittke, M.: Ar in der pkw-entwicklung bei volkswagen. In: Schenk, M. (ed.) IFF-Wissenschaftstage -Virtual Reality und Augmented Reality zum Planen, Testen und Betreiben technischer Systeme, 4. Fachtagung zu Virtual Reality, Fraunhofer IFF, Magdeburg, 27–28 June 2007
11. Ye, J., Badiyani, S., Raja, V., Schlegel, T.: Applications of virtual reality in product design evaluation. In: Jacko, J.A. (ed.) HCI 2007. LNCS, vol. 4553, pp. 1190–1199. Springer, Heidelberg (2007)

Evaluation of a Vehicle Exterior's Sportiness Under Real vs. Virtual Conditions

Max Hoermann[1(✉)] and Maximilian Schwalm[2]

[1] AUDI AG, Ingolstadt, Germany
max.hoermann@audi.de
[2] RWTH Aachen University, Aachen, Germany
schwalm@ika.rwth-aachen.de

Abstract. In order to identify a customer's liking, original equipment manufacturers (OEMs) in the automotive industry conduct so-called car clinics. Contemporary car clinics, however, generate great expenses as real prototypes are required.

Considering these facts, car clinics with virtual models would help to solve this problem. To this end an empirical study was designed and conducted to address the question whether the perception of the overall sportiness of a vehicle's exterior can show the same results for virtual as well as real vehicle models. Due to the fact that until today no standardized instrument was available, we evolved a questionnaire designed to capture a vehicle exterior's sportiness by six depending factors.

Results revealed that the assessments of real and virtual vehicle exteriors correlate highly but do not match exactly.

Keywords: Virtual reality · Car clinic · Vehicle exterior · Questionnaire · Sportiness

1 Introduction

As over the course of time original equipment manufacturers (OEMs) in the automotive industry have assimilated their technical properties, design has become the most important factor leading a person to the decision of buying a certain vehicle. [2, 5, 7, 9] Consequently OEMs - especially within the premium sector – put huge efforts on the topic of exterior styling.

In order to match a customer's liking, OEMs conduct so-called car and concept clinics. [8] These clinics are head-to-head comparisons of competing vehicles wherein target-market consumers are recruited to evaluate the upcoming models and indicate preferences. The clinics' results are of high interest as OEMs take high risks by introducing a new vehicle concept or a newly designed model without a quantified consumer feedback, [6] however, contemporary car clinics generate great expenses as real prototypes are needed. Furthermore, these required prototypes are available quite late in the development process in order to implement distinct changes potentially causing high investments. [6] As a result, OEMs investigate intensively how to integrate and advance customers' feedback within the development process at an earlier stage. [17]

R. Shumaker and S. Lackey (Eds.): VAMR 2015, LNCS 9179, pp. 470–479, 2015.
DOI: 10.1007/978-3-319-21067-4_48

Considering these facts car clinics with virtual models would help to solve these problems and would bring a huge benefit regarding timing, logistics and costs as they only require a digital model of a new concept or design instead of an actual, real prototype. [3, 8] However, until today – to our best knowledge - only the scientific research by A. Erdmann [8] and M. Söderman [15] have covered the concrete question whether or not virtual car clinics could replace real car clinics. Within his doctoral thesis Erdmann concluded that virtual vehicle models would provide the same output as real vehicle models but it has to be stated that a mostly qualitative questionnaire was applied which was not assured to be capable of differentiating. [8] In line with Erdmann's thesis Söderman also only operated with qualitative questions, he, however, concluded that real and virtual prototypes do not provide the same results. [15] According to these diverging conclusions and lack of standardized instruments further investigation on this topic is required.

Analyzing the scientific approaches of how the customer's perception of automotive design is constituted, sportiness is always a recurring aspect. [12, 14, 16] Referring to A. Oehme attractiveness and dynamics contribute significantly to the overall judgment on aesthetics. [14] Furthermore, several premium OEMs maintain sportiness as one of their central brand characteristics, e.g. Audi, BMW and Porsche. Taking these findings into account perceived 'Sportiness' of a vehicle exterieur was chosen as the central aspect for further investigation.

Hence, the following empirical study was designed and executed to address the question whether the perception of the overall sportiness of a vehicle exterior can show the same results for virtual as well as for real vehicle models. Due to the fact that there has been no standardized instrument available yet to describe and to measure the concept of a vehicle exterior's sportiness [1, 5] this had to be developed and validated first.

2 Development of the Instrument

2.1 Method

In order to develop the standardized instrument a three-part approach was chosen. Firstly, a survey was conducted to gather all items which are related to a vehicle exterior's sportiness. In the second step, raw data was edited and finally an extensive empirical study was executed to analyze the data and to identify the latent construct with its relevant factors concerning the perception of a vehicle exterior's sportiness.

The approach's first step was collecting the items. In this context, the main goal was to carve out all attributes which are exclusively linked to the sportiness of vehicles and not beyond as the item-set influences the final results of the exploratory factor analysis [10]. This means the resulting item-set as well as the factorial structure differ depending on the input of variables. [1] For this purpose the data collection was divided into three perspectives. The first part resembled the perspective of an original equipment manufacturer, the second one of the automotive press and the third one of the customer. Relating to the automotive press 300 articles were scanned for expressions considering descriptions of exterior's sportiness. The perspective of the OEMs was simulated by reviewing 60 OEM model pamphlets for sporty items. At last the customer point of view had to be analyzed what was done by an online panel with 115 test subjects.

After data collection the selection was enlarged by items gathered from scientific literature concerning existing questionnaires about related aspects of automotive forms [1, 10–14, 16]. The final item pool resulted in an entity of 150 items.

In order to detect very similar or even redundant attributes, four experts were instructed to perform card sorting independently of each other. The final item-set consisted of a total of 103 items which were the basis for the following study.

Considering the perception of a vehicle exterior's sportiness the main goal of the following investigation was the identification of the latent construct (see Fig. 1). In this context an online-survey was designed and conducted wherein the subjects were asked to assess one stimulus on the basis of the item-set preliminarily defined. The link was distributed via e-mail and social media. By clicking on the link the subjects were randomly directed to one of the different stimuli and asked to assess the exterior using a five point likert-scale for each of the items. All in all 108 items were integrated into the survey in random order including additional antonyms. The stimuli presented were nine images of vehicle exteriors which can be classified into the categories van, station wagon and sports car: Renault Kangoo, VW Caddy, Mazda Biante, Mercedes-Benz C-class T-model, Volvo V70, VW Golf Variant, AUDI R8, BMW i8, Mercedes-Benz SLS AMG. These vehicle categories were chosen as they were supposed to differentiate distinctly considering the vehicle's sportiness. Regarding participation during three weeks of activation 301 subjects attended the online panel. 79.1 % out of them were male and the average age was 32.79 years.

Fig. 1. Screenshot of the online panel

2.2   Analysis

In the context of data analysis the first calculations concerned the specific item values. Relating to these computations, items were excluded which did not differentiate or measure the same property as the remaining item-set. Before starting the exploratory factor analysis the criteria KMO, MSA and Bartlett's test on sphericity had to be checked. [4] As all quality criteria were achieved the dimensional reduction could be performed.

After confirming the data set to be valid the most suitable approach of exploration had to be determined. In line with determining the general methodology the main axis analysis was chosen as it is best for tracing relations between items. [4]

Before fixing the rotation methodology the number of factors had to be defined. Summing up the different approaches – Kaiser-Guttman, Screeplot, MAP and Parallel-Analysis according to Horn – three to seven latent factors could be anticipated.

Regarding the rotation technique orthogonal methods were not applied because they did not fulfill the requirement of an easy structure. So the most common oblique rotation – the Direct-Quartimin method was used. [4]

The structure chosen explains 65.6 % of the variance and consists of six depending factors which are relying on 33 items. Regarding the item clusters the next step was defining suitable factor labels which clearly describe what is measured – see Fig. 2 with the original German items and their translation.

The six depending factors were labeled as 'attractiveness', 'aggression', 'modernity', 'perfection', 'premium' and 'functionality'. Regarding other approaches to describe general automotive design their factors are closely related to the concept of sportiness, e.g. 'attractiveness', 'emotionality', 'innovation', 'quality' and 'dynamics'. [12, 14]

The next step implies the questionnaire's derivation from the online panel's methodology. In order to stay consistent the five point likert-scales and the final item-set were adopted. Regarding the questionnaire's analysis an unweighted approach which results in one value per factor has been chosen. These values are based on the calculation of the factors' arithmetic means which depend on the associated items. This approach provides a subdivided image of a vehicle's exterior sportiness which needs no more interpretation because the higher a rating the higher the perception of the vehicle exterior's sportiness.

3   Assessing a Vehicle Exterior's Sportiness in a Virtual Car Clinic

After defining an instrument for measuring the subjective perception of a vehicle exterior's sportiness the following research concentrates on the question whether the evaluation of virtual and real vehicles provides the same results based on the developed questionnaire.

3.1   Method

The survey was designed against the background that the conditions match in the real and virtual environment. In order to grant identical stimuli all vehicles used in the

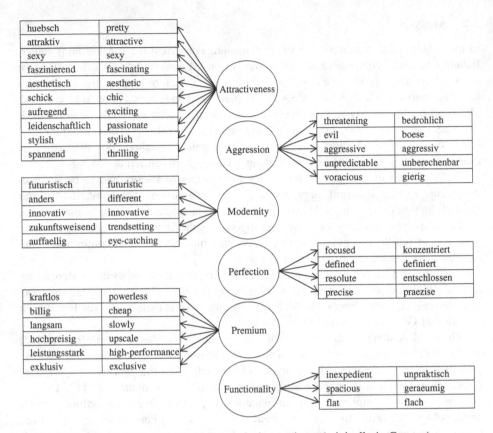

Fig. 2. Construct of a vehicle exterior's sportiness (originally in German)

current study were by Audi. This decision was based on the fact that the required virtual holistic vehicle models are only available at Audi in-house. In accordance to comparability the vehicles chosen were of the same concept. Finally, two current Sport Utility Vehicles (SUVs) were selected, labeled as model A and model B.

Regarding the survey's design a within-subject design was set. Each test subject had to assess all four vehicles, two real and two virtual models. Based on a middle-sized effect the a priori calculation provided a minimum sample size of 36.

As the clinic's location a spacious hall on neutral terrain, outside Audi's premises was chosen. The room was lined by molleton and was divided into two areas according to reality and virtual reality. The virtual models were visualized on a scale of one to one on a 2D back-projection screen which also served as camouflage between the two areas. The back-projection was chosen as it avoids shading by test subjects. A 2D projection was applied based on the determination that the entire exterior should be visible at any time. This constraint led to a minimum virtual distance of the subject to the screen which measured about two meters. According to Audi's experts these conditions supersede 3D visualization as the 3D effect gets lost. A head mounted display (HMD) was also neglected as HMDs can increase the probability of cyber-sickness and unforeseeable effects might arise as most of the subjects have no experience with HMDs. [8]

In order to grant similar conditions in reality and in virtual reality the virtual vehicle presentations were based on pre-rendered high definition images which replicated the subjects' trajectory when walking around the real vehicle on a specified distance. This correspondence was realized by the fact that the test subjects were asked to follow a taped line on the floor while examining the real vehicle. This oval line around the real vehicle with a constant distance of two meters represented the virtual trajectory. In order to completely define the virtual trajectory the eye height of a 50. percentile man was set. Figure 3 shows the survey's setting from above.

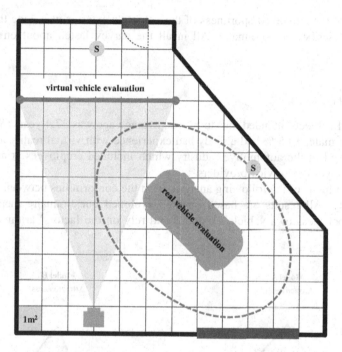

Fig. 3. Setting of the study ('S' represents the subject)

In line with immersion an application was implemented which enabled the test subjects to 'walk' around the virtual vehicle. The interaction of the test subjects with the virtual model was carried out by the arrow keys of a keyboard provided. Pressing the arrow key to the left let to the virtual vehicle turning to the right which conveyed the operator to walk clockwise. On the one hand the application allowed to rotate the vehicle fluently and on the other hand subjects could stop at any point. This should simulate the natural exterior examination (see Fig. 4).

The study itself started with the instruction of the test subjects whereupon it has to be stated that the survey was always performed by a single person and they were not informed about the research's purpose. In order to avoid any order dependencies the order of stimuli presentation was permuted for each subject. After the instruction the

Fig. 4. Comparison of the subject's perspective: real vs. virtual

assessment of the perceived sportiness of the vehicle's exterior was done through the previously described questionnaire. All in all the survey lasted about one hour per person.

3.2 Results

In the end 41 subjects attended the study. The average age was 37.4 years $(SD = 15.8)$, 73.2 % were male, 19.5 % had already had experience with virtual reality and 48.8 % were employed in the automotive industry which included employees at an OEM as well as employees at service providers.

The main focus of the following analysis is on the conformities between reality and virtual reality. All results are based on the developed questionnaire measuring the perceived sportiness of a vehicle's exterior and rely on the factors' arithmetic means (see Fig. 5).

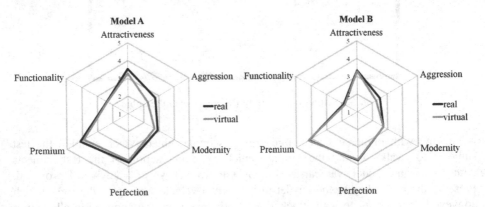

Fig. 5. Results of model A and model B: virtual vs. real

When comparing individual ratings aggregated on factor level high correlations can be found between real and virtual conditions (r = 0.675). Separating the models' results for further investigation the analyses between virtual reality and reality show strong effects – see Table 1.

Table 1. Correlation between reality and virtual reality separated by vehicle and factors

Model A	r(41)	Model B	r(41)
Attractiveness	.622*	Attractiveness	.726*
Aggression	.542*	Aggression	.721*
Modernity	.724*	Modernity	.740*
Perfection	.545*	Perfection	.560*
Premium	.508*	Premium	.672*
Functionality	.610*	Functionality	.618*

In addition an ANOVA with repeated measures on the three factors 'Vehicle' (Model A vs. Model B), 'Condition' (Real vs. Virtual) and 'Dimension' (Attractiveness, Aggression, Modernity, Perfection, Premium, Functionality) was carried out to investigate the ratings' absolute differences. In the following analysis only those effects will be discussed which are relevant to the current methodological contribution.

For the factor Vehicle a just significant main effect was found, $F(1, 40) = 4.10$, $p = .050$, $\eta_p^2 = .093$. For the factor Condition the main effect also reached significance, $F(1, 40) = 16.4$, $p < .001$, $\eta_p^2 = .29$. For the factor Dimension a significant effect was discovered as well, $F(5, 200) = 114$, $p < .001$, $\eta_p^2 = .74$.

For the interaction between the factors Condition and Vehicle a small effect was detected on $\alpha = 5\ \%$ level, $F(1, 40) = 4.15$, $p = .048$, $\eta_p^2 = .094$. As this interaction indicates that the ratings under virtual vs. real conditions differed between the two vehicles, a Post hoc test (Newman-Keuls) on this interaction was executed. Results show no significant differences in the ratings between virtual and real conditions for model B but for model A, $p = .001$. Referring to model A, virtual vs. real, the Post hoc test (Newman-Keuls) revealed significant differences for the dimensions Attractiveness ($p = .008$), Aggression ($p < .001$) and Premium ($p = .003$) but no significant differences for the dimensions Modernity, Perfection and Functionality. If differences occurred ratings under virtual condition were lower than under real condition.

4 Discussion and Outlook

In the current contribution an empirical study was designed and executed to address the question whether the perception of the overall sportiness of a vehicle's exterior can show the same results for virtual as well as real vehicle models. In order to measure the subject's perception of sportiness a questionnaire was developed and validated first. Its final concept describes six depending factors based on 33 items: 'attractiveness', 'aggression', 'modernity', 'perfection', 'premium' and 'functionality'.

Within the empirical study the subjects had to evaluate two current Audi SUV models under real and virtual conditions. Results show that the overall ratings under real and virtual conditions correlate highly. Still absolute differences have been identified between the captured subjective ratings of real and virtual models, especially for one of the observed vehicles and under certain dimensions. If absolute differences occurred evaluations under real condition revealed to be higher than ratings than under virtual condition.

It could be assumed that the application of a virtual presentation lowers the intensity of a visual impression compared to the real world. In line with these findings it has to be hypothesized what might have influenced this. Firstly there is the survey's setting with its 2D back-projection, the projection's resolution and the pre-defined subject's trajectories in reality and virtual reality. For all of these three parameters more extensive alternatives could have been applied, e.g. 3D projection, 4 k resolution, higher degree of freedom by real-time rendering and a higher level of immersion by a HMD. While absolute differences were dependent on stimulus set and results were diverging between model A and model B, this dependencies have not been fully understood yet. In order to grant assured knowledge the parameters listed need to be objects of further research.

All in all the results of the current study could show a high potential for the application of virtual car clinics especially for the assessment of perceived sportiness of a vehicle's exterior in the future. This contribution also shows the need for a methodically developed questionnaire in order to define and measure a certain latent construct relevant for customers' perception of a product – here the perception of a vehicle exterior's sportiness. It could be shown that the developed instrument can show very similar results for virtual as well as real vehicle models.

Regarding virtual car clinics it can be assumed that the current approach could be applied to other areas of customer perception as well – given the existence of appropriate instruments/questionnaires to access the relevant constructs. In the future virtual car clinics can enable OEMs to advance customers' feedback early within the development process. This shift is highly requested as it saves time and money and will allow faster customer centered redesign iterations in the future.

References

1. Dorothee Augustin, M., Wagemans, J., Carbon, C.-C.: (2012): All is beautiful? generality vs. specifity of word usage in visual aesthetics. Acta Psychol. **139**, 187–201 (2012)
2. Bloch, Peter H.: Seeking the ideal form: product design and consumer response. J. of Mark. **1998**(59), 16–29 (1998)
3. Braess, H.-H.: Seiffert, U.: Automobildesign und Technik. Formgebung, Funktionalität, Technik. Wiesbaden: Vieweg & Teubner (ATZ/MTZ-Fachbuch) (2007)
4. Bühner, M.: Einführung in die Test- und Fragebogenkonstruktion. 2., aktualisierte Aufl. München, Don Mills: Pearson Studium (2006)
5. Carbon, C.-C (Ed.) Design Evaluation: Zeitliche Dynamik ästhetischer Wertschätzung. With assistance of Géza Harsányi, Fabian Gebauer, Peter Kraemer. Lehrstuhl für Allgemeine Psychologie und Methodenlehre. Universität Bamberg, Bamberg (2013)
6. Daecke, J.: Nutzung virtueller Welten zur Kundenintegration in die Neuproduktentwicklung. Eine explorative Untersuchung am Beispiel der Automobilindustrie. 1. Aufl. Wiesbaden: Gabler (Gabler Research : Schriften zum europäischen Management) (2009)
7. DAT Welche Kriterien sind Ihnen bei der Anschaffung eines Neuwagens wichtig? Edited by Deutsche Automobil Treuhand GmbH (DAT) (2014). http://de.statista.com/statistik/daten/studie/223037/umfrage/hauptkriterien-bei-der-anschaffung-eines-neuwagens

8. Erdmann, A.: Verminderung des Produkteinführungsrisikos durch Virtual Reality-unterstützte Konzepttests. Eine experimentelle Studie zur Durchführung von VR-Car Clinics. Lohmar, Köln: Eul (Reihe: Marketing, Bd. 8) (1999)
9. Esch, F.-R.: Strategie und Technik des Automobilmarketing. Springer, Wiesbaden (2013)
10. Frey, B.: Zur Bewertung von Anmutungsqualitäten. Köln: Förderges. Produkt-Marketing (Beiträge zum Produkt-Marketing, Bd. 22) (1993)
11. Hsiao, K.-A., Chen, L.-L.: Fundamental dimensions of affective responses to product shapes. Int. J. Ind. Ergon. **36**, 553–564 (2006)
12. Kohler, Thomas C.: Wirkungen des Produktdesigns. Analyse und Messung am Beispiel Automobildesign. 1. Aufl. Wiesbaden: Dt. Univ.-Verl. Forschungsgruppe Konsum und Verhalten, Gabler Edition Wissenschaft (2003)
13. Köprülü, S.: Relevancy of bipolar word pairs across product: A comparative study between automobiles and the iphone. dissertation. Middle East Technical University, Ankara. Industrial Design (2010)
14. Oehme, A.: Ästhetisches Verständnis und ästhetische Wertschätzung von Automobildesign. Eine Frage der Expertise. With assistance of Reinhold Prof. Kliegl. Potsdam: University-Verl (Potsdam cognitive science series, 4) (2013)
15. Söderman, M.: Virtual reality in product evaluations with potential customers: an exploratory study comparing virtual reality with conventional product representations. J. Eng. Des. **16**(3), 311–328 (2007)
16. Yao, X., Hu, H-y., Li, J.: User knowledge acquisition in automobile engineering styling design. Syst. Eng. Procedia **3**, 139–145 (2012)
17. Zimmermann, P.: Virtual reality aided design. a survey of the use of vr in automotive industry. In: Talaba, Doru, Amditis, A (eds.) Product Engineering, pp. 277–296. Springer, Netherlands (2008)

Theoretical Foundations for Developing Cybersecurity Training

Eric C. Ortiz[✉] and Lauren Reinerman-Jones

Institute for Simulation and Training,
University of Central Florida, Orlando, FL, USA
{eortiz,lreinerm}@ist.ucf.edu

Abstract. Cybersecurity is a computer term regarding the detection, anticipation, and prevention of computer technologies and peripherals from damage, attack, or unauthorized access. These technologies include the monitoring of networks, programs, applications, and personnel. Cybersecurity can be viewed from both an offensive or defensive posture involving maintaining and proactively assessing security vulnerabilities. In 2013, Edward Snowden used his position as an infrastructure analyst to leak thousands of top-secret classified documents detailing the U.S. Government's global covert surveillance and eavesdropping undertakings to the public. This incident identified the human threat as a contributing factor that highlighted several weaknesses in the present state of U.S. cybersecurity affairs. In efforts to strengthen cyber defenses, a solid theoretical research foundation regarding cyber vulnerabilities is warranted. Building upon that foundation, training and experimentation can provide insight into current cybersecurity training methods and how they can be transitioned and implemented into future training regimens.

Keywords: Cybersecurity · Human component · Virtual and gaming environments

1 Introduction

In 2013 an employee of Booz Hamilton, Edward Snowden was a federal contractor for the National Security Agency (NSA). The NSA is a United States (U.S.) Government agency responsible for worldwide monitoring of data and information for both counterintelligence and foreign intelligence needs. Snowden used his position as an infrastructure analyst to leak thousands of top-secret classified documents detailing the U.S. Government's global covert surveillance and eavesdropping undertakings to the public. The Snowden incident is considered one of the biggest leaks in NSA history. It is also a prime example of a cybersecurity breach on a national scale that threatened to expose U.S. secrets and intelligence [1].

As information technology expands, the data accumulated and maintained on such technology must be protected. Cybersecurity is a term regarding detecting, anticipating, and preventing information technologies and peripherals from damage, attack, or unauthorized intrusion from cyber-criminals often called hackers [2]. Cybersecurity also includes the monitoring of networks, programs, applications, and personnel.

© Springer International Publishing Switzerland 2015
R. Shumaker and S. Lackey (Eds.): VAMR 2015, LNCS 9179, pp. 480–487, 2015.
DOI: 10.1007/978-3-319-21067-4_49

A cybersecurity intrusion or threat can present itself in multiple ways from malware and viruses, to disgruntled employees [3]. Cybersecurity is important for every person and organization to recognize and become educated on, but is absolutely essential for the Government to stay ahead of the curve for national security, public safety, and economic stability.

Critical incidents such as Snowden [1] have led to the U.S. Government creating laws and regulations regarding information security systems. A National Institute of Standards and Technology (NIST) special publication states "Information technology is widely recognized as the engine that drives the U.S. economy" [4]. The e-Government Act of 2002 makes clear the significance of cybersecurity and national defense. The Federal Information Security Management Act (FISMA) is title III of that act. FISMA states federal agencies must create security management systems adhered to by all other federal agencies [5]. These programs must offer security for the information systems supporting operations of federal agencies including those managed by other agencies. In an effort to achieve these objectives, the NIST was tasked by FISMA to create a standardized framework for FISMA implementation of security controls based upon security classifications. FISMA is effective for providing guidelines that private industry can use to secure information systems and establish relevant training environments, protocols, and practices.

Such laws, policies, and guidelines resulted in cybersecurity viewed from an offensive and defensive perspective involving maintaining, protecting, and proactively assessing security vulnerabilities. The Snowden incident is an example of an attack causing the U.S. to take a defensive posture and identified the human threat as a major contributing factor highlighting several weaknesses in the present state of U.S. cybersecurity affairs. In many organizations, cybersecurity is not given top priority until a cyber-incident occurs forcing a reaction from a defensive posture. This defensive reaction is to prevent further damage and to determine cause and impact of the breach [6]. An offensive position is different from a defensive position because it involves initiating cyber-attacks or proactively monitoring and protecting data or information [7]. An offensive stance can include a concept called penetration testing, which many organizations conduct to self-test and assess vulnerabilities before a hacker has the opportunity [6].

The present paper focuses upon the human component of cybersecurity with particular emphasis given to environments supporting training and experimentation. The benefits and limitations of available simulations and training protocols will be discussed followed by a call to action for informing the development of cybersecurity training and experimentation environments.

2 The Human Component

In keeping an organization safe from cyber-attacks, most attention is placed on technology. Organizations focus on enhancing firewall protection or selecting the best anti-virus software. However, one of the biggest vulnerability points is not associated with technology sustainment, but rather the human component. Ahmed, Sharif, Kabir, and Al-Maimani [8] maintain that in information technology, the human element is frequently referred to as the "weakest link in the security chain."

The threat from the human element can be either unintentional or intentional stemming from people with various reasons. Anyone attacking cyber defenses from outside an organization's networked perimeter is considered an outside hacker, while anyone attacking from within an organization is referred to as an inside hacker. Insiders have multiple advantages over an outsider including knowledge of where critical data exists. Insiders can include past employees and one-time collaborators [9]. Individuals are considered insiders if they presently have the ability to or at one time had permission to access an organization's data or network structures [10]. However, insiders are not limited to individuals bent on accessing network infrastructures for purely malicious purposes.

2.1 Human Vulnerabilities

Both unintentional and intentional vulnerability exposure is equally as damaging and can be carried out by individuals or teams. In the instance of unintentional vulnerabilities, the cause of a critical system or security breach is frequently simple human error [8]. Well-meaning employees can unintentionally make their organizations vulnerable because they may be careless at following security protocols [9] like forgetting to log off of a computer before walking away or allowing tailgaters into a restricted area without using proper credentials to enter.

Intentional vulnerabilities range in motivation from financial to revenge. These individuals typically want to hurt the organization for personal reasons. This form of exposure is challenging because it can stem from anyone within an organization willing to take advantage of accessible information. For example, a disgruntled employee that was fired and now wants to exact revenge by giving sensitive data to the competition or the office secretary with access to a manager's credit card information. Another instance is an employee stealing intellectual property (IP) or trade secrets. Stolen information might consist of price listings, business plans, and proprietary software. This information is typically taken in hopes of gaining an advantage or feel it is owed to them since they were a part of the development team. IT sabotage occurs when former employees or business partners take advantage of their access to network infrastructures for the purpose of disrupting operations. One instance of this situation is a terminated IT manager that will not relinquish his administrative passwords, thus holding an organization hostage until certain demands are met.

These instances of unintentional and intentional vulnerabilities describe insider threats, but perhaps the most commonly thought of intentional threat is a hacker.

2.2 Hacker Types

Hackers can be categorized into three groups: white hats, black hats, and grey hats [11]. White hats are akin to law enforcement agents and generally work to help maintain security and expose security flaws. Black hats will typically have an extensive knowledge of computers and thrive on the ability to infiltrate network defense systems. Black hats are the types that have garnered the most publicity because they believe they are above the law and advertise their hacks to gain notoriety. A grey hat is a relatively new term and oftentimes described as "ethical hackers." Grey hats will only hack into an organizations network as a way to check for vulnerabilities and usually report their findings as way to make sure the organization is aware [12].

In 2013, grey hat hacker Ahmed Al-Khabaz, a student at Dawson College in Montreal, Canada, was expelled for discovering a security flaw in the college's computer system [13]. This flaw compromised the personal information of over 250,000 students. Al-Khabaz was a part of the software development club at the College and was developing a mobile app allowing students easier access into their personal accounts. He described the discovery as "sloppy coding" in the schools Omnivox software, stating the vulnerability allowed users with basic computer knowledge access to personal information of any student in the system [13]. Based upon the publicity garnered from the expulsion and his ability to successfully hack into the system, Al-Khabaz was offered numerous job opportunities including from the software initially hacked.

2.3   The Impact of Human Vulnerabilities

Richard A. McFeely, who testified on June 12, 2013 before the Senate Appropriations Committee in Washington, D.C., stated our enemies in cyber space can include spies from other countries in search of business secrets and IP [14]. It can be criminals interested in stealing money and identities. It can include terrorist that want to attack critical infrastructures, and even "hacktivist groups" interested in delivering "social or political statements." This testimony inferred the U.S. is losing money, data, and ideas to a vast array of cyber threats. As such, the human is an important factor in cybersecurity because it is individuals and their actions committing these behaviors. Vulnerabilities caused by the human element can and do affect all aspects of any organizations infrastructure whether unintentional or intentional.

To illustrate, a virus introduced by a disgruntled IT analyst with full rights to the network for the purpose of crippling the network infrastructure, or a user downloading software to play music containing malware causing system outages. Additionally, it can also come from an overworked IT manager that forgets to install software patches leaving network systems vulnerable. Unfortunately, cybersecurity vulnerabilities are not limited to network infrastructures. The effects of the human threat can also be felt down to the component level. This includes malicious code integrated into computer chips during the manufacturing process by individuals with the ability to intentionally alter them. The code can be designed to sit idle until prompted by an event (e.g., calendar date) to launch an attack [15]. All these events, whether unintentional or intentional, and the widespread damage they cause, create a rippling effect that impacts the whole organizational structure from revenue, organizational productivity, to trust by business partners and consumers such as the Target breach of 2013 [16].

It is apparent that the human component is a critical factor in cybersecurity and its implications can be felt in all aspects. It is for this reason that cybersecurity policies, training, and education based upon sound science all play an important role in understanding and reducing cyber risks. Leaders in organizations may have difficulties conceptualizing that as technology advances so does the human vulnerability. Platsis [17] maintains, "if one chooses not to implement effective and efficient cybersecurity policies, the vulnerability is human, not technological." Users are often naïve in cybersecurity, therefore, training and education is imperative, and this is not only limited to entry-level users. The need for training and education also applies to those responsible for policy implementation and especially those involved with organization-wide security efforts. Deciding on an acceptable level of risk, which is only accomplished by informed leadership, determines the strategies implemented, policies pushed, and training possibilities made available [18].

3 Cybersecurity Training and Experimentation Environments

One of the greatest challenges with training on the human component of cybersecurity is that environments are limited in the ability to convey the complex and dynamic situations for which cyber vulnerabilities occur. Beyond this, effective training curriculum is limited by the inadequate environments available for cybersecurity experimentation, which leads to valid training materials.

3.1 Current Environments

The U.S. military training communities are major contributors and proponents of utilizing VE's and games to enhance performance and increase training retention. Warfighters regularly utilize and conduct multifaceted training simulations equipped with physics and high fidelity 3D components to practice various tactics, techniques, and procedures [19]. These Warfighters are provided with state-of-the art VE's to train in an effort to provide essential skills necessary to successfully execute duties. This virtual training can range from basic marksmanship to advanced combat operations trainers. Naturally, then, the implementation of similar training environments is expected for such an important duty as cybersecurity, but that is not the case.

The current training and experimentation environments for cybersecurity vary in sophistication and are generally delivered via basic multi-media formats. They are usually self-paced and primarily include text-based informational pages followed by evaluation forms to assess information retention. PowerPoint slide shows or low-fidelity case studies, developed in Flash or Java applets, explaining the cyber risks an organization may face and associated IT mitigation strategies are often used. Examples include the DoD Cyber Awareness Challenge Training created for the U.S. Army as an annual requirement for anyone accessing Army networks [20] and SIMTRAY [21].

A few, slightly more advanced environments have been developed. In 2009 the Air Force Institute of Technology developed a virtualization platform for courses in cybersecurity education in an effort to offer more usable, reconfigurable, and practical training environments [22]. They specifically focused on utilizing existing technologies, such as "operating system virtualization" techniques, to redesign network infrastructures containing multiple nodes on simple hardware applications. This enabled a number of operating systems to run virtually and allowed a greater usage of resources and flexibility including reconfiguration. This flexibility gives courses in network security the advantages and benefits virtualization offers. In 2012 an online assessment for cybersecurity training in a virtual lab was developed to offer software that accesses training exercises in an online lab utilizing virtual machines [23]. The concept was to define exercise scenario parameters to introduce a toolkit for virtual machine configuration according to requirements in a training environment. This allowed for dynamic creation of testing options (e.g., multiple choices) for web-based learning environments. In 2014, a low fidelity simulation was developed reproducing features of real-world cyber operator missions of pattern matching and recognition enabling experimentation of cybervigilance [24].

The existing environments described do provide some level of training and ability to test the human component of cybersecurity, but to date do not capture the complexity of cybersecurity for effective, long-term training or experimentation to determine best practices for training. Generally, they also lack in engagement and interaction, reducing the opportunity for retention. A step in the direction of matching current training capabilities used by the military and other domains, while being mindful of cost, is to create a cybersecurity gaming environment.

3.2 Benefits of Gaming Environments and Virtual Environments

The benefits of using gaming environments and VEs to simulate cybersecurity duties include the ability to control and manipulate variables such as graphics, task flow, and logging. The ability to control the variables in an environment for training is important to perhaps provide adaptive training and accurate evaluation of skill and knowledge acquisition. The ability to control variables in an environment is essential for experimentation to enable accurate measurement of a phenomenon. Another benefit for training involves real-time interaction with cyber events, thus providing an opportunity to enhance simulation factors like engagement and flow, and better assess phenomena like vigilance and situation awareness. The immersive nature or competitive components built into a game enable training and assessment of cyber professionals' decision making processes for chosen actions, which impact an organizations ability to function effectively. Gaming components and VEs also include the ability to review past cyber incidents (i.e. after action reviews) in which alternative simulated courses of action potentially mitigate negative outcomes. This capability empowers trainees to see multiple outcomes, successful and consequential, thereby reducing time and cost.

4 Call to Action

Developing environments that are dynamic, controllable, and interactive appears to be the next right step in advancing training and experimentation for cybersecurity, but execution of such a task requires several hurtles to be overcome and warrants multiple communities to do so successfully. The present paper challenges interdisciplinary and multidisciplinary teams to address the following.

- Based upon the complexity of real-world tasks, it is difficult to replicate realistic cybersecurity scenarios. What components of a cybersecurity scenario should be built into an environment? Should an environment be flexible enough to incorporate multiple scenarios?
- A standardization gap exists regarding what elements should be included in cybersecurity training and experimentation environments such as the human component. How do we simulate the human component? Should this be dynamic in real-time or fixed? Should every cybersecurity environment center on at least one same scenario? Should environments be open source or proprietary?
- As cybersecurity continues to expand, it is important to further investigate novel training methods and experimentation. How is cybersecurity evolving? Why is it evolving? Who is affected? How should training and experimentation environments be developed to account for this evolution?
- Relevant information is most often available through media outlets (e.g. newsweek) regarding the present state-of-affairs. Academic journals available are limited or obsolete based upon cybersecurity's ever-changing climate. How should information be distributed publically? How should scientific findings be distributed without becoming a cybersecurity vulnerability for organizations or the Government?

There are a few educational institutes taking steps toward addressing the need for cybersecurity training and experimentation, as well as the development of adequate environments. They are doing this through certification programs (e.g. University of Central Florida's Modeling and Simulation Graduate Program) and degrees for higher-level education (e.g. University of Maryland, and University of Tampa). However, more programs are needed. This is a call to all stakeholders to get involved.

References

1. Greenwald, G., MacAskill, E., Poitras, L.: Edward Snowden: the whistleblower behind the NSA surveillance revelations. The Guardian 11 June 2013
2. Hansen, L., Nissenbaum, H.: Digital disaster, cyber security, and the copenhagen school. Int. Stud. Quart. 53(4), 1155–1175 (2009)
3. McDowell, M., Householder, A.: US-CERT, 6 May 2009. https://www.us-cert.gov/ncas/tips/ST04-001. Accessed 18 February 2015
4. Managing Information Security Risk, U.S. Department of Commerce, Gaithersburg (2011)
5. National Institute of Standards and Technology, U.S. Department of Commerce, 1 April 2014. http://csrc.nist.gov/groups/SMA/fisma/overview.html. Accessed 17 February 2015
6. Vacca, J.R.: Guarding against network intrusion. In: Computer and Information Security Handbook, pp. 86–87. Elsevier, Waltham (2013)
7. Patriciu, V.-V., Furtuna, A.C.: Guide for designing cyber security exercises. In: Proceedings of the 8th WSEAS International Conference on E-Activities and Information Security and Privacy (2009)
8. Munir, A., Lukman, S., Muhammad, K., Al-Maimani, M.: Human errors in information security. Int. J. 1(3), (2012)
9. Kenyon, H.: SMBs Ignoring Insider Threats. InformationWeek, 23 June 2014

10. Greitzer, F.L., Moore, A.P., Cappelli, D.M., Andrews, D.H., Carroll, L.A., Hull, T.D.: Combating the insider cyber threat. Secur. Priv. IEEE **6**(1), 61–64 (2008)
11. Hald, S.L., Pedersen, J.M.: An updated taxonomy for characterizing hackers according to thier threat properties. In: 2012 14th International Conference on Advanced Communication Technology (ICACT). IEEE (2012)
12. Gold, S.: Cyber-psychopathy: what goes on in a hacker's head. Eng. Technol. Mag. **9**(1), 20 (2014)
13. Cox, E.: Ahmed Al-Khabaz expelled from Dawson College after finding security flaw. National Post, 20 January 2013
14. Statement Before the Senate Appropriations Committee. The Federal Bureau of Investigation, 12 June 2013
15. Lynn, W.J.: Defending a new domain: the pentagon's cyberstrategy. Foreign Aff. **89**(5), 101 (2010)
16. Harris, E.A.: Target Executive Resigns After Breach. The New York Times, 5 March 2014
17. Platsis, G.: The Real Vulnerability of the Cyberworld: You and I, Adelphi (2015)
18. Roman, J.: Cost of Mitigating the Insider Threat (2013)
19. Stanescu, I.A., Stefan, A.: Interoperability in serious games. In: The 7th International Scientific Conference eLearning and Software for Education, Bucharest (2011)
20. DoD Cyber Awareness Challenge Training, U.S. Army, 2015. https://ia.signal.army.mil/DoDIAA/default.asp. Accessed 18 February 2015
21. SIMTRAY, University of Maryland University College, 2014. Accessed 16 February 2015
22. Stewart, K.E., Humphries, J.W., Andel, T.R.: Developing a virtualization platform for courses in networking, systems administration and cyber security education. In: Proceedings of the 2009 Spring Simulation Multiconference (2009)
23. Williams, C., Meinel, C.: Online assessment for hands-on cyber security training in a virtual lab. In: Global Engineering Education Conference (EDUCON). IEEE (2012)
24. Sawyer, B.D., Finomore, V.S., Funke, G.J., Mancuso, V.F., Funke, M.E., Matthews, G., Warm, J.S.: Cyber vigilance: effects of signal probability and event rate. In: Proceedings of the Human Factors and Ergonomics Society Annual Meeting (2014)

Investigation of Visual Features for Augmented Reality Assembly Assistance

Rafael Radkowski[✉]

Virtual Reality Applications Center,
Iowa State University, Ames, IA, USA
rafael@iastate.edu

Abstract. The overall goal of this research is to investigate the effectivity of augmented reality (AR) assembly assistance in relation to the difficulty of a particular assembly task since advantages of AR, such as time and error reduction, have not been consequently reported in literature. The research aims to identify additional factors that affect the design of virtual instructions for AR applications. This paper intends to discuss a suggested classification of visual features for AR assembly assistance applications. The classification suggests visual features for different assembly activities and distinguishes significant from less significant parts. It represents a theoretical framework for this research. A user study was conducted to verify the suggested visual features. The results are not significant and do not support the classification. However, observations made during the study indicate additional factors.

1 Introduction

Augmented reality (AR) technology is a type of human-computer-interaction that enhances the natural visual perception of a human user with computer generated information (i.e., 3D models, annotations, and text) [2]. AR presents this information in a context-sensitive way that is appropriate to a specific task, and typically, related to the user's physical location. Viewing devices such as head-mounted displays, tablet computers, or displays are necessary to use AR. The user sees the environment as video that is superimposed with computer-generated information.

An application domain of AR is assembly assistance for manual assembly in mechanical engineering. Manual assembly is a procedural task in which an operator assembles a product from a set of components and assembly assistance are all means that convey assembly instructions. The most important instructions are the assembly sequence, the components that need to be assembled in each step of this sequence, the assembly location and part alignment, as well as the tools that are required. Technical manuals, assembly drawings, and assembly instructors are the classical way provide assembly instructions. Industry already moves to digital instructions using 3D models, animations, and videos to explain the assembly procedure.

© Springer International Publishing Switzerland 2015
R. Shumaker and S. Lackey (Eds.): VAMR 2015, LNCS 9179, pp. 488–498, 2015.
DOI: 10.1007/978-3-319-21067-4_50

AR applications convey assembly instructions using digital 3D models, animations, and text, for instance, referred to as visual features. Figure 1 shows an example of an AR assembly assistance application operating on a mobile tablet computer. A video camera is attached to this tablet, the video is shown on the display. A 3D model superimposes the physical object, which shows the correct alignment of the part to assemble. Several AR assembly assistance applications were already introduced (i.e., [6,18,22,24,30,31]), studies indicate the advantages of AR assembly assistance in comparison to other media [4,5, 20] typically a reduced assembly time and error rate, as well as higher acceptance [14,23].

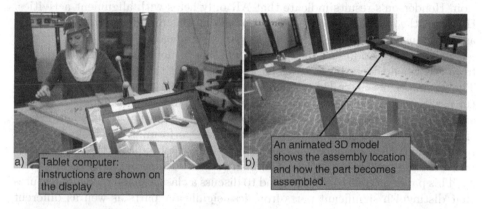

a) Tablet computer: instructions are shown on the display

b) An animated 3D model shows the assembly location and how the part becomes assembled.

Fig. 1. a) AR assembly assistance on a mobile tablet computer. b) The AR application conveys assembly instructions using 3D models of the object to assemble.

A review of the literature unveils a huge diversity among the employed AR applications, study objects, as well as results. Display devices, for instance, range from head mounted displays to handheld devices, and computer displays. The object, the part to assemble also varies between mechanical engineering products (i.e., a pump or combustion chamber), technical consumer goods (e.g., computers), and toys. Most of the studies report several advantages when using AR, advantages such as a reduced assembly time or less mistakes. However, advantages have not been consequently reported. The question here is: why not or which additional factors affect the success of AR? Several studies (i.e. [8,25]) indicate that the difficulty of the object to assemble along with the assembly activities cause a bias, since manual assembly incorporates a wide range of activities and the objects in studies ask users only to perform a few of those activities.

Manual assembly incorporates several different activities such as part identification, handling, alignment, joining, adjustment, and inspection, where all these tasks have a different degree of difficulty. Joining two or more parts with fasteners can be considered as more difficult than pushing a part into position. However, the term "difficulty" is already difficult to define. Agrawala et al. [1] suggest to provide instructions on two levels to address different parts: significant parts and less significant parts & fasteners. Significant parts produce the main function of the product, and less significant parts (i.e. nuts, bolts) are supporting parts. Less significant parts are easier to install than significant parts.

Returning to AR instructions: aligning a part accurately and joining it with several fasteners may be a more difficult task than pushing a part into position. For instance, computer parts and Lego bricks only need to be pushed into position. Thus, they may be considered as less significant tasks. Parts of a combustion chamber or a pump can be easily misaligned - so far, a hypothesis. Research from Wiedenmaier et al. [25] and Henderson [8] indicates the correctness of this hypothesis. The results from Wiedenmaier et al. demonstrate that a user does not gain advantages from AR when parts need to be clipped into position. Henderson's results indicate that AR only helps with alignment activities. However, the authors always used similar 3D models and digital text to convey assembly instructions, regardless of the part's significance.

This research addresses the question whether or not a user gains advantages from AR when the visual features for each task meet the level of task difficulty. The assumption is: significant tasks are more difficult, require more time, thus the user accepts richer information which requires more time to understand. Less significant tasks are simple, the user does not accept instructions when understanding the instructions costs more time than performing the task. Research results, i.e. [12, 13] support this assumption since they indicate that less significant parts do not always require rich instructions such as 3D models.

This paper intends to suggests and to discuss a classification of visual features that distinguish significant parts from less significant parts as well as different assembly activities of manual assembly. The goal of this classification is to provide a guideline for assembly instructions that facilitates development of an AR assembly application. This classification can be considered as a hypothesis that still needs to be proven. Results of an initial study are promising, however, not significant; the study is explained in detail in [16]. Thus, the goal of this paper is to introduce and discuss the addressed research and the classification.

The paper is structured as follows: the next subsection introduces manual assembly and its activities. Section 3 explains the classification and the rational behind the selected visual feature classes. Section 4 summarizes the study that has been presented in [16]. The last section concludes this paper and introduces the future research.

2   Background: Manual Assembly and Instructions

The background information introduces the area of manufacturing and instruction research, which are the foundation for this research. The manufacturing domain uses models to classify manual assembly in order to allow engineers to predict the assembly time and to optimize the workflow on a factory floor. This task classification is the basis for this research since an AR application must support those activities. Instruction research helps to understand how an application can convey procedural information best.

2.1   Manual Assembly

Manual assembly is considered as a procedural task in manufacturing with the goal to assemble a product out of a set of components and/or subassemblies [9]. Manual assembly incorporates different manual activities such as [15]:

- Identification: the operator has to identify a component and/or a tool.
- Handling: addresses the movement of material, parts, tools within the working area.
- Alignment: locating the active surface of a mechanical part to the active surface of a second part.
- Joining: creating a fixed or detachable connection between parts.
- Adjustment: refining the setting of a part and/or of a connection, e.g., change the torque.
- Inspection: assessing the quality of an assembly.

Several additional activities are listed in literature. The list addresses the most important activities that AR can support. The activities are in no order. Which activities an operator needs to carry out and in which sequence depends on a particular product.

2.2   Instructions

The ideal interface is designed in a comprehensible way without overwhelming the user. Thus procedural instructions need to be presented in a most efficient way to not overwhelm a user. The obstacle for understanding information is the limited user's mental capacity. The user requires more time when the information is complex. The theory distinguishes descriptive and depictive representations of information [10,17]. The descriptive information has no visual similarity to the object it describes. Text for example is a descriptive representation of information. In opposite to this, a depictive representation presents information similar to its referent. Depictive information are considered as more concise where descriptive information can be more complete.

In AR assembly assistance research, descriptive and depictive representations are frequently used where the majority of introduced studies focusses on 3D models along with animations, 2D sketches, diagrams, and text. A minority of studies used photos of objects.

Text explains a procedural task by denoting the involved objects and describing the interactions with them. Textual information are omnipresent, which is an advantage. Almost every adult in an educated country can read and understand text without a special training. However, to understand text requires more cognitive processing, which takes more time than understanding an image [7,27].

Diagrams show step-by-step instructions as a sequence of single images, where each image shows one step. Agrawala et al. [1] recommend *action diagrams* which show the activity of the main part. Parts that need to be assembled should be visually disconnected from already assembled parts. Results from Michas and Berry [13] indicate that diagrams can be efficient when explaining simple tasks, such as clipping tasks. To increase the effectivity of a diagram, the information can be associated to a spatial location [21]. Pictograms can be very concise, thus information can be quickly understood [29]. However, a unfortunate design can result in the opposite.

Computer animations and 3D models are the first choice in the AR assembly assistance field. The research in the area of digital instructions underpins the efficiency of 3D models and animations. However, neither advantages nor disadvantages were consequently shown in literature. The research results rather indicate that additional user attributes need to be considered, such as the spatial ability [11], the motor skills [28], the assembly experience [3], and the experience with computers [19], for instance. Research results from Michas et al. [13] and Mayer et al. [12], who investigated multimedia illustrations for learning tasks, indicate that less significants parts and tasks do not always require rich instructions such as a 3D model.

In summary, the research indicates that the assembly activity, its level of difficulty, as well as the user should be considered when selecting the right illustration to convey assembly instructions.

3   Classification of Visual Features

Figure 2 illustrates the classification of visual features for AR assembly instructions. The rows show three different activities of manual assembly: *identification*, *joining*, and *alignment*, which are in focus of this classification since they are the most common tasks that AR assembly assistance supports. The columns show two different visual features for each activity. Each activity can incorporate significant and less significant parts [1]. Significant parts are all major parts, which produce the main function. Only one significant part should be involved in one assembly step, along with several less significant parts, if required. Less significant parts are components such as fasteners, clips, cable ties, etc. It is also assumed that significant parts require more difficult assembly activities than less significant parts.

The two terms *abstract* visual features and *concrete* visual features according to Wilema [26] are used to distinguish visual features on two levels. The concrete visual features utilizes mostly depictive illustrations such as 3D models where abstract visual features use symbolic 2D/3D elements. Concrete visual features convey more information than abstract visual features. Abstract visual features convey little information, however, the user understands them faster.

The rational for the classification is to reduce the time the user requires to understand the information when less significant parts need to be assembled. Following this rational, concrete visual features with rich information should be used for significant parts, abstract visual features for less significant parts. The recommended visual features originate from a literature review in i.e., [4–6, 14, 18, 20, 22–24, 30, 31]. The most frequent visual features that follow the rational of this research have been used to assemble the classification.

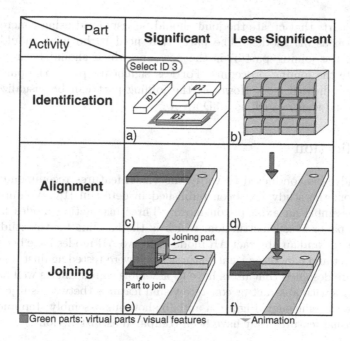

Fig. 2. Classification of visual features for AR assembly assistance(Color figure online).

Identification: the user needs to be able to clearly identify a particular significant part. In opposite, a less significant part is only one part in a group of parts. Thus for the identification of significant parts a) an abstract visual feature should be combined with text. For our tests, we combined a 3D frame, which encases the part to select, as well as text showing an id number. Thus, if the frame does not clearly indicate the part to select, the number identifies the part. Less significant parts b) can be indicated by using an abstract visual feature. We used 3D arrows and/or 3D frames which point to the correct part.

Alignment: to align a significant part c), the user needs to known the correct position and orientation of the part. Therefore, a concrete visual feature is recommended such as a 3D model. For the alignment of a less significant part, the user does not need to know an exact position / orientation because the position and orientation is obvious. For instance, a bolt that needs to be pushed through a hole or a clip that needs to be pushed into location do not require much explanation. The alignment activity is considered as well known. Thus, an abstract visual feature such as a 3D arrow should be used, which indicates the assembly location. The 3D models as well as 3D arrows can be supported with animations, which visually connect a 3D model with the assembly.

Joining: joining tasks typically require to create a fixed or detachable connection between two or more parts using an additional member. To join a significant part, it is assumed that the user is required to know a particular joining method; the joining activity is not obvious. Therefore, the parts that need to be joined as well as the parts that create the joint should be visualized using concrete visual features such as 3D models. The parts that need to be joint should already be aligned, the joining part(s) is the new one which should be animated to demonstrate the joining procedure. For less significant parts, the parts to join need to be indicated, too. However, the joining part can be visualized as an abstract visual feature such as a 3D arrow.

4 Verification

A user study was conducted to verify the visual features recommended in the classification; the study has been published in detail in [16]. Volunteers were asked to assemble an axial piston motor. Three instruction modes have been compared: paper-based instruction, which is the baseline for the study, a concrete AR mode and an abstract AR mode. The two AR modes have been realized with abstract and concrete visual features; each were tested against its opposite: the test were designed that users have to assemble significant as well as less significant parts with abstract or concrete visual features (between-subject design) to compare the efficiency. Figure 3a and 3b show one assembly step and the two different visual features that have been compared as instructions.

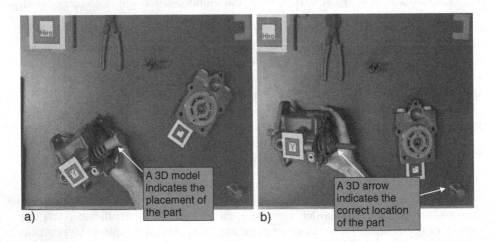

Fig. 3. a) a concrete visual feature (3D model) has been compared with b) an abstract visual feature (arrow).

The piston motor consists of 30 parts; two ball bearings remained on a shaft for this study. To assemble all components, 16 manual steps are necessary. Seven of these steps incorporate significant parts. The assembly of two parts is considered as very difficult: the installation of a swashplate (Step 2) and the alignment of a slipper retainer guide (Step 6). The number of errors the users made and the assembly time were recorded. In total, 27 out of 33 persons were able to complete the piston motor.

In summary, the results do not show significant improvements when using AR in comparison to paper-based instruction. The average assembly time was a) 20 min in concrete AR mode, b) 36 min in abstract AR mode, and c) 21 min with paper-based instruction. The difference between a) and b) is significant. The average number of errors in concrete AR mode is 4, b) abstract AR mode 8, and c) 3.5 with paper-based instruction.

Figure 4 shows the average assembly time for each assembly step. Note, extreme outliers have been removed from step 4, step 10, and step 16. Since a goal of this research is to verify whether or not simplified, abstract visual instructions such as a 3D arrow can better support users when the task is less significant, the assembly times for all steps with significant and less significant parts were compared; all underlined step numbers indicate significant parts.

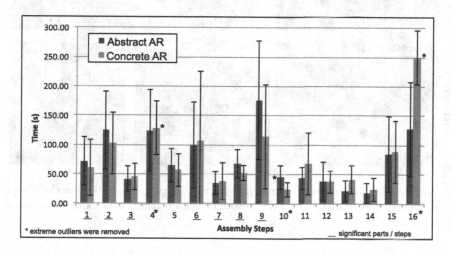

Fig. 4. Time results for all 16 steps in seconds.

The results are ambiguous. The hypothesis expects that all steps with significant parts can be faster completed when using concrete visual features and vice versa for less significant parts. The first two steps, the installation of a piston and a swashplate meet the expectation. However, the third step, the installation of a shaft, which can be considered as the most important part of the pump, can be successfully installed with concrete visual features as instructions and with abstract visual features either.

Nevertheless, some assembly step results and observations made during the study allow to further pursue the hypothesis of this research. Figure 5 shows assembly steps with less significant parts. The upper row shows the part to install, the lower row the AR instruction that were used to indicate the assembly location. The users were able to install part 11, part 13, part 14, and part 16, the bolts, with abstract visual features as instructions. In all steps, a time difference between concrete visual features (3D model) and abstract visual features could be noticed; the time difference is not significant. A surprise is the time difference in step 16, the installation of the pump cap with five bolts. The users need almost half the time when seeing 3D arrows as instructions in comparison to 3D models.

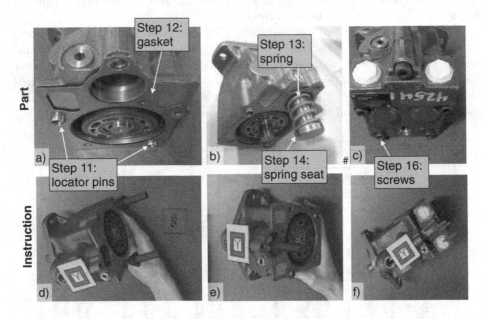

Fig. 5. Positive observations that may underpin the hypothesis. a-c) show the components the user had to install, d-f) the abstract visual features that explain the installation.

This observations may indicate that other factors are more important than the significance of the parts. Two factors have been identified. First, hidden, inlying parts, are difficult to install regardless whether they are considered as significant or less significant. Second, the number of degrees-of-freedom the user has to correctly align when installing a part governs the assembly difficulty. Parts such as the spring (Fig. 5b), the spring seat, and the pins, only need to be pushed into position and only the position along the axis is important to maintain. In future, the research will focus on these factors.

5   Conclusion and Outlook

This research investigated different visual features with the goal to create a classification that facilitate to design an interface for AR assembly assistance applications. Research indicates that AR only helps a user when the particular assembly task can be considered as difficult. Simple assembly tasks, tasks that do not need much time, or where understanding the information requires more time than assembling the part, cannot be supported by AR. However, the hypothesis is that a visual feature that simplifies the information and only gives the user a hint where to install a part rather than explaining or depicting what to install may also support the user during less significant tasks. A user study was carried out to compare two types of visual features for three assembly activities. The results do not support the hypothesis, thus the hypothesis must be rejected.

Nevertheless, the results partly indicate that the difficulty of the task can be important. The observations of the users along with the data of four steps show that simple tasks, which are almost obvious, require only a simple visual indication and no detailed instructions. The future research will focus on the degrees-of-freedom the user has to maintain during the alignment and joining procedure and whether or not the final installation location is hidden.

Acknowledgement. The author thanks Jordan Herrema for conducting the user study.

References

1. Agrawala, M., Phan, D., Heiser, J., Haymaker, J., Klingner, J., Hanrahan, P., Tversky, B.: Designing effective step-by-step assembly instructions. J. ACM Trans. Graph. (TOG) Proc. ACM. 2003 **22**(3), 828–837 (2003)
2. Azuma, R.: A survey of augmented reality. Presence Teleoperators Virtual Environments **6**, 355–385 (1997)
3. Baggett, P., Ehrenfeucht, A.: Building physical and mental models in assembly tasks. Int. J. Ind. Ergon. **7**, 217–227 (1991)
4. Baird, K.M., Barfield, W.: Evaluating the effectiveness of augmented reality displays for a manual assembly task. Virtual Reality 4(4), 250–259 (1999)
5. Boud, A., Haniff, D., Baber, C., Steiner, S.: Virtual reality and augmented reality as a training tool for assembly tasks. In: Proceedings of the 1999 IEEE International Conference on Information Visualization, pp. 32–36. London, UK, July 14–16 1999
6. Chimienti, V., Iliano, S., Dassisti, M., Dini, G., Failli, F.: Guidelines for implementing augmented reality procedures in assisting assembly operations. In: Ratchev, S. (ed.) IPAS 2010. IFIP AICT, vol. 315, pp. 174–179. Springer, Heidelberg (2010)
7. Ganier, F.: Factors affecting the processing of procedural instructions: implications for document design. IEEE Trans. Prof. Commun. **47**(1), 15–26 (2004)
8. Henderson, S., Feiner, S.: Augmented reality in the psychomotor phase of a procedural task. In: Proceedings of the 2011 10th IEEE International Symposium on Mixed and Augmented Reality. Basel, Switzerland, October 26–29 2011
9. Ikeuchi, K., Suehiro, T.: Towards an assembly plan from observation. In: Proceedings of the 1992 IEEE International Conference on Robotics and Automation, pp. 2171–2177. Nice, France, May 12–14, 1992
10. Kosslyn, S.: Image and Brain. MIT press, Cambridge (1994)
11. Lee, D.Y., Shin, D.H.: An empirical evaluation of multi-media based learning of a procedural task. Comput. Hum. Behav. **28**, 1072–1081 (2012)
12. Mayer, R.E., Hegarty, M., Mayer, S., Campbell, J.: When static media promote active learning: annotated illustrations versus narrated animations in multimedia instruction. J. Exp. Psychol. Appl. **11**(4), 256–265 (2005)
13. Michas, I.C., Berry, D.C.: Learning a procedural task: effectiveness of multimedia presentations. Appl. Cognitive Psychol. **14**(6), 555–575 (2000)

14. Nilsson, S., Johansson, B.: Fun and usable: augmented reality instructions in a hospital setting. In: Proceedings of the 19th Australasian conference on Computer-Human Interaction, OZCHI 2007, Adelaide, Australia, November 28–30 2007
15. Nof, S.Y., Wilhelm, W.E., Warnecke, H.J.: Industrial Assembly. Chapman & Hall, London (1997)
16. Radkowski, R., Herrema, J., Oliver, J.: Augmented reality based manual assembly support with visual features for different degree of difficulty. J. Hum. Comput. Interact. (2015, in press)
17. Schnotz, W., Bannert, M.: Construction and interface in learning from multiple representation. Learn. Instr. 13, 141–156 (2003)
18. Siltanen, S., Hakkarainen, M., Korkalo, O., Salonen, T., Sääski, J., Woodward, C., Kannetis, T., Perakakis, M., Potamianos, A.: Multimodal user interface for augmented assembly. In: 2007 International Workshop on Multimedia Signal Processing, MMSP 2007, Chania, Greece, October 1–3, 2007
19. Swan, R., Allan, J.: Aspect windows, 3-d visualization, and indirect comparison of information retrieval systems. In: Proceedings of the 21st annual international ACM SIGIR conference on research and development in information retrieval, SIRIR 1998, pp. 173–181, Copenhagen, Denmark, June 21–24, 1998
20. Tang, A., Owen, C., Biocca, F., Mou, W.: Comparative effectiveness of augmented reality in object assembly. In: Proceedings of the Conference on Human Factors in Computing Systems, CHI 2003, Fort Lauderdale, FL, USA, April 05–10, 2003
21. Tory, M., Kirkpatrick, A., Atkins, S., Möller, T.: Visualization task performance with 2d, 3d and combined displays. IEEE Trans. Vis. Comput. Graph. 12(1), 2–13 (2006)
22. Wang, Z.B., Ong, S.K., Nee, A.Y.C.: Augmented reality aided interactive manual assembly design. Int. J. Adv. Manuf. Technol. 2013(68), 1311–1321 (2013)
23. Webel, S., Bockholt, U., Engelke, T., Gavish, N., Olbrich, M., Preusche, C.: An augmented reality training platform for assembly and maintenance skills. J. Rob. Auton. Syst. 61(4), 398–403 (2011)
24. Westerfield, G., Mitrovic, A., Billinghurst, M.: Intelligent augmented reality training for assembly tasks. In: Lane, H.C., Yacef, K., Mostow, J., Pavlik, P. (eds.) AIED 2013. LNCS, vol. 7926, pp. 542–551. Springer, Heidelberg (2013)
25. Wiedenmaier, S., Oehme, O., Schmidt, L., Luczak, H.: Augmented reality (ar) for assembly processes design and experimental evaluation. Int. J. Hum. Comput. Interact. 16(3), 497–514 (2003)
26. Wileman, R.: Visual communicating. Englewood Cliffs, New Jersey (1993)
27. Wolfe, J., Horowitz, T.: What attributes guide the deployment of visual attention and how do they do it? Nature Rev.Neuroscience 5, June 2004
28. Wong, A., Marcus, N., Ayres, P., Smith, L., Cooper, G.A., Paas, F., Sweller, J.: Instructional animations can be superior to statics when learning human motor skills. Comput. Hum. Behav. 25(2), 339–347 (2009)
29. Yamazaki, A.K., Goto, K., Taki, H., Hori, S.: An effectiveness study of pictogram elements for steps in manufacturing procedures. In: Lovrek, I., Howlett, R.J., Jain, L.C. (eds.) KES 2008, Part III. LNCS (LNAI), vol. 5179, pp. 680–686. Springer, Heidelberg (2008)
30. Yuan, M.L., Ong, S.K., Nee, A.Y.C.: Augmented reality for assembly guidance using a virtual interactive tool. Int. J. Prod. Res. 46(7), 1745–1767 (2008)
31. Zauner, J., Haller, M., Brandl, A., Hartmann, W.: Authoring of a mixed reality assembly instructor for hierarchical structures. In: The Second International Symposium on Mixed and Augmented Reality, ISMAR 2003, Tokyo, Japan, October 7–10 2003

Evaluation of Autonomous Approaches Using Virtual Environments

Katharina Stahl[1], Jörg Stöcklein[1(✉)], and Sijia Li[2]

[1] Heinz Nixdorf Institute at University of Paderborn, Paderborn, Germany
Katharina.Stahl@upb.de, Joerg.Stoecklein@hni.upb.de
[2] University of Paderborn, Paderborn, Germany
lisijia@mail.upb.de

Abstract. In this paper, we address the challenging problem of evaluating autonomous research approaches by the example of an online anomaly detection framework for dynamical real-time systems. We propose to use a virtual test environment that was conceptualized based on the specific evaluation requirements. The architecture is composed of all system parts required for evaluation: the operating system implementing the anomaly detection framework, reconfigurable autonomous applications, an execution platform device for the operating system and its applications, and the device's environment. We demonstrate our concepts by the example of our miniature robot BeBot that acts as our virtual prototype (VP) to execute autonomous applications. With an interactive module, the virtual environment (VE) offers full control over the environment and the VP so that using different levels of hardware implementation for evaluation, but also failure injection at runtime becomes possible. Our architecture allows to determine clear system boundaries of the particular parts composed of perception function, decision making function and execution function which is essential for evaluating autonomous approaches. We define evaluation scenarios to show the effectiveness of each part of our approach and illustrate the powerfulness of applying virtual test environments to evaluate such approaches as the here referred one.

1 Introduction

Nowadays, technical systems consist of components from various domains: mechanics, electronics, control engineering, and information technology. Their interaction is expressed by the term *mechatronics*. The basis of their action is established by collecting information about the system and its environment by sensors, processing and analyzing this information in order to generate a suitable reaction, and adapting the behavior of the overall system. If this behavior is implemented in such a way that no human control is required for system operation, all behavioral intelligence and decisions are performed by the system itself. We call such systems *autonomous system*. Research in the domain of autonomous systems has gained great attention in the recent years.

Obviously the development process of such autonomous systems is different [4] as the key challenge is the implementation of the decision making part.

© Springer International Publishing Switzerland 2015
R. Shumaker and S. Lackey (Eds.): VAMR 2015, LNCS 9179, pp. 499–512, 2015.
DOI: 10.1007/978-3-319-21067-4_51

Because these systems show up their powerfulness primary at their operation, the evaluation of the system in operation becomes essential to enable analysis, validation and performance assessment. In critical (including safety-critical as well as mission-critical) application domains, for example, execution of the system for testing or evaluation purposes may involve high risk with potentials to damage the system itself or its environment or even endanger human life. Additionally, operating the real life system for evaluation purposes might also be expensive, also having in mind potential damages or dangers.

Virtual reality (VR) technology offers an opportunity to manage the execution of such systems and provides visualization techniques that are used to present the system behavior respectively. VR puts the developer responsible for evaluation into a virtual three-dimensional world and enables to use 1:1 virtual 3D model of the product shape and its real environment. The kinematics behavior of the system is visualized using animations or/and further visualization techniques, which may also include the visualization of invisible physical behavior. With all its characteristics, VR provides an adequate platform for the evaluation of a system in operating mode.

2   Evaluation of Autonomous Approaches

Autonomous Systems are computational systems that differ from conventional systems mainly by their decision making process: the decisions made by the system are not human-controlled but are performed by the system itself in an autonomous manner. The autonomous decisions process relies on data obtained by sensing of the system itself and its environment, and is based on predefined rules that may be regulated by random factors also, in order to meet the system's specified objective function. This makes the evaluation of such approaches challenging. The objective of this paper is to examine the evaluation of such novel autonomous approaches by virtual environments.

2.1   Evaluation Target

We have developed an *Online Anomaly Detection* for self-reconfigurable *Realtime operating systems (RTOS)* that operates fully autonomously and is able to cope with dynamically changing behavior caused by self-reconfigurability (which is a property of autonomous systems). The approach of our Online Anomaly Detection was inspired by *Danger Theory* from *Artificial Immune Systems* [1] that have been derived from the behavior of the *Human Immune System*. Danger Theory features adaptability by its nature and can be used for pattern matching, classification, anomaly detection, etc. It introduces so called *health signals* that allow to autonomously classify novel, dynamically generated and previously unknown behaviors correctly, without relying on a clearly separated training phase which usually is required in anomaly detection.

The *health signals* make it possible to implement an autonomous context-related anomaly detection: The *health signals* reflect the operating system state based on an integrated monitoring of the system components and their performance in operation. The current task's and system behavior is evaluated by means of the obtained *health signals*: A behavior pattern is declared as *normal* behavior if the input signals indicate a healthy state of the OS, while, in case of danger signals, the evaluation of behavioral patters lead to an *anomaly* alert. By this approach, also novel and previously unknown behaviors can be classified in a reliable manner, as in contrary to classic anomaly detection, this context-related approach prevents to categorically classify unknown behavioral patterns as unsafe or malicious *anomalies*. Detailed concepts of the approach have been published at IEEE workshops [10] and [9] on self-organizing real-time systems. These concepts require exhaustive evaluation now.

2.2   Evaluation Methodologies

Evaluation of autonomous approaches in not straightforward because of the role of decision making process [8]. Therefore, test methodologies of ordinary systems are not suitable, but no standardized or state-of-the-art method exist up to now. Several publications by Roske et al. [8], Thompson [12], and Garrett [3] analyze the problems and challenges concerned with evaluation and testing of autonomous systems. Pure static evaluation by mathematical methods or formal verification is not sufficient as the strength of such approaches lies in the effectiveness of the approach under operation.

A possible method to evaluate such an approach in operation are model-based testing as proposed by [6]. However, models always provide abstractions that may unintentionally mask some system properties so that the according results will not be able to match the real system in operation. Roske et al. specify the problem of testing and evaluation in more details in [8]. First of all, evaluation requires a *safe* environment because of lower tolerance in terms of unpredictable potential decision errors in real-life applications. Secondly, they propose a clear separation of concerns for testing in order to identify the potential source of inadequate system performance:

1. **Testing the perception function**: Perception is concerned with observing and sensing the environment and its characteristics. The data delivered by perception usually deals as the basis for decision making. Erroneous perception may lead to faulty decisions. The encapsulation of the perception function enables to fully control the hardware and the environment and allows to perform controlled failure injection.
2. **Testing the decision making function**: The decision making process is implemented according to an objective function and operates on the data delivered by the perception function. The evaluation of it mainly addresses to verify the implementation of the autonomous decisions (based on reliable perception data) and the question whether the system behavior approximates towards the objective function.
3. **Testing the execution function**: This is concerned with the testing ability to execute the decisions in order to obtain confidence about the system performance in terms of classical system functions (control performance, protection,

reliability, etc.) as well as physical performance (speed, capacity, resource demand, etc.).

Evaluating the effectiveness of autonomous systems shall be explicitly concerned with testing against a specified set of requirements [12]. These are dictated by test missions set on the system performance (e.g. aspects of objective function) instead of testing the decision process based on assumptions made on decisions. For each test mission, the definition of test scenarios is essential to be combined with scenario parameters and metrics that quantify the satisfaction of the specified requirements.

Thompson suggests to use virtual environments to test autonomous software as they allow a system to be preliminarily executed in a safe environment preventing damage or harm of the target system and its environment. The most important requirement is that the virtual environment is identical to the real application environment in such a way that all essential physical properties and obstacles match the real-world ones. Additionally, the virtual environment must provide all necessary environment information and requires to be interaction-based in order to enable the target system to take all actions specified by its nature. To ensure comprehensive evaluation results, extraction of precise and suitable operation data from the virtual environment must be guaranteed.

2.3   Requirements

Evaluation of an autonomous approach can only be conducted within its application domain. The mission of our evaluation is to verify the anomaly detection approach performance according to its intended properties. Detecting changes in the applications, their parameters, in the environment and the system itself is the crucial task of the anomaly detection framework. Means to induce and control changes in the environment and the system are required to examine the detection quality in order to draw conclusions on the reliability of the detection mechanism. Observed behavior, especially previously unknown, has to be classified and declared either to be normal, suspicious or dangerous on the basis of system health signals provided by the OS. Failures may endanger the entire system and, consequently, shall be detected by the anomaly detection framework. In order to evaluate the classification part of the anomaly detection, unsafe or dangerous system state have to be initiated in a controlled manner by means to inject failures into the executing system. The following requirements on the evaluation environment and architecture can be formulated:

R.1 Reconfigurable Applications and Environment: Our evaluation target is designed to detect unintended and malicious system states provoked by autonomous decisions at the application side. Therefore, an application environment is required that is dynamically changing and executes self-reconfigurable applications as a basis to assess the effectiveness of our online anomaly detection.

R.2 Execution Platform: The validation of the anomaly detection is only possible in the context of a RTOS for autonomous environments.

R.3 Safe Environment: For executing the application, a safe environment is required to ensure the environment to be identical to the real one and to enable full control of the system entities. Full control in this context is related to e.g. controlled initiation of dynamical changes that lead to reconfigurations. Dynamical reconfigurations build up the basis to verify whether and to what extend these changes implicate the target approach in terms of detecting novel behaviors.

R.4 Separation of Evaluation Concerns: Based on the requirements formulated by Roske et al., evaluation environments shall make sure that clear system boundaries can be guaranteed. Considering the evaluation of the pure anomaly detection approach, the RTOS represents the evaluation environment. However, as the evaluation of this approach is strongly related to the application performance, the execution environment has to ensure these system boundaries as well.

R.5 Interaction-based Environment: Environmental changes are foundations of autonomous reactions. Therefore, interaction between virtual environment applied for evaluations and the associated application is essential.

R.6 Evaluation Output: We are mainly interested in whether the intended properties of The main entity of our evaluation is integrated into the OS which is responsible to deliver the results of the evaluation. However, the virtual application environment itself shall provide information to draw conclusions on the system performance from the according evaluation scenarios.

2.4 Applicability of Virtual Environments

VR enables to test mechatronic systems, even in early development phases. Especially, the VP inside a VE provides suitable instruments. For using virtual environments to evaluate such autonomous approaches as introduced above, the requirements imposed for the test environment (namely **R.3** to **R.6**) have to be fulfilled.

VE and VP, by concept, are constructed based on real environment, real prototypes or devices (respective to e.g. the size, mass, physical behavior and so on). Hence, VE and the VP that operates inside act like their real counterparts and fulfills **R.3**. Using a VP inside a VE provides a tool to safely verify all aspects of the mechatronic system without endangering neither the real hardware nor the real environment. Every essential system entity of the real system is constructed independently as an encapsulated system entity in its virtual counterpart with all offered interfaces. By this, decoupled evaluations of individual system parts become possible and allows components to be exchanged by other implementations. This, in particular, forms the foundations for realizing the separation of concerns in the evaluation (see **R.4**).

VEs can provide interfaces for access to system entities and their parameters for analysis, assessment as well as manipulation purposes. Using these interfaces at run-time, changing system components, modifying the VE or even injecting failures into the system can be performed in an interactive manner according to requirement **R.5**.

VEs offer visual representation of the system under execution as well as visualizations of diverse parameters, including values of physical components and parameters of the executed software. Thereby, virtual environments provide facilities to visualize all parameters needed for the evaluation, as defined by requirement **R.6**.

3   Concept of the Virtual Test Environment

As foundation, we use a virtual test environment that has already been applied for the evaluation of other approaches [11]. This virtual test environment consists of a VP in forms of a mechatronic system which in our case is a miniature robot (that acts like its real counterparts, see **R.3**), and its VE being a randomly generated maze. The task of the robot is to find a way through the maze to a dedicated destination in an autonomous manner. The applied algorithm is implemented by an OS task executed on the VP. The randomly generated maze acts as a test environment for the applied algorithm.

In our virtual test environment, virtual (hardware) components and the executed RTOS with its tasks communicate with each other by dedicated interfaces. This enables decoupled evaluations of individual parts, in particular, the VE, the components of the VP, the execution part composed of RTOS and its tasks (and fulfills **R.4**) and, thereby, allows to exchange the execution of system parts, e.g. to execute the OS either on an emulator or on real hardware. **R.5** requires changes on system components, modifications of the virtual environment and failure injection to be performed in an interactive manner. In our concept, we support the system user to implement such interactive behaviors by using a scripting language to specify own interaction methods quickly.

Our virtual test environment offers a visual representation of the scenario execution. Visualizations of diverse parameters, including values of physical components as well as parameters of the executed software, as required for evaluation by **R.6**, are provided by the implementation extensions made on the virtual test environment.

3.1   Evaluation Environment and Prototypical Implementation

Our virtual test environment is split into the virtual execution of application tasks with its OS, and the VE for the simulation of the VP hardware. Using the VP platform, early functional verification tests of newly implemented functions can be performed within its environment without having access to the real hardware platform.

The VE is connected to the OS execution platform by using a network connection which allows a seamless exchange between real and virtual hardware. Our approach proposes a stepwise refinement of the VE towards the real execution environment. In early phases, we are able to test all OS functionalities using a virtual execution platform in connection with our VE. In later phases, we are able to exchange either the VE with the real hardware or changing the virtual execution platform to the real hardware executing the OS. The interface to the real OS is abstracted away by an intermediate layer which will forward all system relevant function calls to the virtual platform.

By using a VE and a VP, we are able to change the behavior of both interactively. In early stages of developing we can disable all random factors like sensor noise or sensor latency for verifying the bare functionality of the algorithm. Later, noise and latency can be enabled to prove the algorithms functionality for the real hardware. Also, disabling specific hardware e.g. sensors to simulate an failure is offered. This helps verifying the fault tolerance of algorithms and respectively, the OS with its internal behavior.

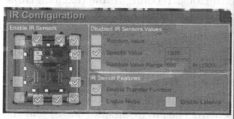

(a) GUI for controlling parameters.

(b) Virtual test environment in action.

Fig. 1. The virtual environment of BeBot and the interactive GUI.

We choose the miniature robot *BeBot* [5] (Fig. 1) for our test scenario. BeBots are small robots serving as a technology platform. They are used for research in the domains of dynamic reconfigurable systems, multi agent systems and swarm intelligence. The dimensions of a BeBot are approximately $9cm^3$ and it provides 12 IR sensors for sensing the environment. Robot movement is achieved by two motors which supports quasi omni-directional movements as it allows the BeBots to turn on the spot. The BeBot itself is controlled by ORCOS, a self-reconfigurable real-time operating system [2].

For the implementation of our virtual test environment and the BeBot as VP (see Fig. 1b) we used *Unity3D*, a professional game engine. To set up the VP we imported the BeBot CAD data used for production and added physical behavior. The maze is build up with virtual counterparts of brick-like plastic elements used for testing the real BeBot. The physical behavior of the BeBot is completely built using the internal physics engine of Unity3D. The IR sensors are realized as a physical ray sent out to the VE. If the ray hits a wall, it returns the distance where it intersects. For realism we added approx. 10 % random noise to the virtual sensor value, which is the amount of jitter we measured on the real sensors.

On the software side, we try to get as near as possible to the real interface of the BeBot. Therefore, the control for the stepper motors, the sensors and the LEDs use the same messages and protocols we used on the real controller. With this approach, we are able to run the same code written for the BeBot platform either on a software or a hardware emulator or on the BeBot itself and combine it with the VP.

4   Implementation of the Evaluation

The evaluation target is the anomaly detection approach presented in Sect. 2.1 and was implemented and integrated into ORCOS, a self-reconfigurable RTOS. ORCOS runs on the BeBot that executes autonomously operating applications and therefore, was chosen as an application platform for evaluation of our target approach. The application running on the BeBot is reconfigurable (exchangeable strategies/algorithms) with respect to an objective function.

4.1   Evaluation Architecture

For evaluation, an architecture is required that combines the VE with its VP and the OS as the execution platform for the BeBot application. Figure 2a shows the architecture which contains the VE representing the environment (maze) and the VP (BeBot). For executing applications on BeBot, we use ORCOS that runs on the emulator *QEMU*. We have customized QEMU for ORCOS by enhancing the communication feature in forms of an *Assistant Communication Module* (ACM) that enables *QEMU* is connected to the VP. Once the virtual test environment is executing, ORCOS starts to communicate with the VP through ACM. The environment data provided by VE is transferred back to ORCOS. A particular BeBot controlling task processes these environment data and commands the virtual BeBot by sending messages to it. This entire architecture of the virtual test environment is implemented to on a Linux system.

The goal of the BeBot in the VE is to reach the destination in the maze in an autonomous manner. We designed several maze-solving algorithms to control the BeBot in order to reach the destination efficiently:

Right-Side Wall Follower: The robot always follows the right-side wall in the maze and must ensure to not lose the wall it is following. For mazes that are not simply connected, this algorithm can not guarantee the reach destination.

Left-Side Wall Follower: This algorithm uses the same principles as right-side wall follower by relying on the left-side instead of the right-side wall.

Random Mouse Algorithm: Whenever the robot meets a junction, the robot makes random decisions on which direction to follow. This algorithm does not guarantee that the robot will find the right solution. However, it can be applied in mazes in which not all the walls are connected and will probably find its destination.

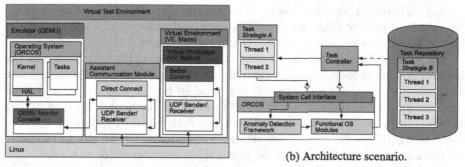

(a) Architecture of the virtual test environment.

(b) Architecture scenario.

Fig. 2. Scenario and Architecture overview.

Parameterized Random Mouse Algorithm: This algorithm is a mean to enhancement the probability of the robot to find its destination by using random mouse. The turning decision are randomized but weighed by parameters reflecting the distance calculated between the robot and its destination.

Each of the maze-solving algorithm is implemented as a single task that performs best in a specific scenario. Figure 2b specifies the application side architecture. The *Task Controller* implements the decision making part to determine the most suitable strategy for solving the maze according to its objective function. If the applied strategy is not suitable to the underlying maze, the *Task Controller* has to choose a better algorithm.

Behaviors of the task are recorded by the anomaly detection framework and analyzed in context of the corresponding OS health state to determine to classify the system behavior as *normal* or *anomalous*. If the anomaly detection framework detects any anomaly associated with one system part (task or OS component), e.g. an unreliable device, the anomaly detection framework forwards these information to the *Task Controller* in order initiate the *Task Controller* to choose another algorithm strategy from the task repository that meets the detected novel circumstances.

4.2 Environment Control and Interaction

For evaluation, full control over the VE and the VP is fundamental. First, we are able to set up the VE and the VP with respect to the evaluation requirements. The BeBot is the unit of the evaluation environment, that is part of the autonomous system and provides the interface to the VE. The BeBot's interface to the VE are the IR Sensors. Our virtual test environment provides different abstraction levels for hardware devices that can be exchanged by the VE. **Simulated *real* IR sensor data** includes the transfer function, the latency and the noise measured in test series of the real IR sensors. ***Pure* distance data** represent the distance of the IR sensor to the detected wall in *cm* without any latency and noise. *User-defined* **data** the interactive control allows to configure the degree of the data interfered with latency and noise as well as the transfer function. E.g. it is possible to set up the distance values with noise added.

With these data abstraction levels, both, the perception function and the decision making process, can be evaluated in a finely graduated manner. Because the BeBot application's decisions are expected to be different in different environmental configurations, in our VE, we can set up the actual maze as well as its type on the fly by using a randomized generation and by switching between different algorithms for maze construction. Furthermore, we are able to configure the start point of the BeBot and the destination position inside the maze.

Second, in our virtual test environment, full control at runtime is presumed and realized by integrating interactive control over VE and the BeBot. Not only the applied model of a device like the IR Sensor is configurable, furthermore, we allow to disable sensors completely in order to enable failure injection. The user can decide interactively between different options for defective sensor values send back to the OS in order to evaluate the reaction of the decision making process.

We have designed a GUI (Fig. 1a) to interactively change all parameters defined above. The great benefit from applying the virtual test environment is the possibility of controlling the VE and the hardware which involves the potentials for simulating failures in various ways. This flexibility offered by the VE cannot be provided by the real hardware or the real environment at the same level of simplicity.

4.3   Evaluation Scenarios

The objective of the evaluation process is to verify the performance and the effectiveness of the autonomous system. We have to deal with autonomous behavior on two different levels: the first is the anomaly detection approach that in fact is our evaluation target, and the second is the BeBot application with its objective to autonomously find a way to a predefined destination in a maze. The autonomous BeBot application builds up the basis (referring to requirement **R.1**) for the evaluation of our anomaly detection framework. Only with a reliable application environment, we are able to examine, analyze and evaluate the performance of the anomaly detection framework. The two different levels in autonomous behavior cause different views on separation of evaluation concerns as described in **R.4**. Considering the BeBot application first, we clearly define system boundaries for the individual system parts.

BeBot Application's Perception Function: The BeBot's perception function is sensing the environment by data delivered from its IR sensors in order to measure the distances to obstacles. Data sensing functions are clearly separated components in the VE and allow separated evaluations. The different abstraction levels determine the accuracy of the perception data and allow to evaluate to what extent the implemented data sensing module matches the reality. In addition, full control over the reliability of the data delivered to the decision making module can be ensured.

BeBot Application Decision Function: In the BeBot application, the decision function is implemented in the software in forms of the task and the *Task Controller*. While the task is executing on the basis of the perception data, the *Task Controller* examines the performance of the task. It is responsible for the decision to either maintain the executing strategy or to reconfigure the application and exchange it by another strategy. A reconfiguration is intended in case of faulty hardware (such as a sensor) or in case the application underperforms the objective function. The decision making process can only be evaluated in separate, if the reliability of the sensor data can be guaranteed. We define test scenarios determined by missions which exhaust and evaluate the specifications set in our decision making process.

BeBot Application Execution Function: The execution function is defined by movement of the BeBot within its environment. This part of the evaluation concentrates on testing the effectiveness of the implemented application strategies and aims to show that the BeBot is able to find the destination. This includes also reconfiguration of the application if configured that did not fulfill the objective.

With these evaluation missions, we are able to evaluate the different parts of the performance of the BeBot application. Even though, we are more interested in the evaluation of performance of the anomaly detection integrated into ORCOS. Now, we examine the system boundaries attached to the evaluation of the anomaly detection approach and verify whether these are realized within our virtual test environment.

Anomaly Detection Perception Function: Our anomaly detection relies on perception of the application behavior in combination with monitored OS health state. The application behavior observation implemented by a *System Call Monitor* integrated into ORCOS that has been evaluated separately in [13]. The OS health state is examined by an *OS Health Monitor* [7] which deal as system-wide input signals indicating the respective heal state of the RTOS for the context-related classification of our anomaly detection approach. Parameters such as processor utilization, memory usage, etc. are examined, but also device drivers which involves the data obtained from the sensors of the VP. IR sensor data represents the perception function of the BeBot device or respectively, its virtual counterpart. Erroneous sensors or erroneous data are intended to identified by condition scenarios specified by the *OS Health Monitor* and are revealed through the system-wide signals. In order to guarantee correctness of the perception function, the performance of the *OS Health Monitor* including the analysis of the IR sensor data has been evaluated in [7].

Anomaly Detection Decision Function: The decision making function in the anomaly detection approach is defined by the classification mechanism for behavioral patterns. It can only be evaluated when variations in system behavior are induced. Here, the functionality of virtual test environment offers great potentials, as it allows to induce dynamical changes into the VP and the VE as well (see Sect. 4.2). Changes in e.g. sensor behavior shall lead to changes in classification outcomes of the anomaly detection approach and in turn may effect reconfiguration initiations. One main objective is the verification of the ability to detect behavioral changes and suspicious OS health state. Related to this, accurate configurations of decision thresholds for detection as well as for classification are examined.

Anomaly Detection Execution Function: This part of evaluation concentrated on the question whether in case of detected dangerous behavior, the information is passed to the *Controller Task* in order to initiate an adequate system reconfiguration.

Each of these separate functions is evaluated within our virtual test environment individually by defined scenarios. The scenarios aim to test only the function concerned while assuming correct functionality of the remaining system parts.

4.4   Output

The anomaly detection operates encapsulated inside ORCOS on the basis of the data delivered by the VE. Its evaluation output is encoded within the RTOS by reporting the results in forms of log files that have to be analyzed after execution. However, decision results directly affect the BeBots performance as a task reconfiguration might have been induced. The BeBot application is executed in the virtual test environment which provides evaluation output related to that. All required information about the performance of the system must be able to be acquired in the VE: With the interaction interface as introduced, we get control over the system entities, but furthermore, this interface reports all information about the state of the system entities at runtime. While the BeBot is driving through the maze, the BeBot application controls the action of the BeBot as well as the performance of the application itself. All decisions made by the application, either BeBot controlling commands or application configuration are displayed at runtime in the VE. Applying the VE for evaluation not only enables to execute the real application within a safe environment in order to asses its performance. Furthermore, it visualizes the performance of the application, so that the developer can directly observe the execution and immediately recognize potential problems. All aspects of the evaluation process are supported by the virtual test environment. The virtual test environment continuously illustrates all evaluation aspects and performance metrics at runtime. Furthermore, what in particular is specific to VE, it illustrates the current execution process with all the associated data in a visual manner. This visualization makes it easier to understand and follow the execution and capture the performance of the autonomous application in order to assess it.

5   Conclusion

In this paper, we address the problem of evaluating mechatronic systems that exhibit autonomous behavior. For these novel research approaches, technologies are required that meet the requirements associated with their evaluation. VEs offer great potentials to satisfy these requirements. The evaluation target presented in this paper is an autonomous anomaly detection framework for self-reconfiguring real-time operating systems. We formulated specific requirements concerning the evaluation of this approach. The evaluation target as encapsulated in an operating system requires an evaluation environment with a concrete (autonomous) application. Virtual reality, in particular VEs and VPs, provide safe environments and full control over all parameters and thereby makes it powerful to be applied for evaluation purposes. We developed a virtual test environment consisting of a VP, an application, controlling the VP, which runs on an emulator that executes our operating system with the anomaly detection. This architecture defines clear system boundaries required for evaluation. The design of this virtual test environment meets all the requirements specified for evaluating autonomous mechatronic systems. Furthermore, the presented virtual test environment allows to interactively manipulate and control all evaluation aspects that are defined by evaluation scenarios. With VEs for evaluation generating variations of evaluation application environments for autonomous mechatronic systems can be done with little effort, therefore VEs will become a general-purpose evaluation platform.

Acknowledgments. This work was supported in part by the Leading-Edge Cluster 'Intelligent Technical Systems OstWestfalenLippe (it's OWL)' and was funded by the Federal Ministry of Education and Research (BMBF).

References

1. Aickelin, U., Cayzer, S.: The danger theory and its application to artificial immune systems. CoRR (2008)
2. Rammig, F.G.: University of Paderborn: ORCOS - An Organic Reconfigurable Operating System (2013). https://orcos.cs.uni-paderborn.de
3. Garrett, S.M.: How do we evaluate artificial immune systems. Evol. Comput. **13**, 145–178 (2005)
4. Gausemeier, J., Rammig, F.J., Schäfer, W. (eds.): Design Methodology for Intelligent Technical Systems. LNME. Springer, Heidelberg (2014)
5. Herbrechtsmeier, S., Witkowski, U., Rückert, U.: BeBot: a modular mobile miniature robot platform supporting hardware reconfiguration and multi-standard communication. In: Kim, J.-H., et al. (eds.) Progress in Robotics. CCIS, vol. 44, pp. 346–356. Springer, Heidelberg (2009)
6. Horányi, G., Micskei, Z., Majzik, I.: Scenario-based automated evaluation of test traces of autonomous systems. In: Roy, M. (ed.) Proceedings of ERCIM/EWICS Workshop on DECS at SAFECOMP 2013, pp. 181–192. Toulouse, France (2013)

7. Li, S.: A Framework for Health Monitoring in the Real-Time Operating System ORCOS. Master thesis, Faculty of Computer Science, Electrical Engineering, and Mathematics, Paderborn University (2014)

8. Roske, V.P., Kohlberg, I., Wagner, R.: Autonomous systems challenges to test and evaluation. In: 28th Conference of National Defense Industrial Association, March 2012

9. Stahl, K., Rammig, F.J.: Online behavior classification for anomaly detection in self-x real-time systems. In: Workshop on Self-Organizing Real-Time Systems. IEEE, June 2014

10. Stahl, K., Rammig, F.J., Vaz, G.: A framework for enhancing dependability in self-x systems by artificial immune systems. In: Workshop on Self-Organizing Real-Time Systems. IEEE, June 2013

11. Stöcklein, J., Baldin, D., Müller, W., Xie, T.: Virtual test environment for self-optimizing systems. In: Conference on Computers and Information in Engineering. ASME, Portland, Oregon, USA (2013)

12. Thompson, M.: Testing the intelligence of unmanned autonomous systems. ITEA J. Test Eval. 29, December 2008

13. Vaz, G.: A reconfigurable real-time monitoring framework for a real-time operating system. Master thesis, Faculty of Computer Science, Electrical Engineering, and Mathematics, Paderborn University (2013)

Appraisal of Augmented Reality Technologies for Supporting Industrial Design Practices

Basak Topal[1(✉)] and Bahar Sener[1,2]

[1] Department of Industrial Design,
Middle East Technical University, Ankara, Turkey
basak.topal@metu.edu.tr, bsener@liverpool.ac.uk
[2] School of Engineering, University of Liverpool, Liverpool, UK

Abstract. Having become widespread and easily accessible with the rapid advancements in technology, augmented reality (AR) offers potential uses for industrial designers, especially for design students. Some design stages, during which traditional tools and methods are used, may not fully communicate the total experience that a product offers. AR can provide a digital layer in which designers can present information and make their presentations more interactive. With this aim in mind, design practice fieldwork with three progressive studies was conducted. The results show that AR can be utilized mainly in presentation and prototyping stages of a design process, to show details such as audiovisual feedback and digital interfaces. With further developments, AR has potential use for several other design activities.

Keywords: Augmented reality · Industrial design education · Design process · Design activities

1 Introduction

To respond to a design brief, professional industrial designers and design students carry out various activities including briefings, field and user research, concept generation, prototyping, user testing, materials and manufacturing selection, and presentations. In representing their ideas, designers use tools and methods such as hand sketches, digital 2D sketches, 3D computer models and physical mock ups. However, the tools and methods traditionally used by industrial designers are not always enough to convey the full spectrum of user-interaction offered through a new product design.

Augmented Reality (AR)a visualization tool that combines digitally created data with the real environment, is a technology that has become relatively easy to access in recent years. Considering that industrial design is a field characteristically open to technological advancements, it can be argued that now is a good time to sample how AR could be utilized within a design workflow. A variety of AR technologies have been developed recently, ranging from room size projections to apps running on smart devices. The literature review carried out in support of this paper revealed that potential uses of AR for industrial design, especially with education, have not been explored adequately.

The aim of this paper is to present the possibilities of AR technology for supporting industrial design practices and to make propositions on how AR can bring

© Springer International Publishing Switzerland 2015
R. Shumaker and S. Lackey (Eds.): VAMR 2015, LNCS 9179, pp. 513–523, 2015.
DOI: 10.1007/978-3-319-21067-4_52

enhancements at different design stages. First, the product development process is explained through design activities and their deliverables. Secondly, the literature review covers commercial and academic uses of AR, alongside related technologies and uses of AR in current design practices. Lastly, fieldwork was carried out to understand whether AR technologies can be reasonably beneficial to industrial designers, and to reach a recommendation on use of AR systems for industrial design education. The scope of this paper is not to cover the whole range of the AR technology, but rather to explore at what stages of design and in which activities AR can be utilized with its current state; and to make predictions on future developments, so as to better fit technological solutions to designers.

2 Overview of Augmented Reality Technologies with Their Relevance to Industrial Design

2.1 The Product Development Process

In a typical design project developed in studio-based industrial design education, the goal is to develop a product from the 'ground-up'. The final year Graduation Projects course handouts offered at the Department of Industrial Design of Middle East Technical University (with student projects winning RedDot, iF Concept awards, and rated by Domus Magazine as one of Europe's top-rated design schools), Turkey in the years between 2012 and 2014 were examined with the premise that the graduation project calendars developed in collaboration with companies are a good representative of new product development process. In Table 1, the design activities and deliverables expected from students are matched with the medium of presentation.

Table 1. Deliverables expected from design students and the medium of presentation

Design activities and deliverables	Medium of presentation
• Project statement	
• Analysis of similar products	• Text
• User group research	• 2D images
• Problem definition map	• Diagrams, charts
• Initial idea workshops	• Sketches
• Prototypes	• 3D mock ups
• Presentation boards	• CAD renderings, drawings

A project statement that sets the criteria for a potential design contribution and defines the problem statement is presented to students in the first step. The user group, the context of use, and the essential requirements for the product are described, followed by user group research that illuminates the characteristics of a potential user. Project-specific research is carried out to gather information about similar products concerning function, usability, aesthetics, usage context, interactions, cost, and material. A problem definition map that underlines the keywords in the project statement that set criteria for design is developed. The first concepts begin to take shape in initial idea workshops, where students are expected to be adventurous and innovative while meeting the needs of the user. To present in the preliminary screening, students keep revising and developing their concepts to a point where they select two preferred and strong design proposals, for which they prepare mock ups and presentation boards. The presentation boards have visualization and details regarding the target group, mood-boards, storyboards that explain usage steps, CAD product renderings, exploded views of product parts, interface ideas, technical drawings, section views, and so on. These details are continually refined up until the final presentation. The presentation boards for the final screening are very specific. Apart from the previously mentioned details, details such as user-product interaction, interfaces, anthropometric assessment, selection of materials and manufacturing processes, mechanisms, and assembly are required to be visualized.

This process and the deliverables from educational design projects are arguably similar to the workflow of an industrial designer working in a professional setting. The physical tools and digital methods used by designers and design students vary in affectivity, and the possible positive outcomes from bringing AR into the design process should be investigated.

2.2 Augmented Reality Technologies

AR is a method to embed computer generated data into real environments with the goal of enhancing human perception [1]. In other words, it is a combination of virtual objects and physical objects that exist at the same time in the same environment [2]. As explained in the mixed reality continuum coined by Milgram et al. [3], AR falls between a spectrum of real environment, which is the physical world that humans live in, and virtual environment, a space that is comprised solely of digitally created elements. AR, therefore, is a combination of real and virtual; interactive in real-time; and, can be observed and/or experienced in three dimensions [4].

AR systems comprise a combination of hardware and software components. The hardware components can include a computer or a mobile device, a monitor or a projector, a camera, tracking components, a network system, and a marker. The software components can include an application or a program that runs locally, web services, and a content server.

AR has been in development since the 1960 s, however, recent developments have made the technology accessible and on demand in commercial and research fields. Examples of AR can be seen in sectors such as advertising, architecture and construction, museums and tourism, medical, mechanics and repair, social networking, entertainment, military, and navigation. As for research, institutions including MIT Media Lab, New Zealand HCI Lab, Georgia Technical University, automotive industry leaders such as BMW, GM, Land Rover, and hardware developers such as Google, Oculus Rift, and Microsoft have developed a number of noteworthy AR applications.

The AR apps that are relevant to industrial design activities are rather limited. The Botta Design mobile app, where users are allowed to 'try on' different types of watches is an example of visualizing user-product interaction. Another example is IKEA's printed paper catalogue, enhanced with the 3D models of the products to show the assembly steps and to visualize the products in their intended usage environment.

Research on the usage of AR in industrial design activities focuses on visualization of products, simulation of usage and ergonomic analysis [5], virtual design environments, hybrid/augmented prototyping, assembly in industrial design [6] and collaboration across design disciplines [7, 8]. The bulk of the findings about using AR in industrial design activities have been focused on augmented prototyping, and virtual design environments.

In augmented prototyping, AR has been considered as a valuable tool for bridging the gap of low quality mock-ups that lack detail. Verlinden et al. has coined the term of augmented prototyping to describe the process of enhancing physical prototypes with virtual details [9]. Some experimental tools for achieving this goal are a system for prototyping interactive handheld products [10], a tool for projecting materials, textures and colors onto surfaces of 3D mock ups [11], a system that combines rapid prototyping with AR based manipulation of shapes, colors, textures and user interfaces [12].

Another utilization of AR into design processes is as a tangible tool for dimensional form-giving, which has been argued to result in more usable and interactive design processes [6]. Likewise, experimental tools such as a system for visualizing and interacting with virtual design objects for reviewing [13], a display concept that uses AR along with haptic feedback for surface creation [14], a concept of using digital tape for freeform virtual geometry design [15], a freeform modeling tool as a virtual 3D workbench [16], a virtual reality environment for creating concept shapes [17], systems for creation of 3D shapes for product design [18] have been developed.

3 Fieldwork for Evaluating AR for Industrial Design

3.1 Planning of the Fieldwork

The fieldwork consisted of three interconnected studies. Study 1, which aimed at creating awareness of AR among industrial designers and was conducted with seven industrial designers, started with a survey about the tools and methods that designers use. The second part of this study consisted of a presentation that showed examples from a wide range of AR applications to participants. The presentation stage was followed by an interview that asked participants to reflect on one or more of their past design projects, to come up with ideas about how AR could have supplemented their design process. Study 2, which aimed at exploring the potential of mobile AR applications in a design project, was conducted with eight graduate level design students in a course project. In the first part of the study, they were shown a presentation about AR and a demonstration of the application Metaio, for the iPad, which were selected because they have free versions and provide the most functionality among content creation AR applications. Then the participants were asked to make use of this application to add interactive content to their final presentation boards of the concept alarm clock design project that they carried out. Later on, they were asked to complete a survey evaluating this application about how they thought it enhanced their presentation, their likes and dislikes of the process. In Study 3, the researcher undertakes an exercise to show the potentials of where AR can contribute in design projects. She uses her already completed projects as examples to reflect on potential contribution of a wide range of AR applications from mobile apps to room-size projections, as well as making suggestions for the future.

3.2   Results and Analysis of the Fieldwork

Study 1. Study 1 started with a preliminary study to find out the following: the activities that industrial design students carry out; the deliverables expected at the end of each of these activities; and, evaluation of physical materials and digital tools used in design projects. The participants were asked to recall their undergraduate design projects to list the stages and/or activities in a design project. The design activities were, with some variations between each participant: project briefing, literature and field research (including a user group review), initial idea generation, sketching and model making/prototyping, user testing, technical drawings, renderings of 3D models and final presentation. During these activities, the participants were expected to present deliverables such as field research results, sketches, usage scenarios, moodboards, interview results, mock ups, CAD drawings and renderings, interface details, manufacturing schemes with material selection, and videos. As mentioned in Sect. 2, these deliverables are produced using a variety of physical and digital tools and methods. When asked to evaluate these physical materials and digital tools, the participants firstly commented that they were not able to represent *interactive* details of the products. These details, such as audiovisual feedback or digital interface content, are not displayed adequately in 2D presentation boards or physical mock ups. The second problem that participants reported to encounter was scaling problems of CAD applications. Because there is no way of realistically visualizing the interaction between the digital 3D model of the product, and the user and the environment, the participants had to create physical models as a parallel process, to determine product size and proportion.

In the second step of Study 1, the participants attended a presentation about AR technology that informed them about usage areas, to inspire them towards fulfilling the third (and last) step of the study: brainstorming about how AR could have been useful if it were to have been adopted during a past design project.

The main design activity that participants thought AR could enhance is *presentations*. The participants mentioned that in stages that they are expected to present details such as sound, light, digital interfaces, user-product and product-environment interaction etc., a 2D presentation board is not sufficient. Being able to use AR to present these details would make their presentations substantially more informative.

Another activity that could benefit from AR enhancement is *scenario building*. While drafting the steps of interaction between the user and the product, traditional methods for visualization are not enough to portray the full range of usage steps, especially for products with digital interfaces.

The participants also thought that AR could be useful for *prototyping* stages of design. Often, product mock-ups are a secondary requirement expected of design students, with time pressures experienced to prepare a realistic physical model that represents details such as textures, materials, colors, and so on. AR could be a convenient and effective way of enhancing a simple physical model, through layering of this additional visual information.

Other activities that AR was found to carry potential are *user tests and usage instructions* (by visualizing the product to testers and showing them how the product is meant to be operated), *conducting research* (by scanning existing products to gather information or creating a material library by taking pictures of textures to later project on physical models), *getting feedback* from instructors (by visualizing a wider range of detail in the development of a project), and possibly for *idea generation* exercises.

Study 2. Study 2 was carried out through the conduct of a design project entitled 'Bedside Alarm Clock' in METU Department of Industrial during the 2013–14 Fall semester on the postgraduate course 'Design for Interaction'. The study aimed to create a hands-on experience of AR during the design process. In the first step of the study, the participants attended a presentation about AR and a demonstration of the AR app *Metaio*. With this information and a tutorial that they had been provided with, the participants were asked to add interactive AR content to the presentation boards of their bedside alarm clock project – the results of which formed the second step of the study. In the third and final step, the participants presented their finalized design concepts with the added AR content in their presentation boards and mock-ups.

The participants enhanced their presentation boards and mock-ups with sound files, video files and 3D model files. As can be seen in Table 2, all of the participants added the sound of their alarm clock in their presentation boards, either embedded in a video that showed interaction details during usage, or separately to show what sound the alarm clock would make when activated. For the videos, which were superimposed on presentation boards and mock-ups (Fig. 1), six of the participants showed the alarm lights and the movements of the products, whereas three of the participants showed the interaction steps of operation. One of the participants chose to show the alarm light glowing (Fig. 1), and another participant decided to present the interaction steps of the digital interface in the form of a video augmented to the surfaces of the physical mock-up (Fig. 2). One participant took it a step further by augmenting the mock-up of the project with a 3D model that showed the true texture of the material of the product (Fig. 3).

Table 2. AR content added to the presentations of participants

AR content	Purpose	Number of participants integrated (out of 8)	Medium of presentation
Sound	alarm	8	2D presentation board
Video	alarm lights and the alarm-clock's movement	6	
	interaction steps	3	
	alarm lights	1	3D mock-up
	interaction steps	1	
3D Model	product form, material texture, graphics	1	

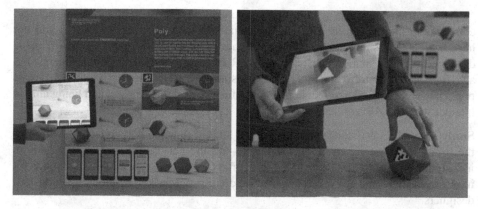

Fig. 1. A participant scans the markers on a presentation board (left) and then the mock-up (right) to show the augmented animation of glowing alarm lights.

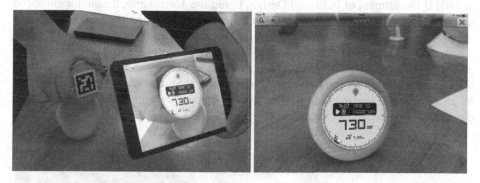

Fig. 2. A participant shows interaction details on a video on the mock-up (left), and the in-app screenshot (right).

Fig. 3. A participant scans the marker on the mock-up to show texture and animation of blinking lights.

The participants had very positive reactions to the *Metaio* software package, commenting that they were able to show details of their projects that they would not have been able to show if they did not have access to the technology. The participants described the presentation enhanced with AR to be informing, surprising, interesting, and fun. Suggestions for improvement in using AR for presenting industrial design projects were: using an app specialized for industrial design purposes, and being able to interact with the AR content.

Study 3. Study 3 was carried out by the first author, to personally reflect – having had the benefit of exposure to Studies 1 and 2 – on the general potential uses of AR in industrial design activities. It included two parts: (i) exploring existing AR solutions for industrial design, and (ii) imagining and predicting future AR solutions for industrial designers.

For the first part of study 3, the author used mobile AR apps to enhance two past design projects, the first being an espresso-based coffee machine completed as part of the postgraduate course 'Design for Interaction' offered in the 2012–2013 Fall semester at METU Department of Industrial Design. Using the *Metaio* app, the author enhanced the presentation board of the project by adding a video showing the blinking lights of the product, a video of the hand gestures that activate the milk steamer, and the sound the steamer makes upon operation. In addition, *Augment* software was used to show the product in its intended usage environment. With these enhancements, seen in Fig. 4, the author was able to show audiovisual feedback of the product, and present the product in its intended usage environment without having to spare the significant effort to build a physical or interactive electronic prototype.

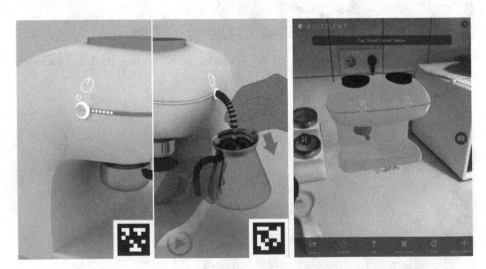

Fig. 4. AR content to enhance the design presentation of an espresso-based coffee machine

Another past design project that the author enhanced with AR is a 'wake up light', completed as a requirement of the postgraduate course 'Usability and User Experience Assessment in Design' during the author's student exchange to Delft University of

Technology. This product aims to wake people in a relaxed, natural environment by mimicking natural sunrise and sounds from nature. For AR enhancement, the plain, white physical prototype of the project was used as a canvas for the projection mapping AR app Dynamapper (by Reotek). With Dynamapper, the glowing warm light of the product and the digital interface was projected onto the surface of the physical model, as shown in Fig. 5. This way, a realistic representation of the final design concept could be experienced in the intended use environment, without the need to create any working electronics inside the model.

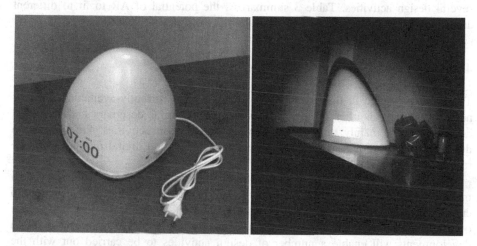

Fig. 5. Physical mock-up of the 'wake up' light project, augmented with *Dynamapper* to show the intended interface and light glow.

Table 3. Potential areas of benefit from AR, based on design activities and design stages

	The Design Process	Project briefing	Research	Initial idea generation	Interim presentation	Development of design concepts	User testing	Final presentation
Currently available (S2, S3)	Presentation				✓	✓	✓	✓
	Physical mock up creation				✓	✓	✓	✓
Suggestions for future use (S1, S3, L)	Scenario building activities					✓		
	User tests and usage instructions						✓	
	Project research	✓						
	Material considerations					✓		
	Mechanical and structural considerations						✓	
	Display and feedback interfaces					✓	✓	✓
	Real-time virtual interaction			✓	✓	✓		
	Product surface creation			✓	✓	✓		
	3D visualization of 2D drawings			✓	✓	✓	✓	✓

S1: Study1   S2: Study 2   S3: Study 3   L: Literature review

The second part of Study 3 focused on imagining and predicting future AR solutions for industrial design purposes, to improve suitability and technology adoption. Firstly, additional interactivity in AR solutions would bring great benefits to existing hardware and software combinations. Being able to interact with the AR content in real time would enable designers to create and modify their own content in a virtual environment. Examples of virtual design environments have been the focus of recent research, but easily accessible solutions are yet to be released. Secondly, an AR solution that is developed just for designers would be very fruitful to enhance the design process. It has been shown through this paper that AR could be useful for several design activities. Table 3 summarizes the potential of AR to fit to different design activities, based on the current availability of relevant solutions.

4 Conclusions

The work presented in this paper shows that amongst currently-available AR technologies, some can offer promising support for industrial designers and industrial design students, mainly through augmenting presentation activities. Product design details such as audiovisual feedback, interaction details and digital interfaces can be readily and effectively shown with AR.

The second most fruitful use of AR within industrial design processes is in physical mock-up creation, where the technology can be used to enhance the mock up creation/prototyping process by superimposing material, texture and interaction details onto a plain (e.g. white, undetailed surfaces) physical model. Additionally, future developments will enable a number of design activities to be carried out with the addition of AR, to make the design process richer and more interactive. The fieldwork for this present study was carried out in an educational setting; however, it is known that the design activities where AR brings benefits in education are essentially the same activities mirrored in professional design practice. Thus, both design students and design professionals can benefit from adoption of AR for future design projects. For further research, keeping in mind the results of the fieldwork, a mobile app specialized in AR for industrial designers, can be developed.

Acknowledgements.   The authors would like to thank all the participants of the fieldwork.

References

1. Van Krevelen, D., Poelman, R.: A survey of augmented reality technologies, applications and limitations. Int. J. Virtual Reality **9**(2), 1 (2010)
2. Azuma, R., Baillot, Y., Behringer, R., Feiner, S., Julier, S., MacIntyre, B.: Recent advances in augmented reality. IEEE Comput. Graph. Appl. **21**(6), 34–47 (2001)
3. Milgram, P., Takemura, H., Utsumi, A., Kishino, F.: Augmented reality: a class of displays on the reality-virtuality continuum. In: Photonics for Industrial Applications, pp. 282–292. International Society for Optics and Photonics (1995)
4. Azuma, R.T., et al.: A survey of augmented reality. Presence **6**(4), 355–385 (1997)

5. Lu, S.-Y., Shpitalni, M., Gadh, R.: Virtual and augmented reality technologies for product realization. CIRP Ann. Manufact. Technol. **48**(2), 471–495 (1999)
6. Ran, Y., Wang, Z.: Virtual and augmented reality applications in industrial design. In: International Conference on Machine Learning and Computing, pp. 252–253 (2011)
7. Shen, Y., Ong, S., Nee, A.: Augmented reality for collaborative product design and development. Des. Stud. **31**(2), 118–145 (2010)
8. Ahlers, K.H., Kramer, A., Breen, D.E., Chevalier, P.-Y., Crampton, C., Rose, E., Tuceryan, M., Whitaker, R.T., Greer, D.: Distributed augmented reality for collaborative design applications. In: Computer Graphics Forum, vol. 14, pp. 3–14. Wiley Online Library (1995)
9. Verlinden, J.C., De Smit, A., Peeters, A.W., van Gelderen, M.H.: Development of a flexible augmented prototyping system. J. WSCG **11**, 496–503 (2003)
10. Park, H., Moon, H.-C., Lee, J.Y.: Tangible augmented prototyping of digital handheld products. Comput. Ind. **60**(2), 114–125 (2009)
11. Saakes, D., Van der Lugt, R.: Relight my model: new media in ideation workshops. In: Proceedings of the Conference on International Association of Societies of Design Research, IASDR (2007)
12. Jin, Y.-S., Kim, Y.-W., Park, J.: Armo: augmented reality based reconfigurable mock-up. In: 6th IEEE and ACM International Symposium on Mixed and Augmented Reality, ISMAR 2007, pp. 273–274. IEEE (2007)
13. Caruso, G., Re, G.M.: Interactive augmented reality system for product design review. In: IS&T/SPIE Electronic Imaging, pp. 75250H–75250H. International Society for Optics and Photonics (2010)
14. Dima, M., Arvind, D., Lee, J., Wright, M.: Haptically extended augmented prototyping. In: 7th IEEE/ACM International Symposium on Mixed and Augmented Reality, ISMAR 2008, pp. 169–170. IEEE (2008)
15. Santos, P., Graf, H., Fleisch, T., Stork, A.: 3d interactive augmented reality in early stages of product design. In: 10th Conference on Human-Computer Interaction, HCI International 2003, pp. 1203–1207 (2003)
16. Fiorentino, M., De Amicis, R., Monno, G., Stork, A.: Spacedesign: a mixed reality workspace for aesthetic industrial design. In: Proceedings, International Symposium on Mixed and Augmented Reality, ISMAR 2002, pp. 86– 318. IEEE (2002)
17. Dani, T., Gadh, R.: Covirds: a new paradigm for conceptual shape design using virtual reality. Comput. Aided Des. J. Special Issue on VR for Desig **29**(10), 555–563 (1997). Elsevier Science Inc
18. Krüger, W., Bohn, C.-A., Fröhlich, B., Schüth, H., Strauss, W., Wesche, G.: The responsive workbench: a virtual work environment. Computer **28**(7), 42–48 (1995)

Advancing Interagency Collaboration Through Constructive Simulation: Results from the 2015 Federal Consortium of Virtual Worlds Workshop

Barbara Truman[✉] and David Metcalf

Institute for Simulation and Training,
University of Central Florida, Orlando, FL, USA
{Btruman,Dmetcalf}@ist.ucf.edu

Abstract. Immersive, 3D conferences are becoming viable using OpenSimulator, open source software. The act of planning for an immersive conference using the software dependent on the conference success strengthens the community of users that participate in the platform. This paper describes three conference events held from 2013–2015 involving an emerging consortium of leading developers and researchers of virtual worlds. The implications of technological success of immersive conferences hold promise for government and military agencies facing training requirements under fiscal restrictions. A workshop was conducted during the writing of this paper establishing the inaugural, immersive workshop for the Federal Consortium of Virtual Worlds sponsored by the US Army and Avacon Incorporated, a non-profit organization producing conference events.

Keywords: Education · Military · Distributed environments · Virtual worlds

1 Introduction

Leadership and technological advancements have enabled online, immersive conferences to become more common occurrences where hundreds and even thousands of participants log into their computers from around the world to interact and learn. Increased access, reduced costs, and benefit to the environment have made online conferences effective and economical [1]. Many professional associations offer online seminars to enable members to access professional development. Such events have become more valued as travel budgets shrank or went away completely during the 2008 economic downturn. During this period, the United States federal government experienced furloughs that required employees to maintain responsibilities in some cases restricted from logging into their computers during unpaid time off. Employees had to compensate to achieve more with less time often for more customers due to interrupted services.

Training was often conducted at a distance requiring time away and travel funding. In person conferences were over relied upon leading to legislation that reduced travel across government agencies by 50 % [2]. Industries, non-profit agencies, and academia

© Springer International Publishing Switzerland 2015
R. Shumaker and S. Lackey (Eds.): VAMR 2015, LNCS 9179, pp. 524–534, 2015.
DOI: 10.1007/978-3-319-21067-4_53

were significantly affected by travel restrictions. In 2013, the U.S. government shut down completely requiring administrators to rethink operational budgets due to new fiscal realities. State funded universities are experiencing program scrutiny to find efficiencies through reorganization and mission realignment.

During this time since 2008, social media use and online professional development offerings have proliferated fueling human networks. The need to keep up with advancements in technologies and knowledge creation propelled and required social learning. University researchers also found virtual worlds to be a low-cost, immersive platform suitable for teleconferencing and research collaboration [3]. Entrepreneurs also engaged in networked communities. Yetis-Larsson et al. reported, "The online economy has made it possible to organize economic activity in different ways by enabling individuals and companies to establish and maintain their businesses through new business models and value propositions" [4].

1.1 Opportunistic Disruption Within Virtual Worlds

Constructive virtual worlds, notable for their community development, were disrupted by the economy too, including the leading platform, Second Life. Since its inception as a means to create new digital realities, users of Second Life began to self-organize and offer online events. The virtual world platform became an engine of collaboration to jointly create experiences. Some universities and organizations, such as the United States Army, made commitments to Linden Lab, maker of Second Life, to participate in a program designed to serve enterprise needs for virtual world use. When Linden Lab cancelled their enterprise program, the open source viewer code was available for use. OpenSimulator was released in 2007 and one of its core developers, Clark-Casey described its broad appeal, "OpenSimulator has two basic architectures, "stand-alone" where the entire simulator and its services are executed within a single process, and "grid", where 1 or more simulator processes and one or more service processes can be run independently, potentially on different hardware" [5]. The open source license enables individuals and institutions to host OpenSimulator themselves, without cost to rent land, enabling integration into existing networks [6]. Medical simulation also found applications in OpenSimulator where the fit for long-term, cost-effective healthcare training increased use for simulating training exercises to improve incident response [7].

1.2 Community and Conferences

As the Second Life virtual platform grew and the economy declined, community conferences were coordinated and became large events with a global constituency. The community was made up of artists, musicians, content creators, educators, and many people who did not want to be known. Mixing at events was not always a positive experience where diversity of interests played out. Entertainment and educational agendas conflicted at times. A subset of the educational community organized its own conference called the Virtual Worlds Best Practices in Education (VWBPE). In 2014, the VWBPE had approximately 4,000 avatars participate from several continents [8].

These conferences were offered at no cost to participants. Sponsors covered costs that were low compared to the overhead of events held in the physical world. Such online events fueled rapid growth of global networks of educators who used virtual environments for many disciplines including global health topics. Umoren et al. asserted, "…when feasible, (virtual environments) should be utilized as a tool for the development of international partnerships [6]. Partnerships do not catalyze without leadership. One virtual world user who took to Second Life and became a leading virtual community organizer experienced the sometimes painful switchover to OpenSimulator as the disruption to Second Life evolved. Chris Collins, also known as Fleep Tuque, helped lead the development of the first OpenSim Community Conference in 2013 [9]. Collins said, "Organizing people & organizing code aren't the same thing, but they both have to work really well for a completely virtual conference to be successful" [10].

1.3   Origins of the Federal Consortium of Virtual Worlds

Like other virtual world communities, members of the U.S. federal government also became networked users seeking collaboration. In July 2007, National Defense University's (NDU) iCollege established the Federal Consortium for Virtual Worlds (FCVW) under the leadership of Dr. Paulette Robinson. Face-to-face conference events were held near NDU that featured several companies that made or hosted online virtual worlds. The FCVW conference offered paid attendees and unpaid online participants the chance to explore virtual world platforms. The 2015 FCVW website was created with permission from NDU after a reorganization prevented the ability to hold the face-to-face conference. The website states:

> The FCVW was created to explore multi-agency and intra- agency collaboration using the robust capabilities of virtual worlds, examining best practices across multiple sectors. The objective of the consortium is to help government agencies to share resources, training, and experience; leverage outreach capabilities and practices; connect to new partners and business opportunities; and demonstrate the benefits for virtual worlds' collaborative capabilities [11].

2   The Military Open Simulation Enterprise Strategy (MOSES) Community

The Military Open Simulation Enterprise Strategy (MOSES) was created by the United States Army's Simulation & Training Technology Center (STTC) as a program to replace the investments made into Second Life Enterprise. In 2011, users from government, other military services, and educational institutions were permitted to request participation. Land was provided for building and in-world meetings were held regularly. Douglas Maxwell, STTC Manager, stated his ambition for the collaborative, MOSES initiative in a conference paper documenting research results, "There is a need for a broader application of simulation-based training systems to train multiple small teams in concert or larger unit operations" [12]. Civilian participants contribute to realism of the virtual scenarios developed for testing. The MOSES community routinely shared experiences creating a cross pollination of knowledge sharing between military, education, and industry members. Administration of virtual land empowered community members whose land called "sims" was configurable for unique needs. Processing capability and dedicated memory are variables left to the administrator for each sim. The variables are highly dependent on user behavior and available hardware resources [13].

Not everyone chooses to participate regularly in the MOSES community where formal protocol is often valued over self-expression common in constructive virtual worlds. Military culture requires hierarchical, professional courtesy that has nuanced translation in virtual worlds, where gender, race, age, and status is permeable. Maxwell reported, "MOSES is not a product, but intended to be a best practice strategy for other organizations wishing to deploy an Open Simulator based virtual world [13].

The MOSES Community was invited to participate in distributed scene graph experiments in 2013 where members role played as civilians or service members in a simulated village. The research was conducted in association with Intel Labs to explore how the OpenSim environment could be scaled for thousands of simultaneous users (see Fig. 1, *MOSES Distributed Scene Graph Load Test.*) Photo credit Barbara Truman.

Fig. 1. MOSES distributed scene graph load test

The Netherlands has an initiative similar to MOSES, and research invited by the European Defense Agency on distributed experimentation with OpenSimulator was found cost effective. A recommendation was made to test larger-scale experiments with more users [14].

A modified version of the MOSES OpenSim configuration was used as part of a field experiment in January 2014 involving guided training. Army reserve soldiers in central Florida participated by accessing the technology in a face-to face lab setting as shown in Fig. 2, *MOSES Field Training Experiment.* Photo credit Douglas Maxwell, Apache Company Armory, Leesburg, Florida. The experiment used an orientation, practice activities, and scenarios similar to those used in physical training. The OpenSim experiment served as an example of new dynamics that may improve training outcomes while saving time and money. The training may be applied for a variety of virtual and physical training needs. A finding from another study on room clearing provided the recommendation, "Rather than substitute VW (virtual world) training for typical live training, augment it, and assess training efficacy" [15].

Fig. 2. MOSES field training experiment

As mentioned in Sect. 1.2, the inaugural OpenSim Community Conference was produced in Fall 2013 through support from the nonprofit organizations, AvaCon, Incorporated and the Overte Foundation. Some members of the MOSES Community participated as well, as speakers and volunteers. Cross-community engagement was found as a characteristic of OpenSim entrepreneurs by Yetis-Larsson et al. where, "Working on multiple teams is also a way for entrepreneurs to explore new combinations, exploit synergies, and transfer best practice between environments" [4]. Core OpenSim developers made thousands of code improvements based on data from weekly load tests. Twenty three regions were created for the OSCC13 and the environment was planned for 220 avatars, but over 400 attendees were able to participate. Synthetic avatars were used to increase the demands on the server as there were insufficient volunteers available any one time to stress the server. Access to the keynote regions were restricted to distribute the highest load. Clark-Casey summarized the sentiment of the conference coordinators, " It also goes to show that in open-source, there's nothing quite like making yourself "eat your own dogfood" – we had committed to put on a conference in OpenSimulator and so were highly motivated to spend the enormous time and effort necessary to get performance to where it needed to be" [16].

A key difference in other forms of open source software is that attendees of the OSCC13 obtained reusable software code. Grid configurations do differ as seen with the MOSES distributed scene graph load tests. In that research, there were also insufficient volunteers to stress the server in specific ways. A key finding of Maxwell et al. reported, "The system and network demands of human agents operating within a simulation-based training system are vastly different as compared to artificial (bot or NPC) agents" [12].

The inaugural OpenSimulator Community Conference was a surprising success. The planning committee made up of members of Avacon Incorporated, the Overte Foundation, and volunteers met weekly on the grid using the OpenSim software as a planning platform. Volunteers were recruited and trained to assist new users. Speakers, moderators, and track chairs had authorization through HUDs built for the viewing during the sessions. Presenters prepared their content for importing into the grid. Videographers choreographed how sessions would be streamed and archived. Eventbright tickets were used to carefully manage registrations and users were placed into groups that dictated how entrance to regions occurred. Very few surprises occurred. Figure 3, *Second Annual OpenSimulator Community Conference 2014*, was taken in November 2014. The event was also a success for the software and community. No incidents were reported. Photo credit Barbara Truman.

Fig. 3. Second annual opensimulator community conference 2014

The majority of users participated via use of the hypergrid where they teleported into the conference grid via other grids enabling them access to some of their inventory. One of the core developers, Crista Lopes, and her coauthors cited the design of the software that makes it suitable for conducting conferences, "The architecture of OpenSimulator is designed to scale to many simulators and their user-driven agents. OpenSimulator provides for managing user data and logins, assets, grid connections, accounts, and inventory" [3]. Hypergridding opens access between OpenSim virtual worlds including the transference of digital content.

3 The Federal Consortium of Virtual World Returns

The success of the OpenSimulator Community Conferences in 2013 and 2014 laid the groundwork for the U.S. Army STTC to contract with Avacon Incorporated to sponsor a similar online event with support of the MOSES Community. Permission was acquired to obtain the name, Federal Consortium of Virtual Worlds for use in the event. References to "conference" had to be changed as many government and military organizations could not get approval to support attendance at a conference, even if it had no cost. The term workshop was adopted. Planning began in earnest in September 2014, prior to the outcome of the OSCC14 event. Figure 4, *Plenary Seating for the FCVW15 Workshop*, shows the venue constructed for the keynote speakers. Dates for the FCVW were selected for March 6–7, 2015 over a Friday and Saturday.

Fig. 4. Plenary seating for the FCVW15 workshop

Scheduling issues surrounding the FCVW Workshop mean that some attendees will not be able to get outside computer access to participate. Saturday scheduling meant that some attendees can get access and attend, but may not want to use their personal time. A key difference in between the OSCC events and the FCVW Workshop involves live streaming. The decision was made to reduce complexity and not overwhelm speakers and volunteers with session logistics. Another key difference in the event was the desire to avoid lecture style presentations favoring interactive sessions with tours and 3D content. MOSES Community members toured regions in advance of the program providing feedback and offering content to fellow members. The MOSES Project provided a packaged platform based on testing and configuration of the grid, complete with voice-over-IP set up and a GUI-based grid manager. The project also provided several regions that were provided as Creative Commons licensed environments [17]. Registration numbers were not finalized at the time of this writing.

Figure 5, FCVW Workshop Planning Team, shows the group meeting on the FCVW grid to discuss logistics of building, sessions, and coordination. The FCVW grid configuration had several differences in configuration compared to the OSCC13 and 14 grids. The database and voice server were notably different creating challenges for staff to manage.

Fig. 5. FCVW workshop planning team

A significant feature of OpenSimulator conferences is the ability to import content for 3D posters or entire regions imported as archive files. In 2014, the Army STTC funded a Lidar scanning project to make a replication of the University of Central Florida's Partnership II and III Buildings located in the Research Park in Orlando, Florida. The building represent a collaboration among the University and military services. The same scanning technology had been used by Dr. Lori Walters for a virtual heritage project. Walters is a researcher with the UCF Institute for Simulation & Training's SREAL Synthetic Reality Lab. Figure 6, *LIDAR Images of UCF's Partnership Buildings*, illustrates a region used for a panel presentation with the Security, Privacy, and Identity Track of the FCVW Workshop. The region will be continued for use in the MOSES Community grid after the workshop for further research and development. The scanning project resulted in identifying scale issues with standard avatars when the avatars entered the lobby of the buildings. A machinima was made to illustrate the process of scanning and conversion into mesh models. Members of the MOSES Community participated in the project to illustrate the ability to go inside the buildings [18].

Fig. 6. LIDAR images of UCF's partnership buildings

3.1   Areas of Future Research

Virtual Conferences enable computer-mediated collaboration and provide the potential to develop virtual community learning organizations that span domains of education, industry, government and military. Future research should explore how virtual conferences using open source software can incorporate crowdsourcing, collective intelligence, and citizen science. Truman's research from 2013 explored collaborative uses of virtual worlds among groups and found, "The use of social media before, during, and after events provides an orbit of activities that also occur within the environment through the use of avatars to build strong relationships" [19]. Figure 7, *FCVW15 Workshop Session*, represents the session that David Metcalf and Barbara Truman presented on the FCVW grid on March 6, 2015. This paper was submitted on the same day so full attendee information was not available, but approximately 120 avatars were present for sessions. The grid performed well. Photo credit: FCVW Twitter account.

Fig. 7. FCVW15 workshop session

The session title was Innovations in 3D Simulation and Challenges of Trust. Examples of mobile use were highlighted for multi-agency collaboration. Integration of mobile devices involving the Internet of Things provides a rich area of future research for the impact on users, business processes, policy, and culture. These dynamics impact research and development of the technological innovations as well.

3.2   Conclusion

The Federal Consortium of Virtual Worlds Workshop was another successful example of an immersive virtual conference using OpenSim software. The event's purpose and transference of brand from NDU to the Army STTC in the interest of collaboration is a success of collaboration. There was no formal ceremony to transfer the changing of the guard. The OpenSimulator platform has proven its potential to host virtual conferences based on two community conferences made possible by a community of open entrepreneurs. The economic and environmental benefits of virtual conferences have been realized. Factors that contribute to the leadership of developing communities within local and virtual environments must be realized to address chronic and acute needs among government, military and academia. "As the line between the physical and virtual worlds continues to blur through virtual world platforms, we observe a tendency among entrepreneurs to embed themselves in both physical and virtual environments leveraging affordances from both spaces" [4].

References

1. Anderson, L., Anderson, T.: Online professional development conferences: An effective, economical and eco-friendly option. Can. J. Learn. Technol./La revue canadienne de l'apprentissage et de la technologie 35.2 (2009). http://www.cjlt.ca/index.php/cjlt/article/view/521/254
2. Bliton, D., Ely, D., Jesukiewicz, P., Norwood, A., Reyher, T.: Applying best practices from industry to your virtual conference. In: Interservice/Industry Training, Simulation, and Education Conference, Orlando, Florida (2013)
3. Gabrielova, E., Lopes, C.V.: Impact of event filtering on opensimulator server performance. In: Proceedings of the 2014 Summer Simulation Multiconference. Society for Computer Simulation International (2014)
4. Yetis-Larsson, Z., Teigland, R., Dovbysh, O.: Networked Entrepreneurs How Entrepreneurs Leverage Open Source Software Communities. American Behavioral Scientist (2014). 0002764214556809
5. Clark-Casey, J.: Transferring a Virtual Environment Client Session between Independent Opensimulator Installations. *VS-GAMES* (2013)
6. Umoren, R., Stadler, D.J., Gasior, S.L., Al-Sheikhly, D., Truman, B., Lowe, C.: Global collaboration and team-building through 3D virtual environments. Innovations in Global Medical and Health Education (2014). http://www.qscience.com/doi/abs/10.5339/igmhe.2014.1
7. Cohen, D., et al.: Tactical and operational response to major incidents: feasibility and reliability of skills assessment using novel virtual environments. Resuscitation 84(7), 992–998 (2013)
8. Virtual Worlds Best Practices in Education. http://vwbpe.org
9. OpenSim Community Conference (2014). http://conference.opensimulator.org
10. Collins, C.: Fleep's reflections on the first annual OpenSim conference. Hypergrid Business (2013). http://www.hypergridbusiness.com/2013/10/44261
11. Federal Consortium of Virtual Worlds http://consortium.militarymetaverse.org/about/
12. Maxwell, D., Geil, J., Rivera, W., Liu, H.: A distributed scene graph approach to scaled simulation-based training applications. In: Interservice/Industry Training, Simulation and Education Conference, Orlando, Florida (2014)
13. Maxwell, D., McLennan, K.: Case study: leveraging government and academic partnerships in MOSES (Military Open Simulator [Virtual World] Enterprise Strategy). In: Amiel, T., Wilson, B. (eds.) Proceedings of World Conference on Educational Multimedia, Hypermedia and Telecommunications, pp. 1604–1616. AACE, Chesapeake (2012). http://www.editlib.org/p/40960. Accessed 8 January 2014

14. Gregory, D., Rulof, F.: A virtual battle lab: enhancing the coordination of distributed experiments. In: Interservice/Industry Training, Simulation, and Education Conference, Orlando, Florida (2013). http://ntsa.metapress.com/link.asp?id=r1xht436733m7569
15. Lackey, S., Salcedo, J., Matthews, G., Maxwell, D.: Virtual world room clearing: a study in training effectiveness. In: Interservice/Industry Training, Simulation and Education Conference, Orlando, Florida (2014)
16. Clark-Casey, J.: Running a Conference in OpenSimulator – The Technical Side – Part 1 (2013). http://justincc.org/blog/2013/10/18/running-a-conference-in-opensimulator-the-technical-side-part-1/
17. Military Metaverse MOSES Website. http://militarymetaverse.org/content
18. Tech Demo of Rapid OE Capture using LIDAR. http://youtu.be/RPJ3NBj-tn0
19. Truman, B.E.: Transformative interactions using embodied avatars in collaborative virtual environments: Towards transdisciplinarity (Proquest 3628698) (2014). http://ciret-transdisciplinarity.org/biblio/theses.php

Study on the Design Characteristics of Head Mounted Displays (HMD) for Use in Guided Repair and Maintenance

Tao Yang[✉] and Young Mi Choi

Georgia Institute of Technology, North Ave NW, Atlanta, GA 30332, USA
tyang81.@Sa.tec

Abstract. Head-Mounted Displays (HMDs) are believed to be extremely useful in industrial applications. However, few studies have discussed the impact of different design characteristics of head mounted displays on task performance. This study aims to find out how different display positions of Head Mounted Displays may affect the performance of workers performing guided repair and maintenance tasks. A set of car maintenance and repair tasks will be performed with the guidance of HMD technologies with 3 different display locations: above eye, eye-centered and below eye, and the traditional paper manual. Time and errors will be measured and discussed, so as the implications of human factors. Designers and engineers may leverage the findings to develop next-generation HMDs that improve the effectiveness, efficiency and satisfaction for workers.

Keywords: Head mounted display · Guided repair and maintenance · Wearable computer

1 Introduction

In the recent years, there have been striking developments in wearable computing. This is a category that includes all kinds of smart devices, such as smart watches, glasses and even ingested devices. Among all the different forms of wearable devices, Head Mounted Displays (HMDs) are believed to be the first seamless way to enable workers with real time contextual information and allow companies to integrate with existing back-end systems. The hands-free features that come along with the HMD also offer advantages over many traditional technologies.

Generally speaking, a Head Mounted Display is a device worn on the head or as part of a helmet and has a small display in front of one or both of a user's eyes. In this paper HMD refers to those which are directly attached to the head, excluding the ones which are worn on or are embedded in a helmet [1].

Consulting and research groups believe that Smart glasses will have great impact on heavy industry such as manufacturing, and oil and gas where they can enable on-the-job training in how to fix equipment and perform manufacturing tasks hands free [2]. The impact on mixed industries such as retail, consumer goods and healthcare, where the benefits may mostly be looking for information via a visual search, are likely

© Springer International Publishing Switzerland 2015
R. Shumaker and S. Lackey (Eds.): VAMR 2015, LNCS 9179, pp. 535–543, 2015.
DOI: 10.1007/978-3-319-21067-4_54

to be medium [3]. Other features such as voice command and video calling also promise easy access to key information and convenient remote collaboration.

There is currently a lack of empirical evidence to support the claimed benefits. It is unclear whether potential benefits arise out of individual design characteristics of HMDs. Even if an HMD system is shown to be better than current technologies, it is not known if other HMD systems with different design characteristics would also perform similarly. The design characteristics of HMDs include but not limited to the display's position, opacity and field of view. Without the knowledge of how individual design attributes affect task outcomes, designers and developers will not be able to identify the best way to customize an HMD system to best match a specific task scenario.

This study explores some of these variables in a controlled set of guided repair and maintenance tasks. Common car maintenance tasks were used and performed in a realistic environment with procedures and preparations that are low-cost and easy to replicate. The goal is to better understand the implications of the attributes that are essential to Head-Mounted Displays, in particular the position of the display.

2   Related Literature

Smailagic & Siewiorek [4] documented the result of engineers of US marines doing a the Limited Technical Inspection (LTI) with VuMan 3, a wearable computer designed at Carnegie Mellon University. They claimed a decrease of up to 40 % in inspection time compared to traditional paper handling and a reduction of total inspection/data entry time by up to 70 %. However, from the screenshot of the display we can see that they just moved the text checklist from paper to the HMD. There was no image of the equipment or visual aid and no sign of task guidance. Therefore, it can't prove that the HMD actually helped the engineers in performing and completing the task. In a later work Siegel & Bauer conducted a field study comparing a wearable system with a paper technical orders on two aircraft maintenance tasks. This time the wearable system was able to give task guidance and allowed more manipulation, but the specialists took on average 50 % more time to perform the tasks using the wearable system.

Ockerman & Pritchett [5] conducted a study to investigate the capabilities of wearable computers, using a case of procedural task of preflight aircraft inspection. They compared three different methods including a text-based HMD system, a picture-based HMD system and the traditional memory-recall method. The result shows no statistically significant effect on fault detection rate, while the videotape showed that those who used the HMD systems had a higher rate of overlooking the items that were not mentioned on the computer than those who did the same inspection by memory.

Weaver et al. [6] in their order pick study however, did find that HMD with task guidance information led to significantly faster completion time and less errors than the audio, text-based and graphical paper methods. A similar work by Guo et al. [7] also stated HMD was better than LED-indicating system. However, both studies were conducted in a layout optimized for the specific task and because the complexity of this task is relatively low, it was remains unsure if the observed effects could be translated to other task-guidance involved applications.

All of the study mentioned above compared only one HMD technology to status quo of the domain and the HMD technology in each study were very different from another, it's unclear whether the result would remain the same if all the factors that differentiate different systems were teased out (for example, the size and position of the display was regulated). And it's even harder to tell which attributes of the HMD technology played the most important role in altering the task performance compared to other methods.

This study aimed to investigate the effects of different display positions – a core factor of HMDs – on guided maintenance and repair tasks. Three HMD systems with highly identical design but different display locations were compared. Cas car repair and maintenance with sufficient complexity were chosen and the study was conducted outdoor in a realistic setting in order to resemble a real life scenario.

3 State of the Art

In recent years many HMD systems have been designed and manufactured in relatively large volumes. These HMD systems are much smaller yet more powerful than the early prototypes which researchers developed for experiment purpose decades ago.

Among these HMD systems, some are specifically designed for industrial application such as Golden-I headset and Vuzix M2000AR glasses. Others systems are more of a combination of productivity and fashion, such as Google Glass and Recon Jet. However, recent trends showed that even those devices originally targeting consumer markets were being utilized for enterprise in the "service and maintenance" [8]. For example, companies like APX Lab and Thalmic Labs had been working on wearable solutions to help enterprises improve efficiency and reduce cost in heavy and mixed industries using a combination of Google Glass, Epson Glass and Myo Armband.

There have been dozens of HMD devices with various input methods (voice control, hand-held control panel, touch pad, etc.) and output configurations (opaque vs. see-through, monocular vs. binocular, etc.) but there's lack of evidence showing which HMD system provide the best results. As more and more companies are starting to realize the potential of smart glasses in industrial applications, there's a growing demand for empirical study on the attributes of HMD systems.

4 Method

The focus of this study is the effect of the Display Position on guided repair and maintenance. Car cars maintenance and repair tasks were used as they were easily accessible to the subjects, similar to many mechanical inspections and frequently performed [9].

4.1 Conditions

Four different conditions were investigated in this study: three of them used HMD technologies and the other used paper manual as a baseline of comparison. The three HMD conditions were operationalized via a customized display system. The system was composed of (Fig. 1) the display of a NTSC/PAL (Television) Video Glass, a Raspberry Pi single-board computer, a modem that provides internal network connection, power supplies and 3D printed housings for other parts to reside in.

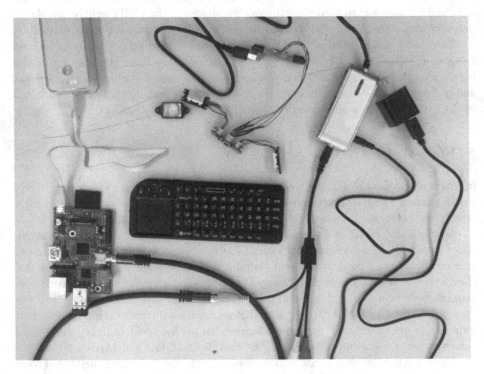

Fig. 1. Components for prototyping the test device

The core display device was mounted onto a headband which the user wore and could be adjusted to different angles and positions relative to the user's right eye. This provided three different display conditions (Figs. 2 and 3): above eye (display is above the line-of-sight), eye-centered (display is centered on the line-of-sight) and below eye (display is below the line-of-sight).

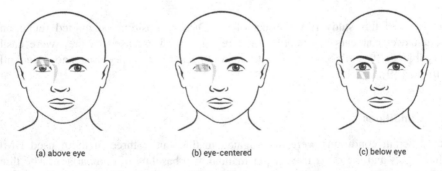

Fig. 2. Three different experiment conditions

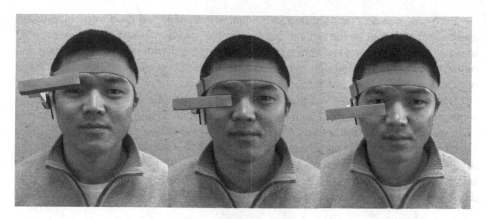

Fig. 3. A user wearing the test device in each of the three test configurations

For the three HMD conditions, the participants had to use voice commands to navigate through the instructions. "Next" to go one step further, and "Previous" to go one step back. The image that the user saw was mirrored onto a monitor next to car and a researcher was controlling from his end while listening to the user's commands: "Next" to move on to the next step, and "Previous" to go one step back. As for the paper condition, same instructions were printed out one on each page of a booklet. Participants manually flipped the page to navigate.

4.2   Tasks and Action Types

Eight tasks with instructions were performed by participants:

- Task 1: Coolant. Participant checks the coolant level.
- Task 2: Cabin Air Filter. Participant checks the condition of the air filter contained inside a housing and change it if necessary.
- Task 3: Engine Oil. Participant checks if the oil level is sufficient using the engine oil dipstick.
- Task 4: Center brake light check. Participant removes the middle brake light assembly and checks if it is burned out.
- Task 5: Fuse (exterior). Participant pulls out a specific fuse from the exterior fuse box to see if it is blown.
- Task 6: Washer Fluid. Participant checks the washer fluid level and add fluid if necessary.
- Task 7: Air Filter. Participant checks the condition of the air filter contained inside a housing and change it if necessary.
- Task 8: Headlight. Participant removes the right front light assembly and checks if it is burned out.

A Training Task was performed before each the main tasks took place. Participants were asked to open the hood using each test condition.

Each task was decomposed into individual action steps and each step consisted of an actual photo taken on the test car and one simple sentence so that novice users could understand. The instructions were screened and validated with official car manual and online resources [10]. Although some previous works also evaluate the interface design of HMD system [11], it is not the focus in this paper.

Based on task analysis and literature review on previous research [12], all of the steps were classified into four action types: Read-Locate-Manipulate-Assess. Figure 4 shows an example of the interface design for the four action types. Locate involves visual search, typically performed to find a specific car component. Manipulate involves physical manipulation such as unscrewing, lifting and removing. Assess involves visual comparison of what is seen in the real world with what is displayed or described on the screen, such as assessing the condition of a car component.

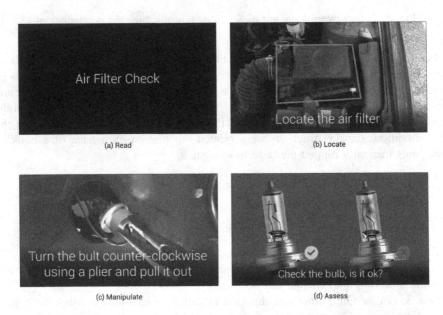

Fig. 4. Instruction examples of four action types: Read-Locate-Manipulate-Assess

The eight tasks were then grouped into four trials (Fig. 5) based on the estimate complexity (one relatively easy task paired with one relatively harder task). By the end of the experiment, each participant performed all the tasks and experienced all the test conditions.

4.3 Experimental Setup

The study was conducted during the day at an outdoor parking deck. The car used for the experiment was a 2007 Toyota Corolla. The tools necessary to complete all the tasks were handed to the participant when needed and consisted of paper towels, a

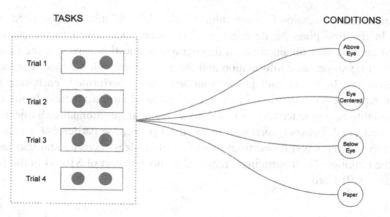

Fig. 5. Eight tasks were grouped into four trials, each participant performed one trial using one technology.

screwdriver, a pair of pliers, and a bottle of washer fluid. Participants were also asked to put on a pair of gloves before performing the tasks.

Three facilitators were involved in the experiment session. A first person who introduced the procedure to the participant and oversaw the performance of the participant. A second person who operated a camera and video tape the whole process. A third person who set up the HMD system and initiated the computer responses during the tests when participants gave voice commands.

20 participants were recruited for the study. The criteria of the recruitment is that all participants must have at least 6 months of driving experience and currently own a car so that they're likely to have some knowledge in car repair and maintenance (not necessarily hands-on experience). All participants must have normal or corrected-to-normal vision while conducting the experiment.

4.4   Procedures

Participants were equally distributed amongst four groups at random. Every group performed the same sequence of trials, but received a different sequence of experimental condition (Table 1). At the end of the experiment, every experimental condition was tested equally often on each task (See Table 1). 20 people ensured 5 people in each sequence of experimental condition, which was sufficient to counter-balance the potential order effects.

Table 1. Test groups and corresponding conditions for different Trials.

	Trial 1	Trial 2	Trial 3	Trial 4
Group 1	Above eye	Eye-centered	Below eye	Paper
Group 2	Eye-centered	Below eye	Paper	Above eye
Group 3	Below eye	Paper	Above eye	Eye-centered
Group 4	Paper	Above eye	Eye-centered	Below eye

An experimental session for each subject lasted 40 to 60 min and consisted of three phases. In the first phase, a description of the study was given to the participant. Informed consent was obtained and a demographics questionnaire was then administered, covering some basic information and the experience with the tasks conducted in the experiment. In the second phase, four tests were performed, each one with a different experimental condition. Each test consisted of an introduction to the experimental condition, a practice task, a trial, and a post-trial questionnaire. Subjects could have a short break between each test. In the third phase, the participant was asked to rank the five systems just tested from most favorite to least favorite and was asked to justify the rankings. Each participant received an honorarium of $10.00 in the form of an Amazon Gift Card.

4.5 Measures

Two kinds of measures were gathered: Objective performance measures and subjective user experience measures. Objective measures included completion time and errors. The completion time is the elapse to complete a step (action). Errors were obtained when participant made a wrong assessment when he or she was performing a Assess action. Subjective user experience measures were gathered through NASA-TLX survey and user experience questionnaire.

5 Discussion

At the time of paper submission, half of the user testing had been completed and the data collected was not sufficient for analysis. The main contribution of this paper was to present a method to isolate the effects of key HMD design characteristics by controlling the effects of other factors in they system, in this case, the interaction method, mounting mechanism, display size, and instruction design, etc. Hence the effects of display positions, tasks, and action types on guided repair and maintenance work can be scientifically studied.

It is anticipated that once all the data are gathered and analyzed, the affect of display position on guided repair and maintenance can be identified. Whether these HMD system outperform the traditional paper-based guidance method will also be evaluated.

Unexpected yet interesting findings have already appeared from the test result and user feedback so far. For example, our decision of not optimizing the interface design and instead using simple still pictures and text was questioned as almost all the participants mentioned the demand of animated instructions for certain tasks such as Locate the brake light assembly. As Towne [13] also pointed out that cognitive time could account for 50 percent of total task time in equipment fault isolation tasks, we are curious to see if adding animated instructions in future study would produce significant difference in completion time.

Acknowledgement. Special thanks to Xianjun Sam Zheng, Cedric Foucault, Patrik Matos da Silva and Siddharth Dasari, Stuart Goose, who conducted a previous work with the first author of this study in a related field. This study was greatly influenced and inspired by the findings of the aforementioned study. However, the aforementioned study was still in proceeding of publication when this study was conducted, which is why we can't directly cite it.

References

1. Mann, S., Lo, R., Huang, J., Rampersad, V., Janzen, R.: HDRchitecture: Real-time Stereoscopic HDR Imaging for Extreme Dynamic Range (2012)
2. Lee, P., Stewart, D., Calugar-Pop, C.: Deloitte Technology, Media & Telecommunications Predictions 2014. Deloitte Touche Tohmatsu, London (2014)
3. Gartner Says Smartglasses Will Bring Innovation to Workplace Efficiency. http://www.gartner.com/newsroom/id/2618415
4. Smailagic, A., Siewiorek, D.: Application design for wearable and context-aware computers. IEEE Pervasive Comput. 1(4), 20–29 (2002)
5. Ockerman, J.J., Pritchett, A.R.: Preliminary investigation of wearable computers for task guidance in aircraft inspection. In: Proceedings of the 2nd International Symposium on Wearable Computers, pp. 33–40 (1998)
6. Weaver, K.A., Baumann, H., Starner, T., Iben, H., Lawo, M.: An Empirical Task Analysis of Warehouse Order Picking Using Head-Mounted Displays (2010)
7. Guo, A., Raghu, S.R., Xie, X., Ismail, S., Luo, X., Simoneau, J., Gilliland, S., Baumann, H., Southern, C., Starner, T.: A Comparison of Order Picking Assisted by Head-Up Display (HUD), Cart-Mounted Display (CMD), Light, and Paper Pick List (2014)
8. The State of Smart Glasses in the Enterpris. http://www.apx-labs.com/2014/08/07/the-state-of-smart-glasses-in-the-enterprise/
9. World Vehicle Population Tops 1 Billion Units. http://bit.ly/1jugNFm
10. carcarekiosk.com. http://www.carcarekiosk.com/
11. Nicolai, T., Sindt, T., Witt, H., Reimerdes, J., Kenn, H., Wearable computing for aircraft maintenance: simplifying the user interface. In: International Forum on Applied Wearable Computing (IFAWC), pp. 1–12 (2006)
12. Neumann, U., Majoros, A.: Cognitive, performance, and systems issues for augmented reality applications in manufacturing and maintenance. In: Proceedings of Virtual Reality Annual International Symposium, IEEE 1998 (1998)
13. Towne, D.M.: Cognitive Workload in Fault Diagnosis. (Report No. ONR-107, Contract No. N00014-80-C-0493 with Engineering Psychology Group, Office of Naval Research) (1985)

Author Index

Printed in the United States
By Bookmasters